PENGUIN BOOKS

Extra Confessions of a Working Girl

Extra Confessions of a Working Girl

MISS S

PENGUIN BOOKS

PENGUIN BOOKS

Published by the Penguin Group
Penguin Books Ltd, 80 Strand, London WC2R ORL, England
Penguin Group (USA) Inc., 375 Hudson Street, New York, New York 10014, USA
Penguin Group (Canada), 90 Eglinton Avenue East, Suite 700, Toronto, Ontario, Canada M4P 2Y3
(a division of Pearson Penguin Canada Inc.)
Penguin Ireland, 25 St Stephen's Green, Dublin 2, Ireland (a division of Penguin Books Ltd)
Penguin Group (Australia), 250 Camberwell Road, Camberwell, Victoria 3124, Australia
(a division of Pearson Australia Group Pty Ltd)
Penguin Books India Pvt Ltd, 11 Community Centre, Panchsheel Park, New Delhi – 110 017, India
Penguin Group (NZ), 67 Apollo Drive, Rosedale, North Shore 0632, New Zealand
(a division of Pearson New Zealand Ltd)
Penguin Books (South Africa) (Pty) Ltd, 24 Sturdee Avenue, Rosebank, Johannesburg 2196, South Africa

Penguin Books Ltd, Registered Offices: 80 Strand, London WC2R ORL, England

www.penguin.com

First published 2008
1

The moral right of the author has been asserted

Typeset by Rowland Phototypesetting Ltd, Bury St Edmunds, Suffolk
Printed in England by Clays Ltd, St Ives plc

ISBN: 978-0-141-03852-0

Contents

1. *Fancy a Dance?*

It was my first real shift after my trial nights at the stripclub a few weeks back, and I was a bag of nerves. I shouldn't have been but I was. This time I didn't have friends close at hand to give me support if I needed it. My first night would be a slow one, I had been told, and I had spent most of it standing in the corner watching, so no wonder I hadn't made much money. But I was determined to give this dancing thing a good try. How hard could it be? Everyone kept saying it had to be better than selling your body, though I couldn't say I really got the distinction. And this was London: surely it had to pay better than working in a brothel in a provincial town?

The keen girls, primped and preened in their tight, sparkly dresses, arrived early. They dashed here and there, smelling of hairspray and stale smoke, trying to look their best so as to catch the attention of any man who came in. Everyone was on a real mission to make money, and it didn't stop at the girls who were dancing. You'd catch a glimpse of the odd waitress liberally applying lipgloss in a passing mirror in the hope of getting even the smallest tip to supplement her low wages.

The girls at the stripclub (sorry, 'gentlemen's club') seemed to be split between the girls who did and the girls who didn't – that is, the ones who would go off with clients at the end of the night for a better tip, and the rather snotty ones who proclaimed that they were 'dancers' and 'artists' and would never stoop that low, bla bla bla. I had gleaned that much from the natter that had gone on in the poky dressing room while the girls were getting ready.

That was the first of many revelations that night. More were to come from a fluffy, sour-faced blonde I soon had tagged as Miss Priss.

I was standing at the side of the main stage in the club. It ran along the back wall of the dark room, with rows of seats and small tables spread before it.

'Hi, you're new here, aren't you, love?' The sour-faced blonde leaned over in my direction.

I looked away from the stage and my view of the girl performing on it. She had big boobs and was shaking them in the face of some poor chap in the front row. He was there by himself, blushing, hands in his lap covering what looked like a prominent bulge.

As it was the start of the night there weren't many girls or guys around. By the look of the near-empty club, not all the girls were in by a long shot, and there was me already dressed and ready for action – if you could call it dressed. I was nervous as hell, as all the girls I had tried to spark up some kind of rapport with in the dingy closet dressing room had just shrugged and pointed when I'd asked them anything, or totally snubbed me. One just grunted at me and flounced off. What a friendly lot!

I looked over at the pouting blonde. She had just asked if I was new, so I smiled and nodded to her, and said, 'Yes, I *am* new here.' I didn't offer my name as she hadn't told me hers. I was a bit wary of her, especially as no one so far had been very nice to me.

She was staring at my chest. I frowned and looked down and then back up at her.

'I thought so, haven't seen you here before. Watch out for Kelly and her mate when they come in later. I'll point them out. You've got even more of a flat chest than they have. If you end up grabbing their few reg clients they'll see you as competition ... Watch out, love, I wouldn't mess with Kelly.'

I nodded my head slowly. I had no intention of messing with anyone. I looked back to the stage and mumbled 'thanks'.

Oh dear, I must have been looking all naive and shocked. People are forever telling me to watch my back, and now they were doing it here too. Well, at least it was better to know I should watch my back than to be stabbed in it, and in this dark environment I wouldn't be the slightest bit surprised if that kind of thing didn't happen all the time.

I was still looking at the stage. The busty girl was now lying on her back, splitting her legs and shoving her shaven naked crotch practically into the face of the gent seated in front of her below the stage. Did we all have to do that? I hadn't seen a girl on stage do it before, not so up close anyhow, but then again, I had spent so much time dashing to the loo on my few trial nights I wasn't often enough near the stage to see much of what the other girls were doing.

The guy who was getting the stage show up close and personal was by this point a very dark shade of beetroot and dribbling drink down his shirt. The girl on stage wasn't even looking at him but at the mirrored ceiling. Somehow she had both her hands round under her legs. From where I was standing at the side it looked like she was spreading herself open for him with her fingers.

I looked over at the blonde girl beside me. Cocking my head in the direction of the girl spreadeagled on stage, I said, 'I thought no penetration, even with fingers, was allowed? A couple-of-foot-distance council-rule thingie.'

She nodded. 'Yep,' she said, looking at the girl on stage and then back to me and shaking her head.

'She's pushing it, just showing him what she's got. No class, that one.' She wrinkled up her nose. 'The rules are very vague. She's one of *those* anyhow.' She virtually spat the words out.

I must have been staring at her blankly. One of *those*? A stripper? A porn star? A contortionist? I must have looked really confused.

The blonde just nodded back at the girl on stage, who was now on all fours with her bum in Mr Beetroot's face, wiggling about like she was having some kind of fit – either that or she was covered in invisible ants.

'You know ... one of *them*! One of the girls who give their number out to guys and go off with them after working here ... You know, the girls who say they are dancers but are actually whores. You can always tell 'em – they dress really trashy and simulate sex rather than actually dancing ...' She went on and on in disgust. I just listened while watching the stage show paid for by Mr Beetroot.

4

OK, I thought. On reflection, I don't think Miss Priss should be the one to ask how I would go about getting extra, after-work clients, or how I would slip them my number without anyone noticing, for that matter. She droned on in my ear as a mental barrier 'CAREFUL WHAT YOU SAY TO THIS ONE' went up faster than Mr Beetroot's erection in the front row.

On the plus side, Miss Priss here can't have thought I looked like a whore. Which had to be good – I hoped.

'See, I know you're not one because you're dressed elegantly and you're not wearing the cheap platform plastic shoes they always do.' She looked me over very intently. 'So where did you work before?'

Oh no. Thoughts were running round and round in my head. I didn't think this girl knew what she was talking about or what I was planning to do, but maybe I was wrong? Maybe she had clocked me and was digging?

I have worked with lots of whores, and only one wore the nasty, ugly plastic stripper shoes Miss Priss was talking about, and that was Suzie, the amateur porn star who worked in brothels on the side – but then again, she *was* a stripper.

I just shook my head. 'Nowhere, I haven't danced before at all.'

I thought telling a little bit of the truth was better than telling a lie. And maybe I'd be able to squeeze other information out of Miss Priss here if she thought I was green and needed her help.

'Look, some guys have just come in. Let's team up and go and say hello.' She sauntered over to two City types in suits, and I tagged behind, putting on my best smile.

'Fancy a dance, gents?' She sidled up to them with a killer-watt smile.

No, they didn't, and neither did the next group of men that came in; they all looked like they needed some Dutch courage before they could ask a woman to strip for them. Either that or two girls approaching them when they had just walked in was a bit intimidating. My new companion in charm Miss Priss made her excuses and suggested that maybe we should split up, as asking the guys if they wanted a dance might be easier to do separately. With that she slunk off to the loos, to 'refresh', as she put it.

I had more luck when she left me to it. Approaching an older gent who was sipping some dark liquid at the bar, I felt more confident than I had.

'Excuse me, can you tell me what the time is?' I queried, tapping him on the arm.

'Sure. It's 9.40 p.m., honey,' he said, looking me over as I thanked him and asked, 'I don't suppose you want a lap dance?'

'OK,' he agreed, 'but just a £5 one down to your underwear. Too much off, and I'll have a heart attack, my love,' he whispered in my ear as we found a table off to the side away from the bar for me to dance for him. At least it was only down to my lingerie. It wasn't being naked that bothered me, but a naked dance had to be done on the big, shiny stage, which could be seen throughout the club and drew most of the men's attention. What if I fell off! Now that *would* be embarrassing.

I was bound to have to do a naked dance some time but as I started slowly wiggling about to the music I pushed it to the back of my mind. Sliding my dress off slowly for half a pop song I didn't even recognize was easy – I had done that before – and in a dark corner with only one set of eyes on me it was no big deal. It was the stepping out of the dress that was difficult. How do you stop a clingy dress pooling round your ankles like a fabric boa constrictor trying to trip you up and wrap itself around your heels? Next time, I suppose I could always lift it over my head, as the girl across the room was now doing in her shadowy corner.

The man sipped his drink. I wasn't paying much attention to him. As I was dancing around him in my black bra, knickers and hold-up stockings, I was still thinking of the other girl who was dancing. Why hadn't I thought of that? Dress over head, genius! Unwrapping would be better, but I couldn't remember the last time I had seen a sexy wrap dress for sale anywhere. Knowing me, next time I danced and tried pulling my dress over my head I would get it caught in my earrings and nearly take an ear off.

The old man held out a £5 note at the end of the song and said thanks as he got up to resume his place at the bar. I hurried to get dressed, tucked the note in my stocking top and started looking for my next paying spectator. Fingers crossed the night would go as fast as that last dance had gone.

A rowdy group of men had come in a few minutes earlier. I had noticed them out of the corner of my eye as I was dancing for my £5 client. They had virtually been jumped on by some of the girls who had just sprung from the changing room. The rowdy men had fended them off until they had settled at a big table near the stage, and now one of the men was gesturing me over, as I was close by from my previous dance. That was handy.

Nodding in his direction, I adjusted my dress and joined their group. I said hi to them, and to two other ladies who were already seated chatting to two of the men at the end. I hadn't seen them come in. They sat there at the end of the huddle of men, talking animatedly, and didn't even acknowledge me. Fine, they weren't the ones who were paying anyhow. I was still trying to pick up the etiquette. How did it all work? No one spoke about it. The girls couldn't all be this unhelpful, surely? Even a whore-house was friendlier than this. The tall man at the end of the table, who was talking to a stunning brunette, was a groom, I gathered, out on his stag night. I smiled as one of the men handed me a £10 note and gestured over the chatter of the excited group to a nearby table by the stage.

Oh dear. £10 meant a nude dance up on the stage. OK, I reasoned with myself, it was only three feet off the ground and the stage was vast – it wasn't as if there was really any danger of me falling off. As we made our way to a front-of-stage seat, I looked over to the two girls on stage dancing. They were not completely naked, which was a relief. It meant they had been paid to stay on stage for at least two songs, so during at least the start of the next song I would not be the only one up there – or I hoped not. I veered off to the side to seat my Mr £10, close to where I was aiming to dance. There was no way I was going to dance at the front of the stage under that strong spotlight – not that the side looked any less bright. OK, deep breath: how bad could this be?

I couldn't see him, but the DJ must have been having a laugh – how can a white girl strip to up-tempo reggae? Idiot. Wasn't there a song about shooting the DJ? Neither of the other girls looked bothered. They just carried on, wiggling away, both of them out of time, and now naked. Any more deep breaths and I was going to look like an inflatable doll. Pull yourself together and get on with it, I whispered to myself. Oh, and smile. With that, and having made it up the steep side steps without tripping over my hem, I sauntered to the spot where my eager Mr £10 was sitting and started to move in time to the music.

Most of the men were looking goggle-eyed at the busty girl I had seen 'dancing' earlier, who was still spreading her legs, now for a different beetroot-faced man on the other side of the dark stage. Good. At least most of the attention would be focused on her. With the lights in my face I could hardly see the rest of the room, so I concentrated on looking at the man seated below me and cut off the rest of the crowd, as if they were not there.

Now even I was dancing out of time, like the other girls. I could feel the music more than hear it as the blood rushed in my ears and blocked out most of the sound.

I stared at the man's nose so as to have something to focus on, and that made it easier. He gulped as I stripped off to the music as slowly as I dared. I nearly tripped myself up, pulling my dress down without thinking.

OK, must make a mental note: over my head, over my head, over my head.

I wriggled out of my knickers but kept my stockings on as they held what little money I had earned so far. I lingered so long over my knickers, I wouldn't have had time to take my hold-ups off in any case. I just managed to get naked before the song ended, quickly whipping off my bra. Ta-dah! I had done it. I was so relieved. The music had ended too quickly, though, much sooner than I thought it would.

The man I was dancing for didn't seem to mind in the least. Mr £10 had appreciated it, and his friends at the table clapped and cheered as he stood up and handed me the money. I slid it into the top of my hold-up, next to the £5 already there. From the patting on the back he got from his mates and the huge grin plastered all over his red face, I think I did fairly well for a first attempt, so I was pleased with myself, and with the fact that I hadn't fallen off either my high heels or the stage, or tripped over my dress – well, I hadn't *really* fallen; stumbling doesn't count. I quickly got off the stage, scooping up my things as I went so I could get dressed at the bottom of the steps at the side, out of the bright lights. But where had my bra gone? I was soon on my knees, hunting for it under a table in the darkness of the front row where I thought I had thrown it. I looked up when I noticed a pair of heels in front of me. My gaze climbed up Miss Priss's legs. My errant bra was swinging from her finger.

'Best to keep your stuff all in one pile on the stage when you take it off, it's easier to find at the end,' she said, handing my bra back to me. 'Why don't you introduce me?' she said, beginning to saunter over in the direction of the man I had just danced for. I managed to catch up with her while at the same time fixing my bra back on and pulling my dress on over it.

I introduced her – not that she needed much of an introduction, as she had got there first and had already said hi and was chatting to the men on the stag night. Ah, so that's how it was done, then? You made brief friends with a girl, and then, as long as you were introduced by her, gate-crashing into a group wasn't so bad. I could see where she was coming from. I needed to make more acquaintances among the girls, then, even if they were only passing ones.

She winked at me as I got a dance with Mr Back-Patter, the one who had congratulated my earlier stage-dancing observer Mr £10 when he had got back to his seat. Mr Back-Patter gave me £20 to dance for two songs for him on stage; I was to 'show him some "ass",' as he put it. I had no idea what he meant, but I had danced once now; the second time had to be a piece of cake. I walked him to the same seat, still vacant from when Mr £10 had sat in it, at the same time as a few other girls were making their way towards the stage ready for the next song, also with men in tow.

I started to dance around near the edge of the stage. I didn't have much of a choice anyway: the stage was big, but six ladies getting naked creates a whirlwind of scattered underwear you need to avoid getting tangled up in, not to mention having to keep well clear of dancing legs ending in killer pointy heels and heavy platform soles. I could see why some of the clubs had separate podiums. I lifted my dress and wriggled my bum in the man's eager face. At least this way I didn't have to look at him drooling in his beer and giving a commentary of 'Oh yes, little girl, work that ass,' and it was easier not facing towards the crowd. It also hid the fact that I winced when I raised my dress over my head: I had caught my hair in my watch strap and had to pull it free, leaving a big chunk hanging from my wrist, which I didn't notice until I left the stage. There was no way Mr Back-Patter had noticed, as he was still intently staring at my bum, and was even more goggle-eyed when I slid my thong down my legs and spread them wide to give him a good view.

Miss Priss was soon up next to me when the second song started, doing the same thing for two more tracks for one of the other men. She was halfway through and making an average job of it as I dressed at the back of the stage from my pile of discarded clothing, the majority of the gyrating, half-naked and fully nude girls still on stage.

As I wandered back to the crowd on the stag do, I felt that it was going to be a long night. No one wanted another dance or was willing to pay me to sit and chat with them.

I went back to the dressing cubby-hole to reapply my lipgloss and gather my thoughts. A lot more girls had arrived by now, and a few were quite pushy with the customers, which I didn't think would work – until it started looking like they were the ones who got the guys to pay for dances. I didn't know if I could be that pushy or aggressive; after all, all the money I had earned in the past had been by being nice. For me, a friendly smile worked to put men at ease, but it didn't look as if it was going to work too well here.

I thought to myself, Just take a deep breath, it will be over soon: it isn't too bad. As I was walking out of the dressing room a girl pushed past me in the doorway in a rush to fix a run in her stocking. I took another deep breath and looked around the main room of the club, making my way towards the bar, where there were a few men sitting on their own. I approached some of them. All of them looked me up and down and said no thanks. That was a bit disheartening. One even looked over my shoulder and said, 'No, thanks, but can you ask her to come over and say hi,' pointing to the busty girl who had pushed past me on her way into the dressing room earlier. I went up to her and said there was a guy at the bar who wanted her, and off she went to say hi, without so much as a thanks in my direction.

But even the men who were turning me down were more friendly than the girls milling around who I was supposedly working with. Fighting for the chance to dance wasn't so much dog eat dog, it was more cat eat cat. I managed to get a few more lap dances down to my undies, after asking most of the men who had come into the club, some of them twice. This went on until a regular at the club asked me to sit and have a drink with him for an hour, paying me to sit and chat, and then he asked for a stage dance. I was beginning to work out that this was the best way to earn, as it paid more. I hadn't made much money, and after having paid the house fee of £40 when I signed in that evening and parking costs, it didn't come to half as much as I had earned in a shift in the brothel.

And it wasn't getting any easier, vying with the bustier girls to dance for drunk men who kept trying for a sneaky feel when you were off guard. It didn't come easily to me, not after the straightforward clients I had normally. I had expected the club to be full of men who would ask me to dance for them; I hadn't expected to have to hustle to get them to show even the slightest interest. Unlike the brothel where I had worked, where friendliness, a fit body and skill with it got you work, in a stripclub it was all about the way you looked, and to me it seemed as if it was the girls with big boobs who grabbed the attention and got the dances. It was all about your body and nothing about physical skill. Girls who couldn't even dance in time to the music got work if they looked good. In a brothel, if a girl couldn't do the job, no matter how she looked, she wouldn't earn as much as one who did it well. There wouldn't be much work for *this* small-breasted dancer unless I hardened up and got a bit more assertive and dirty. It was dawning on me that maybe this wasn't for me, and that it really wasn't as easy as people said or thought it was.

It was now 2.15 a.m. and most of the men had left. The music had been turned off and the house lights were on. It was closing time. As I got dressed in my jeans and top to leave, wrapping my smart jacket around me, I noticed that I smelled of smoke and stale booze. My hair stank and I couldn't wait to get home and have a shower. Miss Priss had already left, without even so much as a 'see ya'. I walked out of the back door into a dark alley with a few of the other girls who were also leaving, all of them hold-ing hulking big rucksacks and holdalls. They looked less like the glam girls I had seen earlier on stage and more like they were on their way to the gym or the laundrette.

A short dark-haired guy I had seen in the club was

outside smoking and he waved to three of the girls as they made their way up the alley. I wasn't sure who he was but I didn't feel he posed a threat; he looked pretty laidback. He nodded to me as I went by. I peeled off to the right.

'You looking for a cab, new girl?' I smiled to him and said no, it was fine, I was driving. 'I'll walk you' was his reply. It was more of a statement than an offer. Before I even had time to think or ask him if he was security for the club I heard 'Wait up' being called from behind, and two girls strode up behind us hauling big bags.

'Chio, aren't you going to wait for us, too?' A tall girl with black curly hair and big spangly earrings trotted up, the other girl at her side.

'Hi, I'm Kelly, and this is Kiki.' The two girls smiled, and Kiki, the taller of the two, put her arm around Chio, the guy in the black suit who had offered to walk me to my car. 'So, sugar, what happened to Annie?' she questioned him.

'Annie? Oh her? She broke my heart and went back to Oz last week. Why? You looking to replace her?' He winked at Kiki, who punched him lightly on the arm.

'Anyhow, you girls don't need me to look after you. I was walking the new girl here to her car, see her safe.'

'Who says we want you to walk us? The new girl might have needed us for protection against you,' joked Kelly, hooking her arm in mine.

They were being nice, but Miss Priss had warned me about a Kelly, and that was enough to put me on my guard. I didn't know who to trust; it wasn't as if Miss Priss had offered to walk me to my car.

I smiled and listened to their banter and introduced

myself. Kelly slowed down, so we were lagging behind, and I took the opportunity as we walked up the alley to the parking area at the end to ask her who the suit was.

'Oh him, he's the boss's son. He manages the club while his old man is away. Always on the look-out for a good time that one, was head over heels with Annie, a tall Australian girl, and more so when he found out she did anal. He likes a tight ass, so I hear.' She just looked at me after whispering that, gauging my reaction I guessed.

'Really' was all I said, leaving her to natter away. We caught up with the other two, and they all waved me off, saying they would see me the next day. I went to pay my ticket so I could exit the car park. I had no idea where they were going, I didn't think to ask, but both the girls went off down another street arm in arm with the owner's son.

I was exhausted when I got back home. Claudia, a Russian girl, was renting out the spare room in her flat and I had moved in a few days ago. The door to her bedroom was closed. I hadn't seen her since the other morning, when she had dashed off to an English language class she was well past needing without so much as a goodbye. She had looked very smart in a nicely pressed suit and a pair of her precious Bally shoes, which were usually all lined up in a neat row by the front door. When I moved in I had been told rather than asked not to leave my shoes next to them, as it would make them look untidy. That put me in my place.

I was so tired I couldn't think straight. I would have to wait until morning to evaluate all that had happened that evening. I had got a bit lost around the London backroads on my way home, not knowing my way very well, so it had taken longer than I thought it would. Now, I couldn't even be bothered to take my money out of my bag, tally it down in my little black book and put it in my locked box. I just flopped down on the mattress that was serving as my bed in my small, poky bedroom, curled up and fell asleep.

In the morning, when I woke up, I was vaguely conscious of Claudia stumbling around fixing breakfast. Ouch, the daylight was bright. I had only just moved in and hadn't even put curtains up in my room yet. There were bags of my stuff all around and somewhere in the mess I knew there was a pair of curtains that matched the duvet I was wrapped up in. I dragged myself out of my pit in search of the coffee I could smell next door in the kitchen.

'Morning.' I rubbed my eyes, gazing up at dressed, washed and nicely smelling Claudia.

'Morning.' She sniffed at me. 'You smell discust-in!' she said, wrinkling up her nose. With some toast in one hand and a cup in the other, she walked past me into the sparsely furnished lounge and plonked herself down on the curving corner sofa.

'Yes, got in late last night. Just fell asleep,' I called after her. The flat was so small you could hear someone talking from one end of it to the other, and I was babbling as I emptied the boiling water from the kettle into a mug that I had found in the cupboard. 'You weren't at the club last night?' I queried, searching for the sugar, to go with the coffee, which I had unearthed in a tin.

'No' was all I got back, as I heard the TV go on in the

lounge. So much for a sociable flatmate. Maybe she was like Layla, my ex-flatmate, who never fully woke up until she had had her coffee fix. But no, that wasn't it; Claudia wasn't any more forthcoming when I sat down with my coffee: black. I mentioned that there was nothing but tofu and salad in the fridge, and that she was out of milk, to which Claudia said, 'Yah, full of food,' adding that I could have the bottom shelf if I wanted. Very gracious of her, I thought, especially considering it was a five-shelf fridge and that, even with the spattering of her half-eaten food, it was nearly empty. We chatted briefly as I sipped my coffee but not about anything much.

Claudia was having some time off from working at the gentlemen's club where I had just started, but it was through the club that I came to be living with her. The day manager who interviewed me had given me her number, as she knew Claudia was looking for a flatmate. Claudia was taking a bit of a break, not to study or go away on holiday but to work for a different one, to see how it was, she said. She was going to start the following week; she 'needed a change'. Well, I suppose it was good for me – at least I would only have to put up with the moody cow at home and not at work too. Maybe if I baked her something, that would cheer her up? It had always done the trick with Layla and Sanita in my old flat – but I only had to give brief thought to how you can make a pie out of tofu before I disregarded that idea.

Claudia got up, claiming she had to meet her man for lunch, and was off in a puff of expensive perfume. I wasn't sure I was warming to her; she was a bit cold, snobby and up herself, the way she looked down at me.

But hey, she *was* nearly six foot tall, she was bound to look down on short little me.

I went back to the club that night after a long morning shower, having fixed up my room a little and stocked the fridge from the supermarket down the road. I didn't care what Claudia said: a girl couldn't live on tofu alone. I had wandered from shelf to shelf in a bit of a daze. Why wasn't I enjoying the dancing job? Why was stripping considered better than being a lowly hooker? Just because you got paid for only being naked and didn't have to have sex with strangers, stripping was apparently OK. I was over-rationalizing, I knew it, but I wasn't happy and felt unsettled. I had passed a special-offer shelf twice and had put two cans of the same thing in my basket before I realized I didn't even like tinned macaroni and put thcm back.

After the poor money I had made on my first night, I was determined to make a go of it. There must just be a knack to it. It was bad enough that I hated every moment. What was the point in teasing men? Taking their money and then not being able to have my wicked way with them? But at the very least I should be earning enough for that not to worry me too much. I could always pick up a man for free sex if I needed it. I didn't like to think I would have to do that yet, but it was always an option.

Maybe I should ask Claudia for some tips – after all, she used to work there, too: she might have some inside knowledge that was evading me. And if I asked her advice it might make her friendlier towards me ... but I just had a deep-down feeling that she would revel in lording her knowledge over me. It wouldn't surprise me at all. I had tried to be friendly to her since I moved in, but to no avail. Wonder if a packet of Hobnobs would cheer her up more than a tofu pie?

2. Come Again?

'Hello, pretty one.' Chio was on the back door when I arrived, early, for work a few evenings later.

'Oh, hi.' I plastered on my cheesiest smile, hoping he hadn't noticed how disappointed I was at having my attention drawn away from the cute black security doorman who had just winked at me over a ledger on a pedestal and turning to look at him. Next to the smart-suited six-foot security guard, Chio looked nothing more than a pale, short, unappealing member of the opposite sex, and standing under one of the spotlights in the well-lit back corridor didn't do him any favours either: his thinning hair and dark eyes were even more pronounced.

I shuffled off quickly, not wanting to get caught between two sparring males, but Chio lingered, tagging along behind me as I dashed into the poky black dressing-hole. It was a far remove from the contract, or agency, strippers' fancy mirrored room down the corridor. I kept hearing about them. Their agents made sure they had the better dressing rooms, and they were also the most glam girls in the club; the others would point them out in passing. For some reason they didn't pay the house fee but they did give a cut of whatever they earned to an agent, who either sent them to different clubs each night or had them contracted to one club for a few weeks and would then transfer them to another. They were in high demand, darting around the club between men. As yet I hadn't had a chance even to catch the eye of one of them, let alone chat – if that was possible without getting a face full of tits, my head being at the same height as their cleavage.

I changed quickly and put the things I might need – really just make-up – in a small handbag. The bag was meant to be for the oodles of cash I was supposed to be making, so that all those notes tucked into the top of my stockings didn't weigh them down. Ha, that was a laugh. At least this time I had remembered to bring it with me, though, not that it was really going to hold more than lipgloss and a few well-palmed notes – if I was lucky. I clipped the bag shut and went off to stash my backpack with the vile house mother, Vera. It held all the things I probably wouldn't need but could retrieve from the locker cum cubby-hole if I did. It contained some normal clothes, a cheap coat, sensible shoes to drive in, a spare dress in case I fancied a change, and a front pocket full of plasters, hair bands and my hair brush. Nothing of value, just in case it was nicked.

Vera was in her cubby-hole when I went past, perched on a stool near the contract girls' dressing rooms reading a book, apparently not too busy. She must have been in her fifties if she was a day, and she had a cold blue stare and a mouth that hardly had a smile. Her short bleached hair was showing its roots, but she wasn't unkempt: you could see that from her gleaming long talons, which were immaculate. In smart slim-cut trousers and a blouse, her glasses on a gold chain around her neck, she held court here, looked after your bag for a tip and sold you over-priced cosmetics and stockings if you needed them. I wondered if she had ever been a stripper. It was hard to imagine it, and if she had, no one mentioned it.

Being new, there was no way I was going to ask her directly, especially as she was a bit pissed off with me. I had taken my bag from the locker cubby-hole last night when she wasn't around, not knowing she wanted a £10 'tip' for watching over it. I had got away with it the previous times because, being a new girl and a new face, she hadn't had time to register me. I hadn't stood out from the crowd, what with all the other girls milling around at the end of the night, rushing about getting ready to go home, wanting to leave as soon as they could. But last night, when she realized the bag she had watched over with countless others belonged to me, she had accosted me as I was getting dressed and demanded her tip in a rather abrupt sort of way, telling me the score, which everyone around me seemed to know but no one had bothered to mention.

No wonder a few of the other girls stacked their cheap bags and even cheaper coming-to-work clothes in the darkest corner of the dark, doorless hole of a dressing room we had to put up with as independent dancers. I didn't want to leave my stuff out in the open like that and thought the lockers would be a safer bet, but now I was on Vera's radar I thought it best to pay her upfront, and for the days I hadn't, just to make her happier with me. I assumed that house mothers at a stripclub were akin to a receptionist in a brothel: if you were nice to them, they liked you and made your life at work a little easier.

'So, anyone shown you around yet?' Chio eased his frame away from the wall as I pushed aside the curtain to come out from the mirrorless dressing room. He must have been waiting to chat some more and, due to the fact it was still early and not many girls were in, he was obviously lacking in people to talk to. Oh joy and lucky me.

'Er, sort of, thanks, yes. I'm looking for Vera?' I asked, hoping the question would give me an excuse to get away.

'Um, she's down there. I think you forgot to pay the house fee when you came in. I can't play favourites, you know, I have to write it in.' He waggled his eyebrows at me as he leaned in, talking lower now. 'Of course, if you sucked my dick for a bit . . .?'

I eased back like I hadn't understood. 'That's OK. I'll see Vera first, drop off my bag and then come and pay the fee at the back door.' I rushed past to get out of his way and to the safety of the gleaming agency dressing rooms, which had a bold sign that said 'NO MEN BEYOND THIS POINT' just outside its door. I had my fingers crossed the notice extended to the boss's son. It wasn't as if it was there for the dancers' modesty; it was more likely that it was there to stop men who had 'got lost' or to keep anyone from wandering in and stealing our bags.

Chio was making me feel really uneasy now. You expect that sort of thing from customers, but not from a manager. Maybe it sounds a bit snooty coming from a whore, no less, but I really think that a good business shouldn't involve its girls giving freebies in lieu of fees. It's just bad form. If the bosses expected it to happen and didn't see a problem in it, then that spoke volumes about the way they ran their business – and it wasn't a business I really wanted to be involved in, especially as that sort of thing tends to cause a bad atmosphere. Any well-run business which looks after its girls doesn't need to do that. Madams might be bitches sometimes, but there's a lot to be said for working for one of them and not having to give freebies to a jumped-up wannabe pimp.

And things weren't getting any better moneywise. That night, I did a few dances on stage, which made up for the money I had given to Vera for looking after my bag, an expense I hadn't expected to have to cover in addition to the house fee and the cost of parking. I had to do quite a few dances just to break even as it was. The evening dragged on. The club was busier but there were more men drinking the overpriced drinks than wanting to pay for dances.

The end of the night came as a relief, especially as I had to deal with a drunk. I did a lap dance for him and he wasn't happy about the fact that I hadn't fully stripped, so he grabbed hold of me by the waist and tried to shove his finger up through my thong for a bit of a laugh. He gurgled as I stamped on his toe with my heel until he let go. A security guard saw what was going on and, as I dashed off to the dressing room to catch my breath, he came over to have a word with the groper, who had stood up and was trying to follow me. But Security didn't throw him out as I had expected they would, even after I told them what he had done. They did keep a watch over him, just in case he did it again – which he didn't, as he was now far too drunk to do pretty much anything at all. I just stayed over at the other side of the club, away from him, trying to smile as best I could as the men got drunker, the smoke got thicker and hands took any opportunity they could to touch and grope.

I didn't feel well at all, a bit dizzy, as I hadn't eaten as much as I should have before I came to work, and I didn't have a snack bar in my bag, which I usually did. I could really have done with a cup of tea too at that point, but the club didn't do coffee, let alone tea. I had chewing gum on my shoe, my hair smelled of stale smoke and all the men ogling me had either bad breath or body odour. It was obnoxious having to dance around them so close. Why was it that I was doing this again? Oh yes, the money – that was it.

Well, I reasoned, it can only get easier. The club was full to bursting with people, but my purse didn't fill up anywhere near as much as I wanted it to. The novelty of having to hustle for money was wearing thin, and the loud music was pulsing through my head and giving me a splitting headache. You had to shout to be heard over it.

At last it was over. It felt good to get back to the flat and, after a long shower, my headache had subsided enough for me to fall asleep as soon as my head hit the pillow. If Claudia came back that night I didn't hear her and, as I slept until noon, I didn't see her for the rest of the day either, which was annoying, as I wanted to ask her how she managed to avoid the drunken late-night gropers.

A week later, and the money I was earning at the club was still not as good as I thought it would be. I was sticking it out – I am not a girl to give up *that* easy: I wasn't going to leave just yet. The money *had* to get better. I hadn't really known what to expect, but I had been reckoning on at least £100 clear, if not more, per evening, and I was averaging £60–£80 if I was lucky. Even when I made a real effort to be friendly to the customers, they didn't want me to dance for them. It wasn't just me, though. Most of the girls at the club were complaining, grumbling that there were a lot of girls on shift and not enough men coming in to give them all enough work during the week. New girls would appear every night to give it a go, never to be seen again. I guess they thought the money would be better than it was, like I had.

And there were so many extra costs on top: house fees, house mother fees, car parking . . . If a man paid by credit card the club took 3 per cent as a transaction fee; even if he paid for a dance with the 'house paper money', which he was overcharged for in any case, we still got £2 less cashing it in at the end of the night. Another transaction fee, so the cashier said. Ironically, in a way I felt I was screwed more working in a stripclub than I had ever been in a whorehouse!

I had tried to make friends with a few girls, but as soon as I did they would leave or begin to get snotty, so I stopped trying. It was the hugely busty women who were the high earners at dancing, and I found I could earn more by sitting and chatting with the men and getting them to order overpriced drinks. Men were always asking me out after hours, but they didn't realize how late we worked; we had to stay until the end of the shift. Even if they were OK with you saying, 'Sure, I can meet you, say, after 2 a.m., I can't leave this moment,' as soon as

I mentioned what I thought was a suitable price, of around £150 for an hour, they tended to walk, saying it was too much. From what I heard from the other girls' chatter £150 was low compared to the high-priced girls working in London they had heard of. No one claimed to know any personally, though, which was frustrating.

There was no way I was going to take such a risk for less money. Just because you could get a nude stage dance for a tenner, for some reason men expected that £100 would secure you for the entire night – mind you, most were so drunk by that point I shouldn't have expected them to be thinking clearly. As yet, I hadn't been able to pick up any after-hours work and, what with the inebriated state of most of the men in the club by the end of the night, I wasn't sure I really wanted any, despite the fact that my funds were running low. After paying to park my car in central London during the day, and for rent and other costs, it didn't look like I was going to save as much as I was used to saving.

And Claudia, my so-called flat 'mate', wasn't much help when I asked her for any tips she might have for stripping. She just looked me over and said, 'Darling, you're short and have no boobs – of course you won't earn that much. If you were as pretty and tall as me, you might have a chance.' And with that she pranced off for lunch. I just smiled, all the while thinking, You bitch. At least steering clear of her in the flat wasn't hard to do: she was never there.

'Hello, hun.' I called Layla, in need of a sympathetic ear to rant into. She was about the only one I could talk to about this stuff, and I explained my issues with the club, how it wasn't as good as I thought it would be and how unhelpful my new flatmate was.

'Sod blooming Claudia. You're not as tall as her – so what? – and you shouldn't make your boobs bigger just for that, that's daft. What about saunas in the area? Why not stick to something you're better at?'

We chatted for what seemed an age. The idea of working in a sauna had run through my mind a few nights before, when the drunken bloke had groped me. I'd thought, I used to get paid better for that sort of thing, and putting up with this was just going backwards.

'I could get a boob job. Lots of girls at the club have had it done, and theirs turned out OK.' I had been toying with the idea, but Layla was horrified. I could hear it in her voice.

'There is nothing wrong with you,' she tutted on the other end of the line. 'You want to look like some silicone Barbie, or what? They always just look real fake.'

We chatted some more and I brushed off the surgery option after having spoken to her. Maybe she was right about looking for another sauna to work for, in London. Finding out if that would pay more would be a better option than having a boob job just to be able to earn more at the club. I could always do short shifts at both until I worked out which was better. I was missing sex, but the money was also a big issue. And there had to be places like the one I worked for before here in London.

Layla didn't have a clue where to start searching, and neither did I. I had only been in London a few weeks and still hardly knew anyone except Claudia. I wasn't going to ask the girls at the club, that was for sure; I didn't know if I could trust any of them. And, after Claudia's useless advice about how to earn more money, I really didn't think she would be much help.

3. Knocking Shops

'So, how's the club you're working at?' I asked. I hadn't seen Claudia in days. I had no idea where she had been, I didn't much care, so I didn't bother to ask. She had been coming back to the flat later than I had, after work when I was tucked up asleep, and then she'd be up and gone before I surfaced. Whenever she was back and around in the evenings, she flounced off to bed before I could speak to her.

It was a Saturday, and I had wandered into the lounge. Saturday was one of Claudia's days off, or so she mumbled. She didn't need to go to her English language class either, so she was lolling around the flat with a mudpack on her face and her brown, bobbed hair tied back out of the way.

'New club? It OK.' She looked up from her fashion mag. 'Why? You not make it work at the club?'

'No, not really. If it was that good, you would have stayed, surely?' I quizzed her.

'It very good, but my man pay me not to dance there any more, he not want me to dance, so I dance somewhere he not know.' She looked terribly pleased with herself.

'Oh, how do you get away with still dancing then?' I sat down next to her with my tea.

'He thinks I have night classes now. Really, my

31

morning classes very short so all good. I can dance at night instead.' She looked happier than I had seen her before. 'He taking me shopping today for more shoes. I meet him for lunch every day. Can you not be here at one? He is picking me up.' She was positively beaming now. 'He thinks I live here alone.' It seemed the shortest path to Claudia's heart was to buy her shoes for her big feet.

'Sure, I'm going out anyhow, to look for some saunas or massage parlours to work at as well as dancing.' I took a sip of tea and watched her expression.

She didn't look that perturbed. 'You have massage certificate? My friend, she does that. She find places in the back of the free paper.' She riffled through a few papers stacked beside the sofa and thrust one at me. ''Ere, you probably do better there than club. My friend, she too short to dance too, she do well give massage.'

I smiled and thanked her for the paper, but I couldn't work out what being short had to do with not being able to dance. I had seen lots of shorter albeit bustier girls in the club make a packet. I had a feeling Claudia wasn't the most clued-up girl on the planet, despite the world we both worked in, and I just knew she had no idea what really went on in a massage parlour or sauna.

'OK, I am off to beauty parlour. I need a pedicure before I go shopping.' Off she strutted to get ready, leaving me to pore over the free London paper for ads in the back. There was only one in the job section advertising for masseuses, and it was asking for certificated women only, which made me wonder if it was a proper massage place rather than a massage parlour, which was

London's equivalent to a brothel in the outer counties. The description in the ad sounded a bit brief and dodgy for it to be a legit massage place, but I was still not too sure.

I went through the other papers and circled any of the massage and sauna ads that looked any good, hoping that an expensive ad would mean an expensive place, one that I could call and ask if they needed any girls. I called five from the paper, and only three picked up. I was briskly given a time to come for an interview. I drew stars against the ones that said, 'Turn up for an interview and we will put you to work.' Only one of the three asked if I had a certificate, and when I said I didn't, the older woman on the other end of the line said it didn't matter and to come anyway, they would sort it out.

All I had to do was wait until I had a day off from dancing to go and check them out, do an interview and see if I wanted to work at any of them.

I drove to the first one on my list two days later, spurred on by still not earning well at the club. It wasn't going any better than it had been; the men were still drunken assholes with wandering fingers who didn't ask or pay. I was really missing the way I used to work.

When I got to the first sauna, I didn't even bother to go up to the door, let alone to knock. It was down an alley and looked decrepit, paint peeling off the door and ripped, dirty curtains in the upper windows. I didn't get a good impression at all, so what would a punter think if he came to call? If he truly wasn't bothered about the state of the place, would he really be someone I would want to meet? Probably not.

The next sauna on my list seemed more promising. It had had one of the smarter ads in the free paper and, from the outside at least, it looked clean. After being buzzed in, I descended to a white, strip-lighted corridor and then walked along it towards a heavy, metal-grilled door. A door on the other side of it swung inward. Now, beyond the bars of the grille, I could see a security guard, who filled most of the doorway behind, and he could see me. Apparently, little me didn't look like much of a threat, because he unlocked the door and ushered me in with a grunt. I was glad I had told Layla where I was going. She was calling me back in ten minutes. The door didn't look as if it was there to keep the girls in; it was more to protect the girls from people trying to get in. And by the look of the bootmarks on the outside doorframe, it seemed that someone had wanted to get in and hadn't been too happy about being locked out.

The disinterested, rough-looking door guard showed me in to a white-tiled reception room and plonked his ample frame back down on his stool, picking up the paper that he had discarded to let me in.

Inside, the place looked a bit worn. It was dotted with cheap plastic patio chairs and tables, and there were a few women draped either over the chairs with their feet up on another or sitting round a table sharing a fag while playing cards, wearing identical grubby lab-coat wraps which had once been white.

The ladies didn't look unhappy; they just wore the bored expressions I had seen before in the faces of other working girls I had come across in the past – the tired expression you had after a long, slow day with little custom.

Some looked up with a smile as I entered, but seeing that I was another woman, who might add to their number, and not a client, the smiles dropped. Uninterested, they went back to their cards, to filing their nails, reading their magazines or watching the caged TV high up on the wall in the corner, its remote control hanging off a chain attached beside it.

The room was whitish and, from what I could see as I stood at the tall counter on the right, it led into a corridor with curtained doorways all along it. One of the white-robed women, who was sitting on a stool at the counter and looked the same as the rest but a bit older and of a happier nature, beckoned me over. I said hi and that I had phoned a couple of days ago for an interview, and she nodded and hopped off her stool, coming around the counter to invite me to sit down for a chat on one of the vacant plastic garden chairs by a wobbly table. I was feeling very uneasy.

The guard on the door was just sitting on his stool reading his paper. He looked a bit miffed when he was interrupted again to open the door for one of the girls, who grabbed her coat and bag and said she was going out for fags and would be back in ten minutes.

I had been right: he wasn't there to keep the girls from escaping; he was just a doorman for their security should they need him. The tired-looking girls didn't even look up from their lounging or TV-watching.

I asked a few questions about the security and was told that it was OK, that it was all very safe and the late-night drunks were dealt with well, as an extra security guard came on shift in the evening.

The fact that they needed two big security guards and a barred door didn't make me feel secure at all. I wasn't surprised though the environment was putting *me* on my guard, so I don't know what it did for the visiting men who, when they were buzzed in, were asked to look at the seated women, pick one, pay the cashier (as my interviewer called herself) and go off to one of the tiny, curtained rooms equipped with a massage bench for thirty minutes.

It became clear that you had to barter with the client in the room yourself to get any money from him for other services, as the fee that was paid to the cashier was the entrance and room fee only. And it didn't cover security, I was told, so both of the guards were given £10 each by every girl who was on shift as a kind of tip. There were no showers and only one toilet on the premises. When I asked where the kitchen was the cashier looked at me strangely and told me that all the girls brought their own food for the whole of the day or ordered take-outs. At that point I left, saying that I would call for a shift, even though I had no intention of doing so; I just wanted to leave.

The atmosphere there was not what I was used to from the other place I had worked in. For a start, I didn't like the idea of having to barter with the men. I already knew I wasn't very good at it, and I would probably end up as miserable as one of the women sitting on the plastic chairs.

*

After these two disappointing parlour hunts, I made a list of a few addresses and drove around the city to check them out during the day, when I wasn't at the club dancing. I thought I'd try and find one that looked better than all the grimy others before wasting time and calling for an interview. In the middle of the week I found a sauna in a part of east London that was smarter than the area the others had been in, with a classy black door with a shiny canopy over it. It looked ten times better than the five saunas and massage parlours I had found closer to where I lived, and the dingy one I had gone to for an interview. From the outside, at least, it looked like it might be one of the better ones in London. The fact that its ad, in the free paper, which I had realized you could pick up outside tube stations, was one of the bigger, flashier ones was also a good sign. Basically, the bigger and more expensive the ads, the larger and more prosperous the parlour, which meant the business was better run and, all in all, it would be a good place to work. Some of the girls I'd worked with the year before, I remembered, had mentioned this logic, and indeed that was how they had found the brothel we were all working in back then and why they had called it for an interview in the first place. The places at the bottom of the scale tried to get away with a brief couple of lines in their ads, and that just showed how small and cheap they really were.

I hung around for a while on the other side of the street, watching to see if anyone came in or out. After half an hour, with no one showing, I gave up. I didn't really know what I was looking for but at least it had given me a good feel for the area. I drove back to the flat in Holborn to get ready for my night shift at the gentlemen's club. When I got back I called the sauna I had just visited to see if they needed any girls and was told, yes, they did, as they had just opened a couple of months back. Could I come in the next afternoon? Of course I was more than happy to, especially since the girl on the other end of the phone sounded friendly, not as harsh as most I had tried to speak to so far. Most of the receptionists I had called to ask for information had dry, rasping voices which sounded suspicious as to why a woman was calling. Talking to the receptionists gave a good indication of what a man would hear if he called. I hedged on the fact that this sauna would be busy because of the way the receptionist sounded.

My interview turned out not to be all that taxing, just a few questions, and the atmosphere most certainly was not as depressing as its 'plastic-chair prison' brother which I'd visited the week before. The receptionist was small, pretty and blonde. Her name was Emma, and she looked around my age. She was more interested in when I could start than in asking about any massage certificate I might have or even for my national insurance number (not that I would have given her the real one), both of which most receptionists had asked about even over the phone.

Emma said that the boss would be coming in later that afternoon if I wanted to sit with the other girls and wait to have a chat. I nodded; I thought it would be a good idea to have a look around and sit with the other three girls, just to see what the atmosphere was really like. The other room was separated from this one only by a swing saloon door, and I had spotted the girls milling around behind it while I was sitting at the desk speaking to Emma. She introduced me to the girls as Shelly, which we had just chosen from a list of names.

I had come up with the names I had used before, and she then went through a list in a folder of girls they had working or who had worked for them to make sure that there wouldn't be a clash. They didn't want to have two girls working there with the same name; Emma said it would be far too confusing for everyone. Shelly was her suggestion. She had rejected the three I had thought up, all beginning with S. I didn't particularly like the name but we settled on it, and so Shelly it was. Who knew I looked like a Shelly?

Emma asked one of the girls to show me around and then dashed off to answer the phone.

Although this place was better than the last one I'd been to see, it was still nothing like the one I'd worked at the year before, which was pretty opulent, with proper beds. As I found out from the girl showing me around, the workrooms in this London sauna were pretty much similar to all the others in London, it didn't matter where you went. They were set out with proper fold-out massage beds, like the ones you'd get in a rather grotty back-street physio's. Apparently, in London, proper beds with a mattress would automatically flag the sauna as a brothel and it would be shut down. As it was, if the council did any checks that fire and safety requirements were being met, this place would pass as a sauna and, as such, get a safety certificate so they could operate under local council regulations. Most places proudly hung the certificate in a prominent place on a wall, mostly so that men would think it was something to do with how 'safe' the girls who worked there were. The receptionists would even use the fact that they had a safety certificate from the council as an extra selling point over the phone if men asked. All it really meant was that the place wasn't crawling with rats and that the fire exits weren't blocked. It had nothing at all to do with the staff, as all the men presumed, but if they asked if we did have a safety certificate we just told them yes and didn't bother to correct them if they had a notion that it was something else. After all, who were we to disappoint them – and our pockets?

So, as long as the place looked like a sauna and actually had a steam room, it was a sauna to the council; otherwise it would just be categorized as a lowly massage parlour like the white-tiled, plastic-chaired one I had already seen and rejected.

After being shown around, I joined the girls, who were all dressed in tight white overall dresses. They perched on a thin, padded bench attached high up a wall in an alcove. It looked terribly uncomfortable, and it was if you sat there for too long, but it was the only seating in the lounge. Unless you sat up straight on the narrow bench you slid off the front and banged your knees on the table in the middle, as I found out, to the cost of my knees.

The girls were a mixed but friendly lot. A tall black girl, a small Chinese girl and a curly-haired New Zealander all looked up and smiled when I was shown in.

When I chatted with them about other places to work in the area they gave the impression that a sauna was a cut above the rest, but not in a snobby way, more in an earning potential kind of way. They made it perfectly clear that saunas were considered much more high class than massage parlours, and a brothel or smaller working flat with two girls and a maid were a step down even from the massage parlours.

It was a bit confusing – after all, a working girl did practically the same thing in each one – however, having seen the places I had in London, I sort of got what they were getting at: nice places to work were few and far between. There were apparently some places where girls aspired to work, and this sauna was one of them. Or, at least for these girls it was. The next rung up was a massage-certificated sauna, and you had to know someone who worked there even to get an interview, and that was after you spent a year at an adult education college learning massage in order to get the appropriate certificate. That was what the girls were saying anyhow. I made the mistake of asking what this 'parlour' was like to work in and was immediately corrected: this wasn't one of those, and it definitely wasn't a brothel either. The cheek of it, this was a sauna! The Chinese girl who had objected looked very smug about this. The other two just raised their eyebrows and looked at her in amusement. Well, at least they had a sense of humour.

The New Zealand girl with curly brown hair was called Zora. She was surprised that I had even considered working at a parlour, let alone a brothel, with the way things were here in London. And given what she thought the brothels in London were like, and what she had probably seen in the past, I wasn't surprised at all at her reaction.

Emma kindly brought me a cup of tea. I thanked her for it and pretended to drink it to be polite. They were nice, and I'm sure the tea would have been fine, but I wasn't taking any chances with people I didn't know very well. I nursed the mug in my hands as Emma took her position back at her desk and I quizzed the others about how they managed on the narrow massage tables. I had never had to work on them before and I was fairly short, so the benches in the rooms were very high for me. No one knew if the council laid down a regulation height for a massage table. 'That is just the way they come,' I was neatly told by the tall, well-built black lady. There was a small collective giggle when I asked, 'The punter or the table?'

Trying to have sex on a massage table that's nearly five feet off the ground and only three feet wide is a tricky business, especially if you're with a fat man. Even a large, tall man would take up the whole table, so it was very precarious if you were on top, as there was nowhere to put your feet, and if he was on top you were likely to be squashed by his bulk. If the man was lying down and you climbed on top it was difficult to balance as all you had were little perches at either side of the table for your feet. If the man managed to get up on the bench and stayed still, you would just end up bouncing around on top till the deed was done – perfect if you were just giving a blow job, as you could crouch between his legs and he couldn't move a lot, so there wasn't much chance of him messing around, poking fingers where they shouldn't go. If he did he would fall off the narrow bench. Sex is far more dangerous on a rickety bench than a BJ could ever be, and you had to be creative with your positions. If you weren't careful, it was a long way to the floor, and usually it wasn't the cleanest of floors you'd ever seen either.

When the boss walked in an hour later it came as a bit of a surprise that she was a woman. For some reason, I was expecting the boss to be a man, but in strode a large, robust-looking lady. She was in her forties and was wearing a suit. Emma, the blonde girl on reception, had called me through when my new Mrs Boss arrived, to go and sit on the sofa in front reception and have a few words with the madam. She was pleasant enough but at the same time she gave off a Don't piss with me vibe. She had pretty much the same kind of attitude as my ex-madam, but this one had better-styled hair and a better manicure. I guessed that she didn't do any work herself but just popped in and sorted out any problems that arose.

She was exactly what I would expect a madam to be. It was Emma who puzzled me; she just didn't 'fit'. To me, she didn't look like a receptionist at all. I sat chatting to the madam, watching and listening to Emma confidently handle an idiot phone call. Receptionists had to deal with the front of house and were the front line in dealing with drunks. In all my experience receptionists had been older women.

Now, if Emma had been a working girl, that would have fitted, but it didn't make much sense that she was having to deal with the wankers on the phone, and to have a petite girl on the front desk who wouldn't physically be able to stand up to any late-night drunks? And it wasn't as if she was covering for an ill receptionist, as

I had already asked her that. She had laughed a little and said, no, she was working there full time. It wasn't a very well-paid job either. She was well spoken and could have got a better job elsewhere. It just didn't make sense.

But hey, what did I know? I was well spoken, fairly pretty (from what I was told to my face anyhow) and had an education. I could have got another job too – albeit a worse-paying one than being in the industry. It wasn't like I would have had to stock shelves at Tesco's; I could manage a team of people doing it, at a pinch. That was if I could have filled in the gaps of over a year on my CV. Other girls had asked in the past why I was a working girl, and I didn't have much of a reply other than the money. Maybe Emma's job paid better than I thought it did.

The madam nattered away, and said she would put me on the rota. I was told to bring a black dress for my first shift, and then she would send a woman to measure me for one of the uniforms the following week if I stayed. The uniform was a fitted white short coat-dress, very much like a proper massage outfit, save for the fact that it was low cut and showed as much cleavage as it could muster – which in my case wasn't much. It was going to cost me £37, but I wouldn't have to buy it or pay for it for a week, or unless I was actually going to stay.

With a date fixed to come back and give it a try, I left, waving to the girls. It was time to go back to the flat and get ready for another slow night at the gentlemen's club. The thought of going there was now filling me with a mix of emotions, all of them negative. I couldn't help mentally counting down the days until I could jack this dancing lark in and actually do something that seemed

44

like second nature to me. At least I was being honest with myself now. Entertaining men can come in all sorts of guises, but my forte was definitely sexual. The sauna seemed like the answer to the boredom and disillusionment I got from the club, and let's not forget the money. It just had to be better than the 'ten cents a dance' experience – or should that have been £10 a dance I was getting? Roll on the Doris Day!

4. *Bitch Mates*

I didn't hear the front door open that morning. I was up early and waiting in the lounge for Claudia to finish in the shower so I could use it. I'd turned the TV on, so the noise of the door, which was right next to the bathroom, was masked by it and the sound of the water. The first I knew that there was someone in the flat other than my sullen flatmate and I was when she screamed and then started shouting over the noise of the shower at a person I couldn't see. I dashed to the lounge door and peered out along the corridor to where the bathroom door was.

I had been drinking my morning tea and I grabbed my empty mug to use as a defence weapon against the intruder, albeit a fairly useless one. The short Indian chap who stood in the open doorway of the bathroom, his hand on the door knob, was now being pushed out by a towel-wrapped and dripping Claudia, who was shouting what I could only guess were Russian obscenities at the mumbling man, who stood at shoulder height to her. He was now being backed up against the corridor wall.

Claudia looked pissed off rather than scared, so I lowered my mug. She was fuming and screaming, 'I don't care. Get out!' at the man, who had obviously just let himself in, as a set of keys was dangling in his free hand. He had raised his voice to protest that he needed to talk.

It caught him a bit off guard when he realized that they were not the only people in the corridor and that I was standing in the doorway to the lounge.

'Who's she?' He nodded my way. By this point, I was guessing they knew each other, but I had never seen or heard Claudia mention him before or known that anyone other than the landlord had a door key. I had asked her about the landlord before I had moved in as I'd had problems with one in the past and didn't want it to happen again.

'She's a friend. Is none of your business,' she sneered at him, while trying to push him back out of the front door.

'I am not going anywhere. You bitch. I need you, I love you,' he shouted back. She froze and started to turn red with visible anger.

It was an unusual sight, tall Claudia in the corridor barring his way, looking down on this skinny, short young man. Bellowing, 'We are over, get out, get out now!', she didn't look as if she needed any help at all. She was really angry, and I felt uncomfortable standing there, caught in an ex-lovers' tiff.

'How dare you let yourself in like that?' The two of them stood in the corridor and carried on screaming at each other for a couple more minutes as I slid unnoticed back into the lounge and closed the door behind me to muffle the argument. I heard a door slam, and just at the same time Claudia swung open the lounge door and marched in looking none best pleased.

'That was Ali. He own flat I rent. We used to date, but it over now. He too stupid to understand.' She was pacing back and forth but finally she came to a stop and stood in front of me. I sat on the sofa and listened to her rant. 'You didn't lock the door behind you when you came in this morning, did you?'

I had popped down to the corner shop for milk for my morning tea, as she had drunk the last of it the night before, and put the empty carton back in the fridge. It was true, I had unchained the door when I left, but I was sure I had locked it behind me when I came back in. I was sure I had.

'Nope. I definitely closed the door behind me. Anyhow he had keys. He probably let himself in!' She flopped down on the sofa next to me as I took a deep breath in order to keep calm. It was far too early in the morning for a shouting match.

'No! You didn't chain the door when you came back!' She was looking at me like it was the obvious thing to have done and I was stupid for not thinking to do it. I could understand chaining the door at night, but during the day too? She had never asked me to do that, and I told her so.

'Why the hell would I have chained the door after me? You never asked! I didn't know you had a stalker for an ex-boyfriend.'

She just huffed at that and flounced off to her room, slamming the door behind her. Note to self: Start looking around for another place to live.

I left a few hours early for work at the club, so that I could avoid Claudia when she emerged from her room. I left my bag in the car and had a very pleasant time looking around the shops for a new dress, a wrap one that

I wouldn't have to pull over my head and so wouldn't make my hair go all static and stand on end throughout the night. After hunting around I eventually found just the thing, and it would do for the sauna too. I made my way back to my car to stash a few bags before parking in the multistorey car park down the road from the club, ready for work.

'Ooh, I like the dress.' Vera paid me the compliment as I left my bag with her. However, I had heard her say the same thing before to a few of the other girls, time and time again during the week. I guess she worked on the principle that if a girl looked happy, she was probably going to earn well and so a nice compliment early on might be to her advantage at the end of the night: she might get a bigger than average tip from a happy, minted girl. Call me a cynic but I reckon she had picked up quick that mostly it worked to her advantage.

I was more pleased by thinking that she might assume from her experience that I might earn well that night than that she claimed to like my dress. I normally hate shopping for clothes, and all the crowds, so unless I really, really had to, I very rarely went, and certainly never to cheer myself up. Today, after the episode of Claudia and the stalking ex, I must have needed the distraction more than I thought.

The night was going well. It felt like my smile was attracting men like flies, but more likely it was the low-cut clingy dress, which did look stunning, I had to admit, and even better with the new heels I had also bought. My purse was starting to fill with £5 notes and all was right with my world. This new satin dress would pay for itself in no time at this rate.

Fuck, fuck, fuck it in a bucket of fuckery. What the hell was that? Not my new dress!

I turned around to find Kiki behind me, fag in hand, apologizing but making out that I had backed into her, when I hadn't moved at all. Well, it was a busy night and a bit crowded but it was Sod's law. I now had a big fag burn in the back of my new dress and, worst of all, with me being so white and my dress being dark blue, it really showed, and my hair wasn't long enough to cover it. My good mood was gone in a flash. I made my way back to the dressing room to change into my spare dress and put an ice cube on the nasty red blister starting to appear. It was just in between my shoulder blades so it was really hard to reach.

An hour later my back-up slinky dress had a hole in the back too.

The house mother Vera had said 'Oh dear' when I walked into the back area the first time to retrieve my bag. The second time it happened, when I was all out of dresses and I hadn't seen who did it in the crowd of bodies in the dark club, she just smirked and said that I should be more careful, shouldn't I, and that 'accidents happen'. Accidents happen, my naked arse.

I wasn't totally dense. Those two, Kelly and Kiki, definitely had it in for me. I wasn't sure when Kiki had done it, but Kelly had a very snide smirk on her face over on the other side of the room as I dashed off to the bathroom. If I had been doing better than them I could have understood. They obviously felt I was stepping on their toes and they were just being vindictive, and the worst of it was that I didn't know why. One new dress couldn't cause that much envy.

One of the professional girls gave me the best advice, which was to avoid them. She said that no one would be interested in a whiny new girl who ran to the bosses because some little thing had gone wrong; it was easier to fire her and replace her with a less accident-prone one. She was one of the nicer, more well-meaning girls I had met, but I got the gist: either I kept clear of Kelly and Kiki or I would have to leave. I wasn't even a contract girl, like she was, so, being independent, I didn't have much say.

I knew, too, that I had no hope of being a contract girl at that time. They were all good dancers and knew their way around a pole, and they were all stunning, with big hair, big make-up and even bigger boobs.

The contract girls made up the main house lap- and stage-dancers. It meant that the club had at least a set number of girls working a night who looked the part. The rest of us were just to fill in really, to make the place look busy. I didn't know that when I answered the newspaper ad; I thought all the girls had got the job through an ad in the paper too. I didn't realize you could work there in a different way. No wonder they hadn't needed much info from me when I started – I doubted I was even officially on the books.

It was starting to feel like, if you didn't have an agent, you didn't have a stripper shoe to stand on. Kiki and Kelly might not have been contract girls, but they had been working at the club longer than I had and knew all the ins and outs of how the house worked. I truly was up stripper creek without a pole.

I lurked at the back of the club for the rest of the night, avoiding Kelly and Kiki, who kept on giving me the evils. I was just waiting for the night to end, and only table-danced for a few men after that, but at least that meant I was away from the stage, where all the action was going on, away from Kelly.

Later, I was on my way to the loos when a girl came out of nowhere and 'accidentally' spilled a drink all down my front. I had seen her with Kelly before, and it was too much of a coincidence for it to have been an accident. Or was it just me getting paranoid?

As it was the end of the night, I hung out in the loos drying off until it was time to go home. I couldn't be bothered to try and plaster on a big fake smile and hustle to get a dance for a measly £5 from a drunk who would blow smoke in my face and try to grope me.

I just wasn't in the mood. I was dressed and away on the dot of closing time, before the other girls had even started to change their clothes. As I drove home I called into the office of the club on my mobile phone to say I was taking some time off. I had two days before I started at the sauna, so I thought I could give that a good go, and if I didn't like it, I always could go back to the gentlemen's club. In a week or two Kiki and Kelly would have moved on, found another target or even left. If it happened again when I went back there, I could always find another club. Claudia would know a few if I needed to ask.

I'd had it! That was it, I hadn't even earned enough to pay for my new, now-ruined dress! I might be running away from the problem and giving up too soon – I had planned in my mind to give it at least a good month or so – but I didn't care. I started to think I had been spoiled working in a brothel; I hadn't felt half as undermined working there as I did working as a stripper. Men going to a brothel went there because they knew what they wanted, they asked for me and gave me the set house fee for my time. I didn't have to handle negotiations or discuss money with them; the receptionist did all that. I didn't have to hustle men and talk them into reaching into their pockets for a few notes like I did in the strip-club. I found it demoralizing. I suppose if I didn't enjoy sex as much as I do, stripping would have been the easier option, but I did. And to add to all that I was feeling unsettled at home too – if you could call a mattress surrounded by packing boxes and bin bags full of clothes home.

I was already living with one bitch. Life was far too short to have to work with them too.

5. *Moan Sweet Home*

Sauna shift 1: 12 noon–1 a.m.

Saturday 15 August 1998

5 clients = £260 (one straight massage only, tipped £15)

– £10 receptionist's tip

– £5 cab

–£37 uniform (paid upfront)

Total = £223

Sauna shift 2: 12 noon–1 a.m.

Monday 17 August

6 clients = £275 (one straight massage, no tip; 3 no sex)

– £10 receptionist's tip

– £5 cab

– £15 straight!

Total = £245

Zora, the New Zealander, and the tall black lady, two of the girls I had chatted to when I came in for the interview, worked nearly every day and told me the score with the rates at the sauna. I soon found out that after the man had paid the entrance fee, it was up to the girls themselves to deal with money for so-called 'services' in the room. Apparently this was standard in all London saunas and massage parlours. It was a bit awkward having to deal with the money yourself, and not very professional on the part of the house, I felt. In the past it had been the job of the receptionist, but this was the way it was done here now. I guess no one thought to do it any other way, as the receptionists pretty much had their hands tied, what with councils in London being more uptight than those in other counties.

They talked me through the fees the first time, but only briefly, as they were not sure if I was going to come back. Everyone (so the girls said) charged a kind of set house fee in the rooms. It had been made up by the girls themselves, according to what they thought the other houses in the area were charging.

£10 just for a massage (£15 for a straight client who only wants a massage)

£15 girl in her underwear giving a massage

£20 for one topless massage on the client

£30 for hand relief dressed

£40 for hand relief undressed

£50 for a naked massage and hand job

£60, the same as for £50, but the client can touch and fondle the naked masseuse

£70 for a massage and a covered blow job (possibly sex, if it was a regular client you liked)

£80 for a massage and sex (possibly a covered blow job, too, if it was a regular client you liked)

£90–£100 for the works: a massage, a blow job and sex
(which was what we were aiming to get)

All had to take place within half an hour of the man
going into the room, and everything was to be marked
on the receptionist's chart. If it took any longer, we just
doubled the price, as we had to pay again for occupying
the room for another half-hour. It was quite a list to
remember but, for the most part, men only wanted a
quickie, a cheap fuck so they could get back to the office
after their lunchbreak. At that time of day you mentioned
the lower prices first, as that's normally what the customer
had in mind and that was their spending limit. The ones
who would stay longer were usually the ones who came
in the evening before going out to a nightclub or the
pub; any later and they had already spent most of their
money and were a bit the worse for wear to last long, or
even to want to stay longer.

In general, the girls would try and get away with doing
as little as they could for the money in any of the price
brackets. It did vary a bit, according to what the individual girl preferred to offer or do, but it was still around
£80–£100 if sex was included. The guys who came in
knew the score and pretty much what they wanted. Some
regulars would hassle for everything for £70 if they could
get away with it and some girls, if they were desperate,
would do it, but at the risk of the other girls finding out
and getting pissed off with them for undercutting.

If a man was new to the area and he didn't look like
he knew the score, you started out by listing the higher
prices, only mentioning the lower ones if he started to

look a bit taken aback. Sometimes you then had to ask how much they had with them. Zora told me it wasn't unusual for a guy to be caught out and think the £10 they paid at reception was for a massage and not just the entrance fee.

Then you had to explain to the man that the house took £15 from each girl as a room fee every time she took a room, which was true, and then you could normally get the guy to stay and at least have a half-hour massage to cover your costs rather than have him walk and ask for his money back. The girls said it didn't happen often, but if it did and the man stayed, he might come back knowing the score another time and actually punt. I didn't know if I believed that, but it was reassuring to hear.

If you had a guy that walked you were out of pocket, Zora was telling me; nice of her to give me a heads-up. I didn't think it was fair that it was all so cloak and dagger, but the other girls said that was just the way it was. You either stuck it or moved on, said Zora. She was what would be considered one of the older girls (not that, at thirty-four, she looked old at all; she could get away with saying she was twenty-six) and had worked a round of saunas in the past. I liked her; she'd even lent me her old uniform, as we were the same size. She was working at this sauna, which had been newly refurbished, as she had worked here before and had liked it better than most. It wasn't great, she admitted, confessing that it used to be the pits, but at least now the new manager was updating the decor and was fair. The updating looked to me as if it only consisted of a cleaned-up shopfront with a new black canopy, a plush reception room with large velvet sofas, a lick of paint on all the walls, some new shower curtains, and some red bulbs in the work rooms, to give 'ambiance'. As all of the five small rooms had a bath and shower as well as a massage bench, there wasn't much room to swing a condom let alone a cat. The place could have had a lot more done to it, but, so I was told, at least it was better than most in the area.

Four of the work rooms were on the top floor and were reached by a spiral metal staircase, and the fifth, larger work room, the one that was used the most, was on the ground floor next to the steam room, just past the girls' lounge alcove. The steam room was a good place to sit if it was a bit chilly and the heating was on low. It wasn't like it was used by the men who frequented the sauna. In fact, I only knew of it being used twice in all the time I was there, which was handy, as most of the time the girls used it as a small laundry room, to dry stockings and such like. They had to be swiftly removed if the boss was around, otherwise she was not best amused.

The first man who came in that day picked me, which was a bit of a surprise. Emma showed him to where we were all sitting, and he pointed at me. I felt quite un-comfortable when I got up, as I had expected that we would each go out one at a time and say hello. I hadn't expected to be confronted with a man walking in to choose as I was filing my nails and chatting to the girls. It caught me a bit off guard, but I showed him to the downstairs room. It wasn't too far along the corridor, so if I needed to shout for help, I could be heard, even with the door closed.

The man was wearing a suit and looked fairly average. He chatted away, asking my name, and saying he had £80 and wanted a BJ and a fuck, with not so much as a blush or a question. He had obviously been here before, so I didn't argue and took his money, putting it in my pocket as he stripped and hopped in the shower without me even having to ask. When he came out, I held out the towel that had been provided and he wrapped it loosely around his hips and jumped up on to the bench, lying on his front and asking for talc, not oil. After standing on my toes and giving him a brief massage, unbuttoning my uniform with one hand as I did so, I stepped away to fold my uniform over the rickety chair in the corner.

My chatty businessman had relaxed and was not so chatty now that he was squirming on his front. I pulled the chair back over to my Mr Erection so I could get up on to the bench to start a blow job and then have my wicked way with him. Time was going faster than I realized. By this time he had turned over to see what I was up to, losing his towel completely along the way and releasing his average cock. I was more concerned about not falling off the chair in my heels and undies than with the cock in front of me, which was standing up like a flag pole, impatient to be sucked. I decided to kick off my shoes. He fondled my breasts and was easing down the lace of my bra to play with my nipples, which distracted him as I straddled him, taking off my bra and slithering down him to suck on the rubber I had just taken out of my stocking top. It wasn't long before I was sitting precariously on top of him with my feet either side on the edges of the massage table. With a few strokes up and down he came. Nice, simple screw. It had been a while but at least I hadn't lost my touch.

He was pretty much an average client, like the ones I usually saw in the brothel, and was all smiles and thanks as he showered, dressed and promised to come back and see me again the next week. My first booking was over. I handed £15 to Emma on the desk after I had shown him out. He was soon replaced by another late-lunch-quickie gent, much the same as the one before, knew what he wanted. A massage, blow job and sex, for £90 this time, which was fine by me and, that being that, he was gone as soon as he had come.

I was bound to get one, but at least it was only one, a walk-in off the street who hadn't realized he would need more money to get what he really wanted. The young man was nervous, I could tell, and nearly walked, until I offered to give him a massage in my undies and stockings. I said he could wank off at the end if he wanted to, which he declined, but he did take me up on the £15 straight massage, I think more out of sympathy and feeling foolish for not knowing the score and coming in with money that wouldn't have paid a street girl, if that, than because he really wanted a massage.

They came and they went, their faces all quickly forgotten by the time I had shown them out. It's hard to remember so many faces, all seen in a gloomy red-lit room, and it didn't matter what they looked like – as long as they put out with money and cock, I was a happy working girl. It had been a good, normal working day, no hassle so far, which I had braced myself for, being new. There was nothing worse than a haggler, pervy newbie-girl hunter or a guy that wants to waste time trying to please you and holds out when you only have less than thirty minutes. A few could be like that, but they were easily dealt with by hand, which was more of a subtle indication that they needed to come because time was up, rather than that they were having trouble getting it up.

You would think most men paying for a screw would just want to get on with it, but on the whole it's rarely like that at all. Ironically, you're more likely to get a roll-on roll-off guy on a date than when he's paying you. If it was as easy as a guy wanting to pay, use you and leave, being a working girl would be so much easier than the flattery, faking and falsehoods we have to deliver to get the job done.

When men pay they in some way consider themselves to be a bit of a stud if they can please a whore. It's perverse: the men who come in the door never consider themselves average punters. Of course they are, but they think, for some reason, what with the media and what they have read, which is mostly salacious tabloid gossip, that all the men coming through the door (apart from themselves of course) are fat, ugly, desperate men that just want to fuck us and leave. And so they think that, as a working girl has sex so often, she must be hard to please and, in turn, that it must be a treat for us to be pleased first. They like to think they are special, that they're doing something nice for you and be able in their heads not to believe they are just using you. But it is actually very annoying sometimes, if they drag it out and you have to fake it for the fifth time, so they think you have had enough and will then come themselves. Men that want to bend you over and just bang away are few and far between, despite what most people think. Average guys still like you to be in charge, though, at the end, to please him back. Great work-out for the thighs, always being cowgirl on top, but bad on the knees after a while.

I took a day off on Sunday to sleep, eat and recuperate. It was wonderful, and better still knowing that my lock box was stuffed with newly earned money. That had been the last thing I had done before crashing out. The day before, I'd worked since noon and had come back just as late as I had from dancing, so it had been a long day, and even just sitting around trying to stay alert gets tiring. The sauna, so far, was so much better than working at the stripclub, but only time would tell if I could stick working every day like the rest of the girls did. I had only worked three days a week before, but here in London they required you to work at least five if you could. If I saw as many clients as I had the previous day, then it si ould be OK. It was only after ten in a shift that I preferred to take the next day off to recover. I probably could do a second day like that, but no more than that in a row. I would be far too swollen by then to be of much use other than to answer wanker phone calls. Layla reckoned she could do at least twelve and work the next day too, but she always was a show-off, and I told her so over the phone that afternoon when she called me and asked how it was going. She *is* nosey – but not as nosey as my family.

I was in a better mood after having had a chat to Layla, so I checked in with my mother next on the phone. She nattered happily away in my ear about news of home and things that had happened at family events, things she hadn't told me about, and then she realized she must have told my younger sister the same thing twice. It was nice to hear her, but an hour of your mother in your ear can make any sane person go a little deaf, especially if yours is deaf herself and tends to shout down the phone. My family aren't the quietest members of the human race; the next-door neighbours could tell anyone that.

I had called and heard my mother's normal response to me – 'So you're alive then?' – on the other end. I hadn't been down to see them in a while, blaming it on moving to London, so she had been bound to call and intrude at some point if I hadn't called her. If I didn't go down there soon, though, she might end up on my doorstep for a visit, and that would never do. Before I knew it, they would all be around, nosing in my business all the time and hard to get rid of, and then they might find out what I was really doing. (I had told them I was working as a night-security monitor for CCTV.) I couldn't see Claudia being at all happy if any of my family descended on us. She didn't like her peace and quiet to be spoiled; she already complained if I had the radio on in my room as I tidied my stuff, still in piles from moving, into bigger piles.

I only managed to escape deafness from the phone call with my mother by promising to go down and visit the following month, hoping she would forget all about it and that I could love my family from a distance and enjoy my own version of peace and quiet, left alone to do what I wished.

*

I'd been at the sauna some time now and, between having to pretty much barter with the clients over rates, which I found a bit degrading, and the fact there were only a few clients for all the girls, the so-called benefits of working in this brothel cum sauna weren't offset by my earning enough to save and become as flush financially as I'd hoped. Let's face it, living in London is never cheap, and even though I was now being paid more for each client, with the cost of living in the capital, I wasn't making or saving any more than I had in the past and, now, I was seeing from three to a maximum of seven clients a day, if I was lucky, so I was earning less than I had before. At least I was earning more than I had been at the stripclub, which was a start, I suppose.

To add to that, I was still feeling slightly unsettled where I was living. I hadn't warmed to Claudia at all, as I had to my previous flatmates; they had been my friends, and Claudia, quite plainly, was never going to be that. The flat didn't feel like home; in fact, it mostly made me feel on edge. The area was all red-brick council flats and it had me on my guard before I even got in the front door. In the past, if I hadn't liked something, I changed it, and it looked like this was one of these times. I needed to move, and probably very soon, since my hackles were up, and for no very good reason that I could see. Looking at it rationally, the rent was very cheap for central London.

I phoned my mum for a chat to see if it would change my mind and convince me to stay put, but it backfired completely. I had thought she would advise me against moving again, as I had just got to London and she could picture where I was in her mind's eye – 'nice and settled again', as she put it – but the damn woman completely floored me by saying she could hear I wasn't happy and maybe I should consider moving somewhere else in London, if it would make me happier. You think you know your mother, and then she ups and surprises you!

To my mother, who lived on the coast, it didn't matter where you were in London, it was all the same. Thank goodness she hadn't yet come up to visit – I could just imagine how worried she would be, going back home having seen the dark and foreboding council block I lived in and the sparse furniture in the flat, not to mention the fact that I was still sleeping on a mattress on the floor. After seeing that she would have called every day to check that I was all right and hadn't been mugged, burgled or murdered. And, to top it off, there would have been frequent visits from various members of the family to make sure that I was OK whenever they just happened to be 'passing by' London. That, I really didn't need. I had always been the sensible one in the family, the one Mum didn't need to worry about or bother, and I planned on keeping it that way.

I pottered off that day to the sauna with thoughts of moving out and where to go and asked the girls if any of them had a flat with a spare room or knew someone who was looking for a flatmate. No one had any ideas, but they all said they would ask around. I then spent the rest of what turned out to be a slow night looking in the papers for flats that were available to rent and within my budget. I would call them the next day.

After much ringing around, I realized that saying I was a dancer was not doing me any favours in selling myself as a tenant-to-be to landlords. It didn't sound too stable a position. One landlady grumbled but agreed to show me around what turned out to be a poky, rundown room on Baker Street. You couldn't swing a cat in it, it had a grubby shared toilet on the landing and she was asking twice the rent I was now paying. The hanging frayed electric-light fixture and the dodgy-looking cooker right next to the bed had me beating a hasty retreat – but I had a feeling most of the flats I would be shown would be similar.

A few days later, trying to reconcile myself to the fact that Claudia's flat wasn't that bad after all for the amount I was paying her, I ambled into work just as Emma was opening up the sauna. I helped her push up the black roller shutters that covered the blacked-out windows and black-plated door. She smiled cheerfully and told me that she had a friend who had a friend with a flat for rent in north London. It was just a bit more money than I had been looking to pay, but it was supposed to be a really nice new one-bedroom flat and was in a good area.

I thought about it all through my shift, sitting perched on her desk in my short massage uniform: it was a lot of money for me. By the time I had drunk the tea she had made and we had munched through half the packet of Hobnobs I had brought with me, I had realized that the new flat was double the rent I was now paying Claudia but, to be fair, cost around the same as most of the flats in central London. Emma prattled on and was just writing down the landlady's number when the buzzer buzzed.

The chap who walked in wanted to see Zora but she

was late in and he didn't have the time to wait. Seeing me, he said I would do. Gee, thanks, buster, I thought, leading him to the closest back room and leaving him there to have a shower. I was still pondering moving as I paid the room fee to Emma out of the £80 the man had given me. I left the £15 on the desk for her, as she was on the phone, and grabbed a towel from the cupboard as I passed.

I went through the motions, rubbing down the middle-aged accountant who was lying quite contentedly on the massage table before me. I asked him to turn over and I undid my uniform, slinging it over the rim of the bath where he had taken his shower, close behind me. My mind was still on the rent for the north London flat Emma had mentioned.

I had a rubber on him as soon as he turned over. I parked his cock in my mouth, sucking him fast to get him hard. *It did sound like a nice flat, and it even had a parking space.*

Percentage-wise, this guy wasn't getting any bigger. He groaned, putting his hand on the back of my head and trying to shove me further down his small semi-hard-on. Even though I knew from experience I was in danger of his choking me, I was not paying much attention. *Percentage-wise, it wasn't as if I was saving what I used to.*

I kicked off my shoes. *It was a big step moving out of central London now I was here and had found my feet.*

I peeled down my knickers, still giving him head and now removing my bra. He was trying to roughly grope one of my small tits with his free hand, which I didn't like. *Even though I didn't like my flatmate, it was still a lot of money to pay just so I didn't have to share.*

67

I climbed on top, tightened my internal muscles and sat down, very slowly, on his under-average cock. 'Mmm,' I mumbled. *Mmm, £150 a week, which is over double what I'm paying for where I'm staying at the moment and four times what I used to pay for rent . . .*

I was now squatting on top of him, my feet either side, and I rose, squeezing his cock tighter as I pushed up with my feet. Ready to relax a bit, I slid down him again, already bracing to repeat the movement. *I had bought quite a few things now, including some bedroom furniture for my room. It would take a few trips up and down to north London to move. Ahhh, now, that might take a few days.*

'Ahhhhh,' I slurred, bouncing around on top of the balding man below me, rubbing my hands over his nipples to see if they were sensitive. *If I did move, at least I would have a flat all to myself, no vain flatmate. If it was as nice as it sounded, my mother, if she did visit, wouldn't feel the need to bother me much or worry afterwards.*

The man drew a breath below me as his nipples hardened at my touch. *I could decorate and sleep when I wanted to – even fall asleep on the sofa and not be bothered by anyone and, more importantly, do what I wanted when I wanted to . . . Oooh, now that was a thought.*

I let out the 'Oooh' as I pinched his nipples. He made a face, shook beneath me and came on time. *Maybe it was about time I did move, after all.*

I climbed off and asked the man if he was OK. I then grabbed a tissue to take off the condom, as I always did, from the box on the windowsill, just to make sure there was no split in the rubber, to check it over. *Right – all I had to do was make contact, check it over.*

I tidied myself up and put my robe back on as the man dressed in a hurry, even more so when he noted the time, which had flown by. I showed him out and he dashed for a cab to catch a morning meeting he was already late for. Emma smiled at me as I turned to close the door behind him. She was waving the phone number she had scribbled down for me earlier.

It was the weekend and I was having lunch in the flat, my sandwich perched precariously on my lap, for want of a better place in our tableless lounge. Claudia was not around, as normal, not surprising, as her lunchtime trysts with (from what I could work out) her sugar daddy always spread into late afternoon. Her sugar daddy was twice her age, if not more, and was supposedly paying her half of the rent, though he thought he was paying for the whole flat for her alone. He was the reason I wasn't allowed to pick up the phone if it rang, or answer the door, which was a moot point as, for some reason, he never came round anyhow. Claudia said that she just had lunch with him and that there was nothing sexual about their relationship – but no girl gets that many shoes as gifts without at least putting out from time to time. She would get really prissy about it all though, so I could never be bothered to bring it up.

Anyhow, lunch was interrupted when a short guy and two larger guys walked in the front door. The short guy was the owner of the flat, and he asked what I was doing there. I said I paid Claudia rent to live there.

The owner said Ali, Claudia's ex-, was his little brother and he had been supposed to look after the flat, rent one of the rooms out and, with that money, pay the bills and do the flat up for his, the brother's, return from working abroad. The landlord had come back the week before to England, rung on the phone a few times and got no answer. Neither me nor Claudia ever picked up the phone. He didn't know that his brother had moved out, and that the flat had been sublet again. The bills hadn't been paid, so he had assumed it was empty. He hadn't been able to get hold of his brother, who had mysteriously disappeared on holiday for a few weeks, so here he was, and he had brought some guys around with him who wanted the flat. They had already agreed between themselves that they could rent the flat and move in the following week.

He didn't look best pleased that his wishes hadn't been carried out and got straight on to the phone to his little brother, who didn't or wouldn't pick up. All dues to the man, he wasn't taking it out on me; if I had been in the same position, I don't know how calm I would have remained, coming into my property to find a drawerful of letter threats from the council over unpaid tax and, to top it off, what looked like squatters, when he thought the flat was empty.

The new tenants looked around and then left. The landlord and I worked out between us that Claudia had been giving his brother, Ali, half the rent and keeping my half. Ali had been pocketing it and not paying the bills either, not that he'd known about them, as Claudia had been putting them, unopened, in a kitchen drawer, thinking they didn't matter. My take on Claudia as an elusive, greedy, money-grabbing bitch hadn't been as far off the mark as it might have seemed. What is it with people!

The landlord sympathized and said it wasn't my fault but, even so, I would have to move out soon. He would look out for another flat for me if I wanted, which I thanked him for, but he said he wasn't going to help Claudia; he didn't trust her. That made two of us then.

We exchanged numbers, but he never did call and, after a few attempts and left messages to see if he knew of somewhere to rent, I gave up.

I told Claudia what had happened when she came back a couple of hours later. She was fuming and tried to call her ex-. No luck: he had turned off his phone. Then, in a sulk, she called her sugar daddy for help finding a new flat.

I asked her casually how much he gave her for the rent, or as casually as you can to a sulking, pissed-off Russian, and she said she had told him it was double what it was so she got to keep half, as he never gave her money for lunch.

I kept my mouth shut about the unpaid bills and worked out that in fact I was paying the rent and she was pocketing the sugar daddy's money and living in the flat for free, lying to me all the while. She was in such a state – worried about being kicked out – I don't think she realized what she was telling me.

I already had a plan but I hadn't yet called the number Emma had given me for the expensive flat in Muswell Hill. It was time to bite the bullet. I had had no luck with the abysmal central London offerings, so I left a message on the number as soon as I could. I wasn't in as much of a panic as I could have been – at least it looked like

I might have somewhere to go rather than being kicked out on to the street.

Where I was now, I was having to pay an astronomical rate for parking. There were no parking spots outside the red-brick block, which was a pain as parking meters in central London just eat money, and even using the option of parking lots a bit out of the centre was expensive. Even if you use the cheaper ones, like those around King's Cross, the costs add up and, with my rent and other outgoings, it was a big drain on my finances. I had to be paying at least £50 a week in parking fees to live in central London, money I'd save living in the smart, modern flat in Muswell Hill with its free parking spot. The money would all even out, and I would no longer be paying to have the sponging Claudia live off me. It was further out of the centre, but I would have a one-bedroom flat all to myself.

As soon as I had the chance, I went up and looked around the north London flat, even though the landlady owner was still living there. I said I would take it but I would have to move in three days' time, on Sunday, as I had to be out of my flat by then. I was thinking I might need to stay in a hotel for a while, but she said that Sunday would be fine; that they – her boyfriend and her – were half moved anyway, into his place, which was a great relief to me.

The flat was at the end of a posh, quiet road of cottages. Inside, it was cosy, with a big floor-to-ceiling window that gave on to a great view of trees in the park below. It was a new housing-association block, and the landlady's one stipulation was that I couldn't open the door to just anyone, because it might be the association checking up and, officially, she wasn't allowed to sublet. That was fine by me. I didn't even answer the door to the postman, let alone to unscheduled and unannounced callers. I was way too paranoid for that.

No one just popped in to see me now that I had moved away. Even good friends like Layla and Sanita, my ex-flatmates and still working girls themselves down south, knew to call before coming around, especially as they knew I had been stalked the year before, and it wasn't like I had made many friends now I had moved to London. The landlady's stipulation gave me a great excuse to tell my family there was no way they could pop around unannounced or without letting me know well in advance. My new landlady didn't need references; she said as her friend knew Emma, the receptionist, she knew where I worked and she had no problem with it, saying that at least she knew I earned well and could pay her, and that was good enough for her. She had met Emma, who, unbeknown to me, had vouched for me, saying in passing that I was a good little earner and no hassle, which I suppose had strengthened my case.

The landlady called me the next day and said they had cleared the lounge already and I could bring stuff around and leave it there if I liked. I liked her. She was pretty easygoing.

I took the next couple of days off work to pack and move, and did ten car trips with my stuff. Claudia was still panicking that her sugar daddy hadn't found her a place to move to yet, and we had to be out by Sunday. Initially, she didn't even ask where I was going. I mentioned it in passing, while taking bin bags of my clothes and stuff out to the car. 'North London' was all I said, when she eventually asked on one of my last trips out to the car. She turned up her nose and said, 'Far too far from shops. I won't move there,' prancing off with her latest copy of *Vogue*. I hadn't asked her opinion, cheeky cow.

Early Sunday morning I left the door key on the kitchen sideboard of the red-brick council flat with a good-luck note to Claudia and drove to the new flat without a backwards glance. I was off to live and settle by myself in a really nice place in leafy north London.

6. Mr Body

I had been at the sauna for quite a few months, and the going was still slow. If five men a day came in during the week it was considered busy. It picked up a bit at the weekend, but it wasn't as busy as it had been. I was working at least five days a week, if not more, and it was all getting dull, just going through the motions.

I was in early, as usual, and was waiting for the other girls to arrive.

'Morning, honey. Looks like we have some new girls.'

Zora blustered in past me. I started filing a broken nail and got up to peep over the saloon doors that separated the girls seated in the corner corridor and the entrance reception room. Sitting there were two smartly dressed, dark-haired girls, chatting to the receptionist and clutching their handbags to their expensively suited laps.

I turned around and followed Zora down to the dark basement room where she was heading. 'Who are they? Social workers? Journos?' I asked her.

They looked too sharp and smelled too expensive to be sauna working girls. I had spotted their smart handbags and shoes, and one of them even had a designer watch glinting on her wrist.

'Escorts sniffing around,' she mumbled, heaving her bag after her and continuing down the stairs to change out of her scruffy jeans and into her white uniform.

'Escorts? I thought they were called call girls?' I was still following her, clipping down the steep steps in my heels.

'Nah, that's Americans on TV. Over here they are called escorts, for some reason. Something to do with paying for their time and not what they do – you know, escorting a punter to functions and stuff,' she muttered, rummaging through her bag in the middle of the floor.

'OK. So what do escorts in London do then?' I leaned against the wall and flipped on another light switch so she could see to find what she was searching for.

'Exactly the same as us; they just have more time to do it and they normally go to the punter on outcalls, so it's more risky. That's why they get paid more.' She fished out her hairbrush and set about her hair with one hand, picking out her shoes with the other. She was late and really in a rush, although I couldn't see why, as there were no clients in to say hello to. It was way too early for that. It wasn't like there was ever a lunchtime rush.

'I'll leave you to it and go and listen in upstairs then,' I said, turning to go back up to see what was happening in reception.

I had heard about outcalls to clients' houses from Layla. No one had called the girls anything as glam as escorts at the time, she said. She had told me all about it the year before, when I had worked with her at the brothel. When she started there, the house had been offering outcalls to men in the local area at £55, which was £15 more than the house rate at the brothel. She had done two outcalls, and they had been OK, but it had taken her a lot longer to get there and back than she had thought it would and Mrs Boss hadn't been too happy. Mrs Boss thought Layla was missing out on bookings during the time it took to travel to the outcall, and the money you got didn't compensate for the time. They had only had three girls working then and were getting busier, as it was a new brothel and the news was spreading.

It wasn't till the third outcall booking, when Layla had been sent to an estate at the top of a hill, that there was a problem. The client, unbeknown to her or the brothel, had locked her in. Outcalls being all new to her, she didn't notice until she was on her knees giving the chap a blow job in his lounge, when she heard a rattle and a bang on the front, locked door and a woman screeching through the letterbox. His wife was shouting how she was going to kill the bitch he had with him and that she had seen what he was up to through the window.

Layla said she was then thankful he had locked the door, but that wasn't the point: she was locked in, and now she couldn't leave, as the bloke's wife was outside, going berserk, thinking he had a mistress on the side. In the end Mr Boss had to go and rescue her out through the back door of the client's house while the bloke opened the front door to the screaming woman and confronted her. I asked her what had happened next, and she said the bloke had called from A&E to see if she had got home safely, as he was nursing a bump on his head and a black eye after being thrown out by his wife. After that, the brothel had decided that it was too dangerous to send its girls on outcalls and that they could make more money by seeing an extra client in the time it took to travel to and fro, so they didn't see the point in all the extra hassle. This story was why I accepted what had been said about girls who didn't work in a house – in my mind, it wasn't safe doing outcall stuff. If Layla, of all people, didn't do it, then it must be on a par with the dangers I imagined girls working on the street would face.

I had never met an agency escort until Sonya, the Slovakian (so she said), and her tall skinny friend had walked into the sauna I was now working at. They had come into reception after ringing for an interview as they had heard you could make money faster in a sauna than in an agency. Sonya said to me that afternoon that she hadn't thought it would be as quiet or as low-paid working here at the sauna as it was. Her friend didn't speak much English, so they huddled in the corner whispering away as I finished painting a snagged nail.

My mind was racing. Why make the switch from an agency to a sauna rather than just going to a different agency? And, if they were complaining at the low rates we charged, and the fact that you had to pretty much barter with the clients (the bit I hated), how much did *they* get paid?

Sonya was going back to her agency in the morning, as it wasn't busy enough for her here, and her friend was going with her. As she was leaving, she leaned in close to me in the corridor. 'Why do you work here? You are not old like the others. Wouldn't you earn more as an escort?' She looked me up and down, a confused expression on her face. 'You would do well.' She patted my arm gently in a friendly way.

I said to her that I didn't know much about it, and

I wouldn't know where to start finding out. It was then I asked, 'Isn't it very dangerous? You hear all the chatter about girls being locked in, gang raped or stuffed in the boots of cars, don't you?' All the horror stories I had heard from the other girls and the madam had stayed in my mind.

'Where did you hear that? Itz not like that at all ... maybe at the cheaper end, but we don't have to works for them, those pimpz.' She virtually spat. 'They take care of you in the good agency.' She was nodding away as she spoke.

'But the newspapers and the girls and the owner here talk about all the bad stuff that goes on. That's why I work here – it's safer,' I carried on. I was still unsure about her. Call me Miss Paranoid, but if everything was great there, why was she looking for work here?

She raised her eyebrow at me. 'Yezz, I think the owner 'ere would say itz bad to be escort, to keeps you 'ere.' She did have a point.

She was busy rummaging in her old Louis Vuitton bag and brought out a bent red card, which she popped down my top before I could take it from her manicured talons.

''Ere, this is where I normally work, a sit-in escort agency. The owner, she is a lush, but itz better than most.'

She winked and dashed off, grabbing her coat and her friend as she went. With that, they cut their losses and left without poor Emma on reception being able to stop them or ask where they were going.

I waited till I was downstairs in the basement before I pulled the crumpled card out of my non-existent cleavage and had a look at it. Written on it in black was the name of the agency, an address and phone number. I put it in the side pocket of my bag and, hearing the door buzz, ran upstairs to say hello. Fingers crossed this one was mine, and then, maybe, it would soon be time to leave and shut up the knocking shop.

The day was bright and I had earned well in the days after my encounter with the escort. My conversation with her was still fresh in my mind. Who knew – maybe you did earn a bit more escorting, but did I really want to take the risk? Probably not. Mind you, having said that, the previous evening hadn't been all plain sailing in the sauna. It hadn't been a day that the madam normally drifted in and, when she did, the girls had to scatter to tidy up and grab their laundry out of the non-used sauna. She had swanned in looking like she had all the time in the world to hang around and chat. There were at least five of us on shift that day and it was a packed house, so she had a full audience. There didn't seem to be much consistency in the rota at the sauna; it looked like any girl who wanted to work could work a shift whenever she wanted. We were supposed to work at least five a week, but it was all very erratic. They didn't have very many girls as it was, so the madam didn't have much choice. Only four of us were fairly permanent, and then there were the odd few girls who started and then disappeared after a shift or two. Today was obviously a popular day to work.

After a ruckus with a late-night drunk the previous evening the boss had come in to check on Emma, who was still more than a little rattled, and to thank Ebony for her help with removing the drunk.

Thank goodness Ebony worked the night shifts was all I could think: she was the only girl big enough, at a hefty six foot, to possibly stand up to or remove a guy from the premises. She didn't get as much work as the other girls, but I was sure the other week she had only given over £5 for her room fee to Emma rather than the obligatory £15 and then had dashed off to tend to her client while Emma put it away in the drawer without making any fuss. I thought it was odd at the time, but now I was wondering if Ebony had an agreed reduced room rate to pay as recompense for being a helping hand. Receptionists were normally burly enough and old enough, with a very sharp tongue to deal with any problems. It was only then it dawned on me that, with Ebony in her corner, the young, petite receptionist had all the help she needed.

Our madam was leaning on the frame of the saloon door and was relating a tale she had heard just recently about a dreadful beating some poor escort had received at the hands of a pimp, much to the shock of a new girl in the corner, especially as the girls then started to speculate about other nasty things they had heard of. I looked up at our boss lady, who was looking rather too pleased with herself at all the horror stories being bandied about, and I couldn't help wondering what had tickled her fancy. The other girls were all too deep in their gossip by then to notice, all talking about how dangerous it was to work as an unprotected escort and how nice and safe we were working here. Looking at the grin on the madam's face, I heard Sonya the Slovakian's voice in my head, saying the other day that of course the boss would bring up things like this to keep us working for her. My previous Mrs Boss had said very similar things about the dangers of working for places in London, that they were all run by pimps who would beat their girls, and that street girls got raped and robbed. She never had much of a good word for strippers either. The brothel had made out that working for a sauna in London was dire, a last resort, and the sauna here in London was doing the same, but giving the impression that it was even worse to work for a brothel, not just in the bad ones in London (which I had a feeling was actually true) but all over England. I was beginning to think that Sonya might be right. Hell, if I was a boss I might stir up the same sort of thing if it meant keeping my girls working for me. It may be sneaky but it was effective.

The stories continued even after the madam had left, but they did start to subside as the afternoon wore on. As there was a lack of seats in the lounge with so many girls on shift, I sat in the reception and chatted to Emma, who wasn't quite her normal bubbly self. While I was talking to her the thought started to niggle at me that she was more one of us than a receptionist. From what I could work out from having talked to her before, she had worked in a sauna some time back but was now happy enough working the desk, even if the money wasn't as good as she used to get. After a while, I left to find Zora, who was sitting in the sauna drying the stockings she had just washed, now that the madam had left.

'OK, I give up.' I kicked off my heels as I opened the smoked-glass door to the four-person sauna. I had been there the day before when the loud drunk had stumbled in, plonked himself on Emma's desk and demanded she suck his cock for a fiver – or something of the sort. I was downstairs when it all kicked off – it had been a slow night and I was watching the clock, getting ready to leave – so I hadn't seen how Emma handled the situation. I heard the shouting in reception from the basement and bounded up the stairs in bare feet, just in time to catch Ebony launching the drunk out of the door with a forceful push. While it was still going on, Emma could have called the police, but they wouldn't have been there in time. The drunk had lost it and was starting to lash out and spit, and when she asked him to leave he had lain on her desk and hung on. That was the situation Ebony had found when she went to help get him out and in the process rescue Emma.

Zora looked up, hanging her last stocking over a towel rail in the wooden box, as I came in and the dry heat hit me. She raised her eyebrows, and I went on. 'You've been here the longest, right? What's the score with Emma? Come on, spill: why is she on the desk?'

Zora pursed her lips and laid back against a towel. I pulled one from the small stack between us and put it down so I wouldn't have to sit on the wooden slats.

'Why? What have you heard, Shell?' Zora stretched her legs out on the bench and leaned towards me. She sounded suspicious.

I shrugged. 'Nothing really. It's just that, between you and me, I don't get it. Why did the boss lady hire her?'

Zora leaned back. 'Ahh, that's between you and me.' She looked over at the glass door and I shuffled closer. Zora was always a mine of information. 'Emma used to work for the madam's son in his Camden sauna last year. She did really well, was one of their top girls. They really liked her.' She looked over through the door again.

'I just bet they did,' I muttered. I could imagine how well a bubbly, pretty blonde like Emma would do in one of the biggest, most popular, cheap saunas in the area. She would probably have been so busy there was no need for her to wear her knickers. Well-proportioned, she was the typical wet wank dream.

'There was an incident with one of the clients. It was a busy night and she was in one of the back rooms which they hardly ever used. The fucking room-security buzzer didn't work; she dived for it and rang it but no one came to help her. The boss had popped out for beer and left another girl in charge, and the dopey girl didn't know that Emma was on shift. The bloke raped Emma, un-protected, at knife point for over an hour, and tied her to the table and gagged her so he could leave without any fuss. The boss came back and found her a couple of hours after that. They never caught the guy and Emma didn't want to report it to the coppers. If she had the son would have had hell to pay, all the heat from the police nosing in. And, of course, his dad's in the slammer, owns the property. They really don't need the coppers sniffing around there.' I shifted in the heat as I started to sweat and fanned myself with a magazine that had been left. I guessed they had made Emma a receptionist here out of gratitude as, from what Zora had said, I doubt Emma would want to be in a room alone with any man any time soon. I was surprised she still had the bottle to work in a sauna at all.

'Guess that's why Emma didn't deal very well with the drunk last night. She's still a bit shaky today.'

Zora nodded. 'Yeah, Shell. She'll be OK though, she's a tough little cookie. Pity she didn't have a safety buddy like I have with Ebony, she could have done with one.' I nodded back. A lot of things were beginning to make sense.

I knew Ebony and Zora came into work together. I had bumped into them as Zora's hubby was dropping them both off that morning. I hadn't realized up to then that neither worked without the other – it just hadn't dawned on me – but thinking back on it, I had never seen one here when the other wasn't. I didn't like to press Zora any further, as I had only found out that morning that she had a husband who not only knew and had no problem with where she worked and what she did but dropped her off at work too, by the look of it. Apparently, it was fine; they swang. I must have looked even more confused than usual. I had the image of some kind of fetish swing contraption in my head and was trying to work out why that would mean that Zora's hubby, a smiling, well-built Aussie, didn't mind his missus shagging men for money. Ebony had shaken her head at my mystified 'Swings?' question and said, 'They're swingers, silly.' Zora had been there and coughed a full-bellied laugh while Ebony chortled.

I left Zora in the sauna as Ebony came in to join her and went off to make a cup of tea, popping my nose round the corner to ask if Emma wanted one, too, rattling my Hobnobs at her. 'Nob?' was out of my mouth before I had a chance to think about it. Luckily, she giggled and said, 'Yes, please.'

*

So now I was settled, earning fairly well, my mother had come up to visit for the weekend and she was very happy that I was happy, and in a nice part of London, so she would leave me well alone, much to my relief. I was still keeping to my night-work story to explain the odd hours I was sleeping and why I looked so pale. After she had left I was on the rota at the sauna nearly every day but, despite all the clients I was seeing, I did notice I was getting a bit hornier than usual. OK, so the men who had come in the past week had all been average massage screws, a few blow-job guys thrown in for good measure; none of them had pressed any buttons for me and, with my vibrator running out of batteries the night before and the ones in the TV remote in my lounge the wrong type to help that morning, I was wound tighter than a spring and had to stop myself driving twice around a round-about on my way into work to perve on a really well-built policeman.

That was probably one of the reasons I took a shine to one of my clients that evening. It was unusual for me to do that. I always liked to keep work separate from free sex. I had seen what happened countless times when girls started to date their regular clients. It always got messy and the girls would get into a state and it would disrupt their earning potential. Anyhow, that evening, a short black bodybuilder, Mr Body, had been dragged in by his mate, whose birthday it was. The so-called mate was white, six foot four, if not taller, with blue eyes and spiky blond hair. He was also drunk or stoned – I couldn't tell which – and looked a bit of a handful. I instantly preferred the quieter, sober black guy. I had had bad shags all that day and I was not really in the mood to deal with another: no matter how much he looked like a Greek god, because he was tipsy I was betting he would have one hell of a yo-yo cock. Unfortunately, the birthday boy was leering at me. Damn, and with only me and the small Chinese girl, who, appropriately, named herself Suk-suk, one of us was bound to get him and, as it was his birthday, or so he said, I was just guessing he would get to pick first. Double damn, especially as Suk-suk was going all giggly over the blond.

We made our introductions and retreated to the lounge benches for them to make up their minds. The silly girl could have him. I got called through first, dragging my feet as I heard the black guy loudly hiss at the birthday boy as he rose from the leather couch they had both sunk into that he didn't want to see some 'Chink'. He looked me up and down with a dark glint in his eye like he had only just really seen me. At my bemused look he strode over and gestured me to show him the way.

Mumbling this and that, we wound ourselves up the slim, tight spiral staircase to find a room on the upper floor. I didn't think the tipsy birthday boy could manage the stairs and so Suk-suk could have the bigger ground-floor room. She would need it, and it was closer if she needed Emma's help. I didn't think I would need any. Following up behind Mr Body on the stairs, I was very nearly drooling, looking at the way his tight trousers hugged his bum. Very nice.

I showed him to a room and said I would leave him to have a shower, as I did all the men. I looked him over as he started to unbutton his shirt. I turned to leave – it didn't mean I couldn't pop back more quickly than normal and catch him in the shower though. He tried to stop me, saying he had just had a shower. I was in no mood for silly games and said, 'Please, out of consideration for my health,' turning to leave before he could get a word in, saying I needed to get more towels. With him being so broad I didn't think one towel was going to be enough to dry him. 'When you're done, just pop up on the bench face down for the massage and I'll be back in to rub you down,' I rambled on, retreating out of the door and shutting it on my last word. I had worked out early on that if I didn't give the clients the chance to speak, then they wouldn't have the opportunity to say no to pretty much anything I asked. It's easier to handle a near-naked man when you're still fully dressed. This one seemed OK, but he was wound tight and a bit stressed, so if I took charge now, he wouldn't be able to give me any bullshit.

I waited outside until I heard the shower running and then left him to it. If a guy was going to be a hassle even when you asked him to take a shower, or refused outright, you knew he was going to be trouble the whole way through. But making a guy get naked while you still had your clothes on put you automatically in control and made him more vulnerable and less likely to try it on and mess you around. To be honest, most guys were fairly clean, and asking them to shower didn't necessarily mean they would wash properly in any case. And I would always have a shower afterwards anyhow, so it didn't really matter much. Asking Mr Body to shower was more about control and, considering his size, I really needed to be more than in control. I like a man to be where I want him, in the palm of my hand, and when they're naked it's so much easier.

I had a feeling he was very nervous. I guessed it hadn't been his idea to come in and play. His friend had already given Emma £200, and she had told us it was to be split between Suk-suk and I before we went in to introduce ourselves to them. By the time I had left my guy in the shower and nipped down the stairs to grab two towels, Suk-suk was leading the blond guy into the downstairs room and looking very pleased with herself. I checked in with Emma and told her to keep hold of my money, minus the room cut, until after I was done, just so I didn't have to worry about it. I rushed back up the stairs to try and catch my guy dripping wet in the shower. The artist in me had already seen that he worked out a lot; he had a very impressive physique. I walked back in without even knocking to see a damp, glistening back stretched out, a towel around the hips.

I had been right, but he was more than just fit, he had muscles on his muscles. No wonder he had looked as if he was tense. I chatted away with him and put all my attention into unknotting the tension in his large back, undoing my uniform as I went. No trouble, no hassle, and with his dry sense of humour, which I could appreciate, we were getting on like a house on fire before I even had him turned over. I stood back and unpeeled very slowly, tossing him my bra as he sat up and unclipping the side fastenings of my knickers as I walked back to him. Upright now, his legs were dangling over the massage table and there was a big grin on his face. I approached and stroked his cock with my right hand, the one I normally use to touch men with.

Drawing my fingers down his length, I looked him in the eye as I tightened my grip. I hadn't expected him to be as huge there as the rest of him was; I had done enough research on the human body to know that bodybuilders' bulk tended to overshadow things in that department. Mr Body wasn't small, but he wasn't a python either. He had promising girth but a fairly average-length cock. I was more than happy with him though and, considering how horny I was feeling, it suited me not having to do yet another boring grey accountant type in a suit. Stroking his cock as he flicked my nipples, I pushed him further back from the edge with a hand on his large chest as I reached for the rubber in my stocking top and sucked it on him. He grunted and leaned back, braced on his elbows, as I sucked him and ran my fingers over his cleanly shaven balls, making him harder.

I kicked off my shoes, withdrawing to climb up on to the seat next to the table. Without the chair it was way too high to get up there. I crawled across the end to where he was propped and knelt up, ready to swing my leg over his lap and slide down his hard length, but just as I was about to do so, he caught my pussy between his fingers and flicked my clit. Before I realized why, I had gasped, and he moved his lips on to the breast closest to him with a wicked grin. His fingers lightly probed, sliding in my lubed-up lips, and fondled as he worked on, licking my nipple. I shuddered at the progress his naughty fingers were making and let him slide one digit up, grasping it with my internal muscles just to let him know how tight I was going to make it for him.

At that, he jerked his head up. For some reason it had startled him. The light grin on his face had all but gone now, replaced with a dark look I could only guess the meaning of. I wriggled on his finger, snug inside, then he withdrew and I took advantage quickly and sat over his lap, hovering over his firm cock with my knees pushed apart, either side of his steel-hard thighs. He gripped my buttocks as I slithered down, tilting my hips to accommodate him easily, until I was in place, ready to tighten up and slide down him. That was all it took for him to buck and lift me into slow thrusts, with his arms under me pulling me in tightly every time.

I let go of the edge, literally as well as physically, which wasn't the best thing to do a couple of feet off the floor on a now wobbly bench, as I nearly toppled off. For such a bulky guy, he managed to swing me under him and carry on his pounding as I wrapped not only my legs around him but my cunt too. He felt so smooth all over and, in the darkened room, with him blocking out the light, my mind was all over the place as I came and came hard. Losing control was not something that was a good idea while at work, but from the feel of it he was losing it too, which made me feel a lot better.

He was rolling around and I was on top. How we managed it without falling off must have been down to his strength as, with my legs wound securely around him, he managed to lift me with him, and around him with one arm, so that as he rolled over I slid my legs from under him and secured them at his sides, squatting over him, cowgirl-style. Sitting on top, my best position to make a man come, I rode him, rocking back and forth and trying to make it last but realizing that time was running out. I made a faster stroke, and he looked like he had been shot when I felt him come. I stretched and slowly wriggled, pulsing my pussy around his hot cock as he gulped deep breaths to steady himself as he came back down. His heart was pounding still. I could feel it in his chest as I lay my hands over the tight, smooth surface. I had needed that, and it took me a few seconds before I could get my own breath back to ease off him and find the tissues.

I hadn't been that breathless in quite some time. I had definitely needed the work-out, I told him, as I tidied up and ran the shower for him. He patted my bottom, and I would have joined him in there but didn't trust my or his hands not to wander and, as time was very nearly up, I was aware that his friend was probably downstairs waiting for him. I quickly got dressed and rubbed him down when he got out of the shower – any excuse to rub a naked man down, I know – but this naked man felt really nice under my fingers. We chatted and flirted as he dressed. He was definitely keen, and said that he worked security on the door of a club and that if any of the girls and I wanted to go clubbing to let him know and he would get us in for free. Nice of him, but I doubted I wanted to let any of the other girls know I might be copping off with a punter, not that he was really a punter.

He said he wouldn't be back, as it was only his mate who liked to come to saunas. I knew for certain he hadn't come in voluntarily. The birthday boy was on 'too many of the wrong steroids,' or so Mr Body said, and having seen the six-foot-plus bulging blond earlier, with his bugged-out eyes, I could fully believe it. His mate had been going on and on all week about coming here, getting on his nerves, so he had finally agreed to a boys' night out. I was grinning from ear to ear as he smirked, saying he was glad he had come – very glad. I'd had a really bad week and he, with his magic fingers, had really cheered me up and, as a bonus, all I'd had to do was sit on his dick – and he had done most of the work! There had been no stopping the man, he was like a jack hammer. I was very impressed. I couldn't help wondering: he had already made me come – with a proper bed and more time, imagine what an orgasm he would give me.

He couldn't give me his personal number, as we didn't have a pen and I couldn't go down looking for one, as time had run out and it would have looked very suss. He gave me one of the cards of the nightclub he worked for and told me to ask for Tony on the front door; that was him. They would call him to the phone and we could swap numbers, if I was up for it? After that performance I didn't want to sound too eager, so I nodded maybe and slid the card into my stocking top as we left the room to find his friend. With me looking around for a better place, I didn't think keeping his number would do any harm as long as I rang it after I stopped working there.

I thought he was single – after all, he didn't mention a wife or wear a ring – but you never really know. He looked as if he would be more than happy if I needed to call him up when I was horny, and it wasn't like he had actually given me any money: his friend had; he hadn't actually placed money in my hand like the others did. In my mind, it was as if he hadn't actually paid me, as if he wasn't really a punter. Mmmm, my own personal sex toy, batteries not included. Hell – they weren't even needed!

7. *Girlfriend Experience*

Layla came to stay during her Christmas break from university. She was still living down south with Sanita and a few others in a big five-bedroom student house. Sanita had gone back to stay with her family up north till uni started again, which we found a bit strange, as she normally avoided them like the plague. She had left the brothel and was no longer hooking, Layla told me with a shrug. It hadn't been long, but it was nice to see Layla again and have her stay and keep me company for a while. The sofa was big enough to sleep on and she was very content to camp in my lounge and mooch around Muswell Hill for a few weeks. She was thinking of going back down south to continue working at the brothel but implied that it was going downhill fast and got me to spill the facts, as far as I knew them, about saunas, or 'fancy brothels', as she called them, here in London. After a chat about my chance meeting with Sonya, the escort I had met, and having shown Layla the card I had been given, her eyes lit up. She said we should at least give it a go but that it would be a good idea maybe to take a look at a few – after all, a girl who had to go and check out work in a sauna as she wasn't earning enough wasn't much of a recommendation for her agency. Added to that, we were very cautious, given Layla's past bad experience, and all the negative things I had heard about escorting.

Looking through the central London papers, we found a couple of likely agencies, and Layla called a few to enquire. One slammed the phone down on her when all she had said was hello. Two didn't pick up. One was really rude and said, no, they didn't need any more girls and then put the phone down. Two, including the one that Sonya had recommended, gave us details and dates for an interview. After a few calls Layla was really eager to go and check them out.

Three days later, at 2.50 p.m., Layla and I were sitting in my car looking over at the office-like front of the building across the road.

We had dressed in suits, with smart shoes, just as if we were going to an office interview. We hadn't been sure what to expect, and that's what the raspy lady on the phone had said to wear.

Layla, with me in tow, pressed the doorbell, which was underneath a little brass plaque on which was written 'International Ltd', at 3 p.m. precisely. It buzzed open abruptly to reveal a bespectacled, bronzed Mediterranean lady in her late forties with a bouffant hairstyle dyed jet-black, and dressed all in black, seated at the desk on our immediate left. I walked in, Layla hanging back.

'Hello. We called yesterday?' I said as I reached over the desk to shake her outstretched hand.

'Yes.' She nodded, and a strong smell of whisky wafted over to us.

'Take a seat.' She gestured to the low Chesterfield couch against the wall on the right behind me. Layla nodded as she closed the door behind her, and we both went to sit on the sofa.

'Can you start this week, either of you?' mumbled the woman behind the desk, rummaging in her desk. We nodded, a bit bemused, because we hadn't even started talking yet.

'Right. You will both have to fill out a form so I can remember who you are, and you will have to sign a contract on the day you start. It's just in case the law gets nosey, it doesn't mean anything really.

'Have you escorted before?' she asked, handing two forms and a pen over the desk to Layla.

'Sort of – we worked in saunas,' said Layla, taking the forms out of the dark-tanned, wrinkly hands festooned with gold rings.

Ms Lush slowly sank back into her chair. 'So, where did you hear of us?'

I took a form from Layla and looked up. 'A girl from one of the saunas I worked at in south London mentioned she had worked here.'

'Who?' Ms Lush leaned closer to us, a puckered, frowning look on her face.

'She was calling herself Sonya?' I raised my eyebrows, hoping Sonya hadn't fallen out of favour.

'Ahh, yessss.' She smiled and put her hand out. 'Give the forms here; I'll fill them out. I only have one pen and we don't have all day – the rest of the girls will be in soon.' Her blood-red talons took back the forms and the pen. 'What are your working names? Real names will just confuse me.' She gestured at Layla, her pen now reinstated in her clutch.

'Layla.'

Ms Lush nodded slowly. 'OK. We had a Layla, but she's left. She was like you – busty, too, and popular – so we can send you out as her if we're asked. They won't know the difference.' Layla just gave me one of her looks as Ms Lush bent over the form she was filling in.

Our interviewer then pointed at me, the pen still clasped in her hand.

'Scarlet?' I shrugged.

She nodded. 'That's OK. We haven't had one of them yet. Goes with the hair, but we might have to change it.' She noted something on the other form.

'Er, my name will have to change?' I was baffled.

Out of the corner of my eye, I could see that Layla was also looking baffled.

'No' – Ms Lush looked me in the eye – 'the hair, your hair. If you were blonde you would do better. Ginger is offputting, guys don't ask for ginger.' With that she swiftly moved on to the next question. I nodded, still a bit confused as to whether I was Scarlet or now called Ginger.

'Now, do you do O level?'

'Errr, well, I have a few GCSEs and a – ' I was quickly interrupted by a huffing noise.

'Nooo. Guys don't really care about your education, not really. What I mean is, do you do oral? It's called O levels, you know, it's code ... so I don't have to say anything about our services down the line.' Again, she leaned closer to us over the desk, and breathed in a whisper, 'You never know who's listening!' She stared at us with raised eyebrows and straightened up. 'Well, do you?'

'Oral on the client, yes,' Layla piped up. I looked at Layla, and the two of us nodded away, both thinking by this point that the woman was nutty as a fruitcake. What was with everything being in code? I thought we working girls were the paranoid ones!

'What about A levels?' Ms Lush peered over her big glasses at us. 'Anal,' she said bluntly.

We must have both looked horrified, because she mumbled, 'I'll take that as a no then. Girlfriend experience?' She looked up at us questioningly.

I looked at Layla who said, 'Uhh, duos?' She looked from me to Ms Lush as she said it, confused, the same as I was.

Ms Lush shook her head, looked back down at her form and huffed, 'Do you kiss?'

She looked up to see two puzzled-looking girls shaking their heads and sinking into the leather couch. 'No?' She huffed again, reached for a cigarette packet on the desk and tapped one out. 'That's OK, they don't really ask for that, if they want that they can get it from the wife ...' She muttered away as she lit the fag now hanging from her lips. 'So that's pornstar experience out then ...'

I mouthed, 'Pornstar experience?' and looked questioningly at Layla. She shrugged and shook her head. We decided it was better not to ask.

'OK. Contact numbers?' The lush looked up, scattering ash from her fag into her lap as she did so.

With that we gave her our mobile-phone numbers and asked about hours of work. She mentioned more than once that the agency was sit-in only and no in-call business; either our clients would come in to pick us and take us out to their hotel or back to their home, paying the fee before they left and us collecting our payment upfront when we got to wherever it was we were taken, or she would send one of us out from a phone description and we would have to take all the fees upfront and return her cut for the agency, before going home, if it was late.

She showed us around the reception room and downstairs to the ladies' lounge, which was not as smart as upstairs but was still nice and comfy and led through into the kitchen as well as having two toilets off it and a further dressing room in the back.

She waved us off, asking us to call in soon saying when we wanted to start and, with that, she shut the door after us as the phone began to ring on her desk.

While I was driving us back to my flat, Layla wound down the window to smoke and I said, 'I'm not sure I like her.'

'You only don't like her because she wants you to change your hair. She's all for the money, that one, but at least you know where you stand.' She took another drag and blew out the window.

'I don't know. It sounds more like working for MI5, with all that code bollocks, than being a whore.' I tapped the steering wheel, wondering if the police really were listening in to the phone calls.

'You want us to go to the other agency we found tomorrow for their interview and check them out too? Maybe they're different.'

I stopped tapping. Perhaps she was right. 'Well, it can't do any harm to go and see.'

Mr Fingers

Thursday: interview
Clients × *1* = *Mr Fingers*
1 × *2 hours* = *£250*
– agency fee £70
Total = £180

Even after finding a place to park and feeding the meter, which took all my change, in a Kensington sidestreet, we arrived half an hour early for our interview the next day. We sat in a pub across the road and watched the door to the address we had been given. A smart older lady in a grey suit and carrying a pink handbag unlocked the door, which had a big swinging plaque jutting out above like a pub sign stating it was an escort agency and giving its phone number below. It was quite high up and not too clear, so I hadn't noticed it was there until we had sat down and were actually looking from across the street. The door was sandwiched between a shoe shop and a pub, and moments after it shut, a light went on above the shoe shop. The grey-clad figure who had just entered appeared briefly at the window and pulled down office blinds, which obscured our view.

'OK, honey, it looks like that's her,' Layla said, draining her fizzy drink very fast. 'Why don't they sell coffee in here? God, I need a coffee.' I checked my cheap little gold-plated work watch as I listened to her ramble. 'Right, nearly time. Better get moving then, better early than late, I suppose.'

We were buzzed in by the lady in grey and sat opposite her in her very grey and dark-green carpeted reception room. It looked like an office and had a smaller, office-like booth on the left side of the wall which contained two grey office chairs. You could just make them out through the opaque glass divide. The room was smart and clean but not as cosy as the other escort-agency office we had been in the day before. This one was slightly sterile-looking. There was also a door behind us, next to the one we had come in through, which I presumed was the girls' lounge.

'Hello, ladies. Five on the dot. I like punctuality in my ladies,' smiled the frail Ms Grey from over the desk. She might have looked small and fragile, but her eyes were like cut glass. Unlike the slightly sozzled Ms Lush the day before, this lady, I felt, saw everything and was as sharp as a tack.

Layla and I smiled back at her.

'So, I take it you have both worked before?' She didn't ask if we had been escorts, so there was no need to lie, and I had a feeling she had said on the phone to Layla that they only took on ladies who *had* worked before. I felt that no wouldn't have been the answer she was expecting to hear and we had both agreed beforehand to lie and be vague if she did ask.

Layla fidgeted and I said, yes, we had worked before, and Layla nodded.

'Right then. If you could fill out these forms, we'll get started. I have a few questions too.' She handed us each a printed list of questions on a sheet of paper mounted on a clipboard with a pen attached at the top.

Layla pulled her chair near to the desk and balanced the clipboard on the edge to fill it out. I saw Ms Grey squint at her as she did so, so I played safe and balanced mine on my knee. It had simple questions such as hair and eye colour, height, age, contact details, real name and work name – none of the personal questions in code we had been asked before. I handed my clipboard over to Ms Grey and Layla followed suit.

Ms Grey looked at them and then at me. 'Sorry – Scarlet? We already have a lady called that. How would you feel about being Suzy? We haven't had one of those.' And she put a line through my name and started to write over the top.

I just shrugged. 'How about Sarah?' I queried. I wasn't going to mention I had been a Shelly. I didn't want to be a Shelly again.

She looked up from her clipboard. 'No. We had one of those a few months back,' she said, and tapped her pen on the desk.

'Always thought you looked more like a Susan than a Sarah to me.' Layla shook her head as she said it.

'Susan?' I queried again.

'That will do, very girl-next-door.' Ms Grey scribbled it down and mumbled away. 'That will go down very well, very well, a Susan I can sell . . .'

As she wrote it down, without even looking at me, I doubted I had any choice now. She looked up and smiled at me. 'You know, if your hair was a bit lighter, you might do better. I'm always asked for blondes. I have quite a few clients looking for a lady like you – if you were a few years younger? You know, you could get away with it.' With that, she drew a line through my '22' and wrote '19'. 'You could get away with eighteen, but we will put you down at nineteen, since you have worked before. How's that, my dear?'

Layla squirmed again in her seat, and I gave her a poisonous look. What was wrong with her? I should be the one who was squirming: I was the one the old bag was calling 'my dear'.

I said that was fine. Then she looked over Layla's form and nodded.

'OK, ladies, it all looks fine. Now, do you do O levels?' She pulled out two index cards from a box on her desk, penned in our new names at the top of each and looked up.

'Yes,' said Layla and I in unison. Layla looked at me all smug, with her told-you-so look, and Ms Grey noted it and asked about A levels. That was a definite no from both of us.

She didn't ask if we kissed, but she did ask if either of us did any hardcore fetish things.

When Layla said yes, that she would piss on men and that watersports were fine by her, Ms Grey wrinkled her nose, scribbled away and then got up to show us the back room where the girls waited, stating they were a sit-in agency only and had no facilities for gents to 'stay', as it were.

The back room was a big black dark hole with a few shabby sofas and side tables. There was also a small, dirty kitchen which had leftover food on the counter and a sinkful of plates and, next to it, a poky little toilet. You had to wash your hands at the sink in the kitchen.

What a contrast to the smart, bright office out front.

The phone rang as she walked us back through from our quick tour and she gestured us to our seats as she answered it, looking at the call number displayed.

Layla and I looked at each other. She fidgeted again in her seat and I glared at her.

'Yes, I think I have the perfect girl for you – new, nineteen, green eyes, five foot five. Jonathan, you'll love her. She's a darling, just your type ... can I call you back in a min? OK, speak soon.' Ms Grey put the phone down with a click and gave me a smile, the biggest one she had given me yet.

'Can you do a booking at 7 p.m.? He's really nice – one of my regular gents, has a house round the corner, so not too far away ... I can get him to come in and meet you, see if you like him? It would only be two hours.'

I was already dressed and had brought my bag full of supplies with me, in case I needed anything, so I thought, why not give it a go and meet him? 'Sure, why not?' I said. I looked at Layla, who gazed at me nonplussed.

'Good, good. You can sign the contract later if you want to come back and work here permanently. Layla can sit in here and wait for you if you want. Neither of you have to start today ... if you want to think about it?' Layla just looked at Ms Grey and then at me.

'That's OK. I have something to do tonight anyhow.' Layla smiled back at Ms Grey and then, looking at me, said, 'Call me when you're done. I'll feed the meter.' I nodded, a hundred things racing through my head at once.

Ms Grey started dialling call-back to the gent I was going to meet. I asked if it was all right if Layla and I left for a while, I'd come back in an hour, I needed to get something from the shops. She nodded and waved us off as she started chatting to the man on the other end of the line, singing my praises.

I poked Layla in the arm as we left and walked back to the car. 'What was with you in there? I know we ran out of coffee this morning, but you're not normally this grumpy or fidgety. Do you have ants in your pants or something?'

'I don't know – they're your damn knickers, the new pair you lent me this morning. I really need to get some laundry done, these damn things are too small.' She gabbled away, pulling at her skirt. 'You and your bloomin' dental-floss pants.'

Yep, someone needed a coffee all right. We emptied all her coin change into the parking meter to top it up and I dragged her to the nearest café for her fix.

'So what do you have to do tonight that's so damn important?' I grilled her as she sipped her coffee.

'Watch after you, you silly tart. I'm going to stand outside and, when you leave, trail you to find out where you end up. Then I can wait until you come out, to make sure you're safe.' She winked.

'You ... are a genie's arse.' I squeezed her arm. Now why hadn't I thought of that? 'What are you going to do for two hours waiting around? You'll be bored stiff.'

'W. H. Smith,' she said, slurping her coffee.

'W. H. Smith what?' I was puzzled. There was one on the corner that sold all sorts, but as we didn't know where

I was going to end up yet, I thought it a bit of a reach to use it as a stake-out point. 'It'll be closing soon.' I raised my eyes at her.

She nodded. 'I'm going to get a book or a magazine, then I'll have something to do while waiting for you. You can give me your car keys and I can sit in there if it gets too cold.' She finished her coffee and waved at the waiter for a second.

'Ahhh. We'd better get a couple of pocket A–Zs from there, too. At this rate, we'll need to know where we're going and where we're going to end up.' It was 5.45 p.m. and I was already a bag of nerves and not thinking too straight. At least someone was thinking about my safety.

After much rummaging through the shelves at W. H. Smith's to find Layla some interesting historical sex-industry-type books and a fashion mag, along with two pocket A–Zs that fit in our handbags, I went back to the agency office and was buzzed in. I took off my coat and sat waiting in the dark lounge with a few other girls who had now arrived.

One of the girls, Samantha, said hi and started to chat and be friendly, while the others sat and read or watched the television. The client I was going to see soon, so Samantha assured me, was a sweetheart, a very nice guy. She wished he saw girls more than just once, as she would have liked to have seen him again; she'd only seen him the once. They called him Mr Fingers, because he was a pianist. The agency sent the new, younger girls to him in order to get feedback, whispered Samantha to me, and then she bounded off to find her phone, which was ringing and had been recharging on a shelf somewhere in the messy kitchenette. Just before 7 p.m. I got a text from Layla, who was sitting in my car down the road: 'I think he's just about to arrive.' I read it as the doorbell sounded. All the girls started to get up until Samantha poked her head around the door and told everyone to sit back down, it was Mr Fingers for the new girl. I smiled, straightened myself up and went to see who this Mr Fingers was. I had had a Mr Magic Fingers before, but I had called him that for different reasons. I wondered if this one would be the same.

He was tall, very tall, but ordinary looking. I had to look up at him as I approached, as at only five foot six in my new heels, he must have been a good foot taller than me, but he looked friendly and smiled and said hello and bent to kiss my cheek. He was in a dark-blue suit and looked very smart even without a tie. I felt a bit uncomfortable in my tight cheap suit as all the other girls had nice dresses on – well, some did. Samantha's was all stretchy and shiny and made of a fabric that clung to every curve and rode up so you could see her stocking tops when she sat down. It looked a bit cheap on her and, as she wasn't the skinniest of girls, didn't flatter her at all.

We didn't chat much, just went through the motions: where I was from (I lied); so I was new? (I sort of lied again – well, I was new to being an escort, so that wasn't really a lie); how old was I? (I lied just like Ms Grey was doing now when she picked up the phone and told someone on the other end of the line that, yes, she had a tall, smartly dressed curvy blonde, called Samantha.)

Mr Fingers was at my side as I half-listened in to the

phone conversation. 'So, do you want to come with me?'

I said I would love to, looking over to Ms Grey, who just gestured that I should go. With that I dashed back into the lounge to grab my coat and bag. I don't know where my nerves had gone but I felt at ease in his company; he seemed OK, no bad vibes. He held the door open for me and led me down the street, chatting about the area and this and that. His house was only at the bottom of the street, and I saw Layla on the other side of the road pop into the same café we had been in earlier and watch me enter his home.

The building was narrow and the whole ground floor was one big, long wood-floored room, with the kitchen running along the right wall, a sofa in one corner and a sleek TV. Apart from that there was no furniture other than a gleaming black grand piano at the far end and a black four-legged stool. Wow! Now I was in mild shock – the place was like something out of one of those architectural books I had on my shelf at home. From the look of it, it had one bedroom on the mezzanine on the upper floor, reached by a winding glass staircase at the end of the room which went up the left-hand wall. I must have taken off my coat and handed it to him, and he got me a glass of water after asking what I wanted to drink. But, for the life of me, I wasn't paying much attention. The feel of the glass as he handed it to me brought me back to earth. 'Er, Susan?' He held out an envelope and I just looked at it.

'You should really ask for the fee upfront,' he said, and laid the envelope in my hand.

'Oh, yes, sorry,' I said, as I stuffed it in my bag.

He chuckled. 'I can tell you're new – you didn't even count it. Come here.' And with that he took away my glass and kissed me, and I ran my hand up his leg until I found a prominent bulge. And that was it. My jacket disappeared and my skirt was around my ankles in no time flat in the middle of the empty lounge. There was classical music coming from somewhere but I couldn't make it out and wasn't really interested. He bent down, scooped me up and strode to the piano, sitting me on the top facing him as he sat on the stool and peeled my knickers off down my legs, leaving my hold-ups on. Then he shrugged his jacket off, letting it fall to the floor. I had managed to undo most of my buttons by then, and my shirt fell open as he watched and he started to undo his too, saying, 'Take it off, and the bra. I want to watch you play with yourself.'

I undressed, watching him, and let my hand travel down my body. With my other hand supporting me, I obliged him, sticking two fingers up myself and panting a little. He unzipped his trousers in no time flat, still watching the progress of my fingers, which by now were wet from all the lube I had used, just in case. I hadn't known quite what to expect. He groaned at the squelching noises my pussy was making and, his trousers still round his ankles, he knelt heavily down on the stool and pushed away my fingers with his tongue and a long, exploring finger of his own. At that point I buckled and nearly slid off the piano and right on his face, in response to which he cupped his hands under my bum and lifted me back up until I was lying down on the polished black surface with my legs dangling down.

I felt dizzy and, after a few minutes of his mouth and fingers exploring, I really needed a good fucking. And really soon. I wriggled down until I was on his lap and kissed him. He was the one panting for breath now. I continued on my way down with rubber in hand from my stocking hold-up top and sucked it on to a springing, more than ready cock. It wasn't anything special, just a normal cock, but his intake of breath told me to take it easy, which for me, a thirty-minute girl, was not what I usually did. OK, slowly, I reminded myself; don't make him pop too soon. I eased down more slowly as he put his hand on the top of my head and shoved himself down my throat further, until I nearly gagged. Luckily, it didn't last until I turned blue, and he was soon trying to stand up and was pulling me up with him. He spun me around and bent me over the piano, running his hands down my legs and lifting me to enter. That was it: less than five minutes of frantic fucking in that position while holding my waist in place and he was spent. He sat down on the piano stool, all red and out of breath, puffing, sorry he couldn't last any longer, he had just needed me there and then on the piano. I stood up and walked over to get our discarded drinks, my knees wobbling slightly, and brought them back. He had recovered some of his breath. 'Sorry. I do make it to the bedroom, as a rule. God, you're tight. Sorry, I just lost it. Are you OK? I didn't bruise you on the hard edge ...' He gasped, looking worried and stroking the piano top.

'No, I'm fine. Don't worry.' I giggled and sat on his lap, handing him his drink.

'I'm exhausted. We'd better get cleaned up and I can

walk you back,' he whispered in my ear. I looked over his shoulder and raised my arm to look at my watch; it wasn't that late.

'You want me to go? I have quite a lot of time left ... I can stay a bit longer. Ms Grey said as long as I was back in two hours ...' I picked up my knickers, which were at my feet, and hung them off my finger.

He laughed. 'No, that's OK. Now we're done you can go, that's the way it works. Even if it has been only thirty-five minutes. We'd better get you back, pretty one.'

We chatted for a bit about his house, as I was in no rush and he was in no real hurry to throw me out. It was nothing like a sauna or a brothel, where you had to run around and had a time restriction on what you could do. I resolved that I should try and make it last longer with the next one. I didn't want them complaining they didn't get value for money. If I could make a client come and be finished in thirty minutes, then surely I could work out how to make them last an hour or two.

We finished our drinks and he led me upstairs to the marble, monochrome bathroom, then he left me to clean myself up and have a shower and went off to find a bathrobe for himself.

Shortly afterwards Mr Fingers locked his door behind him and escorted me across the road and back to the agency. Across the road, I could see Layla in the front window, her head in her book. We were buzzed in. Ms Grey looked neither happy nor pleased until I walked over and gave her the envelope out of my bag. Then I stepped back, turning to my client and thanking him for walking me back. After that I left him to Ms Grey and slid off to the lounge. As I left I could hear Mr Fingers in the background say in a hushed voice, 'She's a little diamond . . .'

I sat down, still in my coat, and looked around. Samantha had gone but a few of the other girls were still there, so I flicked through a magazine until I heard the door go and my client leave. Ms Grey popped her head round the corner and beckoned me to the office. She looked very happy and handed me back the envelope, saying she had taken out her fee and the rest was mine, and if I wanted to work there she would love to have me. I only found out weeks later that she always gave Mr Fingers back the agency's cut, the introduction fee, as she called it, as thanks for making sure that the new girls put out and didn't just take the money for talking, doing nothing or 'social escorting', as it was called. No client really wanted a social-only escort and no agency could see the business sense or point in hiring one, or so the girls said in the lounge.

My new boss gave me a contract to sign then and there when I said that yes, I would like to work for her. The paper I signed listed ten points about my employment and basically said that I was an independent contractor and that the agency wasn't responsible for my taxes, as well as a few other little details. It was all rather long-winded, clarifying that I was being paid for time and companionship, just to cover the legal ass of the agency, I presumed.

The most ironic line was point 5a: The Escort also confirms that she is not nor ever has been a prostitute –

though it was closely followed by point 5b: The Escort also agrees that under no circumstances will she use the agency's facilities to promote prostitution in any way.

Considering that no escort agency would hire a girl unless she said she had worked before, it was a farce. And Ms Grey sent us to hotel rooms and houses all the time while, according to our contract point 8d: The Escort will not date the client privately nor go to a private residence or hotel room. Failure to adhere to this instruction will result in immediate dismissal. It all meant the contract wasn't really much of a contract.

The only useful part was really for Ms Grey, the agency's information about the girl at the bottom. You had to fill out your 'Full-time occupation' (if you didn't, either 'student' was put in, if you were under twenty-one, or 'secretary' if you were over); 'Status', which had 'Married/Single', and the 'Married' was scrubbed out already on the photocopied document, so everyone who signed it had single status whether you were or not. Then there was a big space for Hobbies and shorter ones for Height/Colour of Hair/Colour of Eyes and a space at the bottom that said 'Signed by'.

After signing in my new name and a scribble as a last name and after much prompting to put 'student' and a fake height of two inches taller than I was, Ms Grey put me down for some shifts that week, starting the next day. I asked whether I should bring a dress in case any of the gents wanted to take me out on the town and after answering she said that I could go home. She said to be back at 6 p.m. prompt the next day and added that I couldn't leave after a booking again unless it had started after 9 p.m. I could come back after a late booking if I wanted to try and get another, but they closed at 1 a.m. With that, she waved me out of the door. I stood on the pavement and looked around, a bit bewildered. I had just earned £180 (he had paid me £250 – I had looked in the bathroom when I had gone to clean up – so the agency or, should I say Ms Grey, had taken £70 out), and I had only gone in for an interview! Not bad for a day's work. She let me keep the money this time. She would keep the fee for my first official client as a two-week deposit, in case I didn't stay.

I walked up the road to fetch Layla, thinking that I was going to like this escort lark. Having glanced at Mr Fingers' front door across the street, I knocked on the window of the café opposite for Layla to come out. She looked all dazed and confused. She had been so engrossed in her new book she hadn't seen us leave the house over the road.

'So, how did it go?' she asked as I drove us back to my warm, safe flat, which was forty-five minutes away in north London. I told her all about it and what had happened, and she was happy for me but said she didn't think she liked Ms Grey that much. She would go and work at the other place, the one we had had an interview at the day before, with Ms Lush. It looked quieter and had less business, we agreed, but Ms Lush paid more. The rate started at £270 and the agency cut was the same at £70 but that still left the escort with £200. Layla said she could always give me the extra for petrol money for driving her to and from the other agency and, as Ms Lush's didn't shut till 2 a.m., it would work out perfectly.

We could test out both at the same time and see which was the better one to work for.

The next day I called the sauna and spoke to Emma, as I wasn't working that day. I fibbed and said I had an emergency in my family and that I had to take some time off and would call them when I was back, to see if they would have me on the rota again. I didn't want to burn all my bridges, in case the agency didn't turn out as I planned. At least then I could fall back on working at the sauna. I certainly wasn't going to extend that bridge back to stripping, that was for sure.

8. *Sit-in Agency: A Bad John*

At the agency, if you went out after 9 p.m. and you had been taken out from the office or the client paid by credit card over the phone (so your fee to the agency had been paid), you were free to go home. If he paid in cash and you had been sent to him, you had to stop by the office and drop off the fee before going home. If you came back to sit and see if you could get another booking, it made the receptionist happy – she would at least have some girls to sell in the evening, when it was busier – but on the flip side, if the other girls hadn't been so lucky to be picked that night, you were considered greedy. Most girls, unless they were really desperate for the cash to pay a standing bill or upcoming rent, didn't come back after a 9 p.m. booking, and if they had had a slightly earlier one and had to come back they normally put on a very grumpy face when they said hello to any gent who came through the door in order not to be picked again. I, on the other hand, unless it had been a hard or long booking, would always go back and sit until closing time. I was doing quite a few early shifts and the girls felt sorry for me; no one gave me the cold shoulder because of it. Who's going to give you a hard time and call you a money-grabbing bitch when you're doing the bad shifts and cleaning up their mess in the kitchen and lounge from the night before?

There were a few things that made the agency happy.

Money, obviously: the more clients you could see in a week, the more money you brought in. Repeat custom: I always gave the gent the agency's card and wrote my name on the back, so when they called they knew who to ask for. It's surprising, but after a few months a client could completely forget your name and then give a description that didn't fit you at all. Another tactic was to ask my regular clients to call before they came in just to check I was there. My name popping up on the phone all the time made the agency think I was in demand. In Ms Grey's mind, popular meant good and repeat custom, so being on the receptionist's mind and in her ear all the time was no bad thing, especially if there were no new girls to push on the phone.

New girls are always popular for the first two weeks – not that they are really new and fresh, as most escorts did the rounds and would work at different agencies in order to cream off from new-girl status. There were very few actual new girls. The agency owner would always push the new girls on the phone and talk them up as a good thing so that the girl was busy and earned enough money to pay her deposit. She would also be more inclined to stay if she was earning well. She would be pushed at every client for at least two weeks or until there was another new girl to take her place. After that, it was sink or swim. She would know the lie of the agency's land by then and, if she was good, she would have picked up some regulars of her own for the weeks or months ahead. If she hadn't got the hang of saying hello, didn't like it or was earning badly, she would normally leave and try another agency or give up altogether.

I had come to hate being a new girl; it wasn't my strong point. Being new girl anywhere is never any fun, is it? And in the sex industry it's twice as bad; you always got more of the grotty clients as a new girl. In the past, that was what had happened in the brothel, then in the sauna and, now, with the agency, it wasn't any different. There are always clients who like new girls and will only see a new girl; they're always looking out for someone who knows nothing, someone they can take advantage of, and they'll try and get things from her that other girls won't do. If a girl hasn't been around a bit, she won't know any different, she won't know that there are certain things you don't have to do, things that other girls don't do because of the health risks.

Kissing was still seen as a big taboo, and no one would do anything unprotected. If they did, the other girls would talk about it in the lounge with disdain and say that they would tell their clients, 'If I wanted to catch something by doing something like that or was that desperate, I'd go stand on a street corner or work in an alley behind King's Cross station.' The common consensus in the lounge was that if you did oral without protection no one would sit near you in case they caught something. It was all very snotty, but it was the same in most agencies, from what I heard; only the cheaper girls did that sort of thing. As the agencies had a pretty fixed list of clients, most of the gents knew the score; it was very rare to come across a client who hadn't been to an agency before. The majority even automatically handed you a £20 tip for cab fare at the end when you were ready to leave, without having to be asked.

If a client was new to an escort agency, he would normally be introduced by a friend; it was unusual to get a walk-in off the street. Clients rarely pushed for a kiss mouth-to-mouth – you were lucky if you got a peck on the cheek – and asking for oral without a rubber was virtually unheard of. With all the government-sponsored information on HIV and Aids over the past years, everyone was very paranoid. One of the girls, who was a nurse, even confessed to using a rubber surgical glove if she had to give hand relief, which, although it raised a laugh or two, wasn't dismissed outright by the girls in the lounge. And I thought I was paranoid about my health!

Bad John

Friday: first shift at an escort agency 6 p.m.–1 a.m.

Clients x 2 = Bad John, Mr Old English

+ cab-fare tip = £20 (Mr Old English)

2 x 2 hours = £500

Total = £520

– agency fee £140

– cab fares + £6 (there and back to Park Lane)

Total = £368

'You have a booking for 7 p.m. with one of our regulars. He wants you at the hotel round the corner. Here is the info ... you need to collect the fees, as he doesn't do credit cards.' Ms Grey handed me a Post-it note with the hotel address, the client's name, 'John', a room number and the time written on it.

'He shouldn't need you long, and I'll need you back

promptly, as I might have another booking for you later.' With that, I was dismissed, and she turned her attention to another girl who had walked in after me.

I left the agency and walked up the street. Ms Grey had given me directions as I headed out and it wasn't very far to the hotel. I turned up at the shabby hotel door at 7 p.m. precisely and knocked, only to be confronted with a stern-looking, broad blond man in his early forties.

'You're late. I said 7 p.m.' was all he said, as he ushered me into the small room and locked the door behind me. I looked at my watch, which took my attention away from the lock. I wasn't late according to my watch, so I looked at the bedside clock, and that said five minutes past.

'I'm terribly sorry, my watch must be slow,' I apologized, even though I knew I wasn't late at all. Getting the time right was something I was very conscious of: one minute late calling in, and it would cost me. As the agency would want another £70 fee off me whether the client paid me for extra time or not, the time was always on my mind. Girls were always trying to diddle agencies out of money, or so the agencies thought (and most of the time they were right). The agency didn't really care, they just wanted the money. I set my clocks and phone to the speaking clock because of it. A good escort was expected to be on time, to call to check in and call when she left a booking so the agency knew she was on her way back and when they could stop the clock, as it were. I got the impression that keeping on a girl whose timekeeping was bad was unprofessional, and that an unprofessional escort was either not very employable, only worth giving the worst shifts to or, even worse, the worst clients, the ones none of the other girls wanted.

He interrupted me with a slight smile, bringing me back to earth. I was hoping he had changed his mind about hiring me. No such luck. He said, 'Well, you're here now. Turn around and let's get a good look.'

I did a slow turn on the spot. I didn't like his tone, but had been told he was a regular, so it was best just to smile. Hopefully, I would be out of there soon.

There was a small shower room at the foot of the queen-sized bed, and not much room around the bed for any other furniture. It was a very small, damp and probably cheap room; it was obvious he wasn't into impressing a girl. His casual appearance, the location and his unshaven face spoke volumes.

He came around and plonked his ample frame down on the bed next to me. I turned to face him.

'So, are you a good girl?' he said, raising an eyebrow and reaching out, shoving his hand up my skirt and poking and grasping at my knickers underneath. That was a bit of a shock, but it really shouldn't have been, considering I had met his type before. He tried to push the folds of my long coat out of the way so he could look at what he was doing and nearly made me topple over, getting his hands caught up in my suspenders as he did so. He didn't look too happy that he was being impeded by my underwear.

I grinned down on his thinning hair and then, looking at the opposite wall, said, 'I hope so. I take it you want me to stay then?' his hand still groping away under my coat and skirt.

He lifted my skirt up as I stood and took a small step back. Soon I was against the wall, and he pinged my suspenders. Ouch, that hurt a bit. My indrawn breath made him grin. It was obvious he got off on it.

'You're new, right?' he queried, and I nodded. 'Yeah, you'll do. Take all that off under there. Leave the skirt on.' He grunted as he started to undo his belt buckle and leaned back on the bed. I really didn't like his tone *at all*. He was obviously looking for a submissive girl and expecting me to do whatever he ordered. I didn't usually mind if a man wanted to be in control, and I had dealt with lots of men who liked young girls before, but I didn't like his rough manner. I wasn't as sub as he obviously wanted me to be, and that was going to mean trouble.

'Umm, sure, but I have to call the agency first to check in and let them know I have the fees.'

It was my subtle hint to him to pay me, but he just grunted and said to make it a quick call. I fished my phone out of my bag, keeping an eye on the door and noting that as he had now got up from the bed and was standing between me and the door, I wasn't in the best position to leave in a hurry if I had to. I smiled again and made the call to check in with my boss, Ms Grey.

'Yes, I'm here,' I answered the disembodied voice on the other end. 'No, he hasn't paid me yet.' I hadn't been asked but had been told to say that by one of the girls in the office to prompt the client to pay the fee.

I turned to my non-paying client and smiled again. He said loudly, so it could be heard on the other end of the phone, 'I'll pay her later.' And he reached for his zip.

'It's OK, I heard. John's fine. He'll pay you at the end.' Having said that, Ms Grey hung up.

I looked at my phone and then back at my unpleasant client, who was now lolling on the bed. Turning my phone off, I slid it into my pocket and started to walk around the bed, on my way to hang my coat up on the back of the door. Well, Mr Fingers had been great and had paid. This one wasn't great, but if she said he would pay, then, fingers crossed, he would.

'Where're you going?' He grabbed for my arm as I made my way past.

'Hang my coat up.' I shrugged it off, and he let go of my arm. I hung my coat up. At least I was on the side near the door now. I put my bag on the floor, again near the door, and pushed my knickers, stockings and suspenders down as quickly as I could to please him. Then I kicked off my shoes, keeping everything in one pile on top of my bag, just in case I needed to grab it all and make a quick exit.

He was now standing at the foot of the bed, towering over me in the small room, his trousers around his ankles.

'OK. Get on all fours on the bed,' he ordered. 'I want to see that little ass in the air for me.' He grinned. 'Let's see what you got under that skirt,' he said, as he rubbed his crotch bulge through his boxer shorts. I reached for the rubber that had fallen out of the top of my stocking before I bent over the bed as he had asked.

'Like this?' I queried, lifting up my skirt to give him a view and tucking it into the waistband.

'Yeah,' he grunted, shoving a cupped hand between my legs. I could feel his weight on the bed behind as he poked a thumb roughly up me. 'Nice tight pink cunt. I'm going to enjoy fucking you open,' he said in a sinister whisper over my shoulder as he bent over me, trying to shove more fingers up me as he did so. I wriggled forward a bit, away from him and his probing fingers, as they were hurting a bit. I hadn't had a rough customer in quite some time. I started to turn over, wanting to divert his attention.

'You want to watch me play with my twat? I'm getting a bit wet.' I grinned up at his expectant face. Two could play at his game.

He leaned back, leering, as I turned over on to my back and started to unbutton my blouse and take my bra off, my skirt still hitched up around my waist.

'You are a bit wet, but we can fix that,' he said, grabbing a fistful of the dowdy bedcover and starting to rub away at my crotch before I could stop him. That didn't make me at all happy, as he was rubbing off all my lube, but he looked pleased at causing me discomfort. Putting his hands down his boxer shorts and pulling his cock out, he played with himself as he watched me finger myself, laid out beneath him on the bed.

'Come and suck it, slut.' He proffered his big ruddy-red cock at me, now standing at the side of the bed. 'Come and suck my big fat cock.'

I crawled across, the rubber still in my hand and, just before I was about to put it on with my mouth and hands, he grabbed my hair and pulled me up. Looking into my eyes, he grunted, 'No, not fucking yet, just want to shove it down your tight throat.'

He let go of my hair and I said, 'Deep throat? Sure, I

love to suck rubber.' I smiled and nodded away as if I hadn't understood that he wanted me to suck it without. 'Go on, make me gag with your big long cock,' I breathed, all the while sucking the rubber on as quickly as I could, so I was mumbling the words over his average-sized dick before he could realize what I was doing.

'That's not what I meant ... not with.' He grabbed the back of my head and shoved his cock further in, slamming his crotch in my face. His balls were slapping me under the chin while he groaned away. 'Yes, you little whore ... ahhh ... going to be your fresh pink twat next ... ahh ... Ooopen you up.' He didn't last long; he was soon on the brink, which was good as I was having trouble breathing. He might not have been overly endowed, but sheer force was knocking the breath out of me.

'Yes, going to stretch you open now,' he grunted.

Yeah, go ahead and try, I thought. He had no chance if I relaxed my muscles; the amount of better-endowed men I have had in the past, it was very unlikely he could stretch anything down there. If he was aiming to hurt me, it wasn't going to work. Flipping me backwards quickly, he grabbed my legs and hauled me to him, impaling me just as quickly and ramming away, still carrying on his tirade of abuse.

'Bet you haven't had big cock like this before ... ahhh ... fresh cunt ... does that hurt? ... ha ha.' He grabbed at my tits and I breathed heavily so he thought it did. He didn't seem bothered that I wasn't moving much, that I was just pinned under him, as he was more intent on what he was doing, as if I wasn't really there at all other than as a hole to fill. He was plain vile. I had met his type in the past, he just wanted a body to use, and I knew the quickest way to get out of there was to give him what he wanted and be shot of him. The more I fought, the more it would turn him on. I groaned as if I was in a bit of pain, even though I had relaxed to stop him hurting me so much. I was a bit numb by then anyway, thank goodness, from the rubbing. I had a feeling I was going to have bruises the next day as it was, and I didn't want to make it worse by tensing up.

I wiggled about and moaned a bit more as if he was hurting me more than he actually was. The sadistic sod seemed to like it so I thought it would make him come quicker and I could leave sooner. I was right.

'Yeah ... ahhh ... serves you right for not sucking my cock right ... ahh ... you're only useful for fucking and coming over, aren't you, you dirty little whore?' With that he pulled out, whipping off the condom, and exploded all up my body across my chest. I lifted my hands just in time to stop it getting on my face and in my hair but it had covered most of me all over.

But that wasn't the annoying bit, the annoying thing was the fact he had taken the rubber off and I hadn't had a chance to 'accidentally' ping it as I took it off his sensitive cock after he had come. My chance of retribution had been lost.

He huffed and plonked himself down on the edge of the bed, wiping his cock on the bedcovers as I sat up and started wiping his come off my body with one hand, the come I hadn't been expecting. He got up and opened the bedside drawer after that, taking out a stack of £20 notes and throwing them on the bed at me.

'There, you can go now,' he sneered, not even looking at me, and fishing up his boxer shorts from the floor and pulling them on.

'OK. Can I just use the bathroom to clean up and – ' I was interrupted with a scowl as I gathered up the cash on the bed with my clean hand.

'No. Just go, get out of my sight.' He reached for the TV remote and pointed it at the TV high up on the wall in the corner facing the foot of the bed. I shoved the cash in my bag and reached in the bathroom for a towel, rubbing myself dry as I picked up my clothes and put them on as quickly as I could. I was glad I had a change of outfit back at the agency, and that I could have a wash there. He took no notice of me, just carried on watching the news as I put on my coat to leave. I just wanted to get out of there, so I murmured a 'Goodbye' as I opened his hotel-room door and walked out without looking back.

A shiver went down my back as I stood in the dark corridor wiping my hands with an antiseptic wet wipe from my bag. He was a regular client? Why hadn't she warned me? She must have known what he was like before she sent me to him. What was this, some sort of escort baptism of fire? Hook you in with a good client and then see if you could stick it by giving you a vile one?

I walked back to the agency feeling a bit confused. I hated to think what he would have done to me or tried to make me do if I had been green and truly new to the game as he had expected. Then again, I would probably have done what he wanted and been a good girl for him, if I hadn't known any better. If that made me a bad girl, then good, at least he wouldn't pick me again.

I was buzzed into the agency and put the £70 so-called introduction fee on the desk.

'OK?' Ms Grey said, looking up from her magazine and seeing my frown.

'I don't think he liked me at all, and he was a bit rough.' I didn't bother sitting down, as I just wanted to go to the bathroom for a wash. I could still smell his sweat on me – eau de vile client is never one of my favourites.

'Umm, yes, he just called. It's OK, you won't be going to him again.' She picked up the money on the desk. 'He can be a bit choosy; not many girls like him or suit his needs.' She smiled up at me. 'Bit of a difficult one, John, but a regular client, like to keep him sweet, always wants to see the new girls.'

She was distracted now by counting the money I had given her and noting it down in her book.

'Oh, you have another outcall at 9.30 p.m., a hotel on Park Lane. Can't have you being late for this one now, can we? Nice old reg, he's a darling, you won't have any problems ... Think you'd better call me when you're there and then call to confirm when you're in the room.' She looked down again at her book and scribbled away. I took the silence as my cue to leave and go and clean up. I didn't bother trying to argue that I hadn't been late turning up, as John had obviously complained to her. Too right I was going to call her when I arrived at the next one – so she knew I wasn't late.

The night dragged on. Ms Grey was right: I had no problems with the English chap later on and was back in time to kick my shoes off and watch some TV before leaving when the agency shut to go and pick Layla up from her agency, which was five minutes down the road.

'So, how was your first day, love?' It was 1.05 p.m. and I was driving us back to my flat in north London.

Layla rolled down the window and puffed on her cigarette. 'Yeah, surprisingly OK. I had an old English guy early on – that made the Lush happy – and spent the rest of the night chatting to a girl called Tandy.' She took another puff and blew the smoke out of the window. 'Smart cookie, that one, was going on about ways to get mortgages, shares and such, very interesting.' She stared off into the distance.

'Hello? Earth calling Layla, you looking to buy a house?' This was the first I had heard of it; she had mentioned renting her own place but not buying a pile of bricks.

She drew on her fag and puffed it out again. 'No, no. It was just that listening to Tandy made me think that I should save more, like you do. Where does our money go?' She rattled on while puffing away the whole trip back. 'I mean, you no sooner make it than it's spent. "The more you make, the more you tend to spend," Tandy said earlier, and I think she's right . . .'

After a week at the agency I was doing well, despite getting some clients I didn't like. I was new, so I was bound to get a few bad ones picking on me; I knew that. Both Layla and I did well; even she was surprised how well. I had earned more in the agency that first week than in two months at the sauna. I was definitely not going back there now. I no longer needed to work like that; I was enjoying working as an escort. I felt I had more in common with the girls at the agency than I had with those at the sauna or the stripclub, or even the brothel where I had started. Unlike at the sauna, in the agency no one thought it was strange that I read books rather than magazines. Other girls were reading even bigger books than I was. It wasn't snobbery; I just felt that I fitted in better. I didn't feel I stood out as much, as most of the girls in the agency were around my age, single without kids and dressed smartly too. I didn't have to dress down or plainly to come into work out of fear I might get picked on or that rumours would start that I was earning too much and probably fiddling the house, because I had expensive, nice-looking stuff.

At the agency, flash was all the rage. Not all of it was elegant, though. Most girls had designer this and that, and the amount of money they earned was a way to show how good they were, and the designer brands a way to show the other girls how much they could afford to spend. Louis Vuitton handbags were rife; no one could get away with a fake, as all the girls knew what a real one looked like, and a fake was worse than a cheap bag, as everyone thought you were pretending to be something you weren't. Shoes and watches, too, were a mark of how well you did. Everyone at the agency knew, for example, that a real Gucci bangle watch was £395, and if you were wearing a fake, they knew it and would take the piss out of you. If a new girl started and had on a real Gucci watch, the girls at the agency would know she was one of them and would be more likely to talk to her. The older girls would be far less likely to try it on. With a non-Gucci new girl, they thought they could get away with hassling her, giving her a sob story and asking her to loan them money, making her go to the shops for their fags, making tea or cleaning up their mess in the kitchen, and so on. They knew they wouldn't be able to get away with it if the girl had worked before and knew the score. Having the same designer things as the other girls made a statement that she would know their bullshite and wouldn't put up with it.

I didn't have the designer flash, I've never really liked it, but the fact that I dressed smartly confused most, and responding, 'Yes, I would love one,' and adding, 'if you're making it?' with a big smile to anyone saying 'Tea?', kept most of the bitches at bay, and stopped them from saying, 'Make me one too,' and leaving me to make it for them. I didn't need a Vuitton bag as protection. It all sounds a bit silly but, when you have a bunch of girls in one smoky room for hours on end, subtle little things like that can mean a lot. I quickly worked out that there was a hierarchy among the girls in agencies too, just as in the other houses and saunas. It wasn't much different. The bling was nothing to do with style or how well off you were and everything to do with an escort's status in the agency. It was more about being bitchy than snobbery.

The girls who had been there longest commanded the most respect from the others. After all, they were the ones you could go to, the ones who had all the information and gossip you might need. The girls who worked more than the others and earned more, the top girls, were given more leeway and better shifts, and the owners were more likely to trust them and stand up for them if anything went wrong, as they were the ones making the most for the agency, too. If you let one girl get to you and walk all over you, then others would too. It wasn't just the clients you had to keep happy and keep an eye on, you had to look out for the girls and the owners as well. Whoever says being a hooker is easy money doesn't know *what* they're talking about.

9. *Things that Go Hump in the Night*

A week flew by and, so far, I had no reason to call my personal sex-toy Tony for physical relief. We had spoken on the phone a few times in the mornings; the phone sex wasn't that great, but I was realizing that, as big, powerful and macho as he made out he was, he was actually more submissive than I thought. It wasn't a bad thing, but it did mean that I did most of the dirty talk, which got him beating off but didn't do much for me. I had an inkling he was hiding something – after all, working and dealing all the time with men who keep the secret of seeing working girls gives a girl a sexual sixth sense of how men lie. I eventually got him to admit that he had a wife. He sounded a bit put out that I wasn't bothered he was attached, which I guess was his male pride needling him.

I saw the fact that he had a missus as a good thing, not a bad thing at all. It meant he wouldn't be bothering me too much or get too clingy. Not that he would have anyway, knowing that I was a working girl and what I did, but him being married meant I had a better hold over him than he had over me. He was in no position to mess me around or tell anyone and – best of all – he was less likely to turn into a stalker. It wasn't like I wanted a relationship with him, it was more his gorgeous body I wanted and, since my previous playmate had disappeared – the last man in my semi-private life had been an older gent, who had taken me to Venice and then disappeared into the phone hell of 'The number you have dialled is no longer in use' – I needed a replacement. This time, rather than intellect, a brain to keep me stimulated, I thought I might as well go for brawn, and Tony, who spent all his time in the gym and had a chest that needed custom-made shirts it was so broad and biceps bigger than my waist, was definitely brawn.

I didn't tell him I was working as an escort until the week after I had started, once I knew I was going to stick at it. He just presumed I was still at the sauna, although he had made some comments about better places I could work and was a bit worried about my safety. When I did tell him I was working as an escort, he sounded quite impressed, as if I had taken his advice, but he wasn't quite so impressed when I said I was too busy to see him for a week or so, and that I would call him at the end of the week and come and pick him up. He didn't have a car.

Layla was going off back down south the following weekend, so it was the perfect time to get him around and have some fun. I was hoping he would take me out of my paranoid mood and, if the week ahead was anything like the last, on my two days off I was probably going to need some good sex to keep me sane.

It hadn't been long, but I had forgotten how big he really was. I picked him up from the tube station, and it was as if a gorilla was climbing into my passenger seat, a huge silverback, and he looked even bigger in the small confines of my hatchback. I was seeing him in the daylight for the first time, and his cheeky killer-wattage smile shone. He was more relaxed, too, which wasn't surprising, considering that the last time we had met was in the sauna, where he hadn't wanted to be in the first place. We chatted on the way to mine, but my mind was elsewhere, especially when he put his hand on my knee. I had to remove it, reluctantly, as it was getting in the way when I had to change gear.

He was looking at me suspiciously out of the corner of his eye. He only stopped frowning when I told him to stop sulking, which, as I was wound a bit tight and thinking only of getting my hands on him, came out as more of a command than a request. That brought an even bigger, pearly-white grin to his face – another indication that he was really a bit submissive. But after a grotty week of being paid to be at men's beck and call, and of getting some of the not-so-nice gents, as I was still being sold over the phone as the new girl at the agency, it made a nice change and it felt good to have a man under my command. At my front door, I dropped one of my gloves on purpose, which had him bending down to pick it up for me before I could open the door. Yep – definitely submissive tendencies.

After a whistlestop tour of my compact flat and a blatant kneading of Tony's shoulders, slyly using the excuse that he felt to me as if he needed a massage, I got him to dispense with his clothing in no time at all. It wouldn't have been difficult in any case; I could have used any excuse. I had his huge black body beneath my hands and at my mercy before I remembered to take more than my heels off.

As I was kneeling at his side, massaging the tight

muscles in his back and sliding my hands along his bulging thighs, his hand snuck under my skirt and one of his sneaky fingers probed at the gusset of my damp thong, stroking along the edge of the fabric and teasing it aside to slip underneath, then fondling the damp lips it found. It wasn't difficult to wiggle back and impale myself on it, which caught his attention and allowed me to turn him over so I could rubber him up to suck his cock. His girth looked eye-wateringly good and, from what I remembered, it would grow from its semi-hard state to become a full, rigid prick in a matter of seconds. If, that was, I could get to it. Tony's attention was at present fully focused on my wet pussy. He licked the finger that had been probing my cunt and was now intent on laying me down and licking me out.

Surrendering was no chore. His huge frame bunched between my thighs and pushed my knees apart for better access, and he covered my pussy with his hot mouth and sucked, then settled to flicking my clit with his tongue, then to probing with more than one finger, stretching my hole as he went, until I came over his face and all over his fingers.

He stretched up, looking supremely happy with himself. I was contemplating jumping on his cock, and I grabbed a rubber from under my pillow, one of a few I had put there that morning, ready. I had him rubbered up in no time and lying beneath me before he realized that I now wanted his cock to fuck and not to suck. After a moment squatting above his erection, it was easy to slide down his girth, as I was so wet. I squeezed my cunt muscles, inching down nearly all the way but holding off, just, to rock forward on my knees and hoarsely whisper that I wasn't going to let him come until I wanted him to. That earned a groan from deep in the tense mass of dark, contrasting body beneath me and a twitch in his cock as he fought to buck up to bury himself further.

Time was a novelty I hadn't had at my disposal in a long time. I had meant what I said: I wasn't going to let him come until I had him where I wanted him, and where I wanted him wasn't just in a position to make me come – I wanted a full, knee-trembling, knock-the-breath-out-of-me, didn't-know-where-I-was orgasm, and that, I knew, took time, time to wind me up a few notches to make me dizzy and make my brain flood with all the dopamine I would produce, so that the wave would wash over me and I wouldn't be able to think straight.

Coming for me is a brief, pleasant sensation of pins and needles that skitters up my body like a wave. It's like being wrapped in a warm blanket that makes my body pulse and the blood rush in my ears. An orgasm is, for me at least, a different sensation, a different kind of climax. It's more like an explosion that makes me convulse and my eyes roll in my head; it makes me painfully sensitive all over. It didn't happen very often – most of the time a quick screw and coming would satisfy me – but even a vibrator can't make me orgasm. Fingers crossed that Tony had the potential I thought he had. Perhaps I would be in luck.

I pinned his arms above his head and leaned over him, rolling my hips, stroking his cock with my internal muscles, gripping hold and riding him, easing back to slow the pace when he tensed and nearly came. As I rocked back on my heels, he felt a good fit beneath me, so I swivelled, sitting on his cock in a reverse cowgirl position, my feet together, heels pressing back on his balls. I lifted up, ready to slide down even tighter than before on his pulsing dick. I felt him push up on to his arms, watching me slide down on him. It wasn't long before he wriggled up on to his knees so I could bend over doggie-style, holding on to the bedhead as he started to pound away.

He had a powerful arm around my waist and was lifting my knees off the bed so that I fit him better as if I weighed nothing at all. I fingered my clit to bring myself off as he pushed harder. 'Harder,' I urged, pushing back as he thrust, and that was all it took before I felt a spark go off. I convulsed and groaned as my pussy tightened around him, locked in the orgasm I wanted. I felt the heat as he came.

It was quite some minutes until we both had our breath back and my knees were strong enough to be able to stand. I stretched like a cat and, as I always did after sex, hopped off the bed to go to the bathroom, not giving it a second thought.

'Where are you going?' He sat up, looking and sounding shocked.

I looked over my shoulder. I shrugged, still a bit dizzy. 'Shower,' I replied. Mmm, a nice hot shower ... after all, he had sweated buckets, all over me, and I felt sticky. I wasn't thinking too clearly. My head was fuzzy with cotton wool.

I turned around to face him, leaning against the door-frame naked, my arms crossed, and only then thinking to ask him if he wanted to use the bathroom first.

He shook his head, still looking put out, as I turned and padded to the room next door, murmuring over my shoulder, 'Put the kettle on, will you, for me? We have plenty of time for round two before I have to drop you back at the station.'

I planned to tie him to the bed next and to tease him into oblivion in thanks. I didn't think he would mind, even if it did take a couple of hours. Now, where was that blindfold Layla had bought me for a funny birthday present?

Christmas Escape

I spent as little time as I could possibly get away with back down south for Christmas with the folks, all so I could get back to the agency for the New Year, as Ms Grey had said it would be busy.

I wasn't used to keeping normal hours now, and I found being up in daylight very strange, much to the amusement of my family, who kept on trying to wake me up at some stupid hour in a normal person's morning, flinging open the curtains in the spare room in which I was sleeping and calling me lazy, which didn't help my mood. Although it was Christmas and I hadn't seen them all in a while, I couldn't wait to leave and get back to my blacked-out flat in quiet north London, where people didn't just drop by without calling first and expect you to be sunny and bright all the time.

I was getting slightly paranoid again. I would avoid crowds if I could, and it wasn't just crowds – going out at all in daylight made me anxious for some illogical reason, and it would take some deep breaths to stop my hand shaking on the outside-door handle before I could open it to get to my car. It seemed the paranoia I used to have when working at the brothel had returned full force, but I hadn't really noticed I was pulling away from people and cutting off friends.

As her family wasn't in England, Layla had stayed in London, which gave me a great excuse to get back. I said I needed to keep her company, but that didn't help much, as my mother kept on saying that I should have brought her down to stay over Christmas too. Talk about fuss and kill you with kindness. And I like Layla far too much as a friend to subject her to my lot. Layla got off easy, staying in town and working at her agency on Christmas Day, not that she was busy.

I was glad when I got back to London. I snuck back before New Year, saying I had to get back as friends were having a party but spending the evening in the dark, reading by candlelight, while Layla was out with a guy she had met in a bar, a musician in a small band who also had a nine-to-five job. It sounded serious. I hadn't known her date before – Layla had always lectured about the evils of giving it away for free, ever since some psycho ex- she split up with after I had met her – so I didn't press and ask her much about him.

After New Year I found that the girls at the agency were just as crazy as those in the brothel, and the clients were even more risky. I never really knew where I would end up after a booking, but it never occurred to me that the agency might not know where I was all the time. The guys I saw may have been pervs, or a bit slimy, but on the whole they were nice enough, and none had been too much trouble. You had the occasional drunk, or one or two you thought might be a bit high, but none had been violent. I was more paranoid that people, my family even, might find out what I was doing. I didn't want to worry my mother.

It was only later that I realized I had started to become agoraphobic and a bit depressed. Just working as an escort and not doing anything other than that can make you go a bit crazy. You keep such abnormal hours, it can be very lonely. It just becomes easier to lock people out, not to do other things that could get in the way of earning money, and that in turn feeds the money addiction. I don't fare well without novelty and change in my life, and being stuck in a rut, being paid for sex night after night, can drive you a bit mad, and you don't even know it's happening. And it wasn't just me; I was noticing it in other girls too.

One late afternoon, as I was watching TV while eating my breakfast, Layla padded into the lounge and said, 'My god, you're white – when was the last time you saw daylight? You look like a vampire.' I laughed it off.

'You're looking pale yourself, missus,' I said, and gave her a poke as she sat down. She was right though, I was looking pale, but that didn't bother me: I was still getting picked. The clients liked me white. Who needed a tan?

But in another way, maybe there was a problem. It must have been at least three months since I'd seen the sun. By the time I left the flat to drive to the agency it was always late afternoon and getting dark, and I went to the supermarket late in the evening. Layla was still sleeping on my couch, and to stop the daylight waking her when she eventually got to sleep, we had taped bin bags over the windows to stop it coming through the flimsy curtains. I'd done the same in my bedroom, and masked off the small window in the front door, which gave the only light in the hallway, so no one could look in. The bathroom didn't have a window and the kitchen was in the shade in the afternoon. No wonder my body clock was totally screwed up.

Layla was trying to earn as much as she could before going back to another term at uni, and I was trying to save up for a boob job. I was sick of all the guys choosing me because they thought I was a very young girl; I wanted to get rid of my paedo client base. A week didn't go by without a client wanting me to put on the little-girl act for him.

I'd been thinking about having a boob job since those few nights I had worked at the stripclub. Girls there had had it done, and it seemed to have worked out all right. I didn't dare tell Layla until I had more info and, until I had the money to do it, I had all the time in the world to research and see what the options were. I had tried different make-up and clothes, and had even thought about having my hair cut, until I worked out that that would made me look even younger, but a boob job was really the only way to stop being picked as a little girl. OK, I might look young even with a boob job, but at least I would get picked by the type of guy who liked the busty look and not the guys who liked the flat-chested little-girl-lost look. Guys tended to go for a certain type, and if they didn't pick me, they'd pick Julie. If he was after one of the bustier girls, on the whole, he'd never choose Julie or I. And then there were the tall, leggy girls. They were a whole different category, and they were the ones who tended to get the more social, 'going-out' bookings, if there were any. It's true what they say: a man is either a bum, a leg or a breast man – or lack of, in my case, and I didn't like that at all.

Even though I was pale, at least I was saving. My little locked box was getting full, which was good: it wasn't just the money for the boob job I needed but also money to cover all the bills for the time I had to take off. I reckoned I needed at least £10,000 so that I could take four months off, minimum, and pay for the boob job, with a little bit spare just in case. It was more than I'd ever had to save before – my car had only been a third of what I needed now – but with the way it was going at the agency, a couple more months and I should be able to afford it – if bills didn't keep on popping up all the time.

'You know, you would do so much better if your hair were a bit lighter.' Ms Lush had said it, and so had Ms Grey, when I had my interviews, and I had heard her say it to other girls who had started after me. Agencies liked blondes – men would ask for them over the phone day in and day out – so you couldn't blame them for suggesting it: it was good business. Ms Grey had mentioned it again the other day, and I had just nodded and said, 'Maybe,' but the next time I was at the supermarket, there was a packet of bleach sitting on the shelf staring at me and, before I knew it, I had bought it. If I went blonde, maybe I would have different clients, or more, and then maybe I'd be able to afford the boob job sooner.

I didn't go totally blonde, as I panicked that I might be doing it wrong – what if it turned green? – so I washed it off too soon, and although I was now a lighter redhead, I wasn't really blonde, just more the strawberry blonde I was always sold on the phone as. I thought it still looked ginger, even if my boss didn't. The good news was that Ms Grey was pushing me harder on the phone now I was 'lighter' and I was getting more work, but the bad news was that I was still being picked by paedo clients. OK, it wasn't as if they all wanted to bounce me on their knee as such, but the creep factor was definitely there and, what was worse, they tended to be repeat clients, so they would ask for me again.

Conversation with Julie

'So, you studying?' I eyed Julie over my tea as she flicked through a huge business manual on her lap. Julie was Czech, blonde and blue-eyed, about the same height and with the same slim figure as me, and she did very well. If I had been the jealous sort, then Julie would have been my competition. Luckily, she wasn't the jealous sort either. If a guy liked her and she wasn't there, he would pick me, and vice versa. We both fell into the petite, young, girl-next-door category and, at eighteen, which was actually her real age from what I could gather, although she was quiet, Julie had her head screwed on.

She was popular with the clients, from what I could see and heard, and Ms Grey liked her too. Her English was very good, but she tended to be a girl who kept out of everyone's way and would rather read than chat, which I could fully sympathize with. Uncannily, we were fairly similar.

She looked up and shook her head. 'Not really,' she said. 'I'm saving for property back home. I reckon if I work a year here, really hard, I can buy a block of sixteen flats with a shop on the ground floor. I will turn that into a beauty salon where I can work, and I will have an apartment on the top floor.' She smiled up at me sheepishly from under her short blonde fringe.

I sat down next to her and handed her the cup of tea I had made her. 'Looks like you have it all planned out.' I took a sip of my tea as she nodded and blew on hers.

'Yes. I am not going to slave all my life washing floors and dying of exhaustion in a poky little room like my mum did.' She looked up as one of the other girls walked by and leaned closer in to me. 'You're not like them' – she looked over to Lucy, who was in the corner with a few of the older girls – 'I like you. Watch your back. They are ... what you call it? Back-stabbing bitch,' she whispered.

I smiled faintly; I got it. Julie was basically saying that I was going to do well, and the other girls might be nice to my face, but I had better watch my back.

Mr Slimeball

Friday 6 p.m.–1 a.m.
Clients x 1 = Mr Slimeball
1 x 2 hours = £250
+ cab-fare tip = £20
Total = £270

– agency fee £70
– cab fare £4 (cab back)
Total = £196

He was sitting in the glassed-off part of the office with a notebook balanced on his knee when I was sent in to say hello.

'Please sit,' he said in a faint Italian accent, patting the chair in front of him for me to sit on. 'You a real redhead?' he queried, cocking his head to one side as he asked.

'Yes I am. Is that a problem?' I probed.

'No, not at all. I love redheads. Are you all over, collar and cuffs, as they say?' Now he was patting me on my knee. 'Ahh, nineteen, she says.' He motioned to the shadow of Ms Grey on the other side of the screen. 'I love the taste of a fresh girl.' He started to slide his hand up my skirt, at which point I stood up and smoothed it back down.

'Do you want me to send in the next girl now?'

He winked at me, got up and walked to Ms Grey's desk. 'I would like to take this beautiful girl home with me,' he said to her.

Ms Grey gestured to me and, taking her cue, I was on my way back to the girls' lounge to pick up my coat and bag while she took security info and his agency fee. He took hold of my arm as I went by and whispered in my ear, 'Take off the knickers, bella.'

He was grinning the whole time we were in the cab on the way to his house, which, considering his bad teeth, some of which were black, was slightly offputting. He spent the journey trying to stick his hand up my skirt under the prying eyes of the cabbie while in one breath talking about art and in the next how he was going to lick me out until I begged him to stop. His English was good but he still got his words a bit jumbled up. It was all I could do to stop him going down on me in the cab.

We pulled up at his very smart address and entered a wonderful apartment filled with antiques from all over the world and dotted with paintings of red-haired women, amongst all the other paintings that covered every available space there was. He offered me a drink and went off to get me some water, leaving an envelope on the side, and me to look around the room and make my security call to the agency to say I had been paid. Turning to look at a painting on the wall, I saw him standing at the door, naked, holding two glasses of water.

'Follow me, bella,' he said. 'I have a more interesting room.' And he beckoned me to follow him to his bedroom. It didn't look any more interesting to me: there were fewer things in it, mainly, a very low big bed.

Putting the glasses down on a side table, he grabbed my hand and slid his own up and down me while slobbering all over my face. I just stood there. Didn't the condemned girl at least get her drink before being jumped on?

'I take your clothes off, yes?' He nodded in answer to his own question and started undoing my dress. That would be a no then.

I just murmured yes in his ear, trying to avoid his bad breath. 'You look like one of my paintings, bella, I wanta munch your pretty pussy. Lie down, lie down.'

I lay down on the bed, and he squatted between my

legs and nuzzled my pussy. I had a dreadful feeling I was going to have to do lots of faking to keep this one happy.

'Ummm, you taste good.' The little Italian licked away and then started sucking.

I don't know what he was up to down there, but it was doing nothing for me. I looked up into his mirrored ceiling and round his opulent red-velvet-draped room and murmured as if I was enjoying myself.

'Wow, you're so wet.' He looked up, amazed, a great big grin on his face, and went back to slobbering in my pre-lubed-up crotch, mumbling away contentedly. There was no other way I was going to get wet, that was for sure. He was down there so long I was getting out of breath faking. I must have faked at least five loud orgasms by then and my time was running out, as I could see from my wristwatch. I had tried to wriggle down and get hold of his cock, but he was having none of it and clamped down in my snatch without coming up for air.

'Sit on my face. I want you to come all over it and wank me off,' he begged, lying down. I did as I was told and sat on his eager face. He came the moment I held his cock. Thank wank for that, I thought, looking at my watch again. I'd have to phone in again soon and, in addition to that, I didn't know how long I could have gone on faking without his neighbours calling the council to complain about the noise.

He got up, with dribble on his chin, looking very pleased with himself. 'I will run you a shower,' he said, and off he went down the corridor to the bathroom, while I hurried after him, picking up my bag and things as I went.

He was waiting by the front door in his long robe when I came out of his marble bathroom, dressed once more.

'Ahh, sorry, bella, I have kept you. You are such a pleasure to please. I hope you not in trouble.' He fumbled a £20 note down my front, then kissed me on the cheek as he opened the door.

'No, I called the agency and said I was on my way. If they call, just say I left ten minutes ago.'

He nodded and waved me off and I hurried down the steps, hailing a passing cab and giving the driver the name of the pub next door to the agency. Just then, my phone rang.

'Where are you?' I had called Ms Grey from the Italian's bathroom just before showering, saying I was already in a cab. I don't think she believed me, so she was calling me back to ask why I wasn't back at the office yet.

'I'm still in the cab, on my way.' I slid down the window so she could hear the traffic in the background. 'Looks like there's heavy traffic tonight,' I said, crossing my fingers and hoping I didn't get stuck in any real traffic in the ten minutes it would take to get back.

I could hear another phone ring in Ms Grey's office. She sounded distracted, saying, 'I'll call you back. Your Italian chap is on the other line.'

I sat back. The cabbie said, 'Traffic?', raising an eyebrow in the mirror at me. Nosey bugger. I laughed.

'Yes. I'm running late to meet friends – it can take a girl ages to get ready, don't you know.'

I dashed into the office. I was fifteen minutes late, but

I was hoping that traffic was a good enough excuse not to have to hand over another fee.

Ms Grey looked up. She didn't look angry. 'Your Italian called to say what a wonderful girl you are. He's booked you same time next week, for longer.' She looked very happy now.

'Oh, right.' I grinned back, hoping the disappointment didn't show on my face. I would have been quite happy to pay her another fee if it meant I hadn't had to see the slimy Italian again. I had spent far too long in the shower as it was, trying to scrub him and his garlic breath off me. I must have done too good a job faking it if he wanted me again. I don't know why he gave me the creeps, he just did.

'He has never called back for a lady before, he does the rounds of the agencies. He must really like you.' Damn, she looked pleased. I doubted I'd be able to wriggle out of double Italian next week without severe repercussions. I stomped off to the girls' lounge to boil the kettle for tea.

10. *Mr Average*

Clients x 1 = Mr Average
1 x 2 hours = £250
+ cab-fare tip = £20
Total = £270
– agency fee £70
Total = £200

You get your freaks and your regs but, on the whole, you get Mr Average. He might be the kind of client you prefer, but he is also the guy you don't remember much about. After all, what's to remember about a guy who causes you no problems and no hassle? If you have to remember details, it's usually those of the men to avoid and warn the others about. Well, I do anyhow.

Mr Average isn't really average as a person, just average Mr Nice Client. He might have some little quirk but nothing that most don't, like liking you to wear stockings. Some ask you to wear them as if it's some naughty request, as if they're asking for A levels or something. Mr Average is normally a middle-aged man in a suit, with or without glasses, maybe with a bald spot just appearing on the horizon, with a bit of a paunch and/or love handles from working too hard at his desk; he doesn't have time for the gym. Medium height, dark hair, works in IT, a bank or has his own company. He's been married a couple of years and the wife, after having a kid or two, has gone off sex. Even the nicest man finds it hard if they haven't had sex in a year, and then he'll wander. I had one who had waited twelve years to get his leg over, but the average was around two years. By then they were wound so tight a smaller head had starting to do their thinking for them. Mr Average still loves his wife but that doesn't stop him having the normal male urges and, rather than having an affair, he turns to the less complicated option – a working girl who's there for his needs and gives him confidence, proving he hasn't lost it.

Mr Average is a nice guy, normally, grateful and no hassle. All the girls tend to like Mr Average. The only problem is that he can be so starved of affection, his wife's having gone from him to his kids, or so he thinks, you have to be careful he doesn't start to believe he's in love with you.

There are so many men with the same MO that, after a while, you tend not to notice much about them, other than remembering which hotel it is and the right room number. In fact, as you see the same type of guy all the time, and Mr Average is easy to forget, he ends up pretty much being just a room number. Mr Favourite Regular Client might be a Mr Average too, but Mr Fave Reg is more memorable; there are some men you just click with, in terms of humour and chemistry. For some strange reason, I always seem to have three Mr Fave Regs at any one time – no, not some orgy!; three men I see separately who I get on really well with. Maybe every now and then one will leave to work abroad, or his wife will get back on track and be putting out again, so they might never call for me again, but they are soon replaced by a new favourite. Some just push my buttons more than normal, but I am a sucker for a gift – what girl isn't? – especially something I've really wanted, like a new book I've been trying to get hold of. A gift doesn't have to be expensive, if it's thoughtful, but every little helps.

Where was I? Oh, yes – a date with Mr Average. A call comes through (Mr Average tends to call rather than come in), then I flag down a black cab outside and go to a nice four-star hotel within the Triangle. The Triangle is a bit like the Bermuda Triangle but, in London, it's the area the agencies consider there to be the greatest concentration of the richest pockets, where money easily leaves men's wallets, leaving them with nothing but a happy smile on their face. It stretches from Marylebone to West Kensington, then down to Chelsea and back up. Most of the top hotels and expensive houses are in the Triangle. Other than that, there's the occasional airport booking. To begin with, I thought that, with the City being the big financial centre in London, we would get more calls from that area. After all, at the sauna, a lot of the men who came in had come in from the City, for a cheap quickie in their lunchbreak. But I soon realized that, as an escort, you were in a whole different league. The men I saw now were more interested in spending £200 for a relaxed two-hour evening booking in a nice hotel than £80 for a half-hour fuck on an uncomfortable massage table. Not that there wasn't money in the City, but if a gent had money to spend on an 'upmarket girl', as they called us, he tended to stay in one of the nice hotels in the Triangle. The City didn't really have any nice big hotels to speak of back then. £200 was pretty much average for an agency – you couldn't really hire an escort in London for less than £180 – but there were agencies that charged up to £300 for two hours. The more they charged, the harder they were to work for; you needed to be recommended or know someone even to get an interview. £200 was still a lot of money, and not something the average working man would be willing to pay, so our Mr Average client normally had a good job, not just an average one.

So, back to the date with Mr Average. I turn up at the hotel and walk in briskly, looking like I know where I am going, and walk confidently but not in too much of a hurry towards the lifts. There is nothing that alerts nosey hotel staff more than someone walking into a lobby late at night, alone, dressed up to the nines and looking around like she doesn't know where she's going. If it's a hotel you haven't been to before, at least one of the girls will generally know whereabouts the lift is in the lobby, so it's worth asking before you leave the agency. The girls even played a game when they were waiting in the lounge between clients. In 'Where The Lifts Are', you have to give directions, such as 'past the reception desk on your right, round the corner, under the arch,' and say whether a card key is needed to operate the lift; even a scribbled diagram is helpful sometimes. If there is a card-key system for the lift, you have to ask the agency to phone the client and have him meet you in the lobby. But, with most, you could just take the stairs and bypass the system that way. Not many hotels do have card-key locks on the lifts – and thank goodness, as it's hard enough trying to enter a hotel discreetly and not give your client away as it is. Not that the hotel could do much about it, but there is always the chance that some snooty bellboy could give you hassle and ask, with a raised eyebrow and a downward look, if he can help you.

Getting to the right hotel door and making a quick note of the time (if I was more than five minutes early, I would hide out in the hotel lobby's toilet), I take a deep breath to calm my nerves and put a big smile on my face to calm his, then knock lightly on the door. I quickly unbutton my long coat, as showing a bit of cleavage and some leg as he opens the door never goes amiss – first impressions and all that.

'Hello, John?' I give the client a hug or a peck on the cheek so I can look over his shoulder; he nods and ushers me into the room, after putting the do-not-disturb sign on the door. I take a quick look around the room to make sure he's on his own and that the room looks safe, keeping my back to the entrance wall as I slide my coat off and let my keys, which I keep gripped in my hand as a form of self-defence weapon, slip back into the pocket, then hand my coat to him when he offers to hang it up. 'Thank you. So, do you have a view?' I ask, even if it's obvious that he doesn't, just because it gives me a chance to cross the room and him to have a good look at me, top to toe. I lean over the windowsill so my stocking tops just show under my tight, short but not too short, dress – that has Mr Average in a good mood from the get-go.

The client usually offers me a drink (I always ask for water) and I find a chair or somewhere to perch where I can see him pouring it. I only ever pretend to drink it, just in case he has slipped something into it.

I ask something along the lines of, 'So, you here on business?', something inoffensive so no uncomfortable silence follows, and then keep chatting away to make the client feel at ease. If after ten minutes or so (I always keep an eye on my watch) he hasn't mentioned or brought out an envelope, I ask, 'So would you like me to stay?', which has Mr Average nodding, 'Oh yes,' and fumbling around for the money, looking rather embarrassed that he hadn't thought of it sooner or hadn't known how to bring it up. If he needs more prompting, I use the 'I have to call the agency as a safety check and let them know you've paid' line.

By this time, I've made sure that my skirt has risen up as I sit, and lean forward so that what little cleavage I have is on view to Mr Average, who generally just looks a bit dense, or else shy and distracted. Next I pick up my bag and motion towards the loo, and the client nods again, and I dial the agency to check in. I close the bathroom door behind me and let the agency know I've been paid, quickly counting out the money. It just doesn't feel right counting it out in front of him. Putting it in the side pocket of my bag, I pick out a standard-sized condom and secure it in the top of my stocking ready for use, then liberally apply some lube, wash my hands and fish my massage gel out of my bag. Meanwhile, Mr Average has been waiting nervously in the room, all sorts of thoughts running through his head about what is going to happen next.

I know what's going to happen next, so I'm not at all nervous. I know I will start by unbuttoning his shirt and undressing him, making him lie face down on the bed and giving him a massage for around fifteen minutes as he is bound to be a bit stressed. I wrestle his novelty boxer shorts off, saying he doesn't need them. He's all too eager and helps me push them down his legs and off the end of the bed.

Mr Average is always a bit anxious: his wife and kids make him stressed, work makes him frazzled, the gym makes him tense and, on top of it all, waiting for some unknown girl to turn up at his hotel door has made him nervy. At this point, around forty-five minutes has passed since I entered the hotel room, and Mr Average is relaxed as I have massaged him from head to foot and back up again, a full-on proper massage, not too hard unless he asks me – none of this namby-pamby business just pushing oil around his back that clients tell me they sometimes get from other girls. From all my hours of experience at the massage parlour and the brothel, I'm bound to give good hand – I learned from some of the best, after all.

The massage is to get Mr Average's blood flowing and to relax him, but by now, with a nearly nude girl at his side rubbing him all over, he has started to get uncomfortable lying on his now prominent erection. If it's not yet prominent, it will be at least semi-hard, and the next stage will have him ready for me. I whip off my bra and, now topless, I finish the massage. He turns over to see why I have stopped and is faced with breasts and prominent nipples (I pinch them to make them look perky when I take off my bra). He eyes me, looks up politely and asks, 'Can I?', meaning can he touch and suck, to which the answer is 'Yes, I love that.'

I stroke up and down his leg, not quite touching his cock, as he sucks and fumbles at my breasts. I suck in my breath and enjoy the feeling of his hands travelling over my body and we roll over on the bed. When he starts to travel further down I push him back a little and kiss downwards from his chest, reaching for the condom in my stockings and checking out his cock so that I can be sure the condom will fit. (If not I dive over the bed and rescue another from my bag.) Mr Average is propping himself up, looking down at me as I roll on the rubber and suck him. I look up into his eyes and, if he wasn't hard before, he is certainly getting that way now as I play with his balls and carry on sucking, making sure that I don't carry on for too long and make him come before we have sex. He might feel cheated, especially as I still have my knickers on.

Facing him, I inch my thong down my legs, still sucking and stopping only to completely remove my thong and squat over his cock ready to slide slowly down it, gripping all the way, so that even if he has a smallish cock he feels every inch. Mr Average watches, holding his breath as I clench tight and push down slowly to draw his cock in. It's now around an hour and a quarter since I entered the room. I don't even have to look at my watch, as I can see the clock in the phone by the bed. If we have sex any sooner, I know we'll be finished too early and he might not feel he's had his money's worth and might not book me again, and repeat customers are what I am aiming for. You know what you're getting with a repeat client, and a Mr Average is one you want to come again and again.

If he's dragging it out, and moving on to missionary hasn't worked because he's trying not to come then doggie-style normally does the trick. If poor Mr Average hasn't popped by then, it's down to the fact that he hasn't had sex in a while and is out of practice. The last resort and a big hint that he should come soon is asking, 'Where would you like to come, what about over my tits?' After that, a lubed hand job over my chest will finish him off and have me dashing off to the bathroom for tissues to wipe us off with. If there is still time, I'll sit, chat and fetch Mr Average his drink or some water before I retreat to the bathroom with my things to wash, shower and re-do my make-up and hair.

I'll be ready to leave then and give Mr Average a peck on the cheek and a wave. He'll be wearing a robe and will pretty much automatically slip a £20 note for cab fare into my hand (the agency would have said on the phone that I would need cab fare to get to him and back, or he would have seen another girl in the past and know the score – even if he claims he hasn't out of some strange sort of desire to spare your feelings). You rarely have to ask Mr Average for cab fare, and even if you do, he's happy to give it, now having a huge grin on his face.

And that's about it for a Mr Average booking – all very convenient for me: some sex, some money and I'm on my way. The door closes on Mr Average, and I go back to the agency, fingers crossed to pick up another that I would have some fun with and forget just as easily.

Mr Paedo Pilot

Monday 3 p.m.– 1 a.m.
Clients x 1 = Mr Paedo Pilot
1 x 2 hours = £250
+ cab-fare tip = £40
Total = £290
– agency fee £70
– cab fare £8 (cab back)
Total = £212

He looked very smart but was a bit on the quiet side
but, saying that, most gents who came in were a bit
intimidated by the surroundings so that wasn't surprising.
Ms Grey had popped her head around the door after
the buzzer went and asked that only Julie and I come
out and say hello. There were other girls the same age
as we were supposed to be in the lounge, so the fact that
she had just asked young, blonde Julie and skinny me
had Julie rolling her eyes at me across the room. We both
knew it meant that the man who had come in had asked
for a younger girl.

Julie went first. 'I've seen him before,' she whispered
ominously when she came back into the lounge. 'He'll
want you this time.'

I walked out and said hello to the chap. He was in his
early thirties and was dressed in a smart suit, and had dark
hair and a neat moustache, which made him look rather
distinguished. He smiled, said a brief hello, then stood
and turned to Ms Grey, getting out his wallet to pay her

the introduction fee, which I took as my cue to go and get my coat and bag. I had pulled.

Julie was waiting at the door when I came back into the lounge. 'OK, what's he into then?' I asked, going over to pick up my bag. One of the girls shushed me, as the other girls were watching the end of some soap on the TV.

'He's OK. Quick booking, just likes a fumble and a feel under the covers. Likes you to lie there and not do or say much. No groaning – he told me to stop last time.' I patted her shoulder and mouthed thanks, even so earning another 'Sssssh' from one of the girls. With that advice from Julie, I pulled on my coat and headed out of the door with my client to catch a cab back to his apartment, which was some distance away, in a posh area. We chatted a bit in the cab and I found out that he was a pilot, or so he said, and he proceeded to talk about flying. He seemed very normal.

It wasn't until after I had taken the money he gave me and phoned in for the so-called security check that his manner changed from quietly confident to just plain quiet. I had just sat down. He had offered me a drink and was just off to the open-plan kitchen I could see around the corner when he asked me to go into the bedroom across the hall and wait for him there.

'Can you take everything off, put on the underwear laid on the bed and slide under the covers for me?' He used a creepy, low-pitched tone which, if Julie hadn't had words with me before I left, would probably have had me freaking out. Getting up and walking into the bedroom, I could have guessed that the underwear was going to be a big white pair of cotton panties. I had changed and was just lying there under the covers as he had asked when he came in and gave me a glass of water. I thanked him and asked him to put it down on the side table. He started to climb in on the other side of the bed fully clothed, but I heard his zipper as he reached to turn the side lights down so that we were lying in the gloom and quiet. He obviously didn't want to talk much. He just whispered, 'Daddy just wants you to lie there ... sssh, there's a good girl.'

My skin was crawling. I just lay there and thought about other things: in a couple of months' time he wouldn't even think of picking me; just a few months and I wouldn't have this type of client. I crossed my fingers as he stroked my crotch in the white cotton knickers. He didn't say very much after that and, after what Julie had said, I didn't so much as moan. I could tell he didn't want me to anyhow. From what I could see from the movement under the covers, he was wanking himself off with one hand while stroking the white cotton with the other. It only lasted a few minutes, then he gave a little sigh, came under the covers and stopped stroking.

I looked over at him. There was just his head sticking out from the covers and he was still an arm's length away. He looked happy enough. 'There's a good girl. You can go in the bathroom now and get dressed,' he said, nodding to the adjoining bathroom. Taking the things I had piled on top of my bag at the side of the bed, I slid the condom I was still holding back into the side pocket without him seeing. He was sitting up now, facing away, as I headed to the bathroom to get washed and dressed. I left the cotton panties on the laundry basket there –

it wasn't like I wanted them: I hadn't worn anything like that since middle school. I didn't take long getting dressed again – my make-up and hair were still fine – and I walked out to find him dressed in a robe and sitting in the lounge as if nothing had happened.

'I'll call you a cab, they're hard to find around here.' Gone was his creepy, quiet voice and back was the confident man who had chatted away earlier about flying. I don't know what I expected, but it was all very strange: most men at least wanted sex, especially the guys who wanted you to act young. I was sent on my way with a £40 tip after some small talk about the weather and was back at the agency within an hour of leaving it. The money was good, but I would have preferred to have normal sex rather than all the creepiness and no sex any day. Getting paid for not having sex is never as easy as it sounds – there is always some nasty catch.

I hoped that this particular nasty catch would pick a different girl next time, like he had after seeing Julie before me. Seeing paedo clients was all very profitable, but it wasn't getting any easier. If I could change my main client base, I'd be so much happier. Maybe if I saw more of the nicer clients I got every now and then, my anxiety attacks – if that's what my paranoid bad moods were – would stop. I did get them more when I had seen a paedo client. The bigger, bustier girls didn't have the problem of being cooed over or bounced on some pseudo-grandfather's knee. If it was going to take a boob job to escape that type of client it would be worth the ten months' solid working and saving I had calculated it would take. It was time to do some more research, interrogate some doctors and surgeons, and talk to some other girls who had had it done. Who says you have to lie back and think of England? I was going to lie back and think of Enlargement.

11. *Spank You Very Much: Fetish Clubs*

Samantha had come into the agency the week before waving a flier for a fetish club she wanted to go to. She was looking for girls to go with her, as she had never been to one before and thought it might be a laugh. Intrigued as I was, I didn't think it was a good idea to go with her: Samantha was a complete space cadet and she got into trouble at normal clubs, being thrown out because she was legless. I had heard the other girls gossiping about it in the lounge. Samantha was a party girl, but one that was forever landing herself in the shit, so I wasn't surprised no one wanted to tag along with her. I'd never been to a fetish club before either and, bar a few clients who had mentioned having been, I don't think I even knew anyone who had. I didn't want to end up in some dark place somewhere with my back up against a wall and no one I could trust to bail me out if everything went whip-shaped. But that didn't mean that I didn't want to go and check one out some time. Layla would be a perfect choice to drag along with me: she was ever so slightly kinky and was always game for a laugh. I'd ask her when she next came to stay for a weekend in London as a break from uni.

Well, that weekend had arrived, and here we were. The fetish night was being held in some dark tunnels underneath some railway arches, and it was all a bit of a maze. I had already lost Layla – one minute she was by my side and the next she had wandered off. Neither of us had known what to expect but, apart from the fact that the crowd was dressed differently, it was pretty much like a normal nightclub but with a bit of kinkiness thrown in and some leather benches and metal-framed contraptions in various corners. I spotted Layla – she hadn't wandered far: I could see her on the other side of the tunnel, chatting up some bloke dressed from top to toe in leather and with rather large spikes on his shoulders.

'Go on, spank me, please. I want to feel what it's like.' A girl of Amazonian build looked up at me with big, pleading eyes from where she was seated. Layla and I had sparked up a conversation earlier in the toilets with some very friendly rubber-clad girls, who had been tottering around on their heels, faffing in front of the mirrors. And for the past hour we had all been chatting, sitting round the bar and people-watching. It was Miss Amazon's first time at the club; her friends had brought her. The girls' dresses were brand-new and shiny, and made them look very fetish indeed. Layla was in a black sari with elaborate glitter make-up and long eyelashes and I was wearing a red-satin corset top, a lace-up thong I had made, red fishnet tights and a pair of shiny red platform boots I'd found in Camden. The other week Layla and I had gone looking for a fetish dress shop there. It had moved premises and we hadn't been able to find it, so we had had to make do – and from the wide range of looks and styles sported by the eclectic crowd, it looked like we had done the right thing. The rubber girls assumed we had been lots of times before; I think we looked as if we belonged.

Some guy had come in bare-chested, wearing black jeans, and a matronly-looking, larger lady in an over-tight PVC dress made a comment to me about him at the bar when I went for drinks. She said he shouldn't have been allowed in, that he stood out like a sore thumb and hadn't made any effort at all. If he didn't have the imagination and creativity to be bothered to dress appropriately, he had to be a really bad shag. I nodded to her and made my escape. She carried on making over-loud comments in his direction, and the people around her started giving the guy dirty looks, until he shuffled off, not knowing what he had done that was so wrong. It seemed that fetish clubs had more rules than I had realized. And it wasn't just the rules on the tickets or the signs in the entrance of a normal club about dress code here; the way you dressed gave a statement about your sexual persuasion. Devil only knew what signals my outfit was giving off then! But whatever statement it was making, it was obviously working. Not a single man had pinched my bum, and all the people who had approached me had been very respectful and polite. From what I had seen, no one grabbed; they always asked first. A leather-masked gimp had been following me around, and I hadn't been able to get rid of him, much to Layla's amusement, and in the end I had told him to bugger off, only to have him bow and apologize, saying, oddly, 'Thank you very much.' Then he just disappeared into the crowd – no getting the hump or all pissy as some men did in normal nightclubs.

There was only a smattering of people wearing rubber, and the four girls we were with were having a few problems with it. It was all new to them – they all had identical-looking black, shiny rubber on, no personal touches – and being on 'a novel naughty night out', as one of them put it, they had not known to powder the inside of their dresses and were now sitting stickily on their stools. Two of the girls were also complaining about aching feet, as they were also wearing new shoes and looked rather uncomfortable in them. Miss Amazon was the only one who looked like she was enjoying the sensation of the rubber.

We had just been treated to a display by a lad wearing only a thong. He was bending over one of the stools next to us and had asked one of the rubber girls to spank him with his leather paddle. She giggled and happily obliged him, giving him ten of the best on his bare bum, teetering on her very high new heels as she did so. Then he dropped his white hankie, which was a substitute for his safety word to let her know to stop. The club was loud, and he might not be heard, he said. He looked very pleased with himself and knelt at her feet, licking her shoes in thanks, much to the girl's mirth. She was still holding his paddle.

What little I knew of fetishes had been passed on from other girls I had worked with, and particularly Bella, a brothel dom I had known in the past. The spanking was obviously a real novelty to the rubber girls, as they couldn't stop tittering, but it wasn't that foreign to me. Having said that, it wasn't something that featured in your normal Saturday night out either, that was for sure, and neither were the setting or the crowd of strangely dressed people.

As the night progressed, people had become more confident. Layla and I watched, nonplussed, on the sidelines.

Layla had corrected the rubber-girl spanker so she was spanking upward with the small leather paddle rather than down, as she had a very heavy hand – either that or she was more tipsy by then than we realized.

'Go on, please spank me, too,' said Miss Amazon, eyeing up the submissive's leather paddle and hankie, which were now lying on the table, abandoned in his pursuit of shoes to lick. The man in the leather gear had come back to chat to Layla, and she passed me the spanking paddle with a wink and stood back to make some room.

'Are you sure?' *I* wasn't at all sure – I might have gently hand-spanked a naughty client before, but I'd never paddled a girl. But, if the other girl could do it and it was her first time too, then so could I. Miss Amazon rolled up her rubber dress until it was around her waist and bent over her stool, hankie in hand and her pink thong showing off a pert bottom. It wasn't surprising that a crowd gathered around: Miss Amazon's bottom was far cuter than that of the skinny submissive. I pulled back and gave her a genteel whack to start with.

I bent over her. 'How's that?' I queried.

'Harder,' came the reply, with a big grin.

Well, she asked for it. I flexed my shoulders, turned sideways on and stood my ground, making sure I had a clear space to pull back my hand. I spanked her harder and she wiggled, so I took a step back for more leverage and hit her harder again. This time a small red line was etched across her left buttock. She stopped wiggling but did not drop the hankie, so I changed hands and evened things out by giving her a whack on the right cheek as well.

It was a bit strange dealing out pain when I generally dealt in pleasure, but she seemed to be enjoying it, because she wiggled to be hit again. I know people can be strange but, to me, pain hurts, it's not pleasurable at all, yet here were people who were enjoying and feeling pleasure in the release of endorphins. I might not get it, but if the pain was pleasurable to them, then dishing it out made me feel good, in a weird sort of way. I hit her harder but consistently. Even so it lasted longer, but she took it, egged on by the crowd, who were enjoying the spectacle. She screamed and panted as her rosy bottom became an even red all over. I couldn't help but think it was a very unusual canvas to lay my mark on, wondering about the way the colour changed, how red it would get, and how long it would last once I'd stopped.

I eased off on the spanking, and stroked her sensitive cheeks with my nails and blew on her flesh. That made her shudder, it was so unexpected – and pinging the elastic of her thong was unexpected, too, as I eased back, kicking her feet further apart, ready to continue adding to the hue on her gleaming rear. Her knees shook.

Unfortunately, white-hankie boy was now pissing me off. He was in the way, and as I stood back I accidentally trod on his hand. I was sure he'd put it there on purpose, because he grinned up at me.

'Oh, go and make yourself useful. Get me a glassful of ice,' I said, rousing him to his feet and pushing him towards the bar and out of my way. I stretched back to give a very hard pelt to the girl's bottom, which was still wiggling and now glowing. I gave her three more slow, very hard strokes of the leather hand paddle, putting all my strength into it and trying not to slide back on the floor in my heels from the forward force, before she whimpered, dropped the hankie and stood, rubbing her hands over her rear. Hankie Boy had been lurking by my side for the last stroke, holding a pint glass full of ice as if it were some sort of trophy. I took it from his hands, ignoring his look of confusion. 'It's not for you,' I said, turning to put a reassuring hand on Miss Amazon's back. 'Bend back over and stay still,' I said, and she complied with another shudder. I slowly placed a cold hand on her pink cheeks and started rubbing ice cubes along the flesh, as Hankie Boy knelt at my side, having reclaimed the glass of ice and holding it for me.

It had all become clear to him now, and he beamed up, a contented lapdog at my feet. An all-too-pleading look of 'Me next' was written all over his face, but I shooed him off to take the glass back to the bar, handing him his paddle and telling him that if he came back in an hour and found me I might spank him too. The girls giggled, and Miss Amazon looked pleased, showing off her red bum to anyone and everyone who passed. Layla was finding it all very amusing.

An hour later, Hankie Boy came back to pester me. I sat and made him lick my boots and let Layla deal with him, and she administered the paddle, much to his delight. Afterwards, we slipped into the crowd, losing Hankie Boy, who was becoming a bit clingy. The rubber girls and Miss Amazon, her dress still hitched up around her waist (she couldn't roll it down or sit), had tottered off to the dance floor. We left before the end so we wouldn't have to wait around in the queue for our bags and long coats.

Recalling the events of that night in the car on our way back to the flat, Layla and I agreed that we'd go again when we next had a chance – and when we had found something else to wear. As far as I was concerned, dressing up to go was just as much fun as being there.

Mr Panic

Thursday 6 p.m.–1 a.m.
Clients x 1 = Mr Panic
1 x 2 hours = £250
Cab-fare tip = £0
Total = £250
– agency fee £70
– cab fare £6 (cab back)
Total = £174

When we said hello in the introduction booth, we weren't really allowed to talk about any sexual act. In the office, Ms Grey was adamant that nothing was discussed; we were selling our time, not sex – but it did make it a bit difficult for the client. It didn't stop some of them from asking all sorts of things, though. If they did, we weren't supposed to say yes but were meant to infer that it was acceptable. 'I think we will have a lot of fun' or 'I might be the girl for you' with a wink normally worked. If the client was being particularly dense and kept on asking sexual questions, a whispered 'I'm sorry but we can't speak about that' stopped him. Men who came in through the door knew the score – the agency had been there for years and most of them had been before – and walk-ins who had never been to an escort agency before were rare. There were pretty much two types of agency: sit-in, like the one I was working in, and a few old-fashioned photo-album agencies, where clients went to an office and picked a girl from a photo and description and she was sent to him. Samantha said she had worked for one but liked sit-in better as it meant she worked set times and didn't have to wait at home dressed up and always ready to go whenever she was called for.

Anyway, as soon as this particular guy came in we had a feeling he was a new walk-in. The routine was that we would all go out one at a time to say a brief hello and then the client would pick a few girls to have a quick chat with in the introduction area before he made his choice – but this gent tried to ask the first girl who went in a few questions.

'Think we have a new one out there,' said Julie. She had been the first one to go out and say hello. Ms Grey had seated him in the glassed-off area and we all went in separately for a chat. The girl before me came back into the lounge shaking her head in my direction. 'You're up next,' she said. She kicked off her shoes and sat down. 'He's not a gentleman, that one – asked if he could fuck me here!' She looked shocked and repulsed. She was fairly new, and I guess she'd never really worked before, or at another agency.

I smiled at her and patted her knee as I passed on my way out. 'Fancy him asking that!'

'So, do you suck without?' I had just sat down, and that was the first thing he had asked me. He looked really nervous, sitting there in his smart, pinstriped suit.

'Er no,' I said, getting up from my seat to leave. 'I don't think I am the girl for you.' So much for that. Pity – he smelled of money, from the expensive Italian shoes to the real-gold watch on his wrist. A girl tends to notice fast what a client wears.

'No, I think you are.' He stood too. 'I don't want a girl who does.'

'What?' I was puzzled. 'Then why ask?'

He smiled, sitting down again and gesturing for me to do the same. I stayed standing, raising my eyebrows, still wondering what he was going on about.

'I want a . . .' he looked a bit stuck for words '. . . a safe girl for a few hours, not one that takes risks.' I had a feeling the new girl before me had given him the 'We can't talk about that' line, so now he was finding it difficult. 'Sorry. I haven't done this before,' he said, looking up at me.

I must have smiled, because he started to look less nervous. 'I think I probably am the girl for you, but do you want me to send in the last two ladies to say hello?'

'Do you have to?' He stood up and looked around as I started to leave. He had jumped up so fast it was like musical chairs.

I turned to reassure him that, no, I didn't have to but it might be best to at least see them. 'Don't want them getting jealous of me, now do we?' I winked. 'You can always ask the lady at the desk for Susan – that's me – afterwards . . . if you haven't changed your mind?'

'Susan. Right, got it. Susan,' he muttered as I left to send in the next girl.

Either the other girls didn't take his fancy or they had answered his questions wrongly but Ms Grey popped her head around the lounge door and told me I'd been picked and to go and grab my stuff while she dealt with the agency fee and the security information of the hotel I was going to.

All the way to the hotel in the cab he hardly said a thing he was so jittery. He was a bit more relaxed back at his hotel room, but even so . . .

I should have named him Mr Bad Shag. He pushed in, pulled all the way out, pushed in again and then all the way out again quickly. He went on and on, doing the same thing. I could feel him pumping me full of air, and it wasn't pleasant. Any moment now and he would be causing a fanny fart. I tried turning sideways, which wasn't easy, as I was bent over the bed. It relieved the pressure a bit, but the thrusting and stabbing with his hard cock was getting a bit painful. Luckily, he came, with a grunt, in no time at all, and spread out, a spent force, over me. He was an OK guy; shame about the bad sex. There wasn't much I could have done about it, though: I had asked him to take it slower and tried different positions, but to no effect; he just kept on drawing all the way out and ramming all the way in again no matter what. If that was the way he went at it with his wife, I wasn't surprised she was refusing to have sex with him, or so he said. I didn't even want to think about what his kissing technique might be. Like most clients, he didn't even try to kiss me. I probably would have chipped a tooth if the sex had been anything to go by.

'OK, I'm done' was all he said as he pulled away, not even looking at me. He went into the bathroom to shower. I sat up and gathered my things, ready to pop into the shower after him. He was in the bathroom for what seemed an age. What was he up to? I thought it was supposed to be women who spent ages in the bathroom? A glance at my cheap watch told me that he had spent longer in the bathroom than he had in me!

I re-did my make-up while I waited, sitting on the side of the bed, and then straightened the bedclothes and spread out his discarded clothing on top. He came out wrapped in his robe, smelling of soap and looking rather pleased with himself.

'All yours.' Mr Panic motioned to the still-running, steaming shower through the open doorway as he made his way to the mini-bar to fix himself a drink. I hunted for a shower cap in my bag, got off the bed and headed towards the steam. I had a quick shower, managing not to disturb my make-up, dried off and dressed ready to leave.

He was grinning as he walked me to the door, shook my hand and proposed a longer booking, with dinner, when he was back in town in two weeks' time. I said he should call the agency and started to hand him a card, but he fended it off. Didn't want the wife to find it, so he said.

He waved me off on my way to catch a cab back to the agency without having given me the usual cab-fare tip. I still hadn't worked out a good way of asking for it without feeling as if it sounded cheeky, especially as he had just handed me what I saw as a lot of money, in comparison to what I had earned in the past. I'd ask Layla – she'd know how to do it nicely without getting the client's back up.

Knickers in a Twist

How do you get your knickers off? Now, you would think that, for a whore, it would be an easy business – a whore's drawers are always hitting the floor, right? Well, not really – especially if they are expensive, pretty ones. You don't want to go throwing those on a patch of baby oil and spoiling the fabric or toss them willy-nilly at some naked tea light and scorch an unsought-after crotchless effect in them, not if they have cost you a shag to buy them. (Hands up anyone who has done either of those two things. OK. That'll just be me then.) Well, back to the problem of getting my knickers out of a twist.

Picture the scene. You're giving a guy a massage, and he has wandering hands, so you leave your knickers on till the last possible point so he won't ram his thick and grimy-nailed fingers, which have been goodness only knows where, up you. Keeping your knickers on means that he can't get that far; they stand guard until you can get in position, ready to sit on his, hopefully, hard cock. You know that, at this point, if you take your hand away for a second or two, you can shuffle your knickers off down your legs, over your shoes if you haven't already taken them off or if he's asked you to keep them on. But maybe you've tumbled around, and he's rubbered up, and you're in some daft position you don't even know how you got into, because he's got an image in his head of some Kama Sutra porno he was watching before you arrived, and you don't know he's been watching it let alone have any idea of the plot . . . And then, to have the moment spoilt because you still have those pesky difficult-to-get-out-of-in-a-horizontal-position knickers on. By the time you get back to the cock ready to do the business, it's been and gone all floppy on you.

When I worked in the sauna, I had noticed that Zora had some knickers with a side fastening. They were a cheap, stripper's pair and looked like bikini briefs. They only unfastened on one side, but she said they did the trick in terms of easy, quick removal if you were straddling some chap who had a yo-yo-dick problem. She said they were really useful, but she had bought them in Australia and hadn't been able to find them in England. You could buy silk side-tie ones in the really expensive shops, but they cost far too much for me in those days for just a work thong – not that I had found any shops that sold such a thing anyway. My only option was to add side ribbons, poppers or a hook to pairs of knickers I already had. That should solve the problem.

Or that's what I thought. But ribbons and side ties are all very well, but getting them caught on a guy's watch doesn't help the mood; they are fiddly and difficult to tie straight; and they give your outline a weird lump on the hips through your clothes. Poppers kept coming undone every time I sat down – providing no end of amusement for the girls one afternoon when I stood up and my thong un-popped and slid down my legs on to the floor. So they were out.

In the end, the only thing that worked was a hook-and-eye fastening on each side. The hook had to face out, as I painfully found out. I'm not surprised people say that whores wear no drawers! It would be a damn sight easier than spending a great many evenings taking apart perfectly good pairs of knickers to sew on fiddly hooks and eyes.

12. *A Miss is as Good as a Mister*

'She's going on about how much she likes anal,' whispered Samantha, who was earwigging at the lounge door, listening in to a girl who had come in late for an interview. 'She's going on and on about it. She sounds Brazilian, wants to do strap-on too.' Samantha flopped down on to the chair next to me.

'I heard Brazilians are like that,' piped up Lucy, sounding all smug. Which, coming from her, was a bit rich, as we all knew it was she who was sent when a client asked for anything back door.

'Afraid she'll take all your business then, are we?' Samantha countered, and Lucy huffed and stomped off to the kitchenette.

'Helloo, girls.' A dark-skinned Brazilian lady dressed in bright colours bounded in through the doorway.

'The Mzzz said I should look around.' She sat down on one of the spare couches, crossing her long legs and tossing her hair extensions back over her shoulder. 'So is this it, sit-in? Just a dark lounge?'

She was very friendly and I couldn't help but smile. 'No, there's a loo and kitchenette over there.' I pointed to the corner.

'Aren't you adorable! So tiny!' She beamed at me. I didn't know if it was meant as a compliment or not, but I took it as one.

'I am now Gina.' She proffered her hand to Samantha and me, and both of us shook it. The only other escort in the room was sliding lower down behind her newspaper in her seat to avoid having to shake hands with our new comrade in charms. 'It's *very* dark in here.'

Gina looked around, and Samantha bombarded her with questions. Samantha always wanted to know everything. Learning about people was better than watching the soaps on the TV, she said. I had taken to Gina, and not just because she was so different to me that there was no way she was going to attract the same gents as I would, but because at least she was cheerful. She looked as if she was a naturally merry sort, unlike Samantha, who was bouncy because of her 'slimming tablets' (code for speed, really), and it lightened the mood and made the nights sitting around in the lounge pass more quickly if there was a cheerful girl around.

Lucy had been lurking in the background holding a cup of tea and came over to say a too-bright hello. Samantha had now run out of questions about the agency in Brazil Gina had last worked at.

It wasn't until Gina was called to the office by Ms Grey to sign her contract to start work that night that Lucy sidled over to me whispering, 'She's a he, I swear.'

'Don't be daft, she's stunning,' said an indignant Samantha.

'She looked like a girl to me! She can't be a man – I couldn't see an Adam's apple,' I hissed back at Lucy.

'You're just jealous. She's Brazilian – of course she's a bit dramatic, with all that Latin-American blood.' Samantha wasn't going to be budged.

'I'm telling you: she's a chick with a dick. I've seen it before.' Lucy crossed her arms.

'She's a man,' piped up the other escort there, who was still hiding behind her broadsheet.

'Well, then, you have nothing to worry about then, do you?' Samantha got up to go and listen at the door again.

Lucy turned to me. 'She still on speed, or is it coke now?' She motioned to Samantha, who was chewing a nail, tapping her foot and fidgeting, her ear to the door of the next room.

I just shrugged and picked up my book.

'Oh, fuck, she's sending her to see Bad John.' Samantha grimaced. 'Got to warn her what he's like.'

'She'll be fine,' grinned Lucy. 'Might even give him what he's asking for.'

'Shit, she's going straight there. Didn't she have a coat to come back and get?' Samantha pushed away from the door frame to pace the room, looking about her.

'No,' both Lucy and I said, almost simultaneously.

'She kept it on, Sam. Will you sit down? You're making me nervous.' I patted the seat next to me.

Gina was back before long. When the door buzzer went we started getting ready, putting on our shoes and re-doing our lipgloss, thinking that it was a client. She didn't know that we all buzzed three times so everyone knew it was a girl coming back and not a client and didn't have to bother getting up and ready. As we were now all assembled near the door, we couldn't miss hearing the conversation in the office.

'He is a nasty pig ... I even suck him off, he kick me

out and he no pay me.' Gina sounded really pissed off. The phone rang and Ms Grey picked it up and began murmuring to someone else on the other end. Over the top of the conversation, Gina was demanding, 'Now you pay me. You sent me, and he have no idea how to treat a lady.'

'Yes, but you're not even a lady,' Ms Grey sneered back, just after we heard the click of the receiver being put down in the office. It must have been Bad John on the other end, telling his sordid side of the story, as he always did after Ms Grey sent him a new girl.

'In Brazil that don't matter. I am more of a lady than any of your sheep escorts in there.' Gina was sounding really loud and nasty now. 'You pay me for the cock I sucked now,' she demanded again, this time with a *thump*, which I guessed was her hand hitting the office desk.

'I don't think so, mister. Now, get out, you liar, and don't come back.' Now it was Ms Grey's voice that was drowning out Gina's. For such a small, frail-looking lady, she had a very powerful voice – it could stop phone masturbators at a stroke – and at that volume, even in the next room I was scared of her.

'See!' Lucy looked so very smug. 'I think the boss might need a hand,' she said, rushing to the aid of Ms Grey. From the sound of the slamming front door and Gina stomping down the stairs, it didn't seem like our Ms Grey needed any help at all. She popped her head around the door before Lucy had even got to it to go and help.

'You are all of you girls, right?' Ms Grey asked with a big grin, not looking as ruffled as I thought she would be. We all looked back at her, stunned, and nodded and giggled. Even Samantha laughed.

Orgy

It hadn't been a great week but, then again, it hadn't been a bad one either. The money had been good – I'd been busy, worked every day and, on most days, had two bookings, but they had all, without exception, been with a Mr Average. All of the clients had been quite old, too, and giving hand relief and compensation sucking to keep them up was beginning to get on my nerves. There hadn't been one good hard shag from one of them, and it was driving me nuts. And it doesn't help when it's that time of month when your hormones are making you crazy.

It was the weekend, and a call to my black bodybuilder was more than overdue. At least he might be able to tide me over until the following week, when, hopefully, I might at least get some good, hard, paid-for sex.

'House party? Why do you want to go to a house party? I was talking about coming around to mine and getting jiggy with it.' There was I, lounging on my sofa, nursing a cuppa in one hand and my phone in the other, wishfully thinking of diverting him from the gym and into my bed for an afternoon of romping about, and he wanted to go off to some silly house party that evening. What kind of man was he! I was not amused.

'It's a kind of open-house party for couples – you know, the ones that want to play . . . a swingers' thing.' He mumbled the last bit, and it all started to click. I must have sat up suddenly as I yelped, spilling tea all down me.

'You OK?' He sounded concerned. 'It's all right, there's no need to yelp. My mate has been before, and the guy who's running it is solid. If you don't want to stay, we can leave.' He was trying his best to sound convincing.

'So it's an orgy then?' I said it deadpan, images racing around my head. My afternoon was picking up, after all, and even though I sat there dripping with tea, I now had a huge grin on my face.

'Well, sort of, yes. I thought we could go and watch. I'm going with my mate – he knows I'm married so I can't join in. Can't have him have that info to use as ammunition against me, now can I?' He droned on about watching, and what his mate had said, and how he hadn't been to one before and wanted to go and see . . . Bla bla bla.

All I could think about was how horny I was feeling and how watching was not going to cut it. 'So,' I butted in, 'what does your friend look like?' I had a niggling feeling this friend of his wasn't so much a friend as an acquaintance, as what kind of mate would blab to his mate's missus?

When evening came I dressed in my silk wrap dress, which I had mended after its fag-burn 'accident', and put on my nice see-through net Agent Provocateur lingerie, which some enthusiastic client had bought me. I was all set. I was trying to figure out how many condoms I could fit in my clutch bag in addition to my make-up, but I gave up and tipped the lot out on to my bed, grabbing my bigger, work handbag, which would hold everything I might need. How many condoms does a girl need at an orgy? Just in case, I put ten in the side pocket. I had no idea if they would supply any at this so-called house party. I added another ten just to be sure. What if they didn't have any there – would others need some too? I settled on thirty of different sizes. That should do it. I was horny, but how much free sex can one girl get at an orgy?

Quite a lot, was the answer to that one, as I found out . . .

The ominous, dodgy-sounding house party was being held in a normal-looking three-bedroom house in a run-down area in east London. It was hosted by a Jamaican gent in his late forties, his body still firm. He worked out in the same gym as Tony did and was very pleasant to talk to. We stood in the kitchen and chatted.

It was still early evening, and quiet. The house was scattered with white suburban middle-aged-housewife types and husbands who looked like bank managers. A couple was making out on a sofa in a dark corner, from what I could see. Our host was about to give us a guided tour of the top floor when we were joined by Desmond, Tony's mate, the one who had invited him to the party in the first place. He was a tall, wiry black guy in his late twenties, nothing special to look at, but from the bulge in his trousers he looked like he had an anaconda down his pants. I was intrigued. He was very friendly and more than interested, towering above me and flirting like mad, making one risqué pun after another, which made me laugh. If Tony was on his best behaviour, then this Desmond might have to do.

Tony had already hinted he would like to watch us. I excused myself to find the loo, and when I came back he grinned at me and suggested that Desmond show me around, as he was still chatting to our host about a body-building competition that was coming up. I was more than happy to do as he suggested and, in more ways than one, explore with Desmond.

I slyly hitched my dress a little higher as I was ushered up the stairs in front of my guide. He now had a good view up my skirt and, from the way he went quiet, I could tell it had drawn his attention. We heard a gurgled scream at the top of the landing and made our way to a doorway at the far end. We sneaked a peek around the frame, and we could make out an older couple going at it on the sheeted bed. The room, like the others, was lit with candles on the side tables and windowsills. There was enough light in the gloom to discern another couple sitting in chairs at the end of the bed, transfixed, watching the older gent slowly fuck, I presumed, his wife, as she gestured to a dreadlocked chap in the corner, who was merrily wanking away, to join them on the bed. He was over there like a shot and, no sooner had he loomed over the bed than the woman being screwed on it hung her head over the side and sucked his cock into her greedy mouth.

'Love a good spit roasting,' or something to that effect, was mumbled in my ear, as I felt the tall, dark, bulging body of Desmond behind me. He slid his hand up my dress and rubbed it over my hip and down my suspenders as we watched as she was rammed into by both men, both ends.

Not long afterwards, we checked out the other rooms. The second bedroom contained another bed and an older man and a chubby woman. They were against the wall, her on her knees giving him head, but the room wasn't well lit enough to be able to perve on the couple. The third room was empty, with a big king-sized bed in the centre with a fresh sheet, and surrounded by more candles. There were a few chairs up against one of the walls. It didn't take long to unwrap my dress and lay it over the table, and to get my rubbers out ready. Just in case, I fished out a bigger-sized one from the pile and slid it into my stocking top. I turned to find Desmond had taken off his shirt and was now hopping out of his jeans, clad in his socks and his boxers. He crawled across to me on the bed. It didn't take him long to peel my net knickers off and clamp his mouth to my crotch and lick away. His tongue darted in and out. Soon, my moaning had drawn the attention of other couples, who came to see what was going on.

Desmond was now on his knees on the floor at the side of the bed and I was sprawled over it. I was pinned down at the waist, exposed to the glances of the couples leaning at the doorway. I wasn't alone for long on the bed. It gave as our host sat down on the corner. He raised his eyebrows questioningly, his hand hovering over my nearest breast, and I nodded. I was happy for him to join in. I hadn't had two men before. Two girls, yes; two black girls, yes, that, too, in the past; but certainly not two black men.

I couldn't see Tony anywhere but I wasn't too bothered. Our host lowered his head and, after pushing aside my net bra for better access, sucked my nipple, only to be joined by another black head, who started doing the same on my other nipple. The third man, I guessed from the looks they gave each other, was a friend of the host. Three men? Why not? I was feeling slightly giddy as it was from Desmond's administrations. He, after some lengthy cunt-munching, had relinquished my now sopping pussy to our host, and I rubbered up the now boxerless Desmond and sucked him hard, trying not to choke on his long cock. At the same time I rubbed the now very prominent bulge at the zip of the third man. Hands were everywhere, stroking me, probing me, plucking me gently.

I was in no mood for being licked out any longer. I wanted the long cock that was trying to choke me to fill another hole, the one that was sopping wet from the licking out I had just endured. They might have outnumbered me, but I was very much in control, which is what I wanted. I wanted them to be at my fingertips. I was flipped over on the shadowily lit bed by all the black hands that were on my skin and was filled instantly with a long hard stroke that made me shudder. I reached for another rubber, ready to suck our host's cock, which had just swum into view. Another cock sprang forth from the third man, next to my hand as he sat on the bed close to me. I was on all fours. I leaned heavily on one arm and used my other hand to pull off the meaty cock below me as I was rammed into from behind and sucked the second man's cock.

It was a jumble of legs and arms, and we were soon joined by a dreadlocked head and a prominent cock on the other side of the bed. I took a liking to it; we had been joined by the young chap who had been in the other room. Four I counted, and that was enough. With me as a satellite in the centre, I took it in turns to fuck, suck and wank each cock until I was done with all of them. As I made the last guy make me come, riding him hard to finish him off, too, I spotted Tony, a huge grin on his face.

Three hours it took, from what I could tell, to finish them all off, and I was thoroughly, literally, knackered. I was surprised I wasn't feeling more uncomfortable. I was content, but I was definitely shagged out. I drifted out of the door on Tony's arm, Desmond following behind and thanking our host briefly as we left. The other men had disappeared into the crowd, both saying thanks beforehand, also with big grins on their faces, which made me feel very pleased with myself.

After dropping Desmond off at a tube station, I drove Tony back to his and sat in the car park wanking him off as a goodbye and thanks for the evening. He looked even smugger than I felt at the fact that I had just tag-teamed the only four black men at the party, and he had been able to watch. That was one unexpected experience that I could tick off my mental list.

13. *Scarlet*

'That is *it*.' I threw my shag bag down on the sofa. I had picked Layla up from her agency, and on the drive back she had been nattering about the goings-on at her work. While I listened I pondered over what had happened at mine. I had kept it in for the whole journey, but now we were back at my flat, I couldn't any longer.

'I have *had* enough, that guy was just creepy. That's three in a row, and it's not even the end of the week yet. If I get any more "Oh haven't you got young girl's tits" I am going to vomit on their cocks.' I looked at Layla as she plonked herself down on the other end of the sofa to kick off her heels.

She patted my knee reassuringly. 'Oh dear,' she said, and gave me a look that didn't reassure me at all. She looked concerned. I was waiting for the 'You still get weirdos even if you do have bigger tits' speech, but it didn't come. She looked me in the eye with a firm frown. 'You're serious, aren't you?'

I was serious about the weirdos who like small, hardly there, child tits: they exist. I sat myself down on the sofa next to her with a thud. It was late and I had spent a good hour being bounced on some old codger's knee and then having my 'little-girly titties', as he called them, spunked over. It wasn't that I minded having them covered in spunk, but the way he went about it grated on my nerves.

Layla turned sideways to face me as I grabbed the TV remote to see if anything was on that might distract me from the thoughts pressing on my mind, hoping to forget the vile client I had just seen. But Layla was not making it easy.

'No, I'm not talking about the weirdos. You're thinking of a boob job, I can just see the cogs in your brain turning,' she muttered.

I muttered back. 'What have you got against boob jobs? All that research I've done has just gone to prove that it's not as bad as either you or I thought.' Layla had grudgingly come with me only the week before to check out a clinic that did the procedure. I'd had a feeling she'd been humouring me, thinking that if I went and heard all the gory details I would change my mind and decide against it.

I had decided against that clinic, but not about having the operation. It had taken five solid months of saving, and I now had a big pile of carefully folded notes sitting ready in envelopes in my locked moneybox if I needed it. It hadn't taken as long as I thought it would to earn the money, and now my mind was set. Having done the research, all I had to do now was to find a good surgeon and a hospital that let you stay overnight and didn't send you home straight afterwards, as some of them did. I didn't like the thought that, if anything went wrong and I was sent straight home, I would be stranded miles away from medical help. North London wasn't the middle of nowhere, but it was at least forty-five minutes to an hour to most of the hospitals and clinics which did the 'augmentation', and that worried me. What if the stitches came undone? Or it popped? Or I passed out, haemorrhaged, and even after Layla had called an ambulance it couldn't get me to a hospital on time? And as I had a rare blood group, what if they didn't have the right blood for a transfusion?

I might be set on having the operation, but I didn't take it lightly. It wasn't as if I had just woken up and thought, Oh I have the money: I want to get noticed and having bigger boobs is a good idea. I knew I didn't want big, fake-looking pornstar boobs and, from all the research, I knew they weren't all like that. I just wanted to look in proportion, look normal. Not all fake boobs were hard balloons, that was only the bad ops; the ones that got capsular contracture, the tightening of the scar tissue around the implant, were the ones that looked worst. If you had a good surgeon, then after a few months of them settling, no one should be able to tell and, if I was lucky and didn't go too big, no one would be able to feel either. Fingers crossed.

So began three weeks of searching, making a list and going to speak to the doctors on it. Some of them kept on and on about the scar being underneath the breast and, as I was determined to have the scar in my armpit so no one would be able to see it, I crossed them off straight away. At last I found one doctor, at a private hospital – I had to pay for a consultation even to speak to him – who had moved on from inserting implants from underneath the breast. Although he could put them in under the arm, for hygiene reasons, he claimed the best way and the way he had been doing it for some time was through the nipple. Then the crescent scar on the edge of the aureola would blend in and nobody would be able to see it. He was also using cohesive silicone, saying it was more stable than the saline. It did feel very soft and strong. Before I left his office he said I really didn't need it done, and I decided then that he was the doctor for me. Layla, after sitting in with me, still wasn't too sure but was resigned to the fact that I was determined now to go ahead and said she would take a week off to look after me.

The big day arrived. I had left the agency, telling Ms Grey that I needed some time off and that I would call her if I needed to come back. Only a few girls knew I was going to have the op, and only Layla knew that, afterwards, if I did go back to work as an escort, I wasn't going to work for Ms Grey. With my new, bigger boobs I would go to work at Layla's agency, as it paid better.

I was all set. I had got everything ready in the flat for when I came back, stocking up on food and other necessities, as I wasn't sure when I would be able to drive again. I did, though, fill the car with petrol and oil, just in case I needed it. I made my bedroom extra comfortable for my return and had packed drawstring trousers and front-fastening tops in my overnight bag, knowing I wouldn't be able to raise my arms above my head for at least a week after the op. Morbidly, I had even written goodbye letters to all my family and left them for Layla in a drawer, to post in case anything went wrong.

I arrived at the hospital in a cab with Layla at 7 a.m., way too early for my 10 a.m. prep time, and waited around nervously until I was shown to my room and settled in, ready to wait, and wait. I wasn't the only patient on the wing – at least eight other women were having the same op that day. 10 a.m. came and went and, after a few emergencies that the doctors had to deal with, I was still waiting. I had gone without food and, with more difficulty, water for over twelve hours by the time it was noon, and in the end I had to wait until 5 p.m., when they were finally ready to send me in. By that time I was too hungry and thirsty to be nervous and just wanted it over and done with. Layla was nervous enough for both of us and kept on disappearing for a smoke.

Next I knew I woke up in the recovery room with the two other ladies who had been wheeled in before me. I had seen them go, as they had been wheeled past my room. I was nearly sitting upright before a nurse realized I had come to from the anaesthetic and settled me back down again. I was a bit disorientated and didn't really even notice the bandage around my chest; I was more worried that I was awake and perhaps I shouldn't have been. But it was nothing to worry about, so the nurse said, I had just fought the anaesthetic off harder than the others. They wheeled me through the corridor and put me in my bed. I drifted off, waking some time later to find Layla watching a game show and eating the Hobnobs she had bought me. She smiled: everything was OK; it all had gone well.

I couldn't feel a thing. I was a bit stiff and my throat was dry because of the tube that had been put down there to help me breathe but, all in all, I felt fine. Wasn't that a bit strange? Everything I had read had said it was going to be painful and that I wouldn't be able to move for weeks.

The bandages around my chest didn't look as impressive as I had thought they would either, although I was wrapped up like a mummy from the top of my chest to around my ribs. Well, at least I didn't look like some sex-toy blow-up doll. That was a relief, especially as I had trusted my surgeon to gauge the right size on the day. Tired, Layla would only leave to go back to the flat and get some sleep when I proved I could actually stand and go to the loo with no effort and could even lift my arms a little. She left, her eyes weary, and waved, claiming she would be back at 9 a.m. the next morning, when I would be discharged, to take me back to the flat to recover.

It was nearly 10 p.m. by the time she left and that was almost my downfall, as I decided that, as I could get up, I would clean my teeth, as my mouth felt furry. Everything was fine – I was able to lift my arm a little and lower my head to clean my teeth, and then I climbed back into bed to get some sleep. I was very excited that I now had boobs, so I didn't drop off straight away. After a good half-hour I found that my right boob was hot to the touch. It didn't feel right: I knew there was going to be some swelling but should it feel like a mini coffee per-colator in my chest? No, I had a daunting feeling that I might be having some internal bleeding. I reached for the buzzer, only to be told by the very unhelpful nurse who turned up in response that swelling was to be expected and to ring again in a couple of minutes if it got worse. Of course it did get worse, a lot worse, and it was becoming very uncomfortable, having swollen in the tight bandage by the time the doctor was called back in. They had to operate again.

I had been given morphine for the pain, so I didn't feel much afterwards, and was just relieved to know that they had fixed the problem. I was pestered throughout the night, with nurses coming in and waking me up every hour to stick a thermometer in my mouth.

When morning came a new shift of nurses came on, and the one responsible for my room hadn't read my notes and didn't know I had been under again. She assumed that, because I wasn't speaking, I was just being difficult and deliberately wouldn't sit up for her. She stupidly didn't realize that I wasn't able to speak because of all the anaesthetic tubes that had been stuffed down my mouth and I couldn't sit up because I was still too weak. At that point, I couldn't raise my hand off the bed, let alone sit up. She gave me my drugs and I threw up all over her as she tried to get me out of bed. She went to get help, and it was only after a nice nurse came in and helped me eat and drink some water that I felt a bit better and was able to talk and tell her what had happened.

By the time Layla walked in I was dressed but still very pale, weak and ill-looking. She didn't know I had gone back into the operating theatre and under a second time and was intent on getting me back to the flat. By then, the wing was clear of people, as all the other ladies had left. None of them had had any problems. I checked myself out, not waiting for the nurse to come around and fit me with a support bra. The doctor wanted me to come back in three days for a check-up as it was. It wasn't as if I was too banged up; I only had a wraparound bandage for support.

I had already seen the small neat scars and my new boobs that morning, when the doctor had unwrapped the bandages. Despite the slight swelling from the right boob, which had been operated on again, they looked great. Even Layla was impressed when she saw them. My new boobs were two cup sizes bigger than they had been but still smaller than hers, but she had just imagined for some strange reason that they were going to look like cartoon boobs.

It was two days before I felt better, much quicker than I thought it would be. I had, against doctor's orders, been moving around and moving my arms too, slowly, as I reasoned I had already had a close call, so if it happened again I would know what to do and, also, I had read an article by some American that said if you didn't move a bit after the surgery, your muscles tightened up as you healed and you might not get back the movement you had before. The swelling had gone down and the scars were healing nicely. Apart from the small plasters on my nipples, they looked normal. I really hadn't expected to heal so fast and have no pain, especially as I had haemorrhaged and had to go under again.

By the second day I could not only push myself up out of bed without any problem, but I had no pain and could raise my arms above my head to put a T-shirt on. My new boobs were wonderful, better than I had expected. All the dresses I hadn't been able to wear before because they looked silly on me now looked great. I filled out the tops as well as the bottoms of things now – all curvy and in proportion. By the third day I could even drive to the hospital with no problem at all. Layla came with me but immediately went off in search of coffee. I sat and waited with another lady, who looked very uncomfortable, so I asked if she wanted a hand taking off her coat. She had had the same op on the same day as me but wasn't healing as fast; she was amazed I could lift my arms. Then she said that we were the lucky ones, as she had heard that some poor girl had had to be rushed back in that night. She was even more amazed to find out that it had been me. A few more ladies came in to wait for their check-up too. They were stiff and looked like they were in pain, and I really began to appreciate how lucky I was to have healed so well.

After being told off by the nurse for moving around as I was, and for having taken off my bandages, and getting an earful for not wearing my support bra, I left, having been fitted by the matronly butch nurse with the most lumpy, uncomfortable sports bra imaginable. It stayed on for all of an hour, until Layla and I had raided every lingerie shop I could find from there back to my flat. With new lingerie and new boobs, I felt like a new woman. And it wouldn't be long before I could start with a new agency, and with a new name: Scarlet.

'You'll like it here,' said Layla. She was showing me around her agency and introducing me to a few of the girls. It wasn't so bad being the new girl here, as at least I already knew someone and, because Layla was such a sweetie, she was well liked, which made it easier for me to fit in.

My first few weeks there were very busy; I hardly

had time to sit down and chat to any of the girls as I was dashing in only to be sent out again.

On average, I was seeing nicer clients here than in the last agency I had worked at, but I wasn't sure if it was because of the agency or because my new boobs were scaring off the nasty paedo clients I usually got.

I was getting a whole different type of gent, one who wanted the busty, bouncy blonde look rather than the little girl next door. I really noticed the change. It was far more fun at this new agency, too; the men were happy-go-lucky rather than demanding and our boss, Ms Lush, didn't send me to clients who wanted things I didn't do.

She was far more on top of her game than Ms Grey had been and noticed and heard everything that went on. It really didn't take long to settle in at all, which was good, as Layla was soon going back to uni again. She had been putting it off, feigning illness, but now it was time to go and tie up a few loose ends there, ready to pack up at the end of her term and come back to stay in London permanently.

Ice Maiden

'I don't get it,' Anita was saying. The tall blonde swung her new Louis Vuitton bag down on to the coffee table and herself into the spare place on the sofa.

Tandy looked up from her newspaper and over in acknowledgement at the glacial Swede who was now sitting next to me. Anita threw her hands up in the air and humphed, obviously wanting everybody's full attention.

''E complained, da bastard,' she huffed again. ''Ow dare 'e!'

Tandy put her paper down. 'OK. We give up. Who?' she asked, trying to contain a grin. Sonya was leaning on the doorframe. We were all now staring at Anita, who was flicking her hair back, away from her new Armani suit.

'Dah last punter, 'e phoned the Lush and complained, and I, I do nothing wrong!' She waved her hand.

It was early evening and, as per normal, Anita, and her perfect long legs, blue eyes and beautiful face, had been picked by the first guy who had walked in, as soon as he had heard she was Swedish – without even talking to her first.

Anita was always a popular pick. She could have gone on the catwalk, with her classic Nordic looks. She had come back from her booking scarcely an hour from when she had been whisked off, and there had still been an hour to go.

'What did he complain about?' Tandy asked warily. Anita shrugged, like she didn't really know.

'So what happened?' I just had to ask. Anita didn't normally talk about anything other than shopping, or how much something she had just bought had cost, other than to whinge that her rent was due and she was short of cash.

At that point the Lush called down the stairs and told me one of my regular favourite Mr Averages had phoned and would be in to collect me. She smiled at me from over the top of the stair rail; she didn't even look at Anita.

Anita straightened her back and fought for attention

as Ms Lush stomped off back up the stairs to her desk in her office.

''Appened, what 'appened?' Anita bristled beside me, looking down her nose. 'Well, nothing that doesn't normally 'appen. We go to 'e'ss, 'e offer me drink, I say no, and find bedroom, I take off my tings, give him rubber to put on and lie on bed so he can do dah business, he do sex, I get up go shower, ask him for taxi fare and come back here.'

She shrugged, and I raised my eyebrows at Layla, who was leaning on the kitchen door stirring her tea on the other side of the room. She had come in to listen.

'I do not understand, I thought this one OK, I thought this one at least might call and see me again.' She turned to me. ''Ow come you get punters that come see you again? What you do?'

Layla pushed off the wall and plonked herself on the arm of the sofa next to me and handed me a cuppa. She looked over my head to Anita and answered, not quite as diplomatically as I would have done. 'She wouldn't give the guy a rubber and make him put it on, for a start, let alone just lie there.'

I nearly spat my tea out, hearing her lord it over Anita.

Anita didn't look at all perturbed. ''Ow else would you get them to wear a rubber, but give them one? Some don't 'ave and I not touch their dirty dick.' She looked disgustedly at Layla. I heard Tandy titter.

Anita looked back down at me. 'You must do some other service to make them come back – what you do? You kiss, do it twice?' Anita looked really baffled, and Layla chuckled.

'Er, no, pretty much the same as you, but we chat a bit first, have a drink, then I give them a massage to make them relax,' I answered.

I was just starting to understand why Anita, as beautiful and perfect as she looked, didn't get call backs like the rest of us did. She survived by being picked first and more often, because of her looks and her nationality, but it sounded as if her cool personality and attitude was something that no one desired twice.

Anita looked at her perfect manicure. 'Who has time to do dat? Chitchat? Massage? They only just paying for a fuck!' She hrumphed again, shaking her head and tossing her long hair.

Tandy winked at me and rasped, 'Yes, they pay for our *time*, but there are ways to fuck and ways to give pleasure.'

Anita didn't sound like she got it. 'But that what I do — they have pleasure from fucking me. I lie there, they fuck me. Sometimes I even get on top, if they not ugly and fat.' I could feel more than hear Layla giggling behind me, as I tried to keep a straight face. 'Humph ... I being serious!' Anita grabbed her gleaming shoulder bag off the table. 'I need box of fags.'

In a puff of Chanel No. 5 she got up and stomped off up the stairs to go to the shop, not even asking if anyone wanted anything — not that she ever did think to ask anyhow.

'Poor Anita,' Tandy tittered as she got back to her paper.

'Poor Anita my arse.' Layla was in tears of laughter.

As soon as the front door closed, we all erupted into giggles.

Tuesday 3 p.m.–2 a.m.
Clients × 1 = Mr Slimeball
1 × 2 hours = £270
+ cab-fare tip = £20
Total = £290
– agency fee £70
– cab fare £4 (cab back)
Total = £216

'Here you are, Susan!' He looked thrilled at finding me at a different agency. 'You know Scarlet?' he queried, and I nodded. He didn't look confused at all, just beamed back at me. Mr Slimeball, my Italian cunt-muncher, had tracked me down from my other agency to this one. And I wasn't too happy about it.

'Puff! You just left. I ring around all the agencies to find you, it take ages. The other girls, they are not you, bella. I missed you!' And on he went, pleased as Punch that he had found his 'favourite redhead', so he said, despite the fact that my hair was now much lighter and strawberry blonde. He didn't even notice that my boobs were bigger – mind you, I doubt with the months that had passed he would have remembered, especially as that wasn't exactly where his interests lay. Had I thought having bigger boobs would have put him off, I would have told him, but I couldn't be bothered. I should have known better than to think that I could lose him just by changing agency. I had told some of my favourite clients at the old agency that if

I left and went to another agency, it would be this one I was working for now. It was Sod's law that the ones I didn't want to see and hadn't told would be the ones who found me.

It wasn't long before I was flat on my back in his bed, at his flat. He had been so enthusiastic about finding me again that I hadn't even had time to take my shoes off, let alone my dress – he had just pushed it up and torn away my knickers, which were in his way, before snuffling between my legs.

'Bella, you know what I would like to do?' His question didn't need an answer; in between dribbling, he was already telling me. 'If I could, I would love to mount your juicy pussy in a frame, with the rest of my art, just your ass and legs apart sticking up, tie your ankles to the corners of the frame, mmmm.' He grunted and rubbed his whole face in my sopping lips, now filled with his drool, and carried on with his mumblings. 'You open, come dripping out, hung in my hall! So I can lick you every time I pass.' He was over-excited now, and more than content at the task he had set himself, which was to make me come at least eight times before I left. I was not best pleased at having to fake it that many times, all the screaming and heavy breathing I was going to have to do, and all to his slobbering and running commentary about what he had wanted to do to me while I had been out of his grasp. I let out a fake gasp to keep him content until he was ready to come.

As ever, there are always the clients that none of the other girls want to see, usually because they are rough, nasty or condescending – not enough to be a risk, enough that no one would choose to see them.

Once, a girl I was working with recognized a voice and then a face through the gap in the door upstairs in reception as belonging to some chap she didn't want to see again and faked stomach cramps, saying that her period had just come on, in order not to have to say hello to him. She told us how rough he had been with her during a booking only four days before and showed us the finger bruises on her thigh to prove it. She'd said she wasn't going to see him again, as rough sex wasn't what she was into – even if her rent *was* due.

And she wasn't the kind of girl to pass up on the pound signs, so after that, we all gave him a frosty reception. He left in a huff, after we each of us mumbled our name and said our hellos half-heartedly and rudely, not making eye contact and looking around the room as if he wasn't really there, hoping he wouldn't pick us.

He left without choosing anyone, to try elsewhere, complaining about the rude reception he'd been given. When Ms Lush heard, she stormed down the stairs with a frown to ask what our little display had been about and looked straight at the girl, who hadn't said even a rude hello.

The girl looked straight back at her, and Ms Lush's eyebrows rose, quick off the bat, comprehension dawning in her face. She asked, 'Is that him?' And when the girl nodded, Ms Lush shrugged her shoulders and said, 'Oh,' before padding back up the stairs to answer the ringing phone.

'Has anyone got any mouthwash?'

Layla and I were sitting on the sofa at the agency watching some late-night movie. We probably weren't going to see the end of it, considering that the phone up in the office was ringing every five minutes. It was going to be a busy night. We hadn't seen the new girl much. Being both new and young, probably all of the eighteen that was on her card, not marked a few years down like most of us (I was currently still nineteen despite another birthday having just passed), she had been very popular. Even that afternoon she had already been whisked off as soon as she had arrived by a regular who wanted to 'try her out'. You can guess that I was beginning to find that phrase a little demeaning by now, can't you? Luckily, I had done my baptism-of-new-girl fire by then. But here she was, asking whether anyone had any mouthwash.

'You didn't let him kiss you?' Sonya had demanded of her as she plopped herself down on one of the chairs. But no, that wasn't it. From what we could gather, she couldn't get used to the condom and its taste. She had tried to suck him without, but the guy had complained he didn't want to catch anything, so she had to use the rubber. When she said that she had tried to suck him without one, the whole room went deathly quiet. Not using a rubber when you gave a blow job was a risk – a

208

smaller risk, but still a risk. A working girl or escort with any sense knew that, and that risks just weren't worth taking – after all, it's not as if this job comes with sick pay. If you get ill, you don't earn and, on top of that, everyone considers it your own stupid fault, whether it is or not.

Any working girl who regularly attends a sex clinic, reads all the info and then gets lectured to death by the nurses is more than clued up. They almost scare you off having even protected sex, let alone considering doing oral without. If you didn't protect yourself, you just had no respect for yourself, was the general view. In a roomful of feisty women, in the clinic or in the agency, you just wouldn't argue the point.

The new girl had made a huge faux pas and she didn't even know it. Even if a girl did give oral without a rubber she would never admit to it. She knew all the other girls would think she was an idiot.

Layla asked what kind of condom she was using and the new girl tipped out the ones she had left in her bag on to the table. Layla sifted through them and gave her a quizzical look: the daft girl had been giving head with a normal spermicidal condom – no wonder she didn't like the taste. Nonoxynol-9 ones are like sucking toilet cleaner. And I thought the spermicidal ones would make your mouth go numb if you used them a lot – not that I ever have: I'm not that kind of girl, after all. I didn't use them and I knew Layla didn't either. From experience, both of us knew that using them more than twice for sex in one day could make your pussy sore and sting. Even for sex, we used the non-spermicidal ones. Anyone who used the spermicidal ones for oral couldn't be very experienced, didn't know her rubbers and probably hadn't even been to a sex clinic. And the blow job she would give using one couldn't be worth a damn. Anyone can give head without using a condom – it doesn't take much skill to dribble on a dick – but they do say it takes a pro to give good head when the man is wearing a condom. And I suppose we do all probably get a lot more practice.

Virtually all of us at the agency went to the working girls' project in Paddington, apart from Anita, who paid a fortune every three months to be tested at a private clinic on Baker Street. She didn't want to mix with street junkies, so she said, although she had never been to the project in Paddington and had no idea what it was like. There was a free NHS-run project attached to the civilian sex clinic, and it might have catered for street girls, but they didn't really see the distinction there – at the clinic a whore was a whore was a whore. Full tests there were even more complete than at a normal GUM (genito-urinary medicine) clinic, appointments were easier to get, they didn't ask your name (you had a number instead), you were given a variety of free condoms (including flavoured ones) and they would even make you a cup of tea in the hidden working-girls-only lounge. Why wouldn't an escort go there? They even gave you free lube in handy little disposable packets!

We had known this girl was new but we hadn't until then realized she was a grass-green uneducated civilian. Poor girl – she hadn't even thought of flavoured rubber. The other girls who had been hanging about got back to what they were doing, but they were still earwigging as

Layla, knowing my passion for rubber, and knowing I had a stock lurking in my bag, got me to dig out some flavoured condoms the new girl could try. I handed over three chocolate-flavoured ones, which I didn't like, and a few tutti-frutti ones I wasn't too keen on either. Layla sat and took her through how to suck a rubber on, demonstrating with a dildo she had in her bag – she had guessed, rightly, that the girl was still doing the civilian roll-on-rubber thing – much to the amusement of some of the other girls who were all covertly watching, and one of whom I guessed was pretty much taking notes, going by the look of intense concentration on her face.

Toy Boy

Typical! Just as I had started to rely on Tony, my personal sex toy, to come over when I called him after a bad week or, rather, like this time, a bad month of sex, he was going to up and leave me in the lurch. I had got used to him being at my beck and call, relying on him coming over and my being able to tie his big frame to my bed and do whatever I liked to him – and now . . .!

'Bodyguard?' I had just rung to see if he would come over so I could have an afternoon of sitting on his face, only to find out he had taken a very well-paid job as a personal bodyguard to someone I had never heard of. He was going to be away a few weeks, he said, maybe more. I wasn't going to hold my breath. 'OK, bye then. See you when you get back.' I must have sounded distracted – I was already thinking about a trip to a Soho sex shop for back-up toys if he was going to deprive me of his body.

'Aren't you going to miss me?' he queried, sounding more hurt than I thought he would – after all, it wasn't like I was the one going away.

'Probably not. Might miss your cock though.' What the hell did he want me to say?

It wasn't as if he was mine or was ever going to be. He was way too spoilt on the woman front. He had told me that his wife did everything for him. As far as I could tell, she was submissive, and that was the wrong way for her to go if she wanted his respect. She slaved to look after him and he said she was a walk-over. She even scrubbed his back and fed him in the bath, for goodness' sake. If he was expecting me to pine for him like his wife so obviously would, more fool him. I was going to need a replacement – and sex toys, now that I myself had been well and truly spoilt, might just fill the gap.

14. *Mr Tux*

Wednesday 3 p.m.–2 a.m.
Clients x 2 = Mr Tux, Elderly gent
1 x 2 hours = £540
Total = £540
– agency fee £140
Total = £400

I had been in since 3 p.m., as Ms Lush always liked
to have at least one lady in at opening time, not that any
men would really come in on the dot, but give it half an
hour and on occasion you might be lucky, like I had been
today, with an elderly gent who was in a rush and had
to get home to be on time for an early dinner. He had
booked, with Ms Lush's help, a tatty room around the
corner in the cheap hotel we all hated because it was dirty
and damp. I was in and out in an hour, so I was back in
the girls' lounge in no time at all. It was quiet, no other
girls around to chat to, so I sat down with a cup of tea
and a good book.

We all had to take it in turns as the early girl, as it was
considered a bad shift, normally an extra few hours just
sitting around pretty much by yourself, twiddling your
thumbs. If you were in Ms Lush's bad books – say, if you
missed a shift or were late paying in a fee – she would add
an early call to your rota every day you wanted to work, or

put you on the quiet shifts at the beginning of the week. There would be no chance of being given the ones you wanted. You had to work at least five days a week for her agency as it was. All the agencies had a compulsory minimum four- or five-day week, basically to stop you working for other, rival agencies at the same time and maybe taking clients with you. They wouldn't employ you if you wanted to work fewer days. The compulsory minimum at my previous agency had only been four days, but I had worked five or six.

I didn't mind doing the early shifts; I don't know why other girls didn't like them. Maybe, as well as it being quiet, they didn't want to be the first one in and have to clean up the girls' lounge from the night before. I would ask for early shifts especially, to the point where I came in at 3 p.m. most days. Ms Lush understood: by taking them I would get at least two or three more clients a week, and that added up. The other girls couldn't understand it, but I figured that I was just going to be sitting around at home reading or watching TV, so why not do it at work and maybe make some money? After all, if you got an early booking the client was unlikely to be drunk, was usually less trouble and, sometimes, you could even be back before the other girls arrived to start their own shift so they wouldn't realize you had just had a booking, and would be less likely to be jealous.

I had already been burnt by other girls' jealousy, and I didn't want it to happen again.

That day, I looked up from my book as two girls I knew well teetered down the stairs. I was a bit surprised as I knew they were not on the rota for that day. I nodded as they walked by to hang up their coats and shouted after them that the kettle had just boiled. That's strange, I thought, as a few more girls swept in, and the room started to fill up. Anita came last of all, dead on 6 p.m. By then there were eight of us, when normally only five were on shift at any one time. We all knew something had to be up. A few of the girls said they had been asked to come in because there was a party of gents booked in. How many, no one knew, but it must be a big group of important gents to get the Russian girls now in the corner to come rushing in on their day off. The Lush hadn't said anything when I came in, so it was news to me, but then again, she had been on the phone and had been talking away ever since – phoning all the girls and asking them if they wanted to come in, it seemed.

The doorbell rang just before eight and we could all hear that a big jolly crowd of men had come in. One was particularly loud and sounded like he had already started off the night with a bottle.

It was all quite exciting, but a bit scary too – we had never had such a big group of gents in before. Typically, they came in in twos; maybe five max for a stag party or a birthday; never as many as we could hear now, stomping around and then sitting down on the three Chesterfield sofas that lined the reception room.

'Bring in the wanton women,' bellowed the loud-mouthed gent from above. That was followed by some hearty chuckles – the men were obviously all in high spirits.

A few girls had snuck up the stairs to peek through the gap in the door to see what was going on. 'So, how many?' whispered Tandy when they were at the top of the stairs. We were deadly quiet getting ready – applying lipgloss, straightening stockings and slipping on heels.

'I see nine. Very smartly dressed – bloomin' bowties and everything' came the reply. The girl who had spoken had come back down and was dashing off to the back room to change out of her short clingy dress. Whisking back in sixty seconds flat, she wore a plainer knee-length red affair, which made her stand out from the other girls, most of whom were in their normal black. I was in my new long dark-blue dress so I didn't bother changing. It was slit to the side, low cut and clung to every curve. The other girls who had been at the top of the stairs were now rushing off to put a different dress on, also hoping to stand out.

Most of the girls would have at least two dresses with them. A short one was fine to say hello in, but sometimes gents liked us to wear something less conspicuous to leave and go to their hotel in, something longer and smarter looking. We all wore long coats which nearly skimmed the floor and hid a multitude of skimpiness underneath – that was only for the client, behind a hotel door for an hour or two – but that didn't matter: it made them feel less uneasy if you dressed a little more conservatively.

With that amount of men up there, it wasn't a matter of competing to get picked like in a normal line-up when you go to say hello one at a time, it was all a matter of catching the attention of the best gent and making sure he would pick you. The best gent was normally the one who had the most money and, on the whole, was the one in the group who did most of the talking. Usually, he had first pick, but that wasn't always the case. Sometimes he'd be paying for a friend, or someone he wanted to impress for some reason, and then he'd let the honoured guest pick first. The pack leader wouldn't always be easy to deal with but, looking at it from the money side of things, he was more likely to come back and pick you again, to tip you better or to recommend you to his mates.

'Right, who's going first?' piped up one of the girls.

OK, even I was a bit nervy as the men were still all rather loud up there, but none of the other girls looked as if they were going to volunteer. I raised an eyebrow, leaning on the newel post at the bottom of the stairs. The girls were by now sitting or standing to the sides of the room, but they were all looking up and straining to hear what was being said upstairs. 'Don't tell me you all have stage fright?' I huffed at them. Where was Layla when I needed her? Great time for her to go off back to uni and leave me to fend for myself.

'I'll go last, I need the loo,' said Miss Red Dress, and dashed off. Even Miss Brazil, who was usually the life and soul, was sitting in a corner painting a nail.

I tripped to the top of the stairs, and the girls fell in line behind me after much beckoning. Ms Lush opened the door and came face to face with me.

'Right, there are a lot of them,' she whispered to me. She looked over to her desk, where the phone had started to ring over the chatter. 'Get the girls to come in in fours and introduce them. Otherwise we'll be here all day, and they'll forget who's who by the time they've seen the last girl,' she said, and with that she was dashing off to her desk.

I took a deep breath. Hell, I had said hello to just as many men in the past, and in my undies – I'd even stripped naked on stage in a room full of them. Right, relax: it's only a roomful of rowdy men – how hard can it be to do it in a dress?

I swept the room with a glance – a bit like the way I clean my flat, really. I took note of the nine gents, all in various degrees of black tie, sitting three to each sofa, some perched on the arms.

'There you go – you love a busty strawberry blonde.' One of the gents nudged the gobby ruddy-faced man next to him, who was obviously the leader of the pack, the one we had all heard the moment he stepped in the door and plonked his big butt down centre stage in the middle of the room.

'Hello, love,' the pack leader said, patting his knee.

I put on my best smile and said, 'You haven't seen the other lovely ladies yet. Let me introduce them.' I turned to the door to introduce the next lady, but someone caught my attention. He was standing there, arms crossed, in a smart black fitted suit, a tenth man to the group.

I'm not normally taken aback by men – I see a lot of them all the time, of all shapes, sizes and ages – but this guy was stunning compared to his counterparts on the sofas. They all seemed very nice, but normal, the type that usually come in, an accountant, banker, a company director or two amongst them – they looked the sort, despite the black tie – and anything from early forties up to the refined-looking old chap on the end, who was easily in his seventies.

The tenth man was late thirties if that. He had jet-black hair, stunning blue eyes and a chiselled jaw, and looked as if he was over six foot tall. He had a smart gold watch on his tanned wrist. It's not every day you see a stunningly sexy gent in a black tux who looks like he's stepped out of a Monaco casino, especially not in our agency. It might have been a smart agency, but it wasn't that smart. I took another deep breath, hoping that my stare hadn't been registered.

Damn, he looked like he had seen a ghost. Oh dear, what had I done?

I looked away and back to the leching john, who was positively drooling now, staring at me and still stroking his knee. Bloody hell, I thought, why does this always happen to me? I bet Anita or one of the snobby Russians gets the guy by the door and I end up being slobbered over by this loud john.

I introduced the first four girls and they all gave their own hello, then went back down the stairs so there was space for the next lot of girls. Everyone made an effort, apart from Anita, who never did and couldn't see why she had to. When they left I followed them, leaving the group of men to the administrations of Ms Lush, who had just put down the phone in order to deal with the smart rabble's requests.

'Miles?' The loud john calling out could be heard through the door as we all gathered at the top of the stairs, once more straining to hear what was going on.

'Of course, dear chap. You still get first pick if you

want. She's on me, after all.' After that came much mumbling.

'They're going to take ages,' Miss Red Dress huffed as she stomped down the stairs. 'And after all that, I bet they only pick one of us.'

'Nah, nah, I looking hot tonight, I got new Louboutins! Ve all look hot. Ve all get picked,' pouted the tall Russian girl, digging around in her handbag to find and reapply her clear lipgloss. Anita grabbed her coat from the back room and draped it over the sofa ready.

We all sat down to wait while Miss Red Dress gave us an ever-developing running commentary on who was picking whom. From what I could gather, Miles, whoever he was, had picked me, and Anita had the loud john, much to her disgust and my mirth. Miss Red Dress was mentioned, and there seemed to be a choice going on between the Tall Russian or Miss Brazil – we could hear a booming male voice from above dithering between them.

The girls who had not yet been picked were then called to go up again so the other men could take another look. I got my coat and got ready to leave.

Four of us having been chosen by the first four men, the six men left only picked another two girls in the end, the older gents opting for a quiet night. We four were ready to go. As we passed the reception lounge I could see that the loud john and three others, including the handsome man in the tux, were no longer there. Apparently the four men who had picked us were champing at the bit, waiting for us outside, ready to catch taxis to the various hotels they were staying at. Their mates were still sitting around, two waiting for the girls they had chosen, and to pay.

The fees for a two-hour booking for the four of us had been paid for by the time we got to the front door, though I was still none the wiser as to which man I was going to go with. As I passed the desk, Ms Lush grabbed my arm to have a word.

'As you've already had a booking this afternoon, and your fees have already been paid, you don't need to come back. I have too many girls on now.' She smiled and gave me a meaningful look as I dashed out. I took it as an order rather than a request – she obviously wanted to keep the peace, and not to have too many pissed-off girls sitting around twiddling their thumbs the whole evening, especially as some of those she had called in specially on their day off had not been picked. She didn't need me coming back; she would have a full house to juggle on what was normally a quiet midweek night as it was.

There were two taxis standing on the kerb when I shut the agency door behind me. Two gents were already in one of them with one of the girls, and the loud john was hustling Anita into the other cab, along with Miss Red Dress and another dinner-jacketed man. I gathered rather than was told to get in the first cab and that I was to go back with the man called Miles. Waving to a disgruntled-looking Anita and Miss Red Dress, I climbed in the cab, sliding into the back seat just as a tanned hand reached over and shut the door before I could reach for it. Sitting in front of me on the pull-down seat was the brooding Mr Tux, although now his shocked look of earlier had been replaced with a soft smile. I smiled back a little and then broke into a full grin as I realized that Miss Brazil had her hand possessively high on the leg of the man next to her on the back seat.

Mr Tux was all mine. 'Hi, I'm Scarlet.' I took his hand and reached across the small gap, moving towards him to peck him on the cheek. 'Miles,' he murmured as I leaned back. My hand was still in his, and he placed it on his knee, stroking it casually with one of his long fingers. We didn't get to talk much, as Miss Brazil was quizzing them both about the function they had been to, which had been some boring business-award thing, which is why they were wearing dinner suits and bowties. It didn't take at all long to reach their hotel, it was only around the corner, and, anyway, I was far too distracted by the long, strong finger that was reeking havoc with the skin on the back of my hand and the sharp blue eyes that kept on flicking over me really to pay much attention. In any case, with Miss Brazil doing all the talking, there wasn't room to get a word in.

Before I knew it we had all got out of the taxi and she and I were being whisked across a shiny lobby floor on the arms of our clients and into the lifts. Miss Brazil winked at me as I followed the broad back of my client out of the lift when it stopped on the fifth floor. I winked back as, after my hunk of a client, she had the next-best-looking guy of the group. I followed my tall dark stranger down the corridor to his room. My palms itched in anticipation: I hadn't had a younger, cute man in quite some time and, after the disappointing sex from the earlier booking that day, I was now horny as hell.

I am the kind of girl who, the more sex I have the more I want, and this time it was working in my favour. If this guy wanted to sit around and talk before getting down to action, I didn't reckon his chances. As he opened the door to his hotel suite, I was already calculating how quickly I could get my dress off. I didn't even want to give him a chance to offer me a drink. He stood aside and ushered me in, and I walked straight over to the window, employing my usual tactic but this time pulling down the zip of my dress and letting it hit the floor before he was even halfway across the room after hanging up our coats. Going by the grin he gave me, he definitely liked what he saw, and he stopped in his tracks, starting to pull off his tie. I bent slowly to pick my dress up, looking up at him from under my lashes as he tugged away at the knot at his neck. I tossed my dress over the back of a chair and ambled over to the side of the big white bed to drop my bag on the bedside table. He followed, kicking off his shoes.

For a brief moment I could smell his musky after-shave, and then his tanned, strong fingers swept up my side and around my waist before I could take a breath and turn to face him. I noted the gold band glistening on his ring finger as I looked down to see his hand's progress, sliding up to cup my bra. The room was lit only by a desk lamp in the corner and, even though it was very quiet, I was being deafened by the pounding in my head, and by the sound of his ragged breath by my ear. Arching my back so my bottom made contact with his lap was all it took to confirm that there was a hard erection straining against his dress trousers. There was obviously no need to talk, our hands were set on exploring; there was no need to even pretend with formalities. In the taxi I had guessed he wasn't the talkative sort. The eyes that had been undressing me had told me all I really needed to know: he wanted me, and he knew I knew.

I turned to him as he unclipped my bra, and the hard, pink points of my nipples distracted him as I flipped the small buttons to undo his shirt, pulling it out from his waistband and running my hands up his muscled chest, which was speckled with rough hair, then over his shoulders, which flinched slightly, tightening, as I kneaded. Even if my mind hadn't been racing at that moment I couldn't have missed his lips as he brought them down and crushed mine in a kiss.

That brought me back down to earth. What the hell was I doing? He was a client – a damn sexy client, but a client all the same. I broke away gently, only to be caught by his firm fingers at my back bringing me down on his lap as he sat down smoothly on the side of the bed. My stockinged legs were either side of his firm thighs as I straddled him. Now that we were face to face, his eyes looked black, searing into me as I slid my hands down his chest, at the same time as he slithered his down my back and cupped my bottom, hooking his thumbs in my suspenders.

The side clips holding my stockings in place were dealt with deftly and, as I tried to focus, fiddling with his zip, he dipped his head and licked one of my now prominent nipples. My wriggling on his lap had made his cock bulge and strain even more to be freed from under the fabric. In the instant I pulled away to kick off my shoes and scoop up the condom that had fallen out of my stocking top, he had slipped out of his trousers and boxers. Propped back on his arms, his legs swinging off the bed, I had the condom on him and his cock in my mouth before he had time to take a steadying breath. He was larger than I thought, the bulge getting bigger as I sucked; even though he had been hard before, he was getting harder still. I eased back. I wasn't going to let him come yet – where would be the fun in that?

Firming my fingers round the base of his shaft with a slight pressure, I sucked more slowly as he thrust up, then swallowed a further few inches, drawing it out as long as I dared. My little black silk thong was still sliding down my leg as I crawled up over him, pushing him into the bed as he tried to move so his legs were on it. I hovered, poised over him, and sat up as his hands splayed over my hips, one finger dipping around and skewering my damp cunt before I had a chance to lean over his cock and have that take the finger's place.

He probed and teased, now with another finger, and I raised a knee and leaned over him, arms propped above his shoulders to hold my weight. He sucked my nipple as it came into his line of sight. The fingers explored and tickled, and his other hand turned my hip to rest on the bed as he struggled up. I forgot my job. I forgot about trying to slide down on his cock, I forgot to keep my eye on my watch, I forgot to keep his tongue out of my mouth. I was under him before I could blink, and his fingers were replaced with a pulsing cock. My eye jerked open, startled, as he filled me up to the hilt.

He was in less of a hurry than I thought and took

his time, slowly screwing me into the bed, every stroke pressing harder. Harder, and harder still, till his chest expanded with the effort of breathing and his body glistened under my palms. I came under him with a shudder, then he fucked progressively faster, soaking his cock as he made me even wetter. My pussy started to tighten from the friction. Frustratingly, he came in a surge before I could change our position so I could have him beneath me, where I wanted him.

It was only now, as he slumped over me catching his breath, that I looked at the watch on my wrist over his shoulder. I wanted more, I wanted him behind me doggie-style too. I peered at the dial. Damn, time was nearly up. He sat up and eased off on to his side, his hand draped over my hip, which was comforting. I tried to take my mind off the niggling thought of what his cock would feel like in other positions, what skill his tongue had and how it would feel between my other lips, as he leaned over to kiss and tease my bottom lip as we propped up on the pillows and began to chat.

Now he was more relaxed he was more talkative. I teased out the reason he had looked like he had seen a ghost when he first saw me. He said I resembled his first wife: I was the same height, had the same colouring: even the way I now wore my hair was the same. They had been sweethearts at school but she had died some years back in a bike accident. He had married again since but it wasn't working out. The business associates he had been with, who were out to impress him, trying to strengthen business ties, always brought him along when they went to pick girls at agencies, but he had never taken part. He had loved his first wife and been faithful to her, so he said, and in the second, rebound marriage, too – until I had walked in and reminded him of his dead lost love.

I didn't want to think about how much of what he was saying was a load of bull. It could have been worse. Reminding someone of a love lost had to be better than them thinking of you as a little girl. He was gorgeous, a good fuck and, to top it all, he was easy to get on with and understood my sense of humour. He looked at his watch, the only thing he was wearing, and commented on the time, saying it was a shame I had to go as I slid off the bed, grabbing my bag and heading to the bathroom to clean up. It didn't take long to shower and comb my hair back into place. It took longer wrestling with my libido: I didn't have to go back to the agency; there was no hurry; would he mind if I stayed longer? Noting the time, I took a deep breath and I fished my phone out of my bag. I dialled the agency as I left the bathroom, wrapped in a towel, to find my underclothes, in disarray all over the floor.

'Hi, it's Scarlet,' I said. I looked over to the bed, where the tanned, naked male body I had left there replete was lying still, arms crossed behind his head, feet crossed at the ankles. He surveyed me as I came out of the bathroom, phone glued to my ear. Ms Lush answered on the other end, a brief, irritated YES? I could hear girls bickering in the background.

'I have left the hotel and I'm on my way home. Yes, he was fine. See you tomorrow,' I went on, noting the time. My mobile went dead after a brief OK on the other end.

I turned it off and dropped it into my bag. Then I let my towel fall to the floor. That caught his eye. He stirred and stated the obvious, that I was still there, with a slowly raised eyebrow and a slowly rising erection. I only had to answer that I was now off the clock and that I couldn't go and leave him in that kind of state to have him easing up off the bed further and pulling me to him as I approached. His hands wrapped around me and eased my crotch to his face. I was soon more than content. I was right about his skilful tongue: it set to work and carried on till my legs couldn't hold me.

Morning came faster than we both expected and I hurriedly dressed and shrugged on my long coat as the phone on the bedside table rang.

I scribbled my number down on the notepad as he picked up the phone, answering and 'yes dear'ing to his wife on the other end. I blew a kiss across the room and pointed to the notepad I had left on the side. He frowned and quietly slid out of the bed, gently pulling the hotel-room door shut behind me so it didn't even click. My phone rang as soon as I was around the corner from the hotel, walking to the next street, where I had parked my car the day before. Fingers crossed, as it was still early, it wouldn't have been towed or got a ticket. We chatted as I walked, finding my car exactly as I had left it, safe and sound. I was so mellow after that, I agreed that we should meet again at some point in the future, much to the disgust of my professional, business-thinking brain – my libido was running amok through that.

Thinking about it logically, the sex had been great and,

what with Tony disappearing with no idea when he might be back, I might just have found a replacement. Mr Tux wasn't a brain, wasn't brawn, but if you can class a man as beautiful, he was it. Oh, and the chemistry helped, too, of course.

Remedy

Wednesday 3 p.m.–2 a.m.
Clients x 0
Total = £0

The girl who everyone affectionately called Gypsy had gone over to the new girl with her Tarot cards. The new girl didn't look happy; did she want her fortune told? She was looking a bit uncomfortable and was keeping herself to herself. She had been crouched in the corner of the lounge for a couple of hours and hadn't even got up to say hello to the last client who had come in. Eventually she told Gypsy that she was constipated, and Gypsy immediately started fishing crystals out of her handbag and coming up with all sorts of weird remedies.

Then everyone started chipping in their own piece of advice on the subject. It was a boring Wednesday evening – hardly any men call in midweek – and all the girls were settled in the lounge, whiling away the time until the next call. Only one man had come in in hours, and he'd changed his mind and 'walked'. The phone was so dead that Ms Lush had got one of us to phone the agency earlier, just to check it was working.

I looked up and over to the corner and added my

tuppence worth: 'Think there is some prune juice in the fridge if you need it.'

'Got some 'erbal tablets dat work,' said one of the Russians, diving into her Louis Vuitton bag.

'Are you drinking water? Try with olive oil in,' piped up the other Russian, watching TV and sitting next to her compatriot, who was now muttering what sounded like Russian swearwords and pulling all sorts of things out of her bag and on to her lap, trying to find her elusive tablets . . .

'Senna pods, she needs senna pods,' said Tandy matter-of-factly, looking up from her copy of the *Financial Times*, which she was reading seated at the table. 'Oh, and some sit-ups – exercise works wonders.'

At a sit-in agency, the combination of sitting around for hours, followed suddenly by a lot of, shall I say, 'action', followed by lots more sitting down, the stress from clients and girls, the odd hours and having to grab any kind of food when you can get it (if you don't manage to bring some in) is not always good for a girl's constitution. It was common for the girls to talk about things like that, and slimming tips; everyone would chip in and try to help. This poor girl had only been working for two weeks, and as a truly new escort, not one touring from agency to agency to cash in on the new-girl trade. And as a newbie, she had not had much luck with the girls who had worked there longer talking to her.

She had survived her first busy two weeks and had been suffering in silence until Gypsy asked if she was all right. I was lucky – it hadn't happened to me yet. I had learned from one of the brothel girls I used to work with, and I never ate anything solid after 6 p.m., just soup, a pot of mashed potato if I was really peckish, or just tea or chewing gum. So far, that had worked a treat for me. Everyone thought it was strange, even Layla – but it did mean that my cans of soup and pots of ready-to-rehydrate potato sat safe in the cupboard, whereas a packet of chocolate Hobnobs never could be.

But thank heavens for the twenty-four-hour Tesco down the road in Knightsbridge! Otherwise I would have been grabbing fast food and eating take-aways like the other girls and ended up being in the same fast-food, slimming-pill, hire-a-trainer-down-the-gym, yo-yo-diet hell as every other girl I knew. Working nights and sleeping days, I tended to do my shopping at night after work. Layla always raided the fridge when she got back to my flat after work, and she was the biggest hoarder of laxatives I knew. She took them when she had problems, and I knew that constipation was a problem for most working girls in parlours. I just hadn't realized it was such a problem with nearly all escorts too, until it cropped up that day.

'Got them.' The Russian shook her herbal pills at the new girl.

I didn't know if the pained look on the newbie's face was because she hadn't been able to go to the loo in three days or how she was going to say 'thanks but no thanks' to the weird-looking, foreign-labelled pills; they could have had anything in them for all she knew. The newbie caught them when they were thrown across the room, not wanting to seem ungrateful, especially to the feisty Russian. 'Err, thanks,' she managed to say, slinking off to the kitchen with Gypsy in tow.

She left early that night after a chat to Ms Lush, saying she would come back when she felt better.

'That's the last we'll see of her. I didn't think she'd cut it,' slurred Ms Lush when we closed up later, and she was right. I didn't see her again after that evening.

Mr Arse-lover

Monday 6 p.m–.2 a.m.
Clients x 1 = Mr Arse-lover
1 x 2 hours = £270
+ cab-fare tip = £20
Total = £290
– agency fee £70
Total = £220

He bent me over the table and unzipped my skirt so it fell to the floor.

Picking up the lube, he squirted it in the crack of my bum and ran his spare hand down the inside of my leg and then up, rubbing the lube over my bum again and again until it was dripping all over his bedroom carpet. He had done a similar thing before, so I wasn't surprised he wanted to do it now. I bent over obligingly.

'There, you should see your arse – it's glistening now,' he said, standing back to admire his handiwork.

He dropped the lube to the floor and slid both hands up the insides of my legs, spreading them apart and sliding both his thumbs up into me. I took a quick breath as his fingers tickled my clit, making me quiver. He was making me come, and I was a bit dizzy as his fingers worked away.

'You have such a beautiful arse . . . did you know that?' He leaned over me, holding me over the desk, my legs splayed apart. 'Such a tight little pucker too,' he continued, sliding one of his fingers all too quickly up my bumhole before I had any idea what he was going to do. He hadn't done that before and it was a bit of a shock! I jumped, letting out a loud 'Ouch, what the fu–', making him topple backwards. I winced as he pulled his finger out.

'Sorry, I couldn't help it. You OK?' I looked over my shoulder and he looked back at me like a naughty schoolboy.

'Yes, I'm fine, just a bit of a shock. I can't do that, it's too small a hole.' I didn't add that it was too fucking painful.

'Yes, just like your pussy . . . tight.' He grinned, turning me on the desk edge and lifting my legs ready to enter me. I put my legs behind him and pulled him to me, sliding back and forth on the desk from all the lube. I was still a bit preoccupied about where his finger had been and I was trying to keep an eye on where it was now. I wanted to make sure he didn't touch my cunt and end up giving me a urinary infection because of it.

'We could do some arse training if you like? I can finger you till you're ready to take my dick, I can get some butt plugs, too, to stretch you. I will pay you an extra £1,000 to be in your virgin hole first. Please think about it.' He puffed as he came.

Ha, that will just have to be his fantasy, I thought! There was no way, even if I was desperate for the money, that his cock would fit. The money was tempting, and I had thought about it fairly seriously, but I wasn't sure I wouldn't pass out from the pain. It was the second time that month that some guy had wanted back door and mentioned the so-called pornstar experience, and that was unusual – it rarely happened or was even asked for. At this rate, it wouldn't surprise me if the clients wanted to kiss next, or that Ms Lush was for some reason sending me to A-level clients. I hoped she hadn't got my index card mixed up with someone else's, or that one of the girls hadn't marked my card out of spite. It wasn't unheard of for a girl's card to be changed when Ms Lush popped to the loo or had left a girl to look after the desk while she popped out to the off licence.

Mr Arse-lover waved me off after automatically giving me £20 for a cab back to the agency. I'd suggested that next time he see one of the crazy Russian girls, who might be more obliging. He nodded apologetically and grinned.

Back at the office, after being buzzed back in and my time noted, I asked to check my Rolodex card. It hadn't been changed. I was still marked as a normal escort and not highlighted in a fetish category.

15. *Lady of the Night*

I had seen him twice before already in the previous weeks. He really didn't want sex, and it was easy to work out that he was more of a voyeur. If he just wanted to watch and only really wanted a blow job at the end, it didn't bother me at all. The second time I had met him, he wanted a BJ in his car when he picked me up from the agency. He had a perfectly nice flat near by, but he confessed that it felt more illicit outside, albeit in a deserted, darkened street. I asked whether he cruised for girls in his posh car, but he said he never had, and made a point of saying that, weirdly enough, he had never harboured any thoughts about picking up a street girl; he didn't want to take that much of a risk. He was in his mid-thirties, just under six foot, fairly good-looking and smartly dressed; his suits were, if I judged correctly, custom-made. He was a nice gent. If he got his jollies in his very swish Lexus, which had tinted windows and an all-black interior, well, fair enough – at least it made a change from the monotonous hotel bookings for vanilla, average, run-of-the-mill sex with middle-aged men with glasses.

That second time, he had driven to the dark sidestreet and I had taken care of his needs after only about ten minutes; he was driving me back to the agency in no time flat. I was checking my hair in the passenger mirror when he mentioned that he wanted to take me to a swinger's club. That caught my interest.

'Aren't swinger's parties for couples only?' I asked, now fixing my make-up in the mirror, thinking happily that, as it was early in my shift, I might get at least one other booking, or maybe two, out of the night, if I was lucky.

'Yes, but they won't know if we don't let on. We could pass as a couple. I'd just like to go and watch, that's all.' He parked up outside the agency.

'So, is it like a mass orgy then?' I queried back, thinking it had to be something like the house party I had gone to with Tony, which was the only thing I had to compare it to. The only things I knew about swinger's clubs really was second-hand info from the girls at work and from a few American movies. No one really talked about it, and even the clients who mentioned them were a bit vague.

'Umm, not really. If you come with me to check it out, you don't have to go off with anyone if you don't want to. I just want to watch and then do this again when we leave,' he said, pointing to his crotch. The guy was all class – as much as a guy that gets his rocks off in lay-bys can be, that is.

I nodded and we talked about meeting up the following week for a party he knew was taking place in a wine bar in the West End. I said he should call Ms Lush and organize it. He kissed me on my closed mouth and got out to open my door to let me out. He drove off as Ms Lush buzzed me in, looking at the clock on the wall and then smiling at me when I told her I had an evening booking the following week. I could see the pound signs in her eyes and wasn't surprised when I got the next phone booking, which came in an hour later. I swear Ms Lush could talk any man into anything on the phone – the gent who had phoned had been looking for an exotic, tall lady and ended up with me – and he gave me a big tip, too, when I left.

Mr Swing booked me for six hours the following Friday, a long booking for my agency, and well in advance, which was very rare. Most men called in at the last minute or, at most, the day before to book the lady they wanted. Ms Lush had informed me that my voyeur Mr Swing used to see one of the other girls, who had left the agency last year. The girl had had no problems with him and had gone with him to the clubs a few times but only for a few hours. She assured me he was a good client, but had only just come back; he'd been window-shopping at the agencies until he came across me.

It would have been nice to have known that before I first saw him, but I had worked out that it was easier to get info out of Ms Lush at the end of the night, when she was a bit pissed from the bottle she kept in her bottom drawer. Because I always drove home, it wasn't as if I had to dash off at the end of the night, and helping her lock up put me in her good books. Calculating? Well, yes, a bit, but if five minutes at the end of the day when all the other girls had dashed off got me the better bookings and meant she pushed me on the phone – hell, I wasn't there *just* for the sex, was I? Ms Lush wasn't stupid, she knew why I helped out. It wasn't quite ass-kissing – not like the girl who bought her a bottle of whisky every week as a gift – but it was noted.

'I like the way you help out, it shows respect. Most girls don't think, they're lazy. I know you'll be the same with clients, and that will bring their wallets back,' she said one night as she was locking the front door, then waved me off to my car.

Friday arrived and I went straight to Mr Swing's hotel, with Ms Lush's consent (Mr Swing had already paid by credit card). I arrived at his door feeling more confident than I thought I would and stood there in high heels and a fitted blue dress. He showed me into the small room, which had some boxes stacked on the bed. He had bought me a set of see-through net designer lingerie, which I was ecstatic about. I know it must have cost at least £200. It wasn't as if I didn't have some nice black satin undies on – I had quite a drawerful of sexy, slinky things by then; but nothing like that, nothing quite so expensive. The bigger box was a designer black silk wrap dress, which he said would make a good impression. I didn't like to mention I was a small not a medium and tied it as tight as I could. He didn't notice that it didn't fit too well. I modelled it for him and then gave him a blow job as a thank-you. I struggled to get his zip undone; we didn't have much time. He kept on saying that he wanted to get to the wine bar that was hosting the club night as soon as we could so as not to miss anything. Sex, he said, could always be taken care of later.

The boutique hotel he had booked was quite a few streets away from where the party was happening, so we climbed into his sleek black car, which was parked out front, drove the short distance and parked up on the street the bar was in. We went in, following a smartly dressed older couple. I felt a bit nervous. Was it going to be like a fetish club? Were there unknown rules here, too, that I should know about? Was it a general swinger's club, or were there, as I was beginning to suspect, different types of swinger's clubs? I knew that fetish clubs varied in the particular fetishes they catered for: there were parties for foot fetishists, gay fetish club nights, events that took place in cafés, without the clubbing atmosphere, rubber club nights – the list was as endless as the list of people's perverted persuasions. If you have a fetish, there's bound to be a club for it. Was swinging and swapping partners a fetish of sorts?

There was obviously quite a range of clubs. The wine bar we were in now was a far cry from the house-party swinger's do I had been to; the bar didn't look as if it had beds, for a start. One of the girls in the agency had mentioned a posh swinger's club she knew of where you were vetted before you joined and were only allowed in if you looked right, and another girl mentioned one that was only for eighteen- to thirty-five-year-olds. Going by the older couple we had followed in, it definitely wasn't going to be one of those.

Although Mr Swing was a member, he didn't know much more than I did – or even that much. I could hear music as I descended the steps into the basement bar, Mr Swing behind me. It didn't sound clubby. I was a bit apprehensive. At least when I went to the fetish club I had known I could leave any time I wanted to; here, on my client's arm, I was a lady of the night, his partner, and would have to stay. We had worked out our stories beforehand: he worked in the City and I did something in the art world.

We signed in, paying some sort of fee to the host couple. The hostess marked a card and put it back in an index box on the desk, and both of them smiled as we handed over our coats and they welcomed us in. Mr Host took us over to the bar, showing us around as he went, all the time looking down my front. The too-small net bra gave me ample cleavage.

'Over there is the snug. It's quieter, just for chatting,' he said, pointing to the corner on our right. There were a few couples there already, sitting on the sofas.

'Over there, behind the black curtain, is the dance floor, and that's where the naughtiness commences.' He winked at me as we approached the bar. My gent was looking around eagerly. I was paying more attention to our enigmatic host – after all, he was running the show, and if anyone was going to smell a rat in his camp then it would be him. I smiled, sweetly content that he wouldn't suss I was a hooker: there were certainly women dressed more sluttily than I was in the room.

The host couple must have been in their mid-forties, and he was very grey, with a shiny bald spot on top which the overhead spotlights bounced off. The hostess, who had slicked-back brown hair and the red lace of her lingerie poking through the deep-cut V of her smart tie dress, was obviously a submissive sort, as she looked up at her husband all the time – not in an obvious way, but you could tell who wore the trousers in that relationship. I was very interested at that point, seeing all the content couples around, how they could have sex with others and not feel jealous and fight about it. In my experience, jealousy was the killer in a relationship. I had been with many men who were scared to death of their wives finding out they had been with other women. They said that their wives would leave them, throw them out or divorce them if they found out they were seeking the comfort their wife was no longer providing elsewhere. For them, seeing an escort was less messy and easier than having an affair. I was very sceptical about what really went on with swingers. From the little I had heard from my clients, it tended to be the last stab at a failing relationship, a means to get the wife more involved and spice up a stagnant marriage.

Mr Host left us at the bar, saying, 'Enjoy,' over his shoulder, and went to attend to another couple who had just come in. I smiled, looking at the curtain over the supposed dance floor, which ran from one wall to the other, and from the ceiling to the floor, and turned to my companion for the night. He was looking at a couple sitting across the room on one of the sofas who were chatting away to each other.

'So, do you like her?' I whispered in his ear, as he tried to get the attention of the barman.

'Her over there? No, not really my thing. Do you?'

I looked over at the couple again. The man had a moustache and definitely a paunch hidden under his smart jacket, but he was OK, looked friendly enough, and she was a curvy blonde.

'She's cute, but he's not really my type either.' I had decided that, as he was paying me, I might as well say I liked the couples he liked. It wasn't as if I was fussy about looks really, especially when I was on the clock.

I caught the barman's eye as I leaned over the bar. I had found that cleavage was a fabulous invention for catching a barman's eye. Hell, any man's eye!

I was wondering what was behind the curtain. No one had come out or gone in yet, despite the few couples who had arrived after we had. As we were there on the dot, I had the feeling it was a bit too soon for anything to be kicking off, let alone the naughtiness implied by our host. Mr Swing ordered our drinks and we took a seat on one of the sofas on the far wall.

'Looks like we are here a little early,' he murmured, reading my mind.

'So, what goes on behind the curtain? You've been here before, right?' I asked, sipping my fizzy drink, and motioning over to the area on the other side of the room as another couple walked in.

'Er, no, I haven't been here before, they hold events in lots of different clubs and bars. The curtain is to stop the bar staff getting embarrassed at the dirty dancing that happens on the dance floor ... Supposedly.'

'Supposedly there's dirty dancing, or supposedly it's there to protect the staff from seeing the couples actually having sex behind it?'

He shrugged. 'There are other clubs outside London which are specially kitted out as sex clubs for swingers. The events aren't held in bars or normal clubs like they are here in the city – or so I hear.' He rambled on about things he had heard as I people-watched and nodded.

Our host was still talking to the couple he had gone to greet. The woman had just taken off her coat, handing it to her casually attired hubby by her side. She was topless, wearing only strained fishnet stockings. Flesh bulged out over her suspenders and big knickers. The flustered host hurriedly said a few words, out of our range of hearing, a strained smile on his face. The hubby put his wife's coat over her shoulders and they headed for the black curtain, chatting animatedly and giggling. After a couple of seconds the hubby came back out and went out to the entrance to hang up his wife's coat.

'That told her,' Mr Swing grunted beside me. 'I'm not sure what happens behind the curtain really, I've never been back there. The lady who came with me before didn't want to, so we didn't. Do you want to?'

I nodded slowly, and that perked him up. He was obviously as intrigued as I was, and he was on the point of leaving the sofa when I put my hand on his knee and said that maybe we should wait for a few more people to arrive so that there was actually something to check out when we did go. He nodded, and we chatted about the other couples in the room. Some of them were looking at us, too. I got a wink from an older lady with a toyboy on her arm. Mr Swing didn't like that at all. He was too young for me anyhow. I smiled to the older woman. She was friendly enough but, I gauged, definitely not at all my companion's type.

The basement room was starting to fill up, to the point where I couldn't see who was going into the curtained-off room. There were couples of all different ages. Most were what I expected, but there were a few attractive couples in their twenties, who were drawing the attention of my thirty-four-year-old companion. We eventually left the comfort of our perving position on the sofa and started to mingle. It was all very civilized – names were exchanged, jobs and interests discussed; the normal sort of dinner-party conversation really. Only one older couple mentioned going behind the curtain, inviting us. They went off, Mr Swing saying we would join them later, but I had the feeling not that he wasn't keen on going behind the curtain but that he wasn't keen on them. He was starting to drool over a pretty, shy brunette on the arm of a rather tall, older gent. Of the two, he was doing all the talking. My gent whispered in my ear. 'She's nice – should we go and talk to them?' He obviously hadn't even noticed the older gent she was with. He looked more like her father than her partner.

'OK,' I said. I smiled at her and started to totter over to them to make our introductions, only to be intercepted by the hostess taking hold of my arm. 'How are you doing? Enjoying yourselves?' she said. She giggled a bit, smiling at Mr Swing and grabbing his arm too. By the time I had managed to pass her off to another couple, the tall man and the brunette had vanished, which meant one of two things: either they had left or, more likely, they were behind the curtain. Before Mr Swing had a chance to state the obvious, I was hooking an arm in his and teetering towards a flap in the curtain. I pushed my way keenly through into the darker, much louder room behind.

It took a few moments to make out what the shapes were in the near dark, but my eyes quickly adjusted. Some couples were slow dirty-dancing in the room and others, in various states of undress, were perched on the few chairs that were dotted around the walls. We took a turn around the floor and caught sight of the naked, fish-netted wife in one corner, her hubby seated beside her. He was talking to another lady, his arm over her shoulder and his hand down her blouse, fumbling in her bra. His wife looked totally unconcerned. It was only as we got closer that we made out a head in her lap. A man on his knees was bobbing up and down between her legs, and the look on her face was actually one of content rather than unconcern.

The dancefloor was fairly crowded, but I could just make out the tall man dancing with his lady. I caught a glimpse of another couple, too, just as the lady touched the arm of another passing couple. The gesture was reciprocated and the four moved off to some vacant chairs to chat. It wasn't hard to keep my dance partner in a position where I could watch what would happen next. I'd quickly clicked that the brief touch was a signal: if someone touched you it meant they liked you, and if you liked them too, you touched them back, basically indicating that you would like to play with them. If you didn't touch back, just shaking your head and smiling, it meant you were not really interested: thanks but no thanks. It also looked as if the ladies were the ones with the power. More often than not it was the woman who approached another woman. I had noticed the odd one or two single men, but either they were there alone or their partners hadn't come into the draped-off area or they were in the loos. In any case the single men had less luck, if any at all, in approaches.

I gained back some of my dancing partner's atten-tion by slowly rubbing my chest up against his. He was watching two couples still on the dancefloor but dancing on the spot. The women were facing each other and kissing. One of them was stripped to the waist and the man from the other couple was handling her boobs. The other man had his hands up the other woman's skirt. I leaned in to Mr Swing and slid my hand down his back, leaving my hand on his bum and steering him towards the tall man, who I could still make out on the other side of the room. We made better progress once my partner had the cute brunette in his sights and realized what I was up to.

The tall man smiled at me as we drew near. They were chatting to a nearby couple as they danced, but it was easy to approach as they drew aside to make room for us. I touched the brunette's arm and introduced us both. There was only a slight hesitation while she looked up at the tall man, and at his nod she put her arm around my waist and I broke away from Mr Swing so that she could lean in close to introduce themselves too. The couple they had been talking to were in their mid-thirties and fairly attractive. They also sidled up and, before I knew it, there were hands everywhere, which gained a brooding look from Mr Swing, still keeping his eye on the brunette. He stroked a hand down her back and she didn't mind in the least.

I was now standing with my back to the tall man. The other woman, a curvy blonde, had managed to untie my dress. The front slid open and long fingers snuck up from behind me to rub my nipples over the low-cut net bra as the blonde leaned in to kiss me. I got a mouthful of tongue as the fingers tweaked my nipples. Out of the corner of my eye I could see that the brunette was getting much the same nipple treatment from Mr Swing. The blonde's partner's hands were around her, and now they were stroking along my sides. I moved down from the kiss to find one of her nipples to suck. I saw a dark grin from Mr Swing. He stopped the brunette from unbuttoning his shirt and turned her towards me.

I had raised my head from the blonde, who was now moaning gustily while someone fingered her, and now both my nipples were being sucked, one by each woman. Hands supported me from behind, and there was a firm erection nuzzling into me as I leaned back. The blonde moved up to kiss me again and the tall man behind me pushed the brunette's head down my body. I felt small hands push my knickers down my legs, and her mouth latched on to my wet lips, now directly in front of her, licking me while her partner's hand pushed her head into me. I fumbled with the erection behind me but he removed my hands and placed them on the head in my crotch.

The blonde had by now made it back down to my nipples. I glanced over to the near wall, where Mr Swing had pulled up a seat and had his hand down his trousers. He looked quite content, watching the goings on, and I slowly moved around so he had a slightly better view of the people pleasuring me and what they were up to. It seemed that hands from everywhere were holding me, nearly lifting me off my feet. The brunette buried her head as I climaxed on her face, loud enough that it drew a tight crowd. The brunette looked pleased as Punch, and the tall man bent to kiss her wet face, escorting her out of the room as she waved to me. I had repositioned myself in front of the blonde, as her husband fingered her roughly. She had his cock in her hand, wanking away. I was aiming to leave them when Mr Swing sidled up and handed me a condom, gesturing to the blonde's partner's cock, then re-took his seat to watch the three of us.

They were more than happy for me to rubber him up and start to suck him. We moved back towards the chairs, and I sat down next to Mr Swing, still with a mouthful of cock, while the blonde's partner continued to finger her, jabbing away, all three of us in a strange sexual daisy chain of motion. My voyeur sat back in his chair and looked on as I sunk my nails in the balls of the cock I was sucking and gently squeezed. With a shudder it came in a hot rush as the balls exploded into the mint-flavoured rubber. The blonde sucked him clean and, after giving us a goodbye wink, they both headed for the loos on the other side of the curtain.

We had been on the dancefloor longer than I realized, and Mr Swing, his trousers looking more than a snug fit, was ready to leave. He'd seen more than enough, he said, to keep him in lustful thoughts for quite some time and he was especially impatient to get back to the car for a blow job. A moment was all it took for us to slip out, retrieve our coats and find the car in order to grant his wish.

Mr Panic: Part 2

He swore loudly and ran from the room in a flap, leaving me bent over the uncomfortable arm of a chair, the very painful position he had put me in. I hadn't had the chance to turn over before he left the room, so I didn't realize why he had. One minute he was bad-shagging away, pushing in, then pulling all the way out, then slamming back in, without a clue where he was aiming, and the next he was gone. I eased myself up, feeling a bit numb and sore, and noticed the blood on my leg. Damn, the man had been too rough again; he had very nearly caused damage last time because of it. It all made sense now: he had seen blood and fled to the bathroom. With him being so paranoid about his health, I could just imagine how panicked he would be at the sight of it. I was more in need of the bathroom than he was, but I could already hear the shower on full blast. I could just bet he was scrubbing himself down. I fished my wet wipes from my bag and tidied myself up.

It was a good ten minutes before he came out, looking ashen-faced. I sat fully dressed on the bed, waiting. I needed more than a deep breath to calm myself as he started to go on and on about how I shouldn't be working if I was on my period; the agency shouldn't let me, bla bla bla. I tried to say that I wasn't due on for ages, and that he had torn me, but he wasn't listening. His mind was ticking over too fast, speculating whether he would have caught Aids or not. Here we go. Any minute now, despite the fact that he was wearing a rubber and, as he himself had said, he hadn't had any blood on him, he was going to demand my clinic results to make sure. If I was unlucky, he would call the agency to complain – not that the Lush would give two hoots: it wasn't as if he was a regular client of hers; he had only come to her because he had found me after I moved from my previous agency. I resigned myself to the fact that I would have to go to my clinic and get them to write a letter or print out a certificate of my last test, a month back, to keep him happy, as he was really working himself up into a state, saying it was God punishing him for some reason or some such religious rubbish. It wasn't going to be good enough, he reckoned, to hear from my clinic. *What?*

I was getting a headache and, not only that, I was starting to sting, and all because he was a lousy lay. And now he wanted me to drag myself out of bed the next morning to go with him to a private sex clinic that could give us blood tests and get the results back to us that day. He would pay for the tests, he said. I took it he wasn't going to pay for my time that night. He was starting to say that I shouldn't really work until I was better, meaning until my 'period' was over, and that if I didn't show up the next morning, he really should, out of duty, phone up the agency and make a fuss; I might be giving other people nasty things too. It sounded suspiciously like a back-handed form of blackmail to me, but I didn't want him calling the Lush and telling her I might be contagious; I didn't want it to go that far.

To my mind, he was being totally illogical. There was nothing wrong with me. I always played safe, even on my occasional weekends with Mr Tux. I hadn't had any accidents and all my tests were coming back clear. I was certainly healthier than the chainsmoking doctor I saw at the clinic. In any case, given the state Mr Panic was in, and if he was intent on making a fuss, it could be very damaging to my reputation. It didn't matter that he was wrong; just the whiff of there being something up could be catastrophic. If it got around the agency and another girl talked, no client would come near me, and even if I went to another agency, with the way girls moved between them, it wouldn't take long for the misinformation to travel. I wasn't happy about it but it had to be done.

I should have felt smug the next morning at the clinic, as he still looked preoccupied, as if he hadn't slept. I tried to feel sympathy for him, but it was difficult. He went in first and, after waiting in a small room for what seemed like an age, it was my turn. The male doctor sympathized with me when I said that Mr Panic had been wrong that I was on my period. Mr Panic had blamed it all on me, passing me off as a new girlfriend.

The doctor proceeded to give me a full exam, rather than just taking blood, which, I gathered, had been Mr Panic's idea. The doctor commented on the small tear he found. I told him what had happened and he was definitely on my side. The only advantage for me in being there and having a full check-up was my peace of mind. I was now sure the damage that had been done had already healed fairly well and, as I had thought, that it wasn't worse.

The doctor was a friendly chap and, after he had finished taking my blood and swabs, he went out into the waiting room as I got dressed to find Mr Panic, to have a 'word', he said, much to my amusement. I could hear the doctor giving Mr Panic a faint dressing-down in the other room, which cheered me up no end, then I joined a sheepish Mr Panic, who bustled us out, saying he would rather phone in for the results that afternoon than wait. He charitably said that he would let me know the result later – the cheek! At that he left me to find my car, heading off in the opposite direction. I wasn't too worried, and I was right not to be, as he called that evening. I was 'lucky', he said; he was clear and so was I.

He was ecstatic about the negative result and even suggested that, now he knew I was 'clean' and because he had my mobile number (I had given it to him so he could call me to arrange meeting up at the clinic), he would be able to call me without going through the agency. He said he didn't like going in there, and now he wouldn't need to again; I would have the dubious honour of seeing him privately. Oh joy!

I had phoned in sick to get off work the night before and taken two days off. I always had to take a few days off when I had tests, as the needle left a mark on my arm. I didn't want to go to work looking like a junkie. I was less than happy about losing a couple of days' work and I was tempted to tell him where to stuff his suggestion. I chickened out in the end. I just didn't want the hassle. I said I couldn't that night but would call him the next day. He rang off, full of the joys of spring, 'happy to still be alive'. Straight away I made a new category on my phone; he was the first on my barred list. I swore never to darken his dick again.

Avalon was a tall bi Australian girl with beautiful eyes and a pretty face. She was curvy, long-legged and big-busted, but by no means looked like any of the other girls. OK, she was really tall – six foot three at least – but for some reason she had shaved her head. She was completely bald and liked being that way. With her long eyelashes and doe eyes, it actually looked good on her. She was the most unusual-looking girl I had ever seen working for an agency.

When she first turned up, Ms Lush was very keen on getting her to wear a wig, as she said no one would pick her if she didn't, but Avalon piped up that she had been earning elsewhere and had had no difficulties with being chosen and, if no one picked her, she would be the one who was losing out, so what was the problem? Ms Lush, having lost three girls to another agency the week before, was obviously keen to make up the numbers, so she said she would give Avalon and her friend a go. We were all mystified as to how the Lush had come to employ Avalon, but a little digging around and a long discussion with her friend Daphne, who was American, had her spilling that Avalon was quite submissive; she liked a bit of pain and so did the 'pornstar experience'. Daphne whispered and winked. 'You know – she likes it up the bum and does everything, hard core.' No wonder the Lush had taken her on then; she didn't have many girls who would do that sort of thing.

The tall Aussie didn't look at all submissive though –

far from it: she was quite dominant-looking, with her hard stare and robust stature. I wasn't into women as such, but if I were, I would fancy Avalon: she was beautiful. No, sod that, she was stunning, hair or no hair – and that begged the question: was she shaved all over? My mind had wandered during the conversation I was having with Daphne. She was explaining that they were on a round-the-world trip, making money any way they could. She'd pretty much come along for the ride.

She was a short, small-busted brunette, so she didn't have much going for her in the escort phone-request department, and she said herself that, with her gymnastic skills, she earned better working with a stationary pole than 'a floppy one'. She didn't really need to say that she wasn't too much into men. Now, women, on the other hand ... Avalon was not so much into making money but was out and out up for experiencing anything she could along the way, the more off the wall the better. Daphne was the saner of the two and, although slight, with nondescript dark, straight hair, she was very pretty in her own right; it was just that she was overshadowed by her friend.

It was a surprise to all of us when Avalon bounded up the stairs and nabbed the first client of the day, much to the bemusement of the Lush. According to her, the longstanding client, who usually booked shorter orientals, had said that he had chosen her for her novelty value, as she was so unusual looking, rather than out of lust. Unlike Layla, with her ample charms, me with my girl-next-door looks or Anita with her Nordic beauty, Avalon was picked from curiosity; it seemed she was larger than life. I guess the fact that she would take it in every hole helped too. I was intrigued: did being so big make it easier for her? She said she liked being submissive, she liked being degraded by men, but somehow I couldn't see how anyone could degrade her – there was far too much to her, in terms of both stature and personality. I could just see her in my mind's eye shagging Daphne senseless with a big strap-on. Now there was a thought. But what was I doing? I was drifting off and thinking far too deeply about a girl I had hardly met or got to know. Maybe I was more into girls than I thought, after all.

Daphne had met Avalon while working in a Vegas stripclub. I asked her if her friend was always hyper, and Daphne said yes, she was like that naturally, as far as she could tell from having travelled with her for a year; it wasn't drugs, if that was what I was hinting at. Daphne wasn't exactly a wallflower herself and, with all the yoga positions she did in the lounge while waiting for the buzzer, she put all of us lazy sofa lizards to shame.

Both of them were settling in well. One day, Avalon made her very kinky hello in the shortest skirt possible and talked the client into a two-girl booking. Daphne had just been sent off to a booking in a Park Lane hotel, and I was surprised to find Avalon dragging me along with her. She was such a force of nature, I had no way of saying no, even if I had wanted to, so gathering our coats and bags, we headed off to the client's apartment, which was three streets away in a smart apartment block.

Now, from what I could gather, the client Mr Lesbian Lover was into watching Avalon and me make out while he wanked; he would join in later. She had told me all this in a rush as we had got ready to leave the agency. It was fine by me. I had done girl-on-girl before – not normally with girls I hadn't known, granted – but I was by now itching to see her naked and I couldn't see the harm. After all, you can't turn into a lesbian overnight, just by looking at a naked lady – can you? Avalon had the bemused client strip her. He took a seat on a chair by the bed. He was goggle-eyed as she unzipped his fly and started to wank him. Then it all kicked off. Despite being so much taller than me, when she was on her knees, the tables were turned from the get-go, as she had taken out of her bag and presented me with the longest dildo I had ever seen. Now, I have seen some long rubber phalluses before, but this thing was a snake, and she was all but waving it at me to use on her. She bent over the client so he could watch me, now in my lingerie, put my hands to her hips and raise her from her kneeling position. She now had a faceful of cock, and I slowly eased her cheeks apart and gently slid in the rubber head of the dildo as she wiggled back on to it.

The erection she was sucking lustily must have almost choked her as the client thrust up to get a better look, shunting her backwards. That rammed the dildo in as far as it would go but, even so, there was a great deal of length left – more than enough for me to play with and slide up too. In a jumble of legs and arms, we were all on the bed, Avalon underneath and somehow the client still pumping away in her mouth. She squeezed his balls to make him shudder, and I pulled the dildo slowly in and out, trying to get out of my underwear and the client out of the rest of his clothes. So much for him watching and then joining in; we were in danger of him popping too soon, at this rate, which would not have been good.

Wrangling the client out of his trousers, I took charge, making him slow down a pace or two. I ordered Avalon to stay on the bed, then knelt so that I was poised over her head. I looked down at her to keep her there. Her cheeky grin was not just for show. She looked up at my now uncovered pussy and the client eagerly looked on, too. I was hoping she would understand that we had to drag the show out for longer than she had been. Almost before I caught the glint in her eye, and to the very appreciative moan of the client, she stuck her tongue out and pulled my hips down to sit on her face, skewering me on her waggling tongue and sucking with her hot mouth.

It was a bit of a shock, as she was the first girl to really go down on me properly. Most working girls normally fake it; I knew all the girls I worked with did. Girls said they were bi, but it was all for show, an extra selling point. It didn't matter if you actually were or not. You might have a girl's head in your crotch from time to time while guys looked on during duos, but no girl actually wet, open-mouth kissed down there, let alone sucked or tongued you. If you could act well, you just didn't need to go that far.

This was different. My shocked intake of breath came from enjoyment, and she set to work, tonguing my clit. She was gorgeous below me, all soft skin and smelling of vanilla. I completely forgot the client was there, wanking away and willing us on. I didn't know what to do with myself; should I reciprocate? Now the client was on his knees and between hers, licking her out as she was me, beating me to it. I was feeling a bit light-headed, which wasn't good at that point; the girl had a mouth like a vacuum cleaner and wouldn't let go.

I ooohed and ahhhhed, and the client was more than happy, playing with my nipples, as I stroked hers below me. Avalon stopped for a moment but only because he wanted her bent over so he could ride her doggie-style. They got into position, but she took me with her, flipping me over easily, as she was nearly twice my weight, and she continued lapping away after we had rubbered him up. He rode her and then me, as she lay next to us, playing with the dildo for us to watch.

The client pounded away in me until he noticed that she had bent the double dildo in two and was now buggering herself with the other end as well. His eyes nearly popping out of their sockets, he wanted to swap again, and he slid up her arse, with her on her back beneath him, and before he had made two strokes he came over her in a shuddering heap. I just sat there and watched, trying to get my breath back. Now that had been amazing: she had just swallowed his cock up to the hilt all the way up her bumhole, and it wasn't as if he was badly endowed either. Amazing, and I was truly in lust with her tongue – it was just the same as when Tony used to lick me out when I sat on his face, but Avalon was all soft curves to his hard muscle. I shivered at the thoughts that kept popping up in my head of her beneath me and me ordering her to do what I willed, then started to get off the bed to clean up, letting her and Mr Lesbian Lover, who looked a lot worse for wear, lie on the bed resting.

The guy lay still, panting, and I had to tug her and make eye signals towards the bathroom before she noticed that time was nearly up. If I hadn't pulled her away, I'm sure she would have pounced on either him or I for seconds – and there was I thinking that *I* had a sexual appetite. I had finally met my match in Avalon, but it wasn't helping us get dressed and back to the agency on time. The client was looking happy. I didn't really notice or remember anything else about him. He was an average type of guy, nothing in particular to note, and I had been more intent on my buxom playmate than on paying much attention to him. He was just another face. She, on the other hand – well, the minx was something else. If she had been a guy, it would have been easy but she had Daphne with her, and I didn't want to step on anyone's toes. Not that I wanted a girlfriend to add to my list of people to call in case of horny emergencies. Or did I? Hmmm, sometimes too much thinking is not a good thing.

I was only going to get into trouble if I wasn't careful. Avalon might have been acting, for all I knew. I was pondering all this on the way back to the agency, trying to keep up with her long strides, as she ambled along chattering away about where she and Daphne were going to go that night. She had just called and, as it was past 9 p.m. and Avalon didn't have to go back to work, they were going to meet up back at the agency and go off clubbing. I was going to see if I could get another client that night.

I liked Daphne; we got on really well. She would natter about working in some stripclub in the US and I would tell her what little I knew about the British ones, as she was interested in going back to stripping; escorting wasn't really for her. She said that she missed dancing but was thinking of going back later in the year when they made it to Oz, if they 'got that far'. She motioned over to her tall sidekick, who was chatting to the Russians, trying to squeeze details of late-night clubs and other places they could go to after work out of them.

I wouldn't want to cross Daphne. She was nice, and I had the impression she liked Avalon more than she let on. You only had to watch her face light up when they were in the same room together to feel how possessive she was of her. Avalon was totally oblivious, caught up in her own world and living a self-centred life of abandon and lust. No one around her really mattered, which was her only fault, as far as I could tell.

'I think I'm a lesbian,' I half joked to Layla after awaking from a torrid dream the next day. It had featured me with a strap-on and a naked, bound Avalon bent over a white-leather whipping bench before me.

'Ha! You? You are NO lesbian.' She said it deadpan, although I could tell she was slightly amused.

'I could be.' I was a bit miffed.

'You are no more a muff-diver than I am, you like your men too much. Don't forget: I've been in a room when you shag them senseless,' she snorted.

She had a point. 'You don't have to be a rug-muncher to be a lesbian, do you? Can you be a munchee? Is there such a word?' I quizzed. I wasn't really looking for an answer. 'Ever thought I could be bi?' Layla chortled even more when I suggested that.

'Ha, titty, ha. I don't think being paid to do it counts, babe.' She was very amused now.

'Why? Wouldn't you love me any more if I turned a little lesbian?' I put on a sulking voice, just for the fun of it.

'Babe, if you turn a little lesbian, for free, let me know her name, and then I will believe you.' She all but smirked.

I tittered and let her bend my ear, talking about her plans.

In the end, I didn't have a chance to get into trouble, as I was busy and it was only a matter of weeks before Avalon and Daphne moved on. They promised to send a postcard from Paris, but we never did get one, if one was ever sent. Like many other girls I had worked with in the past, they just disappeared.

Afterword: Not the End

'So who's with me?' Tandy was waiting by the foot of the lounge steps ready to leave the agency after a particularly slow night.

'Harvey Nicks, fifth floor?' queried Sonya. She and a few of the other girls had been nattering about going to posh hotel bars and hanging around to see if they could pick up any clients. It hadn't just been a slow night but a slow week. It had been getting progressively worse at the agency, with fewer and fewer men coming in. We hadn't really taken much notice at first, and when regular girls from other agencies came in for interviews to work at ours, they said that ours was busier than theirs. The influx of new girls was worrying, though, because when loyal girls from one agency start looking for new agencies to work at, thinking things must be better elsewhere, it's a sign that something is up.

Some of the girls were getting desperate and had decided that, if the clients weren't coming into the agency, they would go and find them themselves. The only person who wasn't worried in the slightest was Layla. She had all but moved in with her musician boyfriend and had been working less and less, until she was only working weekends, just in case her new man found out what she was up to. She had told him what she had done in the past but didn't feel the need to tell him she was working as an escort now, and she had even found herself a normal job working in a posh shop during the week as cover. Now, on the verge of moving in with him, she was thinking of quitting altogether and moving the last box of stuff she had at mine to his. His flatmate had moved out weeks before, so there was nothing stopping her. He was a very nice guy and they got on really well. I was happy for her.

Layla eventually quit one weekend when there were lots of girls on shift and no clients came in. I wasn't surprised. I was still doing well, as I had amassed quite a few regular clients by that point, and they still called for me, so I was busy even though, all around me, girls were getting a bit desperate. We couldn't figure out what was going on. Even Ms Lush was confounded: it wasn't just happening at her sit-in agency; it seemed that men had just stopped going to any agency. Things had been slowing down for a few months, and a couple of agencies had shut, but the long-standing, popular ones like ours had still been doing OK – enough to cover the bills at any rate. There were always slow times, such as just after New Year, and busy times, such as Christmas, and summer, when all the girls out and about in shorter skirts got men's blood up and they came in looking for some fun. We just took this for one of these times, thinking that maybe it was the financial market, which had been rocked, causing a ripple effect. Tandy said she had heard the same thing had happened in the eighties. Girls had been able to charge a fortune, as there were fewer of them, but then the financial market had crashed or something, and fewer men were out spending. The girls, who had been able to live on Park Lane and had shoe-boxes of cash under their beds, they had been so busy, virtually overnight had to sell their cars and move out, dropping their rates to get any work at all. Tandy said that it would pass; men don't stop being horny just because of financial restraint. Things would pick up.

I had been settled at Ms Lush's agency for over a year by then, and had made some good friends and had some good clients as regs. The agency had been going for ten years, so it was a bit of a surprise when Ms Lush told me in confidence when I came in for an early shift that she was going to close it in two weeks' time. The lease was due to run out and the landlord of the property was doubling her rent. As he thought the sit-in agency was really some sort of brothel and that it was raking it in, he wanted £100,000 a year rent, which was just silly. As Ms Lush said, the agency hardly made two-thirds of that amount as it was. I didn't know if I believed her or not, but she said there was no point in starting up elsewhere. She had had enough of working late nights after so many years and was going to move to live near her daughter; running an agency was bad for her health. I suppose it wasn't surprising really, but I was betting that, rather than the late nights, it was more likely the bottle she drank dry every night and the amount she smoked that was bad for her health.

'Don't tell any of the other girls,' she said, 'they don't deserve to know. I'm only telling you because you're the only one that has been loyal to me, and I appreciate it and know you can keep your mouth shut.' I understood what she was saying. Reading between the lines, she was telling me it was OK to give out my number to my regular clients or to keep their numbers, so that when the agency closed they could find me and I would still have work.

'Why don't you tell the others?' I didn't like to think of her suddenly springing it on the girls and them being made unemployed overnight.

'Them? They'll live. If I tell them now, most will go off to work for other agencies, and then I'll have no girls to work for the next two weeks, despite the fact that they have to work two weeks before they get their deposit back. They won't care. I need the money that will come in as there's no way I'm going to get my deposit back for renting here.' She lit up a fag and took a drag.

I only gave my favourite regulars my number in the end, thinking that I didn't want to be bothered with the gents who got on my nerves. That would keep me afloat for a while, until I found another way of picking up clients. It wasn't as if I was going to risk the bars and have to barter with men, I knew I wasn't very good at that anyhow, and the agencies that were still open were in just as bad a state as ours and, after ours closed, they would be flooded with girls; they could take their pick. There was always the option of putting an advert in the paper where the agencies advertised. A few girls did, but I wasn't sure if I wanted to deal with the idiots who might phone up to mess me around. In the past, Tandy had mentioned that if she left the agency she might consider running girls so, if I was desperate, I could always give her a call if I needed to keep my hand in and gain new clients but, for the moment, sticking with the regular clients, ones that had my number and I already knew were safe from seeing them from the agency, was a better bet.

I'd be a sort of independent escort. That would be novel. I hadn't had to deal with clients on the phone before, I had always been sent or there had been a receptionist to deal with them, but in its favour there was the fact that I wouldn't have to give a cut to someone else. Most of my regs, as they called for me to be sent to them and didn't come into the office, hadn't had to pay the agency fee separately, so they didn't know that the agency's cut was around 30 per cent. As far as they knew, all the money they gave me came to me so, being independent, I could pocket the agency fee too and keep all of it, no questions asked. I could also take my time if I wanted to and not have to rush off. I could dress how I liked and even go back to being a redhead. Most of all, I wouldn't have to sit around and wait to be told where to go; I could make my own plans.

The thought of being independent, free to sit at home all day or to do other things until my phone rang, calling me into action, and not having to hang around in a lounge full of bitchy girls and cigarette smoke was an enticing one, at least until I worked out what to do next. I could do with a holiday, too. I had got into the rut of working solidly, nearly every day now. My play companions had pretty much run their course. Tony was still away, and I had had to call an end to my relationship with Mr Tux, too, as I had noticed I was beginning to become far too attached for my own liking. I didn't want him to leave his wife for me and I definitely didn't want to mess my life up and complicate it with a full-blown relationship; there was far too much yet to discover in the world.

Who knew? Maybe I could change my frame of mind, from working for an agency to working for myself. I could go off on holiday with Mr Professor, one of my favourite regular Mr Average clients, for example. He'd pay for an exotic holiday, the tickets and meals – not for my time, but that would be OK. The other girls all said disdainfully that it was like giving a client a freebie, but if it was a holiday I wanted to go on . . .? He was a nice, older chap, and we got along really well. What was to stop me flitting off to the Seychelles with him in a few weeks' time, as he had asked? With an indefinite amount of time off pending, I found myself at a crossroads.

What *was* a working girl turned escort to do when her agency closed? Join another sit-in agency, try one of those new online escort agencies the girls had been talking about or – gulp – take the plunge without the safety net of an agency and fly solo?

Well, how hard can it be to go all the way and be totally independent?

Handy Hints for Hookers

Every escort has a shag bag – her work bag – full of the things she can't do without. What she puts in it depends on the working girl. With everything I take with me, my shag bag is not exactly a small evening clutch but that doesn't mean I take a carpet bag with me either. I use a smart, plain shoulder bag, preferably one with a compartment on the outside, which is useful for holding condoms and makes it quick and easy to find them. I personally have two work bags, the second an exact double also containing everything on my list. I keep them both by the door ready to go, so I don't have to tip out the contents of one to empty it into the other. One bag is black and the other is cream, so they go with everything. (Yes, I really am like this and, no, I was never a Girl Guide.)

If the bag doesn't have lots of pockets inside, I use small clear zip-lock make-up bags to hold things so that they are easy to find and don't get lost at the bottom of the bag. There's nothing worse than having a horny gent champing at the bit and having to tip out everything just to find a butt plug.

My Shag Bag Supplies

*My top-five must-haves

• *At least ten condoms of at least three sizes. (Also needed to cover toys to keep them clean in my bag). Ten, even if I have only one client and he only gets to do it once. I don't give them the chance of using the tired old excuse of 'accidentally' taking a rubber off/it coming off and then wanting you and pushing you to do something without one to finish. (This is mainly tried on new, green girls, who may only take one or two condoms with them to a booking.)

• *Lube. No matter who you are, the wetter you are the better. (Tip: Also good as a dab below the eye for refreshing dry make-up quickly.)

• *Work phone, for agency to call me on and a number to give other girls. Have a cheap phone just for work; there are just too many reasons not to use a personal phone. Have a spare, charged phone battery too. (It is Sod's law that you will run out of juice just when you need it.)

• *£20+ for cab fare. Just in case the client doesn't pay. You don't want to be stranded in the middle of nowhere, in the dark, walking a long distance in high heels.

• *Agency card for client. If you lose your phone or reception, you will still have your agency's number to hand. (Also write your agency phone number and that of your safety buddy in your work shoes, in case your bag is snatched.)

• Pocket A–Z, or map of the area you are working in.

• Small vibe toy. Turn the battery around so it doesn't go off by accident.

• Sewing kit. Have different threads and a safety pin, as a lost button on a skirt or a broken zip can be embarrassing when you are crossing a hotel lobby.

• Spare stockings/hold-ups. Men's unkempt nails can cause havoc with your hosiery!

• Folding toothbrush and small tube of toothpaste. For an overnight or dinner booking. (Do not use straight after interacting personally with client in case of aggravating any small break in skin.)

• Your own bar of soap or tube of bodywash. Using lots of different hotel soaps can give you a rash, and you never know where a used bar has been.

• Shower cap. So your hair doesn't get wet and you can leave looking the same as when you came in.

• Hair band/folding brush or comb. So you don't walk out of the door looking like you have been shagged in a hedge or on the hotel roof's heli-pad.

• Make-up. After hours of sitting around waiting in a black hole, you really need it to freshen up and, of course, after a booking.

• Wet wipes. For all those stains that pop up from nowhere when you really don't have time to change.

• Wrapped and ready-to-use latex blocking sponge. Just in case it's the wrong time of the month or a client is a bit heavy-handed.

• Small bottle of massage oil. For normal body massage, not hand jobs, as it can perish the rubber.

• Small pot of massage powder. In case the client doesn't like oil. There is always one!

• Snack bar/protein bar. You may never know where you will end up or when you will next eat, and having your stomach rumble in the middle of a booking can be distracting.

• Mouthwash/gum. To get rid of bad tastes and freshen breath before and after a client.

• Clear lipsalve. No lipstick. Even lipgloss can leave incriminating marks.

• Lighter or matches. In case the client smokes, so he doesn't have to waste time hunting for a light – or popping out and coming back with maybe more than a lighter.

• Small umbrella. Because at some point it will bloody well rain.

• Small pen and a notepad. To doodle on when bored out of your mind.

Safety Notes: For Out-calls

Before you get in a car with a client

• Note the number plate and text it to a friend or safety buddy if you need to.

• Check how many people are in the car – look over at the back seat and even in the boot if you are suspicious. Men have been known to hide a friend there.

• Do not go with anyone wearing gloves.

• If all your senses are screaming that something is wrong, don't go with the client, listen to your instincts. No amount of money is worth risking your safety for.

Once in a car with a client or anyone you don't know

• Don't let the driver use the central-locking mechanism.

• Keep the window open in case you need to shout out.

• Don't let the driver park with your door next to a wall so you are trapped in the car.

• If you find yourself in difficulty, try talking your way out of it, e.g., 'My friend/agency is expecting me back in half an hour and if I don't return she/they will report me missing.'

• If you find yourself in difficulty shout 'fire' as well as 'help' to attract as much attention as possible.

Visiting private addresses

• Make sure someone reliable has the address, knows when you are going and when you are due back. Making friends with another working girl and having her as your safety buddy is to the advantage of both of you.

• If you go in a taxi, ask the driver to wait until the door is opened and wave to the taxi driver as you go in, so that the client will realize that someone knows you are there and has seen you going in.

• Ensure that the client doesn't double-lock the front door behind you.

• If you can, for your own peace of mind, look around and make sure there is only one person in the premises before anything starts, or ask your client to give you 'a tour'.

• Have a good look round so that you are aware of the layout of the flat or house and possible exit points. If you need to, use a plausible excuse and ask to be shown the bathroom or kitchen.

• Keep clients in view when they make you a drink and never leave your drink unattended.

• Check under the bed, if it's viable, and pillows for hidden weapons/objects. You can do it discreetly and not alarm the client by dropping something and having to search for it or by plumping the pillows/pulling back the bedspread and quickly slipping your hand under the pillows as you do.

• Keep your mobile phone with you at all times and memorize the address before you go in, just in case you need to call for help.

• Have a second, charged phone battery in case of emergencies.

• Keep your clothes in one place with your bag in case you need to make a quick exit.

Hotel visits

• When you arrive at a hotel door, stand outside and listen for a minute or two before you knock to see if you can hear other voices in the room.

• Look over the client's shoulder before entering a room, just to make sure he hasn't got a friend you're not expecting with him.

• Casually check out the bathroom on the way through the room or suite if you can, opening the door if necessary, just so you know no one is lurking in there who might pop out and surprise you later.

• When you visit hotels, try and have something discreet to wear when you walk through reception, e.g., a long coat and non-metal heels.

• Remember that, if you need to shout for help, there are lots of other people around in hotels.

• Again, keep your clothes in one place with your handbag, and somewhere on a route from the bed to the door, just in case you need to make a quick exit.

• Never leave your bag unattended. Always take your bag and mobile phone with you to the toilet or bathroom.

• Keep clients in view and, if they make you a drink, watch them make it and do not leave it unattended.

Extra tips

• As with all sex work, use your own condoms and put them on the client yourself.

• Condoms with the British kite mark are better than most.

• Don't wear clothes that could be used to harm or choke you, e.g., scarves, thick necklaces, etc.

• In case your mobile work phone is taken, use a code-name or a letter rather than, e.g., 'Mum', for certain entries, so that no one, even girls you work with, can call or text your family out of spite.

• Try not to take valuable items with you, and no photos of family or anything with your address or real ID on, just in case they fall into the wrong hands.

• Don't have your address with your keys in your bag. If you have to have your keys with you, just put your work phone number on them in case they get lost. (Non-work-related: put your phone number in gloves, or your coat collar, or slip a card into your coat pocket so that, if the item gets lost in a check-in cloakroom, an attendant can phone you if they find it.)

• Learn to recognize your own limits with alcohol or drugs. If you are off your face or even mildly drunk your instincts and defences will be muddled. Having your safety compromised isn't very professional.

• Always plan your journey to and from any venue with care. Know where you are going in advance.

• Make sure you have enough money on you for the journey to and back from the booking, just in case it falls through, so you won't be stranded.

• As with all sex work, trust your instincts. If you don't trust your client, for any reason, don't get involved. Many experienced ladies will tell you this is your most useful tool for safety, survival and wellbeing. Personal-attack alarms and other people can only help so far.

• Pick up a copy of the 'Ugly Mugs' or 'dodgy' punters list from your local project or check online warning sites to keep you up to date with what is going on in your area.

• Last but not least, before you leave a house or hotel after a booking, it is best to put your money safe in your bra or inner pocket (not in the top of your stockings as it can slide down and show while you walk). If your bag gets taken from you/you are mugged outside/the client grabs your bag as you leave/hotel security want to check, etc., your hard-earned money will be safe.

He just wanted a decent book to read ...

Not too much to ask, is it? It was in 1935 when Allen Lane, Managing Director of Bodley Head Publishers, stood on a platform at Exeter railway station looking for something good to read on his journey back to London. His choice was limited to popular magazines and poor-quality paperbacks – the same choice faced every day by the vast majority of readers, few of whom could afford hardbacks. Lane's disappointment and subsequent anger at the range of books generally available led him to found a company – and change the world.

'We believed in the existence in this country of a vast reading public for intelligent books at a low price, and staked everything on it'
Sir Allen Lane, 1902–1970, founder of Penguin Books

The quality paperback had arrived – and not just in bookshops. Lane was adamant that his Penguins should appear in chain stores and tobacconists, and should cost no more than a packet of cigarettes.

Reading habits (and cigarette prices) have changed since 1935, but Penguin still believes in publishing the best books for everybody to enjoy. We still believe that good design costs no more than bad design, and we still believe that quality books published passionately and responsibly make the world a better place.

So wherever you see the little bird – whether it's on a piece of prize-winning literary fiction or a celebrity autobiography, political tour de force or historical masterpiece, a serial-killer thriller, reference book, world classic or a piece of pure escapism – you can bet that it represents the very best that the genre has to offer.

Whatever you like to read – trust Penguin.

read more
www.penguin.co.uk

America's Backpacking Book

America's Backpacking Book

Raymond Bridge

CHARLES SCRIBNER'S SONS   NEW YORK

3 5 7 9 11 13 15 17 19 V/C 20 18 16 14 12 10 8 6 4 2
1 3 5 7 9 11 13 15 17 19 V/P 20 18 16 14 12 10 8 6 4 2

Printed in the United States of America
Library of Congress Catalog Card Number 73—1342
ISBN 0-684-13370-9 (cloth)
ISBN 0-684-14545-6 (paper)

To my Father,
who taught me to love walking in high places.

Contents

Contents

viii

Contents

Introduction

This book is a guide to some modern techniques of foot travel in the wilderness areas of North America. I hope that it will be of particular use to some of the many people who have become interested in camping in the last few years, and who would like to take up backpacking but don't know where to start. It is not just a beginner's guide, however. I have tried to make it a fairly complete discussion of the techniques and equipment needed for successful travel in all kinds of terrain and conditions that can be traveled without highly specialized skills and equipment. Hopefully, some of the discussions here will be useful to those who are already backpacking.

Although the book is intended to be complete in one sense, it is quite limited in another. American wilderness and semiwilderness areas differ greatly and any one person's experience in them is bound to be limited by the situations he has encountered, by his preferences for particular kinds of country, and by plain prejudice. The methods discussed in this book are those I have found effective and which have resulted from my own experiences and those of many friends and acquaintances. In the final analysis I can only say that they have worked for me. They are not the only techniques, and frequently they may not be the best. As the beginner gains experience, he will probably diverge at many points from the advice given here.

Since the experience with wilderness travel on this continent is quite extensive and has produced plenty of literature, the need for books on "modern techniques" may well be questioned. One justification lies in the great improvements in equipment that have been made in the last few years. The modern backpacker has a much easier time of it than any of his predecessors in dealing with average conditions, if he knows how to use the equipment available to him. He also can safely undertake many types of trips that would have involved serious risks or much more elaborate preparation in earlier years. For the beginner or intermediate backpacker, though, the boom in equipment has resulted in considerable confusion both in selection and use. This book attempts to lend some help in these areas.

There is a much more serious need for "modern techniques," however, resulting from a combination of the capabilities of modern equipment, the great popularity that outdoor recreation has gained in recent years, the increased accessibility of remaining wilderness areas to weekend and vacation use, and from the nature of many of these areas. The long and honorable tradition of camping in this country copied from the Indians and modified by trappers, guides, and other woodsmen has become entrenched in the programs of many youth groups, in summer camps, outdoor magazines, and general mythology. Unfortunately, this tradition is suitable only for a particular type of wilderness camping, a type completely inappropriate for most use of the wilderness and outdoors today. There is a pleasant nostalgia evoked by cutting poles for tents or lean-tos, building bough beds, and the use of similar skills redolent of campfires deep in the north woods, but continued teaching and practice of these methods of camping is destroying a lot of fine camping country.

This style of wilderness living was based on small numbers of campers in vast, heavily forested country. It was always destructive when it was used in areas not meeting these conditions, and for most campers today it should be a thing of the past. If you get a chance to explore heavily wooded regions that are rarely traveled, you may still have a chance to camp in this manner without putting an excessive load on the wilderness, but you'll have to go a long way to reach such an area today.

Most wilderness and semiwilderness areas that can be reached by the average backpacker fall into one of two categories. Either they are subject to heavy use or they are very harsh environments. The beautiful regions surrounding the Appalachian Trail are in the first category. If they don't look heavily used, it is because people have tried hard to leave few signs of their own passage and to clean up the debris left by others. At any rate, if each hiker traveling the trail hacked down a few live trees, trips along it would soon have all the wilderness feeling of a garbage dump.

An even less desirable sort of place to practice traditional forms of woodcraft is in the hard climate of the high mountains, the desert, and similarly harsh surroundings. Such wild and beautiful environments are the most interesting places to backpack, but the living conditions in such places make life precarious for the permanent inhabitants, a fact often missed by the casual human visitor. A small, gnarled alpine tree, half snag and half alive, is not like a low-altitude shrub that will grow back in a few years. It is hundreds, sometimes thousands, of years old. In country like this the backpacker must learn to be self-sufficient. He must not rip up delicate tundra to form a mattress or tear up brush for shelter. Only a boor would use the beautiful snags for firewood, but ignorance often causes people to do all these things.

Modern technique demands that the backpacker be aware of his responsibilities for leaving the wilderness as he found it. Many more people are now making use of a dwindling supply of wilderness. There is room for all of them without a feeling of overcrowding or the destruction it can cause, but only if they use camping methods appropriate to their numbers.

Old-timers will find that in many cases I emphasize the use of stoves over fires and other such unaesthetic substitutions. This is not because I am too lazy to build a fire, but because I think that many of us have to revise our thinking about appropriate methods of camping. In country where there is adequate deadwood, fires are always pleasant, but what happens when the camper relying on fallen deadwood can't find any? Does he eat a cold meal or go hungry? The answer is evident in well used campsites. Every dead branch within reach is broken off the trees, and then work starts on the live ones. In many areas we will have to stop building campfires if we want to preserve both reasonable access and the quality of the land. There are numerous similar examples which will be discussed here and there, but the point is simply that some of us who have been camping for a while need to rethink our own practices. Then we need to teach newcomers how to enjoy the back country without disfiguring it.

The book is arranged in five parts. The first discusses basic camping and trail techniques, the standard repertoire of the backpacker. The second part of the book deals with equipment, and includes general advice on purchasing and making various kinds of gear, together with detailed plans for some items. The third part has chapters on various special problems and skills, some of which are generally applicable, like first aid and route finding, and some of which are much more specialized, like the sections on mountain travel and backpacking with children. The fourth section has a chapter suggesting trips that might be especially interesting and a chapter about preserving some of the wilderness you will need for continued enjoyment of the sport. Finally there are appendices listing suppliers of equipment, some useful books, and other assorted compendia.

The author's debts are particularly difficult to pin down in a book like this one, since the writer draws on a general fund of information that passes among backpackers largely by example and word of mouth and occasionally through magazine articles and books. Some acknowledgments are implicit in the bibliography at the end of this book. For the rest, I would like to thank all the companions and chance acquaintances who have taught me, argued with me, and laughed at or with me on the trail and at home. All of them are really coauthors of this book.

Part 1

The Art and Folklore of Backpacking

Why Go Backpacking? 1

Like many similar activities, backpacking and its particular attractions are difficult to explain to the unbiased listener. One is usually talking either to a fellow believer—a kindred soul even though he may never have ventured into the woods—or to a dubious questioner whose values or prejudices seem to preclude the possibility of common ground for discussion. Hence the wilderness traveler cast up in society and trying to explain his passion customarily retreats either to banal statements ("I like it") or high-flown dissertations on the moral and spiritual superiority of experiences in the backcountry over any that civilization could possibly provide.

Those who already know in their heart of hearts that wilderness tramping is for them can skip immediately to the main portion of this book, which attempts to tell how they can engage in the sport with reasonable comfort. The curious may want to stay with me for a little, while I endeavor to explain some of the attractions of wilderness travel on foot.

Nearly everyone seems to be familiar with Mallory's famous explanation for wanting to climb Everest: "Because it is there." It has always seemed to me that this must have been the desperate reply of a man besieged by the hundredth little old lady at a cocktail party rather than the cryptic and profound statement of eternal verity which it is often taken to be. So, pressed for an explanation of my lust for wandering around the backcountry, I feel it would be cheating to give a similar response. The real reasons vary from person to person and from trip to trip, but there do

3

Why go backpacking? The beautiful and peaceful setting of this typical backpacker's camp in the Rockies is answer enough for many of us.

seem to be some common experiences and motives in heading for the woods, deserts, and hills.

Before stumbling along any farther, it may be well to talk about what backpacking is. I think of it as a way to travel in the wilderness, carrying everything necessary to live in reasonable comfort for the duration of the trip (or leg of the trip) in the country you are visiting. In his chosen environment, the backpacker is a free spirit, subject to all the harsh laws of nature, but otherwise going where and when he will. This is not a definition, but an idea, and its appeal lies in its simplicity. It is a very basic way of traveling—you want to go somewhere, you walk. You go there not because the law says you have to, because it may get you a contract, or because your boss said to, but because you feel like it, or because it looks like a good place to sleep, or because you think you may find water there. If you're prevented from getting there it will be because a cliff too steep to climb bars the way, because you're not strong enough, or because the weather is bad—that is, for very simple and elemental reasons.

I think the fascinating quality of all sorts of wilderness and backcountry travel lies in the reduction of life to its essentials: food; shelter; beauty; the confrontation with forces and circumstances which are at once comprehensible, mysterious, and so powerful that they will not be denied. The technological gadgets we carry with us are sufficient to keep us comfortable but elementary enough to leave us aware of the true dimensions of things; we are protected from the elements but remain acutely aware of them.

When you go backpacking you leave enough of the paraphernalia of civilization behind to make it just possible to achieve some real contact with the rest of the world, the nonhuman part—contact, that is, of a different kind and quality than the kind a bulldozer has with the topsoil it is pushing around. Such experiences can range from a Wordsworthian contemplation of natural beauty to a struggle with precipitous mountain walls in inclement weather, depending on your mood and inclination. The touchstone for all these experiences is that nature sets the terms. Whether you are basking or struggling, you are in contact with the sun, the wind, and the rain, and you must come to terms with them and live with them. If your trip is in the desert, the scarcity and the importance of water become a fiber of your being. It's not possible to unthinkingly turn on a tap, bringing in water from eight hundred miles away, or to turn on the air-conditioner when you get hot.

For me, at least, all this provides a very satisfying atmosphere. There is a harmonious feeling about living and traveling in country that you're not trying to change or conquer. Being at peace with the world around you instead of at war, you can develop a feeling of connection with the natural cycles that go on all the time, but from which civilization usually insulates us. If you insist on finding a utilitarian purpose for traveling in the wilderness, look at it this way: by living with minimal equipment in a wilderness situation, you gain an intuitive understanding of the basic economies of nature, an understanding which man must clearly achieve in a hurry if he is not to make the planet uninhabitable.

On a less weighty level, it's nice to get off to places where you can look at the snow and the flowers, breathe air which is still relatively clean, hear the birds and the wind in the trees, feel the roughness of sandstone or the smoothness of glacially polished granite, enjoy the companionship of people where there aren't too many of them, and taste the cool crispness of mountain water that doesn't have to be chlorinated to make it drinkable. It's even nice to meet a big bear and realize that the only reason he even cares about your existence is that you're in the middle of *his* trail. (Better get out of the way.)

Finally it's good for your ego to get the feeling that you can take care of yourself with minimal help from civilization, computers, nursemaids, politicians, or policemen. Of course, normal backpacking uses a lot of the products of civilization. It must, for reasons that are discussed elsewhere in this book, but the skills used in backpacking are easily transferred to the problems of living off the land, the techniques of which are fun to try once in a while. Even if the feeling of self-sufficiency is only self-delusion, it's a nice illusion to experience, and one that is getting increasingly rare in the modern world. The *freedom* of the wild places is one of their great attractions and always has been. Whatever its overtones of romanticism, heading for the wilderness enables you to go where you want, when you want, circumscribed not by tensions or contrived rules, but only by the realities of mountains, storms, waterholes, and your own abilities. By the time you come back to the everyday world, you should have gained a sense of perspective about your surroundings and yourself, which will serve you in good stead during those surrealistic encounters with what your city-bound friends will refer to as "reality." Put a pack on your back and join those of us who think we know better.

Aside from the many heavy reasons I've talked about, most practitioners of the sport go backpacking because it's fun. Enlightenment, when it comes at all, usually arrives unexpectedly, so I generally leave it to find its own occasion and head for the hills to have a good time. You can find incomparable scenery, get away from everyday pressures and drudgery, and just have some jolly good fun by getting to the nearest trailhead with your pack and taking off. All the things like good fellowship and pleasant surroundings go along with this, as does the perpetually rediscovered pleasure that goes along with physical activity.

Some of the characteristics just mentioned have a lot in common with the reasons that people engage in any sport, but trivial as they may seem at first glance, I think that on reflection you will find that they form an essential basis for part of a whole life. I, at least, find I become slightly unbalanced by unyielding pursuit of more serious activities for too long a time, especially in the uptight atmosphere of our urban centers. Though certain little voices from my cultural background keep telling me it's immoral to do something just because it's fun, I don't really believe them anymore.

CAMPING AS AN ART

In the last few years the word "camping" has been appropriated by the promoters of various styles and sizes of mobile homes, trailer parks, and associated paraphernalia. Now an efficiently designed small house which can be driven or dragged from place to place, hooked up to the standard public utilities, and used as a convenient spot in which to watch Johnny Carson undoubtedly has its place, but living in one is not camping. This is pure prejudice on my part, but it happens to be one of the prejudices I'm fond of and intend to keep. I have no objections to someone spending thousands of dollars on equipment for the privilege of being squeezed like a sardine into a "kampground" which looks like a parking lot with a swimming pool—*if* that's what he really wants. However, I am annoyed when people who would really like to learn to enjoy wild places are conned by the entrepreneurs into thinking that they can't possibly go camping without carrying a ton of junk that will tie them forever to their car and the commercial gravel pads. I become irate and start to froth at the mouth when the same promoters use their ill-got gains to lobby for more roads, more parking, and more development in the remaining wilderness and semiwilderness public lands.

With each type of camping there is a point where an increase in the amount and variety of equipment you carry no longer brings with it a corresponding increase in comfort or enjoyment. Where that point is, of course, varies with many factors, including subjective feelings. In general, whether you're car-camping, canoeing, backpacking, or whatever, the more equipment you have the more you sacrifice mobility and the freedom to see what's over the next hill. Backpacking represents a fairly extreme compromise in the direction of mobility. Equipment is cut down in weight or bulk so much that you can carry it comfortably on your back, so you're free to travel anywhere you can walk.

7

Because of this, backpacking is one of the best ways to learn the art of camping, which is the art of living comfortably in primitive conditions with a minimum of effort. If you learn to do this with equipment you can carry on your back, you'll never have trouble doing it with a car, canoe, or raft available to carry your gear. In most parts of the country, you'll also be freer to choose where you want to go. Car camping is predicated on the existence of a road where you want to go and on a fairly low population density there, and the latter condition is getting rarer every day. The backpacker needs only a trail, and in many regions not even that. An area can tolerate more backpackers than cars, yet still leave the visitors feeling less crowded and the natural setting less affected (a principle discussed in more detail later in the book). Hence the backpacker has more freedom than most other travelers and campers. The main exception to this rule is in those areas of the country replete with waterways and impenetrable brush, but low on trails—there, the canoe is the free man's means of transport.

BACKPACKING AS A SPORT

As I hope I've managed to indicate, backpacking is a fine way to approach the wilderness, to experience nature. It's also a good sport, partly because it can be enjoyed at so many levels. Families with small children can make leisurely trips, perhaps covering only a few miles a day, with side trips to satisfy more ambitious members. At intermediate levels, you can vary your trips from easy to difficult, depending on your mood and aspirations. The ardent athlete will have no trouble at all concocting trips to bring him near or past the point of total exhaustion. Difficulties requiring skill, experience, and daring are easy to find if they're wanted, and these can be nearly independent of the athletic prowess or conditioning required. A young hustler may be able to easily outperform his more experienced companion in the number of easy trail miles he can cover in a day, but their roles may be completely reversed when the two confront the route-finding problems of an intricate set of desert valleys, the balance and confidence needed on a steep snow field, or the difficulties of building a fire in a soggy forest after weeks of rain. Both the challenges and the simple pleasures of backpacking are so infinitely varied that their interest never wanes, especially when all the accessory pursuits of nature watching, mountaineering, skiing, swimming, and several dozen others are added.

Sports in general are commonly pursued for many reasons and at many levels, and wilderness travel has many advantages as a recreational activity. It is inexpensive, since a good collection of backpacking equipment lasts a long, long time, and since there are essentially no additional costs except transportation to and from your favorite spots. Any number can play. Depending on your taste, you can travel alone or with a party of sixty. You can (ugh!) even make a competitive game out of it, if that sort of thing gives you satisfaction. Backpacking is the best and least boring way I know to get into shape or stay there, and for those who like to fiddle with perfection of equipment or technique, there is always plenty of interest.

A MEANS OF GETTING TO REMOTE AREAS

I think very few people backpack because they have to, at least not much of the time, but for some, backpacking is simply a means of transportation. People who have to or want to get into wilderness areas often have to backpack in, because of the nature of the terrain, its remoteness, or regulations prohibiting other means of transportation. Various occupations from geology to forestry may require backpacking into some regions, as may avocations from fishing to technical climbing. Most people I know whose occupations require extensive wilderness travel have picked the jobs for that reason, and so require little advice from me. Participants in various outdoor activities may find their horizons widened considerably with the acquisition of the skills needed to travel and live farther into the backcountry than day hikes, jeeps, or horses can take them. They may also find, like many before them, that wilderness travel itself will become as interesting as the activity that initially prompted it.

Presumably, if you've read this far you're either already addicted or are interested enough to think you might want to try getting away from the roads for a little while to see what it's like. Those who have already been on a few backpacking trips and have most of their equipment may want to skip the following section, which discusses . . .

HOW TO GET STARTED

As I've already said a few times, backpacking doesn't really have to be very hard, though it's open-ended in that you can make it as difficult as you want to. It doesn't hurt to be in good shape when you start, but it's unlikely that you will be, so the best thing to do is to pick a trip you think you can manage and *go*. If you've never done any camping before, pick a very easy trip, then stop in the middle of the afternoon to give yourself plenty of time to make camp and fix supper. These things take about five times as long at the beginning, but you'll find that they go more smoothly on each trip.

I think that if you pay close attention to the details of planning, avoid excessively ambitious projects at first, and try to arrange your first few trips in good weather, you'll find that your troubles will be minor, even if you have to teach yourself everything. The easiest way to start, of course, is by going with an experienced friend a few times. A club is another good way to start, especially at most universities, though the trips run by some clubs are absurdly expensive. You must also make sure the trip you go on is within your abilities. In either case, try to get your friend or the other people on the trip to show you what to do rather than just let them do it themselves. Otherwise you may find when you go off on your own that you know no more than you did before you started.

The main problems for beginners, however, aren't really a matter of acquiring esoteric skills, getting in shape, or that sort of thing. They usually break down into two difficulties: the lack of equipment and the psychological barrier that we all tend to have about doing something we've never done before. This book is an attempt to give you some help with the latter problem; hopefully, by reading it you will no longer feel quite so intimidated by the prospect of walking off into a wilderness or semiwilderness area for a few days or weeks, since you will know a little more about the problems involved. The first difficulty, the lack of equipment, presents a number of facets, which will vary somewhat according to your particular situation. You may not be able to afford proper equipment, at least not all at once, or, if you can afford it, you might not be convinced yet that you're going to like backpacking enough to justify the cash outlay. Even if you have plenty of money and don't mind spending it, you are still left with the problem of deciding what you need.

Obviously, one of the functions of a book like this is to help you solve some of these problems. Part II is devoted to a detailed discussion of equipment, and I hope it will help you to make an intelligent choice among rapidly multiplying commercial lines. This section also devotes quite a bit of

With the exercise of restraint in your ambitions, backpacking is a fine family sport. Children enjoy having their own packs.

attention to the problems of getting things at the lowest possible prices, making them yourself, and other cost-cutting alternatives. Incidentally, making your own gear will often give you better equipment than the most expensively equipped banker, so don't despair if you're a poverty-stricken student. The boom in commercially available equipment is of pretty recent origin, and for a long time the majority of climbers' and backpackers' equipment was scrounged or homemade.

11

For those who have reasonable funds but want to make sure of their tastes first, there is an easy alternative in many areas—rental. These days many stores specializing in lightweight gear will rent most of the major pieces of equipment like tents, packs, and sleeping bags at fairly reasonable prices. (Availability of items like boots and sleeping bags varies a good deal according to health codes.) Renting equipment allows you to avoid a large cash outlay for major items until you are sure you want them. In addition you will get some experience along the way, and you'll be able to make a more intelligent purchase when you get around to it. If you rent several times, try to get different types of gear each time so that you'll get wider experience. Incidentally, if you plan to rent, get in touch with the store well in advance and find out whether you need to reserve equipment to assure its availability when you want it.

Those a bit harder up will prefer to avoid the rental route as much as possible, to avoid draining their limited funds without being any better off next trip. And of course, if you don't live near any stores dealing in lightweight equipment you won't have the option available.

The most inexpensive alternative is to limit your trips, at first, to areas where limited equipment and makeshift alternatives will do the job while you gradually accumulate your outfit. Special sales, making your own gear, judicious secondhand purchases, and plain scrounging can cut the costs of an adequate outfit way down. The various methods of cutting equipment costs are discussed in more detail in the second part of the book.

Once you do get started, it won't take you long to decide whether you like the sport or not, but if you do want to like it I suggest that you take it easy on your first few trips. If you're tough and game, by all means ignore this advice, but make sure the other beginners you're taking along are that way, too. This advice applies especially to those traveling with spouses, boyfriends, girlfriends, and children with whom they want to take other trips in the future. If the first one is an ordeal, you may never get your companions to go again.

Watching Your Weight   2

If there is one key rule in the technique of successful and enjoyable back-packing it is to keep the weight of your pack to the minimum which is con-sistent with safety and comfort. This is especially important for the average backpacker, who is rarely in top condition, but even the athlete in perfect shape will enjoy a trip much more with a thirty-pound pack than one tip-ping the scale at seventy. Since modern frames make it much easier to pack brutal loads, people often make the mistake of doing so for no good reason. Only a few special kinds of trips warrant this kind of hard, tedious work.

The greatest virtue of modern equipment is that it allows the average weekend refugee from the city to hike pleasantly with enough equipment to make him comfortable for a weekend or a fortnight. If you succumb to the urge to stuff your pack with more and more of the proliferating arsenal of gadgetry aimed at the camping market, you will soon find that your load is as heavy as it would be without the boons of convenient dehydrated food, lightweight clothing, and so on. The essence of a good backpacking outfit must be its simplicity and the multiple uses to which each of its com-ponents can be put.

The trick in assembling your gear is to take everything that you *need*, but to leave the things that "just might come in handy" at home, in the car, or on the shelf in the store. Most things in your pack should come in for heavy use, and even emergency items should be multipurpose whenever it's feasible. Proper equipment design and many other factors will affect the

Near the beginning of the Appalachian Trail on the Katahdin Plateau. The key to enjoyable backpacking is keeping the weight of your pack down.

weight of your pack, but the most important method of reducing weight is ruthless paring.

TAKING ONLY WHAT YOU NEED

Suppose you are planning a trip; your first step would probably be to make a list of the things you need to take. Clearly, all the equipment should be as light as possible, a matter which is discussed in some detail in the second part of the book. Before you even purchase, rent, or dig out the gear, however, you should go through the entire list, asking yourself whether you really need each item. Most lists, like the ones in this book, err on the side of completeness, since their authors cannot know the country and season in which you will be traveling. You will not need three extra wool shirts while walking through Massachusetts in August, or your long johns, down parka, or ice ax. If there are no problems in building fires where you are going, you can leave the stove, gasoline, and fuel can at home, and if easily broken deadwood is available, the ax and saw can stay with them.

By the time you have eliminated enough items in this way, you may find that the remainder can be carried comfortably in your two-pound rucksack instead of the four-pound frame pack—another thirty-two ounces eliminated. With the lighter load you may also find that you no longer feel the need for your heavy boots and can wear your light trail boots instead, taking a pound off each foot, which helps even more than two pounds off the back.

The difference between a sixty- and a forty-pound load, or between one that weighs twenty and one hefting at thirty-five, is difficult to describe in words. The distance you can travel, the way you feel at the end of the trail, the sense of freedom and ease of movement that a light pack can bring, are so fine that they are worth quite a bit of care and thought to achieve.

A rest stop. Your trip will be more pleasant if you pare your pack down to essentials.

BORING HOLES IN TOOTHBRUSHES

Once you have mentally eliminated what you can from the list, the next step is to assemble your equipment—all of it—into a heap on the living room floor. If you are wise, this will be done at some reasonable time. If it is now two o'clock in the morning the night before the trip, you may have to weigh the value of further paring against that of a few hours of sleep. For your first few trips at least, it's really a good idea to work this out well ahead of time.

Having assembled all that stuff, put on the clothes you would expect to wear on the trail, pack the rest of it up, and then pick up that pack. Heavy? You haven't finished chopping yet. Dump it out on the floor again and get to work. A whole cake of soap? How long is this trip going to be, anyway? Break off a little weekend-size piece. A complete roll of toilet paper? Come now, take the remains of the roll in the bathroom instead. Put that family-sized tube of toothpaste back in the cabinet and take a little plastic bag with some tooth powder. The stub of a candle is probably quite adequate for a supplemental fire-starter, and it weighs less than that full-sized candle you have. You will be amazed at how much weight you can eliminate with this kind of examination, at least until you've gotten down to your standard pack. When you find yourself sitting up one night boring holes in the handle of your toothbrush to make it lighter, go into the bathroom and look in the mirror. Do you see the gleam of the fanatic in your eyes? Congratulations, you're now a confirmed weight-watcher!

THE LIMITS OF PARING WEIGHT

Though the process of reducing the weight of your pack never really ends, there are certain factors which set the limits for each person and trip. Some of them have to do with the locale and the season in which you do your traveling. The greater and more uncomfortable the range of conditions in the places you frequent, the more extra weight you will probably have to carry to meet them. The next chapter discusses these factors in more detail, but the basic principle is simple. In the high mountains or in the far north, for example, you have to carry more clothing for safety, even when it's hot, than you would ever have to take in more temperate regions. The reason is simply that in some places it can get cold in a hurry.

Safety always has to take precedence over the elimination of a few ounces, so that first-aid and emergency supplies are subject to reduction only when their adequacy won't be diminished. Just what *is* adequate is partly a matter of personal judgment, but most of the principles are straightforward and will be taken up in various later chapters. The circumstances of your particular outing will be the main determinant. The clothing needed under survival conditions in the Yukon weighs a good deal more than that required in Missouri.

The remoteness of your trip is as much a part of the conditions as the weather and the terrain, at least insofar as the emergency equipment you have to carry is concerned. Consider your situation in the event of a broken leg on one of two trips under identical conditions except that on one you will never be more than a half-day's walk from help and on the other a week's walk. In the first case one of your party could be out and back with help or supplies within a day, while in the other you would face a one- or two-week delay. Obviously the weight of equipment required for a given level of safety is very different in the two situations.

In a similar category with the remote trip is the solo trip. In most areas used by backpackers these days it's rare to find a trip that is a genuine week of hard travel from help. On a two-week trip you might follow a range of wilderness mountains or wild canyonland, but by heading out at right angles to your line of travel, civilization is usually not so far. Hence a *group* is never *that* isolated. A man or woman traveling alone is in a different situation, however. A hard day's walk through rough country is a long, long crawl. Breaking your leg when you are alone leaves you in a survival situation similar to that of the party a long way from civilization. This is one reason why most solo travelers prefer to leave word with a friend giving their route and a reasonable date for return. Then, instead of having to carry enough equipment to survive till they can get out under their own steam, they need only carry enough to last until the friend comes looking. In well traveled country, of course, the solo traveler is not so isolated from potential help.

EXTRA-LIGHT TRAVEL

One odd feature of your pack if you really start to go light is that its weight converges with that of a basic emergency kit. For example, I find that my pack for a hard one-day solo hike into lonely parts of the mountains tends to weigh about the same as that for a two- or three-day trip in the same region. The reason is that on trips like this I like to travel light by taking an absolute minimum of sleeping gear, cooking equipment, and food. I can make a satisfactory bivouac with the same equipment I have to carry for safety in the event of an accident and bad weather. For food on such trips, I carry things that can be either cooked or eaten without preparation. Then if I have wood for a fire, I have something hot; if I don't, I can eat cold food, just as I would in case of emergency. The result is that on a three-day trip the only extra weight I have to carry is a few pounds of food. Traveling this light, a person in good shape can cover phenomenal distance in a weekend, especially in areas and seasons boasting clement weather and thus requiring a minimum of clothing and shelter.

This kind of travel requires certain sacrifices in comfort, however, and very few backpackers choose it for a constant diet. Such Spartan fare is, for most of us, a bit like very rich food—it's nice in reasonable doses, but a little goes a long way. Effective bivouac travel also requires more experience and better technique than camping with more equipment, despite the apparent simplicity. A bivouac site that will afford its occupant any ease demands a more practiced eye than is needed to pitch a comfortable tent. Finally, comfort itself can be a significant safety factor, especially for those who are out of shape or who are beginning to feel more like old hens than young chickens. If your body is in good tone, a poor night's sleep won't hurt you, and you may be willing to risk the discomfort for an extra fifteen miles the next day, but if you're in bad condition and suffer a bad night, you won't make the extra fifteen miles because of fatigue, and you *will* run a much greater risk of an accident. More seriously, you'll be very short on the reserves of strength you need in case of an emergency. In short, the amount of safety and comfort you can squeeze from a minimum of equipment will increase with your experience and with better physical conditioning. Bivouac equipment remains a measure and a goal for the backpacker to consider each time he hoists his pack.

COMFORT VERSUS WEIGHT-WATCHING

No matter how skillful you are, there comes a time when reduction in weight brings reduced comfort along with increased freedom. Some compromise between the two is necessary, but obviously the artful backpacker will make as few sacrifices as possible. Despite the moral superiority of the bivouacker's example, the person who comes closest to achieving the best of both worlds is usually the hedonist who loves his comfort so much that he strives for a luxurious bed *and* a luxuriously light pack. Backpackers with a masochistic bent insist on being uncomfortable in camp, on the trail, or both.

The first things to leave behind are the luxuries that aren't really that at all. There are lots of tiny things that may make life more comfortable at home, but contribute little if any convenience for a weekend or a week on the trail. Multicourse meals requiring numerous pots are all right for large groups, but they contribute little except work and weight for one to four people. For most backpacking menus a soup-spoon-sized spoon and the same penknife that is used for a dozen other things serve perfectly well for personal utensils—a fork and table knife will add weight without adding to your comfort. Other examples form a long list.

These are small items, of course, but you will probably find that it is the small items which add up to comprise those twenty unnecessary pounds in your pack. I'm emphasizing this fact here, because in later parts of the book I mention a lot of little convenience items. The point is that they are only convenient in special circumstances and if you carefully weigh the potential value of each one before you dump it in the pack. It's really worthwhile to have a steel skillet (a light one, of course) on a trip when you're doing a lot of frying—say, if you're catching fish for most of your cooked meals. If you get in the habit of taking the skillet on every trip, though, chances are that it's just adding dead weight to your pack. This particular example might not apply to you, but there are almost certainly some that do, especially if you go to different kinds of country at different seasons. In the mountains above timberline you'll probably need to carry poles for your tent, but in the woods a couple of dead sticks or lines to trees will do as well, and won't add weight to your pack.

For each kind of trip that you take fairly often, you'll develop in time what you consider to be a standard pack. In fact, if you usually go to the same general region you may end up just leaving it packed after every trip, washing dirty clothing and replenishing some items, then hanging it in a corner so that you are ready to leave on a few minutes' notice. Whenever you travel to a different sort of area, though, you'll have to sit down and figure things out like a beginner.

Once you've rid your winter pack of the mosquito repellent, your desert gear of the long snow gaiters, and your high-altitude sack of the double-bitted ax, you still have the problems of choices that really do affect your comfort. You have to decide how big a tent you're willing to carry for extra headroom when you're sitting out the rain, or if it's worth carrying a tent at all. Do you want to carry a full complement of rain gear, or will a few makeshift items do? How warm a sleeping bag do you need?

Items like this will require you to balance a number of considerations, many of which will be discussed in detail in the second part of the book. You will sometimes be forced to choose between a light load on your back and a light load on your wallet. Also, though quality and light weight tend to go together these days, even if you should decide to buy very high-quality equipment, you are unlikely to want to buy or make half a dozen different outfits for the different conditions you may encounter. The best equipment is quite versatile, but you may sometimes have to pay for that versatility by carrying a heavier pack than would otherwise be necessary. If you can only afford one sleeping bag, it has to be adequate for the coldest conditions you may encounter. Clearly, a bag even barely adequate for winter conditions on Mount Washington or Long's Peak is going to be a lot heavier than necessary for summer hikes on the Appalachian Trail. If you want versatility at a reasonable cost, you will occasionally have to put up with a few extra pounds.

When balancing the demands of comfort, you should choose equipment to meet the worst conditions which you will *usually* encounter. In considering emergency gear, you have to prepare for real extremes, but in planning for comfort your guide should be the golden mean. You *may* be surprised by a storm dropping three feet of snow in the Rockies in early September, and you should be prepared to survive it, but if you prepare to be comfortable in it, you'll be miserably uncomfortable lugging a heavy pack through the pleasant weather which is far more likely. At the same time, some snow frequently falls in this place and season, so warm clothes and shelter ought to be standard equipment.

Using this principle, I carry a minimum of rain protection for summer trips in the Sierra Nevada—a water-repellent parka and a plastic tube tent would be one lightweight and satisfactory combination. In case of a week of rain, I'd get soaked through the parka, and I'd wish for a real tent even though keeping moderately dry at night, but the week of rain is pretty un-likely. For the high peaks I'd take a waterproof cagoule as well, just to be on the safe side. In New England, however, where a week of rain would be as likely as not, I'd be sure to carry both a full rainsuit—say, a cagoule and chaps—and a good shelter. A poncho serving as both shelter and rain cloth-ing might be a good choice for California summer conditions, but it would be miserable where rain is common and prolonged, because once you pitched your shelter, you'd get soaked every time you had to leave it.

A FINAL WORD

The freedom of the backpacker inheres in his ability to travel at will over all sorts of country, carrying everything that he needs. His equipment must be as durable and as versatile as possible, and one of the most impor-tant conditions it must satisfy to be truly versatile is that it must be very light. Its other characteristics will vary somewhat, but they should be cho-sen to be adequate for any circumstances they may be called on to meet and as nearly ideal as possible for those they will usually meet. A desert rat's equipment will differ somewhat from the mountaineer's, but since each will have items which serve as many purposes as possible, chances are that either kit could be adapted to function fairly well in the other domain. One of the most basic requirements for enjoyable backpacking of all kinds is a light and versatile pack. It is amazing how many purposes a really sim-ple outfit can serve. A few sweaters and a cover turn a medium-weight sleeping bag into a winter one. Many layers of good but inexpensive cloth-ing can be taken or left home depending on the needs of the moment; and skis, saw, ice ax, or water bottles are strapped on the outside to meet the fantastically varied climate and terrain of North America. The freedom of the backcountry belongs to those who keep their weight down.

3 Nature Makes the Rules

One of the great pleasures of backpacking is the direct contact with the larger environment which it both permits and enforces. Realities from which we shield ourselves in daily life press themselves upon the attention of the backpacker. The common delusion of our species that it is master of all it surveys is quickly dispelled when the city and the automobile are left behind.

The wilderness foot traveler has to come to terms with his environment on peril of discomfort or worse, and this adjustment to the larger world begins at the planning stages of any trip. Equipment, ambitions, and attitudes must all take into account the conditions in the country and season where you are going. Clothing which is quite suitable for the moderate conditions of the lowlands is likely to be dangerously inadequate in the fickle weather of the mountains. An itinerary which might be so simple as to seem trivial in areas with good trails and easy slopes will become an endurance trial with the addition of rough terrain, steep grades, or dense cover. Lightweight footwear which is a pleasure to wear on well maintained paths becomes painfully inadequate for extended talus hopping and scrambling. The list could go on forever.

An example from my own experience may serve as a typical illustration of the need for careful advance consideration of the environment in which you are planning to travel. My first trip in the California Sierra was a ten-day backpacking tour in the northern part of the range, where the

A winter backpacking camp in New Hampshire. The backpacker has to learn to accommodate himself to the environment.

mountains are too low to support year-round snowfields. All my previous mountain experience had been acquired in higher or wetter ranges where water is never far away, and I was woefully unprepared for the conditions at the end of a dry summer in the Sierra Nevada. Two of us carried a 1½-pint water bottle and packs rather heavy with equipment and food for two weeks. As it turned out, the five-thousand-foot climb with which the trip began was completely devoid of water, the springs shown on the map having dried up. By the time we reached the lakes on the other side of the hill we were parched, having had a long and sunny lesson in the ecology of the area and in the California rainfall pattern.

The environment is not, of course, an enemy to be conquered or tamed, but it sets the ground rules which will become the facts of life you will live with on your trip. Some consideration of those facts will make the living an enjoyable and worthwhile experience rather than a pointless ordeal. The thoughtful backpacker will be prepared to meet situations that can be anticipated, avoiding survival struggles except in genuinely unpredictable emergencies.

The environment in which you plan to travel will impose the dominant conditions affecting all the decisions you make about a trip, from the equipment you need to carry to conclusions you will draw about dangers and difficulties. This intimate involvement with the world around you is one of the attractions of backpacking. By going into the wilderness with minimal equipment, you accept the terms it dictates and you become more aware of the forces shaping the world around you than you could ever be when your experience of them was filtered through machines. The awareness should start at the planning stages of the trip with a brief consideration of the nature of your destination.

WATER

The availability or scarcity of water, its patterns of precipitation and drainage, its form and potability, give it such importance that it tends to overshadow other factors. In dozens of different ways water sets the conditions of travel and of life for you and your fellow creatures.

Consider a trip in the desert as an example. Observation of the world around you will reveal erosion patterns of both wind and water, but the lives of plants and animals seem dominated by the scarcity of water. Plant life is structured to waste as little water as possible through evaporation and to absorb and store any moisture that comes. Some forms of animal life lie dormant for long periods and burst into brief and frenetic activity when the hard rains of the desert fall. Your own dependence on your water supply will have long since become evident to you.

The importance of water is just as great in regions where it abounds. It may present impassable obstacles like large, fast-falling rivers, or it may provide the easiest means of access, as stream beds in densely forested areas often do. The type and density of the vegetation is, of course, dependent in large part on patterns of rainfall, as is the erosion that governs many of the landforms. The great glaciers in the Pacific ranges from the

Cascades to Alaska are the result of the heavy precipitation that those mountains receive. Ranges further inland receive less snow and thus have glaciers only at higher altitudes and latitudes.

Water as a dominating factor is most apparent to the backpacker in its role in sustaining his own life and comfort. In regions where plenty of potable water is available in many places, he can carry dehydrated food and only the water and containers he feels are needed for his convenience. Where drinkable water is available less widely, containers and foresight are required to have water when it is needed. In most parts of this country, water taken directly from streams, rivers, and lakes is not suitable for consumption until it is boiled or chemically treated. In some regions, though water is plentiful it may be impossible to make fit for drinking by any practical means. This is primarily true where people have fouled the water with chemical contaminants. In desert and ocean regions all available water may be too saline or alkaline for consumption without distillation. Finally, of course, there are desert regions where all the water you require for days or weeks must either be carried or cached in advance.

The absence of available drinking water severely limits the mobility of the backpacker, since the body requires large quantities at frequent intervals, and because the stuff is pretty heavy. A two-week supply of dehydrated food doesn't need to weigh very much, and it can be carried without much difficulty even by an unathletic person. A two-week supply of drinking water would weigh somewhere between 100 and 150 pounds, even without considering the extra requirements imposed by high altitudes or very hot, dry regions—so the availability of drinking water obviously sets a rather short limit to the distance that you can cover carrying your own water.

TERRAIN

No environmental factor is really isolated from all the others, not even such a seemingly fixed entity as the terrain through which the backpacker walks. It results both from the action of great terrestrial forces and from the nibbling of small pushes and pulls over the great reaches of geological time. The backpacker will generally consider the terrain to be set in its features, though occasionally he may become profoundly, perhaps unpleasantly, aware of the processes of change. Watching a landslide, sitting out a sand-storm, or climbing a scree slope will probably convince him of the impermanence of even the landscape.

In planning his trips the wilderness wanderer has to concern himself with both the fixed and the changing aspects of the country he hikes through, and as his understanding of the terrain of a particular region grows, so will his appreciation and his imagination in devising routes. A steep ravine of identical contour will have an altogether different meaning in two different places: in one it may provide a highway of talus blocks from top to bottom, while in another it may present difficult slabs of smooth granite or treacherous heaps of crumbling rubble.

The usual way of getting advance information about the terrain of a particular region is to consult a contour map. The technique of map reading is discussed in detail in a later chapter, and with practice the back-packer will find that an amazing amount of information can be deduced from modern government maps. Supplementary information on the geology, climate, and other features of an area fill in the details on the basic outline provided by the map.

Of course, the amount of information the trip planner wants or needs varies a good deal with the trip he is planning. For a weekend in a new segment of a familiar mountain range he may do no more than glance at a map of the area. A long trip through infrequently traveled and unfamiliar country, however, may require many hours of map study to determine the feasibility and requirements of the proposed route.

CLIMATE AND WEATHER

Climatic influences dominate life in the wilderness and provide much of its interest. For the backpacker, accommodation to the patterns of weather and climate are at once the most challenging and difficult problems of the sport. Since the weather can change in a few hours or minutes, the wilderness walker must be prepared to adapt to widely ranging conditions in a short time. The fickle nature of the weather is the main reason why back-packing equipment needs to be so versatile, suitable for wide ranges of temperature, sun or rain, wind or calm, precipitation changing from rain to sleet to snow.

Climate and weather on the North American continent have an amazing variety, and familiarity with their vagaries is the ambition of everyone seriously interested in wilderness travel. Climate and weather influence everything; the number of possible examples is infinite.

As one instance, consider the influence of snow on your trip. Along the coast ranges in California, you can plan a conventional backpacking trip at any time of the year. In winter you will carry warmer and more weather-proof clothing if you are wise, but except for river crossings, the weather will affect your comfort and speed, not your ability to travel. A couple of hundred miles farther inland in the mountains of the Sierra Nevada the story is quite different. Sierra Nevada means snowy range, and the heavy winter snowfall in the high country often makes travel without skis or snowshoes not just difficult but impossible. The snows in winter make a smooth highway for the passage of the cross-country traveler equipped with skis, covering boulders, small trees, streams, and houses. The same snow arrives in storms of quite amazing ferocity, sometimes trapping even the well equipped traveler for days. The backpacker encountering the first big snowfall of the year in the wilderness had best be prepared for a tough trip out.

In regions where the climate permits snow to rest on the ground throughout the year, permanent snowfields and glaciers may provide the traveler with easy paths or formidable obstacles. Such a climate always leaves us a gift of spectacular and wildly beautiful scenery. Other ramifications range from the fantastic geological effects produced by glaciation to the impenetrable thickets that often result from the fine watering of lower valleys by the snowfields.

Of the many environmental factors which will influence your trip, climate and weather are, along with the availability of drinking water, the most important matters for advance investigation in planning a trip. A misjudgment of terrain may mean that you won't get nearly as far as you expected, but this is usually not particularly important unless you are heading for a cache or rendezvous. A real misjudgment of climatic conditions will probably result in your being pretty uncomfortable, and it may be really serious. There are many instances of campers unfamiliar with severe climates getting into trouble in the high mountains and in the far north, because they were inadequately equipped for a sudden onset of storm and cold.

27

I always try to carry adequate equipment to keep me comfortable in any weather that I might reasonably expect to encounter on a trip and to keep me alive in any conditions that might possibly occur. In order to make judgments like this, however, you must know something about the area to which you are going. Such knowledge must include both average and extreme conditions. Average temperature in arctic and subarctic regions in the summer is pretty high, for example, because the sun is shining most of the time. Things can change in a hurry, though, and you had better be ready if they do.

VEGETATION

The plant cover in a particular region is dependent on many factors, including those already mentioned, and it in turn plays an important part in storing water, holding down erosion of the landscape, and so on. For the backpacker, the vegetable cover is of particular interest for still another reason; it affects his mobility as much as the terrain does. Anyone who has ever bushwhacked through really thick forest or bush will know immediately what I mean. Others may take this as a warning. In some areas working through a few miles of forest may take days, while in others the obstructions presented even by heavy woods may be only minor.

In practical terms the plant cover will determine whether the backpacker can plan to travel cross-country with comparative freedom, or whether he must confine his travel to established trails. Where there are no trails and the cover is thick, route-finding problems center on ways of avoiding brush. Under such conditions even a very long detour may often prove to be a shorter route in time than a seemingly direct way.

THE BACKPACKER AND HIS SURROUNDINGS

Only a few of the many environmental factors which affect the backpacker have been mentioned. There are others, and all of them together are woven into a fabric so complex that the individual threads cannot always be distinguished from one another. The success and ease of the wilderness traveler depend on his ability to understand this pattern and to follow the warp of the weave rather than trying to go against it. As his understanding of a particular sort of country grows, he will learn how to find water, how to make the easiest way across the terrain and through the brush, and how to keep track of his wanderings easily. The greatest aid to understanding a particular environment is an open and observant mind.

This understanding begins long before a properly planned trip, whether through previous knowledge, observation of a nearby area, or investigation of the area of the proposed trip through books, maps, friends, or even a look from the roadhead before you decide what you will need.

Of the many sources of information available to the backpacker, the topographic map is the most useful. Reading one is discussed in a later chapter. An experienced map reader with a little knowledge about the geography of an area can pick out campsites and gauge the length of a day's walk from a topo map.

Some other sources of information are listed in the appendix. Important facts are the average minimum and maximum temperatures in the place and season where you plan to travel, the extreme highs and lows that have been reported there over the last ten years or so, rain and snowfall patterns, and so on. Obviously, the need to look up these items is only important for areas which are strange to you. If you live in Ohio and are planning a backpacking trip a hundred miles from your own home, you don't need climatic summaries to tell you what sort of weather to expect. On the other hand, if you are making your first trip to the British Columbia coast range, you'd better get all the information you can.

In some parts of the country, you can be fooled by very short distances. This is particularly true in and near the mountains, which often make their own weather and drastically influence the weather of other areas. By traveling up the side of a mountain, you can get into a completely different climate very quickly. The climate at high altitude bears great resemblance to that of regions far to the north. For example, the vegetation on the plateau of Maine's Mount Katahdin is similar to that of Greenland. Though effects vary to some extent, a rise of a thousand feet in altitude brings one to a climate similar to that three hundred to five hundred miles farther north. The backpacker can change climatic zones faster by climbing a mountain than he could by flying north in an airplane. He will miss the midnight sun, but may have an even better chance to be caught in a summer snowstorm.

29

In the mountains the weather can change completely in a very short time. Storm clouds building in the Rockies.

Mountains cause many other effects that concern the backpacker. By driving a short distance across even a minor range, the traveler may pass from a fairly wet zone with easily available water into a desert in the rain shadow of the mountains. There are many cases like this where major geographical features produce great discontinuities in climate. The backpacker should be wary of assumptions that a short drive or walk will make little difference in conditions.

The tremendous variety of the American landscape provides challenge and interest to the backpacker that would be hard to equal. A day's hike can take him from lush forests to alpine meadows and snowfields, and another day can have him well out into the desert. Mountains and ocean beaches stand side by side. The wilderness traveler who remains keenly aware of the necessity of accommodating himself to his surroundings can spend a long lifetime sampling these possibilities without even coming close to knowing them all.

The Art of Travel   4

The backpacker travels by walking, an art which is in a severe state of decline these days. Beginners at backpacking are even likely to find themselves in the embarrassing position of having to *learn* how to walk. It is important to admit the need, however, at least to oneself, in order to consciously develop the habits necessary to get you farther than the garage without completely exhausting you. Young people in reasonably good shape can get away with inefficient walking while they unconsciously acquire the habits needed for negotiating miles of rough terrain comfortably with packs, but if you are in mediocre shape, you had better use your physical resources as economically as possible.

LEARNING TO WALK

Walking on even moderately rough terrain can be very tiring to those who have not become used to it. Once some practice has given you the knack, you may find that miles in the wilderness are less of a strain than an equal number on the hard pavement. In any case, the first trick in walking long distances is to develop a reasonable stride. Most people accustomed to walking only to the file cabinet or the refrigerator get used to taking very short steps. Swing your legs out in front and put your body into your walk. Of course, your stride shouldn't be exaggerated, and it is always subject to

Even on a good trail like this one, obstacles are the rule rather than the exception. Footing is likely to seem rough to those used to city walking.

the demands of pace, which will be discussed shortly. Even a very slow walk, however, should have rhythm and spirit—get a little spring in your knee and toe. Picking up your feet is most of the work, and adding six or eight inches to your stride can add up to a lot of extra miles by the end of the day.

Obstacles are not the exception in wilderness walking; they are the rule. Prepared trails wind through many extra miles to avoid them, and for good reason. The constant presence of rocks, fallen trees, stumps, roots, mudholes, and other barriers makes it very important that the hiker trying to conserve strength avoid wasting energy on each obstacle. In general, anything large enough to break your stride should be circumvented if this is reasonably convenient. Stepping over the obstruction is second choice, lifting your body and pack weight as little as possible; and stepping up and climbing over ranks a poor third. It is usually much less tiring to walk around fallen trees than to clamber over them, especially when you are wearing a heavy pack. The combined heights of all the rocks and trees you could have walked around can add up to a lot of climbing by the end of the day. In addition to this energy factor, such obstacles often provide insecure footing and invite accidents.

Obstacles tend to shade into the category of generally rough footing, especially in rocky country. This is where the matter of breaking stride as the dividing point comes into the matter. In rocky areas a trail is often defined simply by a cleared route through the brush or a line of ducks crossing a talus fan, and the hiker must pick his footing over the rocks. Practice will enable the backpacker to balance his way along such routes without breaking stride, picking the route ahead with his eyes to avoid more up and down than necessary.

The key to this and other kinds of walking is *pace*. One of the most conspicuous marks of the beginner is his inability to pace himself properly. An experienced walker, even one who is out of shape, knows how to pace himself to make the most efficient possible use of his muscles (though vanity may occasionally make him forget). The object of pacing is to keep the individual hiker or group going steadily at the fastest speed that can be maintained, giving walking a rhythm which keeps the muscles working well and eats up the miles. The most common mistake of the novice is to try to go too fast, forcing his muscles to work jerkily and necessitating frequent stops for breath and for rest.

The start-stop routine is tiring, inefficient, and unenjoyable. It is characterized by brief spurts and panting halts along the trail, especially an uphill one, and by long and frequent rest stops collapsed by the side of the trail. There are a lot of reasons to avoid this routine. It is slow. Extended and repeated stops will hold you back much more than a slow pace that is fairly steady. In addition, your muscles cannot work at their best with this kind of pace. Long rests allow the muscles to stiffen, so that it is hard to get started again. Pushing on too hard in between stops, though it may temporarily convince you that you're getting somewhere, taxes your muscles in a way which you cannot afford if you're out of shape and trying to get somewhere without having to call for helicopter service.

When the muscles are pushed beyond their ability for continuous effort, waste materials accumulate in the tissue. As the concentration of excess wastes builds up, you get tired and you have to stop until some of them have been carried off. The body cannot get rid of these wastes very efficiently, so you have to rest a long time. Roughly, the harder you push yourself past the capacity of your body to handle these wastes as they are made, the less efficiently your muscles will operate. So unless you are in good enough shape to be well on top of the situation, when you get to that hill don't dash madly for the top and stand there panting; go up it slowly and steadily, using your shortness of breath as a guide that you're pushing too fast.

Though you should avoid going too fast and though this is the most common beginners' mistake, I don't mean to imply that you should avoid making any demands on the body. The push should be in the form of sustained effort, and a pace should be considered too fast precisely because it cannot be maintained. Leisurely walking is fine some of the time, but the body must also work hard to develop reasonable muscle tone and endurance. If you expect to get into decent condition within a reasonable length of time, you'll have to put up with a little discomfort occasionally. See the chapter on physical conditioning for more details.

WALKING UPHILL

Climbing hills requires a slower pace than moving on even ground, and for the most part this just means that you shorten and slow your stride somewhat. Try to maintain a rhythm rather than get into the habit of spurting up a few steps to hang panting on a tree and then repeating the process up to a rock a bit farther up. On really steep and strenuous grades, especially at high altitudes, you may find that you can't maintain a normal rhythmical pace. At this point you should switch to the *rest step*, which enables you to incorporate a rest in each step while still maintaining a steady, even pace.

It's hard to get a feel for the rest step except in hard climbing where you need it; then it becomes quite natural as soon as you get the knack. Suppose you are stepping up with your weight on your right leg. When you put your left foot down, lock your right knee and leave all your weight on the right leg. Pause and rest for a short time before shifting your weight to the left leg and stepping up. After stepping up, lock the left knee, and leave your weight on your left leg for the rest interval. The length of each rest interval will depend on how hard the slope is, but the important thing is to maintain a regularity of pace.

When you are walking in rough country, especially with a heavy pack, learn to walk with your eyes well ahead of your feet. Use the ground to your advantage whenever possible. Watch the trail ahead; climbing two steps here may save five uphill steps a few yards farther along. Balancing along some rocks may save some up and down. Cutting to the left may avoid a fallen tree. Walking with your eyes will eventually become an established habit, but you have to cultivate it at first.

TAKING CARE OF YOUR FEET

Whatever violence you're willing to endure in the rest of your body either on trips or in exercising, you cannot afford to brutalize your feet. As the injunction goes, "Be kind to your ass, for it bears you." The backpacker's bearers are his feet and they will make him rue any unkindnesses. In real wilderness areas, whether in summer or winter, the mark of the "tenderfoot" is his sore, blistered, or frostbitten feet, which result from improper care.

The first rule in taking care of your feet is simply to prevent common foot ailments from occurring. Corns, bunions, and ingrown toenails are really serious matters on the trail, the more so because there's not much you can do about them the night before the trip. All these ailments can be prevented and cured, and it is foolish to allow them to occur or to neglect them if they do. The most common cause is improper footwear. Fallen arches are a different problem, and they may require special arches in your hiking boots. If you ever have trouble with painful arches, try your boots well in advance, and get special arches put in if you need them. The strain on your feet is much greater on long walks with a heavy pack, though wilderness footwear is generally better for the feet than city slickers' pointy shoes.

Getting your feet into shape is at least as important as preparing any other part of your body, especially if your first trip in the season is to be a long one. Breaking in a new pair of boots (discussed in a later chapter) will help toughen your feet as well. In general, walking with proper footwear is the best way to toughen your feet, but many people also find it helpful to bathe them in alcohol or alum solution as an aid to toughening. If they are tender, bathing them when the opportunity arises, using foot powder, and changing the socks frequently are all helpful measures. If you bathe your feet at rest stops, an excellent and refreshing practice, be sure they are dry before putting your boots back on.

BLISTERS

However tough your feet ought to be, proper care during trips is mandatory. A hot spot or chafing feeling on your foot is a warning that a blister is forming, and it must be heeded soon in order to head the blister off. Blisters should be prevented rather than treated. If the chafing is caused by loose boots or by wet or dirty socks, tightening boots or changing socks may solve the problem. Otherwise, the irritated spot should be covered, preferably with moleskin, which can be obtained at any drugstore and which ranks as one of the hiker's best friends. Adhesive tape may also be used. If you wait too long and get a blister anyway, don't break it unless you have to—that is, unless you've let it get so bad that you can't fit it and your foot both into the boot at the same time. In this case lance it with a sterile needle or knife point, making only a small hole at the side for the liquid to drain. Whether the blister is intact, broken, or lanced, wash the area well, paint it with antiseptic, cover with a small, thin piece of sterile gauze or cotton made slippery with ointment or Vaseline, and then cover with moleskin or adhesive tape. On a long trip keep this spot scrupulously clean, since if you get an infected foot you may really be in trouble.

At the risk of being pedantic, I reiterate: don't get blisters in the first place. Prevent them by keeping your feet clean, taking care of them on the trail, carrying enough socks to be able to change them when necessary, and using proper socks and boots.

SORE FEET

Unless you have been doing a lot of hiking and backpacking recently, you can expect your feet to be tired at the end of a day on the trail—you might even consider them sore, under any reasonable definition of the word. Really sore feet, though, are bruised badly enough to prevent your walking on them without a good deal of pain, and they can be avoided with boots that fit properly and are sturdy enough for the terrain. Wearing footgear that is too light over very rough country with a heavy pack is a good way to get sore feet. The chapter on footwear in the equipment section goes into detail on the choice of boots and socks. A backpacker wearing sneakers on the trail should be wary of punishing his feet too much, unless they are well toughened.

Keep your toenails trimmed to a reasonable length for hiking. Downhill walking with long toenails can create some very painful bruises. It is also a good idea to tighten your boot laces a bit before starting long downhill sections to prevent your feet from sliding about too much.

Your feet will be much more comfortable if you change socks frequently. Dirty socks are uncomfortable, and they provide less insulation in cold weather. Usually it is convenient to wash your dirty socks out when you change them, hanging them on the outside of your pack or somewhere in camp to dry. In wet weather wring them out as much as possible and hang them in the peak of the tent. Of course, where water is scarce, as it is in desert and winter camping, you may be unable to wash socks, and under these conditions you may want to carry a few extra pairs.

EATING ON THE TRAIL

Whenever you're demanding that your body produce a lot of energy, especially in sustained effort, don't neglect its need for food. Hauling yourself and your pack to the top of a ridge requires a good deal of work, and your muscles won't do that work without fuel any more than your car would without gasoline. The fuel can come either from recently digested food or from the body's reserves of fat. Even though most of us can easily afford to lose some of our fat reserves we should recognize that they are not readily available to the muscles on an instant's notice. If you starve your body in order to force it to use up last month's beer, you'll have to pay the price of a slower climb up the hill and slightly shaky knees at the top.

If your main concern is to make your body run as efficiently as possible between the roadhead and camp, you will have to see that it has fuel available the whole way. Most backpackers do this by eating small snacks throughout the day, beginning at breakfast and nibbling at rest stops or sucking on candy along the trail. This is a particularly efficient way to keep the muscles supplied with energy, since it both maintains the level of immediately available nutrients in the blood and avoids the need to eat large midday meals, which require that much of the blood supply be shifted from the muscles to the stomach. Instead of a major repast, lunch becomes a slightly larger snack eaten in a longer rest period than the others before and after.

The body is really quite capable of adjusting to widely varying styles of eating, so my advice of frequent snacks is merely suggested because it seems particularly suitable for the weekend backpacker whose system is not tuned for sustained effort day in and day out. Frequent small snacks keep usually sedentary muscles operating in an efficient way on the trail. On long trips it's easy to get your digestive system used to whatever regimen seems desirable.

Food is discussed in more detail in Chapter 6, along with various ways of keeping your body fueled without too much trouble. In choosing trail food remember that when you are pushing your muscles hard, you are less likely to become fatigued if you keep your blood sugar up, which is easily done by drinking a sweet beverage or sucking on a piece of hard candy. Fats and proteins "stick to your ribs" because they take longer to digest, but they are less useful for quick energy.

WATER AND SALT

Drinking water is much more critical for the backpacker than food, since the body can function with no food for much longer than it can do without water, and since the weight of a day's water is much more than that of food for the same period. Fortunately, in many backpacking areas finding drinking water presents no problem. Frequent stream-crossings often bring the wilderness walker into almost continuous contact with better drinking water than that available from the tap at home. Where this is true, there is no problem, and you can simply have a drink when you feel like it.

The blissful situation of having readily available pure water is confined to quite limited regions, however, and in large areas of the country there is virtually nowhere left with a pure stream. Any vestige of civilization upstream makes all water (except tap water intended for drinking) suspect. Besides the problem of contamination, in many regions surface water is un-

Drinking water is more critical for the backpacker than food.

common enough to make you pretty thirsty between creeks and springs.

General precautions about the potability of water and methods of purification are given in Chapter 6. It is important to remember that one drink of bad water can ruin your trip, and it may get you in serious trouble if you are far away from medical care when you come down with the bug you drank. In some kinds of places the water can safely be assumed to be pure, but when there is any doubt it must be purified. In areas with suspect water this generally means carrying a water bottle with treated water. When you reach a stream, drink your fill from the bottle, refill it, and drop in the required purification tablets. Don't try to drink the water before the chemicals have had time to work.

Travel in dry country requires carrying enough containers for an adequate water supply between resupply points, including provision for emergencies. The actual quantities you will need depend very much on temperatures, humidity, the difficulty of the terrain and weight of your pack, and various individual factors like physiology and personal stoicism. See Chapter 6 for details.

One of the best ways to save yourself from having to pack too much weight in dry country is to learn to "tank up" when water is available. People used to nearby water faucets generally drink only until their thirst is satisfied, but the body can comfortably absorb a good deal more water than that. Once you get in the habit it is a simple matter to sip your way through a quart or two of water while you are puttering around in the morning or at a lunch stop near a waterhole. After I learned this trick I found myself more comfortable after a day carrying only a quart of water when I used to be carrying a half-gallon.

Other tricks for conserving water are well known: sucking on hard candies or pebbles, taking sips and washing them around rather than drinking in swallows, and so on. You can learn to get along on less water, but there is definitely a limit to this. For one thing, most of these methods assume you'll reach water at lunch or the end of the day or some time soon. Tanking up isn't a way to get along with much less water, but simply a way to consume it at more convenient times. Your body needs a lot of water in hot weather, and except in survival and endurance situations, it is senseless to deprive it unnecessarily or to experiment too precipitously with reduced supplies. In hot weather evaporation is the way your body cools itself, and without enough water it can overheat dangerously quickly. Also, as a practical matter, if you become too dehydrated, you will have to spend some time restoring your body's water reserves. You'll travel faster by carrying more weight in water than if you carry less but have to stop for several hours when you come to a spring just because you've allowed yourself to get too dry.

It is obvious that in country where water is scarce, its location pretty well governs one's line of travel, stopping places, and general view of the trip. One travels from Big Water Spring to Little Fork Creek to Jackson's Well. Trail food in country like this should be chosen to go down easily with small quantities of water. Save the peanut butter and Logan bread for a wetter trip.

Not all thirst in dry country indicates a need for water, though. Whenever you do a lot of perspiring, whether aware of it or not, you need to replace the salt lost in perspiration as much as the water. Heavy perspiration uses up more salt than you normally get in your food, and the deficit has to be made up. Oddly enough, one of the signs of a need for salt is often an insatiable thirst. More advanced signs include muscle cramps. In general, you can expect to need extra salt if you are drinking a great deal of water.

Some people like the simple expedient of taking salt pills to replace what they sweat away. These are hard on the stomach, though, and I prefer to just use ordinary table salt, putting extra in my food, sprinkling a little in my water, or licking it in small amounts from the back of my hand. If you use tablets, take them just before drinking or eating to avoid nausea.

CLOTHING

The importance of your clothing depends mainly on the kinds of places where you plan to go. In other words, it depends on whether the main function of your garments is to protect your anatomy against the elements and the hazards of the trail or to satisfy the needs of propriety and your ego. I know very little about either your ego or propriety, so I will confine my remarks to those situations where protection is important.

You may want your clothes to protect you from scrapes with brush, thorns, rocks, and the like, to ward off the rain, to shade you from the sun, to keep you warm, to break the wind, or any combination of these. The equipment section of the book goes into considerable detail on choosing and making clothes to do these things, so all we're really concerned with here are a few principles for making the best use of your clothes when your body needs shelter from one of the beasties just mentioned.

There's not really much to say about protection from cacti, scrub oak, sharp volcanic rock, and such. The first principle is to stay away from all that stuff, and if you can't, have smooth, tough clothes that keep you from getting all scratched up and which don't get immediately torn to shreds. Move slowly and smoothly through brush so that when your clothes do snag you'll be able to stop before you rip the seat off your pants. Good luck!

WALKING IN THE RAIN

Much of the time, rain really doesn't present much of a problem to the backpacker, providing he is properly equipped and has the right philosophical attitude. On some occasions, however, wet weather makes a state of reasonable comfort so hard to achieve that the most skillful wilderness traveler is likely to be challenged.

41

The main problem with rain is, of course, that it tends to get you wet. Worse, as the days and weeks of rain wear on, it gets everything you are carrying with you wet, too. It requires a true act of will to smile and hold forth on the joys of backpacking without heavy sarcasm when, after slogging through two weeks of rain, you set about pitching your soaked and muddy tent at least high enough above the water line to ensure against your drowning that night, all the while trying to decide whether it would be warmer inside or outside your sodden sleeping bag.

Aside from the misery it can inflict, rain can also be really threatening under certain conditions. Probably the most dangerous kind of storm one can encounter in the wilderness is cold rain driven by high winds, followed by a drop in temperature. If the rain destroys the insulation value of your clothing, the cold wind can easily kill you unless you find shelter.

The methods of handling rain are: (1) avoid it, (2) stay dry despite it, (3) at least keep your spare clothing and sleeping equipment dry, even though you get wet, (4) maintain an ability to dry yourself and your gear out, even if you get soaked, or (5) endure it. You may select your own order of preference. Conditions will probably dictate the choice anyway.

Whether and how hard you try to avoid traveling in the rain depends on your aesthetic sense, the depth of your masochism, and the area you travel in. When you get caught, of course, you have to be prepared with the right equipment and philosophical attitude. Some areas get so much rain that there simply isn't any question of picking a dry weekend—there aren't any. Similarly, on long trips you just have to take the weather as it comes, after the first few days. All this being true, let's suppose you have carefully chosen storm gear appropriate to the place and season—what to do when the rains come?

The first thing to do is to *do something*, even if it is only to decide that you are dealing with an afternoon shower and would just as soon get wet. Don't walk along for a while waiting to see whether it's really going to rain and allowing your clothing to be gradually soaked because you're too lazy to get out the poncho. If you need rain gear, get it out when those first few drops start coming down, or before. Staying dry is generally easier than getting dry. If your pack needs some kind of special cover to protect the contents, it's important to take care of this right away, lest your spare clothes and sleeping bag get wet.

If the weather is warm enough, the simplest way to keep your clothes dry is to put them in the pack, and just wear your boots and a bathing suit, shorts, or whatever, enjoying the shower. It isn't always warm enough for this method, so generally you'll have to put on your poncho, cagoule, parka, or whatever. Try to allow as much ventilation as possible, since all waterproof garments tend to condense moisture from your body on their inside surfaces, soaking your clothes with your own perspiration. This problem is particularly acute in cold weather, precisely when you can least afford to get your clothes wet. Don't draw the openings at the neck, bottom, and sleeves of a rain parka tight unless this is necessary because of wind-driven rain. Avoid sweating when you are wearing rain gear by slowing down if necessary.

Don't forget about your pants when it starts raining. Weather permitting, shorts work well in the rain, with long pants staying dry in the pack for the evening chill. A similar effect may be achieved by simply rolling up the trouser legs. If you're wearing long pants, though, you'll probably need to put on rain chaps or pants. Wet brush, water dripping from cagoule or poncho, and wind-driven rain will often soak your pants in no time unless they are protected.

When the rain first starts it is time to think about fires if you're in wooded country and you want a blaze later. It's much easier to gather kindling for an evening or lunchtime fire before everything on the ground gets wet than to wait until later. By the same reasoning, if you build a lunchtime fire, use it to dry some kindling for the evening one.

Reasonably comfortable travel in the rain demands the same foresight and common sense that is the secret of all effective wilderness travel. On a Sunday walk it is largely a matter of taste how much trouble one bothers to take to keep dry, since wet clothes can soon be shed for a hot bath. You may just not worry about keeping dry during a summer afternoon thundershower in the southern Rockies if you are sure that the dry evening winds will take care of your wet clothes anyhow. On the other hand, on long trips in humid areas where the duration of rain is unpredictable, a great deal of care is often needed to avoid getting any wetter than necessary, and this is particularly true at high altitudes or in spring and fall when falling temperatures may follow the rain. For mountain travelers especially, staying dry is very important. Backpackers who travel in adequately wooded areas may want to use fires to dry themselves and their clothes out. Fire building is discussed elsewhere, but it is worth mentioning here that a small fire in front of a tarp or poncho quickly pitched as a lean-to can do wonders to raise flagging spirits on a rainy day. A little hot soup for lunch is never more welcome.

WALKING IN COLD WEATHER

Except for deep snow, which is discussed elsewhere, the only real problem presented by backpacking in cold weather is the need for special care in the choice and the use of equipment. Warm clothing and shelter must be carried and they must be kept as dry as possible. The principles of insulation and the choice of clothing will be detailed later in the book, but the best available equipment may become quite useless if it is allowed to get wet.

The first principle of cold weather walking is *don't sweat*. The colder the weather, the more important this injunction becomes. The most common mistake of the beginning cold-weather walker is to steam up a hill with all his warm clothes on, not realizing that he is working up a good lather. When he reaches the top of the hill, ready for a rest, he is hit in the face by an icy wind which chills him to the core because of his sweat-soaked clothing. The cold-weather traveler has to maintain adequate ventilation to carry away any perspiration and to keep adjusting the layers of his clothing to keep his body from becoming overheated or chilled. As soon as you start to warm up on the morning trail, take off your hat or unzip your parka. When you stop to rest put on the hat and zip up the parka, since you will cool down as soon as you stop working.

Food is more important in cold weather. If your blood sugar supply runs low in normal temperatures, you will probably find that you are tired and have less stamina. In cold weather when your body runs out of easily available fuel you may not be able to maintain your body temperature properly, so make sure to keep yourself supplied with food.

The rules and techniques for cold-weather travel are discussed in detail in Chapter 20, and there is a long discussion in Chapter 9 of the body's thermostat and the clothing it needs for help in cold weather, so no more detail is given here. Remember, though, that cold weather requires somewhat more careful preparation for safe travel. Cold is deceptive because some cooling factors can change so quickly. *Rain and wind combined with cold are very dangerous to the unprepared.* Don't be caught by surprise.

CARRYING A PACK

Traveling easy terrain with a pack of reasonable weight is not very different from walking without it, except that you will go more slowly and get tired sooner. It is important to choose your pack carefully if you want to be comfortable on your first few trips, though if you're willing to make the effort you can train yourself to carry any kind of suitable pack. The chapter on packs discusses this choice in detail, but most beginners will finally decide on a contoured aluminum or magnesium pack frame with a mated bag. The key to using this type of pack effectively is the waist belt. Make sure you have a good one, and then learn to use it. Get into the shoulder straps first and hunch your shoulders up to raise the pack; then cinch the waistband just above the hips. When you let your shoulders down, most of the weight of the pack should rest on your hips. If it doesn't or if the waistband is uncomfortable, either the pack needs adjusting or something is wrong with it.

Most of the time the weight of the frame pack should rest almost completely on the hips, and the shoulder straps should serve mainly to balance the pack. If you tip the top of your body back and forth a bit you should pass a balance point where no weight at all is on the shoulders. Of course, in a day's walking you will shift the load to the shoulders on occasion for relief of the hips or for other reasons. The fact is, though, that the hips are much better supported for load carrying, providing the load can be got on them without forcing the rest of the body into an unnatural position, and this is what the contoured frame pack permits. The shoulders and the neck require a lot of training to develop the musculature needed to haul heavy loads.

One of the purposes of the contour frame pack is to raise the center of gravity high on the frame, which makes for easy carrying but also for unstable balance. In most situations this is really not much of a problem, and you will soon get used to it, but there are occasions when you will not appreciate this characteristic of modern frames. This high center of gravity makes balancing across slippery log bridges even more delicate than such maneuvers already are. Successfully negotiating these obstacles with a loaded contour frame requires that you develop a new set of reactions, keeping the top of your body carefully erect and making any violent adjustments of balance with your legs and arms. Do your fancy footwork while keeping your torso sedately poised directly above the place you want to be.

A difficult choice faces one in places like this: whether to remove the waistband or not. Leaving it on generally ensures surer footing in slips, but if you are crossing a dangerous spot, you may want to unhitch the belt so that you can get rid of the pack in case you fall in.

The most awkward spots for the wearer of a contour frame are places that require ducking forward, because the high center of gravity is then trying to pitch you on your nose, while at the same time the top of the pack is trying to catch on every available nubbin and branch. This often occurs in bushwhacking, and in passing under fallen trees and boulders overhanging the trail. It is often easier in situations like this to take off the pack and carry it ahead of you.

Carrying rucksacks, older types of frames, and other kinds of packs presents no particular problems other than getting your shoulders strong enough to carry the required load. More care is needed when placing equipment in those packs which don't have a frame holding them away from the back. A pot edge digging into your spine will become intolerable very quickly. Make sure things are packed comfortably before you leave, or you will have to repack on the trail. All packs should be loaded so that the center of gravity is as close to the back and as high as possible. The only exception is that very high packs like contour frames may need the center of gravity lowered for difficult terrain. Special care is needed in packing old-fashioned large rucksacks which hang low and protrude far out at the bottom. Skill is required to get the load close to the frame in such packs, since the big, heavy objects always gravitate to the projecting bottom. If this is permitted to occur, the load will pull you backward, requiring you to lean so far forward that you'll be doing more work holding the pack over your legs than carrying it up the trail.

Some types of frame rucksacks allow some of the weight to be shifted to the hips with the frame and perhaps a waist strap, but most of the load must usually be carried by the shoulders. Waistbands on rucksacks are generally intended to keep the pack from shifting and throwing you off balance on difficult terrain.

LAKE, STREAM, AND RIVER CROSSINGS

Since prehistoric times, one of the great problems of foot travelers has been the crossing of streams, lakes, and rivers, and such crossings remain one of the most formidable difficulties for anyone traveling away from areas frequented by bridge builders and tunnel diggers. If you are following a standard trail, you can usually expect at least crude bridges to exist where there are no good fords or stepping stones. If you are traveling across country without benefit of trails, though, you have no such guarantees. Even the trail traveler in an unusually wet year or in an off-season may find that the usual crossing of a difficult river has been washed away or is under several feet of very fast, cold water. Finally, there are many trails which include fairly difficult stream crossings that may be beyond the skill of many backpackers.

The most obvious way to get past a body of water is to walk around it, a method suited mainly to lakes but sometimes necessary with fast mountain streams in spring. A look at the map may give a helpful hint on the practicality of such an enterprise. In difficult wilderness travel, days or weeks of travel may be needed to get around water obstacles.

A lake on a large river may in fact be the best place to cross, since the problem of fast currents is eliminated. Lake crossings can be accomplished with rafts or by swimming, or through some appropriate combination dictated by the temperature and size of the lake, the availability of materials for a raft, and the skill and ambition of the traveler. In any case, a conservative attitude should prevail, especially if the lake is large. A lake that looks only a mile or two across may actually measure ten, and an improvised raft is not the best vessel to get caught with on a windy afternoon in the middle of a large lake. Improvised rafts are not suitable for crossing really big bodies of water.

Rafts may range from full-sized platforms big enough to carry everything and everyone high and dry to a two-log affair which will keep the top of your pack dry and with which you can swim across a warm lake. For the two-log kind lash the pack between the logs with the logs spread far

47

enough from one another to prevent tipping. Rafts made with three or more logs should have a cross-pole lashed diagonally across as a brace.

On any trip where possible rafts or float crossings are anticipated, a sturdy air mattress should be preferred as a bed to a foam pad, because it can be blown up to make a good float if you choose to swim your pack across. It should be inflated and tied to the pack on a raft trip in case of accident. Large plastic bags closed with rubber bands will protect your sleeping bag, clothing, etc., inside the pack and will also make the whole load quite buoyant.

Long poles are usually more effective for propelling rafts than paddles, but some sort of improvised paddle should be taken in case the lake gets too deep for poling. Lashing the raft should be done with nylon parachute cord, and you should make sure that it is absolutely secure before risking your life by trusting it. Similar care is necessary in preparing a float for your pack if you plan to swim across. Depending on a cheap plastic air mattress that might be punctured halfway across, for example, would not be very prudent.

Rivers can sometimes be crossed using a raft or swimming your pack across, but even more care must be exercised than in lake crossings. Don't rely on your estimate of the speed of the current. Smooth-flowing water is often very deceptive. Throw in pieces of wood and watch how fast they go. Throw some of them as far out as you can—the current may be much faster on the other side. Be particularly wary if there is a cutbank on the other side or if you are on the inside of a curve. Whenever feasible, you should walk far down the river before attempting a crossing, in order to find out about any dangerous spots you might be carried into by the current. The inspection may also reveal a ford that will enable you to walk across. Don't be in too much of a hurry to get across; floating or swimming big rivers is serious business.

Under no circumstances should you attempt a raft or float crossing unless you are a strong swimmer; it is foolhardy. No matter how good a swimmer you are, be extremely careful, and don't go unless you are sure of the safety of the crossing. Improvised rafts are not good white-water craft. Be particularly wary if the water is cold. No matter how good a swimmer you are, really cold water will reduce you to numb incompetence incredibly quickly. If the water is cold, don't make any crossings that might result in a spill.

Raft and float crossings of large rivers and of lakes can make a trip into a real adventure, but they demand a lot of extra care. If the water is too fast, the wind too high, or the rapids too close, spend an extra day or week making a safe crossing, or turn back.

More common ways for the backpacker to cross moving water are to leap across on stones, ford at a shallow spot, walk across on fallen trees, or use some combination of these. In winter or spring snow bridges may be used. The great advantages of stones and logs are evident, especially when the snowmelt streams of the mountains are encountered—you don't have to get your feet wet. As you become more experienced, you will become more adept at leaping across on rocks. With a big, fast stream this can be a real test of confidence and balance. The main trick is to plan your route ahead of time so that you can keep moving during the actual crossing. A continuous series of linked jumps is easier than separate leaps and gives you a better chance to recover if a rock rolls or proves slippery.

With relatively small creeks, the decision on whether to try a series of boulder jumps is really a matter of taste, since a slip just means a cold bath or perhaps a broken leg. As streams get larger and colder, however, this is no longer the case. Especially in the high mountains in the spring, established trails often cross quite dangerous torrents. A fast, deep, frothing meltwater stream is one of the most dangerous features of many a mountain, all the more so because it may not look as hazardous as a cliff.

Remember that rock and tree crossings are likely to occur where the stream is fastest and deepest. If you are not reasonably confident about the safety of a crossing, it might be safer to look for a better crossing or a ford. If you are nervous about walking a log, straddling it may be wiser, although less elegant, especially if the log is greasy. Snow bridges are discussed in a later chapter.

Fording is often the safest way across fast mountain streams, and even in relatively simple creeks, you may speed your progress by fording instead of walking a half-mile through the brush looking for a dry crossing.

The best fords are usually at wide spots in the river, where the current is least forceful and the channel shallowest. At bends expect the fastest current along the outer bank. On an easy crossing of clear water with a good bottom, you may just take off your boots and hang them from your pack or your neck. (Don't just drape them; tie them so that they won't be lost in a slip.) However, if the crossing is hard, if there are sharp rocks on the bot-

And then there are log crossings. Get your practice on easy ones like this, and you'll be ready for the slippery ones inclined over raging spring torrents.

tom, or if the footing is insecure, it's best to take off your socks and wear the boots. This prevents foot injuries, and it gives you better grip on treacherous bottoms.

A lot of rivers can be waded with little problem, but many are difficult because of the current and depth. The waistband of the pack should be taken off and the straps loosened so that you can dump it if necessary. If the weather is chilly, it will probably be warmer to roll up your pants legs or to carry your trousers across in the pack and have them dry at the other side. Beware of fast water swirling above your knees; fast water deeper than this is dangerous. Move very carefully on difficult crossings, and use a pole or an ice ax for a third leg on the upstream side. Try to shuffle across, but don't push too far. A very unpleasant situation can develop in which you can retain your stability with both legs where they are—in the middle

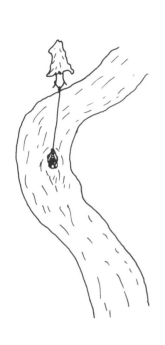
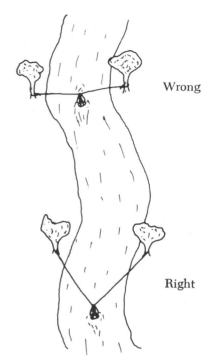

Wrong

Right

Crossing fast water with the aid of a handline. Light nylon line is strong enough, but only if used correctly. In the left-hand illustration the line is rigged so that the pull is as direct as possible, making footing easier and putting minimum stress on the line. In the right-hand drawing, one person has gotten across and rigged the line for the others. The top method is very bad—perpendicular force on a tight line creates tremendous stress, and the line may break. In the lower example, the slack in the line will greatly reduce the stress. The cord should be padded where it goes around rough objects like trees to prevent abrasion from cutting it.

of the river—but you cannot move either of them without upsetting yourself.

A party may be able to cross safely when a single man could not by firmly linking arms, each man holding the wrist of the next. This is useful mainly when only a few feet of channel are really difficult, but it may allow one person to gingerly test a stream while the end of his chain of companions remains firmly attached to a tree on the bank. Mountaineering parties can often make good use of their rope to make crossings safe which would be impossible without it. (Belay the leader from as far upstream as possible.) Nonclimbers should not place too much reliance on such aids, but with a bend in the river, a length of parachute cord may serve as an aid to balance and provide a safety factor, as shown in the diagram. Do *not* rig parachute cord as a tight handline across the stream; it is not strong enough. If you use a handline for members of a party after the first, it must be very slack. See the diagram.

Finally, remember that rocks are buoyed up by the water, and therefore their effective weight is much less in the river than on the bank. Very large rocks may be easily dislodged, so watch your footing.

Most stream crossings are not difficult at all, involving damp feet at the worst. Like other aspects of backpacking, you can find the degree of challenge that you want. A look at the map before you go will usually warn you of the possibility of difficult crossings, which would be more likely after heavy rains or when a heavy winter snowpack is melting quickly in the spring. You need rarely worry about crossings on well-traveled trails except under special circumstances like these. Remember that special conditions can often be waited out. A stream which starts in melting snow is lower in the morning and higher in late afternoon. A creek swelled by rain will drop a day after the rain stops. Sometimes a camp in the afternoon will allow an easy crossing next morning.

Walking in the wilderness is largely a matter of physical conditioning and practice. On your first few trips you may find even easy boulder fields and stream crossings tiring and perhaps a little scary, especially toward the end of the day. By the end of the season you'll be hopping across them without a care, wondering what you thought was so hard. Acquiring this assurance is definitely worth the effort.

Living on the Trail 5

Camping for the backpacker is necessarily a fairly simple affair. Since all the equipment he uses has to be carried along, he has an incentive to stave off the gadget onslaught, a motive which most of us lack in everyday life. Even among backpackers, however, one finds a great variety in life-styles and their practitioners; they range from the vagabond who never carries more than a poncho for shelter and a tin can for cooking to those who would not think of being caught without an expensive tent and a reflector oven for baking apple pie and blueberry muffins. In fact, an attractive aspect of backpacking is its offer of so many alternative ways to approach open spaces and wilderness. There are enough techniques and modes of living to suit the most diverse personalities and the strangest landscapes.

Camping moods and methods result from an interaction between the personality of the traveler and the nature of his environment rather than from either of them alone. The blueberry muffins demand both an ambitious cook and adequate firewood. The techniques that you develop will depend on your own tastes and on whether you camp in the New England woods or the southwestern desert.

Many of the basic principles of wilderness living are the same for any environment and any style of camping, though there are numerous possible variations on the main theme. In general, as surroundings become harsher, they allow less room for individual choice of methods, with the most efficient possible technique and equipment demanded for the most severe conditions. Even the most confirmed poncho camper would not try to use this sort of shelter in regions where rain and snow driven by extreme winds are prevalent.

Within limits technique can be substituted for equipment, and to reverse the same coin, reducing the amount of equipment you carry below a certain level demands improved camping skill. A campsite for pitching a closed tent does not require so artful a choice as one where a poncho or tarp is to be used for shelter. Another less desirable substitute for equipment is fortitude in the face of discomfort, but personally I prefer to endure misery only when it is forced on me by circumstances or difficulty.

The requirements for living in reasonable comfort when you stop walking at the end of the day are an adequate water supply, a good meal, a comfortable bed, and shelter from whatever elements nature might bring along to disturb your night's rest. Water and food will be discussed in the next chapter; bed and shelter are our main topics in this one. In addition to these essentials there are certain amenities like campfires that are so pleasant as to be worth considerable effort when circumstances permit them. Finally the camper has always to concern himself with the problem of leaving his site in the best possible condition for himself and others to use in the future, and the importance of this matter should make it *the* overriding consideration for all of us whenever we are camping.

CHOOSING A SITE

The first order of business in setting up camp for the night is to find a good campsite. The amount of thought that goes into the choice may range from long, advance study of maps in search of suitable spots to simply collapsing in the nearest clearing when it's time to stop, the standard method in open, dry-floored pine forests well supplied with streams. More commonly, the situation is at neither extreme. Good campsites are easily found, but they may be infrequent enough to require that you start looking an hour or two before you definitely want to stop.

It is usually a good idea to decide on quitting time well in advance to ensure that you start looking for a good place early enough. Some situations dictate the need to get to a certain spot. If water is scarce, for example, you may be planning to camp at the crossing of a particular creek, and you might feel the need to get there even if you have to travel after dark. On long trips, planning may have to be tight enough to require that you make a certain number of miles each day. If the primary objective of your trip is a mountain or some other spot, you may have to get to a particular campsite in order to be within striking distance of your goal the following morning.

Barring special circumstances, however, it is almost always best to plan on making camp before dark, and it is definitely more pleasant to be able to hunt up firewood, cook, and get through other camp chores while there is still light. Circumstances may not always permit this, especially with the tight schedules of many weekend trips made by people trying to squeeze long distances into the space between Friday evening and Monday morning. You should beware of just continuing your city habits in the wilderness, though. "Early to bed and early to rise" may not make you healthy, wealthy, or wise, but it will allow you to travel farther, more pleasantly than late starts and late arrivals. Whatever the exigencies of a weekend trip beginning and ending with a long drive, when you go off for a few weeks in the summer, try to cultivate the habit of making your schedule compatible with that of the sun. Among other advantages, you won't have to carry as much power for artificial lights. I used to use my headlamp to wash dishes every night and often to cook supper, too. Now I find that I often go on several trips in a row without ever using a flashlight at all. By the time dark rolls in I try to be sitting back lazily with camp all fixed and stomach full, leaving me free to poke the fire and watch the stars come out.

A good procedure is to figure out how long it will take you to set up camp and do whatever else you want to do before dark. Subtracting this time from the hour of twilight, you have a stopping time you don't want to pass. You may want to stop earlier, of course, and beginners particularly should allow themselves plenty of daylight to set up camp.

The actual mechanics of choosing a site are simply a matter of considering your needs, comfort, and equipment, and matching them with the terrain around you. Easily available water is usually one of the determining factors. Quite aside from convenience, the aesthetic qualities of campsites near brooks, streams, rivers, and lakes are often enough to justify an extra effort in pitching a tent or clearing stones for your sleeping spot. Practically speaking, it's a pain in the neck to have to carry water long distances up- and downhill.

Certain care has to be observed about choosing campsites close to water, however. If there is a chance of rain, it is unwise to bed down either in the drainage system from higher ground or on spots over which your stream or lake might rise when it begins to accommodate the larger flow of water. Such spots are easily recognized if you look for them. Lakes and marshy spots are often breeding areas for insects, and since they may also be poorly ventilated, it's best to be wary of camping in a mosquito hollow. A breezier spot on the slightly higher knoll may be free of pests that infest the bowl just below.

In thickly wooded regions you may also need to exercise care in avoiding noctunal disturbances by larger local fauna. If there is only one clear path down to the water, it is often tempting just to bed down in the middle of it. Before you do, take a look and see whether it is the main highway to the old waterhole for every deer, moose, and bear in the region. Narrow game trails are not likely to provide you with uninterrupted rest.

In some areas, one rarely finds good campsites at convenient distances from water. If you anticipate this situation, carry a couple of big jugs (gallon bleach bottles are light, convenient, and free). When the time comes to start looking for a campsite, fill the jugs at the next watering place, and you will have your water available when you find a place to camp.

Obviously it is advantageous to camp near potable water rather than polluted or questionable sources, if you have a choice. The problem of the purity of drinking water is discussed more thoroughly in the next chapter.

A good campsite should have a fairly flat spot for sleeping, as free as possible from large projections that cannot be smoothed out, such as the pointed tops of large buried boulders. Be particularly careful of sharp objects if you are pitching a tent with a floor, since they will leave holes as a lasting memento to your neglect. Whether your sleeping space also needs to be soft depends on the adequacy of your sleeping pad. If you are sleeping without a pad or air mattress, test the ground carefully. With a good mat, small irregularities are not important, but a level spot is. A tilt that seems slight on cursory inspection is likely to wake you up a half-dozen times during the night to climb back up the hill.

The site itself should be as dry as possible, and if there is any possibility of rain, make sure it has good drainage. Even a good, coated tent

This erosion scar began when someone dug a small trench around his tent near a sub-alpine lake. It has only begun to erode; it will get bigger and uglier until it becomes a gully. Please don't trench a tent unless you know it won't damage the environment.

floor is going to fill up eventually if it is sitting in the middle of your own private lake. In most places you are likely to camp, trenching is *not* an appropriate way to ensure drainage. On forest floors with deep beds of pine needles or humus, trenching may be perfectly all right, and it certainly is on sand or similar surfaces. However, trenching mountain meadows, grassland beside lakes, the sparse soil near trees around timberline, vegetation on dunes, hillside plant cover, and similar spots is foolhardy, irresponsible, and often illegal. Particularly in alpine regions, such trenching, even if it is filled in, may result in severe erosion damage, and at best leaves scars that take a long time to heal. Shortsighted abuse of this type often necessitates the closing of backcountry areas to camping by the responsible authorities, since there is no way to police backpacking campers.

If you are going to pitch a tent or other shelter, you will have to examine prospective sites with your anchoring needs in mind. A tube tent requires two fairly tall objects with a good sleeping spot on a direct line between them. Alternatively, poles must be available for holding a line up. If you were using a tarp or poncho instead, you might prefer a spot farther down the trail with a well-placed boulder against which the tarp could be easily pitched. With a mountain tent you would probably be more influenced by the ease of driving stakes or the presence of strategically placed natural anchors. One simply learns to examine a possible camping place with his own shelter in mind.

If you plan to build a fire, whether for cooking, warmth, or general good cheer, this may be the most critical factor in the choice of a site. Availability of fuel is an obvious factor, and availability will be determined by your equipment as well as by external matters. A saw will enable you to get wood from large pieces of deadfall, while an ax will make it possible to split dry wood from the centers of wet chunks. A suitable spot in which to build a fire is also needed. Fires must never be built on ground which consists mainly of built-up vegetable matter. Former bogs and forest floors with heavy accumulation of debris are the most common examples. A fire built on such a base will often establish a deep bed of coals and continue to burn no matter how carefully you attempt to put it out later. It may flare up and cause a forest, brush, or grass fire weeks after you have gone. If you intend to build a fire, your site must have a spot with a good mineral base.

There is some discussion in the next chapter of limiting fire building because of limited fuel, but there are now also many areas where you should confine your campsites to established spots if you want a fire. In an effort to leave things unspoiled for others, many of us for years have built our fireplaces and then carefully scattered the rocks before we left. In some places this is a good idea, but in many areas it is becoming a self-defeating tactic. Around the attractive campsites surrounding many lakes in the Sierra Nevada these days, there is not a loose stone to be found that is not fire-scarred, nor a boulder without its smoke stains. Clearly, before this point is approached, it is best to leave fireplaces built, and for anyone who wants a campfire to use those already made.

A final point on the influence of fires in the choice of campsites is simply to note that in many wilderness areas there are regulations on both the permissibility of fires and their required location. In some areas you may camp where you choose if you use a stove for cooking, but you may use only designated sites for wood fires. It is important to obey these rules when they apply, both because they are often made for good reason, ena-

A perfect campsite. It has clean water nearby, a view, dry, level ground, and a breeze to carry off the mosquitos. Please don't build a fire unless there is dead wood on the ground, though. This sub-alpine environment is fragile, and plant growth is slow.

bling fire lookouts to identify your column of smoke as a campfire, and because too many violations will force the rangers in charge either to close the area or to impose a host of unpleasant regulations and restrictions on access.

You should also examine your prospective campsite for advantageous situation. There is often an amazing amount of variation in temperature, wind, and ventilation between two spots which are very close together. The most obvious example of this is the sheltered side of large objects. Less widely recognized are the differences resulting from the fact that cold air sinks and tends to follow drainage patterns like water. If you expect the night to be cold, and your sleeping gear is somewhat inadequate, don't bed down in a low hollow—it will probably be the coldest spot. In the mountains, aside from storms and large weather patterns, each night the cold air from the high hills usually rolls down the slopes. This cold wind tends to concentrate in gullies and ravines. On cool nights you would be warmer if you camped above the valley and gully bottoms, but on hot, still nights, you might want to seek out these same places.

Shelter from wind is even more important than temperature if you want to stay warm. Both weather-system winds and the local winds mentioned above will chill the camper with marginal equipment. Many shelters are not suited to withstand high winds either.

PITCHING CAMP

Having settled on a campsite and perhaps taken a swim or a walk if the hour is early, you have to get your camp ready. The order of tasks will depend on whether you are alone or with friends, on the lateness of the hour, and on your own proclivities. If I am building a fire, I prefer to gather enough wood for the night and the next morning as a first order of business, because it's easier to pitch my tent in the dark than to find good pieces for the fire. Next, I get water, unless the source is close and the footing easy. If it is almost suppertime, I may start heating some water while I prepare my bed and pitch any required shelter. Obviously circumstances change the order of preference. In rain you might want to pitch a shelter first, allow the ground under the shelter to dry off a bit, and get your things out of the downpour. In winter the first priority may be to stamp out a platform in the snow for your tent.

Depending on the situation and your preferences, you may have to decide whether to set up a shelter at all or to sleep out under the stars. Some people always sleep in tents or under tarps as a matter of habit, and this may be necessary if your sleeping bag is not quite warm enough. I never sleep under a shelter unless I have to. If the weather is good I always sleep under the open sky, which is far more interesting to watch than any tent roof. I want to be able to lie in my nice warm bed and watch Orion climb up into the October sky. On a good night I also save myself the trouble of setting up a tent at night and the trouble of breaking it down the next morning. Of course, this saving may be counterbalanced by the need to get up and pitch a shelter in the middle of a freak rainstorm at 2:00 A.M., but the risk is worth it.

One can always pitch a tent and then sleep outside, of course, with a readily available retreat in case of rain. I do this occasionally when the weather is threatening. An easy hedge is available to those using tube tents, tarps, or ponchos for shelters. Simply prepare your bed and use the shelter for a ground cloth, but string out all the necessary pitching lines to the surrounding trees or bushes. If rain does come up, it nearly always begins with mild sprinkling, which is sufficient to wake you before you even get damp. All you have to do is toss your sleeping bag and belongings inside, pull the lines tight, and crawl into bed before the cloudburst starts in earnest. This method is really quite effective and not much trouble.

Whether you are putting up a shelter or not, spend some time getting the spot ready for your bed. Pick a level place, or one as level as possible. Pick up all the rocks, branches, pine cones, stones, and other hard, irregular objects, and toss them somewhere else. It takes less time to do this *before* you lay out your ground sheet or tent, and is much less irritating than searching for the lump under your spine after you have gone to bed. Remember that small, sharp objects are hard on tent floors and ground cloths. If you are sleeping without an air mattress or pad, or if you are using a thin, closed-cell pad, pay particular attention to the ground underneath you—you have to live with it all through the long night. A mattress of dry pine needles, well smoothed and spread out, is very pleasant when available. So is sand, but be careful to smooth and shape it well before laying out your bed.

If you use a ground sheet, one side will get dirty, especially when the ground is damp. Always lay the dirty side down and keep your sleeping things clean. If it is windy or gusty, weight the edges of the sheet so it won't blow away, and do the same with your pad and sleeping bag. Fluff the sleeping bag so that it will recover its loft and warmth. If it is still afternoon and is not too damp, it's a particularly good idea to get your sleeping gear out for airing while you go about fixing camp.

Pitching tents easily and quickly is largely a matter of practice. Circumstances vary, but as a general rule the entrance should be pitched into the prevailing wind in order to reduce flapping in the night. If your tent has a floor, simply stake it out around the edges first, or attach floor ties to available anchor points. Most tents are provided with more anchor points than are normally needed, but they should all be secured in windy conditions. A tent without a floor does not have a shape built in to determine the position of the stakes. So with this type you must be particularly careful to check the angles when you stake out the bottom, otherwise the tent will be distorted, wrinkled, and less stable when you raise it. With most tents the next step is to secure all pullouts, side ties, and guy lines to appropriate anchors. Sometimes the proper length for lines can be determined even before the tent is up, but normally these are tied with some sliding tension knot or mechanical fastener and left loose until the tent is raised. Finally, the poles are inserted and raised, and everything is tightened properly.

In forested areas be careful not to pitch the tent under any large dead branches which might be brought down by wind during the night. Such branches are ruefully known as "windowmakers." The great number of available anchor points provided by the woods will often make it possible for forest campers to dispense with carrying of poles. Generous lengths of parachute cord tied to the anchor points of a tent will substitute, except with some of the newer tents that depend heavily on curved poles to hold their shapes. One problem often encountered in using a line to hold up the ridge of a tent is that the center of the line and hence the ridge show a pronounced sag. A second line attached to the center of the first can often be tossed over a tree branch and used to straighten the curve. A guy line which needs a high anchor can be directed across an appropriate tree fork or branch by tying the end to a stone and throwing it over.

Open-fronted tents and shelters are often pitched facing fires for good cheer, comfort, and convenience, especially in bad weather. This is a good and time-honored practice, but care is required to prevent stray sparks from damaging the tent. Usually, the most effective arrangement is to build the fire against a good back reflector, large enough to control the smoke and draft. (See the discussion of backlogs, stones, and such in the next chapter.) Very small cooking fires are usually not much of a problem except in bad wind, but a larger warming fire should be a safe distance in front of the tent. Be conservative in using this technique until you gain experience with it.

Judicious use of natural anchors and weather breaks is important when you are establishing any camp, but it is of especial concern to those who use tarps, ponchos, or plastic shelters. Tarps and ponchos are most comfortable when they are used to form an extra wall in combination with a large log, a natural rock overhang, or other natural shelter. This combination will give you more room and better protection than the tarp alone. Don't get carried away when you find a nice roof, though. Not all overhanging rocks shed water; on some it just runs down along the inside of the roof, pouring off everywhere. Streams draining under the rock or log aren't very pleasant to discover in the middle of a nighttime storm either. A careful inspection before you settle down will avoid most such errors.

Try to determine how the prevailing winds blow when you set up camp. If you pitch your tarp as a lean-to, and have the open side facing into the driving rain, you'll be soaked in no time. The same consideration applies to large ventilation openings in tents, and to the ends of tube tents. The latter can be controlled to some extent if you bring along some spring-loaded clothespins for controlling the opening and anchoring the tent to the line. The best method is to place your shelter well, to begin with. Pitching in a naturally protected spot makes any shelter work better. Lean-tos don't get soaked inside or blown away, plastic shelters are less likely to tear, and tents will not have to shed so much rain and are thus less likely to leak.

GETTING YOUR BED READY

Whether you pitch a shelter or just throw out a ground cloth, it's usually a good idea to get your bed laid out as soon as possible. The insulation in your sleeping bag will work better if you give it time to recover from the compression of packing, and if the air is warm and dry enough an airing will allow some of the previous night's body moisture to evaporate from the bag.

In extremely moist and humid conditions, as in a snow shelter or in a wet tent after a week of backpacking in the rain, it is better to keep the sleeping bag in a waterproof stuff sack or plastic bag except when you are in it. It will stay drier if it is not allowed to cool off in damp conditions, so in these circumstances it is best to get the bag into the stuff sack as soon as you are out of it in the morning.

When you get your ground cloth down or your tent pitched, lie down on your proposed bed, and make sure that there aren't any unpleasant bumps you missed or a slope you didn't notice. Remember that a good night's sleep is important for an enjoyable trip, and it's worth a lot of trouble to make your bed comfortable. Do an especially good job if you are not using a pad. Get the cones out of a pine-needle bed. Scoop or find hip holes if you will sleep directly on the ground. If you are camping on the sand, you will have a comfortable mattress, but only if you shape it well beforehand. It's not as easy as it seems to scrunch the sand to your shape through the sleeping bag and tent floor.

If there is some question about the adequacy of your sleeping bag for cool evening temperatures, try to have some shelter from the clear night sky. If you are not sleeping in a tent or under a tarp, sleep under the branches of a tree. The intervening surface cuts your radiated heat loss, which can be quite high if you sleep out under the heavens on a clear night.

CAMP ROUTINE

There are a lot of details that have to be managed in a backpacking camp. None of them are very difficult under normal circumstances, and in good weather even the beginner will have a pretty easy time taking care of them. What throws some novices into a state of confusion is simply the large number of small tasks that have to be organized. Unsystematic beginners are usually best advised to make things easy on themselves by taking their first few trips with someone who knows what he is doing or with another beginner who has a knack for handling details. Programmatic types have less difficulty adjusting to the new routine of living from a pack.

The experienced backpacker works all the chores and necessities of camping into a routine, so that he is free to enjoy the experience at a leisurely pace when it suits him and he is capable of getting everything done in a hurry when he needs to. He can put up his tent almost unconsciously while keeping his cooking fire fed, dropping ingredients into the supper pot, or whatever. This facility is simply a matter of practice, technique, and organization, but these should be cultivated by anyone who wants to enjoy the sport. Sooner or later nearly anyone who travels a lot in the wilderness is bound to have to put up a late camp in miserable weather, and when he does he will appreciate being able to do it quickly and well.

Developing an efficient camping method is first a matter of getting the necessities straight in your mind. Get used to pitching your shelter in various circumstances, and think about what you need to do at any particular sort of site. Add ties to your tent if they will make it easier to pitch in some places. Get used to setting up your shelter efficiently when there isn't any wind, so that you won't have a lot of trouble when there is. When you use fires, accustom yourself to lighting them with the first match and without fire-starters, so that you'll be able to get them going in bad weather. (Fire-starters are not immoral, but if you get used to using them in relatively easy circumstances, you'll never develop the skill needed to start a fire in a difficult situation, with or without aids.)

Systematic packing is also a great help when you get to camp. When you're tired it's very annoying to have to dig through the pack for twenty minutes to find the salt. With good packing everything you need will be at your fingertips. There isn't much room in a rucksack, but it's amazing how well you can lose something in such a small space if you just toss it in without thinking. It is ordinarily best to try to pack things so that the items you will need first are on top, providing you can do it without unbalancing the pack. In general, trail items go into the most accessible spots, and the camp gear goes in so that the last-needed equipment is buried the deepest. Food especially, which becomes the heaviest and bulkiest part of the load on long trips, should be parceled into packages by the meal, day, or week, and the meals for later in the trip should be at the bottom. This avoids the necessity of unpacking your whole load at every stop, a particularly unwelcome chore when the rain is pouring down while you are trying to fix supper.

If you can develop a more or less unconscious procedure for unpacking, getting your camp up, fetching water, and cooking supper, you will have more time to enjoy the lake and the sunset, and you will also get more pleasure out of the physical activity involved in the chores themselves. Dozens of small matters contribute to this efficiency and confidence. If you always put your flashlight and glasses in the same place, you'll be able to find them easily and without irritation when you need them in the middle of the night. Best of all, you'll feel at home on the trail, not like an unwelcome guest in a strange house.

RUBBISH DISPOSAL

The problem of keeping the wilderness clean is one of the most obvious difficulties presented by the new influx of people into the backcountry. Trash,

An efficient camp routine will leave you more time to horse around. The author mugs for the typical summit picture.

litter, and pollution are already very real problems in many wilderness areas, even in some that are remote. The offensiveness of the junk that is left almost everywhere is obvious. Much of the litter from modern packaging is practically impervious to the natural processes of disintegration, except over a long time. Shreds of plastic from discarded wrappers or ground sheets keep whipping around for years. Tin cans at least rust away eventually, but their aluminum replacements stay shiny through the seasons. The only way to avoid having our woods and mountains turn into monstrous junkpiles is to leave none of our trash in the backcountry. This means either burning or packing out every single bit of your debris.

If you use fires, you can burn up paper and plastic bags. Don't bury the rest—carry it out. Animals dig up buried cans and trash, and erosion often uncovers it. If you can manage to carry a full container into the wilderness, you can certainly carry it out empty! Fixed camps and ski cabins may require refuse pits to be dug, but this is a different matter. Such pits can create various erosion and pollution problems, and anyone placing them should acquire sufficient knowledge beforehand to be able to do it right. For backpacking situations the answer is to burn it *thoroughly* or pack it out. Remember that wrappers made partly of foil, orange peels, and cans don't burn and must be carried out.

Long-distance travelers using caches, rendezvous, relays, or airdrops for supply have a slightly different problem with trash, but this is not an excuse for littering either. Unfortunately, expeditions have long considered themselves privileged to dump in a way that they would allow no one else to do close to home. Where fires can be used, good planning will simply dictate packages that can be disposed of by burning. With a rendezvous, you can always have your support team carry out your junk, an extension of the principle that you can carry out empty anything you can carry in full. Only with caching and airdrops do problems become more difficult, since both methods often require metal containers to prevent damage from the drop or from visiting animals. In the case of caches, you can always plan to revisit the sites at the end of the trip to get the junk out. If you do, don't just *plan* on the return—*make* it.

There are still a few situations where burying rubbish may be justified, perhaps at some semipermanent camps with Forest Service or other approval, or on long trips in some regions. Even in these circumstances everything possible should be burned. Anything to be buried should be burned or washed thoroughly, because if food remains on containers, animals will dig them up. Cans should be flattened so that they take up less space. Tin cans or containers should be burned before burial to melt off the tin; the cans will rust out much faster if this is done. The dump itself should be dug as deep as possible, away from water, some big rocks should be thrown in to make animal excavation less likely, and the vegetation cover must be replaced as well as possible. Anyone traveling in alpine, arctic, or desert environments should be particularly reluctant to leave junk, since natural processes of degradation operate very slowly in such conditions. There is no excuse for dumping in areas within the range of a weekend trip from civilization.

SANITATION

The problem of trash is a simple matter of people accepting responsibility for their own junk. Some pollution problems result as much from ignorance as irresponsibility. Heavy use of many wilderness areas, particularly those in fragile environments, places pressure on natural cleaning systems that they are not capable of sustaining. Besides actual pollution, there are problems of aesthetics that should be a concern of everyone who does much backpacking and which require some changes in current attitudes. Around some popular high-country lakes, one can hardly turn over a stone anymore without finding someone's latrine. Some people don't even bother with the stone. This kind of behavior is simply not tolerable anymore. Where there is earth, take the time to dig a decent hole, well away from any water runoff. For a latrine at camp, the hole should be of a size commensurate with the length of time you plan to stay. For one-time use, the hole obviously should be filled when you leave, but at camp, a moderate amount of dirt after each use will be adequate until you vacate. If you are using a wood fire in camp, bring some of the ashes up and use them in the hole to speed up deterioration of the waste. In places where adequate holes can't be dug, try to find the best possible spot, and carry matches to burn up your toilet paper, which deteriorates rather slowly.

The distance of a latrine from camp should be far enough away to prevent circulation of flies when they are in season, but with a deep enough hole and the use of dirt or ashes for cover, this won't be too much of a problem. The main requirements are that it be well away from water (not just downstream from you!) and that it be in a spot where no one else is likely to want to camp. It is an advantage to have it at a convenient distance from camp so that no one will be tempted to neglect it at night, but self-discipline is a remedy for that problem. Anyone camping on snow should be particularly careful in locating a spot and in firing toilet paper, since the contents of snow holes merely freeze until the summer melt drops them in pristine condition on the ground below the spot where they were deposited.

For the backpacker, garbage should be minimal or nonexistent, because it represents wasted weight and probably wasted food. Burning is the best way to handle any that you have. Small bits of food can be scattered for animals and birds. When this isn't feasible, it's generally all right to bury garbage, but not together with trash. Animals may dig up the garbage and will scatter any trash that is with it.

Washing out clothes and dishes is fairly straightforward, but it should not be done in streams or lakes. Take a pot down to the lake if you are washing in cold water, and do the actual washing and dumping of soapy water at least a few yards away, and farther with a small water supply. It's even better, especially in heavily used areas, to take the water back to camp and do the washing there. Dishwater disposal is not usually much of a problem in backpacking camps, since quantities are small and stays usually short. One or two stray noodles are not going to hurt anything, and they will probably soon be picked up by a bird or chipmunk. Long stays, large parties, or heavy use may dictate more care, though, and so would large amounts of grease from frying bacon or something similar. For better disposal dig a hole, put some rocks and large gravel in it so that it will drain well, and cover the top with dead grass or pine needles. Dishwater is poured into the hole, and the grease and detritus is caught by the grass or needle trap, which is then burned and replaced by a fresh one. Fill the hole before breaking camp.

WASHING

Your own tastes and those of your companions will be the main determinant in the frequency and thoroughness with which you wash yourself and your utensils, but the climate and the length and difficulty of the trip should also be considered. Except for socks and underwear, there is rarely any need for laundry except on trips of more than two weeks.

The face and hands tend to get pretty dirty, except on winter trips in the snow, but beware of too much washing. Removal of the natural oils from the skin promotes chapping and sunburn. People with sensitive skin may need to bring along a skin preparation to replace some of that oil. On dusty trips you may find that you need a bath, or at least want one, every day, while on jaunts across nothing but rock and snow you may well find that you stay cleaner than you would at home. Except where water is scarce and in really cold weather, there really isn't any problem bathing as often as you want to, although you'll probably have to get used to sponge baths. Luxury lovers with adequate fuel can heat up water for theirs, while more Spartan souls can search for fresh snowmelt and top off their bath with a dive into a mountain tarn where ice cakes still float. In either case, though, do your washing and rinsing away from water to keep your contribution of detergent and soap to a bare minimum. Lakes take a long time to turn their water over, and in many of the best backpacking areas, biodegradation takes a very long time. Keep your suds out of the lakes and streams.

What soap you use is partly a matter of your own preference, but if you're washing much in cold water, find a soap that will work up a decent lather at that temperature. Some campers like to carry a very small bottle of liquid detergent for both the pots and their hands, and it works very well. I like a small piece of soap for sponge baths and something stronger for sooty hands. For the latter, you can use a little hunk of gritty laundry soap, some powder like the kind you find in gas stations, or some mechanic's hand cleaner, which works without water and has the extra advantage of leaving an oily film on your hands to prevent chapping.

Scrubbing pots and pans is one of the less attractive chores in wilderness camping, and quite a few backpackers don't usually even bother until they get home. Except in winter I prefer to scrub mine, but I am lazy enough to try to keep the work to a bare minimum. There are a number of tricks to doing this, and one of them coincides with keeping your weight down; that is to use as few pans and dishes as possible. In cooking for any reasonably sized party I rarely use more than two pans, never more than three. One of those pots is usually used only for water, so the inside doesn't get dirty. Parties relying on stoves won't have to worry much about soot, but for others it is very helpful to have an individual sack for each of the nesting pots. Each sack keeps the sooty outside of the pan from soiling the inside of its larger neighbor, obviating the necessity of cleaning the outside of the pots. If you must clean off the soot, a layer of soap spread on the outside of the pan before it goes on the fire will make your job simpler.

There are several kinds of scouring pads which make the pot-scrubbing job easier, though sand and crusty snow also do a fair scouring job. Water should always be heated for dishes if you are using soap, especially in very cold weather. A lot of cold-weather campers would rather scour their pots with some granular snow and forget them on the assumption that a little grease carried over to the next meal won't hurt. This is reasonable, because if you use soap without a thorough rinsing it will mix in with the grease for an unpleasant and unhealthy addition to tomorrow's menu. If you're going to be sloppy about dishwashing it's best to leave detergent and soap out. A small amount of hot water can be used for all your dishes, pouring it from the largest vessel to the progressively smaller ones, and this is the usual dishwashing method for individuals and small groups. Large groups usually prefer a big pan for dishwashing. Remember, if there is much waste in the dishwater it should be burned, and a grease trap should be used if there is much oil.

SLEEPING IN COMFORT

I've already mentioned the importance of preparing a comfortable sleeping spot, but it's hard to overemphasize the point. The art of backpacking is in making yourself comfortable with a minimum of equipment and effort, not in seeing how much misery you can stand. Save the discomfort for extremely difficult trips where it is impossible to avoid, and learn how pleasant most seemingly hostile environments can be.

It is a continual source of amazement after long sojourns in the civilized world to find just how few things we really need to be comfortable and happy. This is the discovery always awaiting the backpacker along the trail. The farther down the path you go, the more clearly those essentials will stand out. One of them, you will find, is a good night's sleep. You'll probably never learn to enjoy long backpacking trips unless you learn how to sleep comfortably.

The first priority for a decent bed is a spot which is reasonably level and free from hard projections digging into your anatomy. In some kinds of country you may sleep with your bag separated from the ground only by a waterproof sheet, but it is usually more sensible to use a foam pad or an air mattress, unless one is included in your sleeping bag. This subject is discussed in the equipment section, so for now I'll just say that with most sleeping bags economy of insulation and comfort dictate the use of a pad of some kind. Springy carpets of pine needles and some meadows may be comfortable, but they are not always available. The famous bough bed of legend cannot even be considered in most places these days—it requires a great volume of live boughs—and besides, it takes quite a bit of time to put together and often gets rather uncomfortable at around three in the morning.

Air-mattress users should beware of inflating their beds too much; this will make them uncomfortable, easy to fall off, and more prone to puncture. Proper inflation will barely keep your hips from touching bottom when you are lying in the bed. Check all your favorite positions when you are testing. I generally fill the air matress and then lie on it, releasing the air slowly until I sag to the proper level. Pads just need to be rolled out early so they will have time to expand completely before bedtime. Thin, closed-cell foam pads are good insulation, but they provide minimal padding, so if you have one, be particularly careful when fixing your foundations.

Most backpacking pads and air mats are the short type, extending from the hips to the shoulders or head. You should take a little time fixing a pillow, if you need one, and providing padding and insulation for your feet and calves when the spot calls for them. On a soft forest floor, your feet probably won't need padding, but they will on gravel, and insulation is needed in cold weather no matter what the surface. Use your pack, spare clothes, and the like to make the lower part of your bed. I make a pillow from some of my clothes rolled in the sleeping bag stuff sack.

Some people like to wear all their clothes to bed, and some do not. It doesn't matter unless the weather is cold enough to push your sleeping bag to its lower limits. Dry clothes may be used to keep you warm and comfortable. If you're wearing damp clothes and it's chilly, though, better change to dry ones. It's true that you can dry off your clothes inside the sleeping bag, but the heat needed to evaporate the water has to come from your body, and if you're cold you won't be able to spare the warmth during the night, when your body produces its smallest quantities of heat. A good night's rest will make you better equipped to dry them out on the trail tomorrow, and wet or frozen clothes in the morning are preferable to a night of wakeful shivering. If you're warm enough you can suit yourself on the question of whether to dry clothes inside your bag. The advantages are obvious; the penalties are some discomfort and some extra moisture in the bag, which will result in reduced efficiency and greater weight. In general, the colder the weather, the more circumspect you should be about drying clothes in your sleeping bag.

Putting on any available dry clothes is an obvious measure to take if you are cold in your bag. Other important steps for a warm sleep on a cold night are to stay warm before you get into bed, to have some food before going to bed, and to fluff your bag up well. If you are cold when you climb into the sack, you will take a while to warm up, because you'll stop most of your heat-producing muscular activity. The food helps because you produce heat in digesting it, and the fluffing gets the maximum amount of insulating dead air into the bag. Pull all your drawstrings tight to prevent the air you do warm up from escaping, but keep your mouth and nose free to breathe outside the bag—you don't want all that moisture in the insulation. If you need more clothes, put on a hat first, since your head radiates a lot of heat.

Isometric exercises are good for getting warm, allowing your muscles to generate heat without stirring up air currents to carry it away. They are especially useful just after you get into the bag on a very cold night, because it takes a few minutes to warm up the inside so that it can start insulating. If you wake up cold in the middle of the night, have a candy bar and do some more exercises. (Isometric exercises are done by tensing up muscles against each other, without moving them significantly. Any muscles will do, but for warming up, tense one set for a few seconds, then another. The abdominal muscles are the most effective for getting warm.)

You won't actually be very likely to need any of these warm-up tricks unless you start doing cold-weather camping or bivouacking with minimal equipment. Backpackers with adequate sleeping bags generally sleep better in camp than at home. The only precaution I usually take when I go to bed is to leave my glasses on for a while so that I can watch the stars from the comfort of my warm bed.

Before you turn in at night, try to put everything you may want to get from the bag within easy reach and in a place where you can find it. Boots beside the head of your bed make handy repositories for pocket items, glasses, and a flashlight. Clothes you need for the next day should be placed within easy distance too. Leaving the pack outside your shelter is all right, providing everything in it is adequately protected against the weather. Try to avoid leaving everything strewn all over camp, though. A surprise rain coming up in the night will leave you the miserable job of stumbling around with a flashlight, trying to find it all. (You won't—the matches will be discovered in a puddle the next morning.) Don't leave out anything that will be damaged by rain or blown away in a hard wind. In cold seasons don't leave things where they might be covered by snow.

MIDNIGHT MARAUDERS

After licking your lips over the last morsel of your gourmet supper, you should spend a few minutes thinking about local residents that might have an interest in your remaining supplies. The possibilities for uninvited evening guests range from mice to bears. As you are the prospective host, you would be discourteous and unwise not to prepare for your visitors.

The safest way to make sure of undisturbed slumber and a full larder next morning is to get all your food out of reach of the local denizens. Some fairly elaborate safety devices are often needed in semipermanent camps, but the backpacker rarely needs to worry about really devious attempts. I usually put all my food in a stuff sack, tie the top to a length of parachute cord, and suspend the whole business from a tree branch well out of reach from the ground, tree, or branch. To get it up, all that is needed is to tie a stone to the other end of the cord, throw it over the branch, and haul the sack up to a convenient height.

In deciding whether you actually need to take this precaution, you simply make an informed guess. Factors to be considered are the amount of use of your campground, availability of other food, the season, and the consequences of losing your larder. On a long trip with tight provisioning, the prospect of an extended trek without food should make you conservative enough to take all possible precautions. In general, animals are more likely to come around looking in frequently used camps than rarely visited ones.

They also become less wary of people and more clever at getting into containers, though at big campgrounds they may prefer the garbage cans to more widely dispersed food caches. Be particularly wary in spring and after early fall snows, when animals need more food and the supply is scarce.

Whether or not you hang your food, there are a few precautions you should always take. Don't let your pack become soaked with food remains. Wash it if a chocolate bar melts through. Small rodents will eat a hole right through the stain, an efficient cleaning job, but one that creates some other problems. Don't put your food in a place that would force a bear to go through you or the wall of your tent in order to get it. The foot end of your sleeping bag or tent is not a good place for a food cache. It will discourage some bears, but will make your encounter with a more determined one rather trying. If you want to risk having a bear carry away your store, leave it where he can get it without bothering you.

Leather boots tempt some rodents, and they should be kept close at hand. Where this seems to be a real problem, watch out for your pack, too. Porcupines hungry for salt will sometimes eat up your sweat-soaked pack straps, whether they are leather or nylon. Swing the whole pack if they are a problem. Where there are porcupines there are trees, but remember to suspend the parcel well out in the air, since porky can climb the trunk.

Where there are no trees, marauders tend to be less of a problem. Small rodents are foiled by simply putting the food in a covered pot, and wiring it shut will stop a raccoon but not a determined bear. Trees too small for limb-suspension systems may still foil bears if they are high enough to get the package out of reach and too skinny for the bear to climb. Steep-sided boulders may also suffice for bear protection.

INSECT STUFF

Smaller marauders, which are more interested in eating you than your supplies, have already been mentioned in connection with the choice of a campsite. In areas and seasons where they cannot be avoided mosquitoes and their allies must be dealt with. If there aren't too many bugs and you're not especially sensitive, you may choose to ignore them. A warning, though—my own worst nights have resulted not from the heaviest concen-

Another kind of backpacking campsite. The salt marsh is beautiful, but in some seasons you had better be prepared for the local insects or you may fail to appreciate the beauty the next morning.

tration of bugs, but from occasions when they didn't seem to be thick enough to require repellent; by the time I woke up covered with bites proving my poor judgment, it was too late to salvage a comfortable night's sleep.

The old standby for insect control is a net bar, cither on the tent door or draped over the sleeper. These are satisfactory for most insects if they are made and draped properly. Take the time to kill everything already in the tent before bedding down. Bars over the sleeping bag should be held up away from your skin, or the little monsters will just sit outside while they feed.

Recently, fairly effective insect repellents have become available which are also relatively inoffensive to humans. Government studies have shown that these work not by smell or taste, but by being unpleasant to the insects' touch. The same studies show that for a given amount of compound, the most effective repellent is diethyl toluamide, so I would recommend picking whatever stuff gives you the greatest amount of this substance for the least money. Aerosols are generally poor buys for carrying on a trip, but they are useful for spraying clothing before you start. Repellent applied to clothing lasts quite a while, but on the skin it goes much more quickly. Personally, I rely almost solely on repellent now, rather than bothering with insect bars. In the worst places and seasons you will need to use both. Some kinds of flies pay little attention to repellents, requiring the use of head nets by day and netting by night.

In tick country you can prevent becoming an involuntary host by arranging a seal between pants legs and boots—with anklets for example. Then add repellent around the ankles and check your clothes every half hour or so. Alternatively, you can strip down and inspect each other a couple of times a day. Children should always be checked.carefully, since they periodically charge through the bush, and often a lot of bushwhacking adults need the same treatment. Hair and ears should receive special attention. Ticks take a couple of hours to really attach themselves, so remove them before they have a chance.

BREAKING CAMP

If you have a destination or distance in mind for the day's hiking, you should remember that an efficient departure is as important as economy in setting up camp. Think about the time you can spare for morning sluggishness the night before. Then pack up and get ready to go before you start lying around in the sun; breaking camp always takes longer than you think it will. When your pack is tied up next to the trail, you can look at your watch and decide whether you have time for another half-hour of basking. This may sound merely puritanical, but every experienced backpacker knows (whatever his practice) that a lot of energy and pleasure is wasted by getting into camp late at night because of a dilatory start.

How long you actually spend getting going will depend a lot on your morning routine, a very subjective thing. The ambitious souls who have scrambled eggs and muffins just have to get up earlier than the vagabond who munches a piece of Logan bread while he packs up. This is very much a matter of personal taste, one about which it is wise to reach an understanding when traveling with new companions.

If the sun is up and you have other chores, open your sleeping bag and air it on a sunny rock or log so that it will dry as much as possible before packing. The same advice may apply to tents also, although this is much less important. In good weather roll your sleeping bag as the last item before leaving in the morning. If the air is damp and soggy, roll it as soon as you get up, before it loses your body heat.

Eating on the Trail   6

Food for backpacking can be about as simple or complicated as you like, and tastes vary in this area of lightweight camping more than in most others. I like to keep things simple most of the time, so if you would prefer to prepare six-course dinners in the backcountry, you can take the advice given in this chapter with a grain of salt. Your pocketbook is also likely to influence your attitude toward camp cooking a good deal. A good sleeping bag is worth making sacrifices for, but expensive freeze-dried meals aren't. Meals for backpacking don't have to be expensive.

FACTS OF LIFE FOR THE CAMP COOK

Regardless of the style of cooking that attracts you, there are certain basic requirements for cooking from a pack that you will have to get used to. Weight is a problem. On a weekend trip you can ignore it if you want to and carry almost anything. Your pack will be heavier than necessary, but it won't be unmanageable. On longer trips, however, it is quite impossible to tote along cans of beef stew and marinated artichokes for your basic diet. The weight of the containers and the moisture in the food rapidly add up to prodigious weights. Next time you come home with a full-week's groceries, think about tossing them into your pack and heading down the trail. For trips of a week or more, bulk can also be a problem. A reasonably compact pack is necessary for efficient walking, and very bulky items won't usually withstand much banging around.

Backpacking foods have to be protected from spoilage. On a weekend trip you may be able to use some fresh foods without much thought to preservation, but in general this is not the case. Only foods which will keep for some time without refrigeration can be carried for consumption after the first day or two of a trip. Winter trips in cold weather can be an exception to this rule, but it applies to most backpacking trips.

Ease and method of preparation have to be considered in planning your menu. If you want to bother to make an apple pie, you can manage it, but you'll have to bring a reflector oven. Length of cooking time can be an important factor, especially at high altitudes, where water boils at a lower temperature than at sea level so that food cooks more slowly, when it cooks at all.

Waste should be kept to a minimum in any foods chosen for backpacking. Carrying ten pounds of garbage a hundred miles into the woods only to be faced with the problem of getting rid of it is rather silly. You might even have to carry it all the way out again.

Finally, food for backpacking has to meet the same nutritional requirements that any other food does, especially since it is usually fueling bodies doing work to which they aren't accustomed. On short trips, a little common sense usually takes care of balancing meals, but on long journeys the need for eliminating all waste and avoiding cumulative deficiencies requires more careful planning.

BASIC COOKING FROM A BACKPACK

The heart of most meals for the backpacker is a casserole-type dish which is boiled rather than baked. Call it stew, soup, or glop, the basic method is to combine a starchy base (rice, noodles, potatoes, etc.) with some vegetables, a source of protein, and some flavorings, and cook it in a single pot until it is done. Sophisticates carefully regulate the timing of each addition and may add touches like dumplings, but the idea is to cook everything in one pan whenever possible, or to use two at the most.

A dish like this can provide everything you need for supper, even if you choose to add side dishes. I nearly always stick to the basic one-pot meal unless I'm having trout or eggs for dinner. When I feel creative, I try to make it a very imaginative one-pot meal, but I stay with the method because it is so well suited to the problems of fixing meals for backpacking.

My own preparation goes like this. Before the trip, I scoop out the ingredients of my meal from my box of camping food, mixing everything that can be mixed, and packaging things that have to go in the pot at different times in different plastic bags. The whole thing goes in one plastic bag, along with a slip of paper telling me any directions I need, like the amount of water to use or cooking time. I have a bag for each cooked meal. On most trips things like coffee go into single bags for the whole trip, but on a long journey, daily rations can go into the meal bags.

At the same time that I pack up my meals I fill my salt and pepper shakers, replenish my bags of sugar, coffee, tea bags, hot chocolate, bouillon cubes, and cream substitute. I make sure that I have the right number of breakfasts and suppers, and that I have enough trail food for lunches. On a long trip I might ration lunches, but usually I don't bother. I'm generous with trail food, and that also provides my emergency reserve. If I am using a stove, I fill my gasoline containers with enough fuel for the trip.

Tea, coffee, and the like go into my cook kit, along with the stove, soap, pot-scrubber, matches, pot handles. The other things are packed in order so that the first day's rations are on top. That way they aren't too hard to find even in the dark, and I don't have to rearrange the whole pack during the first couple of days.

When I get into camp, I get a full pot of water and put it on to boil. When it gets hot I dip water for some drinks right away, pour any extra into the second pot, and start the meal cooking in the remaining water. If I have a fire, I'll start two pots, but with a stove I'll have some soup or something to sip while the meal is cooking by taking the hot water out before adding the meal ingredients to the pot. With instant suppers I may only have to pour hot water from the pan when it has begun to boil.

If I am alone, I eat directly from the pan, putting the second pan on the stove with water for drinks and washing, or moving it to the side of the fire where it can simmer. If I am with others, I dish the food into bowls. With one-pot meals each person needs only a mug and a bowl. Some people just use a mug.

There are lots of special dishes and tricks which can be used in backpack cookery. Some of them will be talked about later in this chapter, but I think the one-pot meal is basic. It allows preparation of appetizing meals in an orderly way on a single stove. Most of the preparation—measuring, mixing, and figuring—is done at home. Only a small fire is necessary if one is used. The amount of liquid can be increased if the party needs liquids, as in winter camping. Both preparation and cleanup are simplified. The method is easily adapted to any size group. It is also adaptable to widely varying tastes and pocketbooks. You can throw some stuff together or make a gourmet meal, according to your propensity.

COOKING UTENSILS

Another advantage in cooking in this way is the simplicity and light weight of the equipment needed. A couple of pots holding around two quarts each will serve a party of four very nicely. Lids should be included to conserve heat, especially for cooking over a stove. If you plan to do much frying, you should take a spun-steel fry pan, which is much superior to aluminum. Some cook kits have lids meant to double for frying made of steel, but most are thin aluminum, good for nothing but burning. A spatula should also be included for frying.

Normally, a soup spoon is all that is needed for tending a one-pot meal. I use a pot gripper available in backpacking stores, and swear by it, but some people manage quite nicely with the cuffs of their shirt sleeves. Pots with locking bails are easy to handle, but they are generally more expensive.

The only other necessities are a spoon, a cup, and a bowl for each person. Avoid aluminum for these purposes: it burns your lips when the contents are hot but cools the food too quickly. The stainless-steel Sierra Club cups are nice and are multipurpose. Enameled ware also works well. However, although I have always hated plastic eating equipment, I have finally become a convert. It doesn't burn you, it packs easily, it doesn't dent, and food and drinks stay hot for a reasonable period of time. A plastic cup can be marked to double as a measuring cup with the aid of a hot knife. The only defects of the plastic items are that they can't be used for cooking and they must not be left too close to the fire. If you opt for plastic get the soft kind that will bend in your pack without breaking, and try to find a design that nests well, so that two bowls or cups take only a little more room than one.

If you are cooking over fires, a grill and a couple of pot-hangers are useful. The grill should be a very light kind made for backpacking, and it should have a case. Sooty pots are more easily taken care of if each has a fabric or plastic bag, keeping the carbon away from other items in the pack, and from the inside of the neighboring pot. Many people who cook over fires like to carry a single cotton work glove for handling sooty pots.

FIRES AND STOVES

I feel very strongly that the attitude of wilderness travelers toward fires has got to be changed. With proper use even delicate wilderness areas can stand quite a bit of human traffic, but subjected to the pressures resulting from the combination of numbers and misuses many areas are suffering badly. Some of the worst abuses are connected with fires. Hacking live trees with hatchets because of a mistaken notion that that is what camping is all about is inexcusable. It is possible as well as desirable to camp without burning everything in sight.

In some areas of heavy use, especially in alpine and subalpine environments, fires are simply inappropriate—any fires. I know how nice it is to sit around the fire, but if you cannot get wood without ruining the spot, use a stove. There is simply no excuse for the kind of self-indulgence that breaks off every beautifully weathered snag and mutilates every tree, just so that someone can toast marshmallows by a lake in the Rockies.

Modern equipment and modern food allow the backpacker to do his cooking on small fires—the kind that old-time woodsmen used to build for making tea in the afternoon. You can make fires from small dead sticks that can be gathered and broken without the aid of saws and axes—fires large enough to cook your supper and give you good cheer without burning up a cord of hickory. Older camping methods used fires to keep people warm all night, to cook beans all day, and for other similar purposes. Such methods still have occasional place, but as a general rule they should be relegated to the past.

In frequently used campsites with established fireplaces and plenty of wood, the camper can build a fire to suit his taste. But in relatively unspoiled sites, he should leave no sign of his passage, and that usually means a small fire, carefully built and eradicated with just as much care.

FIRE BUILDING

For small fires designed for boiling water and being put out fairly soon, there is little need for the elaborate structures which fill the literature. Care is needed for safety, but otherwise, the building can be a simple thing. Fires should not be built on peat, forest duff, or other soils filled with flammable vegetable matter. They should be built on an absolutely fire-proof mineral base or on wood laid on snow. Fire can smolder and travel in peat, duff, and tree roots for weeks before bursting out twenty feet from the original site. Sand or gravel near water is a good place to build a fire. In forested areas it may be possible to remove the duff in a circle and set it aside for later replacement. Be sure to get down to mineral soil if you are building a fire on the forest floor.

One can always build a fire on a rock base, but this practice should be used only when good taste will permit it. Too many areas have been de-faced by having every natural rock formation covered with fire scars. Pick a flat rock that is largely concealed, cover one with sand or soil to protect the rock, or use someone else's spot. Remember that fire scars last a very, very long time. Soot and charcoal are practically indestructible. If the only available fireplace is a beautiful rock formation which is unscarred, have the grace to move on, use a stove, or eat a cold supper.

In a reasonably dry forest, building a fire is so simple as to be almost trivial, even if an afternoon thundershower has wet the wood lying in the open. One has merely to get a few rocks to contain the fire and to hold up the grill and the larger pieces of wood. Kindling can be collected along the last few miles of trail if it is at all scarce. Start picking up dry twigs when you start thinking about stopping. A few dry pieces of deadwood which are protected under the branches of trees can be whittled into fuzz sticks, two or three of which make excellent kindling. A collection of broken up pieces of deadwood (not rotten) ranging in size from the diameter of a pencil up to the largest size you can break completes the fixings. These should be arranged in a loose pile with lots of air space and plenty of wood above the point of ignition in progressively larger sizes.

Practice makes perfect. If you don't know how to build a fire, practice lighting them with a few matches in all kinds of weather. Spend plenty of time laying the fire. That is the key. Once it is burning well, even most wet and green wood can be burned—within reason. Candles make good fire-starters, as do various chemical tablets and pastes, but practice without them.

Fire building only really becomes a test in wet weather that lasts long enough to soak things down. Saving kindling over from one fire to the next is a help, and usually dry wood can be found in protected spots, but it must be admitted that when the weather is wet enough for long enough, you'll only get dry wood by standing it in front of your fire or splitting it out with an ax. If you have an ax and the use seems reasonable, there is always dry wood in a standing dead stub that isn't rotten.

As a general rule, it is far better to collect wood with your hands than with an ax or saw, which leave their telltale marks and add weight that isn't usually necessary. Except in wet weather there is almost always enough wood lying around for a cooking fire, if fires ought to be built at all. If there isn't enough deadwood, then there either isn't enough wood growing or the camping use in the area is too high. Use a stove.

In windy weather don't build a fire unless you are sure it is safe, and if the forest is dry it probably isn't safe, especially with softwoods that spit large sparks. During the day, the sparks may not be noticeable, but take a look at your fire at night to see how far the sparks can travel. If the fire is safe despite the wind, you will probably need to build a small windbreak to protect it.

Beginners commonly make the mistake of not providing for enough air. They pack their wood too tightly and protect the flame from the breeze that would fan it to life. Remember that the fire needs oxygen to burn as much as it needs fuel.

FIRE DISPOSAL

If you make a fire, you must also put it out, and unless a permanent fireplace is to be left, you must also eradicate the signs of your fire. The most important step is putting the fire out, especially in true wilderness areas. In Alaska and wilder parts of Canada like the Yukon Territory, there is no hope of fighting large fires except where they menace settlements. The fires simply burn themselves out, destroying tens of thousands of acres of forest, wildlife, and soil. It is sickening to watch such fires, with the smoke darkening the sky for hundreds of miles. True, such fires used to burn occasionally before the coming of man, but they were relatively rare, even serving a function, and nature had time to repair the damage. People are now setting fires so quickly that reforestation can never keep pace. No one who is careless with fire has any business in the wilds. Take care of your own fires, and if you see someone else who doesn't, do something about it. They are your woods, and there won't be anything left of them if too many idiots are allowed to burn them up.

Make sure your fire is *dead out* before you leave. Drown it with water, except where there isn't any available, in which case it must be spread and smothered far enough in advance to let it cool before you leave. Stir it and feel it after you're finished. If you burn your hand, you'll have learned a worthwhile lesson in what it takes to put out a fire. Don't leave a fire that isn't cold to the touch, even after stirring.

Burning the fire out will simplify the job of putting it out and cleaning up afterward. Ashes disintegrate readily; charcoal and soot last and last. Pick out the remains of any of your trash which didn't burn and take it with you in your trash bag. Scatter the rest of the fire and the fireplace as inconspicuously as possible, and replace the duff if you removed any. The exception in heavily used spots may be to leave a permanent fireplace so that every stone around the lake doesn't eventually become sooty. If you do, build a good fireplace, so that others will use it. If one is already built, use it yourself rather than make a new scar.

Spare wood should be scattered, too, unless a fireplace is left. Leave the site at least as unspoiled as you found it.

STOVES

Stoves for the backpacker are amazingly efficient devices, though they tend to suffer somewhat by comparison to campfires. The surroundings have to be pretty bleak to make snuggling up around the flames of a gasoline pressure stove sound romantic. The food, however, tastes just as good, and the woods around often look a lot more romantic than those which have supported too many campfires. Some beautiful areas that have been closed to backpackers because of excessive population could be opened with the proviso that stoves and tents would have to be used instead of fires and "natural" shelters.

Stoves have other advantages. After a long rain, you don't have to spend an hour hunting up or chopping out enough dry wood to get a fire started properly; you just pitch your shelter, crawl under it, and start cooking supper. In winter, cooking inside the tent or snow cave over a stove is often far more practical than building a fire outside atop green wood laid on the snow. Though every outdoorsman should know how to light a fire, in a lot of places he should *use* a stove.

Cooking over a stove requires several tricks. With a large party you may carry more than one and divide the labor, cooking a main dish on one stove and heating water or cooking a second dish on the other. For parties up to four, though, and sometimes larger ones, if only one stove is carried things must be cooked one at a time. This is really no hardship, once you get used to it. Try the stove out several times before you really need it, and if special accessories like prickers are needed, find some way to make sure that they are always with the stove. The merits and disadvantages of some types of stoves are discussed in some detail in Chapter 13, but the most obvious difference is between bottled-gas and liquid-fuel versions. The bottled-gas types are very easy to light, and there is little to be said about using them. You light a match and turn on the gas; that's all there is to it.

Liquid-fueled types are trickier, because the tanks aren't under pressure, and because the feeding apparatus has to get hot before the fuel will come out as a gas rather than a liquid. These problems are solved in several ways, depending on the brand, the size of the stove, and the fuel. The stove may have a pump to pressurize the tank. With a pumped gasoline stove, you pressurize the tank, open the valve so that some raw gas comes out, light it and allow it to burn and heat the generator, and finally you open up the valve all the way, and off she goes—hopefully. Kerosene stoves all have pumps, and the operation is the same, except that an alcohol primer has to be used to heat the generator. If the pressure starts to get low with a pumped stove, you just pressurize it a bit more.

The really small gasoline stoves which are most suitable for the single backpacker or small party are not equipped with pumps, and there is a certain amount of black magic associated with bending them to your will. The first thing to do is fill the tank, since they are a nuisance to relight in the middle of cooking. Opening the filling cap also assures you that you aren't fighting a slight vacuum in the tank, which will develop as the stove cools. The next step depends on the temperature and on the style of black magic you subscribe to. The idea is to create enough pressure in the tank to force some gasoline through the valve. Once the initial pressure is created, things are fairly simple. You open the valve and allow a little fuel to collect; then you close the valve, light the gasoline, allow it to burn almost out, and then open the valve again. If you give the proper incantation, the stove will now roar to life and will keep going until it is empty. If it isn't quite hot enough it may sputter for a little while, sometimes blowing itself out, but it will soon settle down to a steady roar, and after this it is rarely temperamental.

The trick is getting that initial pressure. Though it may seem odd, I have always found these stoves very simple to light in cold or cool weather. You just warm the stove with your hands (if it's really cold, put the stove in your jacket for a little while so that it doesn't freeze to your hands). After you've warmed it, open the valve and see if the gasoline comes out; then proceed as outlined above. In warmer weather your hands will not warm the stove above the air temperature enough to pressurize it, or else it will happen so slowly that you'll begin to feel like a fool sitting around clasping your stove to your heart. At this point you can heat the stove by pouring a little gasoline into one of the many recesses provided by the manufacturer and igniting this primer. Some schools of sorcery believe in pouring on gasoline and setting a match immediately in all cases, never using their hands to warm the stove. This works, but I avoid it when I can; I think this treatment tends to bring on stove trouble at a much earlier date than normal. Either way, it's an article of faith rather than reason, so suit yourself. One can also hold lighted matches or paper under the stove to heat the tank. Personally, I like to carry a cigarette lighter, which is handy for lighting fires or pressurizing stoves.

If all this seems a bit more trouble than it's worth, you may prefer the simpler bottled-gas stoves. Once you're used to them, however, the gasoline types are not really very troublesome. Don't forget to be careful with the gasoline. Frustration and cold hands should not lull you into lighting the stove while the open fuel can is sitting nearby. I always fill the stove outside the tent, and I light it there if possible.

With gasoline stoves, *use white gas* or one of the special fuels sold in camping stores at ridiculous prices. *Do not use leaded gasoline,* whatever the stove instructions say. The fumes from leaded gas are poisonous, and the effect is cumulative, so it is a good rather than a bad thing that most stoves won't function with leaded gasoline. With any stove inside a tent, make sure there is adequate ventilation, since there will always be some carbon monoxide produced. Take care about tipping, too, especially when snow camping. With a snow base, the stove can melt itself down and tip over. Besides losing your stew and making your sleeping bag uncomfortable, someone could be badly burned if the apparatus tipped over.

Stoves, whatever the type, should be protected from the wind. Whether the stove keeps burning or not, a strong breeze will blow most of the heat away before it reaches your pot. Some kind of windbreak is necessary, whether one carried for the purpose, your tent, or something improvised on the spot.

FOOD FOR WEEKEND TRIPS

Some people like to spend a lot of time planning menus for weekend trips, but I've never had enough self-discipline to bother. For longer travels, one really has to plan pretty carefully, but I generally just make up a menu for two or three days in my kitchen or in the supermarket on Thursday night. I simply count the number of meals of each kind I have to prepare for and then start mixing and filling until I have the right number of bags sitting on the counter.

Beginners may prefer getting started with the meals prepackaged for backpackers which are available at the same place you bought your sleeping bag, pack, or stove. I've always found it easier to pack my own, for a number of reasons. For one thing, most of the packages are allegedly quantities for four people. Either the manufacturers don't go out enough to know that the average party is not four, or they know they are misleading about quantities. If I have to repackage for one or two anyway, I might just as well do it myself to begin with, for a fraction of the price. The price is the second problem. With rare exceptions these foods, although quite good, are priced outrageously. Third, they are usually packaged with big air bubbles in the packages, which help cushion the food but take up a lot of unnecessary space.

As I've already said, proportions are unreliable. If you stick to one brand for a little while, you will find out how to compute portions, but every brand is different, and I find that the effort is not worth the reward. That is, once I find out that their four-man meal is really good for two, I not only have a hungry weekend behind me, in the future I know I will have to pay twice the already high price.

Some of the portions verge on the absurd. There are one-pot meals purporting to provide a serving for one and weighing one ounce. Presumably a one-pot meal is designed for supper, which certainly ought to provide a third of the day's rations. Now, even if the stuff were pure fat, which has the highest fuel value per pound, it would contain less than 260 calories, which would be a tenth of a rather thin diet for a small woman. With meals like that you can lose a lot of weight, but you may not get far. Some brands have generous portions, but you'll have to experiment. For these reasons it's pretty hard to shop by price until you've already tried nearly everything on the market and made notes on it.

My own solution is to get a lot of my supplies from the market, especially for weekend trips. I order my specialized dehydrated foods in bulk from one of the manufacturers, which makes it a great deal cheaper. When I want to use them, I dip the amount I want from a large container into my stew sack.

A lot of foods that are very suitable for backpacking are available in the supermarkets these days. For bases, there are instant whipped potatoes, which I often use when I want to be able to produce a meal by just pouring in hot water. There are also rice, noodles, macaroni products, bulgur wheat, flour, and various other things. These form excellent bases for one-pot meals or for more imaginative concoctions. They are the main ingredients of most ready-packaged camping foods, anyway.

The essential basis for a good cooked supper is to use a starch like the ones just mentioned, add any seasonings and vegetables that you think would go well, put in some margarine or butter for flavor and calories, and finally add a good source of protein: meat, fish, cheese, dried eggs, dried milk, or a proper combination of vegetables (see pp. 103–104).

You can carry a few fresh vegetables along if you like, or you can save weight by taking the dehydrated kind. Dehydrated vegetables can be bought quite inexpensively in bulk, or you can sometimes get some good combinations in packaged soups. Cheese travels well and isn't too expensive as a source of protein. Dried eggs and milk are nearly perfect backpacking foods in all respects. Sausages can be cut into a stew as well as eaten at lunch. There are also various vegetable protein additives, with beef, chicken, and bacon flavorings, which can be added to one-pot meals like meat. Various dried meats are also available in bulk.

Many weekend backpackers use canned meats and fish to finish off a one-pot meal of dehydrated starches and vegetables. The additional weight of a can of tuna, boned chicken, luncheon meat, or corned beef is relatively small on short trips, and they are inexpensive and easy to get.

The suggested recipes later in this chapter should give you a good idea of starting quantities, and you can make your own adjustments as you go along. More detailed information on nutritional requirements is also discussed, but one really doesn't have to worry much about them on short trips, unless it suits the fancy. The only requirements for weekend backpacking meals are that they keep until they are eaten, that they taste good, and that there is enough to go around.

BREAKFAST

There is probably less agreement on the subject of breakfast than in any other area of backpacking. Men who use the same kind of equipment and make suppers that are nearly identical will practically fall to blows over breakfast. In the interests of party harmony, if you plan the meals, check with the other members of the group and try to come up with a solution which won't offend anyone's preferences too much.

One solution to the breakfast problem is the full-scale, no-holds-barred, cooked breakfast. Bacon and eggs, pancakes, or both, are made up, and the most extreme members of this school will even get out the reflector oven and bake muffins or coffee cake. Now, I am at the other end of the breakfast spectrum, so I have to work pretty hard to give these methods a fair presentation, smacking as they do of unseemly fanaticism. Actually, it's not so difficult to make breakfasts like this, and I don't mind eating them. It's just that you have to get up at least an hour early to have that kind of meal, and I would rather stay in bed.

An intermediate course of action is to make a good cooked cereal, which doesn't take too much time and dirties only one pot. This is a fairly good technique for relatively large groups with a central commissary, providing you can agree on a cereal. Liberal lacing with raisins, nuts, butter, milk, and brown sugar increases the food value and makes most gruels palatable.

The instant hot cereals are a good possibility for people who have to have hot food but are as lazy as I am in the morning. These can be bought in bulk or in individual packets. Since they only require the addition of hot water, there is no need to dirty or clean a pot or to watch and stir the stuff. When you wake up, you put on a pot of water to heat, and this is used for cereals and hot drinks according to taste. Have a good selection of drinks and goodies to add to the cereal, and your breakfast problem is solved. Everyone can go about the business of breaking camp, waking up, and thinking his noble or ignoble early-morning thoughts with a minimum of friction and effort.

I have found that every year I take less trouble with breakfast, unless I have a bacon-and-eggs type of companion. I prefer to get on the trail fairly quickly, rather than spend a great deal of time fixing breakfast and cleaning up. Usually, though, I have some cold cereal, into which the powdered milk is already mixed, so that I just add water. Sometimes I use a commercial cereal like Grape Nuts, adding raisins and nuts. Here is the recipe for a very pleasant and highly nutritional cereal you can make up at home.

GRANOLA

½ cup honey	½ cup sesame seeds
¾ cup oil	½ cup shredded coconut
½ cup dried milk	(unsweetened)
(¾ cup if instant)	½ cup raw cashew pieces
4 cups rolled oats	or other nuts, more if
¼ teaspoon salt	you like
1⅓ cups wheat germ	

Warm the honey and oil in a pan, stir in the other ingredients, and then spread in a thin layer in shallow baking pans or cookie sheets. Roast at 350° F., stirring every 5 minutes, until lightly browned, around 10–15 minutes.

Ingredients for granola can be varied to taste. Add raisins or chopped dried fruit if you like. For breakfast I add more powdered milk when I bag the granola. Without added milk or water it makes a tasty trail food.

Another fast breakfast advocated by some of my lazy compatriots is the commerical "instant breakfast" drink. One simply shakes up the powdered milk and the contents of the envelope the night before and drinks it in the morning while rolling the sleeping bag and tent.

A final method which I recommend on those mornings when you really want to get off in a hurry is to simply start taking lunch breaks as soon as you get on the trail, forgetting about breakfast as a separate meal altogether. You can make up a quart of orange juice for liquid, as a bow to convention. This allows you to pack away all the cooking things the night before. You just drag yourself out, roll up the sleeping bag and the tent, and start walking. About the time you've waked up enough to realize that your boot laces need adjusting and your shirt is inside out, you can stop for a breather and the first of many snacks.

LUNCHES, SNACKS, AND TRAIL FOOD

Most backpackers keep themselves fueled during the day with a long series of snacks. The only distinguishing feature of "lunch" is likely to be that it gets a longer break than ten minutes, and that it is slightly larger. If the stove is handy or fire-building materials convenient, it is often pleasant to have a cup of tea or soup with lunch, especially in raw weather, but few trail walkers actually bother to cook lunch. Instead they carry various sorts of trail food in their pockets or in an accessible corner of the pack. This is eaten cold and requires little or no preparation.

There are many popular·kinds of trail food, and you can adjust yours to suit your taste, mood, finances, and metabolism. From a practical point of view, when several people travel together, it is usually most convenient to prepare supper and perhaps breakfast together. Trail food is best left to the individual, though, except for very long trips when each ounce must be planned and rationed meticulously.

I plan my trail food fairly generously, allowing some flexibility, and also taking care of my emergency food supply by simply carrying a little extra salami, chocolate, nuts, and so on. This also allows for daily variations in need. I don't begin to parcel things out into daily portions until the length of a trip exceeds one week. Suit your own taste. Trail food is a good place to adjust for individual needs, simply because amounts and frequency of eating are easy to leave to each person, when all carry and purchase their own. Variety can be achieved by the age-old method of barter.

Possibilities for trail food are almost unlimited, except that most such food should be concentrated and fairly durable. Banging around in a pocket or a pack simply destroys some types of food pretty thoroughly, and the number of special protective containers you carry should be limited. Some people take the trouble to protect a few delicacies, though, whether they lean toward tomatoes, deviled eggs, or nondurable breads.

Good trail foods that will keep for the required time are the long-lasting hard salamis and sausages, candy, nuts, cheese, hard breads, jerky, pemmican, peanut butter, butter or margarine, mixes for fruit drinks, dried fruits, and special commercially made trail rations.

Some details are given below concerning nutritional requirements and packing the most energy into the least weight, but with experience, you will be the world's greatest expert on the way your body functions best. With all the modern knowledge about nutrition, there is still an incredible amount of hogwash written. A good many studies, applied to the history of the species, would conclusively prove that we could never have survived to modern times. In fact, the body is amazingly adaptable to different eating regimes, but periods of adjustment are required. Most backpackers have strange requirements, because they spend much of their lives in relatively inactive work and head for the hills on weekends. The body never really gets in proper tune for this change. A common pattern is to feel really ready to go on Monday morning, when you are back at the desk; by the following weekend you're tuned up to get as far as the coffee machine when you're trying to push up a few thousand feet with a pack on your back, and so it goes. Some people handle this transition best with a lot of small meals of sugars and starches, while others do better with less frequent doses of protein and fat. Use what works best and feels best for you, especially on short trips. On longer ones, when your body will adjust to the exercise and diet, you want to plan your menu with at least an eye to nutritional requirements.

As one additional suggestion for trail food, here is a recipe for a version of the very durable, edible, and long-lasting Logan bread. Don't plan on eating it in the desert when water is low.

LOGAN BREAD

5 cups water	2½ cups raw or dark brown sugar
4 pounds whole wheat flour	firmly packed
1 pound soy flour	1¼ teaspoons baking powder
	1½ teaspoons salt

1½ cups honey   2 cups melted shortening
1½ cups blackstrap molasses

Mix all this stuff up thoroughly. Do not use a weak spoon or try this when your arm is feeling ineffectual—this dough lets you know it's substantial food right from the start. It should be tough stuff; if it isn't add some more flour. Flours do vary in the amount of liquid they absorb. When it is all mixed, bake it in 2-inch deep baking pans for an hour at 350° F. Cut it into 2-inch squares while it is still warm. Set the oven for warm, put the bread in to dry with the door left ajar, and leave it for 8–12 hours. Time depends on temperature, humidity, and your taste. The longer you leave it, the tougher it will get. As long as this bread is dried fairly well, it keeps for a long, long time.

FOODS FOR BACKPACKING

However they are prepared, foods for backpacking have to contain plenty of nutrients in a small amount of weight. Since a lot of our foods contain large amounts of water, one of the best methods to reduce the weight of your menu is to dehydrate it. Drying has also been used for thousands of years as a method of food preservation, so that it often solves two of the backpacker's problems simultaneously. Most menus for long trips will consist primarily of dehydrated foods.

Fortunately, modern methods of dehydration have made the selection of foods available to the outdoorsman much wider and improved the quality of many items. The old-timer stuck to the 3B's—beans, bannock, and bacon, and if he was a sophisticate he added some rice for variety. World War II brought some nutritious, but often revolting, additions. The selection is now so vast that no one is likely to try all the available brands and varieties of dried food.

Besides being dried, foods may also be completely or partially precooked. Some taste very good, while others suffer somewhat from the processing. But precooked foods can often be a real boon to the backpacker for various reasons that will be discussed later in the chapter. Take a look at the label to distinguish between various types. "Instant" foods are completely precooked and need only the addition of hot water for reconstitution to a ready-to-eat condition. Read the fine print to see whether this is the case or whether a few minutes cooking is required. This latter type has also been precooked and is almost as useful for the backpacker. Foods which require fifteen minutes or more of cooking are probably not precooked. They sometimes taste better, are often cheaper, and they may be very satisfactory, but they present some problems for the camp cook.

There are several ways of dehydrating food. The oldest uses low heat, as with drying in the sun. Food can also be cooked and dried at the same time, with a higher heat. Variations of these techniques stir, flake, or somehow agitate the food so that it will reconstitute more easily when water is added. Vacuum drying works to this same end. The most modern method is freeze-drying, in which the food dries in a vacuum at temperatures below freezing. Freeze-drying maintains the original cellular structure of the food more or less intact, so that it will usually reconstitute faster and more completely than things dried by other means. This method usually preserves the texture and flavor of the food better than any other. It is also more expensive, and the food is much more fragile and more bulky, generally requiring protection by elaborate packaging.

Some types of food meet the requirements of the backpacker quite well without special processing, and these are very useful. Peanut butter, some cheeses, some sausages, nuts, and many other foods have been favorites for a long time.

NUTRITIONAL REQUIREMENTS

Even the backpacker who lives to eat rather than eats to live has to combine business with pleasure if he plans to carry a couple of weeks' food around with him. He can't afford too many pounds of food with little or no nutritional value. The first thing he needs is plain, ordinary fuel. To hump a pack up a mountain or keep warm on a cold day you have to burn up lots of digestible food. The amount of energy available in a piece of candy or a stick of celery is normally measured by nutritionists in calories, the weight-watcher's bugbear.

You are not suited, as plants are, to get energy directly from the sun, so any work you do has to be powered by burning the food you eat. Your body can store some of that food as body fat, giving you reserves, but ultimately all your energy comes from food. People's needs vary depending on many things, but you can expect to use between 3,000 and 5,000 calories per day, depending on body weight, metabolism, physical condition, air temperature, and the amount of work you do. Probably your needs will be between 4,000 and 4,500 calories for a day on the trail.

Foods are divided into three main categories: carbohydrates, proteins, and fats. Some of each category is necessary for a good diet, as are certain minerals and vitamins. First, though, let's consider these three main categories: Carbohydrates—sugars and starches—generally provide around 1,600 calories per pound, and protein used as fuel has a similar value. Fats provide over twice as many calories, about 4,000 per pound. All these values are reduced by the presence of moisture or indigestible bulk in the food.

From these figures it is obvious that fats provide far more energy, pound for pound, than any other food, and the backpacker planning a menu should make use of this fact. The most concentrated foods available do have a high proportion of fat, but most of us would not relish drinking cooking oil for an entire week, so there are limits to the amount of fat that can be used. Fats have other special virtues. More heat is produced in digesting them than other foods, and they take longer to assimilate, so they have special value in helping one to stay warm and in "sticking to the ribs." They should receive special emphasis in cold-weather diets. In cold weather most people will happily eat far more fat than they will when temperatures are warm. On the other hand, fats do not produce much quickly available energy, and they require a good blood supply in the stomach for digestion. Hence they are likely to be unappetizing, indigestible, and even nauseating under circumstances when circulation to the stomach is poor, for example when you are at very high altitudes or when you are quite cold and exhausted.

Proteins, as a fuel, have a caloric value similar to that of carbohydrates but some of the other characteristics of fat. They, too, produce more heat in digestion and take longer, so that they "stick to the ribs" and help the body stay warm, although not so much as fat.

Carbohydrates are generally the most quickly digested types of food, so they are far better for quick energy or warmth than either fats or proteins. This is especially true of glucose (dextrose), which can be used by the body without conversion.

Some carbohydrates and fats are generally desirable in a diet, and they present little problem, since almost any menu concocted by the backpacker will have more than ample quantities for nonfuel needs. Proteins, on the other hand, may present a bit more of a problem, especially to the impecunious.

PROTEINS

Carbohydrates and fats really provide much better fuel than proteins, the former being more easily assimilated and the latter providing a maximum in calories per pound. Proteins, however, are essential for another reason—they are used by the body to build new tissue. A good protein intake is essential for the sedentary city-dwellers taking to the hills on the weekend. You need proteins to allow the body to rebuild those aching muscles.

When protein is used as fuel, it does not matter much whether it is animal or vegetable in origin. Like carbohydrates, there are some proteins that humans can't digest, but most are equally suitable for getting you up the hill. For rebuilding muscles, however, all proteins are not equal. Proteins contain varying quantities of different amino acids, and eight of these acids must be present in certain proportions to be used as building blocks by the body.

Since protein to be used for tissue replacement must have all eight amino acids in the right proportions, any protein which doesn't meet the requirement will be used as simple fuel. All the amino acids must be present in the right quantities at the right time, since the body cannot store them up. If only half the right amount of one acid is present, only half of each of the others will be used for tissue replacement; the rest will go for fuel.

All this detail is given because it has an important practical consequence—expense. Proteins which naturally have approximately the right proportions of amino acids are the various animal foods: meat, fish, and dairy products. Vegetable proteins are generally low in some of the essential amino acids.

To have adequate protein in your diet, you must include reasonable amounts of meat or dairy products in the menu, or alternatively, vegetables used in quantities and mixtures that assure an adequate supply of usable protein.

VITAMINS AND MINERALS

The propagandists of the pill industry have educated us all to our need for many essential vitamins and minerals. Fortunately, almost any reasonable menu provides an adequate supply of them and you are unlikely to need any supplementary supply. Some backpackers on long trips prefer to take pills to ensure against a deficiency. There are also advocates of supplements of the water-soluble vitamins even on short trips, since these cannot be stored by the body and may run short when unusual strain occurs. Follow your own prejudices.

FILLING YOUR SHOPPING BASKET

What you buy for supplies will depend to some extent on the length of your trip, how often you go off, and what sort of cooking you plan to do, but it will probably depend mostly on how much money you can afford to put out to keep body and soul together during your trip.

The freeze-dried meals which are now readily available from many suppliers are often very good and convenient. The biggest problem with them is cost, which is sometimes just high and sometimes ridiculous. Another problem with them is bulk and poorly conceived packaging. But basically, they are very good if you can afford them. Their greatest advantage is that most of them need very little cooking—you can pour in hot water and they're done. This has special virtues in some situations, which will be discussed later.

There is little need for instructions if you are buying any of the ready-made meals from backpacking suppliers. Once you've decided the true proportions needed for each person, the directions on the package will take care of you. An increasing number of such meals are available in supermarkets, sometimes costing less than the ones at the specialty shops, but not always offering greater value.

The beginner looking for an easy introduction to camp cooking should pick meals with one or two hearty courses rather than the six-dish ones that take too much time and too many pots to make a bad reproduction of similar meals at home.

If you buy foods at the supermarket or dehydrated foods in bulk, they will often need repackaging. Dried food can be packed simply enough in plastic bags sealed with rubber bands. Peanut butter, butter, margarine, jams, and similar foods can be carried either in screwtop containers made to be tight or in plastic squeeze-tubes with removable sealing strips. Both types of containers are available in backpacking shops. Eggs can be broken into these same containers, and hard-boiled eggs can be carried in special cases made for them.

Most backpackers soon find that the biggest problem in shopping is protein. Good starch bases have been available for years, and there are even more available now. A good instant base is even available in the supermarkets in the form of mashed-potato flakes. Rice, spaghetti, and noodles are old standbys, and many more exotic grain products can be found to satisfy the most jaded palate. Vegetables are also pretty easy to get at reasonable prices, although you may have to go to a special supplier for these. I order about a year's supply at once from a large supplier of dehydrated foods.

Flavoring is also easy to manage. Judicious use of spices will get you off to a good start, and you can get interest and variety by using various kinds of sauces. Many are available in packages at the store or, more cheaply, from a mail-order supplier. Open the packages at home and dump the contents into your stew bag. You can get by even more cheaply by using some of the extracts and flavorings available in larger quantities at reduced prices, especially since you'll probably repackage the stuff anyway.

The actual protein is the expensive part if you stick to meat products. You can buy dehydrated ground beef or chicken or ham pieces, freeze-dried patties or steaks or chops. One of the best ingredients for stews is Wilson's meat bar, and if you can afford it this is a good alternative. They cost about $1.50 each for a three-ounce bar, which works out to $8.00 per pound. Although each bar is the equivalent of about ½ pound of raw meat, it's still expensive for my budget. If the price seems cheap to you, read no further. Wilson's also makes a bacon bar, at a slightly lower price.

Some alternatives have already been mentioned. Working powdered milk into your menus will give you lots of high-quality protein. Cheese is an excellent flavoring and protein source, and the harder cheeses keep very well. Dried cheeses keep best, and for long trips dried cheddar can be got from specialty houses to supplement conventional dry jack, Parmesan, and

Romano. For economy, though, vegetable protein is the best solution by far. In the proper mixtures, vegetable protein is as high in quality as meat protein, and with the proper use of flavorings, it tastes just as good in one-pot meals. You can buy vegetable protein concentrates, already mixed in the proper quantities, either in meal form (often called multipurpose food, or MPF) or in a textured, flavored form designed to replace meats. Some of the dehydrated-food suppliers carry these.

Another alternative is to simply make dishes with approximately the right combinations of sources of vegetable protein. See the reading list at the back of this book for a good book giving lots of combinations.

A list of a few good backpacking foods follows. It is far from complete, but it should help you to get started. Cooking times have to be adjusted for altitude. See the discussion on high-altitude cooking (page 108). Look at the directions on the package. Products vary, and the comments on preparation here are meant as a rough guide to help you plan meals and order food.

STARCHES, GRAINS, AND SUCH

Dehydrated potatoes have become one of the most widely used bases because one simply adds hot water. Repackage the potatoes before the trip, adding 2 tablespoons of powdered milk to each cup of flakes. Use 1⅓ cups of water for each cup of flakes. Dehydrated potatoes are also available in nuggets and slices, neither of which reconstitutes right away. Plan on cooking these about the same length of time as other dehydrated vegetables. The mashed potatoes go well with cheese, gravy, and some meat or meat substitute, or made in a fairly dry mixture and fried as potato cakes, perhaps with a bit of bacon.

Noodles of various kinds and shapes make an excellent start for innumerable one-pot meals, and they are one of my favorite bases. They cook in about 8 minutes of boiling, and they are quite nourishing, since they are generally made with egg as well as flour. For camp cooking with limited amounts of heat, I generally cook them in just enough water to cover them all through the cooking. Frequent stirring keeps them from sticking. Then other ingredients for the meal can be added when the noodles are done. If vegetables are part of the dish, they may need to be cooked for a while before adding noodles. Noodles go with almost any sort of protein and sauce combination. If you are cooking over a fire and have plenty of water, it is a good idea to cook them in more water and drain some of it. The main defect of noodles is their bulk; they take up more space than spaghetti or macaroni, and this may be important on long trips.

Spaghetti, macaroni, and other similar products have always been favorites for the camp cook. They generally require more cooking time than noodles, around ten to fifteen minutes, but this is not excessive in most situations. Tomato sauces are traditional, but macaroni products go very well with many flavor combinations. Cook them the same way as noodles, only longer.

Rice is an old wilderness standby. It tastes good for supper and even makes a good breakfast cereal. It is compact and almost indestructible. Plain rice requires about twenty minutes to cook. Pour the rice into twice its volume of boiling water, cover and keep barely boiling with the cover on for the required time. If other ingredients are to be added, more water can be used. Rice goes with nearly everything. Quick-cooking and instant rice are available, and are useful to the backpacker who needs their special features, although I don't like the texture as well as that of plain rice. Brown rice is usually not suitable for general backpacking menus because it takes twice as long as white rice to cook. You might plan on using it occasionally where this wouldn't matter.

Various other grains make good bases and provide variety, but unless you can find quick-cooking kinds, they are usually impractical for the backpacker, requiring at least forty-five minutes' cooking time. Health-food stores are often good shopping places for foods like this, and if you can discover a source for quick-cooking wheat or other grains, you will find them pleasant. (Quick-cooking grains are simply those which have been precooked by one of several processes.)

One very good grain product that cooks rapidly enough to be useful to the camp cook is bulgur wheat, a very old wheat preparation that is readily available in health-food stores and in many supermarkets. It is wheat which has been precooked, dried, and cracked. Cook it and use it like rice. Cooking takes about fifteen minutes.

Legumes like beans, peas, lentils, and garbanzos are excellent food, and were the staple of most of the trappers, prospectors, and other assorted pioneers. They provide lots of protein, especially when combined with grain products or animal protein. They also have almost any other virtue that the backpacker could wish, except that they take so long to cook that they are nearly useless in their normal form. You can, however, get several kinds of precooked beans which cook quickly and can be used in innumerable dishes. Bean and pea flours make fine soups or thickeners if you can find them. They are usually marketed now as soup mixes. There are good instant pea-soup mixes which are filling and which provide a good source of protein, especially if rice, noodles, or some other grain is included in the meal.

Flours are actually merely other forms of grain, but they cook more quickly than whole grains, so they are useful to the backpacker who learns to cook with them in camp. The various wheat flours are the most common, but almost any other flour you can find can be used in the same ways, and will provide interesting variety. Soy flour, made from soybeans rather than grain, is particularly useful for its nutty flavor and its richness in protein. It can be used for thickenings or added to other flours. Flour can be used to thicken gravy. If you buy a gravy mix in the store you will get meat flavoring and flour. You can make the same thing with instant bouillon, flour, and water. I use a lot of flour for dumplings and bannock. Both of these can be made from the same mixture, which you concoct at home in short order. At camp, just stir in water and add to stews or bake in a pan or on a stick. See the recipe later in this chapter.

VEGETABLES

A great variety of vegetables can now be bought in good dehydrated versions. Freeze-drying produces the best taste, and also makes vegetables which reconstitute more quickly, but it is expensive. Quite a few vegetables turn out very nicely with less expensive processing. Cooking time can be reduced by carrying a wide-mouth screwtop container. When you stop at a stream around lunchtime, put the evening vegetables in the container with some water to soak. They can then be cooked that evening almost like fresh vegetables. Dried green peas, onions, flaked cabbage make excellent material for stews or soups. Carrots, green beans, beets, and corn are also good, but they take somewhat longer to cook, except for freeze-dried varieties. Flaked green peppers and onions make good seasonings and can be added to nearly anything. Powdered yams cook instantly, and mixed with some butter and brown sugar, they make a very good second dish for occasional variety. Tomato flakes mix with water to make paste, sauce, or juice. They are one of the best flavorings available to the camp cook for many kinds of dishes. When buying dried vegetables, check the label for cooking times and make sure that they are suitable for the dishes you have in mind. Different processing methods make a lot of difference in cooking times. Aside from freeze-dried vegetables, you will find that some carrots take four times as long as others to cook. Certain vegetables need to be partially pre-cooked to be practical, since they aren't very suitable for backpacking meals if left raw. If you're buying in bulk, be sure to ask about cooking times when you write a processor for his price list.

FRUITS

Dried fruits make good trail food eaten as they are, and they can also be used at supper and breakfast in various other ways. Raisins, dried apricots, dried apples, figs, prunes, and dried peaches are familiar items in any supermarket. All can be stewed or eaten in cereals, besides being used as trail food. Many backpackers like to stew some for desert at suppertime, making extra to be eaten cold at the next morning's breakfast.

Quite a few other fruits can be bought from houses that specialize in dried foods. Banana flakes are useful crunchy trail food, and they can be added to other dishes. Various fruit mixtures are available, some of them quite tasty, including citrus fruits, strawberries, and fruit cocktail, good for a treat at the end of a week on the trail.

Dehydrated citrus juices are also very good and not terribly expensive when they are bought in quantity. Dehydrated orange, lemon, lime, grapefruit, and pineapple crystals produce a beverage at least as acceptable as other means of preservation.

Oranges are one of the most popular extravagances of weekend backpackers, and there is no doubt that an orange is a particularly fine way to finish a lunch on a trail or the top of a peak. You should carry the peels out, however. The refuse from most fruit is easily disposed of—if it is not burned or eaten by animals it returns quickly to the earth. Orange peels don't burn, and they seem to last almost forever, so don't toss them on the side of the trail.

BEVERAGES

Instant coffee has gotten better, and outdoorsmen have gotten lazier, so few backpackers carry ground coffee anymore. Pack a bag of your favorite instant and make it by the cup. If you are like me and drink it black, don't forget your companions' preferences when you are packing. After spending one trip facing cream-and-sugar drinkers in the morning with no cream (substitute) and sugar, I've always remembered to ask. If you really want to make coffee from scratch you can avoid taking a pot by making "boiled coffee" in a regular pan. Bring the water to a rolling boil, dump in the proper measure of coffee, put on a cover, and set aside for a few minutes. Add a little cold water to settle the grounds. It takes a little while to get the technique, and there are variations in method, but you can make very good coffee this way.

Tea, for some reason, is a much more popular beverage in the woods than coffee. You'll have to experiment, but as a rule take more tea and less coffee than tastes at home would lead you to think you will want. You can make it by the pot, but most people handle the beverage problem with hot water and a choice of additives. Tea bags permit brewing in individual cups.

Hot chocolate is another good wilderness beverage. Though the "real" kind is certainly nicer, a bag of instant hot chocolate allows people to make their own from the common hot-water pot.

Bouillon is another excellent beverage for the woods, especially just after getting into camp. For one thing, it helps to replace the salt you have been sweating away, and so it often stops a thirst that other drinks won't quench.

An unlikely hot drink that is particularly fine in winter and popular with some at other times is gelatin desert. Make it according to directions, but don't bother to cool it; drink it hot instead.

Cold drinks are popular but optional. They consist of things to add to your water bottle, contributing flavor and sugar to lunch. Citrus juices have been mentioned already, but there are also numerous artificially flavored drinks ranging from lemonade to iced tea. Many are good, particularly if water-purification tablets have left a flavor to be covered.

MISCELLANY

There is a long list of popular condiments, spices, side dishes, and so on, which are popular with many backpackers. Only a few will be mentioned here, and you will find many of your own.

Margarine or butter or a substitute is essential. Add to everything, especially one-pot meals and hot cereal. I use margarine because it is cheaper and keeps better. Either can be carried in a screwtop or tube container, but in hot weather make sure it is tight and cover with an extra plastic bag for extra protection. Some backpackers prefer to use a bottle of liquid oil instead of margarine or butter.

Carry salt and pepper in a shaker which has covers. On longer trips carry extra salt, which you will use heavily if you are perspiring.

I add my spices to dishes at home and rarely carry any loose ones on the trail. I use many, and you should suit your own taste, but a few that are especially useful to me are: garlic powder, oregano, sage, marjoram, parsley flakes, freeze-dried chives, cayenne, chili powder, and cumin.

Sweet condiments can be added to beverages, eaten at lunch, added to cereals, and even combined with snow to make sherbert. Take a few that are appropriate for the trip. Sugar and brown sugar are the most convenient to carry, but some people like to carry syrup, molasses, jam, or honey.

If you like desserts, you can use a bit of candy or some fruit, or you can take some instant pudding. Those who like to produce culinary masterpieces at camp can make a tolerable apple pie in a reflector oven, using reconstituted dried apples. The affluent looking for something original can try one of Trail Chef's dried cheesecakes. (I'm not kidding; they make up quickly and taste fairly good.)

THE WATER PROBLEM

There are several different kinds of water problems: the no-water problem, the frozen-water problem, the saltwater problem, and the downstream water problem. Right now we're talking about the last. Mountaineers may not have to worry about this one, but most other backpackers do. The problem is that most of the water in this country is now in such condition that if you drink it you'll get very sick. You may be in a real wilderness, but if there is a human habitation upstream, chances are the water is unfit to drink. I know of rivers in Alaska in very sparsely populated areas, which in a sane world would certainly be good, drinkable water. They aren't, because although there are very few people living on them, they dump their sewage directly into the river.

You must purify water if there is any doubt about its potability. Contaminated water can be really debilitating, so it is important to be sure. Most water can be assumed to be safe if there is no human habitation upstream. Stagnant water or other water supporting much algal growth is immediately suspect, but don't assume the water is good just because it looks that way. Although a stream will purify itself after some distance, there is no practical way to test it in the field, so if there are people uphill, even hundreds of miles away, you must decontaminate the water.

There are several ways of purifying water: boiling, chemical treatment, and microfiltration. The last is of interest mainly to expeditions in primitive areas, and will not be discussed here. Boiling water for twenty minutes will kill all harmful organisms, and this is obviously very convenient for cooking water. *Boil*, don't simmer. For purifying drinking water on the trail, boiling may be inconvenient, and either iodine or chlorine is used to kill any microorganisms likely to be found in North America. The most convenient way to carry these purifying agents is in soluble tablets: Halazone tablets liberate chlorine and Globaline tablets release iodine. In either case, dissolve one tablet per quart of clear water or two tablets per quart of murky water, shake until the tablets are dissolved, and leave for a half-hour before drinking. Water containing a lot of sediment should be filtered before adding chemicals. Several layers of cloth will clear heavy sediment.

Remember that decontamination of doubtful water is very important in the backcountry. Intestinal disturbances are especially common results from drinking tainted water, and they will put you flat on your back, which is not a good place to be if you are a week's walk from help. With virulent organisms, a small amount of bad water is sufficient, so swish the cover and lips of the container with treated water, use good water for brushing teeth, and heat your pans after washing them with suspect water. Being overcautious is worthwhile in this area.

COOKING AT HIGH ALTITUDES

Camp cooking is generally done by boiling, and the boiling temperature of water drops around 2° F. for every thousand feet of altitude gain. This may sound rather abstract and unimportant, but for the backpacker at high altitudes it is critical. I still remember very vividly a trip I took when I was ten years old with a friend at an altitude of eleven thousand feet. I was the perpetrator, and we camped around sunset in some army-surplus horror with the cold rain pouring down. We were undaunted, since we would soon have some hot supper. We built a fire in front of the shelter and started to cook the staple of the stew—fresh carrots. They boiled and boiled and boiled and the damned things stayed as hard as they had been in the store. We finally gave up and ate hot, raw carrots. It must have been a useful experience, because I haven't forgotten the effects of altitude on cooking since. I hope you won't either.

As a rough guide, you can figure that the cooking time for food will double with every six thousand feet or so of altitude. This is only a rough guide, though. Some foods require a relatively high heat to cook at all, and one finds that above, say ten thousand feet, you can boil them till doomsday, and not a blasted thing happens. If your trip calls for a campsite at eleven thousand feet, get quick-cooking or instant foods. Look at the label. If 45 minutes is tolerable cooking time, the label should call for 20 or 24 minutes if you're going to six thousand feet and 10 or 12 minutes for twelve thousand feet. The actual cooking time will be 45 minutes or so in all these cases. All the cooking times mentioned in this chapter are *sea-level cooking times*, as are most times you will find on packages. If you camp atop a fourteen-thousand-foot peak and try to cook some brown rice, you'll have an interesting way to spend the night—watching it boil.

Quick-cooking foods are the favorite solutions to the high-altitude cooking problem, but there are a couple of others. Frying is not much affected by the altitude, and trout caught in a lake at ten thousand feet will be ready to eat just about as fast as those hooked at sea level. Another solution which is rarely considered by backpackers is a pressure cooker. A four-quart model only weighs about 2½ pounds and generally comes equipped with separator baskets which weigh another eight ounces or so. Though not worthwhile for the average backpacker, a pressure cooker can actually mean a considerable saving in weight for a long trip at high altitude. The fuel used up in boiling water away is saved, and at the same time one gains great versatility in the variety of food available. Cooking time is greatly reduced, and in cold weather one saves condensation on tent walls. By allowing one to use ordinary foods instead of expensive freeze-dried menus, a pressure cooker can even save money. All this is not meant to recommend a pressure cooker to the camper who occasionally crosses a ten-thousand-foot pass, but for an extended trip above eight or ten thousand feet, it would be worth considering.

FRESH FOOD SUPPLEMENTS

In this book I have generally put down the idea of living off the land, both for practical reasons and from the point of view of a conservationist. I don't mean by this that you shouldn't make use of available foods, but that one shouldn't plan on living on them exclusively. A little study of local plants will often satisfy your lust for a salad or some fresh greens. In lake country, you may be able to dine on trout every night, carrying fat, flour, or corn meal, and side dishes to supplement fish suppers and breakfasts. In season, berries may liven your diet or even provide a significant amount of it. Used judiciously, natural foods will provide a welcome garnish to your meals. In some places and seasons, with the right knowledge of the country, you might be able to plan on getting most of your food from the land, but this is rarely possible in popular backpacking spots. More commonly, one would have to break the law, wreak ecological havoc, or spend all the time one planned on traveling, simply collecting food.

RECIPES

Following are a few recipes which I like. They are intended as suggestions; one-pot meals are a good place to exercise your own creativity. They are also varied in their applicability to different kinds of camping. On a weekend trip tuna fish would be a satisfactory protein source, readily available and not too heavy, but on a long trip the can and water content would rule it out. Dumplings, on the other hand, can be added to virtually any stew or soup.

CORNED BEEF AND CABBAGE (FOR ONE)

    2 ounces dried flaked cabbage
    2 ounces dried potato slices
    1 ounce dried onions
  2–4 tablespoons margarine
       salt and pepper to taste
    ½ can (12-ounce size) corned beef

Put everything except the meat into 4 cups of boiling water, and cook until tender, around 15 minutes. Pour off any excess water, dice the beef in and serve.

DUMPLING MIX

    1 cup flour
    2 tablespoons soy flour
    2 tablespoons dehydrated eggs
    2 tablespoons dried milk
  1½ teaspoons baking powder
    ½ teaspoon salt
    1 tablespoon shortening

Mix the ingredients at home, cutting in the shortening. In camp any amount you like can be mixed with enough water to make a soft dough. Then drop spoonfuls into the top of a cooking stew or soup, cover, and allow to cook 20 minutes. The same dough can be baked in a pan or twisted on a stick over a fire to make bannock.

STEW (FOR ONE)

    4 ounces dried vegetables
    4 ounces macaroni
    2 ounces beef-flavored vegetable protein or freeze-dried ground beef
    2 tablespoons soy flour
    2 tablespoons margarine
    1 tablespoon instant beef bouillon
       salt, pepper, oregano, sage, garlic to taste

Drop everything into a quart of boiling water and cook until done, depending on the longest cooking vegetables.

110

BULGUR AND CHEESE (FOR ONE)

1 cup bulgur wheat
1 tablespoon dried minced onion
1 bouillon cube (2 if you like)
2 tablespoons margarine
¼ pound cheddar cheese
2 tablespoons Parmesan or Romano cheese
  salt and pepper to taste

Mix the first three ingredients in advance. Cook 15 minutes with 2½ cups of water, and then add the cheese, salt, and pepper.

Part 2

Equipment: How to Buy and Make It

General Considerations 7

Since the backpacker's comfort and safety depend on his equipment, it obviously deserves careful choice. Good equipment is a bargain, even when the initial price is high, because it will last for years of hard use. Still, the beginner with limited finances cannot always afford long-range economy, at least not for everything. In this chapter, I will try to introduce some of the materials used for good backpacking equipment, the factors involved in choosing them, and the ways you can get equipment. Fortunately, good equipment isn't always expensive.

THE MATTER OF QUALITY

I've said that a high-quality backpacking outfit is a bargain, but this does not necessarily mean that high-priced gear is. Quality and price *do* tend to correspond better in lightweight camping equipment than in many other areas of the consumer economy, but there is plenty of room for intelligent shopping, and there are some tricks for getting bargains, for those to whom the savings are worth the effort.

The word is now out that backpacking has become big business, and the predictable flood of junk on the market has probably only begun. A lot of time will be spent in this section describing ways to cut corners and keep the expense of equipment down, but I have done this simply because a lot of people just can't afford to plunk down the amount of money it costs to completely outfit themselves at a good store. Still, don't be deluded; the bargains usually take some work to get, because good-quality equipment requires good, expensive materials and a lot of careful work, and these require money.

The ways of saving money and still getting good quality involve getting around these problems somehow, and this requires a little more trouble than walking around town and finding the cheapest stuff you can. Recently, a flood of aluminum contour packs, small tents, down equipment, and the like has started to hit the "surplus" stores, the discount houses, and the mass catalogue stores. I haven't seen them all, but in a number of searches I have yet to find a bargain among them. This merchandise is generally shoddy and overpriced. It's possible, of course, that you might find a deal, but let the buyer beware.

I really believe that if you are going to buy new merchandise off the shelf at a store, you will get a lot more for your money from one of the stores or catalogue businesses that specialize exclusively in lightweight camping equipment for wilderness travelers. They take pride in their equipment, and if something goes wrong with it, I think almost any of them will give you satisfaction. There are bargains to be had in "surplus" stores, but the bargains are in real government surplus, not in the junk specifically made to be sold at these outlets. The reason surplus can be a bargain is that the government sells it at a fraction of the original cost. Actually, it isn't a bargain at all, but since you have to pay for it on April 15 whether you get any benefit or not, you might as well recoup some of your losses.

Remember that the wilderness is a poor place to find out that your equipment is poorly made. The greater your ambitions, the more true this is. Badly made equipment for wilderness travel can ruin your vacation and even threaten your life. Personally, I put my equipment to some pretty severe tests, and I want to be sure it will stand up. I think it is far better to economize on other things than quality. I would rather have a couple of good wool sweaters and a tough, water-repellent wind shell than a poorly made expedition down parka. The reason is that they are dependable, and this is important in the backcountry.

For all these reasons, if money is not too much of a problem for you, the best way to get equipment is probably either to buy from one of the backpacking-mountaineering stores or to order from the catalogue of one of the mail-order specialists listed in the appendix or advertising in a magazine that caters to wilderness travelers. Send for a number of catalogues if you want to comparison shop; you can save quite a bit that way and get better equipment in the bargain. You may be able to get significant quantity discounts, especially if you get together with friends.

Some of these stores and manufacturers make better equipment than others, and prices vary somewhat, but you can be fairly sure that they won't sell you junk. Buying elsewhere will require that you know a great deal about construction to buy intelligently, and this isn't always possible. You can learn a bit by studying the sections here on the construction of equipment and choice of materials, but you can't see into the insulation layer of a sleeping bag—you have to judge from outside details. Shortcuts like using low-thread count nylon materials are becoming common in cut-rate sleeping bags. Buying from a store that caters to wilderness travelers will save you some of these headaches.

SAVING MONEY ON EQUIPMENT

False economy has been mentioned, but there are a lot of perfectly good ways to save money on your equipment if you need to. Buying surplus has been mentioned. Many former good buys are no longer available, but there are still some bargains to be had in the surplus market. The best one is in clothing. You can buy good wool clothing on the surplus market for a tenth of the cost of equivalent quality anywhere else. In a pinch you may have to pay a quarter of the ordinary cost, but this is still one of the best bargains around. Depending on the garment and your size, you may need or want alterations, but these are usually of a simple kind, requiring little skill. Some other good deals are available in surplus stores, and a few of them will be mentioned elsewhere in this section of the book. A couple of trustworthy mail-order outlets are listed in the appendix.

A few cautions are in order for shopping at surplus sources. The first is to beware of imitations. I have nothing against things made in Japan, but the imitation surplus gear which finds its way across the Pacific to the "surplus" outlets is rarely even worth inspecting. Equipment which bears all the litany of government codes may be surplus or it may be a rejected lot containing defects. These rejects may be fine for your purposes, but careful inspection is mandatory. The same caution applies to used surplus. Some very good items are available only in used condition, but make sure you check everything carefully before buying. Surplus stores are rarely the kinds of operations which will cheerfully refund your money if you find the trouble later.

Another good way to get equipment cheaply is to buy it secondhand. Bulletin boards, want ads, and garage sales occasionally offer good equipment at low prices, especially in college communities. Obvious cautions apply in buying secondhand equipment, but as more and more high-quality gear enters the market, this becomes an increasingly good way of saving money. The brand name and a few current catalogues will tell you a lot about the value of your prospective purchase.

The best deals of all result from the entry of the lightweight equipment stores into the full swing of the American economy. With yearly model changes, catalogues to get out on schedule, and so on, most dealers in backpacking equipment now have periodic sales of last year's models, items with slight defects, rental equipment, discontinued styles, and similar stuff. This is when the poor but knowledgeable backpacker gets his gear. The down jacket with the off-color pockets or the crooked seam goes for half-price, as does the parka with last year's snap pockets instead of this year's Velcro. The main problems with these sales are that you have to be in town, instead of mail ordering, and you often have to get to the store early. It's usually possible to find out well in advance when the sales will be held, and if you are convenient to a store you may be able to save a lot on your equipment this way.

Finally, comes the old-timer's favorite route—make your own. The cost of materials for good equipment is high, but the cost of labor is higher still. Lightweight gear demands lots of sewing time, and you can save money by doing the construction yourself. Doing your own sewing has other advantages, too. It often allows you to save money on materials, a possibility discussed below. It also can be its own reward: there is a particular satisfaction in designing and making your own equipment, especially when you can create it to suit your needs better than any commercially manufactured gear.

There are several possible methods for making your own outfit. You can start from scratch, designing and executing everything to meet your particular needs. You can follow someone else's pattern, modifying particular features if you want to. You can remodel a piece of equipment designed for some other use—surplus, for example. Finally, you can buy a kit, and put it together yourself. Which method you choose will depend on circumstances, including your own experience and feeling of confidence.

Kits are now available for many of the more difficult types of equipment, which formerly struck fear into the hearts of all but the most experienced. Even down bags of sophisticated design are available with the pieces precut and marked for sewing and the down packaged in separate bags for each compartment, a most welcome innovation. For someone who feels nervous about the very idea of sewing his own equipment, this is certainly the ideal way to get started.

Patterns for some items are included in this book. Many patterns and recommendations on designs and materials are to be found in Gerry Cunningham and Margaret Hansson's *Light Weight Camping Equipment and How to Make It*, a really useful book for anyone interested in making his own equipment. Various older books include some designs, especially for tents intended for use in the forest. One of the best and easiest ways to get patterns is from old equipment. If you have a parka or tent of an ideal design which is finally giving up the ghost, you need only rip out the seams to get a pattern for a new one. For clothing, the same method can be used to get a correct fit in basic pants and shirt patterns. Go up to your local secondhand clothing store, find an item of clothing with the correct generous dimensions for outdoor use, and you have a pattern which can be used with any material by just ripping out the seams.

Materials can be bought from many of the catalogues of lightweight outfitters, but before you pay full price, check your local mountaineering outlet and see if they have any remnants for sale. Most companies that make their own equipment periodically sell discontinued colors, small pieces, and bolts with discolorations or other unimportant defects. Such materials can often be bought at well below cost, especially when shops are having regular clearance sales.

PATTERNS AND INSTRUCTIONS FOR HEAVY-DUTY SHELL PARKA

The parka described here is constructed with a double layer of fabric throughout. If you make it with fairly heavy 60-40 cloth (60 per cent cotton

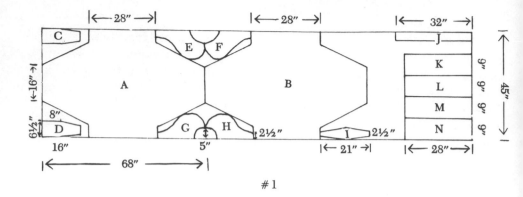

#1

and 40 per cent nylon), it should be quite durable and weatherproof. Basically, two parkas are made, and these are sewn together at the cuffs, the front opening, the bottom, and the drawstring at the waist. Seams joining the two are avoided elsewhere to make it more watertight. Many modifications are possible. The front can be cut only part way down the throat to make the parka a pullover. A rain parka can be made from this pattern by using coated fabric, either in a double or single layer.

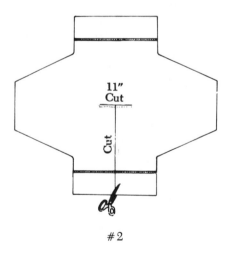

#2

MATERIALS: 4⅓ yards 45″ wide 60-40 fabric, 100″ drawstring cord, 30″ zipper for front, opening at both ends, snaps or 15″ of ½″ wide Velcro tape for storm flap closure, other closure hardware as desired for cuffs and pockets.

INSTRUCTIONS: Lay out the pattern on paper, lightweight plastic, or some other material, cut it, put it together, and check for fit. It should fit loosely. Be sure the hood fits well, and make any necessary adjustments in the length of the arms. Then lay the pattern out on your material, check carefully, and cut it out.

Sew C, E, and F into a hood, using finished fell seams; the narrow end of C faces forward. Assemble, D, G, and H in the same manner.

The 28″ edges of A and B will form the waistline of the parka. There are four such edges. Sew K to one of these edges with a finished

This type of cuff has a drawstring and a leather friction tab.

fell seam lapped so that it will shingle downwards on the final garment. Sew L, M, and N onto the other three edges in the same manner.

Cut the two resulting pieces as shown. The crosswise neck cut (11″ long) should be at the same place on each large piece, equidistant from the skirts. The long cut running up to the neck opening is for the front zipper, and it goes straight up the front.

You now have two parka bodies. Fold each one over, so that the skirts and sides are together and the creases run in the same line as the neck cut, but keep the two bodies still separate. On each one, sew the sides and lower parts of the arms together with finished fell seams (two seams on each of the two bodies).

Fit one of the parka bodies inside the other, and sew the bottoms together with a finished seam. Two grommets may now be installed on the inside layer of the jacket at the waistline, each two inches back from the still unfinished front, to provide for a drawstring. Make sure you pick a waistline low enough to leave the top of the parka loose and roomy. Sew two seams around the sides and back of the jacket along the waistline, forming an envelope for the drawstring running between the two grommets.

The cuffs may now be completed, using Velcro, buttons, snaps, elastic, or whatever sort of closure you prefer. One method I like is shown in the illustration. The drawstring goes around through the cuff and through the stiff leather friction tab cut for the purpose from a scrap of leather.

The hood should now be sewn in. First cut the neck opening out slightly to round off the corners, then pin the hood in before sewing. Sew the inside hood to the inside jacket body with a finished seam. Then sew the outside hood to the outside body with a finished fell seam lapped downward. Check the fit. Install a grommet 1½" from each end of piece I, for the hood drawstring. Fold I down the center lengthwise, pin it onto the hood to form a visor and to finish the edges around the face of the hood.

The parka is now finished except for the front zipper, installation of the drawstrings, and installation of any pockets you may want. Piece J is a storm flap to cover the zipper. Iron a crease in it down the middle lengthwise to make pinning simpler. Pin the two sides of the zipper and the storm flap into the front opening of the jacket, with the fabric edges going between the jacket layers. Start pinning from the top on each side—a few inches space is deliberately left at the bottom to prevent excessive strain on the zipper. The jacket edges should be folded in while you are pinning, so that all seams will be finished. The storm flap is pinned along one side with the zipper, so that it will extend across the entire zipper when it is closed. Install Velcro or snap closures for the storm flap, removing and replacing pins as you go. Sew the front of the parka, and finish off any details at the top and bottom of the opening that may have been left.

The drawstrings can now be cut to length and installed by attaching a small safety pin to one end and working it through the pocket. Tie large knots to prevent the ends of the strings from being pulled through the grommets.

Whatever pockets you want can be installed quite easily, using scrap material for either the entire pocket or the flap only. Pockets can be made by sewing the two shells together and then making a slash opening. Pockets like this can be made in the upper front and the back by sewing two seams from the armpits down to the waist and making slash openings in the sides of the front of the jacket and one side of the back. Pockets between the waist and the bottom of the parka can be made in the same

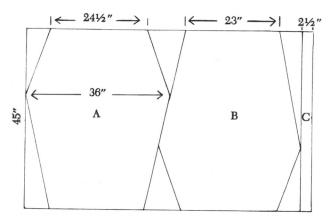

Rain or Wind Pants Pattern

way. Pockets can also simply be sewn onto the outside of the parka, but if they will carry much weight, they have to be sewn through both layers.

PATTERN AND INSTRUCTIONS FOR RAIN OR WIND PANTS

The pants shown here can be made of 60-40 cloth for a very tough set of overpants which will shed wind and quite a bit of rain, or they can be made with a coated fabric for true rain pants. For a very tough set of rain pants, the fabric can be doubled, with the coated sides facing one another.

MATERIALS: Two yards 45″ fabric, one yard elastic for waist, six inches 1″ Velcro tape for cuffs.

INSTRUCTIONS: The pattern is quite simple, but those who aren't confident should still lay it out first on paper, light plastic, or scrap, cut it out, and check it. A and B form the body of the pants, while C is the waistband. Several dimensions should be checked by everyone. Make sure the 22" cuff will fit over your boots—it is annoying to have to remove them to put on rain pants. Make sure the pants will be long enough. They will fit average-sized people, and shorter backpackers can cut them down, but tall hikers may need to change the pattern a bit. Remember that if you are working with coated fabric, you must avoid unnecessary holes; use paperclips rather than pins, and remember that the coated side faces *in*.

For assembly, sew the inside seams on the legs first, that is, the longer diagonal edges of A are sewn together with a finished fell seam. Then sew the long diagonal edges of B the same way. You now have two leg tubes. Next sew the two tubes together into pants with another finished fell seam. Sew the seam very strongly at the bottom of the crotch.

Now check the pants for fit. If the waist is too high, you should adjust it when the waistband is sewn on, because otherwise the crotch will be too low and will tend to bind. Lay the waistband along the waist and make corresponding chalk marks on each at 4" intervals. Ascertain how long the elastic should be to hold the pants up without being too tight. Make ink marks on the elastic to show the section you will need. Now stretch the elastic out on a yardstick so that the ink marks are stretched to the length of the waist band. Fold the band in half lengthwise, put it over the elastic, and sew an envelope around the elastic down the middle of the band. Overlap the ends, sew everything together securely, and cut off the extra elastic. Sew the waistband to the pants, using your chalk marks to line things up so that the tucks are evenly distributed all the way around.

Check for fit again. The cuffs should be about the right length so they won't bind when they are closed tight and you take a high step, but they should not drag on the ground if you open them for ventilation. When you get the length right, make a small finished hem on each one, and sew the Velcro strips on the bottom so that they will close tightly over your stockinged ankle or your heaviest pants and boots.

DESIGN OF EQUIPMENT FOR BACKPACKING

The main requirements for backpacking equipment are fairly obvious, after a little consideration. It has to be tough and durable, since it will necessarily receive rough use and has to withstand the knocks and snags of the trail. It must be as lightweight as possible consistent with reliability and durability. Bulk must be controlled along with weight, so most equipment should be designed to pack into a compact, convenient bundle. Finally, it is nice if things don't cost so much that no one can afford them.

There is a good deal of contradiction in these requirements, but not so much as there used to be before the advent of plastics and modern fabrics. Even now, a certain amount of balancing is necessary, between weight and durability, for example. Rain gear that is used only occasionally can be much lighter weight than designs for constant use.

Other requirements will be discussed in the sections on specific types of equipment, but one consideration should always be the impact that a particular type of equipment will have on the wilderness. Tents that need trenching are becoming less and less appropriate, as are those which require the cutting of poles on the site. All the backpacker's equipment should be as self-contained as possible. Requirements vary with the country in which you camp, but the most versatile equipment is that which requires no materials from the surrounding woods.

In designing and choosing equipment for the wilderness, simple, old-fashioned, durable designs and construction methods should be given preference. Seams should be well sewn, with finished methods that leave no edges to ravel. Synthetic threads are stronger, and are always preferable. Hardware should be simple and strong, and should function smoothly. Unnecessary gadgetry which would be hard to repair ought to be avoided. Outside clothing and packs should be reasonably smooth, snag-resistant, and tough.

Avoid designs whose essential functioning depends on an easily broken or lost piece of hardware for which a replacement cannot be improvised. Tents with oddly-shaped, easily bent frames, stoves with removable valve knobs which fit into inaccessible recesses, and all their cousins should be looked on with a jaundiced eye.

FABRICS

Most camping equipment is made primarily of fabric, and the quality and durability of the finished product depends on the cloth that is used. There are many different kinds of weaves that are useful for lightweight equipment, but only a few will be mentioned here. The material used can also vary, and there are various ways that the cloth may be treated after weaving. Synthetic fabrics are generally much stronger and more durable than fabrics made with natural fibers, so equipment made with synthetics, particularly nylon, can be of lighter weight than cotton. Natural fibers also have certain advantages, however, which are not matched by the synthetics.

Nylon has become standard for many types of lightweight camping equipment. It is very strong and elastic, so that very lightweight nylon fabrics are resistant to both tearing and abrasion. But because each filament of the nylon is round and hard-surfaced, it is difficult to weave into tight fabrics, and good nylon cloth tends to be quite expensive. Nylon also will not absorb liquids, and it is very difficult to treat nylon so that it is water-repellent enough for outer garments that have to shed any rain. Making nylon waterproof is done by coating the whole surface of the fabric with urethane or other flexible plastic substances. In either case because of the smooth surface of each filament and the conductivity of the cloth, nylon fabric tends to condense moisture on its surface easily, and since the fabric is not absorbent, the condensed moisture is cast off quickly. In a tent, that means it drips in your ear.

Cotton still has a strong place in equipment manufacture because it can be easily made into a tightly woven cloth that is relatively watertight, though it will still breathe. Cotton will condense less moisture than even uncoated nylon, and it is absorbent enough to take waterproofing compounds well. Thus cotton is very useful for equipment intended to shed some rain, because those items will still breathe and pass out the water vapor evaporated by the body. Cotton is also considerably cheaper than nylon. Sometimes cotton is mixed with nylon to make a fabric with many of the wearing qualities of the synthetic and the water-resistant qualities of the cotton.

Wool has a special virtue when used for garments like pants, sweaters, and shirts, because it retains some of its insulating quality even when it gets wet. No other fabric or insulating material will do this nearly so well. Synthetic fluffed *Orlon* has this virtue to a lesser degree, and it is sometimes used as a substitute for wool.

INSULATING MATERIALS

Insulation in clothing, sleeping bags, and similar items is provided by air. Air is an excellent insulator, providing it is broken up into small cells and protected from disturbance by outside air currents. Gerry Cunningham is fond of pointing out that the material which cuts the air into cells will work as well whether it is goosedown or steel wool. Wool has been mentioned as a good insulator for a specific purpose. The other insulator that has special value to the backpacker is *down,* the layer of water fowl that grows under the feathers. It consists of many pods, each of which has a central nucleus with many filaments radiating from the center. It doesn't have a quill like a feather, though you may be misled because a few feathers are always mixed with down, and it is the feathers that tend to work through the fabric. Down is special because it will deaden a larger volume of air, and thus provide more insulation than an equal weight of any other material. It will also compress to a very small volume, but will pop quickly back when the compressing force is released. These two characteristics make down nearly ideal as an insulating material for sleeping bags and some other items. Special methods of construction are needed with down, and they are discussed in the chapter on sleeping bags. The best down is plucked from mature geese that have been raised in a cold climate.

In the last few years a combination of increased demand and market changes have made the best down very hard to get. Geese for the meat market are being killed at a younger age. The down from these birds is greatly inferior in quality. Modern culling methods have made it possible to extract fairly good down from this lower grade, and the same culling methods can be applied to duck down. The upshot of all this is that you must increasingly rely on your source for down quality. A label such as "goose down" no longer means what it once did.

CONSTRUCTION

Most camping equipment is put together by sewing. Synthetic thread is stronger than that made from natural fibers, so it should be used throughout. Nylon is the most common material for thread, but some people who have trouble adjusting their sewing machines to work with nylon use Dacron instead. Dacron doesn't have the stretchiness that is the troublesome

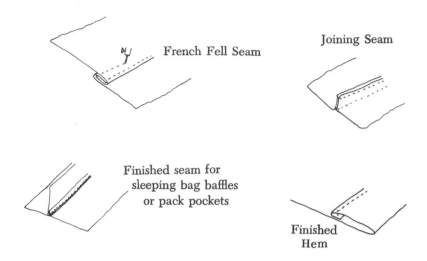

French Fell Seam

Joining Seam

Finished seam for
sleeping bag baffles
or pack pockets

Finished
Hem

A few useful seams for the construction of backpacking equipment.
The French fell seam is the most commonly used for joining pieces
of cloth.

quality of nylon. Anyone willing to spend the time to learn to use a sewing
machine can successfully make many items of equipment, and a home sewing machine will do most of the work quite successfully. Some parts of
packs will require hand sewing with a heavy sewing awl, an item that can
be purchased inexpensively from many backpacking stores.

Seams on backpacking equipment do not have to be pretty, but they
should be sturdy and stay sewn. To prevent raveling, they should be finished seams, that is, double sewn. Fell seams on garments and tents should
be lapped downward to prevent their catching the water. Any garment
meant to shed water should be sewn with the smallest practical needle, and
care should be taken not to make extra holes. This is especially important
with coated fabrics, since the coating is punctured at each needle hole.

You should make a full-size pattern before you cut any expensive fabric. The pattern can be made from newspaper or old worn cloth like ripped
sheets. Pin it together and make sure everything fits. Then lay the pattern
out on your cloth, and figure the most economical way to cut it. With
coated fabrics remember that there is an outside and an inside. The coated
side of the fabric should usually be faced so that it receives the least wear.
Friction will eventually rub the coating off and make the garment leak.

Boots, Socks, and Other Footwear   8

On a backpacking trip you travel on your feet. During a fairly level fifteen-mile hike each one of your feet has to be picked up and put down something like sixteen or twenty thousand times. This fact provides ample justification for special attention to your footwear. If you are careless enough to get a blister on one heel halfway through the hike, that still leaves eight or ten thousand times you have to come down on that heel before the day is out. If your boots are each a pound heavier than they need to be, you have to lift an extra pound thirty or forty thousand times on your hike, which is a lot of work, in case you haven't tried it.

The function of your footwear is, first, to protect your feet—from sharp stones, cold snow, hot sand, wet water, stinging insects, the broken glass of some fisherman's beer bottle, and a host of other hazards. Second, you may demand extra duties from the same footwear, such as boots stiff enough to kick steps in firm snow. You may want the soles to grip well on sloping rock. You should consider all these functions before buying footwear, because they are important. Cheap socks or poorly chosen boots will make your trip miserable and possibly hazardous as well.

Obviously, the same kind of footwear may not be ideal for every kind of terrain, but there are quite a few common characteristics that should be discussed before we consider special requirements. In general, since increased protection usually results in heavier boots and socks, you simply choose the lightest footwear you can find which also gives you the protection and secondary qualities you need. Foot protection together with qualities like good traction and durability come first, and when your real needs are met, you should go to great lengths to avoid every extra ounce on the feet. Remember that, unlike an extra weight in the pack, excess boot leather has to be lifted at every step, even on flat ground.

Good-quality heavy wool socks are even more important for foot comfort than boots.

SOCKS

The characteristics of good hiking socks are pretty much the same, regardless of the season or the terrain. Heavier socks are used with heavier boots, in colder weather, or to provide better cushioning, but otherwise there really isn't much difference between a good hiking sock for summer or winter, desert, beach, or mountain. The socks need to absorb perspiration without becoming matted or soggy, they should cushion the feet from the pounding of heavy packs and rough terrain, they have to protect the skin

130

from too much blister-raising friction, be free of irritating spots themselves, and finally, keep the feet warm in cold weather.

Traditionally, two pairs of socks are worn to help perform all these tasks—usually a lightweight pair next to the feet with a heavier pair worn over them. Many materials have been advocated for the inner pair: silk, nylon, wool, and so on. Try various kinds and find out what suits you best. I prefer a soft wool or bulked Orlon inner sock; they're cheap and comfortable. If you're hooked on "space-age" developments, you might want to try the special "wick-dry" inner socks, which are reputedly quite good and cost about twice as much as wool or bulked Orlon. Avoid cotton like the plague. It becomes soaked with sweat, clammy, uncomfortable, and is almost guaranteed to cause blisters as it rubs, rubs, rubs on your feet.

Outer socks should be much heavier than any normal street sock or most athletic socks. Exactly how heavy they should be depends on the various considerations already mentioned as well as on personal preference. When in doubt, it's better to get heavier socks than lighter ones. Quality is even more important than weight. You don't need to get expensive socks, but you must absolutely get good ones. Socks that are scratchy, mat easily, have sloppy weaves, and so on are a curse to the hiker. A good thick sock feels firm, resilient, and even; the pattern of the weave should not be easily felt by squeezing the sole or the heel with the fingers—if you can feel it with your fingers, you'll feel it with your feet.

I am an unreconstructed wool man when it comes to hiking socks, at least for the heavy outer pair. Wool stays springy, and thus warm and cushiony, even when it becomes wet from water or perspiration. A good pair of heavy wool socks can be wrung out and worn even after an accidental dunking in the river. Other fibers are often added to wool socks to make them wear better, but these should make up no more than 15 per cent of the fiber content. There are several types of good heavy wool socks. I prefer the Norwegian "ragg" type, which are very good and quite cheap. A more expensive type is the "thermal" sock, which has a smooth woven outside and a terry woven lining. The thermal type is fine, but check the fiber composition, and don't get one with a lot of cotton. Finally, for a summer heavy sock some people like the new "wick-dry" ones. They are made with two layers. The inside wicks the moisture to the outside, keeping your feet fairly dry. Thus, through the miracle of modern technology, you have a sock that does what a wool sock does—almost. As I mentioned, I'm prejudiced. Those allergic to wool may want to try the synthetic socks, but Orlon liners generally protect the feet pretty well from wool outers.

Buy your socks first, because you'll need them when you get around to trying on boots. Most good stores have a box of heavy socks around in case you don't bring your own, but until you get used to buying boots it's best to be able to tell exactly how they're going to feel with your socks. Never try to fit boots with street socks; you won't be able to judge either size or comfort.

BOOTS

Boots that are going to be used for a lot of hiking and backpacking are similar in design regardless of where you hike. A good heavy-duty mountaineering boot looks pretty much like a beefed-up version of a good lightweight trail boot. A few kinds of specialized footwear will be discussed later in the chapter.

A hiking boot stands five to eight inches high from the floor to the top of the upper, with six inches a good general height. High boots, especially if they are over ten inches, are heavy without providing additional protection, support, or durability. They restrict circulation of air, cramp the calf, and, as they get older, are likely to fold at the back of the ankle and irritate the Achilles' tendon. This last item is more serious than it sounds. It can keep you flat on your back for weeks and leave the spot sensitive for months.

I suppose there are a lot of good reasons for wearing high boots if you want to lead a cavalry charge, a paratrooper squadron, or a bunch of Hell's Angels, but I have been unable to discover any good reason to wear them hiking. More ankle support can be built into a low boot, because the ankle of a high one has to be made very flexible. Stones and snow can be kept out with anklets or gaiters, which are discussed elsewhere. Only a few of the specialized boots mentioned later in the chapter may need to be made higher.°

The most satisfactory boot sole is made of hard rubber with molded lugs. (Vibram is the trade name of the most common brand, but there are many other acceptable ones.) These soles wear very well, absorb shock satisfactorily, and are good insulation for walking on snow. They give excellent traction on dry rock, and they are as satisfactory as anything except nailed boots on various other surfaces. They are superior to nailed boots in so many respects that they have replaced the latter even among alpinists. Incidentally, hiking boots should have raised heels; the light heelless boots you may see in backpacking stores are designed for technical rock climbing.

Proper height, good soles, and a comfortable fit are the most important requirements in boots designed for backpacking, but there are various other desirable features that are worth looking at when you buy boots. Most of the best models are completely lined with smooth leather, and they are often padded, especially around the ankle and the tongue. The importance of these features depends to some extent on the general design of the boot, and they are more important with heavier boots. Padding generally extends only through the ankle and does not make the boot warmer. Some people avoid padding because it retains water if the boots get wet.

Check the tongue of the boot and the fit around it. Gusseted sides which will exclude water and dirt are desirable, but if they are not included be sure the tongue is sewn on straight so that it won't flop to the side and admit debris while you are wearing it. If it tends to move to the side it won't get better; it will get worse and be a pain in the neck until the day you junk the boots.

Obviously, good leather is important to a good boot. Leather of high quality is recognizable because it *feels* good: tough and dense, not dry and papery as though it was overprocessed reject material from a ladies glove manufacturer. A really well-made boot will have good leather, since manufacturers of good boots are not stupid enough to waste their labor by the use of shoddy material. For this reason, perhaps the easiest way to guess leather quality is to inspect the construction details of the boot.

° One other excuse sometimes given for making boots higher is for use in snake country. Personally, I prefer to watch my step (and reach, and seat) in country frequented by poisonous snakes, but if you're really worried about that sort of thing, I suggest that strap-on shields for the calves would be as good as high boots in very dangerous areas, and they could be taken off when they were not needed, unlike the tops of high boots.

The type of leather which should be used is a more complicated question, since it depends largely on the uses to which you intend to put the boots. Most lightweight trail boots and rock-climbing shoes intended for dry regions and seasons are made from a good-quality thick suede. It is cheaper than other boot leathers, breathes well, and is very tough and abrasion resistant. Its use is restricted in the ways mentioned because it cannot be made very watertight. Boots made with top grain leather can be constructed with the rough side facing out or in. Construction with the rough side out unquestionably gives much better resistance to abrasion, so it is usually the choice for boots that will be used for a lot of rock climbing or scrambling in talus and scree. Leather with the smooth side out is generally tighter against water penetration, and so it is frequently chosen when this quality is important. However, boots of very well-tanned rough out leather have been manufactured which can be made quite water resistant, combining the advantages of watertightness and abrasion resistance. This rough out design is preferable to having the smooth side out where it can be scraped off, eliminating the boots' resistance to water.

It is convenient to have loops attached at the back of the ankle to help you pull the boots on, and these become particularly important in cold weather, when you may have to pull on frozen boots in the morning. One other item worth considering in boots which are expected to be used a lot in wet conditions is the placement of seams, which are the natural weak points to water seepage. The fewer the seams on the lower part of the boot, the better. Check the hardware for leak points, too. On boots intended mainly for dry hiking this is of no consequence.

WHAT KIND OF BOOT?

Despite the fact that the signs of good design and quality are similar in all hiking boots, you must still make the choice of the general type of boot you want before you start hunting for a good fit. Do you want a 6-pound pair of heavy-duty mountaineering boots, a 2½-pound pair of trail shoes, or something in between? Do you expect a lot of wet going or snow so that you have to worry about watertightness, or will you encounter only occasional stream crossings and small snow patches? Finally, are there any special characteristics your boot will need? If you expect to do rock climbing in your boots, you need to take their feel on rock into account. Mountaineers need boots tough enough for step kicking in snow and rigid enough to protect the feet from crampon straps.

The main principle of selection has already been mentioned: get the lightest boot which will fulfill your needs. If you need a heavy mountaineering boot, then nothing else will do, but unless you expect to be doing a lot of work on snow, or generally to be giving the boot such a workout that a lighter boot wouldn't take the beating, you would be better off settling on a boot of moderate weight.

Unfortunately, it is difficult to define "heavy" or "light" meaningfully in terms of exact weights that would be of any use to the prospective boot buyer. Different suppliers use different sizes to figure their "average weight" listed in their catalogues, and only a few bother to tell you which size they use. This allows you to compare weights among their offerings, but not to judge them easily against anyone else's selection. Two catalogues frequently list the same boot with weights varying by more than a pound. Added to this situation is the notorious inconsistency in the ideas of sizes held by various European boots manufacturers; a Pivetta size eight is about the same as a Galibier size nine, and so on. If you decide what general type of boot you need, heavy, light, or medium, and there are two types which seem otherwise comparable in features and fit, you can always ask the store(s) to weigh them.

A medium-heavy pair of mountaineering boots with the smooth side of the leather facing out. Though this pair has had only moderate wear, the leather looks quite worn, a common problem with boots having the smooth side out.

135

Heavy-duty mountaineering boots are the sovereigns of wilderness travel, since they will carry you over almost any sort of terrain and will withstand an unbelievable amount of punishment. They also have the stiffness and ponderousness suited to their regal status. Like kingly robes, they are likely to be a heavy burden to bear. A man's size-ten pair is likely to weigh over six pounds. Choose them only for trips involving a lot of travel in very rugged terrain without trails. Stiff steel shanks that prevent the boots from bending are good for certain kinds of mountaineering, but they make the boots less comfortable for backpacking. Heavy boots do not have to be too stiff for walking.

Medium-weight mountaineering boots, rough side out. This pair is on its third set of soles.

Medium-weight mountaineering boots are lighter and more flexible than their royal cousins and are much more suitable for general backpacking use, since they are easier on both the legs and the feet, require much less breaking in and will still do anything the average backpacker will ask of them. The beginner will still find them rather stiff, but both the sole and the upper are much more flexible than those of a heavy mountain boot, allowing for more comfort on the trail, but still providing enough support to prevent the feet from being bruised in talus hopping with a heavy pack. This type of boot is ideal for the backpacker who expects to be doing a lot of cross-country traveling in rugged terrain or making spring and fall trips where lots of snow and meltwater may be encountered, but who is willing to sacrifice the ability to do extensive cramponing and step-kicking for a little comfort on the trails he'll be walking 90 per cent of the time. A man's size-ten pair generally weighs four or five pounds.

136

Two types of light trail boots, excellent for summer hiking in relatively dry country.

Medium-weight trail boots or light mountaineering boots are much more suitable for most backpackers than the heavier boots just mentioned. Hikers staying mainly on trails or moderate cross-country terrain do not usually need the support and protection of a mountaineering boot. Good medium-weight trail boots give plenty of purchase for climbing occasional rock slides or walking through patches of snow that does not lie at a steep angle, yet they are much lighter and more comfortable than mountain boots. Many trail boots can be made to shed water quite well, and these are good in wet areas like New England or the Northwest. The weight range for a man's size ten is around 3½ to 4½ pounds.

Light trail boots have the same advantages as medium-weight ones, except that they can rarely be waterproofed well, and are best restricted to summer hiking in fairly dry country. They will not last so long as equally well-constructed boots that are heavier, but the cost is correspondingly less. Trail hikers who avoid snow and continuous rain will prefer this type of footwear for inexpensive and comfortable service. Light trail boots are most frequently made of a tough suede which is comfortable and long-wearing. A man's size ten weighs around three pounds.

CHOOSING YOUR BOOTS

Plan to spend some time buying your boots. If you know what you're doing, you may be able to pick a sleeping bag or a tent in ten minutes, but the more experience you have, the more time you are likely to take choosing boots. If you have to buy your boots by mail, follow the directions of the catalogue carefully. Most suppliers have you trace the outline of your sole with your socks on and half your weight on the foot. Using this outline, they can often give you a good fit, but since boots are made differently, it is always easier to get a proper fit by trying the boots on. If you buy by mail, don't hesitate to send the boots back, and keep sending them back until you get a good fit. *Never* buy a pair of boots from anyone unless they will take the boots back, providing, of course, that you haven't worn them outside.

The most critical requirement for boots is that they fit. There are enough different stores and manufacturers around so that you should be able to get a pair which has all the features you want and which also fits well. If you're in a hurry and you have to choose, however, remember that a good fit comes first. A leaky boot will make your feet uncomfortable when it rains, a pair that is too light will be uncomfortable on rough ground, but a pair that fits badly will hurt all the time.

The first rule in fitting boots is that they should be large. After you have pounded along the trail for a while your feet will get bigger because of increased blood supply. They don't just seem bigger; they really are, even if you don't have any extra swelling from injury, bruises, and the like. People who hike a lot every day will have their feet expand permanently to a constant size, but weekend tourists should expect some swelling during the day. Boots that fit like gloves will feel like sophisticated instruments of torture by the end of a hard day on the trail.

The extra room is needed around the front of your foot. The heel should be snug, though not constricting. The front part of the boot should be roomy enough so that when it is laced firmly it does not bind anywhere and allows enough room for your toes to be curled up. Try to push your foot forward inside the boot when it is properly laced. If your toes can touch the toe of the boot, it is too short. Especially after expansion of your foot, when you are going downhill your toes will hit at every step, which gets to be pure agony after a while. The boot should be long enough and

138

hold your foot firmly enough to prevent your toes from hitting even when you jam your foot forward—that's just what you'll be doing on a steep downhill trail. The only people who may want to modify this rule are mountaineers who want to use their boots on difficult technical rock or ice —this means roped climbing of sustained difficulty, not an afternoon scramble—and they will have to decide whether the added security of shorter boots is worth the torture going downhill and some extra risk of frostbite.

Roominess in front doesn't mean sloppiness, however. If your feet slide around inside the boots in any direction, you'll have blisters for sure after a couple of miles. These requirements may sound contradictory but they are met by well-designed and properly fitted boots. Don't settle for less.

If the boots seem to fit, put them both on and walk around the store (or your living room if they are mail order). Any reputable boot supplier wants you to do this. Wear them for a while, scrunch your feet around in them, jump up and down, and try them out on something that slopes so that you can feel what they'll be like going uphill, downhill, and sidehill. Heavy boots will feel stiff since they are not broken in, especially if you're not accustomed to wearing boots, but they shouldn't hurt or irritate your feet anywhere. If they do, reject them and try another pair. If the store doesn't have another pair, go somewhere else, order from a catalogue, or order from another catalogue. Good boots last a long time and they will either become cherished friends or hated possessions before you wear them out.

Remember, a pair of boots that fits well will feel good. A pair that doesn't feel good will feel worse and worse and worse as the miles add up. *Do not* fall for any stories to the effect that the boots will stretch if they are too small or have a tight spot. Boots do stretch in spots as they are broken in, but there are limits and force is required. If you set up a competition for toughness between a pair of boots and your feet, the boots will win.

Do not get roped into buying a set of unsatisfactory boots because they are all the store has. Even assuming the store is fully stocked, everyone has feet that are shaped differently and that move differently, and boots are made with widely varying shapes and designs. It is not rare at all to find that one make of boot just won't fit you properly. If Jones's won't fit, try Smith's. I usually have trouble getting a good fit because my feet are

139

wide, but my latest pair is a French design that is too narrow for most people and fits me perfectly. It just happens to be wide where my feet are and narrow where other people's feet are wide. Keep trying.

The final step in fitting the boots is to wear them around for at least a couple of hours. If you've bought them by mail, this is no trouble. Just wear them while you're walking around the house doing chores. Any reputable backpacking or climbing store will let you bring the boots back if you take them home and find them unsatisfactory. Psychologically, though, I think it's better to make this check at the store, before it becomes inconvenient to decide that they really don't fit so well. Just try on boots when you first go into the store, and do your browsing while you're trying them. The idea of wearing them for this length of time is that stiff new boots gradually feel better or feel worse. If they feel better, clutch them to your breast and buy them. If they feel worse, start over. Choose your boots with the care you would like to use in choosing a spouse or a roommate.

BREAKING THEM IN

The only way to break in boots is to walk in them, preferably in small enough doses to avoid much blistering of your feet. If your feet are tough enough, you can just start wearing them on trips, but remember to take some moleskin. The amount of walking it takes to break in a boot depends on how tough it is and how tough the walking is. Some of the lightweight trail boots require practically no breaking in, but heavy boots can take many miles to reach an understanding with your feet. Actually, breaking in is less important with heavy boots than it once was. Heavy boots have to fit properly to begin with, since they will not move around very much to conform with your feet. If it should turn out that your boots don't quite fit, you might try finding a ski shop with a boot stretcher. Failing this, you may finally find that you have lost the battle to the boots—sell them to someone they fit, and buy another pair—carefully.

TAKING CARE OF YOUR BOOTS

A good pair of boots will stand an almost incredible amount of rough treatment, lasting through several pairs of soles, providing they are given reasonable care. The greatest single enemy of boot leather is heat, and this is the most frequent cause when the soles part prematurely from the uppers. Leather is damaged by excessive heat just as your skin is, but it lacks nerves to warn of burning and has no recuperative powers. Holding your boots near the fire or leaving them to dry in the heat is a sure way to shorten their life. Boots should be allowed to dry at normal room temperature. If possible, it is a good idea to stuff them with newspaper or special drying packets when you get home. Resist the temptation to speed up the drying process by warming them next to a stove, in front of a heat vent, or in the sun. Boot trees are not necessary, but they do prevent curling soles if your boots are very wet.

Boots should be cleaned of mud and dust. When mine are wet and muddy, I sponge them off when I get home. A stiff brush will remove most dry mud and dust. If the dirt seems to have worked into the leather, the boots should be cleaned with saddle soap before applying any waterproofing or preservative, otherwise these will just imbed the dirt deeper, to the detriment of the boots. There is no need to be fussy about all this, but occasional cleaning is needed.

All boots need to be treated occasionally to restore oils that are washed or dusted out of the leather on the trail. Generally, the same compound is used both to preserve the boot and to waterproof it. The amount and frequency of treatment depend strictly on the conditions in which you hike. For summer hiking in dry areas, a few light applications will get you through a whole season. In wet country, as much preservative as possible is rubbed into the boots whenever they manage to dry out long enough. (There isn't much point in treating wet boots.)

Excessive applications are undesirable except in very wet conditions, since the pores of the boot are closed off, making it hotter and more quickly soaked with perspiration. Where you are slogging through rain, mud, and snow all the time, however, you want a practically waterproof boot, and you should use as much waterproofing compound as the boot will hold. For intermediate conditions, simply try to find a happy medium.

There are several good waterproofing and preservative compounds for boots, but greases and oils should not be used. They soften the leather and cause the boot to collapse and lose its shape, which is undesirable in hiking and climbing boots. Liquid compounds penetrate the leather most easily, but check the container and steer clear of anything that purports to soften leather. The most popular compounds are silicone-based waxes like Sno-Seal, which are readily obtainable in climbing and ski shops. For a light coat, just rub the stuff into the outside of the boot, concentrating on the seams and around the welt. A cloth will serve, but the warmth of your hands works the wax in better. For better penetration, melt the wax first and then work the warm liquid into the boot. Whatever the directions on the can say, don't heat up your boots in the oven, heat the wax instead. Suede boots are best treated with a silicone liquid or spray prior to the use of wax preparations.

Good boots in normal use should need no care beyond that already mentioned until the soles wear out. If they need resoling or repairs, it is best to take or send them to someone with experience in working with lined boots. In most areas such bootmakers are a rarity, and you may have to either gamble with a local shoemaker or send your boots to one of the people listed in the appendix. Generally, someone who is competent will have lug rubber soles in stock, but these can also be purchased through many catalogues.

When your boots need resoling, don't put off the day—wear off the rubber, but avoid eating into any of the leather foundations. Most good boots have narrow welts, and there is very little leather to spare for sewing the uppers to the middle soles. Heavy wear of these middle soles is likely to result in extensive repairs or premature retirement of the boots.

For climbers and other rough country travelers whose boots suffer a lot of abrasion from rocks, there are a few additional precautions which will prolong the life of boots and avoid some repairs. All spots which are subject to a lot of rubbing and cutting can be coated with a thin layer of epoxy glue, especially along any stiching which gets chafed by the rocks. This technique is particularly helpful on boots used for technical rock climbing.

BOOTS FOR SPECIAL CONDITIONS

While some version of the standard mountain boot is suitable for nearly all situations likely to be encountered by the backpacker, a few special conditions may call for other kinds of footwear or for special considerations in buying regular boots. I'm sure that there are many such instances I have not run into, and there are certainly many outdoorsmen who wouldn't agree with my choice of equipment anyway. Still, all in all, in my own experience mountain boots are by far the most versatile hiking footwear made, and since the backpacker normally encounters widely varying terrain, he should think twice before sacrificing this jack-of-all-wilderness-trades for shoes specially adapted for wading swamps, running up good trails, skiing, or walking on snowshoes.

Climbing boots. Many of the best mountain boots are specifically made for difficult climbing, but there are many which are not. The average backpacker doesn't care whether his boots are good for edging on small holds or not, but anyone who ultimately wants to use his boots for difficult climbs as well as backpacking has to look at a few extra features. A climbing boot should have a very narrow welt; that is, the soles should not stick out beyond the uppers; such protrusions will increase adverse leverage on the feet and will also tend to roll off small holds. For climbing which involves steep snow, the boot must be fairly heavy and have a stiff sole. In any case, boots intended for difficult climbing must feel secure while the wearer edges on small holds, and this should be tried out in the store. Technical rock climbers who practice their art in areas free of snow and ice usually don't try to combine the requirements for a comfortable hiking boot and climbing footgear. They wear hiking boots for the approach and then change to very tight-fitting lightweight rock-climbing shoes.

Waterproof boots are preferred by a few backpackers who do a lot of hiking in marshy, flat country, especially in spring and fall when wetlands become passable to the walker, but where frequent breaks through the ice into a few inches of cold water make rubber-bottomed boots more comfortable than conventional lightweight hiking boots. The biggest difficulty with rubber boots is that they become clammy inside, hot in summer and cold in winter. They should be worn roomy, with heavy socks and insoles. Except where deep water may be encountered, the rubber-footed, leather-topped variety invented by L. L. Bean is more comfortable than the all-rubber kind. Either type can be bought insulated for cold weather, and either can be found with a Vibram sole for better traction. (You may not be able to find a Vibram-soled pair that fits, however; I can't.) In any case, don't expect to be able to use this type of footwear as a substitute for mountain

143

The rubber-bottom boot is good for hiking in very wet country with easy footing.

boots on difficult terrain. It is treacherous on steep slopes and should not be taken in rough country.

Sneakers are still used by some backpackers who appreciate their light weight and low price, and their use is certainly preferable to not going backpacking for those who can't afford boots. In the long run, however, they aren't cheaper, since they wear out much faster than boots. They are hot, get wet easily, dry out slowly, are brutal to the feet on rough ground with a heavy pack, and they are impossible in snow or cold weather. You may want to use them to put off the expense of buying boots in July, but don't risk a mountain trip with them in October—they might cost you your feet if you are caught in a snowstorm.

Some backpackers like to take lightweight sneakers or *moccasins* along for comfort around camp at the end of the day. They are a welcome luxury, but I prefer to save the weight, and instead I change socks and loosen my boots. Suit yourself. In a similar luxury category are *down booties and socks*, which are very nice to wear for lolling around on chilly nights and for warming your feet in the sleeping bag. They are one of life's little luxuries, but don't forget to worry about the necessities first.

Cold-weather footwear has to suit your means of transportation when deep snow requires the use of skis or snowshoes, but heavy or medium-weight mountain boots do very nicely if the snow permits hiking. Winter boots must be of a type that is easily made water repellent and they must be large enough to allow the wearing of heavy socks without cramping the feet. Remember that if an extra pair of socks makes the boots feel too tight, wearing the additional pair will make your feet colder rather than warmer, because circulation in your feet will be impaired.

The weather likely to be encountered by the normal backpacker does not require specialized footwear. Technical climbers often wear *double boots* in winter, but these are needed partly because of the need to stand for long periods on cramped spots. The backpacker's walking will enable him to cope with fairly cold temperatures without special footwear. An inner boot like that used in a double boot can also be bought separately, and it is an excellent addition if your boots are roomy enough to accommodate it.

Walkers in flat country often prefer insulated boots in cold weather, often combining the advantages of insulation with waterproof bottoms for early-spring and late-fall backpacking. Insulated boots are available with Vibram soles and all-leather uppers, with rubber bottoms and leather tops, or with all rubber from top to bottom. The all-leather type is the only one suited to walking in rough country. Of the other two, the leather-topped kind is much more comfortable to walk in.

Insulation in these boots must be examined with care, since many cheap and rather dangerous types are made. Condensation of perspiration from the feet can easily soak conventional types of insulation and render them useless, so any boot using this sort of material should be made with removable liners, of which at least two pairs should be carried. Another solution is the use of insulation completely sealed between two layers of rubber, the double-vapor barrier principle used in the U.S. Army Korea boots (Mickey Mouse boots). Finally, the method used in many of the best insulated boots being made now is to insulate with closed cell foam like Ensolite or Thermobar, in which each air pocket is sealed and thus cannot absorb water or perspiration.

For very cold weather, an alternative to insulated boots is the *overboot*, a fabric cover for the feet and lower legs with pockets for insulation, which can be put on over normal boots when the need arises. They are similar to mukluks, except that they are worn over boots. *Mukluks* are like thick, insulated fabric or skin boots, and are used in extremely cold weather in the far north and for snowshoeing in dry, very cold weather. The backpacker without skis or snowshoes would be unlikely to encounter conditions requiring mukluks.

Overboots generally have leather bottoms which are slippery on rough ground, but some new types that do not cover the soles will become available about the time this book is published. These should present a less expensive alternative to double boots.

Special footwear is often needed for snowshoeing or skiing in winter, but for normal hiking, the need for it is really quite rare. The only really troublesome conditions are those mentioned earlier when cold has arrived in wet areas, but ice is not yet thick enough to prevent occasional breakthroughs. Similar circumstances sometimes prevail in winter along rivers in the far north when running water may flow over the thick ice layer but be concealed by snow. Frequent hikes in these conditions make an insulated waterproof boot welcome, because feet soaked by ice-cold water are undesirable at low temperatures. An occasional break through October stream ice is adequately handled by extra socks, though, so that marsh hikers are the most likely customers for insulated rubber bottoms.

Except in these conditions, the backpacker does not need to be much worried about a little cold or snow if he has proper clothing and roomy, sturdy boots. If he is caught by the first big snow and really cold weather while wandering the backcountry in the fall or early winter, proper observation of cold-weather rules will be more important than carrying special boots.

Clothing 9

Clothing for backpacking ought to be reasonably practical, loose, and strong enough so that your pants don't split the first time you squat down to light a fire. Roomy clothes are more comfortable than tight or binding ones. Sturdy outer garments will come through bushwhacking or rock-scrambling in a lot better condition than clothes that were never designed to take much abuse.

The importance of choosing your clothing depends pretty much on the type and duration of your trip. Where the climate is harsh it can be a very serious matter indeed. A lot of people die in the mountains because they are caught in bad weather with inadequate clothing.

Like everything else used by the backpacker, clothing has to serve as many uses as possible. A large wardrobe of specialized clothing can't be carried for different kinds of weather. If the elements might turn wet and cold, you should wear pants suitable for the possibility rather than blue jeans.

Leaving questions of modesty, morality, and vanity aside, the function of your clothing is to protect you from the elements and the critters you might meet on your trip. The threats to your epidermis might include hot sun, cold wind, rain, sleet, snow, hail, abrading stones and brush, insects, or all of the above. If you figure out which are likely, choosing clothing becomes relatively easy.

DRESSING IN LAYERS

It is usually best to carry a number of layers of clothing that are of light and medium weight, rather than concentrating everything in a few heavy garments. There are several reasons for this principle. It gives you better control over warmth, ventilation, and other factors. If your windbreaker is a big, heavy jacket, you'll find it isn't very versatile. When you are pulling up a long slope in the sun and a cool wind comes up, all you need is a windbreaker to stay comfortable. The heavy jacket's insulation will just make you sweat like a pig, leaving you damp and cold at the top of the hill. By the same token, in cold, still weather, a fuzzy sweater providing just insulation but no wind protection is often the most comfortable thing to wear —light and unconfining, but allowing a cooling breeze in when you start working hard.

Dressing in layers also gives you more insulation for a given amount of weight. Two light sweaters are warmer than one heavier one, because the layer of air trapped between them gives you additional insulation. Obviously, having your clothing in layers also gives you more control over what you take on a trip or a side trip. You can take one light sweater, but not half of a heavy one.

The layer principle allows you to adapt the same basic set of outdoor clothing to widely varying climates. You start off with underwear, a hat, sturdy pants and shirt, shorts, if you like, for summer hikes, and a good tough windbreaker to go over everything. You can add as many extra shirts and sweaters as you might need to keep warm where you are traveling. You may also carry lightweight rainwear to go over it all. For more severe conditions you might add a pair of windpants, which is a windbreaker for the lower part of your body, long underwear, and so forth. When you head for the desert, you leave the rain gear (sometimes) and take your wide-brimmed hat. The layer system is generally cheaper, more efficient, versatile, and comfortable than heavier, more elaborate clothing.

UNDERWEAR

Suit yourself, unless the weather is very cold, in which case you should use wool underwear. Tight, binding clothing of any kind gets quite uncomfortable, and underwear is no exception.

Net underwear is pleasant and versatile, and you might want to try a net shirt. The idea is that when you open your outer shirt for ventilation, the net allows plenty of cool air in for ventilation, but with the outer layers of clothing closed, a warm insulating layer of air is held near the skin. Even more important is the fact that the net gives the body some air space into which it can evaporate perspiration, so that your clothes don't tend to get soaked with sweat quite so quickly. The net mesh should be widely spaced.

PANTS

They should be loose, comfortable, and tough. A hard weave will shed more water and snags. If you like jeans, they are fine, except when there is a possibility of rain, wind, and cold. Wet, cold blue jeans are one of the most sophisticated instruments of torture known to man. Some wool or Orlon in the pants material is good if wet, cold weather might be expected. Excellent pants can often be gotten surplus. Just remember to keep away from cotton except for warm-weather use.

Two types of cuff closures. A snap fastening and a drawstring.

Knickers are good, the only trouble with them being that in cold weather they require expensive long socks. Their advantage is that they allow free leg movement. You can get them ready-made or easily convert a pair of trousers.

Pockets get a lot of use for odds and ends, so they should be sturdy. It's nice if at least some of them can be closed with zippers, buttons, snaps, or Velcro. If the pockets are hung from the belt rather than just sewn into holes in the fabric, they will last longer and be more comfortable. Pockets on the legs of pants, like those on some fatigues, should not be used. If you have them, don't put anything heavier than a bandana in them. Your legs lift them at every step, and it takes a lot of energy to lift all your pocket junk at every step.

Cuffs can be left plain or they can have some arrangement for closure. A closure is handy for plodding in snow, on dusty trails, and in tick country. For ventilation in hot weather, something that can be opened is nicer than a knit cuff.

SHIRTS AND SWEATERS

At least some of these should be wool if there is a possibility of cold weather. In winter they should all be wool. In summer you can take what you like, but if you are going to do any bushwhacking, wear something strong enough to survive the brush. Even on summer nights, a heavy shirt can be useful to discourage mosquitoes, and long sleeves are nice protection from both brush and bugs. Button pockets are nice.

For extra insulation, concentrate on fuzzy, bulky sweaters rather than tight, heavy ones. They are less resistant to abrasion, but they are warmer, and you can put on your parka for wet weather or rough rock.

HATS AND SUCH

I am not a hat wearer, but in the wilderness one is often essential. When it is cold, a hat is your most important item of insulation. Circulation, and thus heat loss, is not cut down to the head, as it is to the other extremities in cold weather. It is possible to lose over half the body's heat production

A balaclava helmet made of wool can be worn as a cap or over the whole head. It makes an excellent cold-weather hat.

When the weather gets bad, your shell clothing protects you and your insulation from the elements.

through the head. There is an old adage, "If your feet are cold, put on your hat." It happens to be true. If you are cold, put your hat on, and if you get hot, take it off.

A good hat for moderate to cold temperatures is a wool balaclava helmet. It folds up into a watch cap, but will also pull down for a face mask and neck covering when the snow really starts to blow. A watch cap is smaller. Either works well in conjunction with the hood of your parka.

Hats are just as important in hot weather. When the sun really starts to beat down, you need to keep your head cool and the sun out of your eyes. A light-colored, wide-brimmed hat is what you need. The crown should be well above the top of your head, and the more ventilation holes it has, the better.

A bandana is often handy for long sweaty climbs. Worn tied around the forehead, it keeps the sweat from running into the eyes and acts as a headband if you have long hair.

SHELL CLOTHING

Perhaps the most important clothing for the backpacker is his outer shell, which must protect him from wind, rain, snow, thorns, and horseflies. This layer is supposed to keep the inner one working by preventing shirts from being ripped, holding the layer of warm air in a fuzzy sweater despite a howling wind, and keeping insulation dry and warm.

The most important single item of clothing is a shell parka or anorak, made from a tough, windtight fabric. Such a parka should be roomy enough to allow all the insulation you might wear to fit underneath comfortably. It should be water repellent enough to shed a shower, but not waterproof so that it will trap perspiration and soak your insulation from within. It should not restrict movement. It can be a pullover or have a front opening, but any fasteners and hardware must be dependable and should be easily operable with numb or mittened hands. At least one large pocket is needed for odds and ends.

Windpants, when they are needed, should have similar characteristics to the parka. They are meant as a shell. They should go on and come off easily over boots, and they shouldn't weigh too much.

Material for parkas has always been the subject of considerable controversy, because of the many contradictory demands that are made on them. The best water-shedding material which still breathes is long fiber cotton in a suitable weave. Nylon is tougher, but it is impossible to waterproof it well without coating it completely and is harder to pack into a good wind-proof material. A good compromise is 60–40 cloth, which is woven with nylon in one direction and cotton the other. A well-made version of this mixture has many of the advantages of each of its components: tear strength, abrasion resistance, and water repellency.

A parka for all-around use should usually be made with two layers of fabric, at least on those sections subject to wear and heavy beating by the rain. Seams should be kept to a minimum, especially on the shoulders. Seams are the most common places for leakage.

Pullover and jacket-type parkas each have their advocates. The pull-over has the advantage of simplicity and lighter weight. If the zipper fouls at the worst possible time, you still have some protection, whereas the jacket type flaps uselessly in the wind. On the other hand, the jacket design, opening all the way down the front, gives better ventilation control, espe-cially on the trail, and I prefer it for general year-round use. Make sure the zipper is a good one, operating smoothly and without jamming.

RAINWEAR

Rain gear also falls into the category of shell clothing. You may not need to take separate rain clothing, depending on the weather where you are hik-ing. Staying dry is pleasant, however, and it is important if the weather should turn cold and windy. If you have to worry about no more than a summer squall, you might just rely on your parka, but no fabric which breathes will turn the rain forever. I carry a very light rain shell in most re-gions.

The problem with all rain gear is to keep the rain out without keeping all your body moisture in, a dilemma which you can never solve with com-plete success. Especially in cold weather, your perspiration will tend to condense on the inside of a waterproof garment.

The condensation problem can be reduced by providing adequate ven-tilation inside the garment in order to carry away the moisture before it condenses. This purpose is best served by a poncho, which is essentially a

A poncho turns the rain well where wind isn't too much of a problem. A long one can be worn over the pack, which helps provide ventilation. This one is made of inexpensive plastic, suitable for occasional use.

waterproof sheet with a head hole and hood in the middle. Some ponchos are made with an extra-long flap in the back which will drape over the pack frame or snap up when not in use. This type serves to keep the pack dry and improves ventilation, too.

A poncho is clearly superior to any other type of rain protection until the wind starts blowing or you are beating through heavy brush or scrambling on steep rock when the skirts get in the way or it just blows around your neck. In these circumstances a waterproof parka is much better. Choose the one which suits the kind of walking you do most. If you expect to meet the rain on a forest trail, get a poncho. If you would be more likely to find rain on a windswept mountain ridge, get a parka. A long, very roomy rain parka is called a cagoule, and I prefer it to a short parka. You can pull your knees inside it in a bivouac, and it hangs down far enough so that full rain pants aren't necessary.

Whatever kind of rain top you choose, make sure that you can get as much ventilation as possible. Cuffs should have fasteners which allow them to be opened, rather than elastic which keeps them closed tight. The neck should have some means of getting air in and out, a drawstring, zipper, or

A rain parka or a cagoule like this one is better protection from wind-blown rain. Rain pants or chaps protect the legs.

Velcro flap. The bottom should be wide and left open except when the wind necessitates pulling it tight.

For any extended walking in the rain, you will also want protection for your legs. Even if you aren't pushing through wet brush, enough rain will drip off your poncho or parka to soak your trousers. The same water-tight material as is used for a top can be used for rain pants. They should be fairly loose. If you wear a parka, you will need full rain pants. Generally, with a poncho or a cagoule, rain chaps are adequate, and they are lighter and take much less space. Rain chaps have no seat or crotch. They consist just of the legs with loops to tie onto your belt.

Material for rainwear should be of coated nylon. There are many good types. The heaviness of the material and the number of layers simply depend on your planned use. Lightweight material made into a garment of single thickness is very compact and will turn a lot of rain, but it is not so durable as heavier material or two thicknesses of lighter material without overlapping seams. I use a single layer of coated ripstop nylon for light-

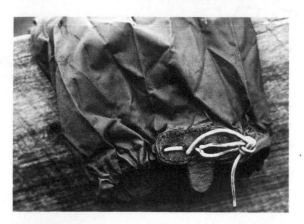

A good home-made wrist closure for rain gear. The leather friction tab holds the cuff at any diameter.

weight garments. Seams should be painted with a sealer. For more durable items, I use two layers of the same material with the uncoated sides facing out, the coating sandwiched inside where it cannot be abraded. Plastic rain gear is inexpensive and adequate for infrequent use.

A hat somewhat like those in the old sou'wester outfits is sometimes more pleasant to wear than the hood of a parka or poncho. It sheds water away from the face and allows more ventilation around the neck.

DOWN CLOTHING

In other chapters the special advantages of down as an insulator are pointed out. Down provides more insulation with less weight and in less packed space than any other material. It is the ideal insulator for use in sleeping bags and also for clothing to be used in extremely cold weather and at very high altitudes, where sufficient insulation in traditional form would be too bulky and constraining and where there is little danger of the clothing getting wet.

Down clothing is also a pleasant bit of luxury. A down vest or jacket brings a lot of warmth with little weight and bulk. It is unsurpassed for comfort in lounging around camp. For most general backpacking, however, down items are unnecessary, and they should be placed well down on the list of things to be purchased or carried. Lighter down items like vests and light jackets are usually more useful than big expedition parkas.

Too many people in the last few years have been relying almost completely on down clothing for warmth, ignoring the fact that down becomes absolutely useless when it gets wet. Some basic wool clothing should be carried wherever there is danger of wet, cold weather. Use down clothing for supplementary warmth, in really cold weather, or as a substitute for a sleeping bag. Down clothing is pleasant and convenient, but get a wool sweater, wool pants, and a good shell parka first.

Construction methods with down are described in the chapter on sleeping bags. For supplementary garments such as light jackets and vests, the most useful pieces of down equipment for backpacking, sewn-through tube construction can be used. Heavier down clothing requires full use of differential cut and baffling to prevent compression of the down. Proper tailoring in down parkas is even more important than in sleeping bags, because body movement will compress the down unless the design prevents it.

Since basic design and construction methods for down clothing are the same as in sleeping bags, there is little need to repeat them here. Material should be tightly woven nylon, but it should be the lightest weight consistent with durability. Heavier weight fabrics will tend to compress the down. Down garments usually need more down than sleeping bags to fill a given amount of space, since they have to withstand compression by wind.

MISCELLANEOUS ITEMS

In cold weather *gloves* or *mittens* are essential. Gloves allow more dexterity, but mittens are warmer. Wool liners and overmitts or overgloves are good, and surplus ones are inexpensive. Various other types are also available.

Gaiters or *anklets* are necessary in soft snow and sometimes useful to keep out scree or sand. Gaiters are long tubes of fabric covering the upper boot and lower leg and closed with laces or zippers. Anklets are shorter versions just covering the ankle and upper boot. Either prevents snow and debris from getting into the boots, and gaiters also help keep the lower leg warm in snow.

10   Packs

Presumably you should have a backpack in order to be a backpacker, and the variety of designs that are offered may be somewhat confusing to the beginner. There are many very good types available at any backpacking or climbing shop. There is also an increasing volume of shoddily made junk flooding many surplus, hardware, department, and sporting-goods stores. Choosing between the better types of packs is largely a matter of deciding what you're going to use one for.

TYPES OF PACKS

In order to consider their characteristics, it will be helpful to break the various packs down into broad categories, although there are some that overlap. All of them are designed to hang on the back, so that the wearer will be able to carry his load and still have a good deal of freedom to move about and use his hands. Only very small loads can be carried practically in pockets, belly packs, shoulder bags, and the like. Modern packs are all hung from the shoulders or a combination of the shoulders and the waist or hips. Tumplines, which hang the load from the head, limit movement of the neck severely, and it requires years to develop the neck muscles to use them properly, hardly a worthwhile enterprise when the loading point can

A simple frameless rucksack. A good, inexpensive day pack or children's pack, but unsuited for overnight trips.

be moved down the spine to the hips. Tumplines still have value to the canoeist for portaging, but they can be ignored by the backpacker.

The simplest pack is the *frameless rucksack*, which in its most rudimentary form is nothing more than a sack hung from two straps. Simple ones can be made from trousers and pillowcases. All the load in this kind of pack is carried by the shoulders, and any waist strap that is provided serves mainly to keep the pack from swinging around. As the most basic pack, the frameless rucksack has the virtues of simplicity but also all the defects that people have tried to correct with other designs. One is that the wearer's back has no protection. Hard, sharp, or irregularly shaped objects will gouge into your back unless you can put them on the other side of the pack. If there are only a few objects in the pack, they fall to the bottom, which isn't always the most comfortable place to carry them. As it is stuffed full the pack will start to bulge in all directions, tending toward the shape of a sphere, or if it is a long pack, a cylinder. Carrying a small, frameless rucksack packed tightly is like carrying a medicine ball hung on shoulder straps. This bulging creates the dual problem of an uncomfortably shaped pack and one which sticks far out behind, tending to pull the walker over backward, and forcing him to lean far forward against the straps.

The bulging problems can be partly solved by shaping the pack care-

159

A compartmentalized frameless day pack. The load is better controlled in this type of pack.

fully, by not overstuffing it, and by making it in separate compartments. Separate compartments control the shape of the pack well—several small cylinders sewn together properly make a pack of the desired shape—and they also allow the wearer to hold objects in particular places, heavy objects on top or hard things in back. Small compartments won't hold large pieces of gear, however, and all the weight of the pack still hangs from the shoulders. Also the frameless rucksack makes your back sweat badly in warm weather because there is no ventilation.

The *frame rucksack* was for many years the main answer to the problems mentioned above. The pack was attached to a large frame, basically triangular in shape, and the frame was hung on the shoulder straps. This solved several problems immediately. Hard objects were kept away from the back, no matter where they were put in the pack, the frame held at least one side of the pack in the desired shape, and the frame kept the pack away from the back, providing an air space for cooling and evaporation of sweat. However, the older rucksacks like the U.S. Army ski-mountaineering pack in the picture still bulge out a lot at the bottom, which forces the wearer to lean far forward against the weight.

Major improvements were made in the frame rucksack when the Bergans Company of Norway began to make frame rucksacks with a narrow

160

A standard frame rucksack. This one is a U.S. Army ski-mountaineering pack, still available at good prices in the surplus stores. Note that the load tends to bulge far from the back, forcing the wearer to lean forward. With careful packing this can be a good pack.

bottom and wide top, retaining the volume of the pack, but preventing the load from sticking so far out from the back. With the load carried higher, a smaller forward lean put the center of gravity over the feet. Since the wearer didn't have to lean so hard against the pack, carrying was easier.

Most of the weight of the frame rucksacks still goes on the shoulders, though some is transferred by the frame to the hips. This limits the load that can be carried by the average person in the frame rucksack. Training the shoulders to carry heavy loads requires a lot of miles and a lot of aches.

An improved frame rucksack, shaped so that the load rides higher, so that the wearer does not have to lean forward so much.

161

The frames of the two rucksacks shown above. The Bergans design on the left is wide at the top, so that the load in the sack can be pushed higher.

Another solution to the disadvantages of the frameless rucksack was the *packframe*, a rectangular frame with carrying straps, generally made of wood. The packframe could be used for carrying all kinds of irregular loads, since they could simply be lashed on, or it could be used with an attached bag. It usually extended above the top of the shoulder straps, allowing the load to be placed higher, so that a slight forward lean would put the center of gravity over the feet. The exaggerated lean required by some rucksacks was avoided. The packframe was also completely adjustable in the volume of the loads carried, because one could simply wrap the load in a tarp and lash it on. A small load could be placed high on the frame or a large one distributed along it in the most comfortable possible arrangement. The load still hung mainly from the shoulders, however, and if the lashing method was used, the whole pack had to be undone to get at anything inside.

It remained for A. I. Kelty to design the closest thing to an ideal pack for the average backpacker, the *contour frame pack*. The original Kelty pack is still one of the best of these, although other manufacturers are now making very good ones. As this is by far the best pack for most of the people most of the time, it is worth considering in detail.

CONTOUR FRAME PACKS

The contour frame is made of aluminum or magnesium tubing bent to follow the contour of the back. The curve brings the load closer to the back and enables the frame to be made longer, so that a pack of the same size can be made thinner while retaining the same volume, again keeping the weight closer to the back. The height of the frame makes it possible to pack the weight very high, putting the center of gravity of the pack over the feet with only a very slight forward lean.

A contour frame pack. Heavy objects are high and close to the back, with the sleeping bag and pad strapped lower down. The whole load can be transferred to the hips with a very slight forward lean.

All of these features make possible the most important feature of the Kelty-type pack, which is the use of a waistband to transfer most or all of the weight of the pack to the hips. This can be done only with the center of gravity high and close to the back and with a rigid frame that extends below the waist. It is a tremendous boon to the weekend backpacker, because the hips are well suited to carrying a lot of weight without special training of the muscles. Thus, with a good contour frame pack, any refugee from the city in reasonably good health can comfortably carry supplies for a week or two of backpacking, a feat which is much harder with a rucksack.

The frame can be used to lash irregular loads on, but it is normally used with a matching bag attached tightly to the frame with metal pins.

A contour pack frame with a 360° belt, far superior to the belt and backband arrangement. The complete belt can be like this one or it can be padded. The width of the shoulder straps at the top is adjustable by moving the clevis pins.

The bag can be full length, but a practical arrangement for most purposes is a bag that extends from the top of the frame two-thirds of the way down. Sleeping bag and pad are then strapped on below. The bags are made in many sizes and with many differences in detail. Shop around with the following points in mind. Get the smallest bag that will suit your purposes. There is a tendency to use bags that are far larger than needed. A narrow bag keeps the weight close to the frame where you want it. An "expedition-style" bag is designed for very large loads, and if you need it for one person's gear on a week's backpacking trip, you are carrying too much.

Dividing the bag into compartments has the advantages of holding the bag in shape and enabling you to control the load, keeping heavy objects up high. On the other hand, compartments that are too small for some of your equipment—cooksets, for example—are a damned nuisance. Many other features that add convenience are pretty obvious. Pockets are nice for lunch and miscellaneous small gear that gets lost in the main part of the pack.

More important in the long run are the details of construction. A pack that is heavy nylon throughout will last much longer than any other material. The hardware attaching the pack to the frame should hold it positively. If the pack can move around, the rubbing will soon cause some points to fail. Seams should be strong and finished so that they won't ravel out. Zippers should operate smoothly and be placed so that they don't bear heavy strains. Check all the construction details. Packs take very heavy wear, and there is no way to nurse them. If there are any weak points in the manufacture, they will cause the pack to fall apart in short order.

The frame itself should be as strong as possible. Check it as best you can, but you might as well recognize that weak points in the frame are not always visible. The belt has to be wide and very sturdy—it will carry a lot of weight. A little, dinky belt will cut you in half before long. Padded belts are nice, but they aren't necessary. A wide, plain belt will do the job. The belt can either extend around the front only, using the lower backband to support the weight in the rear, or go all the way around the hips, with the pack hung on side tabs. The half-belt is all right for moderate loads, but the 360° belt is so far superior that I wouldn't be without it. One kind is shown in the picture. The more common and expensive variety is padded. Shoulder straps should be padded, sturdy, and designed in the standard fashion. Some improved shoulder harnesses have been made, but their importance on contour frames is minimal, since most of the load is transferred to the hips.

OTHER PACKS

Although the contour frame pack is the standard backpacker's carrying case, it does have a few disadvantages, so that other packs are better for some purposes. As a general rule I would recommend that the beginner get a frame pack, adding to his collection as he becomes a connoisseur. A few beginners will have good reasons to choose other packs.

The high, rigid frame of the contour pack will not move around easily with the body. This is no disadvantage on open trails, but if you have to do a lot of bending it can be a real nuisance. The high center of gravity then tries hard to pull you over, and the frame catches on brush, rock outcrops, and fallen logs. For bushwhacking in heavy brush, a frame is a pain in the neck, and a rucksack is far superior. Other places with little headroom are equally difficult to negotiate with a frame. I remember all too well the experience of trying to get through a series of caves with a frame pack.

The extension of the frame behind the head also makes looking up rather difficult, and the climber may find the frame a nuisance in this respect. A final objection made by some people to the frame is that it makes footing a bit more difficult because of the high center of gravity. I find this to be true only in cases where you are forced to lean or bend a lot, in rock-climbing for example. Most of the time you can learn to keep the frame from throwing you off balance, and even use it to advantage, but this takes a little practice.

Frame rucksacks have the advantage when you have to carry quite a bit of weight, if the contour frame has been ruled out for some reason. Skiers, climbers, and those who backpack in brushy country often prefer rucksacks. They are pleasant to carry with reasonable loads once your shoulders are in shape, though with really heavy loads there is no substitute for a frame.

Frameless rucksacks allow even more natural body movement and weigh less than those with frames. They are favorites with bivouac specialists and with many mountaineers, but they must be packed carefully, and the load must be kept to a minimum.

An intermediate pack is the *flexible-framed rucksack*. It allows a little of the load to be transferred to the hips like the regular frame rucksack, and controls the shape of the pack somewhat, but the weight is less, and much of the flexible feeling of the frameless pack is retained. Usually stays of aluminum or magnesium are used for the flexible frame.

DESIGN FEATURES IN PACKS

There are some common requirements in the design of a good pack, no matter what the type. The most obvious is that it has to be sturdy. Packs are almost invariably *stuffed*. Strain is put on the fabric and the seams. If they aren't very tough the pack won't last long. Shoulder straps and waist-bands have to carry the weight of the pack. They must be very strong, and their points of attachment to the pack have to be, too. These points should be heavily reinforced. The bottom of the pack needs to be reinforced, too, if the pack will rest on it when set down.

Shoulder straps also have to be designed for comfort. They should be wide where they pass over the shoulders to distribute the load—narrow straps or straps that curl and become narrow will cut unmercifully into the shoulders. Padding of shoulder straps is very helpful. The straps must taper as they go under the armpits or they will chafe badly. The tops of the straps should be close together, so that they will pass over the shoulders as close to the neck as possible. This is usually achieved by hanging them from a single D-ring or sewn patch. With frames, it is a good feature for the distance between the straps to be adjustable at the top for different builds.

Straps and pockets can be chosen or designed to suit the preferences and needs of the user. They have to be sturdy to do any good, and they should be carefully sewn and reinforced at points of stress.

It is helpful if packs are waterproof, but coating a fabric also makes it weaker, and the coating on pack material has to be fairly heavy or it will be worn off quickly by the constant friction that a pack suffers. For these reasons, pack material that is waterproof has to be made much heavier than equally durable material that is not waterproof. Some manufacturers like Kelty prefer to make a separate lightweight waterproof cover for use in the rain.

USING PACKS

Remember that the best pack has to be used properly to take advantage of its design. Pack it so that the cook kit doesn't dig into your back. The weight should be as high and as close to the back as possible, so that you don't have to lean against the straps in the wasted exercise of simply staying upright. For skiing, climbing, or difficult footing, you want to get the weight lower, but this makes it even more important that it be kept close to the back. A waist strap is essential for these purposes to keep the pack close to the body and prevent it from swinging. On some contour frames the pack can be lowered to bring the weight lower.

SAVING MONEY ON PACKS

It isn't really feasible for you to make your own contour frame, though you can buy a frame separately and make the bag for it if you like, either from your own design or with a kit. Study commercial ones carefully before you design your own. Shop around a little and you'll find there are a few good combinations available at reasonable prices.

Pack Layout

Fabric approximately 42″ wide

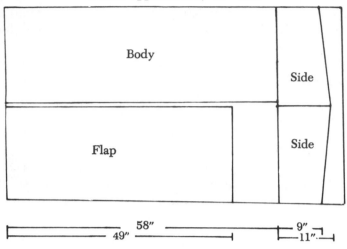

You can make your own frameless and flexible framed rucksacks, but rigid frames are pretty hard. The Army ski-mountaineering packs are still floating around, and they are good rucksacks if they are packed properly, even though they are not so well designed as some modern ones. The price has been going up, but you can still get some good ones for eight dollars or so. Don't get stuck with a bad imitation.

Packs are a good place to tap the used market, especially for frames. A top-brand frame can be gotten for half- or quarter-price, and as long as it isn't bent it will probably be in just as good a condition as when it was new. Frames last indefinitely, although some attachments need occasional mending or replacement.

INSTRUCTIONS FOR MAKING
A FLEXIBLE-FRAMED RUCKSACK

This pack is a good compromise for someone traveling fairly light. It molds well to the body, but is fairly comfortable for carrying loads. In making your own

168

pack, you should regard patterns and instructions as suggestions. Change the pack around to fit your body and your needs.

The design is fairly simple. The basic sack is made by sewing two sides on one piece which wraps around to form the front, back, and bottom. Another piece doubles the bottom and the section which fits next to your back, forming a pocket into which the frame will be sewn, and then it continues over the top to form a flap.

The frame is formed by three aluminum bars 3/4-inch wide and 1/8-inch thick. These are drilled at the ends for machine screws or rivets, and they can be formed into a triangular frame that can be bent to fit the back, after it is sewed between the two layers of cloth on the front of the pack. The machine screws go through the stays and the fabric, with leather reinforcing pieces and washers on either side to prevent ripping of the cloth.

The pack is carried by means of both shoulder straps and a waistband. The waistband is 2 inches wide and sewed to the pack along the lower stay for a length that makes the pack comfortable for you. The shoulder straps go all the way over the shoulders. At the front they attach to the bottom of the triangular frame. At the back each strap attaches both to the top of the triangle and the top of the pack.

Much of the pack can be sewn on a sewing machine, but you will get a stronger pack by stitching throughout with a sewing awl (speedy stitcher) using heavy nylon thread.

The pack is designed without pockets, but they can be easily attached to the sides or back of the pack, if you want them.

When cutting nylon webbing, melt the cut ends to prevent fraying.

MATERIALS LIST

2 yards coated nylon pack fabric
4 feet 2″ webbing, flat type
1 buckle for 2″ webbing
3 aluminum stays, ⅛″ x ¾″, two 17½″ long, and one 13″ long. Round ends with a
    file and drill for ⅛″ machine screws ½″ from each end of each stay.
18 feet 1″ nylon webbing (medium weight flat)
6 buckles for 1″ webbing
2 pieces sponge rubber 2″ x ½″ x 12″
15 grommets and setting tool
6 scrap-leather patches, approximately 2″ square
3 brass, round-head machine screws ⅛″ x 1½″ with nuts

6 ½" washers for screws
1 boot lace, 5 or 6 feet long
sewing awl and thread

1. Sew the sides into the body, making sure that the coated side of the fabric will face toward the inside of the pack. The narrow ends of the sides are at the bottom and the slanting edges at the back. The pattern allows for 1" margins. The coating will prevent raveling, but double-stitching is still wise. Make a narrow finished hem at the top edge of the pack, and install grommets along it for a drawstring, about every 4".

2. Sew the flap onto the pack. Begin at the bottom of the pack, where the flap wraps around to form a double bottom. The flap is proportioned to extend 3" up the back of the pack and 1" up each side. Sew it onto the body of the pack with a single line of stitching, folding 1" of each edge under and making tucks as you go around corners. Sew the flap all the way around the front of the pack, to within an inch of the top. Three sides should be sewn, with an opening at the top between the body and the flap, so that the frame can be inserted. The top part of the flap which protrudes above the pack should be hemmed all the way around.

3. Cut two lengths of 1" webbing, each 50" long. These are to be sewn on the flap so that they will be on the inside of the pack. Each should run 5" in from the outside edge of the flap. Start sewing them so that the ends are 2" inside the space between the body of the pack and the flap. The ends will hang out from the end of the flap. Cut two more lengths of webbing, each 6" long. Sew a buckle on the end of each. Sew these to the bottom of the pack, with the buckles protruding just up onto the back to meet the flap straps. Each will be about 4" in from the edge of the bottom.

4. Screw the frame together temporarily. Place it in the pocket between the body and the flap so that the lower stay is about 1" above the bottom of the pack and the top juncture is in the center. Melt holes in the fabric with a hot knife for the screws to go through. Punch holes in the centers of each of the leather patches. Cut two lengths of webbing each 20" long. Make a small hole in the center of each, about ½" from one end, with the hot knife, and another hole 16½" along each one from the first hole. Cut two more lengths each 10" long, install a buckle at one end of each, and make a small hole in the center, 1" from the opposite end.

Now it is time to install the frame. The bottom two screws go toward the inside of the pack. Each screw passes through the pieces in the following order: washer, leather patch, short buckle strap, short end of 20″ strap, hole in flap, two metal stays, hole in body, leather patch, washer, nut. The top screw goes through: washer, leather patch, long ends of two 20″ straps, hole in flap, two metal stays, hole in body, leather patch, washer, nut.

The 20″ straps should now run along the stays, but on the outside of the pack, with ends protruding from the upper leather patch. The two buckles should stick out from the lower junctures. Position the buckle straps so that they point upward, sticking out at an angle of 20° or so from the pack. Now sew around all the leather patches, going through both patches and both pieces of webbing, and criss-crossing back and forth so that each junction is very strong. Then sew along each side of each of the 20″ straps between the leather patches, sewing through strap, flap, and body, forming an envelope around each of the upper stays. When the frame is sewn in, sew the flap and body together at the top, just below the line of grommets, reinforcing the seam near the flap straps. Tighten the machine screws, cut off the protruding ends, and peen them down with a hammer.

5. With the scrap pieces of fabric, make tubes to sew around the foam-rubber pads. Each tube should be 18″ long and should fit tightly around the pad, with no seams on one side (which will rest on the shoulder). Coated side of the fabric should face in toward the rubber. Place a piece of sponge rubber in the center of each tube, and then sew them in with seams close to the ends of the rubber. Fold the ends of one end of a pad envelope over and sew it to the end of one of the 20″ straps. Do the same with the other pad. Two things should be noted here. These are shoulder straps, so care should be taken to make the sides which will rest on the shoulders fairly smooth— keep the folds and rough spots on top. Also note that the two 20″ straps cross at the frame apex; the strap coming from one side of the pack goes over the opposite shoulder.

Cut two more pieces of webbing each 16″ long. Sew these to the oppo-site ends of the shoulder pads from the pack. They fit into the buckles at the bottom of the frame.

6. Sew the 2″ buckle on one end of the 2″ webbing. Sew the center section of this waistband onto the pack along the line of the lower frame piece. It is usually most comfortable to sew it a total of 11″ to just short of each end junction, but try it out. Sew this firmly, with plenty of reinforcing.

7. Sew one 12″ piece of webbing on the top of each shoulder pad, sewing

about 2″ of an end to the pad, so that the free end points toward the pack. Cut two 5″ pieces of webbing and install a buckle on each. Sew the opposite end of each onto the top of the flap, on the line of the flap strap about 5″ back, with the buckle pointed forward. These can be connected to the straps coming back from the shoulder pads, giving you control over the lean of the pack.

8. Install the boot lace as a drawstring through the grommets. The pack is now finished. Experiment with various packings and loadings, and reinforce any points that seem to come under a lot of strain. Bend the frame to fit your back.

Tents and Other Shelters 11

The shelters used commonly by backpackers vary a great deal. Prejudices play their part, but forms and materials are dictated largely by the conditions that prevail in different seasons and parts of the country. A backpacker may use natural shelters or accommodations already built along the trail. He may improvise a shelter from natural materials or he may carry his house on his back. Semipermanent shelters such as lean-tos have special virtues for areas of heavy use. They lighten the load on the back and confine camping to spots which can be controlled, though by definition they are not wilderness.

In some places natural shelters can be relied on. One camps in the shelter of an overhanging rock if the weather threatens, and that is that. Planning on using a natural shelter requires that there be one and that you know it exists, conditions that rarely occur.

Improvising shelters is rarely practical these days, at least not without using some materials which you carry in. Shingling lean-tos with live boughs in most wilderness areas ought to be punished with thumbscrews and hot irons. Areas and seasons suited to snow shelters are about the only places where one can still plan on using strictly natural materials very often.

We are left with the tents, ponchos, tarps, and plastic sheets the backpacker brings with him, and they are the subject of this chapter. The choice between them must rely first on your particular requirements. What do you need to be sheltered from? Rain? Wind? Sleet? Cold? Insects? A combination? Is the rain of the afternoon-shower variety or of the pouring-down-for-weeks-without-end kind?

Take the California Sierra Nevada Range as an example. It does rain there in the summer, but not very often. One can backpack dozens of times there from June to September and only get caught by rain on a couple of occasions. Insects are not too bad either, and they can generally be controlled fairly well with repellent. In that sort of situation, it is just plain silly to carry a lot of tent around on every trip. Take the lightest serviceable emergency shelter, and be done with it. If I backpacked only in summer and only in that area, I doubt that I would even buy or make a tent. A tube tent would be a fine contingency shelter, except above timberline; so would a tarp or a poncho or a bivouac tent.

On the other hand, winter in the same mountain range brings quite a different story. The storms are frequent, dumping large amounts of snow and bringing respectable winds. If a snow shelter was not to be used, the backpacker would have to carry a good, weathertight tent, capable of withstanding high winds. Summer in other spots requires better protection, too. Rain may come down as the rule rather than the exception. Insects are often as much of a problem as the weather, and a tent may be preferred to a tarp or other open shelter, simply because it can be designed to keep the bugs out.

Like other items of backpacking equipment, shelters are the result of compromise. Pick the best type for your temperament, needs, and pocketbook, and then make do with it in those situations for which it is not ideally suited. You may eventually own more than one type, but the number of well-made tents you can wear out in one backpacking career is quite limited. A good tent lasts a long time.

TARPS AND PONCHOS

The most elementary kind of shelter is a flat piece of waterproof material, usually with grommets along the sides and some ties here and there for convenience in use. If a hole and a hood are put in the middle, the tarp is a poncho and can be worn as well as pitched. This arrangement is still preferred by many experienced backpackers because of its simplicity, light weight, versatility, and low cost. A tarp can be pitched in an almost infinite variety of ways, just a few of which are shown in the drawing. Dimensions vary a good deal, each having its advocates. There are 9- and 10-foot square men and defenders of 7′ x 9′ or 9′ x 11′. For two people 11′ x 14′ works well.

A tarp-tent is very simple to make, requiring only that you sew the material into a square or rectangle, hem the edges and put on attachment points. Along the edges these can be grommets, loops of nylon tape, or D-rings. In the body of the tarp one simply sews on enough tape ties to suit the fancy. A 9′ x 11′ tarp tied to itself the long way also makes a good one-man tube tent. Coated nylon makes the best material for tarps.

TUBE TENTS

The original tube tent was simply a tube of plastic, usually three mils thick. This can be easily pitched by stringing a line between two objects to hold up the tube, which is normally about nine feet long. They are made in diameters for one and two people, weighing about a pound per person.

The tube tent is an excellent emergency rain shelter for relatively sheltered areas. All that is needed is the tube, a length of parachute cord, and

A plastic tube tent like this is a good shelter to carry below timberline in mild weather, in case of unexpected rain.

175

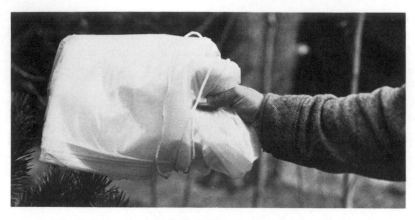

A two-man tube tent folded. Weight is about two pounds.

two objects from which to suspend the tube. The weight of the body holds the arrangement down, so that there is no need for stakes. The arrangement is light, simple, and cheap, and thus has become very popular in regions to which it is suited.

I carry a few spring-type clothespins with the tube tent for use in the wind to partially close an end if necessary and to hold the tent at the proper place on the line. On threatening evenings, when I want to sleep under the stars but am worried about rain coming up in the night, I string out the tube tent between two trees with a sliding friction knot on the line. I leave the line loose, using the tent as a ground cloth. If sprinkling wakes me in the middle of the night, I stuff my gear inside, pull the line taut, and hop back in bed, the whole operation taking no more than a minute.

Tube tents are basically emergency protection against the rain. They are short-lived, are no protection against insects, will not withstand high winds, and are completely unsuitable for snow camping or very cold weather. They require ties, and although one can improvise supports, they are suitable mainly for use in places where there are trees. Used properly, they are a great boon to the backpacker, but they are not substitutes for mountain tents and should not be used as such. During long periods of rain, they will not keep you dry.

176

A tube tent can also be made of light coated fabric which weighs about the same as a plastic tube tent. The cost is much higher, but the product is much more durable. Although these can be sewn with small awnings and other improvements, they have basically the same advantages and defects as the plastic tube tent.

PLASTIC SHEETS

A plastic sheet around three mils thick can be used in the same ways as a tarp, but it will not last so long. Several devices are available for gripping a plastic tarp without starting a rip. You can also simply place a small stone or other object at the place you want to tie, twist it into the tarp, and tie a line around the twist.

Plastic sheets serve as ground cloths and useful emergency shelters, although tubes are more versatile. One plea about both: if you take them in, take them out again. Shredded plastic sheets are starting to appear everywhere, draped over rocks and lean-tos and then abandoned. Really, no one wants to look at the remains of your bivouac next year!

INSECT BARS

If you have an insect problem but you are using a shelter with no closure against the bugs, or no shelter at all, you can either rely on repellents or use an insect bar. This is simply a large piece of netting which you put over your sleeping bag.

There are various ways you can make a bar fasten to your bag, but it is simpler to get a large piece and drape it. A 3-yard piece of nylon netting 45 inches wide will weigh only 5 ounces. The sides can be weighted with stones. Prop the section over your head up with a stick or pack, or tie it up with cord. If you let it rest on your cheek the little beasts will bite right through.

TENTS

Tents are more durable and stable structures than the ones just mentioned. Instead of allowing dozens of forms of pitching like the tarp tent, a normal

A typical open-front forest tent. This one is a modified Baker design with an awning pitched as a double roof for snow camping. Such tents are not suited for use in the mountains or outside forested areas.

tent permits only one or two, but it pitches much more efficiently in that way, excelling in those respects for which it was designed. Most tent designs are very poor, and even many of the good ones are completely unsuitable for the backpacker, so it will be easy to narrow the field down.

There are many excellent designs of tents for forest camping, usually with open fronts, without sewn-in floors, and designed to be pitched from lines tied to surrounding trees or perhaps from poles cut or found in the surrounding forest. The open fronts of such tents make them a joy to pitch in front of a fire, especially during long rains. They also enclose a lot of space for a given weight of material. They are not generally all-weather tents, however, not easily pitched away from trees, unstable in high winds, often unsuitable for snow camping. Moreover, few of them are made in modern fabrics, so that if you want one, you may have to make it yourself.

Most modern backpacking tents are designed to be self-contained, whereas most of the best of the older styles depended on locally cut poles or on guy lines strung between trees for pitching. Such a stable, closed, self-contained tent gives the backpacker a lot of freedom, because it can be pitched almost anywhere without damaging the site. The main disadvantage is that most such tents are somewhat cramped.

THE MOUNTAIN TENT

The prototype for most modern backpacking tents was the mountain tent, itself a more sophisticated version of the pup tent. The cross section of this type of tent is a triangle, and the standard size, perhaps 7½ feet long and 5 feet wide at the front, is about right for two men and their equipment. Originally, one pole was used at each end, but this has been abandoned for the more convenient design using two poles inserted in sleeves and meeting at the top, so that no pole blocks the entrance. Some mountain tents have only one entrance at the front, with a low rear end propped by a single pole at the back. Others are full height throughout, and these often have entrances held up by two poles at either end.

Many modifications have been made in the mountain tent in the last few years, and special features will be found in many versions. Vestibules can be included at one end or both for equipment storage, different kinds of ventilation flaps and accessories can be added, and various types of entrances may be featured. More important developments have used tents designed with semicircular or other modified cross sections which are lighter, require fewer stakes and guy lines, and are more stable in winds than older tents—as well as being considerably more expensive. Most important, however, are certain basic design features that should be considered whenever you are buying or building a tent.

A typical two-man, all-weather mountain tent, made of a nylon-cotton mixture.

FEATURES OF AN ALL-WEATHER WILDERNESS TENT

Some of the requirements for an all-around backpacking tent have been mentioned. It must be self-contained. If you do all your camping in forested areas, you might not need an all-purpose tent. One of the older designs might suit you better. If, however, you expect one tent to serve you in the woods, above timberline, in snow and mountain meadow, in exposed and windy places as well as those which are well protected, you will find that the older designs won't work very well.

A tent meant to meet the requirements just mentioned has to be closed. Whatever side flaps it may have, when the wind comes up and really starts blowing, you have to be able to close everything down. An open-front tent just isn't the thing to have in a windy, exposed place. Poles have to be carried. They may serve other purposes on the way in—ski-poles, for example—but any tent requiring poles so large they have to be found or cut at the site is not an all-purpose tent.

An all-weather tent should have a waterproof floor, and the waterproofing should preferably extend six inches or so up the walls. If both the floor and lower sides are waterproof, all need for trenching around the tent is eliminated. This is essential in soggy mountain meadows and similar places where drainage is poor but trenching shouldn't be used.

There are a great many possible arrangements of poles, wands, and tie-outs, but the net effect should be a tent which pitches with a smooth surface, as little sagging as possible, and a reasonable wind profile. Sagging folds indicate poor design, and large vertical walls will catch the wind like a sail. A less essential feature of some of the best new tents is that they can be pitched with only a few stakes and guys, because of aerodynamic design and superior placement of poles. This lessens the real weight that has to be carried when stakes can't be found locally, and it greatly simplifies pitching the tent on hard ground and on snow and ice. Some of the best such designs require only three or four stakes and no guy lines. Extra staking points should be provided for use in case of extreme winds, however.

FABRICS, FLIES, AND BREATHING

The biggest problem in designing tents is finding a way to shed any rain and snow that fall on them, while still avoiding heavy condensation of moisture inside the tent. Condensation falling three feet from the roof of the tent is every bit as wet as rain coming down several thousand feet. Condensation occurs in a closed tent, because cooking, breathing, and evaporation from the skin make the air inside the tent fairly humid. If the inside of the tent is much warmer than the outside, the tent wall will tend to condense the moisture, just as a highball glass or a cold window will. Many methods are used to try to keep this condensation to a minimum, and they are important, because such condensation can eventually soak your sleeping bag and your clothes, which is a serious matter if they cannot be dried out occasionally.

Adequate ventilation will eliminate the condensation problem altogether. With an open-front tent or a tarp pitched as a lean-to, you won't have any condensation difficulties. The humid air circulates away before it has a chance to cause a problem, so these shelters can be made of coated nylon fabrics that are absolutely waterproof. Unfortunately, ventilation is sometimes too adequate, which is precisely why one sometimes wants a closed tent rather than a tarp shelter.

Proper ventilation can make a closed tent of a single layer of coated

An example of a single-layer tent of coated fabric. Side vents are necessary to minimize condensation. Good for use only in mild weather.

fabric practical, but not as an all-weather tent. Some good inexpensive tents are made with large side flaps that can be opened to give a lot of ventilation. Such a tent can protect you from heavy summer rains, be screened against insects, and provide a good shelter with light weight and low cost. In cold weather, though, condensation will occur even with the vents open, snow will blow through them if they are open, and the ventilation will chill the tent, even though it doesn't solve the condensation problem.

There are two normal solutions used in all-weather tents. The tent can be made of a cotton fabric or a good cotton-nylon mixture. When such a fabric is properly chosen, it will breathe well and will minimize condensation, and yet it will shed most rain. Cotton takes waterproofing well, and the cotton fibers will swell when they get wet, tightening the tent wall. In a downpour which goes on for days or weeks, such a tent will *eventually* leak, but it will keep you quite dry in all but the wettest climates. Because of the conductivity and surface of the fabric, a cotton or cotton nylon surface always condenses less moisture and frost than synthetics, even uncoated ones. A single-layer tent of cotton or 60-40 cloth (with a coated floor) is the least expensive way to make a good all-weather tent.

The second solution to the problem is to make a tent which is really two tents, one pitched inside the other. The inside tent should be complete in itself, with a coated floor sewn in, mosquito netting, and so forth. The top of this tent can be made of uncoated nylon fabric, strong, lightweight, and capable of breathing. When there is no danger of rain, this tent can even be used alone, protecting against wind, insects, and somewhat against cold. For rain protection and additional warmth, a coated roof called a fly is pitched over the inside tent, leaving a space of a couple of inches between the two. The roof sheds the water, but the inside tent still breathes. Since both layers can be made of pure nylon, a lighter fabric can be used than in cotton or cotton-nylon tents, and the whole double tent will probably weigh no more than the single one.

The uncoated tent with a coated fly has several special advantages. The fly need only provide a roof to shed the force of the rain, and it can be used to provide an extra alcove at the front or rear of the tent for equipment storage, giving protection, but requiring little extra weight. Sealing of the seams of the fly is less critical than in a single-layer tent, since a few drips getting through will be shed by the inner tent, rather than falling on your nose. These advantages of the fly system have resulted in its displacing the single-layer tent in most of the best equipment lines in the last few years. Many manufacturers have dropped single-layer tents altogether. This is because of the greater affluence of the clientele, however, as well as the advantages of the double tent.

There are several disadvantages to the uncoated nylon tent with a fly. For one thing, it is expensive. The price of a good two-man mountain tent with a fly is quite high, even if you use a kit. Condensation is greater on nylon than on cotton or cotton-nylon mixture, so that even with the fly, a nylon tent is not usually any better, and in very cold weather frost formation is usually worse. Though wicking will eventually cause leaks in an uncoated tent, especially a small one in which rubbing against the walls is impossible to avoid, this problem should not be overemphasized. My small two-man mountain tent is made of 60-40 cloth, and in ten years of camping over much of the continent, it has kept me quite dry. A large tent which I made of Oxford weave cotton has been through downpours lasting weeks and never leaked. Nylon has tremendous advantages for making light-weight equipment, but if you should decide to make a small tent to save money, you might be better off using a single layer of cotton.

In cold weather, instead of condensing in liquid droplets on the tent wall, water forms frost. This is less bothersome with cotton and its mixtures than with nylon, but it will occur with either. For very cold weather, a frost liner is used to help solve this problem. It is a very light liner hung a few inches inside the main tent. It is not necessary for normal backpacking trips.

DESIGNING OR BUYING YOUR TENT

As with all other equipment, tent selection starts with an analysis of your own needs. I feel that for most people, purchase of a tent can wait a while. Sleeping bags, packs, and boots ought to come first. You can take a lot of good trips in nice weather using a tube tent or similar shelter in case you get caught by the rain. Later you will want a tent, and by that time you will know your needs better. If you camp mostly in the woods and use fires a lot, you may prefer one of the old designs like the Whelen tent. An open-front tent like this is a lot more pleasant to sit in on a rainy afternoon than a cramped mountain tent. See the book list at the end for details on where to find some of these designs.

Most modern backpackers, however, will be happiest with a tarp, tube tent, or a closed tent. A closed tent for one or two people should be a mountain tent or some variation of it. Dimensions depend on your preferences. The most efficient design will be about 7 or 7½ feet long with an entrance in front, but tapering in height and width toward the back to save weight. A tent wide enough for two is best except for inveterate soloers. You don't save that much weight in a one-man tent. A two-man tent which doesn't taper has a lot of advantages for long trips, especially in winter. Two entrances can be included, allowing one man to get in and out while the other is cooking, without kicking over the pot.

A four-man modified pyramid tent on the left, all nylon with a separate fly, and a two-man mountain tent on the right.

Such designs can also be enlarged for three or four people, but some kind of modified pyramid is generally used for these larger tents. A central pole or suspension line is used for the major support.

All tents are made of relatively light fabric suspended from some kind of frame, and certain standard problems in design should be considered by anyone making one or buying one. A suspension line or edge carrying the weight of the fabric, and perhaps strain from the wind as well, will tend to sag. There is no way to avoid some sagging. Pulling the fabric tight enough to avoid most of it requires a great deal of tension force. All such edges and lines need extra strength. A seam which has several layers of fabric folded together can be deliberately placed where it can take one of the lines of strain. Strength can also be provided by sewing tape along such a line. Sag

An example of a well designed pull-out tab. This one is sewn at the intersection of two seams, so that the strain is widely distributed.

These poles fit together at the top and extend through sleeves sewn on the outside of the tent. This prevents sag and leaves the entrance clear.

185

can be reduced by the use of extra suspension points and pull-out tabs to which guy lines can be rigged. A pull-out has to be strengthened or it will rip out on the first gusty night. See the illustration for an example of reinforcement. A ridge line which is not supported by a rigid pole will always sag, and a curve is often cut right into the line to prevent folds in the fabric below. This is called a catenary cut.

All other points subject to strain and wear must be reinforced, just as pull-outs are. Loops for stakes must be sewn so that a large area of fabric takes the strain. Poles should attach to reinforced points.

The bottom points of the poles fit into grommets in tabs sewn to the tent, preventing the poles from sinking into the snow and holding the tent in shape.

Except for pyramid tents, poles are best fitted *outside* the tent. Two poles which join together at the top make a good support for the front of the tent. They can fit into sleeves on the outside edges, and the lower ends can fit into a grommet in a piece of tape (see the illustration). Some newer designs may use poles which fit together to form a curve, which is then slipped into a sleeve. Support for the walls of a tent may be achieved with pull-outs or wands. Wands are like lightweight poles which slip into sleeves along the sides of the tent. They are generally made of light fiberglass sections, like those used in fishing rods.

If you are designing your own tent, get as much literature and go to as many stores as you can. By studying the best commercially made tents, you will get ideas to incorporate in your own tent. At the same time, don't be cowed. A tent made commercially, even by the best manufacturer, must be a compromise which may not best suit your needs. Designing your own

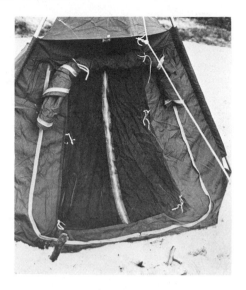

Mosquito netting is a desirable feature in any backpacking tent.

tent can be satisfying and you can often produce a far better tent for your purposes than anyone else.

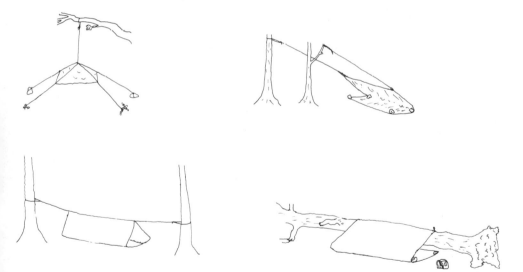

A few ways of pitching a tarp. Methods are limited only by your imagination and by the anchors that are available.

187

12 Sleeping Bags, Pads, and Air Mattresses

A sleeping bag is the most expensive item that most backpackers ever buy, and it is one of the most important. The days of all-night fires to keep warm by are pretty well over, and the sleeping bag is the piece of equipment that enables you to camp in a wide variety of conditions and still sleep comfortably. A night out without one will not kill you, but it will not usually be very cozy either. I like to bivouac without sleeping bags occasionally, but most of the time I wouldn't be without one. With far less bulk and weight than the old blanket roll, a modern sleeping bag keeps you genuinely warm.

HOW MUCH INSULATION DO YOU NEED?

Just as with other equipment, there is no *best* sleeping bag for all climates and all purposes. A lightweight, inexpensively constructed bag would be completely inadequate for camping in really cold weather, but the most expensive bag offered by a mountaineering shop is just as inappropriate for a summer on the Appalachian Trail. The purpose of a sleeping bag is to provide the extra insulation you need to sleep comfortably at night, when temperatures are coldest and the body's production of heat is at its lowest level.

Before thinking about the bag itself, you should decide what you want it to do. What are the warmest and coldest conditions you *normally* want to use it in, and what are the extreme conditions you would like it to withstand? Temperature ranges are very rough approximations, and many factors besides temperature have to be considered. If you do all your winter camping inside well-protected shelters, you may not need as heavy a bag as if you pitch a tent in very windy spots. Protection from wind, overhead shelter, altitude, and difficulty of trips are all important in choosing sleeping bags. Your other equipment and your clothing are important. Finally, *you* are important. The difference in the amount of insulation that people need is amazing. Some "sleep cold" and some "sleep warm," so you will have to gauge your needs from your knowledge of your own body.

My general rule for buying a sleeping bag is that it should be comfortable in the coldest conditions one normally meets, without wearing extra clothing inside. That is, if you sleep in pajamas, you should be comfortable in them; if in your underwear, you should be comfortable in that; and so forth. I save the possibility of donning every last sweater for the times when I meet extremely cold conditions, when I am run down, when the insulation is starting to get damp, and for similar difficulties. Usually, a bag that is just adequate in your coldest normal conditions will be all right the rest of the time, too. Zippers can be opened in warmer weather, or a cover can be used as described later in this chapter. Some may prefer the extra versatility of a double bag, one fitting inside the other. If summer temperatures where you camp are in the 70's at night, but down to −30 in winter, you might need two bags. Get one medium weight one that is fairly roomy, and one very light close-fitting bag for the heat of the summer. The light one goes inside the other in bitter cold.

INSULATION REQUIREMENTS

The backpacker has rather stringent requirements for his sleeping equipment. It must be light. I have carried some of the heavy car camping bags around the backcountry. It's better than not going at all, but it doesn't contribute to the enjoyment of the trip. They are horribly heavy and not very warm. The backpacker's sleeping equipment should provide as much insulation as possible for the least amount of weight. It should also have a reasonably small packed size, since bulk presents carrying problems. This means that the equipment should be quite compressible. The insulation between the sleeper and the ground, however, cannot be too compressible, because otherwise it would do no good. The body weight would squash it down, leaving no protection from heat loss to the cold ground.

The basic principles of insulation were discussed in an earlier chapter, but we might as well recapitulate them briefly here. So much nonsense has been written about sleeping bags that it is important to clear some away right at the beginning. The actual insulating material of any sleeping bag is air. Down, foam, Dacron, or whatever serves to hold the air in small, still cells. The amount of insulation is dependent on the thickness of the insulating layer. Period. There are other design considerations. The bag with the most insulation isn't necessarily the warmest, but the insulation is provided by that layer of air, and a bag with inadequate insulation can't be warm. If the insulation layer is two inches thick it provides twice the insulation of a layer one inch thick.

For all this to be true, the layer of air has to be immobilized to prevent convection currents, so that, for example, one type of insulator might maintain its effectiveness in a ten-mile-per-hour wind, while another might not. There are, however, no miracle insulators that will provide more insulation with less thickness. Thickness is the basic factor in maintaining warmth.

INSULATION MATERIALS

The three main possibilities for insulation in sleeping equipment are down, foam, and synthetic fiber batting. Since Dacron is the most effective of the synthetic fibers for this purpose, I'll stick to that; the remarks about Dacron apply to other synthetic fibers as well. Several types of foam are used for sleeping bags and sleeping pads, with different purposes and priorities in mind. Down comes in various qualities, as discussed earlier, and it may also be mixed with feathers.

Except for special circumstances, down is by far the best insulator for sleeping bags designed for backpacking, throughout those parts of the bag not bearing the body weight. It meets all the major criteria for this insulation. A given weight of down will expand to fill much more space, and thus provide much more insulation than any other material. It will also compress into a smaller space, but it will return to full volume quickly again and again. Down also has minor advantages. Its major disadvantages are in the area of cost. Down is expensive. The best down, that which is plucked from geese grown in a cold climate, is the most expensive. In addition, the characteristics of down make expensive construction necessary to make proper use of the good insulating qualities.

Thus for any given amount of insulation needed, a down bag can be built which is more efficient than any other type. On the other hand, if most of your camping is done in a fairly mild climate, you may want to buy or make a less expensive bag, using Dacron or foam. Before you do, though, be sure that they are adequate to your needs.

Dacron has to be sewn into batts to be used as insulation, because otherwise the material mats and leaves cold spots in the bag. Foam also presents some construction problems, because it is difficult to sew. One solution is to glue the foam into the shape you want and then to cover it with fabric.

THE SHAPE OF THE BAG

The large rectangular shape of most car-camping bags is a very inefficient shape for a sleeping bag. A good deal of the material lies in useless folds and represents wasted weight and money. It also presents a greater surface area to the cold air, and so loses more heat. Thus thicker insulation is needed in a rectangular bag than in a more compact bag. The most efficient bag is one which fits the body closely, following its contours, a shape commonly known as the mummy style. Most backpackers prefer to leave a little room for shifting around and choose some slightly more roomy modification of the mummy design. The bag should be roomy enough to allow you to sleep comfortably without suffering attacks of claustrophobia, but no larger. Most of the standard designs these days strike a reasonable compromise, but several manufacturers carry a special lightweight bag which is cut more closely and efficiently, a true mummy design.

All too often foam and Dacron bags are cut to a pattern which is far less efficient than most down bags. This is silly. Since these bags are colder and heavier to begin with, they need to be shaped properly even more than a down bag does.

ADVANTAGES AND DESIGN OF FOAM BAGS

Several manufacturers are now producing foam bags, although there is nothing particularly new about them. They are especially useful on boats when the temperature doesn't drop too low, since foam bags retain most (not all) of their insulating qualities when wet. The top layer of foam should be relatively soft, so that it will drape over the body somewhat. Draping is often improved by using two thinner layers of foam rather than one thick one. A foam bag should have a drawstring at the top and a zipper on the side for temperature and ventilation control.

In general, foam is stiff enough to stand out from the body and to move as a unit when one end is disturbed. As a result, foam bags tend to pump the warm air inside the bag away and suck in cold air from outside. A foam bag has a bottom which insulates the user better from the ground than other insulating materials, and a foam bag won't require additional padding in warm weather. The same can be said of a foam-bottom down bag, however. The characteristics that make foam a good ground pad make it a poor top.

I don't advise purchasing a new foam bag unless its special advantages are what you need. The current prices will buy you a better bag made of other materials or will get you a kit for a high-quality down bag. It might be worthwhile to *make* a foam bag. An excellent design is given in Paul Cardwell's *America's Camping Book*, pages 139–141. It is inexpensive to make but not anywhere near as warm as a good down bag. I want my bag to be warm enough so that my teeth won't chatter all night when I'm tired and temperatures start to plunge. However, I also sleep very warm, so if I get cold in a bag, most other people would, too. My own preferences probably stem partly from the fact that I often backpack in fairly extreme weather conditions. The claims made for some bags are absurd and are often based on one wearing a lot of insulation inside the bag. With an expedition down parka and thick insulation on my legs I can sleep at $-20°$ F. with a bedsheet over me, but that does not make the bedsheet good down to 20 below. An active man can stay warm in cold weather with relatively light clothing, and though he may carry some extra, the winter camper often depends on his sleeping bag to provide most of the insulation he needs when he stops for the night, when his body is inactive and temperatures are dropping. Furthermore, in cold weather, some emergency reserves are necessary. There *is* a good argument for carrying more insulation in the form of clothing and less in the sleeping bag, but when this is done, it is the clothing which provides the insulation, not the sleeping bag.

The great advantage of foam bags is their performance when wet, but their temperature range is limited, so this only applies in fairly mild weather. The claim that a foam bag acts like a diver's wet suit might be impressive if you want to sleep on the floor of the Atlantic, but it won't help much on Mount Whitney. A diver doesn't encounter subfreezing temperatures, evaporative cooling, or high winds. The backpacker does.

I think that someone who doesn't expect a lot of extreme cold and wants to make an inexpensive, versatile bag for himself should consider Cardwell's design. Before you do, though, compare its cost with that of making a down bag with a foam bottom or foam pad. There is a price difference, but it is not very large when you are using new materials.

DACRON BAGS

A few well-designed Dacron bags can be found on the market for $20–$30. For people who sleep fairly warm, these should be adequate for all conditions short of snow-camping and extreme cold weather. They can be extended to the latter uses with enough extra clothing, but this is a less efficient way of providing nighttime warmth than having a thicker sleeping bag. Dacron bags should probably be used only by those who rarely go out in cold weather or who need a stop-gap until they can afford a better bag. They are also good for anyone allergic to down. I think the better commercially made Dacron bags are a better economy choice than foam bags.

Dacron bags can be constructed by sewing directly through the outside fabric, the batt, and the inside fabric. This leaves cold seams, but these are not as bad as the cold seams in down or down-and-feather bags, because the Dacron doesn't compress so much. A warmer bag can be made by using two layers of batts, each sewn between one of the shells, and a thin layer of netting, then put together with no overlapping seams.

DOWN BAGS

I am giving details on the construction of down bags because I think they are a better choice for the backpacker and because construction methods are necessarily more complicated. Some of these methods are also applicable to the construction of bags using other materials.

A typical down bag suitable for most backpacking. This one has a liner to keep the bag from getting dirty.

Down is made up of tiny nuclei with filaments radiating in all directions. Although all down contains some small feathers, down pods are not feathers. The filaments can be compressed, pushing the air from between them, but when pressure is released they will spring back to shape. To provide an insulating layer, enough down must be stuffed into a compartment both to fill that compartment and to push the sides out to their full extension. Getting the maximum possible insulation from a given amount of down requires careful design to avoid loading the down and necessitating more fill to expand a compartment.

Down also shifts readily, and if it is sewn in large compartments, it will tend to bunch in one corner of a compartment unless an overfill of down is used. For the most efficient design then, many relatively small compartments are required, and they must be designed carefully to avoid loading.

The drawing shows a cross section of a few types of baffling. In the simplest, with sewn-through seams, a cold spot is left at each seam, where there is no insulation. This method of construction is suitable for some clothing but only for the very lightest sleeping bags, designed for warm-weather use. A second method was designed to eliminate this problem, and

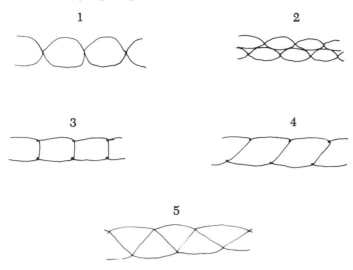

Some methods of construction for down insulating layers.
1. Sewn-through seams, which leave cold spots at the
stitching. 2. Two layers of sewn-through construction, with
the cold seams staggered. 3. Rectangular down compartments are formed by baffles sewn between the two sides.
Baffles are made of very light fabric or netting. 4. Similar
to 3, but with the baffles tilted, generally known as slant-
tube construction. 5. Triangular baffling, which gives the
most efficient use of the down, but is also the most expensive type of construction.

it uses two sleeping bags, either sewn together or not, with the tubes overlapping. It works well, but a lot of weight in fabric is wasted. The third and
fourth methods use baffles sewn to the outside and inside layers of fabric to
form tubes for the down. These are very good methods, but twisting will
still tend to load the down. The best method of all, and the most expensive,
is the triangular baffling method, in which a baffling layer goes back and
forth between the inside and outside layers.

In addition to the methods of forming tubes for the down, the tubes
themselves need to be baffled at intervals to prevent down shifting along

them. The best bags are normally made with the tubes running across the bag horizontally or in a chevron pattern.

MATERIALS

Down bags should be made of lightweight nylon. It is stronger than cotton, more wear-resistant, and lighter, so that it doesn't tend to load the down. The inside of a nylon bag is slipperier and tends to bind less, which is important with closely fitting bags. Baffling material can be made of netting or a very light nylon fabric. The latter is better, allowing less shifting of the down. Thread should be synthetic throughout. Cotton thread inevitably wears out quickly, and the repairs are a nuisance.

Down is available in many grades. Judging among manufacturers is difficult because they rarely use the same systems for describing their down. Northern goose down from mature birds raised in a cold climate produces by far the best grade, but *some* duck downs are better than *some* goose downs. Within a particular line, you will often notice that several grades are used, but this is of limited help in comparing manufacturers. You will have to make a choice using other features as a guide. Remember that the weight of down in a bag means nothing by itself. Construction is more important, and down quality is at least as significant.

Since European poultry farmers are now killing geese at a younger age, the best down is no longer readily available. Quality is now achieved mainly by culling techniques. Goose down is no longer a guarantee of quality, nor is duck down necessarily an indication of inferiority. You must rely heavily on the integrity of the manufacturer.

Zippers and hardware should be of the best quality. Some good metal zippers were used in the past, but most high-quality bags today use oversize zippers of nylon or other synthetic materials, which have less tendency to jam or freeze and which are less brutal to the skin in cold weather.

OTHER CONSTRUCTION FEATURES

Any sleeping bag should have a good hood arrangement for protecting the head and preventing air circulation, while still permitting the sleeper to breathe outside the bag. The design can be simple or complicated, providing that it works. Zippers should not be cold spots, as they will be if they are left open to both the outside and the inside. This is usually solved (sort of) by the addition of a down-filled tube to cover the zipper. The zipper side of the tube should have a good, tough tape attached to prevent the zipper from catching. A better method is to have two closures with a baffle in between, either two zippers, Velcro and zippers, or another arrangement. Unfortunately, I think only one manufacturer uses this method at the moment.

A differential cut is an advantage when it is properly used. The illustration shows how this works. The idea is that if the inside of the bag is cut to the same size as the outside, you will press the two shells together every time you scrunch up or stick out an elbow. With a differential cut the inside is a smaller diameter, so that even when you stretch it tight, you don't press it against the outside and compress the insulation. The contour should be sewn in at the sides of the bag to prevent the bag from barreling and standing away from the body.

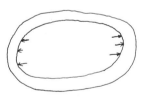

The advantages of a differential cut. At the left, the bag uses inside and outside shells of the same size, and when the body presses against the inner surfaces they are compressed against the outer ones, forming cold spots. At the right, the inner shell is cut to a smaller diameter, so that pressure cannot push it against the outer bag.

Generally, bags for the backpacker are constructed with down insulation throughout, even though the down which is compressed below serves no useful purpose. This practice is simpler to use than building ground insulation into the bag, and it prevents the bag from sustaining ground wear. Some manufacturers have started to build ground insulation directly into the bag, using a foam pad or shredded foam in the bottom part of the bag instead of down. This results in a more efficiently designed bag if it is done well. Make sure there are no cold seams at the juncture of the two forms of insulation. If a pad is included in the bag, the material surrounding the pad should be of waterproof-coated material. Material coated on one side only should be used on the inside, with the coating facing the pad (plastic coating is most unpleasant against the skin). A hole for the air to get out and into the pad area must also be included.

The standard practice in making down bags is to use permeable (uncoated) fabric both outside and inside the bag. The idea is that water vapor from the body passes out through the insulation to the outside air. The body is always evaporating some moisture even without the sweating that you feel. Sweating occurs when the body becomes too hot and perspires to cool itself by evaporation. Insensible perspiration, which you do not feel, occurs simply because your skin is more moist than the air around it.

The difficulty with permeable materials is that when moist air works out through the bag it reaches colder and colder regions, often condensing as dew before it gets out of the bag, causing the down to become damp. This particular problem is worst in extended periods of cold weather. One solution is used by Stephenson's. They make the inside of their bags from impermeable fabric so that moisture from the body cannot filter into the down. This keeps the down dry and also reduces evaporative heat loss. It is an interesting method, not yet used by anyone else. A great problem with the technique is that if heavy clothing is worn inside the bag in cold weather as supplementary insulation, moisture will condense in the clothing. For some purposes, however, this innovation offers much promise.

In any case, impermeable materials must *never* be used on the outside of a bag to make it shed water. Moisture moving through the bag from the inside will then condense on meeting the outer surface, soaking the insulation in short order.

Zippers or other closures are essential in any bag except an ultralight one designed for a very narrow temperature range. When the bag is too warm, the zipper can be opened for ventilation. For this reason, I have always preferred side zippers, which allow ventilation without causing the bag to fall off your chest. Top zippers allow less expensive construction, however, so you might prefer one. A full-length zipper makes the bag slightly heavier and less efficient, but it allows making zip-together bags, permits easier drying on sunny mornings, and allows the bag to be opened and used as a quilt.

Zip-together bags are pleasant for couples, although they are not as efficient as they seem. They require more material than one bag made for two people, and their gain in efficiency is nearly always lost by extra ventilation around the neck. Various methods have been tried to control this, but no one has come up with a good one yet. Double bags, made for two people, are more efficient, and the neck closures are usually a little better. They can be used only by couples who are truly inseparable, though.

COMPARING BAGS

In buying a sleeping bag, it is often difficult to compare the bags made by different manufacturers, since everyone uses different standards in describing comparable features. The first thing you might do is to send for catalogues from a number of mail-order houses. A few that don't make their own bags will have useful comparisons among bags made by different suppliers. Temperature ratings will give you a rough idea of the differences between the bags of a single manufacturer, but they don't help much in comparing one maker's with another's.

Look at the construction, baffling methods, size of down compartments, and amount of down. The amount of *loft* is useful. It represents the thickness to which the insulation expands, but some companies quote the thickness of the whole bag, top and bottom, while others refer to the top alone. Also, don't compare lofts too literally; there are different ways to measure it.

Since you can't look at the internal construction of down bags, you will have to judge it by externals. Be especially careful to examine workmanship. Bags with sloppy outside construction will be even sloppier inside. Beware of the new bargain bags appearing in stores that don't specialize in supplying backpackers or mountaineers. Many of them use inferior cloth (a lower thread count per inch which won't stand up to wear), and their materials and workmanship are often sloppy.

AIR MATTRESSES AND FOAM PADS

Unless you have a bag which includes a ground pad, you will have to get a separate one. They are more comfortable than sleeping on the hard ground, but this is not really the main point. If you sleep on the bare ground in a down bag, you have essentially no insulation on the bottom, so you have to have a lot more on the top, and that is a waste of money and weight. There are three commonly used types of ground beds: *air mattresses, open-cell foam pads*, and *closed-cell foam pads*.

Three types of ground beds: an air mattress, which folds to a very compact size; an open-cell foam pad with a coated fabric cover, a light and very comfortable bed; and a closed-cell foam pad, which provides maximum insulation for the least weight and expense.

Air mattresses are convenient some of the time, but they are used much less than they used to be. A few people find them more comfortable than foam pads, but most find them less pleasant to sleep on; it's mostly a matter of what you are used to. There is no question that they are colder than foam, because air currents carry heat rapidly through the mattress, and so they should not be used for snow-camping. The greatest advantage in an air mattress is that it deflates into a more compact package than a pad. Unfortunately, it may occasionally do this in the middle of the night.

If you get an air mattress, make sure that it is of good quality, made of coated nylon fabric. The plastic kind will not stand up to the rough use a backpacker gives an air mattress. The heavy rubberized fabric kind is strong enough, but is rather heavy. Be sure to carry a repair kit. An air mattress is most comfortable when inflated just enough so that no part of your body touches the ground. Overinflation makes the mattress uncomfortable and increases chances of puncture.

An open-cell foam pad is more comfortable to most people than an air mattress; it is lighter and warmer. The pad can be 1½ or 2 inches thick, depending on the amount of padding and warmth you want. It should be covered with fabric to protect the pad from dirt, abrasion, and moisture, and the covering should be waterproof on at least one side. A 2-inch foam pad is a real luxury bed.

Closed-cell foam, such as Ensolite, Thermobar, or Voltek, provides a slightly more Spartan bed than a regular foam pad. Closed-cell foam is blown so that each air pocket is closed from all the others. Thus there can be no air circulation through the foam, and a thinner bed will provide more warmth. A closed-cell foam pad is less bulky than an open-cell one that provides the same warmth. It weighs less and is cheaper because no cover is required (it can't soak up moisture). A thickness of ¼-inch will do, but ⅜-inch is warmer and gives more comfort.

Whether you use a pad or an air mattress, get a short one. There is no need for a full-length ground bed, even in the winter. Put some of your clothing in the sleeping bag stuff sack for a pillow, and use your parka, pack, or some combination for your feet. A bed around 20 inches wide and 40 inches long is adequate; get one a little larger if you like.

OTHER SLEEPING ACCESSORIES

Unless you are camping in a tent with a floor, a *ground sheet* is essential to protect your pad and sleeping bag from moisture and dirt. You can carry a sheet of coated nylon, but most people use a plastic sheet, which is discarded after it starts to wear out. Such sheets can often be gotten as scrap, eliminating cost and waste. It is not generally a good practice to use a poncho as a ground sheet, because small holes will soon develop.

A *sleeping-bag liner* is very worthwhile to help keep the bag clean. The less often you have to wash your bag, the longer it will last. Some manufacturers sell them to go with their bags, or you can make them yourself. A flannel liner will add warmth. I prefer a very light nylon ripstop: it weighs almost nothing, is slippery and doesn't bind, and it is so sheer it can be washed on the trail and dried very quickly. The cheapest liner is made from bedsheets that have worn out in some spot—usually enough material can be salvaged for a sleeping-bag liner. Sew ties into your bag and matching ones on the liner, and make sure that the head of the bag, which gets the most dirt, is well covered.

A *sleeping-bag cover* will substitute for a ground sheet, protect the bag from dirt, extend the temperature range about another 10° F., and will serve as an emergency shelter bag. Some sleeping-bag covers are fitted to the bag. I prefer a big, loose-fitting sack, which can be held up to give me some breathing space and which will accommodate my equipment as well. The ground side of the cover should be waterproof, and the top should breathe. (Unless you have a sleeping bag with the inside of impermeable fabric, in which case a completely coated cover could be used.) Plans for a cover are included in the patterns. In warm weather you can use the cover to sleep in, with or without the bag as a blanket.

MAKING SLEEPING BAGS

A down sleeping bag is probably the most difficult project you could choose to undertake, so unless you have already had some practice or are very confident, it is best to use a kit for this one. Excellent kits are available at a moderate price. A good foam-bag plan can be found in Cardwell, and Gerry's book gives an excellent general discussion and fine plans for Dacron bags and lightweight down ones. The plans presented for foam and down bags should be studied carefully before any cutting is done. Make a mock-up and check the size first, altering where necessary.

Miscellaneous *13*
Equipment

There are a host of small items which, if not essential to the backpacker's existence, at least help keep him comfortable and happy. Some of them are required for safety, some for bodily well being, and some to preserve the character of the wilderness. This chapter is a sort of buyers' and users' guide, designed to help you to get the things you really need into your pack without breaking your back or your wallet in the process. A number of improvisations are suggested for temporary or permanent use to keep initial expenses down.

Backpacking equipment should be light and easy to pack. This spin-fly rod has good action, but it weighs only ounces and breaks into a short package.

POTS, PANS, AND COOKSETS

This is a good place to make do when your budget is tight, but it is also an area to exercise care if and when you do get around to spending a few dollars on cooking equipment. Making do can be accomplished by a raid on the kitchen pantry or on your local Salvation Army store, where old pots can usually be got for a dime or so apiece. My personal preference for a cheap cooking set is the hobo's standby—a kit made of tin cans. This method has enough virtues so that I occasionally use it in preference to my regular pots. Tin cans don't last very long, but they are free, can be tossed away at the end of the trip, and they are quite light. They fit well into the pack, and the sizes and numbers of cans can be readily adjusted for the size

A salt and pepper shaker with sealing lids is handy.

of the group. For one person a two-pound coffee can, one smaller can (say a No. 2 or 2½), and a cup make a positively luxurious kit. You might have to pay for the cup, but the rest is free. Utensils consist of your pocketknife and a soup spoon—you certainly should be able to scavenge a soup spoon. Salt and pepper can be carried in plastic bags or in the little paper packets dispensed by hamburger stands, airlines, and other gourmet establishments. Tin-can pots should be equipped with wire bails after punching holes on either side of each pot. You make the wire bails out of wire, the kind without insulation. If you go out and buy a cookset, make sure to get one that will fit conveniently in your pack. Short, wide pots are more stable and heat more efficiently. They also slop water all over the place while you are carrying them up from the stream, and they don't always fit into the

The wide bail on this pot locks into position so that the pot won't tip when it is hanging and pouring is easy. The cover fits in either way and also serves as a dish.

pack compartments where you want them. Tall, narrow pots have the opposite set of vices and virtues. Two pots holding about 1½ or 2 quarts each do nicely for parties up to about five. Covers which double as plates and makeshift frying pans are a good idea, but if you plan to do much frying, make sure you have a steel frying pan. Thin aluminum burns but does not cook well. A Teflon lining is not a bad idea either.

There is a real virtue in pots with bail handles that lock in place. They can be hung over the fire without the danger that they will suddenly decide to tip, and they are easy to handle without a special gripper. The one shown is excellent—and expensive.

I always carry one or two of the aluminum pot grippers, and I maintain that they are a necessity of life, but some people manage very well with a long shirtsleeve as hot-pan holder.

Pots that are used over fires are much more conveniently handled if you have a little sack for each one. The soot doesn't get spread over the inside of the pack or smeared on the inside of the next pot, yet you don't have to wash it off either. You don't need to buy the sacks; they can be easily made of scrap cloth. The kind of material is unimportant, since they are only covers.

For cooking primarily with a stove, you may prefer a cookset designed to stack in an efficient combination. The one shown in the illustration in-

Pot grippers like this clamp onto any pot or cover, greatly simplifying the handling of hot pans.

cludes a stand for the stove, a windscreen, two pots, and a cover. These work very nicely, and they are recommended for high altitude and for winter especially. If you buy one, check the joints between each of the sections, especially each of the pans and the stand. Don't buy a set that has any tightly fitting joints—as soon as wear dents them a bit you will find them stuck together while you are trying to get a hot pot of stew off the stove. You can buy these sets with the stove included, but I think it is better to buy them separately. Though you pay a little more, if you buy the stove by itself you get a cover and windscreen so that you can use it with other pans when you like.

This type of cooker fits together into a compact unit and makes cooking with a stove very efficient. The second pot can be stacked in also.

STOVES

Though many types of stove are available to the backpacker, the choice for most purposes can be narrowed to that between those burning unleaded gasoline and those using propane or butane cartridges. I suspect that most newcomers to backpacking will pick the propane or butane types, because of simplicity of operation. Gasoline stoves take some getting used to and have certain disadvantages, but they are also superior in some respects. Before discussing individual models, I'll summarize the pros and cons of each of the two types of stove.

Stoves using unleaded gasoline. Advantages: fuel is readily available— even in remote localities; the fuel is inexpensive; large containers of fuel can be carried on long trips, saving weight, and the exact amount of fuel needed for a trip can be measured into the can; the stove burns at full pressure and temperature until it is empty; it can be filled at the beginning of a meal, so that it doesn't go out in the middle of cooking.

A typical backpacking stove. This one is fueled with white gasoline and generates its own pressure once it is burning.

Disadvantages: gasoline stoves are tricky to light, especially if the wind blows the flame out; they are especially inconvenient if you should just want to light one for a few minutes to reheat food or fix a hot beverage beside the trail.

Stoves using propane or butane cartridges. Advantages: the stove lights easily and quickly—you just hold out a match and turn on the burner, and it can be turned off and relighted with no trouble; putting on a new cylinder is simple and requires no careful pouring of a flammable liquid.

Disadvantages: fuel may be impossible to obtain except at specialized stores, unless you get a stove using standard propane cylinders, and the stove is absolutely useless without the proper cartridges; the fuel is considerably more expensive than white gasoline; a cartridge that is half-empty cannot be filled at the beginning of a trip or a meal; the stove runs poorly during the last ten minutes or so of a cartridge; the empty cartridges have to be carried out—they have become a new source of joy for the litterbug.

Essentially, the cartridge stoves are clear winners for convenience, but gasoline stoves are cheaper to run, will usually result in a smaller load in your pack, and it will be a lot easier to get fuel for one in that small town near the trailhead in Wyoming.

Except for large groups, gasoline stoves for backpacking should be the kind that generate their own pressure instead of using pumps. The ones with pumps put out more heat, but they are much heavier. Some gasoline stoves are Primus (the old standard), Svea, and Optimus, all of which are very good. There are dozens of models. The champion for weight and output is the Svea 123, which packs stove, windscreen, stand for a pan, and even a tiny pot into 18 ounces. The Primus 71L and the Optimus 80 weigh a couple of ounces more and have a bit more fuel capacity, which can be an advantage in winter and with larger parties. I also like the Optimus 8R and Primus 8R, which sit flat and are more stable than any of the upright stoves just mentioned. They weigh about 8 ounces more than the Svea.

The cartridge stoves are latecomers, and there are new entries every year, all the more complicated because each one manages to bring its own type of cartridge with it. The first one to become popular in this country was the French-made Bleuet, which burns butane gas and uses its own special cartridges. It is rather tall, and hence somewhat top-heavy for cooking in tents. This would probably be the best choice for a butane stove, because cartridges are available at nearly all mountaineering and backpacking suppliers. Other entries that burn butane are likely to cause you trouble unless you carry a lot of cartridges on any trips away from the store where you bought it.

Primus makes stoves called "Grasshoppers" for both propane and butane. Propane has the advantage in cold weather, because it becomes liquid at a much lower temperature. In winter you may have to warm a butane stove before lighting it. The Primus Grasshopper that is made for use with propane also uses standard cylinders, which are generally available in hardware and department stores. It gives more burning time for the weight than the Bleuet, and the cylinder can be removed when half-full, so you can take a full cylinder on a week trip or a partly empty one for a weekend. The cylinder is heavier but the stove is lighter, so that on the return trip a Bleuet with an empty cartridge weighs about the same as a Primus with an empty cartridge. The Grasshopper is also more stable; it rests on the wide tripod formed by two folding legs and the cartridge. Of the two, the only real disadvantage of the Primus is that with a full cylinder it weighs more than a Bleuet with a full cylinder. However, the Primus cartridge lasts about a week to the Bleuet's three days. And the Primus cylinder can be removed.

Whatever kind of stove you get be sure to get a windscreen if it comes separately (as it does with the Bleuet, for example). Most of your heat will be blown away by a light breeze without one. Even with it, you must use any backpacking stove in a sheltered spot if you want to cook your food rather than simply heat the outdoors. You should also be sure to carry any prickers that might be necessary to clean the burner-jet. Don't let prickers or valve stems get lost. If a funnel is needed for filling, pack that with the stove, too.

Keep any stove clean, so that it will work when you need it. Empty the fuel tank if you are storing the stove for the season; otherwise varnish tends to form inside. I don't know about the butane and propane stoves, but eventually, after long use, the gasoline stoves start to get cranky. When this happens, buy a new one. I know from personal experience that when they start to go you'll have nothing but trouble, and one of my friends had one blow up because he tried to nurse it too long. Luckily, he managed to throw the flaming mess out into the rain before it caused real trouble, but you might not be so lucky. These stoves last a long time. When yours decides to retire, give it a decent burial.

FLASHLIGHTS, CARBIDE LAMPS, AND CANDLE LANTERNS

A flashlight is one of the essential pieces of equipment, even if you become a devout early-to-bed-and-early-to-riser. There is always the possibility of

Various flashlights. A headlamp, which can be strapped on the head with the batteries kept in a pocket, freeing both hands; a penlight; and a small Mallory flashlight. Tape must be kept on the switch of the Mallory when it is not in use to prevent accidental discharge of the batteries.

an emergency or unforeseen contingency that will make it necessary for you to follow a trail in complete darkness. The size of flashlight you choose will depend on the length and circumstances of your trips.

The amount of light that a flashlight puts out is determined by the bulb and the voltage of the battery combination. Most flashlights use two 1½-volt cells in series, giving a total of 3 volts, whether the size is AA, C, or D batteries. The amount of light getting to the ground where you are looking for the dropped matches is determined also by the design of the reflector.

Of the normal flashlights the Mallory lights are currently the best around for putting the most usable light where you want it with the smallest amount of weight. The reflectors are efficient and the case and switching gimmickry is light in weight. Unfortunately, the switches get cranky after a while.

If you are using a flashlight much, getting into camp late every night so that you have to cook by artificial illumination, for example, a headlamp is a lot more convenient than a flashlight. Trying to serve the stew or tie a guy line with a flashlight clamped between your teeth is really annoying after a while. A headlamp has an elastic band that holds the light and reflector on your head, with a wire going to the battery pack in your pocket. Anything that requires using both hands is a lot easier to do with a headlamp. The main trouble with them is that most currently available ones are too heavy, because they use three or four D cells. The most commonly available one is also notorious for its sloppy construction, but for some reason the backpacking stores continue to carry it.

You can find a lightweight headlamp if you look for it. If you decide to buy a heavier one, get the kind with three D cells lined up side by side—there are a couple of good ones on the market which use this design. Do *not* get the kind that uses four cells in two stacks of two each. The springs in this model are too weak, and the light will go off and on in rhythm with your step—until it quits altogether.

The length of time your flashlight goes on shining depends on the kind of bulb and the size of batteries you use. It also depends on the kind of batteries and the temperature. The bulb part is simple: the brighter the light, the less time it will last. A PR-4 bulb requires about half the current of a PR-2, and it will last about twice as long; it will also give less light. The useful life of batteries increases with their size, unless you also increase the bulb size, and hence the drain on the batteries.

Alkaline batteries last many times longer than regular batteries, though exact figures mean little because of the many variables involved. The alkaline types cost more initially, but less over their total life. They also work better under heavy load (as when you are following a trail at night), have a longer shelf life, and are not as affected by the cold. They last somewhere between five and ten times as long as regular cells.

Always carry a spare set of batteries and a spare bulb for your flashlight. In situations where you have to use the batteries for long periods, they will last longer if you switch the two sets of batteries every hour or so, allowing one pair to rest. They will also last longer if you keep them warm. Really cold weather can make regular batteries stop working altogether, and it affects alkaline batteries as well. This is one advantage to a headlamp. The battery case can be kept in an inside pocket to keep the cells warm.

Always inactivate the flashlight before you put it in your pack or your pocket, unless you're going to use it again soon. A flashlight accidentally switched on in the pack will nearly always prove a source of considerable annoyance, and it may be a really serious mistake. With a standard type of light reverse half the cells; with the Mallory or other light, where taking the case apart is inconvenient, use a large piece of tape to immobilize the switch.

For summer trips when I don't plan to use a light very much, I now carry one of the small Mallory flashlights with one spare pair of AA cells, using a PR-4 bulb. When I tested this combination, two fresh pairs of alkaline batteries switched every hour lasted ten hours in reasonably warm weather. That would enable me to walk all night even after some previous use of the light in camp. On trips when I expect to be on the trail in the dark, and on winter trips, I generally carry a headlamp using larger cells.

Some people like candle lanterns, and they are pleasant to light a tent with on a long winter night. They are nice for romantic suppers or to light your way out of camp on short journeys in the night. They won't substitute for a flashlight, though, and I find that I rarely carry one.

A carbide lamp is a much more practical alternative to a flashlight, although most people aren't familiar with them. It is the lamp often used in caves and mines, where an electric light might cause a dangerous spark. A carbide lamp has a small pressure chamber which is filled with dry fuel, calcium carbide. When water drips on this fuel, acetylene gas is released, and this escapes through a jet in the center of the lamp reflector. A small sparking device like the one on a cigarette lighter is attached to the reflector. You simply rotate the wheel, the jet lights, and you have a very brilliant light. The flame is not very hot, so it doesn't pose a fire hazard.

A carbide lamp produces lots of light, and the fuel is much lighter than batteries, so for some kinds of trips it might be a very useful substitute for a large flashlight. It can be hung in the tent and will produce enough light for reading. There are some serious problems, however, which make it quite impractical in winter and in the mountains. The lamp requires water and is made of metal, and in cold weather the water freezes and the lamp stops working. Strong wind also makes trouble, because it affects the gas jet. If you're making long trips in forested areas, though, and you would like to have a good source of light in the evenings, a carbide lamp is ideal. A standard one weighs about 7 or 8 ounces. If you use a carbide lamp, the fuel must be kept absolutely dry. Pill cases make good waterproof containers, and some sizes are just right to carry a filling for the lamp. Keep the parts properly cleaned, replace the felts when necessary, and carry a cleaning brush for the jet.

MATCHES AND FIRE STARTERS

Get wooden kitchen matches—the big, nonsafety kind. If you find match-books convenient to carry, they're all right, but when the weather turns damp and the wind starts blowing, they get wet and worn, and the flame won't hold long enough, so have some kitchen matches, too. Carry plenty of matches in several waterproof containers distributed in different places. You can use plastic pill bottles, double plastic bags sealed with rubber bands, or a host of other containers. Unless you have something on your person that makes a good striking surface, pack a little piece of fine sand-paper in each container (everything around always happens to be wet when you need to light a fire). Matches can be waterproofed by dipping them in melted paraffin. A few of the windproof kind with long-burning heads may be helpful in some circumstances. They can be purchased in backpacking stores.

Many commercial fire-starters are available. Carry a few in your emergency kit, if you like. I have a candle stub which will serve as a light or get a fire going easily. Some people carry hexamine tablets or rolled-up newspaper soaked in paraffin to get the fire going in wet weather. The hexamine is available in surplus stores at a dime for a tube of five or six.

For lighting fires, a cigarette lighter can be very handy. It's easy to light and keeps burning like a candle rather than a match. Carry a few matches, too, just in case. A lighter is also good for getting a gasoline stove going. You just hold the lighter under the stove for a minute, and you have your needed pressure.

Flint and steel kits are now available in a variety of very good small designs that throw a fine, hot spark. If you want to carry one for emergency fire making, by all means do so, but don't bother unless you are going to take the time to learn to use it. There is a knack.

A piece of steel wool makes excellent tinder for emergencies, as well as being useful as an abrasive. It burns only once, so make sure everything else is ready before you use your only piece.

CONTAINERS

At least one water bottle is usually necessary, depending on the availability of water. It is convenient to have a fairly wide mouth on the bottle so that you can get it full in shallow streams and trickles and so that you can pour things like dry milk or instant breakfast in if you want to. A quart- or liter-size polyethylene bottle is tough and convenient. You can mark measurements on the side with a hot knife (not too deep!). You can save money by salvaging a bottle that contained dishwashing detergent or some similar stuff. In the desert, make sure any bottle you are going to stuff in the pack is tough.

For large containers for water, half-gallon and gallon plastic bleach bottles work fairly well, or you can buy tougher polyethylene jugs. Make sure they include some way to attach them to your pack. Treat bleach bottles with reasonable care when they are full—they aren't thick enough to stand a lot of beating.

A wineskin (bota) is a good substitute for a bottle. Wineskins are available in one- and two-quart sizes. They are flexible and pack easily, and in

A wineskin is a handy container for water. It is especially good in cold weather, when the water bottle has to be taken to bed to prevent freezing, being a more comfortable sleeping companion than a canteen.

cold weather they are lots more pleasant to sleep with than a bottle. I wouldn't trust one in the desert, though. Modern ones are manufactured using cheap split leather on the outside and a thin plastic liner inside. When the plastic liner finally goes, there is no warning—and no water.

For gasoline, a metal container is advisable. Two types are generally used: a round anodized aluminum bottle or a rectangular tin-alloy fuel can with two spouts. Get the rectangular kind. It is impossible to pour from the round ones without spilling until they're partly empty. (A new pouring

One type of fuel can.

spout has just been put on the market to correct the trouble, but you might as well get the rectangular kind with spout attached). The rectangular ones also fit into pack pockets more easily. They are available in 1-, 1½- and 2-pint sizes. The 1½-pint can plus what is in your stove should get you through a full week easily, unless you are melting snow.

KNIVES

The backpacker can get along very nicely with a small pocketknife. Get a good one; that is not the same as an expensive one. All that is needed is a pair of decent carbon steel blades that will hold an edge. If yours has a can opener, that's fine, but you can get a teeny, super-efficient GI can opener for fifteen cents and use it for a zipper pull. There are good three-dollar

A good pocket knife like this can be quite inexpensive.

pocketknives that will hold a fine edge and twenty-dollar pocketknives that won't. Try yours out in the store.

The backpacker doesn't really have much need for a sheath knife, but some people do prefer to carry them for help with kindling. There is absolutely no point in having one with a blade longer than four or five inches. You can do anything for which a camp knife is needed with that length, in-

An excellent design for a sheath knife.

cluding skinning out a grizzly bear. The swords that some people carry on their hips might be good in hand-to-hand combat, but they are certainly useless in camp. If you want a sheath knife, the rules about prices and knives apply here, too. The knife shown in the illustration is an excellent design for a sheath knife, and I have seen knives on this pattern selling for eighteen dollars. Mine cost two bucks, plus a dollar for the sheath.

Outdoor knives are best made from carbon steel rather than stainless. Stainless is hard to sharpen, and usually doesn't hold an edge particularly well.

SHARPENING A KNIFE

Dull knives aren't much help in building a fire or repairing a ski, but they are very dangerous. A dull knife requires too much force to cut, so that you

Sharpening a knife. The blade is drawn in
the direction shown by the pointing finger.
A much smaller stone can be used.

tend to lose control. It also tends to glance off tough spots in wood, and
with all your extra pushing behind it, it is likely to end up in your leg.
Keep your knife sharp.

Sharpening a knife is simple enough. You need a sharpening stone.
The best ones are made of a fine artificial stone on one side and "soft Arkansas" on the other, but these are getting expensive and hard to find. Don't
get just a "hard Arkansas" in any case; it is a finishing stone designed to
put a razor edge on an already sharp knife. A pocket double stone of medium and fine Crystolon is good. Most people will probably be satisfied
with a little pocket carborundum stone for a pocket or sheath knife. You
can use a fine cutting oil or just water on it. Lay your knife diagonally
across on the coarse side. Lift the back of the blade about a quarter-inch
for a sheath knife or an eighth-inch for a pocket knife. Grind the edge with
a pulling stroke for about twenty seconds or so on each side, depending on
how dull the blade is. The cutting action is diagonal. Then turn the stone
over and repeat the process on the fine grit side of the stone. Now pull the
knife straight along the stone, as if cutting, with the blade at the same
angle, two or three times on each side to remove the wire edge. The knife

217

should now be fairly sharp; you can test it lightly against a fingernail. If you want it really sharp, strop it on a belt or a leather pack strap. Strop in the opposite direction from cutting. This will remove the last traces of a feather edge.

AXES

The ax is the traditional woodsman's tool, which is one reason there aren't as many woods as there used to be. For most backpackers today, there really isn't much need for the ax, but if you go off on a trip into seldom traveled woods and you want to split logs for all-night fires, you might want one. Similarly, if you do a lot of camping in a very wet, wooded region, you might only be able to get dry wood out of the deadfall by splitting open good-sized logs. The ax is the tool for this kind of job, but it is heavy enough so that it isn't worth carrying unless you really need it.

Many disagree, but I haven't any use for hatchets. (An exception is for clearing trails, but that isn't our subject here.) The heavy part of an ax is not the handle, it's the head. If you are going to carry all that weight

An ax and a folding saw. A saw like this, a pruning saw, and a saw with a rectangular frame can be used for any wood-gathering chores except splitting, but they are much lighter than the ax.

218

around in the head, it's ridiculous not to have a handle long enough to use the weight effectively. A 28-inch handle is long enough to enable you to get a full swing. With a 2-pound Hudson's Bay head the ax will weigh about 2¾ pounds, but it will be a really effective ax. A 1¾-pound head will bring the weight down even further.

An ax is dangerous. It requires practice to learn to use one well, and only one mistake can bring an accident that is really serious in the wilderness. A 28-inch handle is short enough to cause the head to bounce into your leg unless you position yourself carefully. Learn to swing the ax in a relaxed way, and let the head do the work. Clear away anything that might catch the ax before you start swinging; many accidents are caused by the ax deflecting on a branch that the chopper didn't notice. Don't hold the piece of wood you are splitting in your hand or try to hurry your swing because it is falling. Practice with the length handle you will use. Suddenly switching to a shorter handle can be dangerous unless you are careful. Finally, keep the ax sharp. Using a dull ax in the wilderness is an excellent way to commit suicide; it's dull enough to glance off a knot, but plenty sharp enough to go halfway through your leg.

SAWS

A saw is generally a far better choice for the woodland backpacker than an ax or hatchet. It is lighter and more effective for getting firewood from deadfall, except in very wet places where dry wood has to be split out of logs.

Hacksaw blades and wire saws can be carried conveniently and are very light, and they are good emergency tools. If you really plan to use the saw to get wood, though, you should get a pruning saw or a frame saw. The pruning saw is cheap and light. You can get one with a folding handle that will cut wood up to 4 inches in diameter easily, weighing about 7 ounces with a 10-inch blade.

For larger wood, you can carry a folding saw that uses a flexible bow saw blade. Frames can be triangular or rectangular. The rectangular type may not be as strong, but it will cut a larger log. You can pay six or seven dollars for this type of saw, weighing from 12–18 ounces, or you can make one of about the same weight for two or three dollars.

MISCELLANEOUS MISCELLANY

You should carry sunglasses or goggles unless you know from experience that you won't need them. Snow, sand, and high altitude are especially hard on the eyes. Prescription sunglasses are a lot more pleasant for those who need glasses. On snow, side visors are desirable.

I wear glasses, and they do create some special problems. If you can get used to the kind with wire loops behind your ears rather than the regular plastic kind, you'll find that they do better at keeping the glasses from sliding down your sweaty nose. In some situations you'll probably want a safety band. You can buy them in sports stores or make your own. Safety glasses are a wise precaution.

Fogging is always a problem, especially when you're pushing up a long trail in cold weather. There are several antifogging compounds available that help a little. Finally, depending on how bad your eyesight is and the nature of the trip, you should consider carrying a spare pair of glasses.

Part 3

Special Skills

Finding Your Way   14

Finding one's way in the wilderness has a traditional and almost mystical significance attached to it. According to the romantic notion, if you can find your way through the great north woods and build a fire in any weather you are a woodsman. If not you are a tenderfoot. Despite this, backpackers often have only rudimentary skill at route finding. For many people, even experienced campers, getting lost in the woods is a rather terrifying possibility, the more so because route-finding techniques tend to be neglected. The modern backpacker generally follows trails which are fairly well marked, and he may have only the foggiest idea of how to use a compass. His map reading is likely to be a transposition of methods from road maps to trail maps: "Turn left at the next fork, Mabel."

Actually, backpackers in many areas have little need for general path-finding techniques, so the neglect of these skills is understandable. Still, your freedom of travel will always be limited if you stick to trails cut and marked by others. So will your confidence in your own ability to cope with some emergencies and your performance if you are actually confronted with them. You can get along as a beginner with simple route-finding skills, but you won't really achieve the freedom of the wild places until you learn to find your way around them.

The basics of making your way around the woods or the mountains are the same as those used in steering a path through the streets of New York City. They consist of ways of relating your own position to various features of your surroundings. If you want to go somewhere, you must know the relative location of that spot, a feasible path around intervening obstacles, and some way of guiding yourself along the route.

People who are very much at home in a particular environment often find their way without paying any conscious attention to their methods. It is important to note that this is an acquired skill. No one has any "natural sense of direction," or any other kind either, except for a false sense of confidence. It has been proven on numerous occasions that without some reference to the outside world, people circle aimlessly while convinced they are walking a straight line. Many "old woodsmen," dumped in an unfamiliar environment, would have just as much trouble finding their way as a city slicker. An old-timer may have literally hundreds of tricks for getting around, but they are all based on reference points in his surroundings. It is these reference points that you learn to use in finding your way, together with the description of them we call a map and the direction-finding tools you may carry, especially the pocket compass.

MAPS

Maps are *the* basic route-finding tools in wilderness travel, and learning to use them skillfully will contribute greatly to your freedom to move about easily in wild areas. You will probably rely heavily on them, from the rudimentary inspection of a road map that will place you at the trailhead to the planning of trips over trackless regions. The amount of detail you inspect will vary with the kind of trip, but journeys that don't depend on some map use are rare indeed.

All maps are designed to represent the features of the earth's surface graphically, but there are as many kinds of maps as there are purposes for using them. The first consideration in map making is *scale*. A small-scale map covers a lot of country on a small amount of paper, and so it is obviously the most convenient and inexpensive to use, providing it conveys all the necessary information. Larger-scale maps include more detail, but are more cumbersome. If you want to find out where Chicago is located in the United States, you would look on a map of the country, but if you wanted to find your way to the Field Museum, you would want a street map of the city. Neither map would be of much use for the other purpose.

Fairly large-scale maps are generally most suitable for wilderness use, since the backpacker covers ground rather slowly and needs to know about detailed landforms in planning and executing trips.

Aside from scale, different maps also vary widely in the information they try to convey and the methods used. Road maps show roads, but they generally include very little information on the land surrounding automobile corridors. Maps intended for canoeists give great detail on rapids, portages, dams, and so forth, but they too are apt to be scanty on landforms. Very good maps exist for dozens of other purposes, showing the geology of an area, the legal ownership, or the tribes of Indians that once inhabited it, but none of these is of much use in planning a backpacking trip.

The most suitable maps for the backpacker are the topographic ("topo") maps published by the U. S. Geological Survey. They show the outline of terrain by means of contour lines, are drawn on a scale appropriate for the wilderness traveler, and can often be obtained in editions showing vegetation patterns as well.

READING A TOPOGRAPHIC MAP

There are a number of ways to show the general relief of the land on a map, all designed to give a three-dimensional view on a two-dimensional surface. Various relief shadings are easy to visualize, but the most accurate way is to use contour lines. Once you have learned to read contour maps, you can visualize terrain you have never seen with relative ease, and you can get precise information on grades, watersheds, whether one point can be seen from another, and a host of other questions, the answers to which can greatly simplify route finding.

The map in the illustration is part of a U.S.G.S. topo map. Designation of lakes, trails, snowfields, administrative boundaries, and so on is fairly standard and obvious. The lines are contour lines. They are lines of constant elevation—that is, if you were to follow one of these lines as though it were a trail, you would never go up or down. On a hill, you would stay at the same height and eventually walk all the way around the hill to arrive at your starting point.

The edge of the ocean forms a boundary at zero altitude above sea level, ignoring the variation of the tides and waves. Looking at a map of

A section of a topographic map published by the U.S. Geological Survey. This one is in the fifteen-minute series, and the scale is approximately one inch to the mile. The area shown is rugged and mountainous, but gradients are not nearly as steep as some others near the area shown. The contour interval is fifty feet. There are numerous lakes and a flat, marshy meadow in the upper center at Washakie Park.

226

the shoreline, the water's edge would form a contour line. Now, if you imagine the ocean rising, say fifty feet, a new contour would be formed representing an altitude fifty feet above sea level. In some places with long sloping beaches and marshes, the water would come miles inland, and the contours would be quite far apart. At cliffs or bluffs they would be packed close together. High points in the land would form islands, and these would appear as closed curves describing the new shorelines. If we kept raising the ocean fifty feet at a time until all the land was covered, we would have a contour map of the area. Of course, there might be depressions protected by hills which would have to be filled to the proper levels at the same time the ocean was raised, with a siphon if you like.

This analogy may help you to visualize the terrain represented by a contour map, since any contour line can be thought of as an imaginary shoreline. Naturally, if we are standing on a hill, and there is another one across the valley, it will have a shoreline corresponding to ours, a contour at the same level.

The illustration shows a few common contour patterns and the features they represent. Note that the contours don't just tell you that there is a slope or a hill; within the limits of scale, they show you the shape and gradient of the slope or hill. The closer the lines are together, the steeper the slope, and the farther apart, the more gentle the slope. If the lines get closer together toward the top of the slope, it is concave; if they get farther apart, it is convex.

A few facts about contour lines follow from the description of them. Followed out, a contour line always meets itself eventually, forming a closed curve. Thus each line will either disappear off the edge of the map or will double-back on itself.

Contour lines cannot normally cross one another. If they do, they show an overhanging cliff. When the lines get so close together that they cannot be distinguished they represent a near-vertical cliff, and some U.S.G.S. maps leave such a space blank instead of dark. The meaning is always clear with a little study. This is only a printing problem; the actual contour extends across the cliff.

SCALES, INTERVALS, AND SUCH

As mentioned previously, the scale of a map must be appropriate to your purpose, and for the backpacker the usual rule is that the larger the scale,

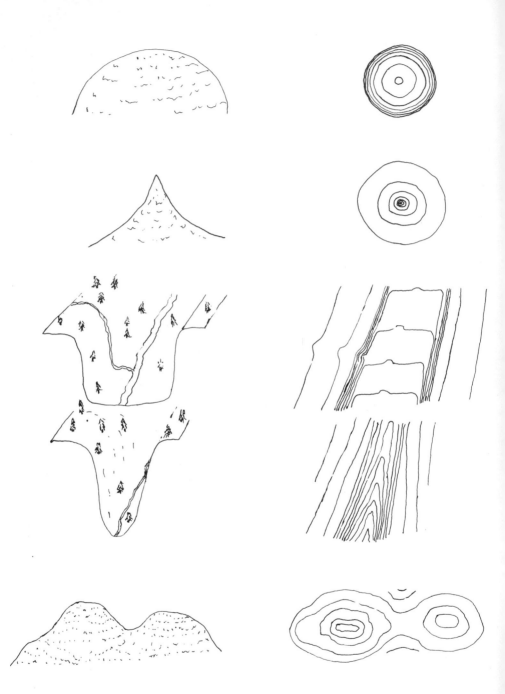

the better. Most of the United States is now covered by the new 15-minute quadrangle maps series, the 7½-minute series, or both. These cover areas of 15 minutes of longitude by 15 minutes of latitude (or 7½' by 7½'), and they both show admirable detail with the tremendous accuracy allowed in trackless regions by the wonders of stereoscopic aerial photography. The 15-minute series is drawn on a scale of 1:62,500, that is, one finger width on the map equals 62,500 finger widths on the ground, not counting ups and downs. The scale works out to be very close to 1 inch: 1 mile (1:62,360 for the precision minded), close enough for the difference to be ignored by backpacking types. This series is quite adequate for most wilderness travel, showing considerable detail, but covering enough country so that the maps don't become unmanageable.

The 7½-minute series is on a 1:24,000 scale (1 inch: 2,000 feet) and it sometimes seems so detailed one could find an anthill. These maps are excellent, but for longer trips they can become both cumbersome and expensive. Even here, though, the expense is only comparative, since all the U.S.G.S. maps are bargains. Maps from either of these series are all the wilderness traveler could ask.

For those areas where the 7½- or 15-minute quads are available, they serve the purposes of the backpacker so well that there is rarely much point in considering other maps, except supplemental trail guides. There are, however, some parts of the country which are not yet mapped in these series, and many of them have great interest for the wilderness traveler. This is not coincidental, because wilderness regions tend to rank low on the list of bureaucratic priorities (mercifully), so they have been left until last for mapping. In such places wilderness travelers have to depend on various other series. In Wyoming, for example, the new series are far from complete, but the whole state is mapped on a scale of 1:250,000 (1 inch: 4 miles). These small-scale maps are very well done, but they necessarily give considerably less information than one might wish. The old 30-minute quads, which are somewhat more detailed at a scale of 1:125,000, are being allowed to go out of print by the Survey, though some are still available.

Some simplified contour patterns. The top two contrast the appearances of convex and concave slopes, and the next two show the different representations of U- and V-shaped valleys. At the bottom is a typical rounded hill or mountain with two summits separated by a saddle.

These were made around 1900, and they must be treated much more circumspectly than the modern maps made with aerial photographs, since the guesswork which often went into them did not always correspond to the realities of the landforms.

Various special prints are available from the U.S.G.S. on some regions of particular interest to backpackers, especially of the national parks and of various river systems. The scales vary considerably.

Contour intervals—the changes in elevation represented by successive contour lines—vary just as scales do, and the interval used depends on the map scale, the surveying method, and the terrain. A smaller-scale map necessarily has larger contour intervals, because it becomes difficult and pointless to fit many lines into a small space. Surveying methods influence the contour interval and have differing allowances for error, although on older maps the contours are frequently interpolated by informed guesswork. Finally, terrain affects the choice of interval. Precipitous terrain would make 2-foot contour lines run together into a continuous blur, while some parts of the country are so flat that a 200-foot interval would never show from one end of a map to another.

Most of the new 7½-minute series use 40-foot intervals for mountainous terrain, and they may use 2-foot intervals for gently rolling country. Thus one of the first things to look for in reading a map is the contour interval. Do those closely packed lines represent a 50° face or a gentle slope? The answer is a function of the scale and the contour interval.

Usually, contours are arranged in groups of five for convenience in reading the map. Every fifth contour is heavier and is marked somewhere with its altitude. With 40-foot contours each heavy line represents a 200-foot change in elevation.

In regions with extreme variations in terrain, say a quadrangle where mountains meet plains, supplemental contours may be used to show detail. These are usually shown by dotted contour lines between the solid ones, and they simply represent intermediate elevations. In the example mentioned, the steep mountain slope might make contours closer together than 40 feet impractical to use, while 20-foot levels are required to show some hills on the level land below.

Another important type of information on the U.S.G.S. maps is shown in the cultural features. These include buildings, roads, trails, and other man-made additions to and subtractions from the terrain. Clearly, the cultural features are those most likely to be out of date on an old map, so the survey date is important in evaluating the accuracy of such a map. A separate date may be shown for an updating of cultural features. Buildings may have been built or demolished. Trails and roads may have been cut or grown over since the survey was done. One other change which is less obvious is the addition of lakes to some regions. As you puzzle from a mountaintop over the identity of a large lake in the distance, don't forget that it may have been created by a dam since the mapping was done.

Unfortunately, one special problem for the backpacker concerned with trails is that the Survey is rather inconsistent about the ones it shows. Mappers are faced with the problem outlined above—namely that the maps, once made, are likely to remain unrevised for some time. Obviously, the surveyor does not want to include a path that will be obliterated within a couple of years. The judgments made vary a good deal from map to map, and as a result the hiker will find that on two maps of recent vintage, one will show every trail while the other shows nothing less substantial than a well-established, graded road. The only safe rule is that in a recently surveyed area all the trails shown on the map will exist.

U.S.G.S. EDITIONS

Various editions with different overlays are available for the standard U.S.G.S. maps. The most common are the contour and the shaded relief editions. The contour edition is far more useful, once you have taken the time to learn to read it. For beginners it may be helpful to pick up both editions for some area and compare them. The shaded relief is a bit easier to read at first and may help you to learn to interpret the contours.

Different overlays may also be available, but the only important one is the green woodland overprint. If the map you want is available with this overprint, it is to be preferred, since it shows which portions of the area covered by the map are forested.

OTHER MAPS

There are many other kinds and sources of maps, and only a few will be mentioned here. Since the U.S.G.S. maps are so well suited to the purposes of the wilderness traveler, they are usually preferred. Even in areas where the final editions have not yet become available, preliminary working editions can often be purchased from the Survey. If the region you are interested in is not covered by current large-scale maps, you can find out the status of the mapping by requesting status maps (free) from the U.S. Geological Survey, Washington, D.C. 20242. Ask for "Topographic Mapping— Status and Progress of Operations," which is updated every six months.

Aside from Survey maps, there are many other government agencies which publish maps of the areas they administer. The ones of most interest to backpackers are the Forest Service maps, but these vary tremendously in quality. There are rumors that high-quality maps made from aerial surveys and with a large scale are going to become available for sale, but so far only those for a few forests in the Northwest have appeared. Most of the current maps are rather small in scale. Some are useful supplements to the U.S.G.S. maps, showing trails more accurately. Since these maps are less expensive to make than detailed topo maps, they could be updated regularly to provide current trail and road information, and that would be really useful. The real situation, however, is that the trails shown are less reliable than those on the Survey maps. In some forests, they are generally accurate. In others you may find the trail shown has been overgrown for a couple of decades, while in still others the carefully drawn trails are proposed routes to be built and maintained if money and manpower ever become available. In defense of the Forest Service, it should be noted that most of these problems stem from lack or misallocation of money and manpower, problems which will be resolved only as a result of your pressure.

The situations in different wilderness and recreation areas are so variable, that it is impossible to generalize. Good trail maps are available from park departments, state conservation agencies, and so on, but you may have to write some letters to find them. Frequently, "sportsman's maps" are available in stores. These vary in quality, since they are usually copies of the maps of some state agency, which you can get free elsewhere.

Generally the best source of trail information for the backpacker is the trail guide or trail map published either commercially or by some local club. These are available for many popular hiking and climbing areas. In some cases these maps and guides are so good that no supplementary information is needed. Those published by the Appalachian Mountain Club are a good example. More commonly, the guides are designed to be used in conjunction with topo maps. The guide or trail map tells you where the trails are cut, but gives only enough detail to enable you to locate it on a U.S.G.S. map.

Finally, there are still areas in this country for which no good guides or U.S.G.S. maps are available. If you want prior information for a trip in one of these, you'll have to work just a little, getting a sampling of the uncertainties, joys, and frustrations of having to dig what information you can out of old accounts and inadequate maps. The U.S.G.S. may still be able to help, however. You may be able to get advance proof maps. These have unlabeled contours and elevations and the outlines of lakes and snowfields, but that's all. You have to fill in names and other information yourself. They are also subject to correction. Failing even advance maps, you can purchase aerial photos. Information on available aerial photographs and photomaps can be had free by writing the U.S. Geological Survey, Washington, D.C. 20242, and requesting "Status of Aerial Photography" and "Status of Aerial Mosaics" maps.

LEARNING TO USE MAPS

If you're one of those rare souls who was taught to use terrain maps as a child, you won't need any practice, but otherwise it's a good idea to spend some time learning the skills before you really need them. This can be done on a Sunday walk in some local hills or on a leisurely weekend backpack along well-marked trails. Get topo maps of the area beforehand, and then keep them handy while you're walking. Look at the features around you, and match them up with their representations on the map. Try to visualize some of the landmarks ahead from the map, and then see how far off you were when you reach them. Keep up your map practice on subsequent trips, and you will be able to use the map effectively when you need it.

KNOWING WHERE YOU ARE

Having obtained a decent map of the region in which you're traveling, you're ready to start the business of skillfully piloting yourself across vast and trackless regions without getting lost. Only start with small trackless regions. Oddly enough, it's sometimes easier to get lost when you're following a trail than when you really are in a pathless area. The reason is simple —when you're following those trail markers you don't really pay any attention to where you're going, and if you lose them you don't know where you are or which way is up. The obvious conclusion, for all types of hiking and backpacking, in true wilderness or on the trail, is to know where you are.

There are a lot of ways to keep track of your position, using a trail or topo map, drawing your own map as you go along, or simply keeping a mental map. In all three cases, you have to relate your own route and position to the terrain through which you're traveling. If you do this well enough, along your entire route, you can retrace it whenever you choose to do so. Being able to do it well is a matter of training, though, and training yourself requires some self-discipline. This can be as true for the experienced walker as the beginner, since when he steps into a new sort of country he may get lost by not going back to basic rules. The mountain man may get so used to working by well-defined watersheds that he gets lost after walking a mile in level forest.

With a topo map in fairly well-defined terrain, you can use the easiest and best way of knowing where you are just by occasionally glancing at the map and keeping track of your position. If you're traveling up a long valley, you simply note the landmarks as you pass by them. Having a topo map, knowing that you're traveling northwest in Big Water Valley and that you passed Bareface Bluff forty-five minutes back is as good a location as you could ask. If a blinding snow or fog suddenly appears, you can pull out your trusty compass (about which more later) and steer from where you are to where you want to be.

In the absence of such strongly delineated landforms, or a good map, or both, things get a little more complicated. If, for example, Big Water Valley is just a wide trough filled by a meandering stream and Bareface Bluff is ten miles off to one side, your casual attitude of thinking you know where you are may turn out to be quite unjustified when the fog rolls in. Even if you find the stream you won't know which direction it is traveling at that point, since it curls back and forth.

There are a host of position-finding methods, and in any particular situation only some of them will be applicable or necessary. It is important to learn to apply them and to always be aware of what you would have to know to get out of any difficulties that might occur.

The first and most satisfactory position-finding method has already been mentioned, that of keeping track of your location on a good map of the region. It is easy to do in many sorts of country, requires little or no written record-keeping, and except in difficult terrain it will enable you to steer your way out with a compass in case of need.

Lacking an accurate, detailed map or the sort of landforms that can be constantly matched with it, one method of keeping track of your position is simply watching your own trail. You may draw a crude map, keep track of walking times between landmarks or locations on the topo map, and write or mentally record various identifiable features along the way, especially at junctions.

Several rules are frequently missed by beginners in watching their own trail. The first is to *look back over your shoulder.* Any route looks very different when approached from the opposite direction. A second is to *write things down.* Memory may be relied on in many cases, especially when it is well trained, but we all tend to place far too much faith in a recollection which is likely to be under considerable strain when it is actually needed. The next day or week, with a storm raging and the fear of being lost added to natural forgetfulness, you may find your critical gully to be much less distinctive than you thought. Writing down your trail signs is also salutary in forcing you to *pick really distinctive features.* A tree that seems unmistakable when you first see it may well merge its image with hundreds of others by the next day or week. By trying to put its unique qualities on paper, you may find out just how easy it will really be to recognize them.

There are a number of special techniques for finding your way, and most of them rely on one additional piece of information to those we have already mentioned—direction. For the backpacker the normal direction finding device is a pocket compass.

DIRECTION FINDERS

The basic element of a pocket compass is a magnetized needle or a magnet attached to a face, either of which is free to rotate on a pivot. The magnet aligns itself with the earth's magnetic field, and thus tells us the direction of the field at the point where the magnet is situated.

There are a few standard fallacies about the earth's field and about compasses which we have to get out of the way, since they are rather widespread. The earth's magnetic field is not perfectly regular. Though it has a north and south pole, these do not happen to coincide with the geographic poles, and they are large shifting areas rather than well-defined points. Even if you consider the needle of the compass as pointing to the magnetic pole rather than the geographic one, you will be ignoring the irregularities in the earth's field owing to mineral deposits and other influences. Remember that the field is somewhat distorted and that it changes slowly. Remember also that the field is greatly distorted in the vicinity of iron or steel. Almost everyone knows that a compass will not point accurately if it is laid on a car fender, held next to a steel belt buckle, or rested on the pack just over the steel frypan, but people keep making these same errors anyway.

The normal way to find out the direction of the earth's magnetic field in the area where you are is by looking at your topo map, which should have a declination diagram along the margin somewhere.

DECLINATION

By declination we mean the amount that a compass needle declines from pointing true north in a particular place. It is not negligible and should not be ignored. Within the contiguous United States it varies from over 20° west, to over 20° east, and in Canada and Alaska it may be even greater. For example, in the Indian Peaks in Colorado the declination is 14½° east, which is not especially large. Even so, steering a compass course for only five miles and ignoring the declination would have you 1¼ miles off your intended route, quite enough to get you thoroughly lost. The error might be even greater, because in this kind of country one usually steers by watersheds, and the common use for a compass would be to get you down into the right one from a peak or a ridge, after which you would follow the slopes. Coming down in the wrong drainage system can head you off in the opposite direction from the one you want to go, and it may lead you to impassable cliffs.

Proper use of a compass is really an important skill for a backpacker to master. In some kinds of country the compass will be in daily use. In many other regions you may go for years without taking it out of your pack, but when you do take it out your life may depend on it. Backpacking in the Sierra Nevada range in California, I can remember few occasions when I used my compass. At least one time, however, as I was coming out of a large round valley in blizzard conditions, the difference between magnetic and true directions was also the difference between hitting the route out on the other side of the ridge or climbing a local peak. The storm was severe and the wrong route would have been extremely dangerous. The difficulty in judging distance in such conditions makes it doubly important that directions be correct and that you have the confidence to know they are correct.

Back to declination then, a confusing correction until you are used to it, but one that is important to understand. You can think of your compass needle as aligning itself with a magnetic line which itself is wandering, with an occasional drunken stagger, toward the north magnetic pole. The

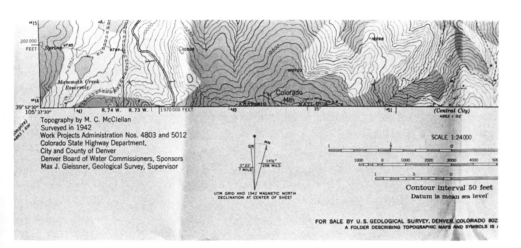

Various information is given in the margins of the U.S.G.S. maps. In the center here is the declination diagram. The star indicates true north. "MN" means magnetic north, and this angle is the declination. The arrow to MN shows the direction your compass will point. "GN" refers to the direction of a grid system which is of no particular use for backpacking. To the right are graphic and ratio scales and the information on the contour interval used.

difference between the direction of this line and the direction of true north is the declination. If the declination is 17° west, then the compass needle will point 17° to the west of true north.

In the eastern parts of the United States and Canada declination will always be west, but in the western parts of those two countries it will be east. For the inexact purposes of the backpacker, the declination can be considered constant within the limits of a 15-minute quadrangle map, and the declination at the center of the map will be shown in the diagram at the border. On some larger-scale maps or on maps of areas with wide variations in declination, a diagram showing declination at various points on the map may be substituted for the single value of center or average declination.

Though declination varies with both time and distance, the changes are generally of little consequence for the foot traveler except on very long trips or in unusual regions. You can check your maps beforehand to see what the total change in declination will be over your route, and then if it seems necessary make daily or weekly adjustments. It will rarely be necessary. Variation with time is a problem only with out-of-print maps, since on current maps declination is generally brought up to date periodically even on an old survey. Thus, on a U.S.G.S. map you will often find a more recent date under the declination diagram than under the map name. Declination changes slowly enough so that the variation is unlikely to be a problem for the backpacker.

All the foot traveler generally needs to do about declination is to make sure he knows the proper figure at the beginning of a trip. If his compass allows mechanical correction, the adjustment is made at the trailhead and can then be ignored. With less elaborate compasses the adjustment must be made in readings each time the compass is used. We'll go into more detail on this adjustment later in the chapter, but to make it you ought to know the declination of an area before you take off. This will usually be shown on any adequate map, but there are exceptions. You might have unthinkingly made one yourself by cutting off the margins of the map at home. When you do that, make sure you have all the information you need first.

WHAT THE COMPASS TELLS YOU

Even though the actual information given by a compass is pretty well understood by most hikers and campers when they are pressed, it's amazing how many of them harbor a kind of mystical faith in its abilities. People wander off into the woods with only the foggiest idea of where they are or where they are going, and they expect their native instincts and their compasses to lead them back if they get lost. When they realize they *are* lost panic sets in.

A compass gives you a directional frame of reference independent of your map and of your ability to see landmarks or celestial directional guides. Since it is independent, the compass can be used separately from the map or to supplement it. The compass can be used to orient the map when this can't be done visually. It can be used to keep you on a specific course independent of visible, identifiable, well-placed landmarks. It can be used for readily choosing natural landmarks with which to set a course. It can be used for keeping track of your route over confusing terrain or for drawing your own map of your trail, which can then be retraced if the map was properly made. The compass can be used for fixing positions, providing appropriate distant sighting points are available.

A compass is a directional guide. It can't tell you where you are, where your compass is, or where a road is. You must have other information to tell you those things, and the only way to make sure that you have that other information when you need it is to make sure you have it all the time. In one fashion or another you have to keep track of where you are and how you got there whenever you are traveling in wilderness or semiwilderness areas.

KEEPING TRACK OF WHERE YOU ARE

There are lots of ways of knowing where you are, all of them relative and useful only some of the time. The trick is to be aware of lots of ways and to choose those most appropriate to a particular situation. One of the best has already been mentioned. You carry a topo map, and in a more or less formal way, you follow your progress on it. In regions where this method works well, it is easy, fast, and interesting. It requires no tedious sightings and recording of compass readings. If the fog comes in and obscures everything more than twenty feet away, you dig out the compass, figure your desired course on the map, and start walking in the right direction.

Generally, this method is used in mountainous regions effectively, and it is often applicable in other places like deserts, where visibility is good and landmarks available.

Things are different in heavily forested regions, especially those which are relatively flat, which have confused drainage patterns and the like. Tundra, prairie, rolling fields, featureless deserts, and a host of other such places do not lend themselves to this kind of route finding. One can't keep continuous track of where he is from the map, because there is not a continuous set of natural guideposts for him to use for reference. All but the most skillful map readers may have this same difficulty in some hilly and even mountainous country, where each rise looks much like every other and a single missed stream can throw one off completely. In adverse weather conditions, landmarks disappear in any terrain.

Think a little about the ways you can keep track of where you are in a city. You can carry an adequate map, and providing you know your home address, you can wander aimlessly as you choose. When you want to go home, you find a street sign, establish a direction from numbers or the sequence of intersections, and figure out the way back. With a less adequate map you might simply find one main artery which extends a long way in either direction. Knowing a nearby number on that street you can simply wander about to one side of it or another, keeping track only of the direction of your base street. To return you simply have to cut across to the artery and follow it home. With an identifiable skyscraper or two as guide, you might choose to wander at will, heading back for Old Faithful Bank Tower when your feet got sore, knowing that you were living at the opposite end of the park from it. With a city set in a grid, you could simply keep track of the number of blocks in each direction and come back the same number by any route. Finally, in a strange city with no map and irregular streets, you might just keep track of your path—left after two blocks, right after three more, 45° left at a star intersection, and so forth—retracing the sequence to come back. A long walk by the latter method would probably require taking a few notes.

Most of these methods have corresponding wilderness techniques, although there is no friendly cop or taxi stand on the corner in case you get mixed up. With some care and a good mixture of methods you can find your way around the woods without much difficulty. The terrain is more rugged, of course, and you might have to walk farther to get around a river than a freeway. On the other hand, you won't get mugged while you're trying to find the ford, you won't have to walk five miles in discomfort to find a place to go to the bathroom, and you won't get arrested if you get tired and lie down to go to sleep.

BASELINES

One of the most useful ways to orient yourself in the backcountry is by using a baseline of some sort. This is the method which corresponds to finding a long street in the city to which you can always cut over. In the wilds a baseline can be the road where your car is parked; it can be a long river, valley, or creek; it can be a ridge, a power-line cut, a railroad track, a trail, a lake shore; it can be an imaginary line between two landmarks or a compass bearing on one; it can even be a line which you temporarily mark yourself.

The advantage to the baseline is pretty obvious. Even in dense forest, you don't have to keep careful track of every twist and turn in your wanderings. You only need to glance at the compass occasionally to maintain a rough idea of the direction you are going, and when it's time to go back, head for the line. When you hit the line you follow it back to camp or to your car.

There are some fundamental qualifications in using a baseline for your wanderings. To begin with, the baseline has to be long enough in proportion to the distance you're going to go, and it should run more or less perpendicular to your line of travel. A mile-long trail is a fine baseline for an afternoon's berry-picking expedition, but it's not so good for a three-day trek. This may seem obvious, but remember that unless you *know* your road or lakeshore extends five miles past your car or camp, you had better make sure. I know people who have planned to hit roads which made right-angle bends half a mile past where their cars were parked. One of them got very tired indeed going through five miles of heavy snow as he walked parallel to a road a hundred yards away. When the road finally turned again and he hit it, he had to go back the same five miles. Winding roads, lakeshores, and rivers can be very confusing if you don't know about the bends.

In addition to being sure your baseline is long enough, you must learn

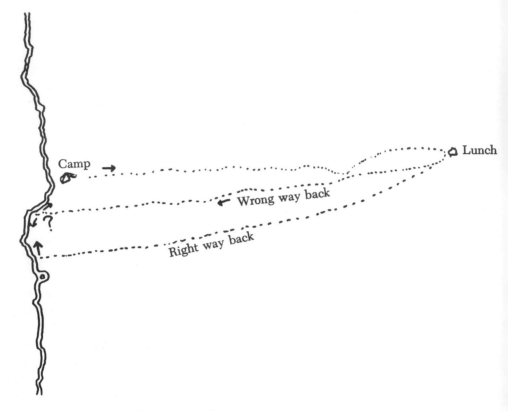

Using a creek for a baseline. The party follows a general bearing on a day hike, and then tries to retrace the bearing. When they get to the creek, they don't know which way to turn for their camp. By intentionally bearing slightly left of the proper route they would know that when the water was reached, a right turn would get them back.

to locate your objective along it. If you are familiar with the baseline in both directions, you may hit it anywhere, knowing which way to go. More commonly, you would be in the position of the party whose route is illustrated. Camped along a creek, they steer back to their camp, but on reaching the creek have no idea which way to turn. The proper method is to aim deliberately to one side. Then the direction of camp is known when the baseline is reached.

242

TAKING BEARINGS

Taking bearings means using the compass (or some other method) to determine the direction of an object from your position. Determining that Mount Highspire is due north of your camp is done by taking a bearing on Mt. H. The normal method of listing directions these days is to use the *azimuth* system, which simply divides the compass face into 360 degrees, running clockwise, with north $=0°=360°$. Thus east is $90°$, south is $180°$, and west is $270°$. There are other methods, of course, but if you want to get into working with bearings like *north-northeast by east,* you're on your own. For more precise measurements degrees can be divided into mils or minutes and seconds, but for work with a pocket compass, you don't have to worry about them—working to an accuracy of $\frac{1}{2}°$ would be exceptional.

The mechanical details of taking a bearing are different depending on the type of compass you have, but the process is fairly simple in practice. Let's suppose you have a very simple kind of compass. The kind shown in the illustration is the sort that is most familiar. (It is not the easiest to use.) The first thing you have to do to get a bearing is to orient the compass. Suppose you are in the Colorado Rockies where the declination is $14°$ east. That means the needle on this simple compass points $14°$ east of true north. If you turn the compass so that the north-seeking end of the needle is on 14, the compass face will be properly oriented. All you need to do now to take the bearing is to sight across the face of the compass and read the number of degrees. Since the compass shown does not have a sighting device, you might use a couple of matchsticks or pine needles to get the most accurate possible reading. Place one above the center of the compass and move the other around the edge until they line up with the distant object. Then you can read your bearing.

TYPES OF COMPASSES

While normal backpacking trips do not require the precision of surveying instruments, a rugged, fairly accurate hand compass is really worthwhile. The example just given referred to the sort of pocket compass which lacks any means for sighting, but these are not really good instruments for the outdoorsman. Any compass *may* be better than none, but not if you rely on its presence only to find it broken and useless in the bottom of the pack when you really need it.

In my opinion any compass that is going to be used for route finding ought to have some provision for sighting, even if it is only a lubber's line (see the illustration). Sights and a sighting mirror are an advantage. The compass has to be ruggedly constructed. You might bang it around for years before you really need it, but if it isn't working when that time comes, you might just as well have not bothered. You should be able to take azimuth readings to within a degree or two to provide reasonable accuracy. The little things that can't be read closer than five degrees may help guide you to a baseline, but they are inadequate for many jobs. As a final minimum requirement, the needle or compass card (moving face) must be either liquid damped or held rigid when the compass is not in use, so that the bearing is saved excessive banging and wear.

There are a lot of other desirable features for compasses; the ones listed above are minimum requirements. Before going any further in listing special attributes, though, we need to look at some of the types of compasses that are made. The most basic one is the one we used for our bearing. More adequate compasses will have some provision for making sightings. The most obvious way to do this is to attach sights to the simple pocket compass used for taking bearings in the example above. This solution will cause certain complications in calculating bearings, though, as we will see. These problems have been solved in several ways, and probably the easiest way to explain the problem and solutions is to show how a bearing would be taken with each of several types of compass.

In the illustration a bearing is being taken on a mountain at azimuth $36°$ in an area with a declination of $14°$ east. Compass A is a standard pocket compass with a sight attached so that it is aligned with the north-south markings on the face. This is a very common type of compass. When the sights are pointing at the mountain, the bearing is obtained by the following process of calculation: the north-seeking end of the needle points at $338°$, but since the needle points $14°$ east of true bearing, a needle pointing true north would point $14°$ farther west, or $338° - 14° = 324°$; the bearing is the same number of degrees clockwise from zero as $324°$ is counterclockwise, so the bearing is $360° - 324° = 36°$.

Now it is possible to train yourself to make these complicated corrections automatically, but it really shouldn't be necessary, and it isn't. The

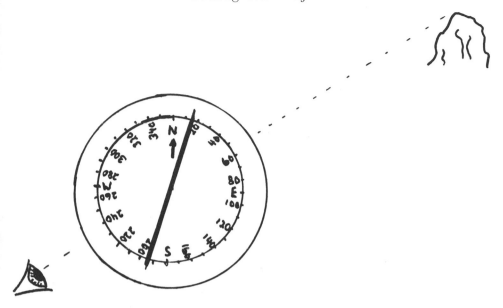

Sighting a bearing with a very simple compass. The compass needle is set on the declination, 14°, and a sighting taken across the compass. It is impossible to sight with much accuracy using this arrangement.

first thing to eliminate is the need to make the correction 360° minus the true needle reading equals the bearing. This can be done in several ways. The first is that used on compass B, a cruiser's compass. The azimuth readings run counterclockwise instead of clockwise on the dial.

The bearing calculation would go this way for compass B: the needle points to 22°, but since it is pointing 14° too far east, the true azimuth reading is 22° + 14° = 36°. We are still correcting for declination, but things have gotten a lot simpler.

A second method for simplifying bearing calculations is to use a compass card instead of a needle, as on compass C. A compass card is simply a calibrated face with a magnet permanently attached, which is free to turn on the pivot in place of a needle. The sights are still fixed to the case, but the azimuth scale is not. Again we can read the magnetic bearing directly, add the declination, and have our true bearing: 22° + 14° = 36°.

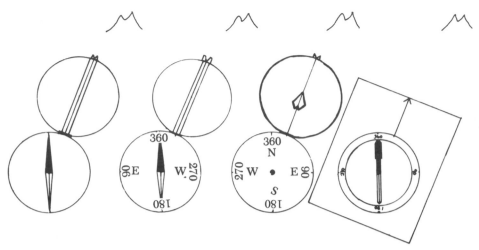

A simplified drawing of the method of reading bearings with four different types of compasses. See the text for explanation.

The third method of eliminating this calculation is to add an additional moving part to the simple compass, giving a system with a magnetized needle free pivot inside a clockwise azimuth scale, with a sight attached to the scale but free to turn around it. A compass of this type is shown in figure D. With this system, we simply turn the scale so that the needle points at the proper declination, 14°, and then we turn the sights to point at the mountain and read the declination directly, 36°.

OTHER COMPASS FEATURES

All these types of compass are made in more expensive versions which have provisions for setting off declination. A screw may be turned or another mechanical device set at the trailhead, so that you don't have to worry about declination until you've traveled far enough for it to have changed, something you won't do on a weekend backpack. This adjustment is helpful in preventing confusion in difficult situations when your mind may be a bit fogged.

A few other compass features need to be mentioned as particularly worthwhile. Walking on a bearing is much easier to do if the needle

A good hand compass. This one is rather old-fashioned, dating back to the early part of the century, but it is more effective than many modern compasses. The mirror in the lid reflects degree readings from the face (written in mirror-image figures) so that a reading can be taken at the same time as a sighting. The brass case and dial lock make the compass sturdy enough to ensure that it will be working when you need it. The line across the cover is called a lubber's line, providing a rough sighting device if the compass is held at waist level.

doesn't joggle with every step, requiring five minutes to settle down. Liquid-filled compasses solve this problem best, providing they don't contain any bubbles to interfere with the action. A cheaper method of damping needle motion is effective, though not quite as good. It is called induction damping and uses the electromagnetic field generated by the moving needle to damp it.

A map can be oriented much more easily if some kind of straight edge is fixed on the compass. The same purpose may be served by scribed lines on the bottom of a compass with a transparent plastic base. Such transparent bases are a fine feature anyway, allowing the compass to be used as a protractor, and eliminating several steps in various triangulation procedures.

Small mirrors and lenses are often attached to sights so as to allow the compass dial to be read while the sight is being taken. If mirrors are used, the dial is usually printed with both normal and mirror image figures. Large mirrors, which may be attached to the top or bottom of the compass, serve this purpose and also make bearings more convenient and accurate. With such a mirror, one can take sightings forward and backward along the trail without moving the compass placed on a steady surface, since the mirror can be angled to allow sighting from a wide range of angles.

Two recent compasses use a completely different sighting system than any normal pocket compasses, eliminating the major problem with most of them—the difficulty of getting accurate readings from the hand-held compass. It often is impossible to rest a compass on a solid object when you are taking bearings in the field, yet most compasses require the eye to focus on several points in different places to get a reading. With a hand-held compass, the needle always moves while your eye goes from the sight to the numbers, resulting in an inaccurate reading. The new Wilkie bearing compass and the Suunto KB-14 eliminate this problem with a lens allowing you to read the bearing while sighting, and they are accurate to under a degree even when hand held. The Suunto is better, since it also has a straight edge, but the Wilkie costs half as much. If you're buying a new compass one of these two would be by far the best buy for wilderness use.°

Other conveniences such as measuring scales may be included on the compass, and their utility is obvious, but beyond this point we begin to enter the regions charted by the secret rings you used to get for fifteen boxtops. Any day I expect the advent of a compass with a secret decoder and a concealed poison dart for subduing grizzly bears.

MORE ON DECLINATION

Declination tends to be more confusing to beginners than any other feature of compass work. Since the needle may point east or west of true north, one may have to add or subtract the declination figure. Most of your trav-

---

° A recent article by D. B. Richards, which appeared in the January 1972 issue of *Wilderness Camping*, after this was written, finds the Wilkie greatly inferior. Apparently Mr. Richard's sample had an inaccurately set face, indicating poor quality control. I agree with him on the Suunto, and interestingly he found the old U.S. Army Corps of Engineers compass more accurate for hand-held readings than anything but the Suunto. This is the compass shown in the photograph, one I've carried and relied on for years.

Compass sightings usually have to be taken with the compass held in the hand, and one should be bought with that fact in mind. Systems which require you to focus on several places at the same time are impractical.

eling will probably be in the same general region, though, so you shouldn't have to go back and forth every weekend. In any case you should try to get used to adjusting for declination in the same way each time, whether it is by making a mechanical adjustment on your compass at the trailhead or making a final addition or subtraction at the end of each bearing. Adjusting for declination at the end of a calculation may be the easiest way to handle declination arithmetically. To do this you take your bearing as if the needle pointed to true north, making whatever other calculations your compass technique requires. This gives you a *magnetic bearing*. Now if you are in the East, having a *west declination*, *subtract* the declination figure from your magnetic bearing. If you are in the West, having an *east declination*, *add* the declination to your magnetic bearing. Always adjust for declination at the same point in your calculation to avoid confusion.

If you are simply recording a series of bearings along a trail in case of storm, or making your own map as you go along, you may choose to use magnetic bearings exclusively, ignoring the problem of declination. This is all right, because the problem of declination only arises when you have to relate your directional system to a map or the stars or some other outside frame. Assuming you don't travel far enough for declination to change significantly, it isn't important if you use *only* magnetic bearings. If you do use such a method, however, I suggest you label all bearings to prevent later confusion. One can use *m* and *t* to indicate magnetic and true bearings. Then if later comparison with a map is needed, there won't be any awkward questions.

WHAT BEARINGS ARE GOOD FOR

Having gotten through some of the confusing preliminaries, we can go on to the actual use of map and compass as guides for travel over terrain with few landmarks or poor visibility. Perhaps the most obvious such use would be to pick out one's location and a goal on the map and to use the compass to steer the course between them, ignoring intermediate features. In practice, this method is avoided whenever possible, because of the difficulty of doing it with accuracy. Obstacles intervene and require detours, staying on a compass direction is hard while one is bobbing along on his feet and trying to watch his path, and continuous observation of the compass is irritating even when it is possible. This method is used in some circumstances, though, and many variations of it are frequent. So to begin with, the map procedure for this method will be described.

In the illustration the goal is Walleye Lake, and fortunately the end of the road is shown on the map. A line has been drawn between the two places and another line due north, so the bearing can be easily measured with a protractor or transparent-bottomed compass. In this case the proper bearing is 45°. One possible method of getting to Walleye Lake would be to follow a compass bearing of 45°. The declination diagram at the bottom of the map shows that the compass will point 17° west of true north. Thus magnetic bearings will be 17° greater than true ones,

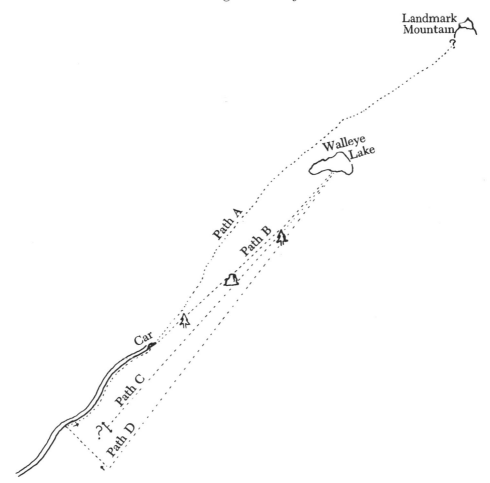

Steering a course with a bearing on a distant landmark. Using intermediate features in line with the mountain ensures a straight course. On return, deliberately heading to one side of the road is wise, so that one knows which way to turn in order to find it.

and to follow a true bearing of 45° to Walleye Lake, a magnetic bearing of 62° will be required.

The backpackers who want to go to Walleye Lake don't want to try to watch their compasses every second, so they would normally try to pick the most distant visible landmarks along the bearing 62°m. It is best to pick out two marks that line up, rather than only one; this method gives a continuous line of correction to the hiker as he weaves around obstacles. Also, if two points on a line are picked, as the nearer one is approached it may be possible to pick another landmark along the line without the need of a new compass bearing.

In the illustration, there is a large mountain on the other side of Wall-eye Lake from the car, and we'll assume that it is visible most of the way. Of course if the mountain was right behind the lake, the backpackers might simply be able to head straight for its summit and be assured of hitting the lake on the way. Landmark Mountain is really a good five miles on the other side of the lake, though, and if the hikers head for it, they might well take path A. Their detours around obstacles have caused them to miss the lake altogether even though they had a landmark. The way to follow path B instead is to pick intermediate landmarks, perhaps trees or rocks, to line up with Landmark Mountain. As each intermediate point is approached another farther one is picked which lies along the same line with Landmark Mountain. Occasionally the compass may be pulled out to make sure that there hasn't been significant drifting.

This same basic method might have been used if no particular goal was intended and the party was just off for a few days in the woods. A course of 62°m might have been followed, using the same method of staying on course. When the time came to return, the bearing would be reversed (62°m + 180° = 242°m).

Actually, to hit the road end the hikers would not want to try to follow an exact course of 242°m the whole way, because it would probably lead them on a course like C. It would be unlikely that they would hit the end of the road exactly, and when they realized they had missed it they would have no idea which way to turn. Instead, they should bear intentionally to one side or another. The party following course D figured that they had traveled about ten miles from their car along a fairly accurate course of 62°m. Instead of following 242°m, they took a course of 237°m, figuring that the 5° difference would leave them a little less than a mile from the road. When they were sure they had gone far enough (by traveling 1 hour longer than they had taken on the trip in) they turned right and soon hit the road. Turning right again on the road they were soon back at the car.

If they had been less sure of their accuracy going in they might have allowed a 10° leeway instead of a 5° one.

The examples given so far have been concerned with situations where a compass course is being followed, but there are many other more common occasions when compass bearings are used. When following a topo map, the experienced wilderness traveler is likely to notice certain places along the route where the returning party might have difficulty. On rounded summits above timberline, for example, the rocky terrain takes on a confusing sameness in snow or fog. In weather that is even slightly threatening, it is often prudent to jot down a bearing on the summit from the point where the route would become recognizable if the party returned in bad weather. If this has been done, clouds closing in quickly at the summit need not bring apprehension. The party can simply reverse its compass course to get back to the trail or gully.

There are many similar situations when individual bearings may be needed, even though the party is not following a continuous compass course. A portion of a trail may be unclear. A route down a hill which avoids cliffs may not be visible from above. Several watersheds may take off from one point, and a bearing may be required to get started down the right one.

ESTABLISHING A POSITION

Especially with the availability of modern maps, the main problem in finding your way is often determining where you are in the first place. You may be able to establish your own location by the use of a topo map alone, but this is not always possible; many kinds of terrain just aren't that distinctive. In the example used above, the road on which the car was parked was clearly shown on the map, but many approaches follow networks of logging roads that are unlikely to be accurately represented. You cannot determine a good bearing to follow from a map if you don't know where your starting point is. Trying to follow terrain is even more confusing when you start with a misconception of your position.

Position can be determined in a number of ways. If you are camped beside a lake, you can follow the shoreline with confidence in your ability to return, because your position relative to the lake is clear. A more general reference system will give you far more freedom to travel, though, and this is why orienting oneself on a map is generally preferred.

The principles and information used for orientation are easily listed. You may have a map, and if you do it tells you the relative position of a number of features on the landscape. Sitting out in the landscape some-where, you will have some information about the relative positions of any existing landmarks because they are there, too, and even their absence tells you something. If the map shows a mountain beside Lake Enigma, but there isn't any mountain near the lake where you're sitting, it isn't Lake Enigma.

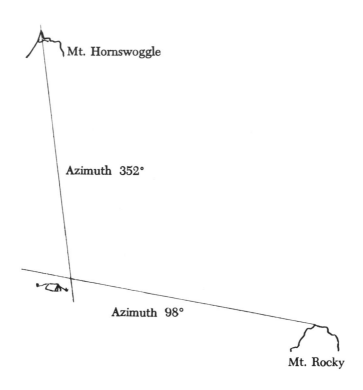

Triangulation enables you to determine your position from bearings on two known landmarks.

You have a device which gives you a directional frame of reference, your compass. (Make sure you carry it—always. Some natural direction finders will be mentioned elsewhere in the book, but depending on them is foolish. If you have limited space in your memory, fill it with the imperative ALWAYS CARRY A COMPASS IN THE BACKCOUNTRY, rather than the fact that the first star in Orion's belt rises in the east.)

The final item in your route-finding bag is simply your knowledge of elementary geometry. From it comes the method of *triangulation,* which establishes your position from the direction of two landmarks. Triangulation is used in many ways, one of which is shown in the illustration. The camp shown is within sight of two easily recognized mountains, Mount Hornswoggle and Mount Rocky. Taking bearings from camp, the backpacker determines that Hornswoggle is at azimuth 352° and Rocky is at 98°. Since there is nowhere else except the spot he is standing from which the two peaks will appear at these angles, the position is established. The backpacker can wander around as much as he likes within sight of Mt. H. and Mt. R., and he will always be able to find his way back to camp within the error limit of his compass.

If the backpacker wants to fix his position on a map, he can draw in these same bearings, using a protractor and straight edge (some compasses will serve both functions). Through the point on the map labeled "Mt. Hornswoggle" he draws a line 8° counterclockwise from due north and through Mount Rocky a line 98° clockwise. When these two lines are extended they will intersect at the campsite.

Positions are generally fixed through the use of several methods. If one is traveling along a river, a bearing on a distant landmark often gives a well-defined position along the river. The same is true of any other baseline combined with a bearing. Bearings in fact establish usable baselines. If only one landmark is visible from a distance a bearing on it may be used as a baseline to which one can always return after travel roughly perpendicular to it.

It should be apparent that proper use of a compass will allow almost complete freedom of travel in any area where there are a reasonable number of recognizable landmarks. These do not have to be continuously visible. One might confidently travel a considerable distance on a bearing with no visible landmarks, as long as he knew that Mount Hornswoggle and Mount Rocky would eventually show themselves.

The use of bearings as guides requires an understanding of their limitations, however. Any bearing includes some error. With precise surveying instruments this error is very small, but even a good pocket compass used carefully is not a precise surveying instrument. It is worthwhile to try to find how accurate your sightings are. With a very good compass, readings can be obtained which are accurate to within less than a degree, but most compasses and operators are less exact than this, and readings which are consistently within a couple of degrees of true are fairly good for most purposes. Such an error would amount to one-third of a mile in each ten. In country where landmarks are visible for long distances, you could depend on keeping within this error, but if new bearings were being taken every few hundred yards, a much larger error might accumulate.

Errors can be reduced in many ways. Multiple sights on one point will reduce an individual error on that sighting. Triangulation errors are reduced by sightings on three or more landmarks. Triangulation with only two landmarks is most accurate when the sightings are approximately at right angles. The reason for this is shown in the illustration. The best way to reduce errors in following courses or mapping your own is by periodically establishing new starting points and thus reducing errors to zero.

WALKING A COURSE

Suppose you are camped in a wooded area and you are planning to climb a mountain on a day trip away from camp. Finding your way to the mountain is simple, since it is frequently visible through the trees. The only route-finding problem will be in making your way back to camp, because there are no very good landmarks nearby. The mountain is seven or eight miles away, and if you simply take a bearing on it in the morning with the idea of reversing that course on the way home, you will probably miss the camp on the way back.

You can improve your chances of hitting the camp enormously by marking out a baseline perpendicular to your line of travel. From a standard red bandana I've torn enough strips to mark a line every hundred feet for a mile. Anyone coming back to the camp and getting within a half-mile of it would pass within fifty feet of one of these markers. With careful compass work, it is fairly easy to hit a mile-long target.

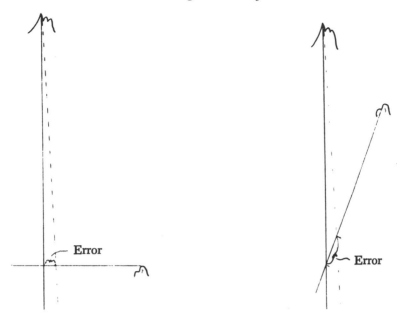

Triangulation errors from the same degree inaccuracy are much less when landmarks are roughly at right angles to one another.

An even shorter line would probably do, however, if the groups made frequent zeroing operations, an easy matter in most terrain. If, for example, a creek was crossed a couple of miles out of camp, it could be used as a new baseline. A cairn or some other marker is placed beside the creek, a new bearing taken on the mountain, and on the return the creek is crossed at the cairn, rather than wherever it is reached. When you get to the creek, you find the cairn before going on. By thus separating the journey into a number of legs, large errors are not generated. In areas with good visibility and much featureless ground, one can accomplish similar ends by traveling from one landmark to another or even building cairns.

There are times when there is no alternative but to stay on a compass bearing with no visible landmarks available. In heavy snowstorms, for example, or in fog, it may be impossible to see any appreciable distance. In such cases, if one is traveling with others, the last one in line holds the compass and directs travel. The line should be stretched out as far as visibility permits. The compass man then sights along the line at the front man, directing him whenever he begins to veer off course. On flat ground without obstacles an amazingly accurate course can be steered this way. You can even keep fairly good track of distances if you learn a pacing stride and find out what its length is. More commonly, one simply keeps track of the time he took to cover a distance over similar terrain before and estimates the distance covered by the time taken, with any needed allowances for wind, new snow, or other factors that may slow the pace.

Rounding obstacles is the usual source of error when a party is trying to walk on a particular bearing. The remedy is simply to make accurate

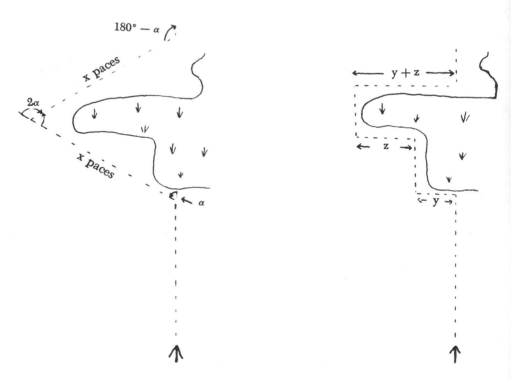

Using combinations of right angles greatly simplifies the problem of rounding obstacles. You need only keep track of a distance figure.

marches around the blockades, whenever this is possible. The illustration shows two ways to turn an intervening obstruction. The shortest way is to angle around as shown in the first example, but this requires some care in keeping the deviation and the return leg symmetrical. For foggy minds the right angle turns of the second example are simpler, and the central leg of such a course doesn't have to be paced off. For crossing ponds and creeks, one can simply take note of a landmark on either side, returning to the proper point on the opposite shore without the need for keeping track of turns along the way.

MARKING A TRAIL OR BASELINE

One occasion for marking out a line was mentioned above, where an artificial baseline was mentioned as a method for finding a camp on the return journey from a long hike. One may also wish to mark trails, junctions, or landmarks for a return journey. This is commonly done for you on maintained trails, especially in areas where the path would not show, above timberline in rocky areas, for example. On some occasions you may wish to follow suit by temporarily marking your own route or a few spots along it. While this is rarely necessary, there are occasions when it can save a great deal of time and trouble.

The traditional means for marking forest trails is by blazing trees. It is a good method for permanent routes, but it has no place in the methods of the backpacker marking a temporary passage. You should aim to leave as few signs of your visit as possible, rather than a record that will last for decades or centuries. Obviously the same comments apply to paint marks on rocks and similar defacements.

In open rocky places, ducks serve the backpacker's purposes well. A duck is simply a small cairn, a little pile of stones set in a prominent place. These show up remarkably well, and the only caution that the user may have to observe is to beware of old ducks set by others. In some places you may wish to make larger cairns and to travel from one to the other by compass bearings. Notes and bearings will help when there might be confusion in your mind on return after several days absence. Ducks and cairns are particularly useful in finding return routes down mountains topped by broad rocky plateaus but surrounded by steep sides.

In forests the best temporary markers are brightly colored plastic strips like those used by surveying parties. They can be quickly tied to twigs and are visible for long distances. I admit to writing this paragraph with trepidation, though, with visions of fluorescent orange forests dancing in my head. For God's sake take any of those things you put up back home with you. They are useful markers, but as trash left in the woods they are both obscene and everlasting. Pull them all down on your way back, and stow them carefully in pack or pocket. One substitute for plastic strips has been mentioned—a shredded bandana. You can think of others if the need arises.

WORRYING ABOUT YOUR COMPASS

There *are* places where the compass is unreliable, but they are really pretty uncommon, and "something wrong with the compass" usually translates accurately as "creeping panic and confusion in the operator." If you are planning on a trip in the regions near the magnetic pole where a normal compass is useless, you'll have to use specialized instruments, but elsewhere you are unlikely to run into areas of magnetic irregularity. Your map may make note of any that exist within its boundaries.

If you do have doubts about the compass, try to pick landmarks a couple of hundred yards apart. Take a bearing from one to the other, then walk to the second and take a back bearing. If the two bearings are 180° apart within the normal accuracy of your readings, there is no magnetic irregularity causing problems, and you can trust the compass readings.

In case you are having compass trouble, make sure you are not causing erratic readings with a piece of iron or steel on your person or somewhere else near the compass. Another possible source of error is a lock on the face or needle which is not releasing completely.

True magnetic irregularities rarely extend very far, so there is a good chance of leaving them behind by simply following a straight course in the direction of your best guess. A straight course can usually be maintained by lining up trees, rocks, or your companions. Back sights along the course can be taken periodically, and when they begin to agree, the compass can again be trusted. If you have paced off the distance traveled, this information can be combined with the backsight to give you a good estimate of the direction and distance of your blind march.

Remember, 99 per cent of all erratic compass readings are due to erratic readers. Trust your compass unless you have carefully tested reason not to; in a contest between your instinct and the compass, always assume your instinct is faulty.

NATURAL ROUTE FINDERS: STARS, MOSS, AND ALL THAT

There is a common assumption that route-finding ability starts with vast stores of information about moss growing on trees, shadow sticks, and such. It doesn't. Spend your time learning to use maps, compasses, and your own eyes, and when you've learned, spend some more time learning to use them better. Obviously, it is possible to use natural route finders to get around— people did it for millennia before the discovery of the magnetic compass, and the stars are still the most accurate directional indicators. For precise position finding when large distances are involved, specialized instruments for celestial navigation are needed. The reading list at the back of this book will tell you where to get more information on the use of transits, sextants, and similar instruments. Celestial route finding with a transit or sextant is a different matter from picking your way along by the sun and the tree rings, however.

The reason I am cynical about such methods is that they are all very unreliable. The first difficulty is remembering them. If you can't remember to bring a compass when you head for the woods, you'll probably forget which way to point your watch, especially in the panic that usually accompanies the realization that you're lost. Such methods are even more unreliable because all the good ones require fair weather, and in my experience the time you really need to know which way is north is when the visibility is poor. If you're in a comfortable enough position to wait out the snowstorm and watch for Polaris, chances are you don't really need to anyway.

There is a function for such knowledge in survival manuals, and some of it is nice to know, but although a prisoner of war will not have a compass and may need to follow the sun, you should have a compass and map that are unaffected by the cloud cover.

Without a compass or map one generally does have to use celestial bodies as guides. There may be land features which will give you directional hints, but they are of a local nature and are not likely to be of much

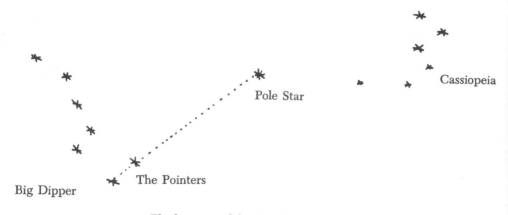

The location of the North Star, Polaris.

use unless you are quite familiar with the area. Such signs include water flow, topography, wind direction and signs of it like blown snow or plant growth, and pattern of vegetation growth.

The best celestial guide is the North Star, Polaris, which is never more than about one degree from true north. The drawing shows the common methods for locating it, but the more familiar with the night sky you become, the better able you will be to interpolate on evenings when clouds or hills obscure parts of the sky. Another possible guide at night is Orion. The star on the front of his belt is on the celestial equator, so it rises in the east and sets in the west. However, in the wilderness you are unlikely to see the rise over a true horizon, so this is a rough and unreliable guide. Those really familiar with the night sky can find other rough directional signals, but since travel at night is usually inadvisable, all you can do is set two sticks in the ground sighted at Polaris and wait until morning for some landmarks to appear.

Many methods of getting the direction from the sun have appeared from time to time. Most of them are useless, either because they are not reliable (the watch method, for example), or because they use up long periods of time, usually at a particular time of the day. The only method worthy of much attention is the one devised by Robert Owendoff.

THE OWENDOFF SHADOW-STICK METHOD

For the Owendoff method you need the shadow of some object with a steady point three or more feet above the ground. The shadow point should fall on a spot that is fairly level for a few inches around. A shadow can be that of a rock or tree (one not being moved by the wind) or one can be made by planting a stick in the ground. A stick around four feet long is a good size. Mark the point of the shadow with a twig, a matchstick, or something similar. Wait until the shadow has moved a couple of inches and mark its position again. A line between the two points you have just marked will run roughly east-west with the east end at the second mark.

Like all rough shadow methods, the Owendoff technique is subject to considerable error, but it will give an approximate direction fairly quickly. It is most accurate around noon and least accurate around sunrise and sunset. It is accurate all day around the spring and fall equinoxes, while maximum error is reached on the summer and winter solstices. If you're going to get lost and break your compass on a sunny day, make sure to pick one of the equinoxes. Owendoff also points out (Robert S. Owendoff, *Better Ways of Pathfinding*) that his method has the advantage that the errors in it will cancel out to zero through the day, a characteristic not possessed by some other methods.

In using any celestial method, try to set your course with landmarks that will carry you in a straight line for good distances between checks. Line up two trees along the course, for example, and before you reach the nearer one pick another along the same line.

TRIANGULATION WITHOUT A COMPASS

If you think a little about the method of triangulation, you will realize that it does not depend on a compass for accuracy. If a compass is used to orient the map, then only two landmarks are needed to determine your position. If you have no compass you need three landmarks. I think the easiest method is by using a piece of tracing paper, which I carry with my map. The tracing paper is laid on a flat spot from which three landmarks are visible. I then take sights using needles from the repair kit, but matchsticks, pine needles, or twigs will do. One needle is stuck at approximately the center of the paper. Another is lined up between the first needle and a landmark and stuck in the margin of the paper. A line is drawn between the two needles. The outside needle is taken out, and without moving the paper it is lined up with the center needle and the second landmark. A second line is drawn, and then the procedure is repeated for the third landmark. The paper now has three lines on it, intersecting near the center of the paper where the central needle was.

The tracing paper can now be laid on the map and moved around until each of the three lines passes through the landmark it represents. (The landmarks will not be at any particular distance along the position lines.) There is only one position that this will occur, when the intersection rests over your location on the map.

The tracing paper method can be used even if you are not certain which landmarks you see, providing you have some notion of where you are. The paper can be moved around to test different combinations. When you find one that seems to fit, you can orient the map with one landmark and test the hypothetical position against the terrain. More than three landmarks can be used when they are available.

GENERAL

Finding your way in the wilderness, at least for reasonable distances in regions mapped by modern methods, isn't really very difficult. Exploration in remote areas where maps are inadequate is another matter, but even that shouldn't intimidate anyone who has come to feel at home in wild places.

The fundamentals in getting around beyond the well-marked trails are the training of your own powers of observation, learning to write important things down, developing skill at reading maps, and learning to use a compass properly. With those skills, you'll have little difficulty in meeting emergencies. The likelihood of breaking your compass at the same time that you can't get out using a map alone is pretty small. Besides, the more experience you get in guiding yourself around through the woods, with and without trails, the fewer the occasions will be when you don't know just where you are. Personally, I get lost a lot, but somehow it always happens on the roads leading to the trailhead rather than in the paths and gullies beyond.

Emergencies and   15
Survival Techniques

There is an emphasis throughout this book on intelligent preparation as the best way to avoid serious trouble in the wilderness. This readiness is more a state of mind than a particular piece of equipment or safety precaution taken in advance. Wilderness travel is an activity that depends for its enjoyment and safety on the self-reliance of the people or person doing it. Equipment of a particular kind may be necessary or desirable, but it won't make you safe. The determined idiot can manage to get hurt anywhere, and the wilderness will provide him with plenty of opportunity for getting lost, breaking a leg, or having his strength sapped by weather conditions.

STAYING OUT OF TROUBLE

The way to stay out of trouble in the backcountry is to get to know yourself and the wilderness you are traveling and then to confine your travel to situations you can handle. When you won't know what you're getting into, make your decisions in a conservative frame of mind. In the mountains, don't try to explore a long and possibly impassable route when you don't have adequate food and clothing. In the desert, don't push on to an uncertain waterhole when you are carrying a minimal supply of water. In the woods, don't take strong chances of breaking a leg when you are a long way from help.

It would be pointless to catalogue a great list of possible mistakes that one can make in the woods; they are numberless, anyhow. Following good camping and hiking practices will keep you out of most trouble. If you are to avoid getting lost, you need to use good route-finding methods. Adequate clothing and shelter will protect you from the weather, while poorly chosen equipment will not. If you don't take enough food, you may expect to get hungry.

SOLO TRAVEL

The rule that one should "Never travel alone!" has been written many times. I can't very well repeat it because I frequently travel in the wilderness alone. Personally, I think it is a silly rule. It is important to recognize the element of truth in it, however. Solo travel away from the beaten path requires far more care than trips with other people. The lone traveler must rely on his own resources without help for an extended period. This self-reliance can be very exhilarating, but it can also be burdensome.

Most of the North American wilderness is quite hospitable in temperate seasons. If you are traveling with a friend and you slip and break your leg, the situation isn't usually serious. He can help you to get comfortable and fetch whatever you might need during his absence, and then he can go out for help. Your situation when you are alone is quite a bit more serious. You have to splint the leg yourself and to manage water, food, and shelter until a search party comes on you or until your leg has knit well enough to allow you to get out.

If you think a little about situations like this, you will realize that the solo traveler often has to carry far more equipment and supplies than a member of a large party. He must not only take all his own basic equipment, he must also carry larger reserves. This is particularly true when the environment is inhospitable—in winter, in the desert, on high mountains.

In referring to solo travel here, I'm talking about trips into true wilderness, on infrequently traveled paths, or wandering out of season. You don't need to take company on popular trails in the summer to have the advantages and disadvantages of other people. The John Muir or the Appalachian Trails on an August weekend are well enough traveled so that you would have help in short order, and thus you would not need to apply more caution than if you were traveling in a group. The equivalency applies only as long as you are on the traveled trail, though. A side trip of a couple of miles changes the picture completely.

Traveling by yourself in the backcountry can provide some of your most memorable wilderness experiences, but reasonable safety requires that you be aware of the special dangers of being alone. You have to use more care in planning trips and choosing equipment and provisions. You must leave wider safety margins. Finally, you should pay particular attention to the advisability of leaving word of your plans with someone in case of accident, a subject discussed in more detail later in the chapter.

EMERGENCIES

One thing that every sensible wilderness lover has to realize is that no matter what precautions are taken, the possibilities of an accident always exist. Life in the wilds is at least as uncertain as it is elsewhere. That is the reason for taking various precautions to ensure that one is fairly well prepared for contingencies. The best mountaineer can be caught by a storm and the best woodsman can slip and break a leg.

One of the implications of the discussion at the beginning of the chapter was that it is generally possible to prevent emergencies by avoiding accidents. It is equally important, though, to prevent difficulties and accidents from becoming emergencies. Getting lost is not an emergency. Many outdoorsmen have become temporarily lost. At worst, the result is a chilly night and a growling stomach, and in return, the lost man has received a few good lessons. Getting lost only creates an emergency when combined with other problems: panic, accidents, and so on. The additional ingredients which create the emergency usually result from the actions of the people in trouble.

The one essential ingredient in every formula for dealing with difficulties in the backcountry is a cool head. If you keep your wits there is rarely a serious problem and almost never an insurmountable one. If you lose your good sense, you can get into real trouble in a woodlot. A second very useful quality for dealing with difficulties is a sense of humor. If you can sit down and have a good laugh (not to be confused with an hysterical giggle) at yourself for getting into your predicament, you have practically guaranteed that you will follow a sensible procedure in getting out of it.

An evaluation of your situation is important if you want to follow a sensible course, and that evaluation has to include all the information you have, including that about yourself—you are, after all, the most important ingredient. The need for haste is rare in the wilderness, whether in emergencies or not. Timetables are usually determined more by when you have to be back at the office than they are by your surroundings, and when real problems arise they have the virtue of enabling you to forget external irrelevancies. In difficulty in the wilds careful consideration is usually far more valuable than a thirty-minute head start.

People usually fear their problem to be much greater than it actually is. The body will stand a good deal more punishment than its owner generally thinks, and a bit of hunger, cold, or thirst, uncomfortable as it may be, hardly makes an emergency by itself. Even injuries are not always particularly serious. A broken arm can be set just as well in five or six days as tomorrow, providing its owner acts sensibly and avoids breaking a leg in his panic to get out.

The other side of the coin shows itself in the underestimation of certain kinds of trouble. Wet clothing in cold weather is a more serious problem than many others which appear much more alarming. A deep snowfall can reduce travel without skis or snowshoes to a tenth or twentieth of the speed of the party before its occurrence. Careful evaluation is the key to getting out of trouble in the wilds. Panic and the calm bred of ignorance are the main pitfalls to avoid.

SURVIVAL

Remember that whenever you get in trouble in the woods, survival is not usually the issue at hand. You can live and function for quite a while in most wildernesses with adequate clothing, even if you are completely out of food. With care you can even last for some time without water.

In either case, though, you cannot afford to squander your body's reserves of food, heat, and water. If you spend the night out, don't get cold and wet when you can easily build shelter and a fire. If you are in the des-

Survival depends a great deal on the equipment you carry with you. A waterproof cagoule like this covers the whole body with the knees drawn up. It can be a lifesaver in wet, cold conditions.

269

ert without water, travel when the sun is down to conserve your body's moisture. Such advice follows from common sense, but don't forget to use yours when you need it.

The problem in most emergencies in the backcountry is getting out, not surviving for months at a time in the same place. Most of the survival literature is designed for the military and has only slight relevance to the problems faced by the outdoorsman in trouble. You will not have your parachute or the fuselage of your plane handy. It will do you little good in British Columbia to know which part of a cashew to eat, and hopefully enemy troops will not be searching you out. Thus while it is understandable that an escaping prisoner of war will not have a compass handy, there is certainly no reason why you shouldn't. The principles of travel and survival in the wilderness in case of trouble are pretty much the same as they are when you're just having a good time.

A word about finding food is in order here, but I am not going to give a list of drawings and designs for snares, as I think they would be a waste of time. Living off the land is a fascinating technique to learn, but I don't believe that it has much to do with the survival problems faced by the average wilderness traveler in trouble. If you're traveling for months at a time in the far reaches of the north woods and you're living off the land, fine. Just keep doing it. Similarly, if you have fishing equipment along and your trip out from a fine chain of lakes is slowed by a sprained ankle, you would be a fool not to keep on fishing.

The methods for finding and getting hold of wild food in a particular kind of country usually require detailed local knowledge. You may learn every edible plant in Pennsylvania, but the knowledge will do you no good if you are stranded in the mountains of Colorado. The study of edible plants is worthwhile, but you should start with a guide for the region where you live, and not expect to apply the same guide to a different region.

The advice to try a little of an unfamiliar plant has been frequently repeated. If your problem is truly that you are starving, this might be wise, but under most circumstances I think it would be stupid. There are several plants in North America besides mushrooms which are highly poisonous even in small quantities and there are many others which can produce quite disagreeable effects. Aside from the possibility of killing yourself, the last thing you need when you are trying to walk out of the wilderness is an energy-depleting digestive upset. If you find a patch of raspberries, that is dandy, but I think that experimenting with unfamiliar plants is one of the more foolish courses of action in the emergencies you are likely to encounter. If you want to learn how to live off the land in your area, you had better get some plant guides and start learning.

Animal life, including insects, is generally safer and more nutritious than plant food for the neophyte suddenly thrown out on his own, providing he avoids sick animals. He generally won't have much trouble avoiding them, however, because they will avoid him. You may be able to net fish, snare rabbits, and beat porcupines over the head with clubs, but you may not. If it's only a forty-mile walk out, you'd probably be better off using your energy to do that. The most likely source of concentrated food is the insect population, but even that depends very much on location.

It has always seemed to me that the biggest problem with living-off-the-land techniques as an answer to wilderness emergencies is that real trouble generally occurs when they are not very applicable. If I am caught by a deep early snow, I am not going to waste my energy trying to dig out some miner's lettuce. Blizzard conditions are a time to hole up, not to go out tracking rabbits that are sensibly curled up at home. At the times and places where food is relatively simple to scrounge up, there is rarely any real need to do so. When the woods are friendly and the food is flitting around, you aren't likely to have an emergency. When the wind is howling and the sleet is blowing and freezing and you slip and break your hip on the icy rockfield you're crossing, *then* you have an emergency, and also more important and useful things to do than setting snares. That is the time for which I carry emergency food.

INJURIES

First aid is discussed in another chapter, but some of the difficulties surrounding an injury will be considered here. Once the necessary first aid has been given, one is faced with the question of what to do next. Is the injured person well enough to walk out with or without help? Will he be well enough tomorrow or the next day?

There is no way to set up a formula to deal with the problems created by an injury, but some general principles can be mentioned. Complicating factors need to be taken into account, as do the consequences that can be expected from the delay in obtaining medical care for the injured person. The effects of shock and cold in particular must be anticipated. In a wilderness situation, where blood transfusions and warm rooms are not readily available, vigorous treatment to prevent shock and body chilling have to be started as soon as possible.

Once first aid has been given and the victim made as comfortable as possible, the problem of obtaining help or evacuation arises. With a large group the problem is greatly simplified. The group may be large enough to evacuate the victim without outside help. This should be done in an orderly fashion, avoiding any unseemly haste that is not required by the condition of the victim.

Smaller groups are placed in a more difficult position. The number of people required to carry an injured man out should not be underestimated, although it will vary with the situation. Sending for additional help or waiting a few days until the victim is well enough to aid in his own retreat should be considered.

In case of trouble on the way out, two people should be sent out wherever possible. In their haste they must take especial care that they can find their way back and that they do not become totally exhausted. They will need to bring back help besides reaching it. A man going out for assistance is also obviously not doing his injured companion any good by breaking his own leg. Will power needs to be exercised to prevent carelessness during emergencies. More care is needed, not less.

With a party of three, one of whom is severely injured, obviously one person goes for help, while the other stays with the victim. The most difficult decisions must be made by the person whose single companion has been badly hurt: whether to stay and nurse the victim or go for help—the decision must be made on the basis of whatever knowledge of the situation he has. It may be possible to get food, water, and fuel in sufficient quantities for the person to take care of himself if he is not too badly hurt; the judgment has to be made on the spot.

Fortunately, the kinds of injuries that result in such dilemmas are rare in the backcountry. A sprained ankle, broken leg, or flesh wound would be far more likely. Wounds heal themselves if they are kept clean, and infecting bacteria are much rarer in the wilds than in civilization. A victim of a broken leg will usually be able to take care of himself while waiting for help, once the leg is splinted and supplies are gathered and conveniently placed.

GETTING LOST

The first thing to think about when you find you are lost is that this state is always only relative. You will invariably know *something* about where you are. If you sit down and think about it, you will probably find that you know a lot more than you first realized. Narrow your position down as much as possible, and figure out any information you have about landmarks and boundaries and watersheds in the area in which you are lost. Very often the idea of following water out works very well, though following the *watershed* would be a better way of putting it. This is because in many kinds of country following the ridgelines will get you out much faster than fighting along the creek bottoms. In any case, don't blindly follow either one; think about the area you are lost in first.

You are unlikely to travel very far between the time you feel you know where you are and the time you decide you are lost. Figure out a systematic way to return to your position. Use your map and compass if you have

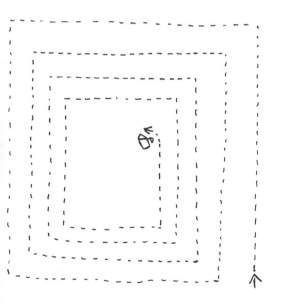

A search pattern which can be used if you are near camp but visibility is poor. Make the initial square much larger than you think necessary, so that you can be sure the perimeter surrounds your camp. Make the reduction in size on each sweep small enough so that you won't miss the camp.

them. Do not go running back trying to find a familiar place, which will probably just leave you more confused. You are almost certain to have enough information to find your way back—*if* you proceed systematically and avoid attempted shortcuts. If you are near your camp in forest or similar terrain, follow a search pattern like that shown in the diagram.

Don't guess where you are or what direction you should go and then gamble heavily on that guess. Allow yourself the widest possible latitude for error, and then follow a plan that allows for it. Don't thrash around for two days looking for a trail when you are not sure you're even in the right valley. Instead, head for a road that you can't miss, and then follow it out.

Remember that the general principles of route finding are the same whether you are lost or not. Keep a record of your bearings on the way out, so that you won't get more confused. Without a compass, you can still maintain a straight line of travel by lining up two objects at different distances. Find a third object on the same line before you reach the first.

WALKING OUT

If you get lost, lose your equipment, run out of supplies, or have some similar crisis, don't immediately start working up images of the Donner Party trapped by the great blizzard in the Sierras. The North American wilderness is generally a fairly friendly place. In the woods, you can build a fire every night and stay reasonably comfortable even without food for a few days. You can walk a long way in that time if you keep your wits about you. In really remote areas, you could start eating grubs, lizards, frogs, or something else easy to trap, and keep going for the better part of the summer. The point is simply that in most wilderness in temperate seasons, a sensible person will always manage to get out—a little the worse (or better) for wear, perhaps, but he will get out.

In difficult environments and seasons you may have to be a little more clever. If you are lost in the desert and you find a nice waterhole, don't take a drink and wander on—at least until you have planned out a good course of action. If you leave it, mark your trail back. In winter with a broken ski or snowshoe in a storm, dig yourself a snowhole for a shelter, and then stay where it's warm while the storm blows over and you fix your transportation. A good shelter in a bad mountain storm is the place to stay while the weather is bad, unless you're well equipped for anything. In all these cases, remember that your body has a good reserve supply of essentials, but they can be depleted in a hurry by the weather. If you can outlast the elements, do so rather than trying to challenge them at their worst. When you are in difficulty don't try to fight nature; you will lose. In the desert, for example, if your water container is too small and you get dehydrated making it to your waterhole, spend a day there tanking up and allowing your body to recover before you try to make another leg of your journey.

All this desperate-situation advice is quite unnecessary for the well-prepared wilderness traveler under most circumstances. Follow normal safety rules in preparing your trips, and you are unlikely to run into such problems. Most such survival crises don't happen to backpackers but to mechanized travelers when their machines break down.

LEAVING WORD WHEN YOU GO IN

It is only prudent and courteous when you head for the backcountry to leave word with some responsible person. Tell him where you are going, side trips you might make, when you plan to be out, and when to assume you are in trouble. This precaution should not be ignored unless your passing would never be noticed. If your wife or your job is expecting you on Tuesday, they will let someone know when you don't get back. If your car is left sitting by the trailhead, someone will eventually come looking. Be reasonable enough to let them know where to look, so that they won't have an army searching an area of hundreds of square miles. Also, as long as they're going to be looking anyway, why not give them a chance to find you in a day or two, instead of your body a month later?

Backpackers tend to feel naturally reluctant about cramping themselves with registration systems, but the proper response is to improve the methods rather than ignore them and provoke responsible authorities into tightening up. Personally, I think there is a lot to be said in favor of removing the responsibility for rescues from the shoulders of the Park Service, the Forest Service, and similar administrators—it too often tempts them into promulgating books full of rules, and every citizen over the age of consent ought to have the right to be a fool and get killed if he wants to. However, as long as administrators are expected by the public to mount searches and rescue efforts, it behooves those of us who want to roam to make those rescues as inexpensive as possible. The alternative is idiotic regulation like that in Grand Teton National Park, where travel alone off the trails is illegal.

A solo traveler especially, might want someone to know where to pick him up in case he should happen to break a leg. If you know that a friend will come looking when you're not back on Tuesday, you can lie back and relax and eat your spare food while you wait. Allow enough leeway in your schedule to take care of unforseen delays, and be sure to mention all possible changes in plans. Don't forget that if you change your mind at the trailhead, all you have to do is leave a note with the car.

Besides calling friends or family to leave word, there are various formal systems of reporting. The oldest is to leave a note on your automobile. Many wilderness areas have registration systems along the trail, but these don't allow for much detail and they aren't usually checked in the off seasons. So leave word somewhere else, too. Registration with the rangers is a common system, especially in the national parks, and this is one of the methods which arouses the most opposition among climbers and backpackers, creating many unfortunate hostilities and misunderstandings. In remote areas, leave word with law-enforcement officers or a storekeeper in the last town you pass.

Objectionable registration systems need to be changed, but their virtues and purpose in aiding rescues ought to be mentioned here. Try to cooperate with the rangers where registration systems exist, and if you ignore them, at least leave word with a friend who can tell someone where you went in case you get hurt. Some registration systems also have the admirable purpose of preventing excessive pressure on delicate areas. Cooperate, please!

One of the best systems going is the kind operated by the Rocky Mountain Rescue Group in Boulder, Colorado. There is a phone number with which one can register at any time of the day or night. This is cheap, since it can use a recording, and it doesn't require anyone to drive a hundred miles out of their way to register somewhere. You just call the number when you wake up at four in the morning and decide to climb a mountain, and then you call back when you return. It is particularly worthwhile in a town where there are many college students or out-of-town visitors who don't have any friends to leave word with.

However you leave word of your intentions, don't forget to let whoever was responsible know when you are out. Every rescue group remembers a few thoughtless individuals who got back from the mountains, forgot to let Aunt Tillie know they had come home, and took off for a wild weekend in Mexico with six-dozen searchers and four helicopters combing the hills in blowing sleet.

EMERGENCY SUPPLIES

The equipment and provisions which you will need in case of an emergency vary with the sort of trip you are taking, its remoteness, the kind of country, and the season. Potable water is plentiful in some places, but not in others. Low temperatures that might be expected will obviously influence your choice of basic and extra clothing. Even on day hikes, however, there are essentials you should never travel without:

    First-aid kit
    Pocket knife
    Matches in waterproof container and candle or other fire-starter
    Compass
    Map
    Flashlight
    Extra food
    Windtight parka
    Rain gear where needed
    Water bottle(s)
    Water-purification tablets where needed

Each person will add his own essentials: a whistle for signaling, parachute cord for many purposes, and so on. I include some of these in my first-aid kit. A generous emergency supply of matches should be carried separately and must be left untouched by daily needs. Even if you're a great fire builder, wet and windy weather combined with cold hands can use a lot of matches getting a flame going. Special equipment like skis may require special repair items, and these are obviously essential for emergencies. Extra food should be of a type which can be eaten uncooked if necessary. A piece of steel wool makes very good kindling. Use it well—it only goes once.

In some places—the mountains, for example—sunglasses and sunburn preventatives rank as essential, since snow blindness or serious sunburn may result from forgetting them. A suitable hat is vital in the desert, and extra clothes are important survival items whenever the weather may turn cold.

First Aid and Emergency Medicine 16

It is a cliché that the best cure for accidents is prevention, but it is true nevertheless. I don't happen to believe in safety at any cost, but anyone who does a lot of traveling in the wilderness will take his risks with some premeditation rather than out of sheer ignorance. Five days travel from the road is a long way from help.

There isn't much reason to be frightened about wilderness travel. The hazards to a healthy person in most types of terrain are pretty minimal. The point is simply that self-reliance applies to medical problems as well as other aspects of life when you are in the backcountry. The more that you and your companions know about first aid and subsequent care the better off you will be. You may never have to use what you know, or the use may be confined to patching up the victims of auto accidents while you are driving to and from the hills. But you'll never regret any time you invest in learning first aid.

PHYSICAL CONDITION

Sensible backpacking requires that you have some idea of what shape you are in before you start. A checkup by a doctor from time to time is a good idea, and it is mandatory for older people who are taking up backpacking after a long sedentary period. A remote wilderness peak is not the place to find out that you have a heart condition. If you have any unusual problems which require special attention or drugs, it is important to carry whatever you might need on the trip. It is also essential that your companions know about your condition and what to do in case of difficulties. A diabetic, for example, needs to pay special attention to his diet on a strenuous trip, and it is important that his companions be able to recognize and treat coma and insulin shock. Someone allergic to bee stings might have to carry adrenalin, and again his companions should know what to do in an emergency.

There is very little information in this chapter on the treatment of problems which might arise from a preexisting condition that would have been detected in a physical examination. Ask your doctor, and tell the other members of your party anything they might need to know. With limited space, it's impossible to discuss all the possible accidental injuries that might arise in the woods with normal, healthy people. While at the doctor's you should get a tetanus booster. Trails traveled by animals are full of the microorganisms that cause tetanus.

I strongly recommend that anyone interested in wilderness travel learn as much first aid as possible. Take the Red Cross courses, and check with any mountaineering clubs in your area to see if they give advanced courses beyond what the Red Cross teaches. The Seattle Mountaineers give a particularly outstanding course, and the textbook for it, *Medicine for Mountaineering*, edited by James A. Wilkerson, is excellent.

First aid is what you do under normal circumstances until the doctor comes. Since no layman has enough training to understand all he should about injuries, the Red Cross courses wisely limit themselves to the care that would be advisable under the assumption that a doctor will be available in a short time. Obviously, this is not the case if you are thirty or forty hard miles from the nearest road. Under such conditions, you must at the very least plan on nursing a seriously injured person for some time.

CARING FOR AN INJURED PERSON

Some general principles apply to the care of anyone who is sick or injured. The first is to think. Obvious as this may seem from the vantage point of an easy chair, it often takes a good deal of self-discipline in an actual accident situation. The first thing you have to do is to evaluate the situation, which may take a matter of an hour or a few seconds. In case of severe persisting danger, the first thing you might have to do is to get yourself and the victim to a safe place. Such situations are rare, and it is never good to move an injured person before examining him carefully. But if he has been hit on the head with a rock you will do him no good by getting knocked on the skull yourself.

Aside from dangerous positions, the thing to check first is the possible presence of one of the medical emergency cases: severe bleeding, cessation of breathing, or poisoning. The last is unlikely in wilderness circumstances, although it happens. The first two are quite possible, and they require immediate action on your part—stopping the bleeding and giving artificial respiration if breathing has stopped.

Having taken care of the emergency cases and removed yourself and your victim from imminent danger of lightning strikes, drowning, or falling off cliffs, take a few minutes to really take stock of the situation. There are a lot of things you are going to have to do, and your patient will be better off if you take time to plan them. You have to:

1. Thoroughly examine the injured person to find out what is wrong, as best you can.
2. Get help, send someone else for it, or decide that circumstances make this unnecessary or impractical.
3. Give whatever first aid is necessary to the injured person, splinting broken bones and so forth.
4. Give supportive care to the injured person, and perhaps move him to a better spot, especially if the weather is cold or stormy.
5. Talk to the victim, who is presumably your friend; calming him and comforting him is as important as taking care of physical injuries.
6. Write down all pertinent information, including what happened, what you found, what you did, and when each occurred. The sequence may be very important to the diagnosis of a doctor taking over. Don't rely on memory.

Deciding on the order of these steps, priorities, and thoroughness is a matter of judgment and the particular situation, but make sure you exercise that judgment rather than simply go on at random. If you are dealing with a serious injury but have plenty of people, and help is a couple of hours down the trail, you should have a couple of people on their way as soon as you've taken care of the hurry cases. On the other hand, if there is only one other healthy person and help is a long way off, you may need his assistance in moving the victim and getting him into a shelter before he goes for help. Variations are infinite, and you are bound to make mistakes. The important thing is to think everything out before you go off half-cocked and make the situation worse. Force yourself to be cool and methodical.

TRAUMATIC INJURIES

Most people engaged in backpacking are fairly healthy, whether they are young or old. If someone does get suddenly sick, it is usually from the kind of infectious diseases that don't flourish in the wilderness. After one has walked into the woods for a week, any medical problems that arise will probably be from falling off a cliff, being hit on the head by a branch, cutting oneself with an ax, or something similar. Such injuries are *traumatic* injuries, those which result from some violence done to the body.

Traumatic injuries are also the cause of the major first-aid *emergency*, severe bleeding. Blood is essential to the body's functioning, it is under a good deal of pressure as it leaves the heart, and there is a limited amount of the stuff in the body. It follows that SEVERE BLEEDING MUST BE STOPPED RIGHT AWAY. Get something on the wound and apply pressure with your hand. Sterile dressings are ideal, but they are rarely at hand, and stopping the bleeding immediately is more important than sterility, so grab anything, slap it on the wound, and clamp down. Then hang onto it, and the bleeding will stop. *Don't peek.* Maintain the pressure without trying to look for around fifteen minutes after the major bleeding stops. Otherwise you will dislodge the clot that has been forming, and you'll have to start all over.

There are a lot of suggested ways to tell the difference between venous and arterial bleeding, but direct pressure is the way to stop either one, so if you are in doubt, don't worry about it, just put pressure on the wound. The essential difference is clear: arterial pressure is much greater.

An arterial wound spurts hard, and you have to press hard to stop it. It may squirt a considerable distance with each beat of the heart. Venous bleeding is slower, steadier, under much less pressure, and much easier to stop.

Remember that *the treatment for bleeding is direct pressure with whatever is immediately at hand.* Elevation of an arm or a leg will be of some additional help. Unless you know the pressure points from lots of practice, don't worry about them; you'll just waste time. Everyone has learned something about tourniquets somewhere. Don't use them. The need for them is rare, and they are very dangerous. It is unlikely that you would ever have to use one.

While you are holding onto that wound, or after you have found that there isn't any severe bleeding, you can start thinking about the other things that are or might be wrong with your friend. Traumatic injuries include burns, wounds, broken bones and injuries to the joints, and various kinds of internal injuries. If you are hurt, or if someone you are backpacking with is hurt, you probably already know a lot about what happened, so you should be able to tell what sorts of injuries are likely. Have a talk with your friend and see what he can tell about what happened and what is the matter. Even if he is unconscious, you know a lot. If he fell off a cliff and he isn't conscious, chances are pretty good that he hit his head.

SHOCK

One of the common characteristics of traumatic injuries is shock. Basically, traumatic shock results from a loss of blood pressure, and you can expect some shock with any injury. It is vitally important that you treat for shock from the very beginning. Shock is no joke—it is what kills most people who die from accidents. In a wilderness situation rapid treatment is even more important than on a city street, because no blood transfusions are going to be available an hour later. Shock is the kind of disorder that keeps building and feeding on its own symptoms, so you have to stop it as soon as you can.

Since there is a drop in blood pressure with shock, it stands to reason that not as much blood will get up to the brain of a standing person. One way or another, he is quite likely to go down, so you should get him to lie down before he falls over and hits his head in the bargain. Feet can be

283

raised slightly unless you have reason to suspect head or internal injuries. Keep the victim lying down.

Again, if blood pressure is lowered, you can expect that circulation is going to be impaired and that he is going to have a hard time keeping warm. You have to help him to retain his body heat. How vigorous the treatment should be depends on conditions. If it is a pleasant temperature out, just cover your friend with a couple of sweaters, but if there is snow on the ground and a cold wind is blowing, you may have to get into a sleeping bag with him inside a tent. You don't want to make him hot and sweaty, but it is vital that you keep him from getting chilled. A person in shock is likely to be thirsty. He has usually lost blood or fluid from the blood, and his body needs to replace it. If your friend is conscious, let him have sips of water or (better) warm bouillon or soup. If you use water, put a pinch of salt in each cup. Don't give any liquids orally to an unconscious or semiconscious person, who may inhale them. Also avoid giving liquids to anyone who is nauseated (common in shock) or if you suspect internal injuries. If the liquid makes him throw up, he will lose more than he has gained.

Finally, psychological factors are very important in shock. If your friend is really hurt, he isn't going to be too happy. It is up to you to reassure him and give him confidence by talking to him and handling the situation calmly and well. Don't make tactless comments which will make things worse, and don't let anyone else do so. If you have a hysterical type in the company, get him away from the injured person. On the other hand, don't make inane comments to the victim like "Everything is okay." He may be woozy, but he knows everything is not okay. Tell him what you're doing, and be sensibly optimistic.

Symptoms of shock include general pallor, cold skin, sweating when the person isn't hot, fainting, a panicky, alarmed, incoherent state of mind, listlessness, dilated pupils, and a weak, thready pulse. However, don't wait for symptoms to appear. Treat for shock in the case of any traumatic injury.

BURNS

Burns other than minor ones are not very common in the wilderness, but they do happen. Treatment is simple, although the injury is not. Minor burns can be immersed in cold water until they feel more comfortable, and then bandaged. With serious burns, expect severe shock and treat for it. Burns are very painful—and this alone can induce shock—and fluids from the blood are lost in quantity through the damaged cell walls. The burn should be covered with a sterile dressing, and the victim should be gotten to medical care as soon as possible.

WOUNDS

Wounds are the most common sort of injury in the woods. The major danger is bleeding, which has already been discussed. Some bleeding is a good thing. With puncture wounds, it may be a good idea to induce bleeding to clean the wound out, particularly if the puncture is from some object that may have come in contact with animal dung.

Once the bleeding has been stopped and the victim is under care for shock, you have to worry about infection. This is one area where the wilderness has good advantages. Harmful bacteria are considerably less common than they are back home, but they are around nonetheless. What you actually do will depend on the wound. The best first step is probably to wash your hands well. If the wound is dirty, wash it too. The body can handle a certain number of outside bacteria, but large quantities of germs are carried in with dirt, and the dirt particles are irritants in themselves. Get the wound clean as soon as possible. There is some natural anesthesia at the beginning, and cleaning will hurt more later. Once the wound is clean, cover it with a clean sterile dressing and fasten that with tape or bandages. If you don't have a sterile dressing in the first-aid kit, make one from the cleanest lint-free cloth you have. You can sterilize it by boiling or singeing it in a flame for a while. Don't get a lot of fancy ideas about stitching up the wound. That is a good way to seal in pockets of infection, causing them to spread. The wound will heal faster if it is stitched and *if* there is no infection, but it will heal more surely if it is left open and covered with a dressing.

BROKEN BONES

Besides wounds, broken bones, sprains, and other joint injuries are the most likely medical problems in the backcountry. First aid is treatment for shock and immobilization of the injury. If a bone is broken completely the rigidity of the limb has been destroyed, and motion will cause the jagged ends of the bones to injure the surrounding tissue. A splint should hold the limb rigid so that this can't occur. There are many bones and joints in the body and many kinds of injuries that can occur. A few general rules apply.

Some fractures are open, that is, the skin has been broken either by the end of the broken bone or by the impact that caused the break. In either case infection is a strong possibility. You should treat the wound like any other wound, stopping any bleeding, cleaning, and applying a sterile dressing. At the same time, however, you should recognize that this is an especially dangerous wound, since an infection could involve the bone, and bone infections are dangerous. If the bone end is protruding, it is not generally advisable to pull the bone back under the skin, but this will be necessary if you can't get the person out within a day or two. Clean a protruding bone end off with a sterile pad and Phisohex or Zepharin. Once the wound is dressed, a compound fracture should be splinted like other fractures.

While splinting a fracture, move the affected part as little as possible. Don't try to set it—that's what doctors get paid for, and they can do it just as well next week if you don't get out today. You may have to straighten a limb to splint it. Do the moving gently and slowly, with some tension on the end of the limb. It will hurt the victim, but use his pain as a guide to whether you are doing more damage. Extreme pain means you're injuring tissue. Finding splints where you are may require some imagination on your part, but it usually isn't too hard. The basic principle is to immobilize the joints above and below the injury, so that the fracture won't be moved around. Other parts of the body can be used as splints. A leg can be splinted to the other leg, a finger to another finger, the arm to the upper part of the body, with the upper arm along the side and the forearm and hand across the chest—the same position as in pledging allegiance to the flag. You can use sticks, air mattresses, ski poles, and pack frames for splints. Get the limb in a position that is fairly comfortable for the victim. His pain is your best guide to whether the bone end is pressing somewhere it shouldn't. Try to splint things in their normal positions of rest. Fingers curve and elbows and knees are slightly bent, not straight. If you splint to another part of the body, have some cloth preventing two layers of skin from touching, and pad joints where they press together—knees, ankles, finger joints.

Severe sprains and joint injuries should be treated like fractures. They may be breaks, and you can't tell. The general rule is to treat any suspected fracture as though it were one. Dislocations should generally be treated the same way. Fingers and shoulders are the most common. Fingers can just be splinted and left alone. A dislocated shoulder may need treatment. If a doctor can be reached by hiking on out, just put the injured arm in a sling and walk. If you won't get out for a few days and the circulation to the hand is impaired, you may have to do something to prevent damage to the limb. Have the victim lie down, and sit down on his injured side facing him. Take off one of your boots, put your foot in his armpit, and pull on the arm. Just pull steadily, and look at the scenery or something. You have to overcome his muscle spasm. This won't occur until *his* muscle gets tired, and that won't occur until *your* muscles get tired. Keep pulling, and after around ten or twenty minutes his joint will pop back in and he'll heave a sigh of relief. Then put on the sling. Don't ever try to reduce a fracture like this unless you have to. A bone can be chipped or a nerve pinched.

Whenever you are applying a splint, allow for adjustments of the ties or tape in case of swelling. Swelling will normally occur after a fracture, and you don't want circulation to be cut off. If possible, you should be able to get at the toes or fingers occasionally to check for circulation problems.

Fractures of the spinal column are very special cases. The spinal cord runs down the middle of the spine, and if this cord is severed, the victim will be permanently paralyzed. If the injury is in the neck, he will die. If you have any reason to suspect a back injury, you must not move the person in a way that could cause further injury. Very careful movement and splinting is necessary to prevent possible severing of the spinal cord.

Symptoms of a back injury include local tenderness, inability to move one or both the lower extremities, inability to feel your touch or pinch on one or both of the lower extremities, a prickling sensation on one or both of the lower extremities. The abnormalities just mentioned occur when the spinal cord is already damaged or under pressure, but their absence does not mean there has been no back injury. It simply means that the spinal cord has not yet been damaged. Don't be the one to damage it. If you sus-

287

pect a back injury, assume there is one and splint it. All this applies even more to neck injuries. A neck injury must be supported with a small pad behind the neck, about the size of a pair of street socks rolled up, and then the whole head must be held immobile. The sleeping bag makes a good splint for the head. The victim has to be placed on something rigid like a pack frame. His head goes on top of the middle of the sleeping bag on top of the frame. Don't forget the pad under the neck. Then half the bag can be rolled on each side of his head to form a large pad. The head and chest are then strapped down so that the neck cannot be moved. The greatest care should be taken in moving the victim onto the splint. Several people are needed to raise the person a few inches while the pack frame, pad, and sleeping bag are slid under him. One person should hold the head, very carefully and under slight tension as the lift is made together on his command. The same sort of procedure and the same rigid splint are needed for any back injury, and a pack frame with a sleeping pad is an excellent splint.

Rib fractures are rarely serious, and they don't require any splinting. Normally, the chest muscles become rigid around the injury and splint it fairly well. If the victim is in considerable pain from breathing, but isn't short of breath, you can tape along the line of the ribs from breastbone to splint, just below the nipple and just after the victim has exhaled completely. This prevents the injured side of the chest from moving so much, but for this reason the tape should be removed after a day or so if you are still in the backcountry.

Don't forget about shock with fractures. Even without an open fracture, there is always bleeding—that's what the swelling is. Loss of a quart of blood is normal with a break in a large bone like the thigh or pelvis. Multiple breaks cause a lot of bleeding. In a wilderness situation you must be very careful of this. Your friend won't die of a broken leg, but if you aren't careful he might die of the resulting shock.

INJURIES TO THE VITAL ORGANS

Traumatic injuries can also result in damage to the organs in the body cavity or to the head, with or without an outside wound. Such injuries are not common in normal backpacking circumstances. You may slip and break your leg on the trail or open up your hand with a knife, but unless you took a long fall, you would not be likely to suffer internal injuries. You should recognize the possibility, however, if someone has received a bad blow to some part of the body. Chest and head injuries will be considered separately.

The symptoms you should look for in circumstances that might result in internal injury are pain, nausea, bloody excretions or vomit, and most important, shock. Internal bleeding is just as serious as external, but there is nothing you can do to stop it. If an internal injury is indicated your friend will need surgery. Treat him for shock, don't give him anything by mouth, and do something to get him to a hospital.

Chest injuries other than a broken rib are also pretty unlikely. In rare cases a broken rib may penetrate into the chest cavity and puncture a lung, causing severe pain, some difficulty in breathing, and coughing up of frothy blood. Have the victim lie on the *injured* side. If he lies on the other side, the blood will run into the good lung and cause trouble there. Another uncommon chest injury is caused by a complete puncture of the chest wall, say by a ski pole or ice ax. This causes what is known as a sucking chest wound. The action of the breathing muscles forces air in and out of the wound, and the victim cannot get any air into the good lung. The hole has to be sealed up so that the victim can breathe. Use a piece of plastic, a gauze pad covered with Vaseline, or something, but don't delay. One final injury about which you can do something is known as flail chest. If the chest receives a massive blow in a fall, the ribs on one side may be so shattered that the whole chest wall loses its rigidity, even though there is no puncture. It flaps uselessly in and out, and again the victim can't breathe. Roll him onto the injured side, with a rolled-up jacket or a day pack under the injury. The other side of the chest will then be able to pump air in and out of the lung, and the breathing difficulty will decrease.

There are some other types of chest injury which won't be mentioned in detail here, because there is nothing you can do except to get the victim in a position where breathing is most comfortable. With any chest injury, the victim must have medical help quickly.

HEAD INJURIES

The brain is a unique organ both because of its function and the way it is enclosed in a rigid case of bone. The skull is intended as protection for the brain, and obviously any injury to it is a matter of concern. Basically, there isn't anything you can do for skull or brain damage except to get the victim evacuated, but there are a few special problems you should be aware of. If a person receives a blow to the head and is unconscious, this is a sign that his brain has been injured. Like any other part of the body, the brain may swell up after an injury, but since it is encased in the skull, there is no place for it to swell, and pressure will build up. For this reason, a person may be unconscious from a blow to the head, recover completely, and then start showing signs of a head injury again minutes or hours later. After any period of unconsciousness, this should be watched for, since it indicates a very dangerous situation.

Normal signs of head injury include irrationality, grogginess, nausea, unequal pupil size, complete or partial paralysis, or leaking blood or straw-colored liquid from the nose or ears. Bleeding may be local however, rather than indicating skull damage.

CARE OF AN UNCONSCIOUS VICTIM

Unconsciousness may result from head injury, electrical shock, suffocation, or various other things, but the first concern of the person giving care (after severe bleeding) must always be the victim's breathing. If he isn't breathing, you have to give artificial respiration. This is simple enough with the mouth-to-mouth method, but you ought to practice it on one of the Red Cross dummies. To perform resuscitation, turn the victim on his back, clear any vomit or other debris from his mouth, get the tongue away from the back of the throat by tilting the head back or pulling the jaw forward, pinch the nostrils shut, and blow into the victim's mouth. Remove your mouth, take another breath, and do it again. You should hear the air coming out of his lungs, and see his chest rising when you blow. If you don't, something is stuck in the airway. Roll him over, hit him in the back, clear the mouth, and try again. Continue artificial respiration as long as there is any chance the victim is alive.

Even if the unconscious person is breathing, you must still worry about the airway. In a coma, the muscles may relax more than in sleep, and the tongue may drop to the back of the throat, suffocating the victim. Place the unconscious person on his side, the head tilted down to prevent the tongue dropping, and to allow any vomit to escape without choking the victim. If the victim must be kept on his back, he should be attended all the time. Don't forget to keep him warm.

HEAT AND COLD

The temperature of the environment can cause problems for anyone who is caught unprepared. Too much sun can cause overheating. If you're out in the sun too long, you or one of your companions may start to feel faint and look pale, suffering from heat exhaustion. Skin temperature will be about normal. The solution is to rest in the shade, drink some liquids, and get some salt. Heat exhaustion is not serious, and a little rest will bring you back to normal. Heat stroke is very serious and must be treated immediately. The victim collapses or feels dizzy, and the skin is hot, red, and dry. Heat stroke is fatal unless the victim is cooled off right away. Wet cloths or immersion in cool water would be possible methods.

Don't get sunburned. Use a skin preparation and put on clothing before you burn. For complete protection of exposed parts of the body zinc oxide ointment can be used.

Cooling of the body can also be a problem. Inadequate clothing and not enough food can easily result in chilling when a cold wind comes up, especially if the clothing is wet. If the body core becomes chilled, the victim can die from exposure. Watch your companions, and be especially alert to someone who has suffered an accident. If the person starts to become short-tempered or irrational, look for signs that he is getting cold, perhaps bluish lips or nails. He needs warming and some sugary foods. As the body temperature drops, the victim will start to be clumsy, will become listless and incoherent, and will finally start to cough up froth and become unconscious. He has to be made warm. Get into a sleeping bag with him. Give him warm sugary liquids if he is conscious. This cooling of the body core is known as hypothermia, or exposure. For an accident victim during cold weather it is an especially dangerous possibility in combination with shock.

Frostbite will not occur in backpacking situations, unless the victim is already suffering from hypothermia or from another injury that has affected circulation to a limb. The best cure is prevention, warming extremities when they start to feel numb, changing socks, and so forth. The old advice to rub a frostbitten part with snow is so grotesquely absurd, I can't imagine where it started. Rubbing shouldn't be used at all once a part is actually frozen. Proper treatment of frostbite is rapid rewarming in water of 108°–112° F., but it must be no hotter and checked with a thermometer, and possibilities for this treatment in a backpacking situation are limited. Usually, it would be best to walk out on a frozen foot and get to a hospital. After thawing, a person whose foot was frostbitten is a litter case. Any friction will cause severe tissue damage. True frostbite with deep freezing is quite unusual and unnecessary in any normal backpacking situation. Frostnip of the face, ears, and nose in very cold winds should be watched for, and warmed right away without rubbing.

BITES

There are a lot of little critters out there waiting to bite you, but fortunately most won't do you any permanent damage. Snakes and black widows get the most publicity, but the species in the United States are rarely lethal. Multiple bites or bites of children account for nearly all fatalities. Carry a snake-bite kit in snake country and season. A small incision is made over each fang mark with a sterile razor or knife blade, and as much venom as possible is drawn out by suction. Meanwhile, spreading of venom should be slowed by keeping the victim quiet and tying a wide constriction band above the bite. The constriction band is not a tourniquet and should not cut off circulation. As the swelling moves up the limb, another set of incisions can be made four inches or so above the first and suction applied there, but don't do any more cutting after that. Infection is likely to be a worse problem than the bite if a long line of cuts is made.

Remember that poisonous snakes in the United States are not terribly dangerous. Keep the victim calm and reassure him. Incisions should be only about one-half inch long and the same depth. On the hand or foot, they should be even shallower, and great care should be taken to avoid cutting nerves or blood vessels. There is little chance of death even with an untreated bite. Keeping the victim quiet is probably more important than incision and suction.

Scorpions and black widows are also not likely to be lethal in this country except rarely to children and older people. Again the victim should be kept quiet and given care, and medical help should be sent for if spasms and other symptoms indicate the bite or sting was poisonous. But incision and suction will not help and should not be performed.

Ticks can carry several diseases. In tick country, keep pants legs tucked in or closed and use repellents. Alternatively, the body can be inspected every few hours, since ticks take some time to settle down and start biting. In removing a tick, the head of which has become imbedded, be sure to get the whole tick out by pulling very gently, and then wash the wound well. If any parts of the head are left in the bite a doctor should be visited when you return from the trip.

Animal bites carry the danger of rabies, and the animal should be captured if possible, followed by a visit to the doctor. Even though the chance of rabies may be remote, it is fatal once it appears, so this is not an area to take chances.

CARE AND TRANSPORTATION

No hard and fast rules can be laid down for the problem of how to get an injured person out of the woods. A few general comments are worth making, however. The first is that haste is only rarely necessary. If your friend breaks his leg, take care of him. Don't try a lot of breakneck heroics. He will be in a lot better shape if you nurse him for a week where you are than if you try to pick him up and carry him out that night. Internal injuries and the like are urgent, but there is still the matter of balancing the advantages of speed against the damage that may be done in getting the victim out a day earlier. Don't underestimate the difficulty of carrying out someone who is really hurt.

A man with a broken arm isn't an emergency at all. Get a good night's sleep, and then you carry the gear and he can carry himself. Someone who can't walk will have to be carried out on a stretcher. If you have a large party, you can improvise a litter out of packframes and manage all right, but with a small party, send for help. Sloppy transportation is the cause of more injuries than any other mistake in first aid. Back and neck injuries especially demand getting help if at all possible. You can splint them with packframes, but getting the victim out should be done with proper equipment and methods. A treated wound or splinted fracture can wait. Internal injuries or head injuries may require fast treatment.

293

If you have to care for an injured person for a few days while someone goes out for help or while you wait to be missed, you have a lot of work on your hands. Cleaning a wound and changing dressings daily are important. You will probably have to sterilize cloths to do it, since your first-aid kit is bound to be of limited size. An injured person may repress the need to eliminate because of the problems involved, and extra difficulties will arise. Ultimately, for example, he won't be able to urinate if he waits too long. Ask him if he needs to go to the bathroom, and figure out a system for managing it with some kind of improvised bedpan.

Bed sores and pneumonia have to be prevented with an injured person. Lying on the same parts of the body for long periods cuts off circulation and ultimately results in tissue death and severe open sores. You will have to help your friend shift position every two hours, without fail, if he is laid out so that he can't move. At the same time, you should make him cough, especially if chest pains cause him to resist the need to do so. Fluids accumulating in the lungs make a good place for bacteria to grow, and they will cause pneumonia if they aren't coughed up.

A FINAL NOTE

Despite the many horrible possibilities discussed in this chapter, most injuries in the backcountry are not serious, and thoughtful action will take care of the situation. Panic and hasty action cause more trouble than the accidents that precipitate them.

FIRST-AID KIT

The items listed here are far from definitive. Make up your own kit and use whatever training and experience you can get as a guide. Prescription drugs are often advisable for wilderness travel, but since you will have to see a doctor for them anyway, no advice will be given here. See the book list at the end for more information:

elastic bandage—good for bandages as well as minor sprains
adhesive tape, 2"–3" wide—the cloth kind that can be torn into narrower strips

sterile dressings
sterile razor blade
aspirin
Band-Aids
a few cotton-tipped swabs
tweezers
small bottle of aqueous Zepharin—antiseptic which doesn't sting or
 leave red coloring that masks infection
snake-bite kit (when needed)
needle
moleskin (for blisters)
soap

17   *Physical Conditioning*

Typically, at the beginning of the season the backpacker drags his winter-softened and beer-sodden body through several agonizing weekends before he begins to feel human in Saturday night's camp. One solution would be to stick to very easy trips during the first month of summer, but that would require one to make an embarrassing admission that he has fallen apart and would also severely curtail the summer program. So one puts up with aching muscles and near exhaustion.

Common as this syndrome is, nobody really advocates practicing it. So there are the annual resolutions to "stay in shape this year," sometimes carried out, but more often dropped by the wayside. This chapter is written for your time of trial—the first morning you decide to skip your situps until tomorrow. It also offers some suggestions on getting in shape for wilderness travel.

BACKPACKING AS A CONDITIONER

Backpacking itself is a good exercise, especially since it can be enjoyed at many levels of difficulty. The only problems with it are that most of us don't manage to get out often enough and that a lot of people like to do backpacking at a much more strenuous level than the one for which their daily routine prepares them. If you're satisfied with walking a few level

296

miles to camp a couple of times a season, then you shouldn't need to undergo any special training to get in condition beforehand.

More fundamentally, most people (at least the kind of people likely to read this book) would like to stay in good physical tune. When you are out of shape, you get tired quickly, you can be injured easily, you don't feel as well, and you are subject to various unpleasantries like premature aging and heart attacks. Many sorts of exercise programs are suitable to keep you in shape, but it's more pleasant if you follow one that you enjoy. You are also more likely to keep it up. Though backpacking to me is a good deal more than a way to stay in shape, it serves that function, too.

RUNNING YOUR BODY EFFICIENTLY

Like most machines, the body operates most efficiently when it is functioning at a level well below its greatest capacity. Your car uses less gas traveling a mile at 30 mph than covering the same mile at 75 mph. Your body works the same way. A person in good shape uses fewer calories to carry a forty-pound pack ten miles than someone in poor condition does.

Both for enjoyment and safety, it is worthwhile to be in good enough shape to undertake the kind of trips you like without pushing yourself to the limit. Maintaining an extra reserve ensures that you will be able to go as well Sunday as Saturday, that you will be able to enjoy the scenery at stops instead of just lying exhausted on the turf, that the hard parts of the trip will be enjoyable rather than a torture, and that you will have a reserve in case of difficulties.

Clearly all these adjectives are relative. What is difficult terrain for the family backpacker may be an easy morning stroll for the fanatic peak bagger, and similarly what is good physical condition for one is soft for the other. This is as it should be. The governing factor is how you feel. If you're forty pounds overweight and never walk farther than your car, you have a good chance of having a cardiac arrest at an early age, and you should certainly work into backpacking slowly. If you're fit and you feel good, you can backpack as fast and as far as you want to without overtaxing your body.

STRENGTH AND ENDURANCE

The definition of good physical condition should be largely a matter of common sense. Someone spending most of his time doing hard work in the outdoors doesn't have to worry about it. He gets in good condition for his work by doing it, and he stays in condition by doing it every day. The work that most of us do these days, however, is good physical conditioning for nothing so much as lying quietly in a coffin, perhaps with martini in hand. Most people know they're in rotten shape and have a vague desire to improve. Someone is always willing to sell them a way to do it without expenditure of time or effort.

A lot of schemes that have been promoted recently of the "six-minute-a-day-do-it-in-your-office" variety are simply ludicrous. Others are all right for building up a little muscle strength, but the amount of good that this will do you in backpacking or similar activities is limited. When we talk about physical fitness we really mean many different things including strength, endurance, and flexibility. Endurance is much more likely to be a problem for the average person than strength is. He can pick up a fifty-pound pack, but he is ready to collapse after carrying it for a hundred yards.

Isometric exercises—those which build strength by contracting a muscle completely for one short period a day—have been demonstrated to be as effective as anything in building muscle strength. Such exercises are easy and take very little time, but they don't build a capacity for endurance at all.

Endurance is built up by forcing the body to develop improved capacities for breathing and circulation in the lungs, heart, and muscles. The only way to build up endurance is to engage in activities which require you to endure. There is clearly an overlapping area of activity increasing both strength and endurance, but the two are really distinct. Doing isometric exercises or heavy weight lifting won't help you climb two thousand feet on a mountain trail, because the muscles have been pushed only in short spurts.

EXERCISE FOR THE FITNESS YOU WANT

The body follows rules so in tune with common sense that our habit of looking for tricks makes them seem too straightforward to be true. Exercising in a certain way prepares the body for the same kind of strain. If you want to be able to lift a heavy weight, train for it by lifting progressively heavier weights. If you want your spine to be flexible, bend it. If you want to be able to hike over the hills for hour after hour, do work which pushes your muscles constantly over an extended period.

There is no cheap and easy way to train for endurance. There are lots of enjoyable ways, but they all require that you keep your body working continuously for at least an hour per exercise period. You may jog and walk, run and jog, play tennis, bicycle, or climb a local hill, but you have to keep your muscles working all the time. You don't have to maintain the same pace for the whole period, but you have to keep going. Run until you're out of breath, and then slow to a fast walk, or bicycle at full tilt and then slow down a little for a while. Don't collapse for five of each fifteen minutes. It is better to keep going at a lower level of performance than to push as hard as you can and then drop. Endurance training requires you to keep working.

You may feel that you need extra strength in particular muscles, that you aren't flexible enough, that your balance is poor, or what not. It is easy enough to work on any particular deficiencies in the course of almost any exercise program. If you are training for a really long backpacking trip on which you will carry brutal loads, you can always do some jogging with a heavy pack occasionally. Jogging on rough ground will do wonders for your balance and agility. You can interrupt a bicycling trip for some one-legged deep-knee bends to improve the strength of your legs or pull-ups for your arms. Put in some occasional stretching and bending exercises for flexibility.

BY THE SWEAT OF YOUR BROW

There aren't any really hard and fast rules about what kind of exercises you have to do to get fit. They don't have to be the same ones every time. If you're training for endurance, though, you can always count on the rule that you are going to have to do some work to do any good. Increased capacity for any physical activity results from taxing the body. If you can lift a 150-pound weight in a press, regularly pressing 75 pounds will not persuade the muscles to become stronger. Similarly, running at an easy pace will not force the body to improve its capacity for sustained exercise.

When you finish a training session, you have to feel as though you have been pushing yourself, if it is to do you any good. If you haven't even worked up a sweat, you won't have worked up any more endurance either. You get what you train for.

HOW FAST

People who are young and in good physical shape can push themselves as fast as they want to. If they go too hard, they'll suffer from aching muscles for a few days, the body's way of revenging itself on excess. But this really doesn't matter much. Older people and people who are terribly out of condition should take things more slowly. The older you get, the longer your body will take to respond to training, an excellent reason for staying in shape once you get there.

Have patience. As your body develops an increased capacity, increase your demands on it. A little common sense will tell you how to balance things. You should feel tired after training, but if you don't bounce back after a reasonable amount of time, you're pushing too hard.

It should go without saying that a physical examination is mandatory before you start a program of hard physical conditioning when you are out of shape. This is especially true for people over forty. People who are overweight and in poor muscular condition should get medical advice on a combined program of exercise and dieting.

HOW OFTEN

If you're trying to build yourself up, a good training session every other day will do nicely, while two sessions a week will keep you at a given level of fitness. Whether you use a rigid schedule or a less regular one is unimportant providing you can keep it up. Some people work best by scheduling an exercise period every day or every other day. Others do better by taking opportunities that arise, sometimes going out for a run and sometimes just taking the bicycle on a thirty-mile errand instead of the car. The important thing is not to let the sedentary days drag into weeks, working out three days in a row and then stopping for ten. Good results do depend on *regular* exercise.

If you go on a backpacking trip over the weekend, two more sessions of exercise on Tuesday and Thursday will keep your capacity for work building up without costing you too much time. Weekends alone produce results much more slowly. The body is all tuned up on Monday morning, but by Friday it has lagged back into the city patterns and requires the whole weekend to get used to hard exercise again.

Another season. Backpacking on skis in the winter is a good way to stay in shape, besides having a special fascination of its own. On a ski mountaineering trip in Rocky Mountain National Park.

DO SOMETHING YOU ENJOY

Those endowed with Puritan ethics and iron will can keep up the most boring exercise routines every day for their whole lives, and I applaud them. Their superior moral fiber is an inspiration to us all. But I find that daily setting-up routines lasting an hour or so are a colossal bore. I need exercises with some inherent interest or I soon stop doing them. The trick is to find some things you like to do that are also good training, and then do one of them at least every other day.

Running and jogging are great exercises if you like them enough or if you have someplace to go that is interesting enough to keep you happy. Beaches are fantastic conditioners and interesting enough to make running a pleasure. Running to or from work is great, providing you can manage the practical problems of dressing and showers. Bicycling on some of your regular trips tends to be even better, because the bicycle has a much greater range.

Variety helps the jaded muscles to keep going. Go swimming on Monday, bicycle on Wednesday, play tennis on Friday, and go backpacking over the weekend. It's more interesting than setting-up exercises every morning, anyway.

You can avoid the winter doldrums by not putting your equipment away during the cold months. Try cross-country skiing or snowshoeing. You may find that backpacking in winter is even more enjoyable than in summer.

Mountain Walking 18

The mountains provide one of the most interesting and challenging environments for the backpacker. My own vision of paradise would not be complete without a range of jagged, snowcapped peaks. The basic principles of backpacking are the same in the mountains as anywhere else, but a little extra care and equipment may be needed by those whose experience is limited to the flatlands. Also, on more difficult mountain terrain, special skills are essential for safe travel.

THE MOUNTAIN ENVIRONMENT

It is characteristic of all mountain ranges to have weather conditions which are more variable and harsher than the gentler country around them. Higher altitude means colder temperatures, but it also means less atmospheric protection from the rays of the sun. Even more important, mountains present a barrier to catch weather systems moving toward them. By forcing the air in those systems to go over or around them, the mountains are likely to produce turbulent winds, rapid temperature changes, and often storms. Mountains may even generate their own miniature weather systems, producing thunderstorms, and then attracting the lightning from them.

Mountain terrain is generally more rugged and difficult than that of

303

the land surrounding it, although there are exceptions. Difficulties may range from steep trails to glaciers, snow slopes, and cliffs. As a general rule, travel in mountains is slower, because of the need to do a lot of climbing. My own general rule is that each thousand feet of altitude gain takes about as much time and energy as three miles of horizontal progress. If you need to go over a couple of passes during the day, rising and dropping several thousand feet for each one, you may have a long, hard day even though the distance you cover is only five or six miles.

Since the mountains in this country range from wooded hills to sandstone monoliths and glaciated crags, generalized statements about them are hard to make, but as a rule, one can say that in the high country the weather will be rougher and more erratic, the environment will be consistently harsher, and the ecology will be more fragile than in the surrounding country.

THE VARIETY OF NORTH AMERICAN MOUNTAINS

The meaning of the word *mountain* is rather varied, depending on what part of the continent you happen to be occupying. The ancient and worndown mountains of Virginia would be foothills in some other states. From the point of view of technique, backpacking on a mountain which is wooded all the way to the top is not very different from traveling in the surrounding country, except that the going is slower. Timberline is a good dividing point, indicating that the conditions above are too harsh to permit tree growth. Above timberline the weather is harder, shelter may be difficult to find, and fuel is generally unavailable.

Where mountains are wooded and rounded off, there is really not much need to consider special techniques. Hills are longer, weather patterns may be influenced by the mountains, and of course the tops of the hills will be cooler and more exposed to wind or snow than the country below. It is above timberline, though, that these differences in degree generally amount to a difference in kind.

Harsh mountain conditions result from a combination of altitude, latitude, and situation. Timberline in the Colorado Rockies will probably be reached between eleven thousand and twelve thousand feet; in the White Mountains of New Hampshire it may be below five thousand feet. In British Columbia and Alaska, glaciers may drop all the way to the sea. The mountains of North America are as varied as the continent itself—no book can list enough rules to cover all the situations. Watch for the special problems presented by the mountains, and avoid them if you are not equipped to cope with them. This applies to every backpacker from the rank beginner to the most experienced mountaineer. The key to safety in the mountains is respect for their power and variable temperament. As you get to know them better, you will be able to undertake more difficult routes with confidence and safety, but as you do you will gain more and more respect for mountain hazards.

DANGERS IN THE MOUNTAINS

The greatest danger in the mountains is bad weather. Anyone can fall off a cliff, and even experienced travelers do so once in a while, but only in very unusual circumstances. Bad weather can claim the lives of careful and intelligent people, because it is hard to foresee. Even the best mountain weathermen are sometimes fooled. Most important, weather is too familiar, and people tend to discount the need to prepare for it. Most backpackers have enough native good sense not to attempt a traverse of a steep snow gully without the proper equipment and experience. The mere thought of an uncontrolled slide to the rocks a thousand feet below is enough to make them think twice. Unfortunately, a cloud does not evoke the same caution. Yet it is just as important to be properly dressed when the weather deteriorates as it is to have an ice ax for arrest of a fall on a snow slope.

Weather is exceptionally dangerous in the mountains because it can change greatly in a very short time and exposed peaks may not offer any shelter or makings for a fire. Thunderstorms, for example, are very dangerous when they catch climbers high on peaks and ridges.

Besides the hazards of deteriorating weather, many mountains present the more obvious worries associated with steep terrain. If your mountain has steep rock walls and snow or ice slopes, you must either avoid them or have the equipment and knowledge to travel past them in reasonable safety. The dangers of rock walls, glaciers, and snow slopes include not only poor footing, but rockfall, avalanches, and crevasses. The experienced mountaineer is usually far more fearful of stones falling from cliffs above than he is of falling from his own stance.

Mountains, especially steep ones, are subject to tremendous pressures from the many erosive forces of weather. In terms of geological time precipitous mountains are very young, and the adage that what goes up must come down is quite true of the high peaks. Long before they even reach their greatest elevation, the mountains are being worn away, eroded, and broken down by the wind, gravity, running and freezing water, avalanches, and the pressing, exploring roots of the plants. Every mountain is always in the process of falling apart, and it is a good idea to be somewhere else when some of the pieces decide to make their downward trek. Rockfall can threaten the hiker as much as the rock gymnast, if he is standing under a loose cliff.

So much for the itemization of mountain dangers. None of them need cause particular worry if you pay adequate attention to safety during mountain travel. Like other wilderness dangers, they are generally easy to avoid.

SPECIAL EQUIPMENT FOR MOUNTAIN TRAVEL

The changeable weather of the mountains has already been mentioned, so it should be obvious that the high-country walker needs to carry spare clothes to keep reasonably warm and dry in case of a sudden storm. The principles of clothing were discussed in Chapter 9, so there isn't any need for repetition here. The point is to be alert to possibilities and to prepare for them. In the high ranges of the United States and Canada snowstorms can occur in any month of the year, and the even more dangerous combination of cold rain and high wind is common. Allowing the warm sun to persuade you that shorts and a light shirt make an adequate outfit is asking for trouble. You'll probably get away with it many times, but one day it may kill you. Wear what you like, but always carry clothing for conditions that may come in later. What is needed will vary with the range and season, but a minimum should include some woolen clothing, together with wind protection and perhaps rain gear. Wool is the only fabric that retains significant insulating power when it gets wet.

Camping at high altitudes requires warm sleeping gear or a fire, and fires can never be depended on above timberline. Cooking above timberline demands a stove and fuel and often shelter from wind. In most ranges, camping above timberline requires a mountain tent, even if it is not used on warm nights. Bivouac equipment may be substituted, but shelters that cannot be pitched in a high wind are not dependable above timberline. Mountain boots need to be sturdy and have good traction.

Most specialized climbing equipment is outside the province of this book. Climbing on rock steep enough so that a minor slip would be dangerous requires sophisticated technique and equipment, beginning with a rope. Even more elaborate methods are required for safety on extreme climbs, with various types of climbing "hardware" used to protect against the consequences of a slip and sometimes to aid the progress of a climb. This kind of mountaineering is generally categorized as *technical climbing*. Those interested in this sport should refer to the bibliography at the end of this book for literature. Serious study of technique is required for safe travel on technical terrain.

Between the worlds of the backpacker on the trail and the serious technical climbers, there is a vast amount of mountain terrain which can be safely traveled without using a rope. It is the proper province of the adventurous backpacker and also the ideal training ground for those who want to go on to bigger things one day. This is the province of the rock scrambler and the snow slogger. Rock scrambling requires no special equipment, but the backpacker venturing onto steep terrain where there are stretches covered by snow will feel the need for an *ice ax* and perhaps for *crampons*, and some of the uses for these tools will be discussed later in this chapter.

MOUNTAIN WEATHER

As with all kinds of weather prediction, local experience is invaluable for the amateur in the mountains, as is a check with TV or radio or a call to the weather bureau before departure. Despite all my cautionary notes, I don't believe in carrying stuff I don't have to, and calling the weatherman sometimes saves me a few pounds. If I really don't expect rain, I carry only emergency rain gear, whereas if I plan on it I carry the equipment I need to be comfortable.

The mountains, though, have wiles of their own, which will never be mentioned by the forecaster talking to the millions down in the flatlands. An acquaintance with the weather patterns of the ranges you frequent will mellow through the years into warm friendship and also contribute a lot to your comfort.

The first thing to remember about mountains is that they stick up a long way out of the ground. Suppose you are a reasonably friendly mass of air, rolling peacefully across the country at a sane and moderate speed. Then you come to this mountain. It is in your way, and since there are other masses of air traveling along behind you, jostling if you slow down, somehow you have to get past the mountain. You can either push up and over the barrier or perhaps around it and through a pass; in either case you'll have to speed up to maintain your rate of progress and keep from being pushed too much. Anyone on the mountain will experience high winds and air turbulence. Furthermore, you'll expand and cool in the higher altitude and lower atmospheric pressure as you go over the top of the mountain, and if you are carrying a lot of moisture most of it will fall as rain, sleet, or snow. Thus the mountain backpacker is struggling in a very real storm, despite calm, sunny weather on the plains.

Mountains also generate their own weather. The slanting rays of the sun often strike the mountainsides straight on, warming them more than the ground around them. The mountainsides, in their turn, warm the air nearby, and when this air is warmed it expands and rises. An updraft of air is created around the mountain, and it is often quite strong. Depending on the air currents involved and the moisture content of the air, winds, clouds, and thunderheads may result. A thunderhead can often be recognized as a

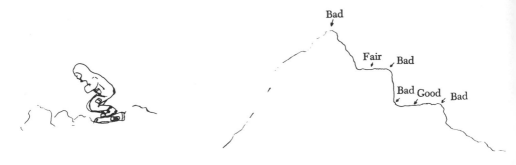

The crouching position with the feet close together is the safest one in a lightning storm; a pack under the feet helps insulate the backpacker from the ground. The cross-section of the mountain shows the relative danger from lightning strikes at various places.

billowing, heavy cloud which expands upward, often very rapidly. When it reaches its height, the top flattens off against a higher atmospheric layer, and the cloud takes on an anvil shape. Large fronts of advancing clouds also bring thunderstorms, and either kind is a signal to get off the peaks and ridges in a hurry.

The cold winds, fog, rain, and snow of an intruding frontal system can be just as dangerous to the ill-prepared, but they are no real threat to the well-equipped party. They also usually give more warning than the rapidly building summer afternoon thunderstorm. Lightning from either an isolated thunderhead or a frontal system can only be avoided, so first consideration will be given to this threat.

LIGHTNING

Electrical storms are among the most feared hazards of the mountains among experienced backpackers and climbers, not because they claim large numbers of lives, but because they are among the *objective dangers* of the mountains. Objective dangers are those which, like rockfall, can only be escaped by being somewhere else when they occur. They have frightening inevitability about them, and though the danger is not great, it can be reduced only by learning enough to take evasive action.

Lightning is a very rapid electrical discharge resulting from a large voltage between two clouds or between a cloud and the ground. Lightning bolts from the ground are the ones we are concerned with. Prior to the strike, a large difference in charge has built up between the cloud and the earth. The only way the difference can be balanced is for a current to flow between the two, but it will not flow easily, because the air between is a good insulator. The discharge only takes place when a tremendous voltage has built up, enough to overcome the insulating layer. When this happens, the lightning bolt follows the path of the least resistance, generally from the point closest to the cloud, perhaps the peak of the mountain or some sharp point along a ridge. As the discharge takes place, currents flow along the surface of the ground to the point of discharge, also flowing along the path of minimum resistance, and these ground currents are just as dangerous as the lightning bolt itself. Ground currents become stronger and more hazardous close to the strike point.

If a thunderstorm is threatening, the first thing to do is to get down off the mountain as quickly as possible, short of taking a fall. For example, suppose you have climbed a mountain along a ridge several miles in length. Another route drops off a saddle to your right, but it goes off the wrong side of the mountain. If a thunderstorm is threatening, the worst place you could possibly be except for the summit itself is along that ridge. Take the saddle route down even if it means a long walk home. If the storm clears, you can always backtrack.

Once the storm begins, it is best to find the safest location nearby and to protect yourself as best you can. If lightning is striking or threatening, continuing your climb down is likely to be dangerous if you are still high, and descending would require you to cross exposed places. The diagram shows the most dangerous and the safest places. Ridges, summits, outer sides of ledges, and outcrops are the likely strike points. Depressions and places on the inside of wide shelves are fairly safe. On a shelf, the safe spot is as far in as possible, but still well clear of the inside cliff. (See the diagram.) If a strike occurs nearby, remember the surface currents. They will not hurt you while flowing past the soles of your feet, but if your feet and hands, or both hands, or feet and head, touch the rock, your body may be the path of least resistance for the current. The best position is a squat, with only the feet touching the ground. If a rope, pack, rolled tent, or something similar is available, squat on that to get a little extra insulation from the ground. Keep your feet close together.

A cave provides excellent protection from lightning as well as rain, because the currents flow along the surface. Great caution is required here, however, since a hollow or a shallow cave is very dangerous. *Do not get under an overhang for shelter from the rain during a thunderstorm high on a mountain.* A current running along the surface and trying to get past a shallow cave or overhang will use your body as the route of least resistance from the floor to the roof. This is unhealthy. A good cave must be quite deep with no crevices in the rock running to the back of the cave.

A few warning signs might be mentioned, although they may or may not occur prior to a strike. When the charge is building up on a mountain on which you are standing, it will build up on you, too. When your hair stands up on end, you have good cause to worry. I have experienced this sensation and have no wish to repeat the experience, but I've never heard what the French call "the buzzing of the bees," a humming sound which often precedes a strike.

The most obvious warning signs are threatening clouds, and they give much better notice than the last-minute frights mentioned before. It is almost always possible to see storms building up well in advance, and being caught by surprise is usually the result of not paying attention. Watch for the buildup of thunderheads on nearby peaks, and don't underestimate the speed with which they can form once they have begun to mushroom upward. Keep an eye out for approaching frontal systems; a little study of the area will tell you the direction they usually come from at a particular time of year. Breakneck retreats off the summits should be rare. They indicate you are pushing your luck and cutting things too close. There is an occasional unavoidable situation when all the visible sky looks beautiful, but you meet the storm system coming from the other side of the hill at the top of the ridge or peak.

RAIN, SLEET, DRIVING WIND, AND ALL THAT

Although lightning tends to be the most feared element of mountain weather among experienced backpackers and climbers, far more people run afoul of the other ingredients of mountain storms. No one really knows how many deaths occur each year in the mountains from body chilling, but it is probably the most frequent form of accidental death in the high country. The chilling effects of sudden storms deserve the utmost caution of anyone who wanders in the mountains, and one should always carry adequate clothing and supplies to meet the danger.

Rules for proper clothing are simple enough, but on sunny summer days they are too often forgotten. Even in winter at high altitude, the sun is often deceptively warm when the wind isn't blowing, and the cool air is still enough so that its temperature isn't noticed. With the muscular exertion of hiking up steep slopes, the traveler will probably be sweating, and the dangers of chilling will not occur to him.

The wind alone may chill the mountain walker to the bone. Coming down from his mountain in the afternoon with his clothing soaked with sweat and his body reserves depleted by hard work, the combination of the afternoon wind and creeping shadows may chill him severely. If a cold rain is added, he may never get back.

The effects of storms carrying freezing rain and then snow are much more serious than this, especially if they catch the hiker above timberline and shelter. Without proper clothing even the strongest hikers are quickly chilled. The principles discussed in the clothing chapter are important for the mountain traveler more than any other. Windtight shell clothing is essential for mountain travel. Shell clothing is light and easily carried. Enough insulation should be taken for reasonable comfort in any weather that might blow in. Obviously, quantities will vary with range and season, but the rule remains constant—don't be lulled into a false sense of security by the weather at the trailhead or at camp in the morning. The most characteristic feature of mountain weather is rapid change.

When wet weather is a possibility, water resistant or waterproof shell garments are needed, the choice depending on various considerations mentioned elsewhere. Finally, to harp on my favorite rule, when wet, cold weather is a possibility, carry some *wool* clothing. With the affluence of many backpackers now hitting the trail, a lot more down clothing is being carried, and it is so warm that people carrying it tend to rely completely on its qualities, which are great indeed. But, when down gets wet, it is completely useless. Basic insulation in the mountains, except in places and seasons where there is never any rain or sleet, should be wool, which is the only material retaining much insulation power after it gets wet.

Clearly, it is especially important in the mountains not to get your clothes wet in the first place if you can help it, unless a change will soon be available. Take off your sweater before you soak it with sweat, and stop to get the rain gear out of the pack as soon as the drizzle starts, not after you're already beginning to feel soaked. By the time your skin starts feeling wet, your clothes are already pretty damp. Stay as dry as possible.

ROUTE FINDING IN THE MOUNTAINS

Basically, finding your way in the mountains is easier than in most terrain. Visibility is usually good, terrain and landmarks are well defined, so that following progress on a topo map is quite simple. Only a few special tricks have to be learned. The first is to avoid terrain that is too difficult. Both in planning trips on the map and looking at the scenery ahead, it is important to consider your abilities, time, equipment, and party, so that you avoid getting into trouble. Remember that there is a lot of terrain in the mountains that is impassable to the backpacker. This is especially important when you plan routes which take a different way down a peak or a pass than up. If you aren't sure of the feasibility of a route, allow enough time and energy to search for the way and turn back if necessary.

Get in the habit of planning your routes in the mountains well in advance, or at least looking for them. You can often tell a great deal from the map and from distant views about features which will be obscured once you are close to a mountain. From the trailhead it may be quite obvious that a particular ridge is easy or impossible, while from below the same ridge will be invisible or completely distorted. It is especially difficult to see the route ahead from above, and if you make a wrong choice, you have to climb back up, the thought of which may encourage you to take foolish chances.

Guidebooks may be useful for advance information on mountain trips. Once you are familiar with a particular region, maps become more useful, but in an area that is completely new to you, many mysteries will remain until you see the ground. A forty-foot cliff doesn't show on a fifty-foot contour map, and on ridge routes especially, the map may not give you any indication of what to expect.

Always be wary of the consequences of a possible slip in the mountains. Climbing sound faces with proper technique and equipment isn't too hazardous, but scrambling around unroped on easy but loose rock just above a cliff can be very dangerous. Backpackers who wouldn't think of trying difficult rock climbing sometimes manage to get themselves into far more precarious positions than the average rock climber ever does. You can often travel safely on difficult terrain, providing you keep a close eye out for the consequences of a slip. It's quite safe to climb a very difficult step when there is no place to fall, but a loose blocky slope that looks very easy may be too risky when it hangs over thin air. Care and experience are the essential ingredients. Unless you know you can manage a move safely—and come back if you have to—don't try it.

Backpackers should be especially careful about snow slopes. They provide safe avenues for the traveler on many mountains with proper care, equipment, and practice, but without one of these elements they are dangerous. In the spring, many established trails cross snow slopes, and examining them with an eye for the consequences of a slip is vital. The use of the ice ax for self-arrest is discussed later in this chapter. Without an ice ax, stopping a fall on steep, hard snow is virtually impossible. You will go to the bottom in a hurry. Crossing and climbing snow slopes can be completely safe, but get your experience in places where you won't be hurt by your mistakes.

Though trails maintained by government agencies or private clubs are generally safe even for inexperienced walkers, the mountains are not a good place to blindly follow trail markers, leaving good sense behind. Sections of a trail may be washed out, maintenance may have been dropped, or snow or bad weather conditions may have turned a normally simple trail into a route for roped parties only. Cairns and worn trails do not necessarily mark an easy route either. Especially in popular climbing areas, these may simply guide the climber to an extremely difficult route. Finally, on rocky land above timberline, trail markings may be nonexistent or difficult to follow, especially if the weather deteriorates. Keep your common sense in the mountains, and let your own experience guide you in the safety of routes. If things start to get too hard, turn around and go back. There's always another weekend.

CLIMBING AND SCRAMBLING

The principle of watching for the consequences of a slip has already been mentioned several times. It provides the general dividing line between roped climbing and scrambling. Where the line will be drawn will vary with the individual and his experience, but the beginner should be careful to draw it with a generous margin for error. Where the consequences of a slip would be disastrous, the climber should be roped and have the skill to use the rope effectively. Easy footing should not lull you into false confidence—it's what is underneath you that really counts.

The use of ropes and climbing hardware is beyond the scope of this book. In this chapter I've chosen to draw my own line at the start of terrain where a rope is needed. Unfortunately, that beginning is somewhat ambiguous, and I can only advise the reader to make his own decisions conservatively—don't climb up anything unless you're sure you can get safely down. Down-climbing is almost always harder than going up.

314

SNOW

In many mountain ranges permanent snowfields last all summer, and even lower ranges sport them in spring and winter. Long climbs on steep snow are the province of the mountaineer who has practiced proper use of the rope, protection, step-cutting, and other skills. However, the experienced backpacker often makes trips which involve crossing or climbing occasional snow slopes. Learning the use of an ice ax for self-arrest and perhaps a little crampon technique greatly extends the range of possibilities open to the backpacker. Even if only one snow gully ten feet wide needs to be crossed on a particular trip, that gully might be an impassable barrier without an ice ax, if a slip in it would result in an uncontrolled fall.

Actual progress on snow can be made in one of several ways. On fairly flat terrain, of course, one simply walks. On the consolidated snow slopes of spring and summer, though, simple walking will usually result in a slip. If the snow is reasonably soft, steps can be kicked into the snow. One or two kicks make an adequate step if the snow is soft enough for kicking steps at all. Harder snow requires either cutting steps or wearing crampons. Routes requiring step-cutting should be avoided by all but experienced climbers. If the slope requires cutting steps, then a fall would be dangerous, and an ice ax being used for cutting cannot be held ready for self-arrest. A rope is usually required, so step-cutting is not in the province of the backpacker.

Going down should be given more attention than going up. Don't ever go up a slope unless you're sure that you can get down safely. In soft snow, the technique is to face out and walk down, plunging the heel in at each step. The natural tendency of the nervous beginner is to stay as close to the slope as possible, leaning back and almost sitting down. Learn to overcome this temptation. The safe position is standing straight up with your weight over your feet. Come down hard on your heels to dig good steps. Leaning back simply tends to break out your steps.

If you're thinking about climbing a slope, check to see if it is soft enough to heel down first. Unless you have crampons and can use them, harder slopes shouldn't be attempted. Coming down facing the slope, trying to kick steps below you, is no exercise to try without a rope.

Remember that snow conditions change during the day. If the sun is just leaving a snow slope, it is going to freeze harder in a few hours. Are you going to be coming down again? If you're working up a slope that is just soft enough to kick steps in, make sure it will be softer rather than harder on your way down. Remember the slope during the day. If the weather changes and starts to get cold, turn around before the snow gets hard.

In spring and early summer, slopes may get very soft and avalanche. If there is any avalanching on similar slopes, if large balls have been rolling down, if there are any cornices above, or if the snow is very sloppy, *stay off*. It takes years to learn to judge avalanche hazards well. Don't take chances. In winter conditions, before the snow has become consolidated, stay off steep open slopes completely, unless you have studied avalanche conditions thoroughly. Avalanches are killers.

THE ICE AX AND SELF-ARREST

The mountaineer uses the ice ax for many purposes, but only one of them will be discussed here. For the general backpacker the ax is used mainly as a walking stick and occasionally for self-arrest. The walking stick use needs no explanation.

Self-arrest is the use of the ax to stop a slide on a snow slope. In principle it is simple, but it can only be learned through practice. To learn it well, you'll have to go up to the mountains, find a snow slope with a gentle runout so that you can't get hurt, and practice for at least a day. To do any good the arrest has to become a reflexive action. You have to train yourself to use it by instinct, and that does not come naturally. Your natural instinct is to let go of the ax and claw the slope with your fingernails. Long experience has shown this instinct to be unhealthy.

If you decide to learn self-arrest, you must first buy, borrow, or rent an ice ax. Fine points of design become important in step-cutting and technical ice and snow climbing—they need not concern us here. If you expect to go on to roped climbing, I recommend you get an ax with a metal handle, but this is not important for the backpacker. The handle of the ax should be long enough so that the point reaches the floor when you hold the head in your hand. A few inches one way or the other doesn't matter. Don't get an extremely short ax that may be prominently displayed in a mountaineering store. It is excellent for climbing severe ice walls, but you aren't planning on climbing any severe ice walls, and a short ax is dangerous for self-arrest.

A standard ice ax should reach the ground when the head is held in the hand. At the bottom is the spike, or point. The head, at the top, is made up of the pick, extending in the direction of the thumb, and the adze, going the other way.

Once you have your ice ax, take plenty of warm clothes to the hills with you. A day of self-arrest practice means a day of sliding and wallowing in the snow. Be sure to wear a hat and mittens or gloves. You will get wet, and a change will be welcome at the car or in the pack. You need to find a slope that is packed and steep enough so that you would slide if you should slip, but it must run out onto a gentle flat patch with no protruding rocks in case you do indeed slip and slide.

Climb up the slope a little way and hold the ax in the position shown in the illustration. The head is held in the hand with the thumb going around the adze. The other hand holds the shaft just above the spike. The shaft goes diagonally down across the chest, with the pick sticking out away from the body and held just below the shoulder. To arrest a slip, you

The ice ax held ready for self-arrest. To check a slip the climber falls forward on the pick, controlling it with his hand and shoulder.

simply fall on your chest and dig the pick into the snow. For more stopping power, hunch your back up so that your weight is on the pick and your toes. This is simple in principle, but there are a lot of fine points which have to be learned with practice. Try a few practice arrests whenever you have a chance. In soft snow, you start digging with pick and feet just as fast as you can. In hard snow, when you get going fast, the pick has to be edged into the snow very quickly, but smoothly and carefully, or else it is likely to be pulled from your hands and left far above you.

In your initial practice, keep trying the same thing, climbing higher onto steeper ground as you learn the technique. Let yourself slide a little way before you start the arrest, so that you can find what it is like to stop from a faster slide. Learn to really dig in. You have to get your face down to the snow to get your weight on the ax pick and your feet. Your hand controlling the pick must hang on to prevent it from being pulled up above your shoulder, where you can no longer put weight on it. If you start to lose control of the pick, lessen the pressure on it until you regain your hold. *You must hang onto the ax!*

Once you feel you have mastered the arrest while falling forward, try falling a bit to each side. Roll onto the ax and then get your rear end up to put pressure on it. Then try facing downslope and falling forward. Finally, you will get to the point of falling backward. Start low the first few times,

Practicing self-arrest. The sliding person is trying arrest from a backwards, head-first tumble. These people are using a rope for safety because the snow here has rocks at the bottom. Find a place with a safe runoff instead unless you have been trained in the use of a rope.

and then practice from higher up. Roll over on the pick side, hanging onto the ax in the arrest position. Don't roll toward the point. It might catch in the snow and rip the ax from your hands. Once you've rolled onto the pick, a little pressure on it will make it drag, and your body will swing around so that your feet are downslope. Then you're in normal arrest position, and you do the same thing you've been doing all along. On fast snow this all has to be done very quickly or you'll get out of control.

If you manage to get through backward headfirst falls and you're still ready for more, repeat the whole sequence with a pack. Don't get overconfident. Start on an easy slope with each new step and then work onto steeper ones. And *never* practice on a slope without a good runout or one with rocks protruding in the possible line of fall. Learn self-arrest on safe

319

slopes. Once you've become sure of yourself, you'll be able to safely traverse snow slopes that are within your capability for self-arrest. The more practice you get, the better those limits will get and the better your judgment of them will be.

A few special cautions are in order regarding snow slopes. The first is to make all your judgments about them conservatively. An uncontrolled slide down a snow slope or gully could be deadly. There is no reason to be afraid of snow, but there's very good reason not to try anything unless you *know* you can handle it. Pushing your limits is completely out of place without a rope and proper rope techniques.

An arrest requires a certain distance to work. Whenever you're deciding whether a slope is safe, look at the distance you would have available. Make sure that there is a lot more distance than you need to stop before you would reach any rocks or drop-offs. Be particularly watchful for ice patches in the snow. Arresting on snow and ice are quite different matters, and a few yards of ice can cause you to take a spill or throw an arrest out of control. Don't climb or cross any snow slope unless you know you could arrest a fall. Don't forget that it takes longer to arrest if you're wearing a pack.

CRAMPONS

After gaining some experience on snow, you will find that you could easily arrest a slip on many slopes that are too hard to permit step-kicking. Crampons permit easy footing on hard snow. They are steel frames that strap to the boot with spikes bent at right angles to stick into the snow. For short sections of snow lightweight instep crampons are available, with four or five points, designed to strap to the center of the boot. These require considerable care in use, however, and for longer snow stretches full length crampons are required. These should have points 1¼ inches to 1¾ inches long; ten points per crampon, all going straight down from the boot sole are best. Those with points projecting straight out in front of the toe are of use only on steep slopes, where the backpacker has no business.

Crampons are tricky to use until you get the knack, and you should get lots of practice in a safe place before you try to use them where a fall could be dangerous. *They must fit your boots properly.* This means that the

Strapping on a crampon. This one has horns sticking out in front which are not recommended for beginners. A good fit to the boot and secure strapping are essential.

side irons must hold the boots firmly, allowing no side to side slipping. The front points of a crampon should be just under the toe of the boot, not in front of it or very far behind. Make sure the binding is secure. A loose or badly fitted crampon is really dangerous.

In use crampons must be placed with all the points dug into the slope, which means that the ankles have to flex to the angle of the slope. Edging the foot so that only half the points go into the slope invites a fall. Practice going up, down, and across the slope. Be sure to practice switchbacking, the most insecure maneuver you are likely to make.

Be very careful not to catch one of your crampons on the other pant leg. This can cause a fall, a gash in the leg, or both. When they aren't on your feet, crampons should have some kind of guards on them and be put in the pack. They are sharp and dangerous. They should be kept sharp—dull crampons can cause slips.

Practice arresting with crampons on. On hard snow, be careful about digging your toes in while wearing crampons, especially if you have front points that stick out from the toes. A crampon catching suddenly in hard snow can flip you over and cause you to lose control completely. One other caution: soft, wet snow sometimes balls between the points of crampons, which can cause them suddenly not to bite. Be very cautious if snow starts to stick between your points. The problem can be stopped by poking the points of the crampons through a piece of plastic sheeting, and then tying it fast around the boot.

Desert Walking   19

Like the mountains, deserts are extreme environments. They have great appeal for many backpackers, and their aesthetic qualities are unique and immensely varied. They range from great mazes of red sandstone canyons to vast stretches of sand dunes, shifting endlessly in the winds. The special beauty of a shaded waterfall surrounded by cottonwoods and animal trails in the midst of the harsh clarity of the desert is unmatched by anything in nature.

The single characteristic which sets the desert apart is, of course, the scarcity of water. Definitions vary, and they need not concern us here—the essential tone of life in desert country is set by the fact that water is not readily available. There are as many kinds of desert as there are mountains. The climatic conditions which produce deserts may exist over flat plains or incredibly rugged landscapes. Rock may be granite, sandstone, or any of a host of others; plants and animal life vary even more. The saguaro cactus forests of the Sonoran Desert give way to the agave plant to the southeast and the Joshua tree to the north. Further north stretch the endless reaches of sagebrush of the Great Basin.

Common features are equally striking. Life in the desert must suit itself to short feasts and long famines. Like the life of the high mountains, growth is often crowded into one short season, and much of the structure of the plant or animal is built around the characteristics needed for survival during the rest of the year. Conservation is the basic survival requirement in the desert—conservation of water.

The backpacker in the desert has much to learn from the forms of life that survive there the year round. He must be prepared for extremes of temperature, not simply of heat but of cold as well. Without heavy vegetation cover, large bodies of water, or significant masses of water vapor in the air, the desert responds much more directly to the sun's daily cycle than other places. When the sun comes up, its radiation heats things up rapidly, and when the sun goes down, the heat is radiated to the black sky just as rapidly. Blazing days and freezing nights are quite common in the desert. Actual temperatures will vary with location and season, but it is a general rule that the daily temperature range in desert regions will be great. The desert is not the jungle, and you must be prepared for chilly nights as well as hot days.

CONSERVING WATER

The human body will function properly only within a very narrow temperature range, and it will not even survive if the temperature of the vital organs goes much above or below the level it should be. Even so, we can function well in widely varying environments but there is a price.

The price is the need to maintain the right body temperature. When it is cold, you cannot hibernate like a snake; you have to burn enough fuel to keep warm. Similarly, when it is hot, your body must be cooled to keep its temperature from going too high. Cooling is our main concern here.

There is only one way that the body can cool itself in situations like desert walking with no convenient swimming pools or air-conditioned restaurants, and that method is by evaporation. Turning liquid water into water vapor uses up lots of heat, so the body sweats when it gets too hot, and when the sweat evaporates, the skin is cooled. By increasing the circulation to the skin, the body ensures that the blood is cooled.

Clearly, this cooling method requires water—the more cooling, the more water. So if one wants to conserve water in the desert, the way to do it is to minimize the amount of cooling which is necessary and to ensure that it is as efficient as possible. The amount of water needed by the body for its other functions is small by comparison, and the possibilities for reducing it are minimal.

If the body is to remain at a constant temperature, the amount of heat lost must be exactly the same as the quantity of heat gained. If one exceeds the other, the body will get warmer or cooler, and this can go on only for a short time before trouble ensues. For a simple example, suppose the air temperature is exactly the same as body temperature—that is fairly hot, nearly 100° F. Under such conditions, there will be no heat loss or gain from the air alone. Heat loss will be due to evaporation, and heat gain will be from sunshine, touching hot objects, and the body's own heat production.

In the desert, direct sunshine can contribute a good deal of heat. This can be reduced by wearing light, loose clothing, and especially by wearing a hat with a high crown and a wide brim. Obviously, it is even more efficient to stay out of the sun in a shady spot. This may sometimes be advisable in a hot desert during the summer months—one simply camps in a shady spot during the day, confining travel to the evening, night, and early-morning hours.

During the day, hot objects will include anything in direct sunlight. The ground temperature on a hot day in the desert is much hotter than the temperature of the air. Generally, only the feet are touching the ground, so protection is provided by relatively thick lug soles on the boots. Thin-soled shoes should be avoided. If you sit down to rest on hot ground, you may need to protect yourself with your pack or sleeping pad.

Generally, the biggest contributor of heat is the body itself. The body gets energy by consuming food as fuel, but this can never be done with perfect efficiency. Some of the energy from the food is simply generated as heat, so the body is always producing heat as long as it is alive. A certain amount is produced at rest, and the more work the body does, the more extra heat is produced. If the environment is colder than the body, then the extra heat is used to maintain normal body temperature, but in the situation we are discussing, all this heat must be eliminated by evaporation of water. It follows that the more work the body does, the more heat has to be eliminated, and the more water will be required. To conserve water, keep your activities slow, steady, and efficient. Sudden bursts of energy in the desert produce great quantities of sweat which run off the body without doing their job of cooling.

These rules are also sensible for other reasons. When you are overheated, your body does not perform well. Traveling at night during really hot periods will often get you twice as far, besides keeping your water-consumption down. This is true simply because your body functions better when it isn't overheated, even though visibility is poor.

A light-colored hat with a wide brim, high crown, and good ventilation is important to keep you cool and to keep your brains from becoming addled. You need all the good sense you can muster in desert travel, and you'll have very little left after the sun has beaten down on your bare head for a few hours.

Don't risk sunburn. It is a dangerous matter in the desert. Do your sunbathing judiciously, and cover up with light, loose clothing when water is a problem—the water won't evaporate so quickly, the cooled air will remain near the skin for a little while, and your body won't be heated so much by direct sun.

WATER—HOW MUCH AND WHERE

How much water you need to carry depends on how far it is to the next sure supply. You must also allow leeway for unforeseen circumstances. Amounts will also vary with the individual and with temperatures. As a rule, figure on a minimum supply of a gallon per day for each person. Always err on the high side, even though each gallon weighs over eight pounds.

Once you have gained some experience with the amount your body needs, you may be able to reduce this amount of water somewhat, especially where safety is not a problem—hiking in hills above a water source, for example. In any case, learn the trick of tanking up on water when you stop at a supply. Your body can store quite a bit of water itself, and provides the most convenient place to carry reserves. If you are camped at a spring, start drinking as soon as you get up, taking a sip every few minutes. If you get in the habit of drinking a lot when water is available, you'll find you can go a long way before you have to break out the supply in the pack.

Don't try to reverse this coin by allowing your normal reserves to become depleted, unless it is absolutely necessary. It takes more water to replace the body's usual supply after it is overdrawn than it does to keep the supply up in the first place.

The matter of finding water should never be left to chance in the desert. In some desert regions, water supplies are relatively frequent, and practice will teach the desert rat to dig it out, but desert regions are not the same, and your basic water supply should never depend on the uncertain possibility that you will find a waterhole.

Check with someone who *knows* about water supplies. Rangers, ranchers, or other local people who have visited an area recently should be able to tell you whether you can depend on a spring or a creek. Don't depend on maps, which may be inaccurate or out of date. I have found permanent springs shown on U.S.G.S. maps dried up even in nondesert areas. Don't believe everything you hear. "Oh yeah, I was over to Buzzard Spring just last week, and it was running high" may mean just that, or it may mean your informant has never even heard of Buzzard Spring but won't admit it to some cocky city feller. Use your judgment and a large dose of skepticism; your life may depend on it.

If you are in doubt about a particular water supply, you may have to carry enough water there for the outward journey and return to the last source or continued travel to the next sure source. So for a day's journey to Dubious Creek, you would have to carry at least two gallons of water per person, one to get you there and one to get you back.

Water containers for use in the desert must be dependable. Cheap or poorly made canteens and bottles are all right where they may merely mean a couple of hours of dry going, but in the desert there is no room for wineskins with split liners or canteens with leaky rivets in the covers. Always put on the lid securely when you set the canteen down. A careless kick can be serious. Polyethylene bottles must be kept well away from the fire.

You can travel for some distance on your body's reserves of water if you are careful to conserve them in every way possible, but save this sort of endurance trial for emergencies. You will be more comfortable and use less water if you take small sips when you feel the need, rather than holding out as long as possible. Your body does not work very well when it becomes dehydrated either, and you run a much greater danger of overheating. When your mouth gets dry, take a small swig and roll it around for a while to wash away the sun.

Finding water follows fairly obvious rules, combined with any knowledge you may have of patterns in a particular area. Plant life generally indicates water, especially if there are a number of trees growing together.

Unfortunately, the water may be quite a way down, especially in a dry season. If you find good plant growth near a dry wash, try digging at the lowest point.

If you hit damp soil or sand within a foot or so, you'll probably get some water further down. If not, you've had a lesson in how far down tap roots can go. There's water under that mesquite all right, but it may be thirty or forty feet deep. Converging animal trails will also lead to water, if you can find some converging animal trails. Following a gully downhill may bring you to a point where a rock layer carries the water close to the surface. Finally, there are the various survival methods, particularly the solar still. The solar still depends on the plastic sheet trapping moisture, which the heat of the sun evaporates from the soil in which the hole is dug. When the plastic sheet cools, the humid air below condenses dew on the sheet, which then runs into the container. Under the right conditions, this condensation may occur throughout the day, since heat builds up below the sheet as it does in a greenhouse, while the air above tends to cool the plastic. The method works best where there is a wide temperature change during the day. It is a good way of getting fresh water along sunny beaches. It won't work at all if there is little or no moisture in the soil—or no soil.

The method for making a solar still is shown in the diagram. You'll need four to six going all the time the sun is up to get enough water for a day, and this means you'll have to carry the equipment for making them, weighing a pound or a pound and a half. Despite propaganda to the contrary, they do not always work.

You may have guessed that I am generally dubious about such means of finding water. It's always nice to be able to find a waterhole that you weren't anticipating, perhaps by making a short detour to a grove of cottonwoods at the bottom of a bluff, and there's no question that the more you know about finding water, the better off you'll be backpacking in desert country. The fact remains, though, that you may be forty miles from the next waterhole, and whether you can spot it from twenty miles away or not, there is just one way to make sure you'll get there. That is to know where the water is to begin with and to carry a large enough supply to get you there with plenty of room for error. I have never had to try chopping open a barrel cactus, and I don't ever want to—it isn't something you should do except in an emergency. Besides, most of the desert in the

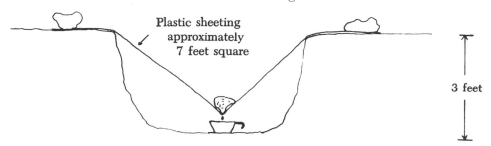

A solar still is made with a large sheet of plastic hung in a freshly dug hole, weighted around the edge with rocks, with one rock holding a drip point in the center over a container. Pieces of moist plant can be cut up and put in the hole to contribute extra moisture. The quantity of moisture that can be obtained is limited and quite variable.

United States has no large cacti. I'd hate to try sucking water from sagebrush. With my luck if I depended on a solar still, I'd actually need it on a solid sandstone rock shelf where it would be absolutely useless.

The best way to handle the hazards of desert backpacking is to be ready for them. Know what you're doing before you leave. Be *sure* to carry enough water in good containers. Take along a map which you've studied in advance, and make sure you have a compass and know how to use it. Don't take chances, and follow the normal safety rules for wilderness travel discussed elsewhere in the book.

WATER FIT TO DRINK

The desert is practically unique in that one finds there a good deal of water which is tainted, not by people but by natural circumstances. Of course, the same caution about possible human pollution applies in the desert as anywhere else. If there is any doubt about purity, don't take chances: boil or use a chemical method to protect yourself from getting sick.

Wherever there is a reasonable amount of rainfall, water collecting in a basin will finally overflow and cut out a drainage system. Thus in most parts of the continent water is running toward the sea—slowly, perhaps, but moving still. In the desert this is often not the case. Where evaporation has exceeded rainfall for eons, the hills surrounding various drainage basins may never have been cut through because water never rises high enough to spill over. In some of our deserts there are vast drainage basins which end in a lake or low point with no outlet. As the water evaporates, minerals it has leeched from the ground are left behind. After many years the deposits build up: salt flats and alkali pools. The very names in many desert regions bear witness to the disillusionment in that sterile water—Great Salt Lake, Badwater, the Alkali Lakes, Arsenic Spring, Salt Wash Valley.

Checking with someone in advance will warn you of bad water. If you do come upon water that is suspect, look around for plant and insect life. Its absence is a sure warning of trouble, and the possibility of arsenic should make you wary. Even where plants are growing, water may be too saline or full of other minerals to be potable, but where other life is flourishing, a taste will not hurt you.

TOO MUCH WATER

In desert regions plants are scattered and there is little soil. When water does fall it is usually in the form of hard thunderstorms, and runoff is rapid, because little moisture can be trapped and stored. This is when the normally dry washes and arroyos are filled with sudden torrents. Watch out for these sudden floods, even though they don't occur frequently. If great thunderheads are billowing over the hills, it is a good time to stay out of that narrow canyon leading up to them—don't forget that it was formed by the water rushing down. Above all, don't camp in the bottom of a dry wash, lest you have a sudden surprise during the night. Debris along the sides of gullies and washes will often show you how high the water rises. Camp a little higher than that.

If you are hiking in a river valley below a control dam, in Grand Canyon for example, be especially careful to camp high or to check with the authorities before you go. Such dams have completely stopped the normal river cycle; the amount of flow is controlled not by the rainfall but by the dam. If a call is put on the river downstream from you, the water level may suddenly go up five or ten feet when the dam is opened. If you happen to be camped by the side of the water when this happens in the middle of the night, you are in for an unpleasant shock.

OTHER CAMPING HINTS

The obvious search for afternoon shade should not lull you into forgetting the morrow. The early-morning sun in the desert gets hot in a hurry. If you want any sleep in the morning, you should take the morning shade into account. You might use the sun as an early alarm clock instead, but personally I hate to wake up overheated and dry. In the absence of natural shade, you may want to pitch a poncho or a tarp as an awning, a particularly useful trick at lunch and during rest stops.

In deeply carved country, cooling generally creates strong downcanyon winds in the evening, so try to pick a campsite that avoids them. If you can't stay away from them, at least weight your gear down so that you don't lose half your equipment if the wind suddenly comes up while you're down at the creek for water.

Be particularly scrupulous with sanitation and trash in the desert. Carry out anything that doesn't burn completely, choose latrines carefully, burn the toilet paper if possible, and don't pollute streams, especially small ones, by washing in them. Carry washing water away from the channel. Water in the desert is rare and precious, and even in sparsely populated country other people and animals will seek out the smallest creek. Leave it clean for them. The same rule applies to campsites. You want to camp near water, and so does everyone else. Leave the site at least as pleasant as you found it.

If you use fires for cooking or warmth, burn dead wood only. Lots of living desert plants look dead and burn easily, but that is not an excuse for breaking them off and using them for fuel. In heavily used areas, use a stove, and encourage others to do the same. Perennial plants grow very slowly in the desert, and it is disgusting to destroy a beautiful campsite for generations just for cooking fuel.

FINDING YOUR WAY

The general principles of getting around in the desert are no different than for anyplace else, but there are a few special cautions worth mentioning. In badlands, canyon country, and similar regions, watersheds and landmarks are often very confusing. One can easily become lost in a maze of gullies or canyons, and special care is needed to prevent becoming lost. The practice of "following water to civilization" is particularly inapplicable in desert regions, unless careful thought is given in advance. Water may lead to a seasonal lake in the middle of nowhere, or it may follow hundreds of miles of impassable canyons. Careful mapwork and advance study of watersheds are essential.

SEASONS

Again like the high mountains, deserts frequently are out of bounds for normal backpacking during several months of the year. Study your particular region for temperatures, snowfall, water, and the like. In general, fall, winter, and spring are the best seasons for desert backpacking. Summer trips in the desert should be undertaken only after careful checking and usually only after you have had some experience. Regions like Death Valley may require night travel in the summer months.

Backpacking in Winter 20

For backpackers whose favorite wilderness lies deep under the snow during the winter months, cold-weather camping can provide a fascination matched at no other time of the year. Snow camping is also more difficult than bedding down in summer meadows, especially for the self-propelled camper, and far more skill and endurance are required than in milder seasons.

In snow country, winter brings peace and solitude to many areas that have become crowded and noisy in summer. The beauty of the winter landscape is the equal of any other season, and the quiet clarity of the air is unrivaled. Winter brings challenge for the competent and potential danger for the careless, both of a much more serious nature than trials and threats that occur in milder seasons.

Because of its unique rewards and difficulties, deep snow country is a special place for the experienced backpacker, a place where true wilderness can often be found even in regions relatively close to civilization. There is a peculiar exhilaration in the winter wilderness that can be found at no other time of year.

Special cautions must be applied, however. Except in a few particularly harsh environments, the summer backcountry rarely presents any serious danger to any traveler who takes the most elementary safety precautions. A couple of nights out in the woods at most times of year will make you hungry, and if you are not adequately clothed you will be a bit the worse for wear, but that's all, providing you keep your head. Even in the mountains in the summer, a person who is properly equipped can generally spend a night out suffering no more than moderate discomfort. In winter things are not so simple. Adequate clothing, equipment, food, and the skill to use them well are often essential for survival, not merely for comfort.

In summer, I really believe that any reasonably healthy person who has not allowed himself to dissipate completely can manage to go on a successful backpacking trip. He may have to limit his goals at first, and he certainly will need to be careful of his equipment and load if he is not in proper physical condition, but normal good health is the only qualification for easy trips. The victim of the idiot box and the reclining chair may be dog tired at the end of an easy day, but he can manage it, and he will feel good on Monday morning.

In winter this is not the case. Some winter trips are easy, and some winter activities are not strenuous. Backpacking in snow conditions that may change in a few hours is a different matter, however. Physical reserves are required that are not necessary in summer. A typical winter trip will require a heavier pack than a summer one. More clothing, heavier sleeping equipment, more food, a more comprehensive emergency kit, and various incidentals must all be carried, and either snowshoes or skis must be worn. Travelers in winter often have to break trail through powder snow or breakable crust, and this is strenuous exercise. On reaching camp, it may be necessary to stamp a platform before a tent can be pitched and before one can stand without the aid of snowshoes or skis. Days are short, weather can be severe, water may have to be melted. Simply getting up after a spill in soft snow can be quite tiring for the novice to wilderness travel on skis or snowshoes.

This partial catalogue of difficulties is not intended to discourage the prospective winter visitor to the wilderness. It is merely cautionary. A rank beginner may well enjoy easy snowshoe hikes or ski tours on trails, perhaps including overnight trips to cabins accompanied by experienced companions. True wilderness travel in deep snow country is not for the neophyte, however. Start backpacking and camping in mild weather, and take to the snowy trails when you feel physically fit and at home in the wilds. If you want to start in winter, begin with short trips of a few hours on skis or snowshoes, *with companions*, or start camping close to home or car. Cold-weather camping, like cold-water swimming, should be approached with caution. It's all right to plunge right in *after* you know you can take it.

WALKING IN THE SNOW

Backpacking with a few inches of snow on the ground is not much different from doing the same thing with no snow. You must make sure that your boots are heavy and watertight enough for the conditions and that your clothing is adequate for the weather conditions. Other equipment must also be suitable. With a light autumn snow cover it is usually best to clear a tent site of snow so that the tent can be pitched directly on the ground, but in spring the snow cover is likely to be more consolidated; a bare spot may be so wet that it is just as well to camp on top of the snow.

Occasions when it is practical to hike with snow on the ground may range from relatively mild spring conditions or moderate weather in places which do not receive a heavy winter cover to the extremely severe cold that may be found in midwinter during a light snow year in the north country. Camping techniques range accordingly between regular summer methods and the snow-camping procedure outlined below.

Besides taking special care that they have adequate clothing, shelter, and food, hikers in cold weather must beware of one particular danger, especially when engaged in fall and early winter camping in heavy-snow regions. They must remember that even though there may only be six inches of snow on the ground when they leave, a storm in the backcountry could easily bring a couple of feet or more, making the trip *out* a very different affair from the one going in. On snowshoe and ski trips when a heavy base has already been built up, an additional two or three feet is of no particular consequence and may even make the going easier, but for hikers caught by the first heavy snow of the year, a pleasant autumn hike may easily be turned into a survival ordeal. Backpackers should be wary of this possibility in fall and in early winter, particularly in the mountains, and they should go prepared. On long trips into deep wilderness, this will probably mean carrying snowshoes even if they are not needed for the trip in. Four days of good going can get you a long way in before there is much snow on the ground, and if you'd like to be sure of getting out again before spring, think about what the same trail would be like after heavy snows and drifting winds.

335

WINTER TRANSPORTATION: SNOWSHOES AND SKIS

In areas where the snow comes and goes and at times when the snow is shallow enough or well enough consolidated to allow normal walking, camping and hiking are simply a bit more challenging than they are when there is no snow on the ground. When the snow pack begins to build up, however, travel becomes impossible without special equipment designed to keep the traveler on top of the snow. In principle this is fairly simple: you fasten something to each foot which increases the area bearing your weight and thus prevents you from sinking too far into the snow.

There is not adequate space here to go into the selection of snowshoes and skis in great detail, and I have discussed this and other winter backpacking subjects in considerable detail in my book on snow camping. Essentially, the choice depends on the sort of country you want to travel. The first choice to be made is between skis and snowshoes. Skis are the more elegant form of transportation, and in country where they are suitable they are much faster. With skis one can slide effortlessly on downhill sections of a trip, while with snowshoes one must still walk. Properly chosen and waxed skis also allow a lot of gliding on the flat and on gentle uphill slopes, except when breaking trail though heavy snow. By comparison, snowshoes require one to slog along. Finally, on many kinds of steep, open alpine terrain, skis are much easier to use than snowshoes, whether for up- or downhill going.

Before you conclude that no one in his right mind would use snowshoes in preference to skis, though, you should consider the other side of the coin. Skis are very awkward to carry when they are not in use, whereas many kinds of snowshoes can be strapped on the back of the pack so compactly that only their weight will even be noticed. Skis require snow deep enough to provide a reasonably clear path, especially on steeper slopes, and to cover rocks and stumps enough to prevent damage to the skis. Snowshoes have considerably more latitude. This difference is of little importance in places like the Sierras which have plenty of snow and open terrain, but can be decisive in regions like the Northeast which have less snow and more brush. Skis are also generally more expensive, less adaptable in use with various sorts of footwear, and demand more preliminary practice.

As a general rule, the hiker who wants to continue backpacking after the snows fall can start snowshoeing almost immediately, and he can become a skilled snowshoer in a fairly short time. Skis take more initial practice and gradual development of skills, especially for steep slopes and alpine conditions. In regions like the Northeast, skiers are more confined in their range. For country with heavy snow cover, though, skis are by far the finest means of transportation in winter.

There are many specialized varieties of both skis and snowshoes, and there is not enough space here to go into detail about choice. For snowshoes the following general considerations apply: (1) Longer shoes are faster

Some good snowshoe designs for different conditions. At the left are modified bearpaws, good in very brushy country, and fairly good for climbing. The long shoes with tails are usually known as Michigan or Maine snowshoes, and they are very good all-around models. Second from the right are Green Mountain bearpaws, a good compromise for mountains and thick woods, but not so good for steep climbing as the regular bearpaws on the right. The latter are worst of all on regular trail travel.

337

and more comfortable to wear in open country and on good trails, but they are not good for steep slopes or brushy, rough country; (2) upturned toes are best in light, powder snow and with moderate slopes; straight toes are good for step-kicking on steep slopes, but are a pain in the neck the rest of the time; (3) tails help the shoes track and reduce dragging, but they become inconvenient in brush; (4) the area of the shoe governs flotation; smaller shoes sink deeper, and more body weight or a heavier pack should indicate a bigger shoe; a long, narrow shoe may have the same flotation as a shorter, more rounded one; (5) all snowshoes should be heavier at the back, so that the toes will lift clear of the snow without special effort; (6) the area in front of the foot which actually bears weight determines whether the shoe will tend to "dive"—the smaller the front area, the more dive; a toe-hole close to the front of the shoe will make the shoe dive and will be better for climbing, but the more true this is, the less comfortable the shoe will be for straightforward going; (7) the awkwardness of snowshoes depends mainly on how far apart the legs must spread in walking, and this depends both on the width and form of the shoes—the Michigan and Maine patterns, for example, are wide in the center, but they fit together in a walking pattern so that the feet don't have to spread far; longer shoes will do the same with a long, gliding stride.

Any well-made pair of snowshoes will do in almost any country, even though each type has particular advantages. My own preference for general use is the Maine or Michigan design, both of which are rather like the old beavertail styles except that they have toes curved up a few inches. In mountain country I use bearpaws, which have no toe lift at all and which have the toe hole well forward. In regions where the advantages of very long snowshoes are evident I almost always use skis, so my experience with long snowshoes is limited.

Like snowshoes, skis come in specialized versions, but unlike good snowshoes, they are not all equally rugged. Most of the ski-binding-boot combinations used for downhill skiing these days can be dismissed out of hand for wilderness use, but with the increasing availability of Nordic touring equipment, the self-propelled skier still has a vast variety of equipment available. Any skiing gear which will be used on the flat and uphill as well as on downward runs must be adjustable to permit the heels to lift and the ankles to move back and forth. Rigid modern downhill arrangements won't do.

Acceptable equipment for wilderness skiing with backpack can range from Nordic "light-touring" gear to slightly modified downhill equipment. The lighter the equipment, the more enjoyable it is to use, but since safety and versatility have to be major considerations for wilderness skiing, lightness must often bow to conservatism. For most backpacking trips regular Nordic touring skis, 60 millimeters (2 ⅓ inches) across in the center, are the minimum size suitable in durability for backpacking in unbroken snow on varied terrain. Experienced wilderness skiers in suitable terrain can often manage with light touring equipment, but one should be wary of using such fragile gear in deep wilderness. For alpine wilderness travel, Nordic mountain skis should be considered the minimum in sturdiness—their steel edges are a necessity on steep and icy slopes. When alpine skis are used they should be fairly soft if possible, since stiffer skis tend to bury themselves in troughs of soft snow. "Deep-powder" types are excellent.

Bindings and boots for wilderness backpacking must be such that the heel will rise easily from the ski during cross-country travel. Boots and socks should be heavy and warm enough for the conditions that may be encountered; neither ultralight Nordic shoes nor alpine molded casts are suitable for the varied demands of the generalist.

My own recommendations would be as follows: for the backpacker on really easy terrain who plans to travel mainly in groups or mainly on day tours with occasional overnight trips in good snow, standard Nordic light-touring equipment with pin bindings and insulated boots; for the person who wants to do a lot of week-long or weekend backpacking on skis, mainly along trails, roads, or rolling country, standard touring skis, Nordic cable bindings, and the best insulated Nordic touring boots he can find; for the mountain tourer who expects to go through a lot of rough country, crusty snow, and icy slopes, but who is willing to sacrifice some downhill speed and control for better mobility, ski mountaineering boots, Silvretta bindings, and mountain touring skis; for the mountain tourer who doesn't want to sacrifice any of the thrills of the downhill run, a flexible downhill ski, Ramy or Eckel bindings, and a good ski-mountaineering boot.

TRAVEL IN THE SNOW

Whatever your means of transportation, on foot, ski, or snowshoe, the most important thing to remember in planning trips for the snowy seasons is the

Ski touring in the backcountry.

variability of the snow cover. The experienced mild-weather backpacker learns to judge his capabilities pretty accurately. With some general knowledge of the country and a map he can plan to get from point A to point B with relative confidence. Except for difficult off-trail routes near the peaks even the weather is not likely to slow him too much. Even the exceptions can usually be anticipated—ridges or valley rims that may or may not turn out to be passable, and so on. Snow upsets all this easy planning: the smooth ski tour of one day becomes a hard three-day slog with different snow conditions; the easy hike through six inches of powder becomes an endurance trial after a heavy night's fall; a little sun changes simple snowshoeing atop a crust into a grueling slog through sticky, wet, soft, heavy slush.

Snow can be deposited rapidly, it can form deep drifts in minutes, and it can change quickly in important ways. This fact, combined with the severity of winter weather conditions and the more isolated circumstances which generally prevail during the winter months, makes it necessary for the wilderness traveler to allow himself much greater margins for error when

340

planning trips. One of the unavoidable consequences is a much heavier pack.

Planning winter trips will depend on your means of transportation and the area where you travel and on information which you must obtain either through experience or research. The depth of the snow cover is often a vital factor in determining what a particular tour might be like, and this will vary with region and year. By midwinter of practially any year you can confidently plan to ski almost anywhere in the High Sierras of California, but that is certainly not true in New England. A late December trip through the Rockies might slide over a snow cover a couple of yards thick or take you up a trail as dry as it was in July.

The most difficult conditions for winter travel occur when there is enough snow to make walking difficult or impossible but not enough to provide a smooth cover over which to ski or snowshoe. The rocks stick out far enough to make skiing impossible, snowshoes take a terrible beating and tend to sink and jam between boulders, and the walker finds himself plunging repeatedly through the unconsolidated snow. In these conditions, all but the most ambitious are best advised to stick to smooth valley trails, where ski touring and snowshoeing are possible long before steeper slopes are filled in.

Depth of snow is relative to terrain. On the plains, fields, and beaches, a few inches of snow makes ski touring with Nordic equipment so speedy and effortless one seems to ski in a dream. Mountain boulder fields will require many feet of snow for snowshoeing and even more for skiing. An open forest floor makes for easy travel with little snow, but brush, small growth, and deadfall take much more snow before easy travel is possible. Whatever your means of transportation, pace and ambitions have to be adapted to the prevailing snow conditions, and plans have to take into account the possible changes that may precede your return to civilization. A change for the worse will cause you to regret running your supplies down to the end.

The most important special feature of the winter trail is the much greater need for regulation of the body's temperature. Cold air requires that you dress heavily at camp and during rests, but strenuous going forces your body to produce lots of extra heat, and you may find yourself sweating almost as soon as you get going. Normal human frailty prompts most people to procrastinate at each step of stripping down—*don't wait*. Take

341

Warm, well-chosen clothing is vital for wilderness travel in the winter.

clothes off before you begin to sweat. Perspiration will soak into your clothing almost unnoticed until you stop, and then the chill wind will remind you that sweat-soaked clothes are poor insulators. Wet clothes in winter are dangerous, and they get wet as often from the inside as from outside.

Clothing is discussed in an earlier chapter, and it is only mentioned here to note that it is important. In summer you can get away with a lot, but cold weather is often unforgiving of such carelessness.

There are several things that summer backpackers are likely to forget when they first hit the trail in the winter. Winter days are short—remember? In summer you may be able to get away with late starts and late camps, but in winter that sun goes down early, and then it gets *cold*. Wilderness travelers tend to become dehydrated easily. You work hard, you may be panting, and you often sweat without knowing it because the perspiration evaporates quickly. Winter air tends to be dry, so that you lose more moisture, and the fact that available water is frozen may make you drink much less than you need. Whether you stop for tea, get lots of liquid at supper, or solve the problem another way, it is important to maintain an adequate liquid intake. Among other things, your body is much more vulnerable to shock in case of injury if it is dehydrated. Also, it is more important to keep the food going into your system in cold weather. If you don't, hard exercise can easily drain your ready reserves, leaving you without fuel for warmth when you need it. Eat fats and proteins for staying power and carbohydrates for quick fuel.

CAMPING ON SNOW

There are several major differences between cold-weather camping and living outside at milder times of the year. For one thing the harsher climate generally makes shelter necessary. It is possible to sleep out under the sky even in winter with sensible and efficiently designed backpacking equipment, but wind combined with cold often makes this impossible. Such shelter must also do more than simply shed rain. Winter camping in the woods may utilize the cheerful combination of a lean-to tent and a fire in front, but if you plan to venture into windswept regions with sparser vegetation

Wind-driven snow makes a closed tent desirable in winter.

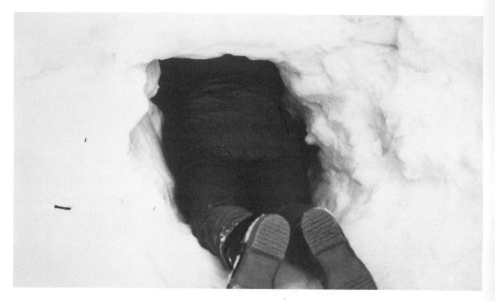

Snow shelters are good protection from the elements, although getting in and out may be chilly.

or into forests where fires would be inappropriate, you will have to build a snow shelter or have a closed tent, preferably one with a floor.

A good snow cover at least minimizes the danger of forest fire, so that there is usually no hindrance to building fires on that account. Other problems do confront the camper who wants to keep himself warm in front of a cheery fire, though. As a start, he should remember that a cooking fire is quite a different matter from a warming fire, especially when it comes to gathering wood. The mountains of wood that a healthy fire can consume have to be collected a few times before their size is adequately impressed on your mind. An ax or a saw is usually mandatory for those depending on fires for warmth in winter, both because dry wood may have to be split out of logs or stubs and because deadfall is often covered over in winter. For this purpose, emergency tools are not adequate—putting up enough wood for a good night's fire requires adequate equipment.

The problem of justification is just as relevant in winter as in summer. In some areas with plenty of fast-growing woods fuel is no problem, but in many regions it *is* a problem, and even in heavily wooded areas big fires are unjustifiable if heavy use in the summer leaves no surplus growth. Since this issue has already been mentioned, I won't belabor it here, but it is important to note that going out in the winter and proving your hardy constitution does not give you special license to cut down live trees where the cutting would be improper in summer. Deadfall may be easy enough to find where the snows don't fall too deeply, but in some places standing dead trees or stubs are the only source of deadwood. These are always good prospects for dry wood, since they will not become wet to the core until they rot out.

Cooking fires don't present the problems of all-night warming fires, and in most forested areas you can get enough wood for cooking from dead branches or deadfall, even without a good ax or saw. Squaw wood *usually* provides adequate kindling, and your pocket knife can be used to make fuzz sticks.

For any kind of fire in winter you will have to worry about the problem of a base. If the snow is only a few feet deep, digging down to the ground is the easiest expedient, but with a deep snow cover this is not practical (you don't want to have to lower pots to the fire with a line). Often the best alternative is to build on the top of a boulder when a suitable one is available, which also puts the fire at a convenient height. When this is not practical you must have a base on the snow to prevent the fire from melting its way out of sight and drowning. The traditional base uses a number of green poles, which is all right if the forest can spare them and you have the means of cutting them. A better alternative when materials are available is to use rotten chunks of logs. These are usually wet and punky enough to hold up a fire for quite a while, but they may also be buried in deep snow where you can't find them.

With a heating fire, a reflector is even more important in winter than in summer. Without a reflector, you'll need a conflagration to keep you warm and half a day to get the wood to feed it. In winter you have a ready material for building the foundation of a reflector wall—banked-up snow works to hold up a wall of logs. The snow also provides an easy method of controlling drafts. With big fire, though, you will find that melting will force frequent revision of fireplace architecture.

Backpackers using stoves for cooking in winter generally work from the comfortable interiors of their sleeping bags. Once the strenuous activity of the trail and setting up camp is over, it tends to get cold waiting around for the snow to melt and the food to heat, and the luxurious warmth of a down bag makes it a nice place to wait. Make sure you get all the chores done first. It's hard to get out of that snug bag once you're in.

When the snow cover is light, it is usually easiest to clear a spot for the tent, but with a deeper layer, a platform has to be stamped out. Start with your skis or snowshoes on; sidestep with skis and just walk around with snowshoes. Be sure to cover a large enough area, since you'll need space to walk around the tent, and you'll want a platform in front.

When you reach the point of diminishing returns with walking, start hopping up and down on the boards or webs until you are convinced that you've done all the packing you can with them on (wearing the pack will give you more oomph). Now try stepping off onto your platform to see whether you've really done all you can with the skis or snowshoes. Pack for a while with your boots. Eventually, you should end up with a fairly stable platform for the tent. Make it smooth—bumps and holes will soon freeze solid.

Set up the tent using whatever anchors are at hand that are appropriate to the snow. Sticks may work as stakes in snow of medium consistency. They can be buried and stamped down in soft snow, with the tent loops tied around them before burial. Skis, poles, ice axes, and snowshoes will all serve as anchors, but think a little beforehand. Don't use your skis to hold the main guys for the tent and then find you need them to go for water.

COOKING AND WATER

Cooking in snow camps should be kept as simple as possible, since it is usually done inside the tent or snow shelter. Stick to one-pot meals. The danger of spilling the stew in a cramped tent is bad enough without attempting any six-course suppers. In very cold weather you may be able to count on keeping some fresh food like meat without worrying about spoilage, but the main problem in winter cooking is that liquid water is often not available. Find some if at all possible. Melting snow is time-consuming and takes a lot of fuel. It takes almost as much to convert the snow to water as it does to heat that water all the way to boiling. If you must melt snow, try to find crust, ice or granular snow. Incredible quantities of light powder snow are required to get any amount of water. Melt a little snow and then keep adding more. If you start with a full pot of snow, you are liable to scorch the pan, giving a burned taste to the water and the stew. With powder snow, you are sure to scorch the pot unless the snow is added bit by bit, because the powder acts like a blotter and soaks up the water as fast as it is melted. Get plenty of liquid at meals to replace what you lost during the day, and fill your water bottle to take to bed.

A few other tips on winter cooking. Use a lot of fat. You will find that it tastes good. You need the calories, and the extra heat that is produced in digesting fat will help keep you warm. Use a cover during cooking, keep the tent door open if you can, and avoid meals that require long periods of boiling. Water vapor inside the tent in winter will condense as water or frost, and some of it will end up in your insulation.

OTHER WINTER-CAMPING NOTES

Use all of your insulation at night. Fluff up sleeping bags carefully and prepare your bed well. You may not wear your extra clothing, but you can put it in waterproof sacks or shells and use it for insulation underneath the legs and feet, as a pillow, or as extra insulation under the upper body.

Do not leave anything lying about loose outside the tent. Even a light snowfall at night will cover it up, providing it isn't blown away. Skis, poles, and snowshoes that aren't used for anchoring the tent should be stuck upright so that you won't have to dig them out.

Snow shelters are warm and protected from the wind. Learn to build them on mild afternoons. It takes practice. Igloos are hard to build except when snow conditions are right. A snow cave is generally best. It is most easily dug into the side of a large drift, preferably with a light shovel carried for the purpose. Wait for consolidated spring or wind-packed snow for your first attempt—powder snow just collapses. Make the cave just large enough to enable you to get in and make necessary movements. Dig the entrance a little lower than your sleeping spot, so that cold air will go down. Punch an air hole above you. Take your digging tools in with you in case of drifting during the night—*this is important!* Don't leave your equipment where it could be buried outside. Take it in or leave it where it could not be snowed into featureless landscape. Practice with snow shelters before you depend on using them. They are very effective, but they require experience.

AVALANCHES

One winter hazard of the mountains deserves special mention—avalanche danger. The mechanical properties of snow vary widely and are constantly changing, so it is always hard to judge the stability of a snow slope. A completely safe snow field of a morning may be very hazardous the same afternoon. Snow obeys the laws of gravity like any other substance; when the forces holding the snow on a slope becomes less than the force of gravity, the whole thing goes down. If you are skiing on the slope or snowshoeing under it when it decides to make its trip to the valley floor, you may not live to tell the tale.

Avalanche problems are too complicated to discuss in any detail here. The Bibliography at the back lists a number of books on the subject which should be read by anyone who travels the mountains in winter. Avalanches and other winter hazards are discussed in more detail in my book on winter camping. The beginner should beware of any slope between about 20° and 45° that is not heavily forested, especially during or after a heavy snow or blowing snow. Lee slopes are the most dangerous. Being in the runout path is almost as dangerous as being on the slope itself. An avalanche will run a long way on flat ground once it is moving.

Finally, remember that winter camping is very enjoyable, but it requires care and a conservative attitude. Allow a large safety margin in winter. The wilderness in snowy seasons is much less forgiving of stupidity or overconfidence than it is at milder times of year.

Long-Distance Walking   21

Certain basic problems become quickly obvious to anyone interested in long trips on foot, whether he inclines toward a summer journey along the Appalachian Trail or a couple of months in the Brooks Range of Alaska. Where water has to be carried it puts a very strict limit on feasible distances, but even if water is plentiful the weight of food begins to damp the enthusiasm when your ambitions stretch much beyond two weeks.

The weekend backpacker can take a fairly casual attitude toward the weight of food, even carrying fresh steaks and oranges if he likes. Long-distance travel, however, really brings him up against the problems of weight and preservation. He must also consider nutritional requirements which are not very important on short trips, ensuring that the normal vitamin and mineral needs of the body are satisfied.

On a long trip, the backpacker will work himself into excellent shape, and it is usually found that his capacity for making use of fuel will increase. During the first few weeks of a trip a caloric deficit will probably even serve the beneficial purpose of burning off accumulated city fat, but eventually an insufficient diet will slow the walker down. Besides, developing a constant craving for food is no way to enjoy a trip, so adequate food is essential.

Finally, I think that it is important to have an attractive diet on most long trips. If you are trying for some kind of endurance record you may choose to live for a couple of months on pemmican, but it's a lot more pleasant to have a varied diet which weighs slightly more per calorie. Chocolate bars and dried salami are all right for short trips, but they get awfully old after a week or two.

On a long trip a man of average size will probably need over 4,000 calories per day. It is possible to provide 4,000 calories of nutritional food with only 1½ pounds, but this requires concentrating almost exclusively on fats and protein. For most people this is likely to be a rather boring diet and also a fairly expensive one.

I would recommend planning on about 4,500 calories per man per day, at least until you are sure you can go for long periods with less—you may even find you need more. Small people may plan on a bit less. Using light-weight food, but with a reasonable amount of variety, this will probably result in a load of about 2½ pounds of food a day for each person. That adds up to 17½ pounds of food a week, and this figure may need to be increased if stoves are used and fuel must be carried.

Taking this figure, we have a load of 35 or 40 pounds for two weeks worth of food, depending on whether or not you have to carry fuel. Piled on top of your other equipment, this load will probably just about set the limit of the distance you will want to travel. It is possible to carry more, but it is not much fun.

REPLENISHING YOUR SUPPLIES

The conclusion of this discussion is that you should try to plan on replenishing your supplies at least every two weeks on a long trip. There are circumstances which may force longer intervals, and there are some methods which may enable you to lengthen your period of independence, but for most trips the two-week cutoff is reasonable.

The question then becomes how to restore your larder in the middle of your trip. This problem of logistics is the one which has always complicated the planning of expeditions into faraway places. Backpackers, like armies, march on their stomachs. Unfortunately, the problem of supply is much easier these days, because wilderness areas are shrinking.

Hikers on routes like the Appalachian Trail can use one of the simplest, cheapest, and most reliable means of resupply, since there are towns within easy reach of most of the length of the trail. One simply packages his gear in parcels of appropriate size and arranges to have a friend mail them to him, care of General Delivery at the next convenient post office. Small towns usually are poorly stocked with backpacking foods, but this system allows plenty of leeway. If you decide you want a little more food for the next leg than you had originally planned, you can purchase a few meals at the local grocery.

It is usually wise, in fact, if you are stopping at towns in this way, to buy the next day's food there. It satisfies the inevitable craving for some fresh vegetables and fruit. This method allows for lots of adjustability in your schedule. When you pick up one package, you send a postcard to your friend telling him to drop the next parcel in the mail.

There are two main defects of this admirable method. One is that the Post Office Department is not so reliable as it used to be, especially for General Delivery. Make sure to allow enough time for the packages to arrive. Sending *Special Handling* will speed their transit, and insuring them may get them treated a bit more carefully. Be sure to carry identification, because some post offices now require it, and have enough cash along to get supplies in case a package goes astray. Have all packages marked *Return Postage Guaranteed* in case you miss one.

The main problem with this method is, of course, that you have to walk into town. In many areas this may cost you a couple of extra days of travel, and in others the distance makes the whole idea impractical. You must also coordinate your schedule with that of the post office. If you arrive in town at one o'clock Saturday afternoon, you'll have to wait a day and a half to get your package. Check on the schedules of rural post offices, and then allow plenty of leeway. Maybe they shouldn't close an hour early, but it won't do you much good to know that when you find the doors locked.

Walking to town from your route may also have aesthetic disadvantages. It's often pleasant to drop off your route and have a beer after a couple of weeks, but there are some times when the continuity of the experience has real importance for you, and then it may take a week to reestablish your rapport with your line of travel. If you feel that this would be the case, use one of the other methods of resupply.

351

CACHING

Another good method of replenishing supplies on a long route which approaches roads occasionally is to establish caches of supplies in advance. During the planning stages of the trip, you simply take weekend jaunts to places along your route to carry in supplies. This technique has many advantages. It enables you to place your food just where you need it, eliminating the need for long side trips during your actual journey. You are independent of the schedules of local grocers and postmen. And you don't need to leave your route unless you want to. You can also establish the cache near the road or close to your path, depending on considerations of time and mood.

The defects of the cache system are fairly obvious. Lots of advance travel is necessary, a minor matter if you live within reasonable distance of the route, but not so minor if you do not. If your trip is in Wyoming and your home is in Virginia, advance trips over weekends in the spring would probably prove somewhat impractical. Under these circumstances, you may have to plant your caches just before the trip, somehow finding the extra time and patience to do it.

Caches also have to be protected from raiders, six-, four-, and two-legged. Any sturdy, tight container will do to keep out insects, but animals and people may be more determined and clever. Hide it to protect it from possible human depredation, unless the spot is exceedingly remote. A note with a moving plea may or may not be effective. Where there are trees or the right kind of rocks, hanging your supplies up should keep out four-legged scavengers. Make sure to arrange things so that squirrels cannot jump onto the top and get in that way. Metal friction-top cans will protect against rodents, and they can be buried or hung, but they are not proof against bears, so in bear country hang them well out of reach. The only major problem with metal cans is getting rid of them. Please don't toss them on the landscape just because you're on a long trip.

The degree of care and protection you give a cache should be in proportion to its importance and remoteness. Don't count on the distance from civilization alone making a food or water cache safe. In many regions food in a moving camp is relatively safe from animals, but when it is stored in one place for some time, especially when it is unattended by people, the local animal life can be expected to make a few attempts. Consider the capabilities of the local denizens when you choose sites and containers.

Don't neglect the possibilities of laying out your caches from the water. A canoe will carry far more than you ever could haul on your back, and if you are crossing rivers or lakes on your trip, you can have a pleasant advance look at the country from another point of view by bringing in some of your supplies by canoe or kayak.

Make sure that you can find your supplies when you need them. Write down the location of every cache, and be sure the location is positive. "Behind a big rock a couple of miles along the ridge north of Rabbit Ears Pass" is likely to prove vague when you come by a month later. Use bearings, markers which won't be obliterated, or some other positive means of locating the cache. All this is more important if you get someone else to lay some of your supplies out.

RENDEZVOUS

You may be able to press some of your friends into service to keep you supplied. Get one of the more dependable ones good and fired up about the trip, and then try: "Say, Harry, how about meeting me at Buchanan Pass on July 10 with a few odds and ends?" Don't tell him what the odds and ends weigh yet. In any case, once you have him hooked, drop the casual air, and make sure he'll come, through rain, sleet, or snow. Joking aside, this can be pleasant for you and your suppliers both, providing all the details are hammered out in advance so there is no chance of a foul-up. Don't pick someone who might change his mind and go on a heavy date instead.

This method can work at almost any level of difficulty and distance, although planning problems get worse as you get farther into remote areas. You might get a friend to canoe into an area with some supplies for you and spend a few days visiting. In remote areas you may be able to hire someone who will contract to bring in supplies and meet you at a certain place and date. Obviously, you have to satisfy yourself that he is reliable.

Rendezvous have great advantages in that they are adaptable to almost any kind of trip, although they require lots of advance arrangement. They provide human contact, something that might or might not attract you. Their main disadvantage is their inflexibility. You have to be there when you said you would be. If you are two days ahead of schedule, you'll have to wait, and you have to plan in such a way that there is no danger of your getting behind.

AIR SUPPLY

Rendezvous can be made with vehicles as well as people on foot, and air supply has obvious attractions for the sojourner in really remote locations. The greatest problems are those of logistics, expense, and possible interference from the weather. In many regions of the North, it is possible to arrange a meeting at a lake where the plane can land readily. This greatly simplifies packaging problems, possible confusion over location, and so on. In forested areas, lakes also provide just about the only reliable places for you and an airplane to find one another. Large snowfields and glaciers can also be used by planes equipped with skis, but this is much more complex.

For wilderness not supplied with convenient lakes, the alternative is an airdrop. You wave *hi* to the pilot from the middle of your great big visible something-or-other, and he drops your stuff attached to a parachute. I've never tried it, but it all sounds very exciting, especially if you've ever attempted to pick out a small object from a few hundred feet up, moving fast. For drops, your stuff obviously has to be packed to stand some banging, and the site and signal method from you to pilot have to be chosen with care.

In either type of air supply, make sure you have a reliable pilot who knows the country and what he is doing. If it's an airdrop, be sure he has made a few. Finding the right pilot is easier in the remote regions of the North, because small planes are more commonly used for such purposes there. A lot of bush pilots are very good, and many of them know the country they fly very well indeed. Just make *sure*.

Once you get a good pilot, don't leave any uncertainties. You're going to meet him at Big Trout Lake on such and such a date. What if he doesn't make it? Planes depend on weather and sparkplugs. What if you don't make it? Does he come back the next day, or what? If he just assures you not to worry about a thing, don't—go to someone else.

Airplanes make a lot of noise. Avoid using them, if possible. But they cost less money than you would expect. Although you have to pay for flying time both ways, from the airfield back to the same airfield, it usually doesn't take very long, and sometimes you can find someone who makes regular runs to a fishing lodge or something and will give you a reduction. Rates vary a lot, somewhere between ten and twenty dollars per half-hour. Arrange everything in advance. If you haven't agreed to pay him to come looking if he misses you, he may not feel you'll reimburse him to do it. Make a definite arrangement.

PLANNING

One of the pleasures of weekend trips, once you've taken quite a few, is that you can do them on short notice. Decide to go somewhere, throw some things in your pack, and go. One of the pleasures of long trips is in the planning. The anticipation can add to your enjoyment, and the planning can be as much of a challenge as the execution. It had better be a pleasure, because there is a lot of it. Mistakes which are minor miscalculations on short trips add up to major ones when the time period extends to weeks or months. Quantities of food, water, and fuel must be calculated carefully. Menus must be planned. Socks have to be replaced and clothing washed. An inadequate sleeping bag becomes a curse rather than a small annoyance. Boots that press on the Achilles' tendons will literally cripple the wearer. Timetables have to be met, so that rendezvous are not missed or supplies allowed to run out.

Planning such a trip requires some knowledge of your equipment and yourself. You can't afford to guess how much terrain you can cover. You have to have a pretty good idea. You must also know a lot about the country to which you are going. Temperatures, terrain, water supplies, mosquito season, and a dozen other factors have to be considered. You have to be prepared for whatever problems you might encounter, so a lack of knowledge means extra weight—things you have to take because you aren't aware that you won't need them. If the snow is melted in July, you won't need an ice ax in August, but unless you find out in advance, you may end up carrying one.

You'll need maps of your whole route early in the game. How much ground are you planning to cover, and how much time do you have? What about vegetation, trails, elevation gain, and so on? Then you have to break the trip down into legs, finding places and ways to get supplies, and arranging the details. Finally, you have to buy the stuff, package it into parcels for days, weeks, and supply points, and get it where it has to go. By the time you finally get off, you'll *need* a couple of months in the wilderness.

Don't leave anything to chance in planning a long trip. Make lists, check them, and double-check them. Pay special attention to your repair kit, since wear and tear that you might normally manage at home will have to be handled on the trail. The same rule applies to certain kinds of supplies. Minor first-aid supplies get used up, as do soap, matches, film, and so forth. Plastic ground sheets wear out. Such items need periodic restocking.

Most methods of resupply can be integrated with safety checks and perhaps with chances to get extra things you might need. If you are stopping at towns, you can obviously write friends, letting them know you are all right, and perhaps requesting they mail more socks or a yellow camera filter to your next stop. A rendezvous will also serve as a safety check, and if there are several, you may also ask someone to pick up an item for you and bring it to the next meeting place. Even caches might be checked by friends for notes if you make advance plans to leave them. Your precautions depend on your taste and good sense, but give the matter some thought. At a minimum, you might leave a prearranged sequence of messages in case a search is necessary, to narrow the range down.

RELAYING

For the completely self-sufficient party, the absolutely self-contained trip or section of a trip, there is one solution other than the native porters of the pukka-sahib set: relaying. The principle is simple. You start off with a mountain of supplies and your pack frame. You pick up as large a piece of the mountain as you can carry, tie it to your frame, and carry it off in the direction you want to go, for a period that suits your taste. You leave the piece and go back for the rest of the mountain. Eventually, all of the mountain has either been eaten or carried to its new location. Repeat.

Eventually, attrition reduces the mountain to a size that will fit into one packload. By this time, if your calculations have been accurate, the remaining supplies are just about enough to carry you to the place you are going and still leave a bit for emergencies. The method is tedious and is used mainly for climbing large mountains, but it has some place in the normal repertoire of long-distance techniques. For trips where the return is over the same route, caches are left along the way for the trip back.

AND THEN THERE'S LIVING OFF THE LAND

For long-distance trips into wilderness far from any roads, the idea of living off the country has obvious attraction. If you could count on getting most of your food from the woods and waters, you could plan on a three-month trip with only what you could carry in a reasonable pack. Sometimes it is possible, but as a rule it isn't.

To begin with, the pressure of population, excessive hunting, and poor conservation has necessitated game laws which are not designed for the pot-hunter. Even where there is sufficient game, seasons are usually very limited. This is sometimes true of fishing as well. Big game is generally out of the question except in rare cases.

For someone who wants to live off the country, the best prospects are fishing, small game, and native plants. All these may be useful to supplement food you carry, but unless you have spent lots of time in a particular area and know food-gathering methods there well, it would be unwise to plan on getting a great deal of your food from the land. You would probably find that you could hunt for food or walk, but not both. In good fishing country, or at a time and place with plenty of berries, you might get a lot of your food from the land, but think twice before you count on it, and always carry a reserve of food with you for scarce times.

Techniques for living off the land should be kept in conformity with good conservation practices, whether these are legally required or not. Especially in harsh environments, the ecological system is often a fragile thing. The fact that an animal is not protected does not necessarily mean that it is plentiful. If you hunt or fish, have some concern for the animals that are providing you with food. Don't violate game laws just because there is no warden around.

Plant hunters can also be destructive. Pick your berries without pulling the plant out by the roots, and don't tear up the plant cover in places like alpine tundra, where it regenerates slowly. Heavy plant gathering should usually be restricted to zones where plant life is abundant and grows quickly.

Living off the land, while it is still perfectly appropriate in areas like northern British Columbia, which are very sparsely populated, is becoming a less and less desirable activity in the wilderness areas which are easily accessible and suffering from severe population pressure. The normal ethic of the wilderness traveler in this day and age should be to leave the wilderness in the condition in which he found it, without a mark of his passage, rather than trying to harvest it. Men can no longer live as predators; there are too many of them.

Bivouac Camping: 22
Going Extra-Light

Personal styles of tripping in the wilderness range over a full spectrum, from the luxury lover who won't move in the morning without his fresh-baked blueberry muffins to the half-mad saints like John Muir who cover hundreds of miles on the bread crusts and tea they carry in their pockets. Both extremes are poorly represented in this book, since I never go to either one.

Bivouac camping tends toward the Spartan side of the continuum, but thanks to modern equipment it is usually a lot more comfortable than the nights suffered by some of the hard men of the past. With down clothing, lightweight waterproof material, aluminum pots, and tiny gasoline stoves, a comfortable night can be spent with amazingly light and compact equipment.

The bivouacker attempts to reduce his load to an absolute minimum consistent with safety and reasonable comfort. The definitions of both "safety" and "reasonable comfort" will vary, but the intent is to shave them down as closely as possible. Though many campers have begun this way through lack of funds, it isn't really a technique to be recommended for the beginner, especially in cold weather, in the mountains, or in the desert. Both enjoyment and safety in this sort of camping depend on skill and good physical condition. Further, equipment for this style of travel may in fact turn out to be more expensive than for more hedonistic methods, because really good quality is essential.

EQUIPMENT

Equipment for bivouac camping must be even more carefully matched with the conditions of the area in which you plan to travel than more orthodox outfits. Generally, when the lightweight specialist sets up his "bivvy" for the night, he puts on every piece of clothing he carries. There isn't any spare sweater for a cold night—the sweater is included in the initial calculations. This applies to each item of equipment. A tent is usually not carried. A light tarp may be used as shelter, ground cloth, and fire reflector, but just as often the poncho, cagoule, or walking tent doubles for rain protection on the trail and at night. In case of rain a natural shelter is found when possible, and if not, one stretches or huddles beneath one's own.

Cooking equipment is kept simple by cooking simply. In forested areas, a coffee can for a pot, a cup, and a spoon do very nicely. Where fires can't be built, food can be eaten cold, a very light gasoline stove can be carried, or chemical fuels like heat tablets can be used for small heating jobs. I feel that fires and gasoline or bottled gas stoves are the only methods worth considering except for emergency kits. If I can't build a fire and don't want to carry a stove, I plan to eat my food cold. Heating tablets aren't worth the trouble.

Obviously the principles of choosing equipment for bivouacking are the same as for any other kind of camping. There are no miracle materials that will buy you luxury at no cost of weight and money. The lightweight specialist cuts extra ounces off by sacrificing other virtues for efficiency, versatility, and light weight. If he travels in cold regions where down sleeping equipment is needed, he may use a down parka and a half-bag for sleeping, getting a jacket as well as sleeping gear into the same package. Otherwise he picks the tightest-fitting and most efficient bag, trading roominess for light weight. Unnecessary extra clothing is left at home. The most rudimentary shelter possible is used.

The equipment needed for bivouac camping cannot be prescribed, because its choice depends on the experience of the camper. In the woods it may consist of a light ax, some matches and food, and a coffee can and spoon for eating and cooking. The mountains in winter will require a light shovel and expensive down equipment with a host of other essential items.

PUTTING UP WITH DISCOMFORTS

The main difference between bivouac camping and ordinary backpacking is that the lightweight enthusiast is willing to sacrifice some comfort in the interests of increased mobility. He may not *always* be less comfortable, but by cutting down on his reserve equipment, he must willingly face the possibility of a few wet, cold nights from time to time. On a really cold night he expects to survive unharmed but understands he will do some shivering. His menu is Spartan, planned for the least possible weight, and it may be eaten cold. He eschews a spacious tent in favor of a cranny under a rock, knowing that he can travel farther without the extra weight.

Bivouacking is not always uncomfortable by any means. Warm nights under the stars and dry nights in natural shelters are remembered with affection by every hiker who enjoys camping with an absolute minimum of equipment. On occasion, however, even the most skillful suffer a miserable night. That's not so bad when the sun rises bright and warm the next morning, but sometimes the night is followed by a raw and cheerless day. Then the bivouac camper is forced to turn philosopher to explain his devotion to the art.

EXPERIENCE AND PHYSICAL CONDITION

Bivouac camping is a delightful style of backpacking. It allows a more intimate contact with one's surroundings than more elaborately equipped methods do. The lightly equipped hiker can cover a tremendous amount of ground in a day, even in rough terrain. However, the line between effective lightweight travel and getting into trouble because of inadequate equipment is fine—that is what bivouacking is all about. The lightweight specialist has to know what he is doing. He may not be able to afford the mistakes that inexperienced people are bound to make. It is important to work into this type of backpacking gradually, as you gain experience and knowledge both of your own ability and the vagaries of the land you travel.

Bivouacking with a real minimum of equipment demands precise knowledge of the area in which you are traveling. How fast can you drop down to timberline? How easily can fires be made in the rain? How cold does it get at night four thousand feet above the highest weather observation station, and how hard do the winds blow? The average backpacker simply takes enough equipment to allow him plenty of leeway, but the bivouacker wants to cut this to an absolute minimum, and he must have a pretty good idea of the answers to such questions. The experienced wilderness traveler in an unfamiliar area will always take more than he needs, because he has to allow room for error about conditions.

The beginner also should beware of leaving basic equipment home too soon. Practice the techniques of improvising a shelter before you stake your life on being able to do it. Bivouacking safely requires skill and judgment on such matters that will come only with experience.

One other factor which is important for bivouac camping is good physical condition. Going extra-light requires a certain amount of gambling with weather conditions. If you lose the gamble, you are thrown on your body's reserves of endurance and strength. The dependability of those reserves and your proper assessment of them are even more important than your equipment as a guarantee of reasonable safety. If you are out of shape, you may be using most of your available strength to cover the distance you have traveled, and a good meal and warm sleeping bag may be essential to allow your body to recover from the day's exertions. If this is the case, a cold night may leave you in poor shape to handle any difficulties. These are the ingredients of real trouble in the backcountry.

Understanding your body is also important. Too many people, especially men, refuse to admit that their bodies have limits. The superman complex often blinds one to information that is critical for successful bivouacs. No two people's bodies work in quite the same way. Metabolism, weight, circulation, and a dozen other factors vary greatly. In consequence, tolerance of cold and different kinds of food is completely different from one person to the next. Such tolerance does not necessarily correspond with general physical condition. Thin, wiry, lightweight people tend to chill more quickly even if they are in excellent shape, because they have little fat under the skin (fat is a good insulator) and because their surface area per pound of body weight is greater, causing them to lose a higher percentage of heat.

Many other factors enter into cold tolerance, however, so that it is impossible for anyone except you to predict how many wool shirts you will need to get through a cold night, even if you use every heat-saving trick known. You will be able to predict such information only by watching how you react in different circumstances. Your responses to different kinds of food in different situations are just as important and even less predictable by an outsider. Some people can sit out a cold night, fueling themselves happily with dry salami and chocolate bars. Others cannot tolerate fats when they get cold—their circulation to the stomach is too poor to digest it —they need sugars and perhaps hot food. Find out your idiosyncracies in advance.

A CONTINUING EXPERIMENT

Though bivouac camping is often comfortable and almost luxuriant, it is also wrapped up inextricably with a kind of self-testing and stoicism. One tests and refines his skills at taking every advantage of his knowledge of the land and the capacities of his body. A bit of care will ensure that this doesn't involve undue risk, but it will inevitably call for endurance of some discomfort. You can't find out how little you can get by with except by trying to get by with less and less. Pushing yourself to the limits is a good thing; you will usually find that they are a lot farther than you imagined. The human body is a very elastic thing, especially when it is frequently stretched so that it does not become brittle.

Still, this kind of testing is not everyone's cup of tea. It is possible for anyone in good health to backpack without sacrificing much in the way of comfort and bodily pleasure. The same cannot be said of bivouacking. If even thinking about a long, chilly night of wakeful shivering bothers you, don't try ultralight travel.

23 Backpacking with Children

Backpacking makes a really pleasant family sport, providing that a reasonable amount of common sense is used in planning family trips. Children cannot be expected to go like adults in their prime, nor can they be expected to want to repeat the experience of an unpleasant first trip. Older kids with adventurous spirits may be willing to put up with quite a few hardships and still enjoy themselves, but younger children require gradual acclimatization to an unfamiliar environment. Don't make their first trip on a weekend in October when the weather looks like it might pour cold rain down for a few days in a row. The same cautionary note applies to older kids who think that a walk in the country means a stroll in the park at the end of the subway line. A lot of young people (like a lot of old people) don't adjust easily to strange surroundings. Take them car camping and on day hikes on nice sunny weekends to break them in.

BACKPACKING INFANTS

In some ways infants are easier to handle on backpacking trips than older children are. They don't want to walk, aren't yet place-oriented, and they almost always love the movement of the carrier. A baby may fuss when you first put him in the carrier, but he will quiet down as soon as you get moving, unless he is really uncomfortable for some reason. Plan your trips in reasonably clement weather, and allow plenty of extra time for feeding and changes, and you should be able to take a pleasant trip with the baby along.

The biggest problem on trips with infants and toddlers is the bulk of their clothing, since you need to carry a lot of changes. If the weather is at all chilly or windy, you don't want to leave wet things on the child. And while the extra clothes and diapers don't weigh very much, they take up a lot of space. They can be put in a stuff sack and be attached to the outside of the pack or baby carrier.

I have little use for disposable diapers at home, but on trips where fires can be built they are a real blessing, simply because you don't have the weight of wet diapers to worry about. I think the best kind is the one without a plastic cover which is meant to go in special pants. These weigh less and take up less space than the full-sized kind, and the lack of individual plastic covers makes them a bit easier to get rid of. While you're on the trail you can drop these into a plastic sack hung on your pack. When you reach camp, set them on a rock or branch to dry as much as possible. After you're finished cooking, build the fire up and burn them. Throw in a little at a time—if you toss three or four wet diapers on top of the fire at once, they'll put it out. This method requires firewood, and in its absence, cloth diapers will probably work better. Carry cloth diapers to use at night, anyway, so that the baby won't soak its clothing and sleeping things and get cold. The cloth ones absorb much more liquid.

If you are using cloth diapers, you may be able to make your stops where water is available and rinse the diapers out (not in the stream, please). Then you can hang them on the pack to dry, and once dry they can be stored in a plastic bag. For trips longer than two or three days, you will certainly have to stop to do washes every couple of days with any child who isn't toilet trained.

Food is really less of a problem than clothing with infants and toddlers. Breast-feeding simply requires the choice of a scenic spot for a stop. For bottle-feeding, carry plastic bottles, which are lighter and don't get broken. Use one of the powdered formula preparations that makes up on the spot, like dried Enfamil or Similac. All you need is a clean bottle with the right amount of clean, tepid water. Since you make it up at the time and don't store it, sterilization isn't necessary. Water will be available at body temperature if you put the water in the bottle an hour or two ahead of time, and then carry it in your pocket.

Other food isn't too much of a problem either, although this will depend on what you are already feeding your child. Lots of dehydrated foods reconstitute in mushy form, and you can try these out on your baby at home first. Banana flakes, pea and bean powders, dried mashed potatoes and yams, puddings, custards, and cooked cereals are examples. Regular baby cereals are as easy to make in camp as at home. If you prefer, it isn't much trouble to carry jars of baby food along.

Sleeping arrangements can be managed with pinned blankets and the like, with packs and other padded objects forming a bed. One of the fluffy synthetic "sleepers" is a good garment to use inside the blankets. As the child gets older, a Dacron-filled mummy-type sleeping bag can be gotten at a reasonable price; down is a poor choice until the child can sleep dry.

SLIGHTLY OLDER

Children are hardest to manage on trips at age four or five. The exact age varies with the child and the parent, but it is reached when he gets too heavy to carry and is still too young to walk very far. You may be able to carry the child some of the time, letting him walk for the rest, but you'll probably have to plan shorter trips. Try to make the trip interesting. Children at this age are rarely enthusiastic about just hiking. They may enjoy playing outside, but they don't want to make headway on a trail. They are capable of walking a long way but get bored doing it. Getting the child interested in looking for wildflowers, insects, trees, or what have you can serve the dual purpose of teaching him something about the subject and getting him pleasantly from point A to point B. Water is a great help. Half an hour playing in a stream will renew flagging spirits.

Don't expect to make very long distances each day with children this age. Plan to stop early in the day, and use up your extra energy taking walks or climbs from camp. Everyone will be happier as a result.

SCHOOL AGE

From about the age of six or eight, children start to become good hikers. The only trick is to keep up their enthusiasm and interest. Try to make trips pleasant and interesting. Some children can take a lot of challenge, but others can't. Don't overdo things.

By this age, children are usually enthusiastic about carrying their own packs. Give them some of their own bulky things, but don't let their packs get too heavy. Kids have plenty of energy, but not too much endurance.

Watch your children's clothing carefully, especially in cold or hot weather. Because their bodies are smaller, they can become chilled or overheated very quickly. A child needs an extra sweater when a cool breeze starts to blow and a hat to protect his head against the sun even more than an adult does. Use sunbonnets for small children in warm weather. A child also needs periodic snacks for energy. These strictures apply even to adolescents. A teen-ager generally does not have quite the reserves of an adult in similar physical condition.

Once children stay dry through the night, sleeping gear can be about the same as adults'. A few economies can be made in that younger children don't usually go on trips where really severe conditions are expected. Dacron mummy bags may be adequate during the years when they are growing fastest. A child's down bag will also double as a footsack for adult bivouac equipment. (Many manufacturers sell the same bag for both purposes.) If you do want a down bag for a younger child, you might want to consider the new kit that is being offered by Frostline. The bag is made so that extensions can be sewn on as the child grows, spreading the weight and expense of the bag over several years.

CARRIERS

Small children have to be carried, at least some of the time, and quite a few manufacturers are now making carriers. Very young infants don't get enough back support from the standard frame carriers. Several solutions are possible. The frameless carrier shown in the picture is excellent for infants, as are other similar ones. Good carriers for very young children can also be made from small frameless day packs by cutting leg holes. Finally, you can make a sort of cocoon for the child in a regular frame carrier by dropping the seat and packing the baby in receiving blankets.

One trouble with the frameless carriers is that they don't allow the child much freedom to move and look around. As the child gets older, a

A frameless carrier like this works well for infants. A shell parka can be worn over the whole thing, baby and all, if a cold wind should come up. A pack can also be carried on the back.

frame pack is more suitable. The parent is also likely to find the frame type more comfortable as the child gets heavier.

Frame carriers are made either so that the passenger can face forward or backward. The forward-facing type is easier to carry, but is a little hotter and gives the child less freedom to kick his legs around. Of the two sets of disadvantages, I prefer those accompanying the forward-facing style. If you buy a frame carrier, get one with the seat suspended in a larger compartment, like the one shown in the picture. These are adjustable, and they give you some space to store diapers, extra clothes, and so forth.

The problem of who carries the child for a backpacking trip of a weekend or a week is largely a matter of balancing weights and strength. All equipment can be packed on one packframe for the man to heft, while the mother carries the baby, or some combination can be worked out. One method is shown in the picture. An extension is mounted on the top of the packframe, while the pack is mounted in a low position. Then the baby carrier can be strapped to the extension. The extension can be purchased, or you can make one out of a couple of pieces of broomstick and a piece of aluminum rod. This arrangement isn't too bad when the child is really young, but it starts to get pretty heavy around age three!

Frame carriers like this are the best way to carry children once they are old enough to sit up well.

When you are picking routes for backpacking with a child in a carrier, steer as clear as possible of thick brush. It becomes quite tricky to get through without scratching the baby. Be careful about leaning forward to duck under brush and limbs, lest you run the baby right into the obstacle. The arrangement with the baby high on a packframe is only for open routes. The child is much higher than your head, and real care is required in watching for branches that might hit him.

OTHER COMMENTS

Younger children generally take to camping quite well, but the unfamiliar surroundings are apt to be rather scary at first, particularly at night. A little time and thought will prevent unpleasant experiences that leave lasting impressions. If you get up in response to the child in the middle of the night, shine the light on your face, not on his. That flashlight coming at you in

The carrier can be strapped on top of an extension on the frame, and the pack carried below. With an older child this makes a heavy load. This arrangement is not for brushy routes!

the middle of the night isn't very comforting. Small children should be very thoroughly diapered and sheathed in rubber pants on a cool night, so that their bedding doesn't get soaked and cold. Above all, don't push the child too hard to match your ambitions for the trip. Make it pleasant, so that he will want to go again.

Watching the World Around You 24

The backpacker has an unusual opportunity to study an environment which is relatively free of people. Occasionally he may even have a chance to see one which shows few signs of human influence, but that possibility is becoming quite rare. You can become absorbed with the natural world around you without understanding too much of its operation or being familiar with many of its other inhabitants. Personally, however, the more I know of the incredibly complex ecological system through which I am traveling, the more appreciation I gain for it.

In the short space of this chapter, it's impossible to talk very much about nature study. One of the characteristics of natural history is that the more you learn about it, the more aware you are of the inadequacy of your knowledge and the better your realization of the complex pattern of interactions that go on even in the tiniest and most barren segment of the world around us.

One of the interesting aspects of nature study in wilderness areas is that many things which might excite your curiosity are not very well understood. This is still an area in which the interested amateur can make real contributions if he is so inclined, although most of us confine ourselves to satisfying our own sense of wonder. There is a special thrill in observing wildlife in its habitat, a particular excitement in spotting a species you have never seen before or which has never been observed in the area you are

traveling. There are also moments of vision, much harder to come by, when a vantage point combines with your own state at the moment to make you really, intuitively understand some great natural process. Whether you are looking at the strata of a mountain from a particular angle, watching a bank of clouds roll in, or studying an insect engaged in his tasks, such a moment of understanding is priceless.

In this chapter I'll try to make some suggestions on ways that you can find out about some of the workings of the country around you when you go backpacking and how to become acquainted with some of its inhabitants.

LEARNING THE NAMES OF THINGS

One aspect of nature study is inevitably the problem of identification. You can study a plant yourself, or watch an animal, without having any idea what others have called it. If you want to be able to look it up later on, however, to find out what is known about its patterns of life as an aid to future observations, you'll have to find out what it is called. Learning to identify shells or birds or grasses tends to be a nuisance and a bore at first, but it usually becomes fascinating after you have passed the first frustrating stages of finding out what to look for.

Naming things in a reasonable way actually requires a good deal of understanding, and taxonomy, the science of classification and naming, is a subject with fascinations of its own. For the beginner, books which use popular names and descriptions that aren't too obscure are obviously preferred. In many areas, this is all that is ever needed. "Red-shafted flicker" is certainly adequate and is comprehensible to more people than *Colaptes cafer* just as "sugar maple" is generally more satisfactory than *Acer saccharum.*

It is worth realizing from the beginning, though, that some disciplines have their own jargon for reasons other than obfuscation. Popular names can sometimes be very confusing because they vary so much. One flower

---

Walking the wild country, occasionally you have moments of vision when you intuitively apprehend the great natural forces around you. Junipers in the Desolation Wilderness.

can have half a dozen names, and each one of them may be applied to completely different plants in other regions. This can have amusing results, as in one argument I remember over whether a tree was a ponderosa pine or a yellow pine (the same thing), but it can be very confusing as well. There is a great advantage to a scientific system of nomenclature which is generally used throughout the literature. The standard system is in Latin, although there are standardized English lists in some specialized fields. (For North American birds, for example, there is the American Ornithologists' Union checklist.)

Amateur naturalists who get interested in certain areas will ultimately have to learn the scientific system of nomenclature for one of several reasons. Popular names simply don't exist for many plants. Conspicuous forms of life like birds, mammals, and wildflowers attract enough attention to have common names, but this is not always true of small plants or insects. The keys and literature used by professionals will be likely to use scientific names. For an introduction to standard scientific nomenclature for the plant and animal kingdoms, refer to the Bibliography at the end of this book.

FIELD GUIDES FOR THE AMATEUR

The beginner does not usually have to resort to the full paraphernalia of technical descriptions these days, because good field guides, written in fairly plain English with useful illustrations, are now available for most things you might want to begin learning about—birds, trees, shells, and so forth. The importance of this for the beginner is hard to overemphasize. Many older guides are overlarge, require a dictionary to use, need long, tedious cross-referencing to find necessary information—the list could go on and on. The best modern field guides are so well done that the beginner can actually *use* one right away.

The backpacker has to be very selective about what he carries, so he must limit himself in the subjects on which he wants to concentrate on a particular trip. You won't get very far if you pack up a geology of the area, a couple of bird guides, a flower book, a manual of woody plants, and half a dozen other volumes. Concentrate on one or two subjects at a time, and then be selective in choosing your guide to each.

374

Some birds are readily identified without guides, like these magnificent Canada geese at mating time.

Invariably, the best way to learn about birds or geology or clouds or trees is to get someone who is knowledgeable to show you. He can work from the specific to the general, and in thrashing through a book you have to go the other way. He can point out the pattern of flight of a flicker or a horned lark, something a book can never adequately describe. He can tell you that the plant you found varies from the norm in a particular way because of its exposure to the elements.

If you can't get someone to teach you, the next best thing is a good field guide. It is also the transition tool for the beginner who has learned the basics and is starting out on his own or the expert on his first hike in a new region. To use a field guide effectively, you have to become acquainted with it. Each guide will have a different system of identification, depending on its purpose and its author. Some guides will require only a cursory glance at the beginning, while with others, long advance study will pay off when you get outside.

The guide must use some kind of a system of classification. A good one will have a system that is easy for the amateur to use in the field. If you're looking for a tree guide to New England for use on ski tours, don't pick one that relies mainly on leaf characteristics. Unless you have achieved some botanical proficiency, you will be better off with a flower guide that makes basic separations with simple-minded distinctions like color instead of anatomical classification. Many plant guides use keys, a programmed system which guides you through a series of questions, each answer taking you to a new question, until you finally arrive at your species, as if by magic. Try the key out on a few things when you first look at the guide. You may find that it works beautifully, or you may discover that it is hopelessly confusing. In general, keys are best used in narrowly based guides—for example, those designed for use in a particular region. Keys to large numbers of species become rather complex. One problem with keys is that if you make one mistake you are led down a dead-end path. Other systems are sometimes better because you end by comparing a number of characteristics.

Field guides to animals are necessarily more complicated than most plant guides. Although one usually has to consider more species of plants, a tree or flower will stand still for examination. A tree guide may be able to rely on one characteristic, say the needles of a pine. A bird guide must show many field marks—a tail band will do you no good if you saw just the front of the bird. A fox may leave only his tracks as a sign of his passage.

CHOOSING GUIDES

A number of general field guides are listed at the back of this book, but often the best solution is a pamphlet that confines itself to a particular region, perhaps even narrowing the field further to a season. For the backpacker a local guide will eliminate a lot of extra ounces, and for the beginner it will limit the headaches. Limitation of scope can greatly simplify a manual. Regional guides are often prepared under the auspices of universities or museums, and their limited scope may keep them out of standard bookstore channels, but they are well worth searching out.

Special regional guides often cover a larger range of subjects than

A lightweight local guide to plants and animals in the Rocky Mountains would enable you to identify the more common and prominent flowers like these columbine.

comprehensive field manuals for North America, the eastern United States, or similar large geographical areas. There are good guides to the wildlife and plants of the southern and northern Rockies, for example, which discuss all the more commonly encountered flora and fauna very well. One small volume thus covers a great deal of the most interesting natural history of a good-sized region.

It is worth spending some time in a library studying various field books. Try to envision their use outdoors, or take them out for a day, if this is feasible. Try to find those which most closely suit your purposes. A field guide becomes an old friend—you get far more out of it because of long acquaintance, so it is worth choosing well. Usually, modern guides are most useful. Improvements in printing technology have allowed much better use

377

of illustrations, and of course, new authors have a chance to profit from past mistakes. Sometimes, though, you will find a very old guide which is far superior to anything recent, especially in the special regional manuals.

Field guides are necessarily very brief in their discussions. The purpose of a field guide is to enable you to identify a hawk, not to delve into its life history. Generally, only those habits will be included which will help in distinguishing the species. You will have to go to other books to make a real acquaintance after you have been introduced by a field manual.

It is usually best to start with an introduction to the natural history of the place you are traveling in. Some broad information about the ecology of the alpine zone or the Great Basin desert will give you a framework into which to fit the life cycle of a particular inhabitant. If you want to find a species, some knowledge of its habits is a great help in deciding where and when to look.

GETTING STARTED

The natural world is a complex and continuous web; there is no starting point and no end. Whatever you begin to study will ultimately lead you everywhere else. If you begin with the landforms, the history of which extend far back beyond the beginning of life and for which a thousand years is a moment, you will still find soil produced and bound together by plants. If you look, you will find great cliffs of rock made up solely of the fossilized skeletons of billions upon billions of tiny animals.

Start at the point that interests you. You might just want to be able to identify the trees in your favorite forest or along a mountain trail. You might want to make a better acquaintance with the hawk that soars on the summer thermals while you take your midmorning break. You might want to find out something about the forces that shaped and sculpted a valley you frequently camp in or to be able to make a better pattern of the stars you watch from your sleeping bag. Perhaps you would just like to find some good salad greens.

A little patience is generally required in many fields of nature study. Bird-watching or track-hunting is likely to be a bit frustrating at first, until you have beaten enough of the basics into your skull, then things will begin

A pair of lightweight binoculars is a great help to the backpacker in many kinds of nature study. These are 6 x 25, meaning that they magnify six times, and the diameter of the objective lens is 25 millimeters. 6 x 15 is even lighter and adequate for most purposes, although they would be poor in twilight.

to come much more quickly. If you don't feel patient, try learning trees or constellations first—a few satisfying results usually come a bit more quickly.

TOOLS OF THE TRADE

Some areas of nature study require nothing more than an alert pair of eyes and an inquiring mind. On the other hand, you may find yourself carrying more weight in equipment for your investigations than for staying alive and comfortable. The backpacker has to make do with lightweight equipment in order to travel freely in the wilderness. Pick your binoculars and other items with an eye toward weight and versatility. When you've learned enough of the basics, carry a notebook and paper instead of a library of guidebooks, and look up that odd flycatcher when you get home.

Very lightweight inexpensive binoculars are now available which are ideal for the backpacking wildlife watcher. The price you pay for the low weight is measured light-gathering ability; in other words, such glasses are not effective in poor light. This is rarely critical in the backcountry, at least in my experience. For even lighter weight, you can carry a monocular instead, although this is less satisfactory for some purposes. Either will double as a magnifier by looking backward through it at close range. Whatever tools you carry, try to keep their weight down while making them serve as many purposes as possible.

The study of your surroundings can enrich your backpacking trips and your life for as long as you pursue it. Whether you limit your study to a hedonistic subject like edible mushrooms or follow an arcane interest in lichens, it is sure to increase your enjoyment of your own trips and broaden your understanding of the balance of natural forces in the wilderness. It is a pursuit which brings its own rewards.

Part 4

Where to Go
and What to Do
When You Get There

Some Nice Places to Backpack 25

There are so many fine places to go backpacking in Mexico, the United States, and Canada, that there is not the slightest hope of compiling a list of a very large number of them here. The best that I can hope to do is to mention a few interesting places for you to consider and to suggest a few spots that you might not think to investigate. Some are wilderness areas and some are not, while some fall in between. By definition a maintained trail is not a wilderness, but it may run through a true wilderness. Some trails, in fact, although they were built by people, are kept open mainly by animal traffic.

Several great trail systems and routes exist which should take precedence in a list of places to go backpacking, the first and best known of which is the . . .

APPALACHIAN TRAIL

The Appalachian Trail is a well-maintained and well-marked trail extending two thousand miles from the summit of Mount Katahdin in Maine to Springer Mountain in Georgia. Hundreds of side trails provide access and additional interest. The trail is described in detail in a series of trail guides describing each section in nearly perfect detail. The country along it varies from deep forests and bogs to the boulder fields above timberline in the Presidential Range. In the country through which it winds travel is often exceedingly difficult without trails. So for the long-distance walker in the eastern United States, the Appalachian Trail and its branches are a favorite refuge from the megalopolis. The fine maintenance is a real blessing in an area where the brush overgrows an unused trail very quickly indeed. There are many lean-tos and shelters along the trail.

Besides the guides listed in the Bibliography, you can get information on the trail from the Appalachian Trail Conference, 1718 N Street, N.W., Washington, D.C. 20036. Many local affiliated clubs cut and maintain hundreds of miles of other trails. Request a list of such clubs from the conference.

PACIFIC CREST TRAIL

Unlike the Appalachian Trail, which was established and is maintained by dedicated hikers on the East Coast, the Pacific Crest Trail varies tremendously in its condition and marking. From available information you could plan a trip over the length of the Appalachian Trail in a week, but setting up for the Pacific Crest would take long and careful checking.

The trail is about 2,300 miles long and traverses some of the most beautiful country in the United States. It begins in the arid mountains of southern California, winds through the beautiful Sierra Nevada Range and then through the Southern and Northern Cascades. Passing the rock walls of the Sierra and the glaciers of the Cascades, this trail presents one of the finest backpacking possibilities in the world. The trail is more rugged and not so well marked and maintained as the Appalachian Trail. Some sections, like the John Muir Trail in the Sierra, are heavily traveled in summer, but some other parts are not much visited. The trail passes through twenty-five national forests and six national parks. A description is available from the Pacific Crest Trail Conference, Green Hotel, Pasadena, California 91101.

THE ROCKY MOUNTAIN ROUTE

The longest route of all, and one which is not yet a trail, generally follows the Continental Divide from Mexico to Canada. The divide separates westward-flowing streams from eastward ones. It extends well over three thousand miles from its entry to the United States in New Mexico, through the high country of Colorado, over semidesert and glaciated peaks in Wyoming, along the Montana-Idaho border for a way, and finally through Montana and Glacier National Park to the Canadian border.

A trail route has been proposed which generally follows the divide, departing from it where it becomes too rugged, but only some sections of the trail actually exist, and the challenge of wilderness route finding is very real for any backpacker attempting a section of the divide route. The route passes through three national parks and many wilderness areas.

OTHER LONG TRAIL SYSTEMS

There are many other trail systems, formal and informal, which can occupy the backpacker for weeks. The *Long Trail* in Vermont is the oldest, extending 261 miles through the state, traveling in beautiful woods, and climbing in the northern section into fine mountain areas. A part of the Long Trail is included in the Appalachian Trail.

You might be surprised to know that the greatest system of state trails in the country is in Pennsylvania, which has well over four thousand miles of state trails. This system includes the new *Susquehannock Loop Trail*, an 85-mile trail within easy reach of New York, Philadelphia, and other teeming millions. You can get a map of the system for seventy-five cents from Keystone Trails Association, P.O. Box 144, Concordville, Pennsylvania 19331.

The *Northville–Lake Placid Trail* is an even better goal for refugees from the megalopolis, passing through some fine semiwilderness in upstate New York. There are about a dozen lean-tos along the route and many fine campsites. You can get a free pamphlet describing the trail from the New York State Department of Environmental Conservation, Bureau of Forest Recreation, Wolf Road, Albany, New York 12205.

AND OTHER PLACES

If you travel a bit farther, to the northern end of the Appalachian Trail at Maine's Mount Katahdin, you will find one of the finest backpacking areas in the eastern United States. Katahdin is in *Baxter State Park*, whose managers have mercifully protected it from would-be improvers, developers, and other assorted vultures, so that it remains a paradise for the wilderness lover. At the height of the summer season, you'll have to make reservations or take your chances, since the rangers will not permit overuse of the campgrounds. In spring or fall, which are nicer anyway, you shouldn't have much trouble. Unfortunately, the park policies toward winter travelers are still rather unenlightened and practically prohibitive of winter travel by skiers and snowshoers who can't afford a ranger as a companion and guide.

One of the most interesting spots in the East, and one of the least visited (believe it or not!), is in New Jersey. The great *pine barrens* stretch in from the shore, covering over a million acres, and most evidence of civilization you will find there consists of ruins dating back to colonial times. Although there are some developed campgrounds along roads, heading back into the woods will soon get you away from your fellow men. There are a few maintained trails, but it is more interesting to follow the remnants of ancient roads.

In Ohio you can follow the 500-mile *Buckeye Trail*, parts of which travel through interesting country. Some sections are rather urban for the backpacker, and permits may be required for entry or overnight camping from various public and private groups. Trail maps and information can be had from the Buckeye Trail Association, 913 Ohio Building, 65 South Front Street, Columbus, Ohio 43215.

Westerners have so much country to choose from that any listing is almost random. California alone has nearly sixteen thousand miles of trails on federal lands and over fifteen hundred miles of state trails. Colorado has over eleven thousand miles of trails and Idaho over ten thousand. These states and others in the West, besides having more trails than you could explore in a dozen lifetimes, have many possibilities for off-trail travel. Even a whole book of selected routes would necessarily be capricious and arbitrary, and picking a few trails and spots for this chapter seems nearly hopeless.

All of the national parks, all of the wilderness areas, primitive areas, and many national forests and national monuments are fine places to back-pack. Some of the national parks are becoming crowded, but getting away from the roads will usually leave the crowds far behind. Even overbur-dened Yellowstone has some wonderful little-used corners, and if you head across the northern park border to the incredibly fine *Beartooth Primitive Area,* you will find one of the wildest and most rugged regions in the coun-try, a true wilderness for the mountain-minded traveler with enough expe-rience to find his own way.

The *Wind River Range* of Wyoming is another of the best alpine wil-dernesses in the West. Many trails and routes are described in Beckey's guide (see the Bibliography), but bushwhacking is common in these great mountains.

The Northwest contains some of the most rugged mountain wilderness in the country. A circuit of *Mount Rainier* is a good backpacking project, and the rugged routes in the *North Cascades* are legendary. A guide to *Routes and Rocks in the Mt. Challenger Quadrangle* is published by the Se-attle Mountaineers, and serves both hikers and climbers. Washington also possesses the fantastic wilderness of *Olympic National Park* and adjoining areas on the Olympic Peninsula. This magnificent region has as much to offer the backpacker as any comparable region of the world, ranging from rain forests and peaks with good-sized glaciers to fifty miles of beaches and rugged coastline, most of it wilderness.

The Southwest offers good possibilities for backpackers in widely var-ied country ranging from desert to fairly well-watered mountains. The *Grand Canyon,* both in and out of the park, offers so many possibilities for the wilderness traveler that one could spend a lifetime exploring it. *Can-yonlands National Park* is fascinating in a different way. In either place it is easy to get off the beaten track if you want to.

Leaving the "lower 48" in either direction by land will lead you to wide opportunities for exploration. Mexico offers many possibilities for combining backpacking with meeting people of different cultures. For the wilderness backpacker, though, the gem of the country is probably *Baja California,* the long peninsula that forms the Pacific coast south of the U.S. state of California. Baja has hundreds of miles of beaches and desert, but it also includes some fine granite peaks. A useful guide to the rarely visited mountain country is John Robinson's *Camping and Climbing in Baja.*

Canada and Alaska have so much wilderness country that listing it is absurd. Nearly all of Alaska is wilderness, some of it quite feasible for back-packing without trails and some practically impassable by foot. A visit to the *Brooks Range* might be the dream of a lifetime for many wilderness backpackers. The Forest Service and the Bureau of Land Management have literature describing some trails maintained within their jurisdictions in Alaska. Canada's national parks are perhaps even finer than ours, and other wilderness areas in the north and the west of Canada are so huge as to boggle the imagination. The average map distorts the north in Canada and Alaska, giving no accurate impression of how vast the country really is.

In eastern Canada there is a great deal of true wilderness, unlike the eastern United States, and although much of it is best traveled by canoe, there is a great deal of fine backpacking country as well. Much of the inte-rior of Newfoundland, for example, is completely wild. There are also some excellent trail systems. The *Fundy Trail* in New Brunswick Province is one, and the *Bruce Trail* in Ontario, 480 miles long, is outstanding. For informa-tion on the latter, write the Bruce Trail Association, 33 Hardale Crescent, Hamilton, Ontario. Ultimately, the Bruce Trail will form a trail over 1,100 miles long with the Finger Lakes Trail in New York, when the latter is complete.

This short list doesn't begin to touch the possibilities open to the back-packer in North America, but I hope that some of the suggestions will get you started. Good hunting!

Saving Your Wilderness   26

Once you become interested in backpacking, you are almost certain to become a confirmed conservationist, but it may take a few years of watching your favorite spots dwindle in size and disappear before you realize how serious the possibility of the destruction of all our remaining wilderness is. Americans still tend to think there is an unlimited frontier out there somewhere, and this illusion is most prevalent around those spots that remain unspoiled. The booster mentality is still very strong in this country, despite current lip service to the environment. Tactics for destruction are sometimes more subtle now—the merits of a proposed wilderness are studied by a committee while the devastation goes on, or the virgin stands of timber are cut down to make way for roads so that more people can enjoy the scenery.

If we manage to overcome our other problems, the need for open places and wild places in this country will grow fantastically in the next few years, just as it has been growing. People from all kinds of backgrounds want to get away from the cities and away from suburbia to visit unspoiled places. Unfortunately, assorted commercial interests are hell-bent to convince them that they can't enjoy the outdoors without buying a half-dozen machines to destroy it. Population in all our parks, forests, and wildernesses is growing, but pressure is growing faster because so many people don't know how to use the backcountry without ruining it.

One of the purposes of this book is to present a method of traveling the open spaces of North America without damaging them, whether you

are walking trails near the great urban centers or crossing the most rugged wilderness. The time for pioneering is over. We have little enough wild country left, and the aim of every wilderness traveler should be to leave no trace of his passage, unless it be to clean up someone else's mess.

The first place to preserve the wilderness is where you encounter it. Carry your trash out. Bring a stove rather than break lovely, century-old snags to make your tea. Help to minimize the damage to delicate environments by population pressure.

Still, although there is some need for improvement in the attitudes and practices of backpackers, they are not the ones who are threatening the wilderness, and it *is* being threatened. Various commercial interests remain the great gobblers, abetted by their bureaucratic allies. The oil companies are busy in Alaska trying to destroy the last great wilderness in the United States. The highway interests have designs on so many places it would take a shelf of books to enumerate them. This kind of list could go on and on, but that would serve little purpose. The point here is simply that every inch of countryside will one day stand in the way of *something* justified in the name of growth and progress. The value of open lands and wilderness should be quite obvious from the current population pressure on them. It is time that we as a nation realized that wilderness is a resource far more precious than a highway right-of-way, an additional tract development, or even a few tons of minerals.

A host of practical arguments for the preservation of wild lands have been elaborated elsewhere, and I will not reiterate them here. One other point that I would like to make is simply that there is a moral issue involved. I don't believe that we have a *right* to destroy every other species and ecological system and place of beauty on the planet because it happens to suit the purposes of a chamber of commerce. During his period of claiming stewardship over the planet, man has been a poor caretaker, a fact that is becoming increasingly clear every time we open our eyes or take a breath. The lesson of the true significance of man's place in the universe is one thing that the wilderness can teach, and it is a lesson far more valuable than any oil field on earth.

Reflections of a more permanent reality. The preservation of the beauty of this wilderness depends on you—both when you go backpacking and when you are acting as a citizen.

DO IT

Those people who travel in the backcountry have learned to value wild places, and if they do not do their best to ensure preservation of our remaining wilderness, no one else will. If you have come this far in this book, *they* is you. Public pressure, if it is strong and determined enough, is a great thing. You can help by joining various conservation organizations, like the Sierra Club and the Wilderness Society, but the pressure you can exert is far more important than money. Use those groups to help stay informed of places where action is important, but don't limit yourself to what someone else tells you. If you hike in the wilderness, you owe it a little protection. If you see someone building a road in it or tearing up the meadows with a trail bike, do something about it besides shaking your head. One of the defects of the Forest Service is that it is subject to local pressure, but this can also be a virtue. If you like the way the Service is handling your favorite area tell the local chief ranger and his boss. But if you don't like it, say so forcefully, and don't let them hide behind regulation books. If you let them clear-cut the finest grove in the forest, you won't get it back.

There are a lot of issues of concern to the backpacker besides the preservation of pure wilderness. I won't go into large problems of the environment and the society, but at the most immediate level of recreational use, areas of heavy utilization are as important as wilderness. They are needed to take the pressure off true wilderness, and they are required to teach citified people the value of a stream, tree, or mountain. A person who loves a city park is going to be a lot more responsive to pleas for preservation of your favorite mountain range than someone who never sees anything but concrete.

A FEW SPECIAL ISSUES

This is a particularly critical time in the preservation of many areas, because many government agencies are now required to make evaluations of lands under their jurisdictions for classification under the Wilderness Act. Recommendation by an agency that an area be considered for wilderness status gives that region protection until Congress has acted, but recommendation that it not be so considered can be disastrous. Outside Alaska, the most important such agencies are the Forest Service and the Park Service. Without public pressure, the Forest Service in some areas will follow the pressures of the local mining and timber interests. There are many glaring examples. Find out the status of wilderness areas that you know. Are they protected? What is their status? What can be done to protect them?

Semiwilderness areas need protection, too. They are often just as fine as pristine wilderness, but show considerable evidence of human habitation and exploitation. They may or may not be suited to heavy population pressure, and they should be managed to retain their quality.

Recreational use can be just as destructive as any other form of exploitation, and this is an area that really needs your good influence. Many national parks are already overdeveloped by bureaucrats who measure their success in managing a park by the number of people they have managed to cram through during the year. This trend can be reversed only by pressure on the Park Service. People who drive through the parks without stopping except at the ice cream stand cannot be blamed—most of them don't know they are being short-changed. If the rangers have a legitimate function besides enforcement of reasonable rules, it is to introduce people to the wilderness around them. That cannot be done from a car, and cars have little place in the parks. Under current circumstances, people may have to use them to get *to* the parks, but the value of creating a miniature Los Angeles within each national park isn't open to question—yet this is what many of the development projects amount to.

The current tendency in the parks is to limit entrances by upping admission prices, requiring reservations, and so forth. These solutions may be necessary, and I would rather put up with them than see a park destroyed. But usually pressures could be better reduced by getting rid of the motor vehicles. A car takes up more space, makes more noise, pollutes more air, requires more facilities, and carries more trash than a person—or a lot of people. Let the visitors walk or put them on bicycles. That is what the parks are all about anyway. Let them stick their noses in flowers, gawk at the cliffs, wonder at the sunset, and get blisters on their feet. But for God's sake, let them leave their gasoline engines somewhere else—we need parks, not parking lots.

Appendices

Where to Get It

All the companies listed here deal in mail orders. Writing for catalogues is a good idea even if you plan to buy your equipment at a local shop. A selection of these catalogues will give you a good idea of what is available and what it should cost. An asterisk indicates a house with an especially good selection of items for the backpacker:

ABC SPORT SHOP, 185 Norris Drive, Rochester, N.Y. 14610

ALASKA SLEEPING BAG CO., 334 N.W. 11th Ave., Portland, Ore. 97209

ALPINE HUT, 4725 30th Ave., N.E., Seattle, Wash. 98105

ALPINE RECREATION, Warehouse, 4–B Henshaw S.E., Woburn, Mass. 01801

BACK COUNTRY CAMP AND TRAIL EQUIPMENT, 8272 Orangethorpe Ave., Buena Park, Calif. 90620

EDDIE BAUER, Seattle, Wash. 98124

L. L. BEAN, Freeport, Me. 04032

BERNARD FOOD INDUSTRIES, Box 487, San Jose, Calif. 95103
Dehydrated food.

BISHOP'S ULTIMATE OUTDOOR EQUIPMENT, 6804 Millwood Rd., Bethesda, Md. 20034

BLACK'S, Ogdensburg, N.Y. 13669

CAMP AND TRAIL OUTFITTERS, 21 Park Place, New York, N.Y. 10007

CHUCK WAGON, 176 Oak St., Newton, Mass. 02164
Dehydrated food.

DRI-LITE, 11333 Atlantic, Lynwood, Calif. 93001
Dehydrated food.
°EASTERN MOUNTAIN SPORTS, 1041 Commonwealth Ave., Boston, Mass. 02315
Also has a new line of kits.
EUREKA TENT & AWNING CO., P.O. Box 966, Binghamton, N.Y. 13902
FROSTLINE, Box 2190, Boulder, Colo. 80302
Outstanding kits for tents, down clothing, and some other items that you sew yourself. Planning and instructions are very good.
GERRY, 5450 North Valley Highway, Denver, Colo. 80216
HIGHLAND OUTFITTERS, P.O. Box 121, Riverside, Calif. 92502
HIRSCH-WEIS/WHITE STAG, 5203 S.E. Johnson Creek Blvd., Portland, Ore. 97206
HOLUBAR, Box 7, Boulder, Colo. 80302
Their Carikit catalogue has their new kit line.
KELTY, 1801 Victory Blvd., Glendale, Calif. 91201
PETER LIMMER AND SONS, Intervale, N.H. 03845
Custom and ready-made boots.
MOOR AND MOUNTAIN, Concord, Mass. 01742
MOUNTAIN PRODUCTS CORP., 123 So. Wenatchee Ave., Wenatchee, Wash. 98801
MOUNTAIN SPORTS, 821 Pearl St., Boulder, Colo. 80302
NORTH FACE, 1234 5th St., Berkeley, Calif. 94710
PERMA-PAK, 40 East 2430 So., Salt Lake City, Utah 84115
Dehydrated food, including good bulk items.
°RECREATIONAL EQUIPMENT, 1525–11th Ave., Seattle, Wash. 98122
Generally the best buys around. Recreational Equipment is a cooperative which gives you a rebate on some of your purchase money at the end of the year. Membership fee is $1.
RICH-MOOR, P.O. Box 2728, Van Nuys, Calif. 91404
Dehydrated food.
SIERRA DESIGNS, 4th & Addison, Berkeley, Calif. 94710
°SKI HUT, 1615 University Avenue, Berkeley, Calif. 94703
SMILIE CO., 575 Howard St., San Francisco, Calif. 94105
STEPHENSON'S, 23206 Hatteras St., Woodland Hills, Calif. 91364
TRAIL CHEF, 1109 S. Wall St., Los Angeles, Calif. 90015

Where to Get It

U.S. GEOLOGICAL SURVEY, Washington, D.C. 20025 or Federal Center, Denver, Colo. 80225

Index maps for any state are free on request.

WEST RIDGE, 11930 W. Olympic Blvd., West Los Angeles, Calif. 90025

Bibliography

This section is included so that the reader who would like to pursue particular subjects or get a different viewpoint will have a starting point. Backpackers disagree on many subjects, because they have different bodies of experience to draw upon. After a few trips, the reader will have his own set of facts and prejudices with which to judge this book and the others mentioned here.

GENERAL

A good basic book on modern camping of all kinds is *America's Camping Book*, written by Paul Cardwell and published by Scribners. The best book about north woods-style camping, far from civilization, is Calvin Rutstrum's *New Way of the Wilderness* (Macmillan). For a book about modern backpacking with a slightly different viewpoint from mine, try Colin Fletcher's *The Complete Walker* (Knopf), an altogether delightful volume. The Sierra Club *Wilderness Handbook* (Ballantine), edited by David Brower, is a paperback version of the old *Going Light with Backpack or Burro*.

FOOD

Those who travel in large groups should consult Hasse Bunnelle's *Food for Knapsackers*, published by the Sierra Club. If you delight in traditional methods, you'll like Bradford Angier's *Wilderness Cookery* (Stackpole). If you like to plan your meals with scientific precision, or if you are going out on long enough trips to be concerned with nutritional requirements, two government publications will provide the information you need: *Food,* the 1959 Yearbook of the U.S. Department of Agriculture, and *Composition of Foods* by Bernice Watt and Annabel Merrill. Both are available from the U.S. Superintendant of Documents.

If you're interested in cooking with vegetable protein, substituting it for meat, eggs, and the like, a good introduction is *Diet for a Small Planet* by Frances Moore Lappé (Ballantine).

ROUTE FINDING

The best book around is Calvin Rutstrum's *Wilderness Route Finder* (Macmillan), including information on the more intricate techniques needed on extended trips in the far North. *Better Ways of Pathfinding* by Robert Owendoff (Stackpole) is worth reading.

FIRST AID AND EMERGENCY MEDICINE

The current Red Cross *First Aid Textbook* (Doubleday) is basic. The best discussion of wilderness medical problems in short compass (assuming you already know your Red Cross first aid) is the *Mountain Medicine Symposium,* reprinted from *Appalachia,* and available for one dollar from the Appalachian Mountain Club, 5 Joy St., Boston, Mass. 02108. *Emergency Care and Transportation of the Sick and Injured,* published by the American Academy of Orthopedic Surgeons, is outstanding and thorough.

Advanced techniques are covered exhaustively in *Medicine for Mountaineering,* edited by James Wilkerson and published by the Seattle Mountaineers.

Anyone interested in mountain or winter travel should try to get a copy of *Hypothermia: Killer of the Unprepared,* a booklet by Theodore Lathrop, published by the Mazamas.

THE MOUNTAINS

The best guides are *Mountaineering: The Freedom of the Hills,* edited by

Harvey Manning and published by the Seattle Mountaineers, and Alan Black-shaw's *Mountaineering* (Penguin).

WINTER

The author's *Complete Snow Camper's Guide* is also published by Scribners. The Sierra Club *Manual of Ski Mountaineering* (Ballantine), edited by David Brower, is an old standby.

THE NATURAL WORLD

It is impossible to even begin to mention the many good nature books that are available. Local field guides are often best, but they are also very numerous, and there would be no point in trying to list them here. A good introduction to the methods of the naturalist and to scientific nomenclature is Vinson Brown's *The Amateur Naturalist* (Bramhall House).

The best field guide to the birds is *Birds of North America* by Chandler Robbins, Bertel Bruun, and Herbert Zim (Golden Press). Two excellent older guides are Roger Tory Peterson's *A Field Guide to the Birds* (which covers the eastern part of the country) and *A Field Guide to the Western Birds,* both published by Houghton Mifflin. Records of songs are available, keyed to the Peterson guides. Peterson has also written a good introduction to birding, *How to Know the Birds* (New American Library).

For mammals, a good guide is *A Field Guide to the Mammals* by William Burt and Richard Grossenheider. Tracks and signs are discussed delightfully in Olaus Murie's *Field Guide to Animal Tracks.* Both are put out by Houghton Mifflin.

Flower lovers have to go to regional guides for field manuals, since no one has yet come out with a book of manageable size that takes in the whole country. A search of the local libraries and bookstores will be fruitful.

Tree guides are numerous. The best one covering all the United States and Canada is *Trees of North America* by C. Frank Brockman (Golden Press). For more leisurely and intimate acquaintance with the trees, try Donald Peattie's *A Natural History of the Trees* (about the eastern species) or *A Natural History of Western Trees* (both Houghton Mifflin).

Many other plant forms are particularly interesting, but available field guides to ferns and such are regional. The gourmet will find Alexander Smith's *The Mushroom Hunter's Guide* (University of Michigan Press) indispensable. Various other mushroom guides are good, but don't ever try a mushroom unless you're *sure*.

Field Book of Snakes of the U.S. and Canada by Karl Schmidt and D. Dwight Davis (Putnam) is a good guide, as is *A Field Guide to the Insects* by Donald Borror and Richard White (Houghton Mifflin).

The patterns of the stars are made easily recognizable by H. A. Rey's *The Stars* (Houghton Mifflin). *The Friendly Stars* by Martha Martin and Donald Menzel is charming; it is an older book brought out in a new edition by Dover.

There are many rock and mineral guides; Frederick Pough's *A Field Guide to Rocks and Minerals* (Houghton Mifflin) is one. Pamphlets and maps on the geology of many regions are published by the U.S. Geological Survey.

A fine introduction to the natural history of the continent is Peter Farb's *The Face of North America* (Harper and Row). Victor Shelford's *The Ecology of North America* is a comprehensive attempt to describe the life of the continent before the intervention of the Europeans.

A few of the really great books about wild places and the intricacies of nature are: *The Life and Death of the Salt Marsh* by John and Mildred Teal (Ballantine), *The Outermost House* by Henry Beston (Viking), *Desert Solitaire* by Edward Abbey (Simon and Schuster), *A Sand County Almanac* by Aldo Leopold (Ballantine), *The Man Who Walked Through Time* by Colin Fletcher (Knopf), *The Forest and the Sea* by Marston Bates (New American Library), *The Edge of the Sea* by Rachel Carson (Houghton Mifflin; Signet), Thoreau's *The Maine Woods* (Bramhall House), *The Immense Journey* by Loren Eiseley (Random House), *The Desert Year* by Joseph Wood Krutch (William Sloane), *The Mountains of California* by John Muir (Doubleday), *From Laurel Hill to Siler's Bog* by John Terres (Knopf), and *One Day on Teton Marsh* by Sally Carrighar (Houghton Mifflin).

EQUIPMENT

The indispensable guide for anyone making his own equipment is *Lightweight Camping Equipment and How to Make It* by Gerry Cunningham and Margaret Hansson, published by Colorado Outdoor Sports Corporation in Denver.

WHERE TO GO

The only comprehensive guide is the *Handbook of Wilderness Travel* by George Wells. The new edition by Colorado Outdoor Sports Corporation has not been adequately revised, but there is still a lot of information.

The Appalachian Trail Council publishes a series of eleven guides to the Appalachian Trail and side trails to it. They cover Katahdin, Maine past Katahdin, New Hampshire and Vermont, Massachusetts and Connecticut, New York and New Jersey, Pennsylvania, Susquehanna to Shenandoah National Park, Shenandoah National Park, Central and Southwestern Virginia, Tennessee and North Carolina to the Great Smokies, and the Great Smokies to Georgia.

The Appalachian Mountain Club publishes comprehensive trail guides to Maine Mountains, the White Mountains, Massachusetts and Rhode Island, and to Mount Desert Island–Acadia National Park. A *Guide to the Long Trail* is published by the Green Mountain Club, and a *Guide to Adirondack Trails* by the Adirondack Mountain Club.

For trips in Washington and Oregon, the Seattle Mountaineers publish many books of short hikes besides the booklet mentioned in the text. For the Glacier Peak Wilderness Area, there is *Routes and Rocks*, also by Tabor and Crowder. The Olympic Peninsula is covered well in Robert Wood's *Trail Country*.

Wyoming is served by Orrin and Lorraine Bonney's *Guide to the Wyoming Mountains and Wilderness Areas* (Swallow), portions of which are also available in smaller editions.

Some of the best trips in California are described in two Wilderness Press books by Karl Schwenke and Thomas Winnett, *Sierra South* and *Sierra North*. Robert Wood's *The Tahoe–Yosemite Trail* and *Desolation Wilderness* cover some of my favorite trails in the Sierra.

Robert Ormes' *Guide to the Colorado Mountains* (Swallow) and Herbert Ungnade's *Guide to the New Mexico Mountains* by the same publisher are not primarily trail guides, but contain a great deal of information useful to backpackers.

Index